Ireland For Dummies
5th Edition

9/1/15

W9-AXA-470

The Ring of Kerry

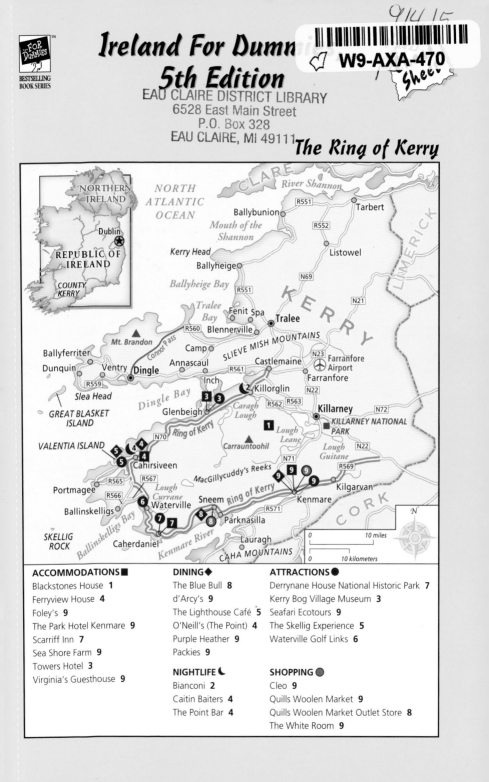

ACCOMMODATIONS ■
Blackstones House **1**
Ferryview House **4**
Foley's **9**
The Park Hotel Kenmare **9**
Scarriff Inn **7**
Sea Shore Farm **9**
Towers Hotel **3**
Virginia's Guesthouse **9**

DINING ◆
The Blue Bull **8**
d'Arcy's **9**
The Lighthouse Café **5**
O'Neill's (The Point) **4**
Purple Heather **9**
Packies **9**

NIGHTLIFE ☾
Bianconi **2**
Caitin Baiters **4**
The Point Bar **4**

ATTRACTIONS ●
Derrynane House National Historic Park **7**
Kerry Bog Village Museum **3**
Seafari Ecotours **9**
The Skellig Experience **5**
Waterville Golf Links **6**

SHOPPING ◉
Cleo **9**
Quills Woolen Market **9**
Quills Woolen Market Outlet Store **8**
The White Room **9**

Learning the Lingo

Refer to this helpful list of lingo while touring Ireland.

An Lar	city centre	**garda**	policeman
bonnet	car hood	**lift**	elevator
boot	car trunk	**mna**	women (Gaelic)
car park	parking lot	**off-license**	liquor store
cheers	thanks	**petrol**	gas
crack, craic	good times, fun	**quay**	waterfront (pronounced *key*)
creche	day care	**quid, or bob**	pounds, or money
deadly, brilliant	great, excellent	**ring**	to telephone
fa'ilte	welcome (Gaelic)	**sláinte**	cheers or goodbye (Gaelic — pronounced *schlancha*)
fir	men (Gaelic)		
footpath	sidewalk	**take-away**	fast food, to go
		windscreen	windshield

Ireland Mileage Guide

Use this mileage chart to help plan your itinerary.

Belfast

Belfast	Cork	Derry	Donegal	Dublin	Galway	Killarney	Limerick	Sligo	Waterford	Wexford
264	**Cork**									
73	266	**Derry**								
112	250	43	**Donegal**							
104	160	147	138	**Dublin**						
190	130	169	127	136	**Galway**					
271	54	274	235	192	120	**Killarney**				
201	65	204	184	123	65	69	**Limerick**			
128	209	84	41	135	86	213	144	**Sligo**		
207	78	238	222	98	137	120	80	182	**Waterford**	
192	116	235	231	88	157	158	118	191	39	**Wexford**

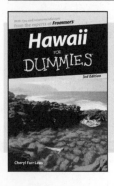
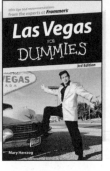

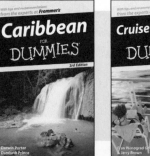

Ireland
FOR
DUMMIES®
5TH EDITION

By Liz Albertson

WILEY

EAU CLAIRE DISTRICT LIBRARY

Wiley Publishing, Inc.

Ireland For Dummies®, 5th Edition
Published by
Wiley Publishing, Inc.
111 River St.
Hoboken, NJ 07030-5774
www.wiley.com

Copyright © 2009 by Wiley Publishing, Inc., Indianapolis, Indiana

Published simultaneously in Canada

For general information on our other products and services, please contact our Customer Care Department within the U.S. at 800-762-2974, outside the U.S. at 317-572-3993, or fax 317-572-4002.

For technical support, please visit www.wiley.com/techsupport.

Wiley also publishes its books in a variety of electronic formats. Some content that appears in print may not be available in electronic books.

ISBN: 978-0-470-42207-6

Manufactured in the United States of America

10 9 8 7 6 5 4 3 2 1

WILEY

About the Author

Liz Albertson worked as an editor for Frommer's Travel Guides for four years before making the leap to the other side of the computer as the author of *Ireland For Dummies*. When she isn't researching and writing, Liz spends much of her time in Ireland sitting in on traditional music sessions, fiddle in hand. She currently teaches sixth grade in Northampton, Massachusetts, where she lives with her fiancé, Hugh, and her adopted African cichlid fish, Rocky. Liz welcomes feedback and suggestions for the next edition of the book at ejalbertson@yahoo.com.

Dedication

For Julie and Kathy.

Author's Acknowledgments

Thank you so much to Christine Ryan for being a wonderful editor. Thanks also to friends and fellow travelers for their travel tips, encouragement, and excitement on my behalf. And, of course, thank you, thank you, thank you Hugh for being you.

Publisher's Acknowledgments

We're proud of this book; please send us your comments through our Dummies online registration form located at www.dummies.com/register/.

Some of the people who helped bring this book to market include the following:

Editorial

Editors: Christine Ryan, Development Editor; Lindsay Conner, Production Editor

Copy Editor: Anne Owen

Cartographer: Roberta Stockwell

Editorial Assistant: Jessica Langan-Peck

Senior Photo Editor: Richard Fox

Cover Photos:
Front: © Gavin Hellier/Robert Harding World Imagery/Getty Images
Back: © Irish Image Collection/DanitaDelimont.com

Cartoons: Rich Tennant (www.the5thwave.com)

Composition Services

Project Coordinators: Katie Key, Erin Smith

Layout and Graphics: Reuben W. Davis, Sarah Philippart, Christine Williams

Proofreaders: Laura Albert, Cara L. Buitron

Indexer: Becky Hornyak

Publishing and Editorial for Consumer Dummies

Diane Graves Steele, Vice President and Publisher, Consumer Dummies

Kristin Ferguson-Wagstaffe, Product Development Director, Consumer Dummies

Kelly Regan, Editorial Director, Travel

Publishing for Technology Dummies

Andy Cummings, Vice President and Publisher, Dummies Technology/General User

Composition Services

Gerry Fahey, Vice President of Production Services

Debbie Stailey, Director of Composition Services

Contents at a Glance

Maps at a Glance

Table of Contents

Introduction

● ●

*R*elatively tiny Ireland (84,434 sq. km/32,600 sq. miles) offers travelers a diverse range of experiences. You find landscapes that range from those famed rolling green hills to stark, rugged cliffs; restaurants that serve the best in modern fusion cuisine and pubs that serve Irish stew made from a recipe that's hundreds of years old; theaters showcasing the best in contemporary dance and festivals devoted to traditional Irish music. This guide highlights the best of Ireland's diverse offerings so that you can plan the trip of your dreams.

About This Book

This guide is designed to help you travel smarter, with a concise, savvy approach that helps you get to the heart of what you're looking for. It's a quick reference guide that includes need-to-know information, from the best online bargains and package deals to helpful tips on how to organize and maximize your time in a destination. Each destination features a selective, streamlined choice of hotels and restaurants in all price ranges. I weeded out the clunkers to focus on the best choices, whether you're looking to splurge on a luxury resort or find an affordable place for a family of four.

I tried to anticipate every question you may have about traveling to Ireland and provide the answers. If you've never been to the country before, I show you what to expect and how to plan for it. If you're an old Ireland hand, you probably bought this book because you don't want to waste a lot of time sorting through a billion different hotels, restaurants, and attractions trying to find the absolute best ones. You want a quick and easy, yet comprehensive, source of information, and that's exactly what I give you here.

Of course, you don't have to read the whole book. And you don't have to start at the beginning, either. This is a reference book. Check out the table of contents, and then read the parts that answer your specific questions.

Please be advised that travel information is subject to change at any time — this is especially true of prices. You may want to write or call ahead for confirmation when making your travel plans.

Conventions Used in This Book

In this book, I include descriptions of the best sights in Ireland; reviews of the best hotels, restaurants, shops, pubs, and more; and all sorts of tips for planning your visit to the Emerald Isle. I employ a few conventions designed to convey critical information in a simple, straightforward manner.

Money matters

For this edition of *Ireland For Dummies,* I used the currency exchange rates of $1.60 to every €1 and $2 to every £1. Exchange rates fluctuate all the time; check www.xe.com for up-to-date exchange rates.

All prices given here over ten euro, dollars, or pounds are rounded to the nearest euro, dollar, or pound. All prices are, of course, subject to change.

In the accommodations sections, the listed price is a *rack rate* (the official rate published by the hotel) for one night in a double room (one room accommodating two people); the actual prices you'll pay are often less than the rack rate.

Each accommodation and dining review is accompanied by a dollar-sign designation designed to help you get a sense of the price category of the lodging or restaurant at a glance. The following table gives you the key to the dollar-sign designations for accommodations and restaurants.

Accommodation Category	Euro	British Pound	U.S. Dollar
$	€110	£88	$176 or less
$$	€111–€160	£89–£128	$178–$256
$$$	€161–€240	£129–£192	$258–$384
$$$$	€240 or more	£192 or more	$384 or more

Restaurant Category	Euro	British Pound	U.S. Dollar
$	€ 15	£12	$24 or less
$$	€16–€23	£13–£19	$26–$37
$$$	€24–€30	£19–£24	$38–$48
$$$$	€30 or more	£24 or more	$48 or more

Other matters

I provide an entry called *Suggested visit* at the end of each attraction listing. This is my estimate of how much time you should budget to do and see most of what's available at each attraction. This length of time is just a suggestion — you may find you need more or less time, depending on your interests.

The following is a list of the credit card abbreviations used in the listings in this book:

AE	American Express
DC	Diners Club
MC	MasterCard
V	Visa

In the dining sections, the listed prices are the range of prices for dinner main courses, unless otherwise noted.

And just in case you're not familiar with the term *en suite,* it means a room with a bathroom connected. In some B&Bs especially, you may be expected to share a bathroom with other guests, so ask for a room en suite if a private bathroom is important to you.

My Assumptions

In this book, I make some assumptions about you and your needs as a traveler. I assume you are one of the following:

- ✔ An inexperienced traveler looking for guidance when determining whether to travel to Ireland and how to plan for it
- ✔ An experienced traveler who hasn't yet visited Ireland and wants expert advice on where to go and what to see
- ✔ A traveler looking for a book that focuses on only the best and most essential Irish sights, tastes, and experiences

If you fit any of these criteria, *Ireland For Dummies,* 5th Edition, gives you the information you're looking for.

How This Book Is Organized

This book is divided into seven parts. Parts I and II whet your palate and get you ready to go, and Parts III through VII deal with what you can see and do while you're there. Each section in the regional chapters has a Fast Facts portion at the end, listing addresses and contact information for visitors' bureaus and tourism offices, Internet cafes, hospitals, local genealogical resources, and post offices.

Part 1: Introducing Ireland

This part introduces you to the splendor of Ireland and helps you get an idea of what you'd like to see and where you'd like to go. The book starts with a chapter devoted to the very best that Ireland has to offer. Chapter 2 includes all sorts of information about Ireland, from a look at the island's history to translations of local lingo to culinary information. Chapter 3 provides brief descriptions of the regions covered in this guide so that you get a sense of where you'd like to go. In Chapter 3, I also discuss various approaches to touring the country, and hash out the pros and cons of visiting during different seasons. I also give you a rundown of the many festivals, events, and celebrations held in Ireland throughout the year. In case you'd like some guidance on how to plan your itinerary, I offer outlines for four different suggested itineraries in Chapter 4.

Part II: Planning Your Trip to Ireland

Part II answers all your practical questions about planning and getting ready for a trip to Ireland. Chapter 5 deals with money, providing rough guidelines on what things cost, helping you decide how to carry your money, and listing 20 (count 'em: 20) money-saving tips. Chapter 6 outlines the different ways to get to Ireland, and Chapter 7 deals with the various options for getting around the island. After you plan how to get there, you can turn to Chapter 8, which gives you the lowdown on the different types of accommodations in Ireland, plus tips on how to save on lodging costs. Chapter 9 includes tips for travelers with special needs and interests, including seniors, travelers with disabilities, gay and lesbian travelers, outdoorsy travelers, and more. Before you go out and start buying your travel-size toothpaste, check out Chapter 10 for information on getting a passport, figuring out your insurance, packing your bags, and staying in touch once you get to Ireland.

Part III: Dublin and the East Coast

Part III is dedicated to Dublin and the surrounding counties: Meath and Louth to the north and Wicklow, Wexford, Waterford, Kilkenny, and Tipperary to the south.

Chapter 11 covers Dublin, the Republic of Ireland's bustling, vibrant capital city. This fat chapter is packed with information on the best restaurants, hotels, attractions, shopping, and nightlife in the city. If the choices overwhelm you, check out the one-, two-, and three-day itinerary suggestions I provide.

Counties Meath and Louth, just north of Dublin, are home to a treasure trove of prehistoric sights, including the remarkable burial mounds at Knowth and Newgrange, and the storied Hill of Tara, ancient seat of the Irish high kings. You'll find more information about these areas in Chapter 12. Chapters 13 and 14 cover the beautiful southeastern counties of Wicklow, Kildare, Wexford, Waterford, Kilkenny, and Tipperary.

These counties offer a diverse array of attractions, including some of Ireland's most beautiful gardens, medieval towns, stunning mountain and coastal scenery, and the popular Waterford Crystal Factory.

Part V: Counties Cork and Kerry

Part IV covers only two counties, Cork and Kerry, which together attract the lion's share of visitors to Ireland, who come for the stunning mountain and coastal scenery in these parts. Bustling Cork City; and the gorgeous sea- and landscapes, and cute towns of West Cork are covered in Chapter 15, while Chapter 16 features the best of beautiful Killarney National Park and the breathtaking Ring of Kerry and Dingle Peninsula.

Part V: The West and the Northwest

This part bundles the entire western and northwestern areas of Ireland into one neat package that incorporates a tremendous variety of landscapes and towns. Chapters 17 through 20 are filled with information on gorgeous natural wonders, including the sheer Cliffs of Moher and Slieve League cliffs; the rocky, wildflower-studded Burren; the beautiful Aran Islands; the wild landscape of Connemara; and much more. You get the lowdown on some of the best cities and towns in this area, including the sweet Mayo town of Westport, artsy Sligo Town, and the "it's-so-great-why-doesn't-everyone-live-here" city of Galway.

Part VI: Northern Ireland

Part VI covers the separate country of Northern Ireland, which may be last in this book but is not least in terms of natural beauty and interesting cities. Chapters 21, 22, and 23 guide you to the most beautiful natural wonders, including the Mourne Mountains and the hexagonal basalt columns of the Giant's Causeway. They also give you all the information you need to explore the hot-and-happening city of Belfast and the up-and-coming historic city of Derry.

Part VII: The Part of Tens

The Part of Tens chapters feature some fun extras, such as Irish food and drink that you shouldn't miss during your trip, and my top ten suggestions of what to buy in Ireland.

You also find another element near the back of this book. I include an appendix — your "Quick Concierge" — containing lots of handy information you may need when planning your trip.

Icons Used in This Book

Keep an eye peeled for these icons, which appear in the margins:

 This icon highlights money-saving tips and/or great deals.

This icon highlights the best the destination has to offer in all categories: hotels, restaurants, attractions, activities, shopping, and nightlife.

 This icon gives you a heads-up on annoying or potentially dangerous situations, such as tourist traps, unsafe neighborhoods, rip-offs, and other things to beware of.

 This icon highlights attractions, hotels, restaurants, or activities that are particularly hospitable to children or people traveling with kids.

 This icon flags bits of information that are important to keep in mind.

 This icon points out useful advice on things to do and ways to schedule your time.

Where to Go from Here

Now you're ready to go! Put a Chieftains CD on the stereo; pour yourself a pint of Guinness; and get ready to fling yourself headlong into the historic, friendly, beautiful experience that is Ireland today.

Part I
Introducing Ireland

The 5th Wave   By Rich Tennant

WHILE ON VACATION IN IRELAND, BILL AND DENISE WATCH A LOCAL FAMILY WORKING ON THE TRADITIONAL THATCHED ROOF COTTAGE, THATCHED ROOF SATELLITE DISH, AND THATCHED ROOF JEEP CHEROKEE.

In this part . . .

*I*reland is a traveler's dream, with diverse and spectacular scenery, vibrant towns and cities humming with activity, a culinary scene that makes the most of the country's delicious fresh produce, a wide array of attractions, great music, and more than its share of superb accommodations, from upscale hotels to cozy B&Bs. Chapter 1 whets your appetite with brief descriptions of some of Ireland's best scenery, restaurants, accommodations, and more.

Read through Chapter 2 for background information on Ireland, including a look at Irish history, Irish cuisine, and local lingo, plus a list of some fun and interesting Irish books, movies, and music.

In Chapter 3, I provide brief descriptions of the regions covered in this guide, discuss various approaches to touring the country, and hash out the pros and cons of visiting during different seasons. I also include a calendar of events so you can schedule your trip to coincide with the festivals and celebrations that interest you.

Overwhelmed by the wealth of things to see and do in Ireland? Chapter 4 includes some suggestions for itineraries.

Chapter 1

Discovering the Best of Ireland

In This Chapter

▶ Enjoying Ireland's best travel experiences

▶ Finding Ireland's best hotels, restaurants, and pubs

▶ Exploring Irish history at the best castles and archaeological sites

▶ Playing at Ireland's best golf courses

▶ Experiencing Ireland's natural wonders

*T*his chapter gives you the lowdown on the very best that Ireland has to offer, from the best food on the island to the most gorgeous seascapes to the best spots to hear traditional Irish music.

The Best Travel Experiences

With all that Ireland has to offer, it's tough to come up with a list of favorite experiences. But here are some of the adventures I keep day-dreaming about long after I'm home.

✔ **Listening to traditional Irish music:** What could be better (or more Irish) than relaxing to live traditional music in an atmospheric pub? The Traditional Irish Musical Pub Crawl (see Chapter 11) is a terrific introduction to the musical style. If you're in the groove after the pub crawl, head to the Cobblestone (also in Chapter 11), which hosts exceptional musicians.

✔ **Taking in the Book of Kells:** This ninth-century book of the four gospels glows with ornate Latin script and stunning Celtic knots and designs. The exhibit about the making of the book is fascinating. See Chapter 11.

✔ **Filing into Newgrange Tomb:** You'll feel like a lucky explorer as you descend into the cool, dim chamber of this 5,000-year-old *passage tomb* (an underground chamber thought to have religious or ceremonial importance), where you'll find ancient geometric rock carvings. See Chapter 12.

Ireland

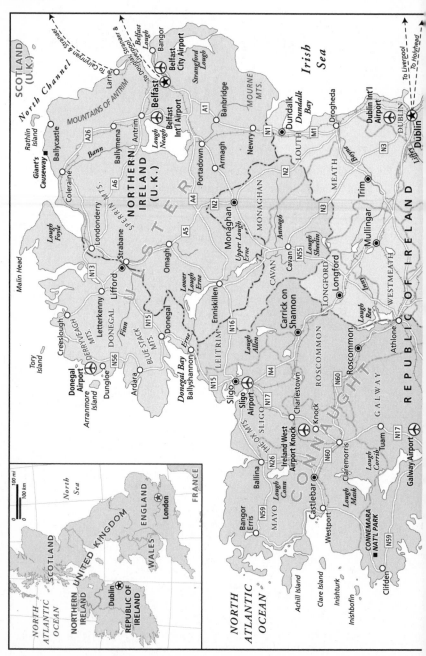

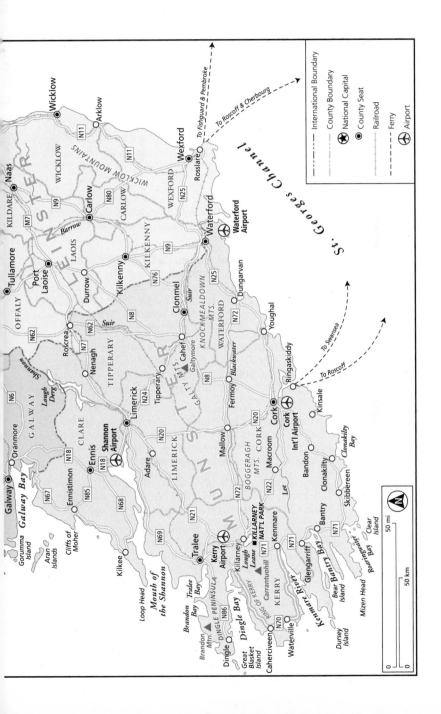

✔ **Strolling through Powerscourt Gardens:** These gardens have many facets, including a mossy grotto, a formal garden with an impressive fountain and statuary, a rose garden that bursts into a riot of color in season, and peaceful woodlands. See Chapter 13.

✔ **Touring the Waterford Crystal Factory:** A fascinating tour takes you behind the scenes to watch the evolution of Waterford Crystal pieces, from their beginnings as molten crystal to the finished product. Naturally, there is a giant retail space on site. See Chapter 14.

✔ **Eating your way through Kinsale:** Not only is Kinsale the picture of charm, with a beautiful harbor and an adorable town center, but it's also Ireland's gourmet capital; you'll find loads of excellent restaurants here. See Chapter 15.

✔ **Exploring Killarney National Park:** Use a bike, horse, jaunting car, or your own two feet to explore the silver streams, sapphire lakes, dense woodlands, and heather-covered mountains here. See Chapter 16.

✔ **Driving the Ring of Kerry and the Dingle Peninsula:** Driving along both of these peninsulas, you'll encounter vista after vista, each more spectacular than the one before it. Seascapes, cliffs, and mountain views are the order of the day on the Ring of Kerry, while the Dingle Peninsula is all hills, covered in a patchwork of farms, plus sandy beaches, craggy cliffs, and more seascapes. See Chapter 16.

✔ **Walking through the Burren:** Walking is the ultimate way to see this strange and gorgeous rocky plateau, filled with wildflowers that poke up through cracks in the rock, shallow lakes and rivers that spring up from below, and ruins from the Stone Age through medieval times. See Chapter 17.

✔ **Exploring Ireland's Islands:** Taking the ferry out to Ireland's islands is part of the adventure. The other part is exploring these peaceful islands, with their different ruins and cultures, by bike or by foot. See Chapter 18 for information on the Aran Islands.

✔ **Taking a hike:** There's nothing like wandering through the countryside to really experience Ireland. One of my new favorite hikes is out of Port, on the peninsula north of Donegal Bay. See Chapter 20.

✔ **Gazing awestruck at the Cliffs of Moher:** Tuck extra rolls of film into your backpack before you head up to these breathtaking cliffs, which plummet down to the Atlantic 288m (760 ft.) below. The vistas are stunning — you can see all the way to the Aran Islands in Galway Bay when the weather is clear. See Chapter 17.

✔ **Seeing the Derry or Belfast political murals:** These murals are moving testaments of the Troubles. See Chapters 21 and 22.

✔ **Clambering around the Giant's Causeway:** You can climb around this natural wonder — a stretch of tightly packed six-sided basalt columns of varying heights — like you're on a StairMaster gone crazy. See Chapter 22.

The Best Hotels

The following hotels made my list of favorites because they offer a unique atmosphere, outstanding service, uncommon luxury, a particularly Irish flavor, or perhaps all of the above.

- ✔ **Number 31 (Dublin):** A country-chic oasis with gorgeous modern accents, this small hotel is a calm retreat in the middle of Georgian Dublin. Good luck pulling yourself away from the delicious breakfast. See Chapter 11.

- ✔ **Waterford Castle (Waterford):** Don your crown and head to this castle on its own island, with an interior featuring tapestries, antiques, and stone fireplaces. See Chapter 14.

- ✔ **Butler House (Kilkenny):** The décor here is a gorgeous marriage of old and new; service is spot-on; and many of the spacious rooms have views of Kilkenny Castle that are so beautiful, they look like storybook illustrations. See Chapter 14.

- ✔ **Killarney Park Hotel (Kerry):** Luxury, luxury, and more luxury are on tap at this hotel, with a gorgeous Victorian-style lobby and spacious guest rooms furnished with antiques and lush fabrics. See Chapter 16.

- ✔ **Adare Manor Hotel & Golf Resort (Limerick):** You'll want for nothing at this castlelike manor house. The public rooms are grand and luxurious, and the bedrooms are filled with opulent fabrics and carved wood and stone. The grounds feature a trout-filled river, sweeping parklands, and a Trent Jones–designed golf course. See Chapter 17.

- ✔ **The G (Galway):** Okay, so it's expensive (really, really expensive), but this place boasts theatrical surroundings, a wonderful spa, friendly staff, and possibly the most comfortable beds on the Emerald Isle. See Chapter 18.

- ✔ **Ashford Castle (Mayo):** Live out a fairy tale with a stay in this luxurious castle. Public rooms hold large gilt-framed oil paintings, medieval coats of armor, and oak paneling, while antiques and carved wood furniture are the order of the day in guest rooms. The hotel offers all sorts of activities, from horseback riding to fishing. See Chapter 19.

- ✔ **Malmaison (Antrim):** I challenge even the grouchiest traveler to find fault with this trendy boutique hotel, where service is extraordinarily friendly, and the warm, spacious rooms are designed to cater to every need. See Chapter 22.

The Best B&Bs

I love bed-and-breakfasts because you get the company and advice of a friendly local along with a homey, comfortable room — and often a good bargain to boot. Here are some of my favorites.

- ✔ **McMenamins Townhouse (Wexford):** Kind hosts, soothing rooms, a central location, and a spectacular breakfast make this place one of Ireland's best B&Bs. See Chapter 14.

- ✔ **Foxmount Country House (Waterford):** It's easy to feel like the lord or lady of this manor as you stroll the stunningly landscaped grounds and settle down in your cozy, elegant room. See Chapter 14.

- ✔ **Ballymakeigh House (Cork):** Dine on a five-course meal made from the freshest of produce before stumbling upstairs to your comfortable room that overlooks the surrounding dairy farm. See Chapter 15.

- ✔ **The Old Presbytery (Cork):** The only way that this place could be more relaxing would be if a masseuse came with each room. The huge beds are filled with snow-white blankets and pillows, many rooms have tubs or Jacuzzis, and the staff is among the friendliest and most helpful around. See Chapter 15.

- ✔ **Milestone B&B (Kerry):** Owners Barbara and Michael Carroll make this B&B a standout, helping every guest to plan his or her perfect Dingle Peninsula itinerary. See Chapter 16.

- ✔ **Berry Lodge (Clare):** The views of farmland and sea are gorgeous, and the bedrooms are comfy and bright, but the real reason to stay here is the unbelievably delicious cuisine served at dinner. See Chapter 17.

- ✔ **Devondell House (Galway):** This sweet B&B is a slice of home (with a terrific breakfast) right outside of Galway City. See chapter 18.

- ✔ **SeaMist (Galway):** Peace and tranquility are the words that come to mind at this B&B in the middle of the bustling little town of Clifden. See Chapter 18.

- ✔ **Templehouse (Sligo):** A stay at Templehouse is what life would be like if you had a close relative who just happened to own a sprawling manor house on 400 hectares (1,000 acres). See Chapter 19.

The best of the Irish awards

As you make your way around Ireland, you discover that the Irish absolutely love awards. Almost every restaurant and lodging has some sort of sign or sticker indicating that the place is lauded by one organization or other. In fact, there are even awards for the best public bathrooms in each county. You heard it here first: One of Ireland's top toilets is in Lismore, in County Cork. The esteemed public bathroom is located at the foot of the road leading toward the castle. As you enter towns and villages in each county in the Republic, you often see awards for the Tidiest Town, presented by the environmental council. If you feel like planning an itinerary through Ireland's tidiest towns, check out www.tidytowns.ie.

- ✔ **The Merchant's House (Derry):** Slip back in time with a stay at this beautifully restored Georgian B&B, featuring high ceilings, intricate plasterwork, and a museum-quality Georgian-style dining room. See Chapter 21.

- ✔ **Ash-Rowan Town House (Antrim):** This serene B&B is a welcome oasis after a long night in Belfast's pubs or a long day exploring the city. Rooms are decorated with country-style furniture, Victorian antiques, and fresh flowers from the garden in back. See Chapter 22.

- ✔ **Slieve Croob Inn (Down):** You can't beat the location of this comfortable inn, nestled in rolling green hills a few minutes away from the Mourne Mountains. Walking trails start practically at the front door. See Chapter 23.

The Best Restaurants

Feel like sitting down to an elegantly prepared seafood entree? Or is meat-and-potatoes comfort food more your style? Perhaps you'd like a fusion meal, featuring ingredients and cooking techniques from all over the world? No matter what you're craving, you won't go hungry in Ireland. Following are my favorite places to dig in.

- ✔ **Mermaid Café (Dublin):** Fresh Irish ingredients and innovative dishes characterize the menu at this buzzy, warm, modern restaurant. See Chapter 11.

- ✔ **L'Gueulton (Dublin):** Come at some obscure time (Tues night at 6:17 p.m., say) to ensure yourself a seat at this casually elegant restaurant, where the friendly staff serves up perfectly prepared dishes made with excellent fresh ingredients. See Chapter 11.

- ✔ **The Winding Stair (Dublin):** Set aside an evening to enjoy the New Irish delights at this recently-opened Dublin restaurant. See Chapter 11.

- ✔ **Ristorante Rinuccini (Kilkenny):** Open the door and slip into Florence at this romantic Italian restaurant with its excellent homemade pasta. See Chapter 14.

- ✔ **Fishy Fishy Café (Cork):** Come here for sparkling fresh fish prepared beautifully and served in a bright, sea- and sky-blue room. See Chapter 15.

- ✔ **Man Friday (Cork):** There's no fancy footwork at this seafood-and-meat restaurant, just excellent ingredients cooked in a way that allows their flavor to shine, such as the black sole cooked on the bone. The interior is warm, romantic, and cozy, lit by lantern-style lamps. See Chapter 15.

- ✔ **Packies (Kerry):** You can't go wrong with any of the dishes at this hip and lively restaurant, from the simple crab claws in garlic butter to the adventurous plaice with orange, lime, and cilantro. See Chapter 16.

✔ **Out of the Blue (Kerry):** In a sea of seafood restaurants, Out of the Blue stands out, offering some of the freshest fish in town in a cheerful, Mediterranean-style restaurant. See Chapter 16.

✔ **The Lighthouse Café (Kerry):** The view from the picnic benches will knock your socks off before you've even begun to dig in to the unbelievable seafood chowder and other casual dishes. See Chapter 16.

✔ **The Wild Geese (Limerick):** Dishes at this candlelit restaurant, all made with local ingredients, are daring, modern, and absolutely delicious. Case in point: the onion-and-Parmesan tartlet studded with raisins. In addition, service is some of the most gracious and attentive in Ireland. See Chapter 17.

✔ **Zucchini (Clare):** Fantastic service, beautifully-prepared inventive dishes, and stylish surroundings should make this Ennis newcomer a star. See Chapter 17.

✔ **Nimmo's Wine Bar (Galway):** The inventive dishes here make use of herbs and spices from all over the world, which complement the flavors of the fresh main ingredients. The restaurant overlooks the River Corrib and has a cozy, eclectically decorated interior with a nautical bent. See Chapter 18.

✔ **Brown's Bar and Brasserie (Derry):** How does honey-glazed lamb with mint jus and a tomato, mint, and mozzarella tart sound? This sleek, modern restaurant has a menu full of dishes like these — imaginative creations that take advantage of local ingredients. See Chapter 21.

✔ **Cayenne (Antrim):** There's a reason that all those decked-out folks are crowded into the entranceway of this restaurant: The fusion cuisine here is daring and luscious, featuring bold dishes such as an appetizer of cinnamon quail with carrot, honey, and ginger salad. See Chapter 22.

✔ **Zen (Antrim):** Though I've tried to rein myself in, you'll probably notice my passion for sushi as you read this guide. Boy, was I happy to find this excellent restaurant, where delicious Japanese dishes (sushi and others) are served in ultradramatic surroundings. See Chapter 22.

The Best Castles

You can step back in time and unleash your inner lord or lady at any of the following castles.

✔ **Dublin Castle (Dublin):** Art and history lovers alike will appreciate a tour of Dublin's castle, which has been used in various capacities for the past 800 years. See Chapter 11.

Travel: A study in serendipity

This is probably the most difficult chapter to write, because some of my Ireland "bests" are one-of-a-kind moments, which lack admission fees and open hours — a late-night Irish music session, a great conversation with a Dublin taxi driver, the sun breaking out of the clouds to illuminate a faraway hill. You will have these "bests" too, experiences unique to your trip. Dog-ear this book, mark off everything you want to experience, and make reservations for the best restaurants, but don't forget to be open to those serendipitous experiences that make travel so magical.

- ✔ **Cahir Castle (Tipperary):** This 13th- to 15th-century defensive castle, the setting for the movie *Excalibur,* is one of the best-preserved medieval castles in Ireland. See Chapter 14.

- ✔ **Kilkenny Castle (Kilkenny):** A storybook-castle exterior, a beautiful interior boasting 1830s furnishings, and expansive grounds are the charms of this medieval castle. See Chapter 14.

- ✔ **Blarney Castle and Stone (Cork):** Does this place really need an introduction? You can explore the impressive grounds and well-preserved ruins of this 15th-century castle. And, of course, you can kiss the famed hunk of rock. See Chapter 15.

- ✔ **King John's Castle (Limerick):** One of the finest examples of a fortified Norman structure in Ireland, King John's Castle boasts weapons of defense in the courtyard and a fully restored interior that's open to the public. See Chapter 17.

- ✔ **Bunratty Castle and Folk Park (Clare):** Built in 1425, and featuring an interior that's furnished as it was in the 15th century, Bunratty Castle is one of Ireland's most popular attractions. For the full castle experience, book a seat at one of the medieval banquets held here. See Chapter 17.

- ✔ **Dunguaire Castle (Galway):** Each floor of 16th-century Dunguaire Castle is furnished to reflect a different era in its history. The view of Connemara and Galway Bay from the top of the battlements is incredible. See Chapter 18.

- ✔ **Dunluce Castle (Antrim):** Perched over the crashing waves of the ocean, the stone ruins of 17th-century Dunluce Castle are some of the most picturesque in Ireland. Window openings and doors frame the sea and sky, and you can still see the remains of the giant stone fireplaces. See Chapter 22.

The Best Ruins and Archeological Sites

History buffs will have a field day at any of the following attractions.

✔ **Newgrange (Meath):** Check out the stones carved with geometric designs before entering the passageway of this 5,000-year-old burial chamber. See Chapter 12.

✔ **Glendalough (Wicklow):** A monastic community founded in the sixth century, Glendalough functioned as a community of learning for almost 900 years. As you gaze at the remains of a cathedral, graveyard, and remarkably well-preserved round tower, you can almost hear the passionate exchange of ideas. See Chapter 13.

✔ **Jerpoint Abbey (Kilkenny):** One of the best-preserved monastic ruins in the country, this 15th-century Cistercian Abbey is home to Celtic crosses and stone carvings of knights and dragons. See Chapter 14.

✔ **Rock of Cashel (Tipperary):** Once the province of the high kings of Munster, many of the ruins on this limestone outcropping are tied to St. Patrick, who is said to have explained the Holy Trinity to pagans on this site. See Chapter 14.

✔ **Gallarus Oratory (Kerry):** This tiny seventh-century church, built without any sort of mortar, is one of the Dingle Peninsula's many interesting archaeological sites. See Chapter 14.

✔ **Lough Gur (Limerick):** Evidence shows that this Stone Age settlement was occupied from Neolithic times to medieval times. You can explore diverse ruins here: burial mounds, a wedge tomb, and an impressive 4,000-year-old great stone circle. See Chapter 17.

✔ **Dún Aengus (Galway):** Set on a sheer cliff overlooking the Atlantic Ocean, this giant, well-preserved prehistoric stone fort stretches over 4.4 hectares (11 acres). See Chapter 18.

✔ **Carrowmore Megalithic Cemetery (Sligo):** A tour of this site, the largest collection of megalithic tombs in Ireland, paints a vivid picture of life on the island thousands of years ago. See Chapter 19.

The Best Scenic Drives

Ireland's landscape is so stunning that almost every drive is a scenic drive. Here's a list of my favorite excursions.

✔ **Cooley Peninsula Drive:** This drive, along the rough Irish Sea and pretty Carlingford Lough, travels past *dolmen* (Neolithic tombs), forests, mountains, rivers, and quaint fishing villages. See Chapter 12.

✔ **South East Coastal Drive:** Fishing villages, seaside towns, and coastal vistas are the highlights of this drive. See Chapter 14.

✔ **The Vee:** This drive provides panoramas of lush mountains and farmland laid out like a quilt below. See Chapter 14.

✔ **The Coastal Drive from Skibbereen to Mizen Head:** Cliffs and seascapes are the stars of this drive, which ends at wild-and-wooly Mizen Head, where the Atlantic waves crash on Ireland's south-westernmost point. See Chapter 15.

✔ **The Ring of Kerry:** Give yourself at least a whole day for this winding drive, because you'll be pulling over every couple of minutes to take pictures of the ever-changing seascapes, mountain views, and charming villages along the way. I recommend getting off the Ring drive at some point to explore the beautiful mountains in the interior. See Chapter 16.

✔ **Slea Head tour on the Dingle Peninsula:** This round-trip circuit will make your jaw drop. Highlights include the towering cliffs of Slea Head, incredible views of the Atlantic Ocean and the nearby Blasket islands, and hills covered in a patchwork of small fields. See Chapter 16.

✔ **The Connemara Drive:** The spectacular drive west from Galway, tracing the Galway Bay Coast, features amazing views of the Aran Islands and passes through some adorable seaside towns. Join up with N59 in Maam Cross, and head out to the west, making a big half-circle on your way up to Leenane. This part of your journey affords picture-perfect views of the silent bogs, lush woodlands, and glistening lakes of Connemara. See Chapter 18.

✔ **Drive around Lough Gill:** Take along a book of Yeats's poems as you make the drive around this peaceful blue lake. The lake itself and its many islands (including the famed Lake Isle of Innisfree) feature prominently in the poet's works. See Chapter 19.

✔ **Clew Bay Drive:** This dazzling drive (one of my absolute favorites in Ireland) takes you past the pyramid-shaped peak of Croagh Patrick, through moody bogland, and along glassy Killary Fjord. See Chapter 19.

✔ **The Peninsula north of Donegal Bay:** Make sure that you find the twisty little road to Port as you cruise around the peninsula north of Donegal Bay. See Chapter 20.

✔ **The A2 along the Antrim coast:** The A2 winds along the Antrim coast, past cliffs, beautiful seascapes, and small seaside towns. See Chapter 22.

The Best Golf Courses

Ireland likes to take credit for starting the sport of golf and boasts over 250 courses within its borders (not bad for such a small country). Following are some of the best.

- ✔ **Portmarnock (Dublin):** A rugged natural course, Portmarnock has been home to a number of championships. See Chapter 11.

- ✔ **The K Club (Kildare):** This tough (and expensive) course was designed by Arnold Palmer himself. See Chapter 13.

- ✔ **Old Head Golf Links (Cork):** This challenging course has breathtaking views of the surrounding Atlantic Ocean. See Chapter 15.

- ✔ **Ballybunion Golf Club (Kerry):** This seaside club features two excellent 18-hole, par-71 courses. See Chapter 16.

- ✔ **Royal County Down Golf Club (Down):** The two tough courses here are full of sand dunes, but if you get frustrated with how your game is going, you can distract yourself with the surrounding views of the Mourne Mountains. See Chapter 23.

The Best Natural Wonders

The whole of Ireland seems to me to be a natural wonder, but for this list I've tried to pick out the most extraordinary sights on the island.

- ✔ **The Wicklow Mountains (Wicklow):** If you want green, point yourself towards the lush and rolling Wicklow Mountains. You find leafy woodlands, shimmering lakes, verdant fields, and plenty of walking trails on which to enjoy the surroundings. See Chapter 13.

- ✔ **The Skelligs (Kerry):** A boat ride is the best way to appreciate these rocks, which jut dramatically from the frothing sea below. See Chapter 16.

- ✔ **The Burren (Clare):** This vast expanse of cracked limestone is a strange and stunning place. Though it looks like a forbidding habitat, the Burren supports a wide variety of flora and fauna. A dazzling rainbow of wildflowers pushes up through the cracks, and the diverse array of plants includes species that are usually seen only in the Arctic or Mediterranean. Twenty-six species of butterfly — plus lizards, badgers, frogs, and birds — call this place home. See Chapter 17.

- ✔ **The Cliffs of Moher (Clare):** These sheer cliffs rise more than 213m (700 ft.) above the crashing Atlantic, providing spectacular views of the Clare coast, the Aran Islands, and, on a clear day, mountains as far away as Kerry and Connemara. See Chapter 17.

- ✔ **Connemara (Galway):** Still glacial lakes, stands of evergreens, towering mountains, quiet boglands, and granite moorlands compose the hauntingly beautiful area of Connemara, populated by rugged Connemara ponies. See Chapter 18.

- ✔ **Slieve League (Donegal):** The cliffs of Slieve League are the highest in all of Europe, towering over the turbulent Atlantic. You can take in their grandeur from a viewing area or experience it yourself with a walk along the ridge. See Chapter 20.

- ✔ **The Giant's Causeway (Antrim):** This place practically defines the term *natural wonder.* The landscape is made up of natural six-sided basalt column of varying heights, cascading down into the sea. See Chapter 22.

The Best Pubs

It's no secret that the Irish have a bit of a reputation for being enthusiastic drinkers. Check out a few of these inviting pubs, and maybe you'll understand why.

- ✔ **Cobblestone (Dublin):** This is the real deal — a cozy pub filled with locals and ringing to the rafters with traditional Irish music played by excellent musicians. See Chapter 11.

- ✔ **Jack Meade's (Waterford):** Crackling fires, loud laughter, a warren of small rooms, and terrific pub food conspire to make Jack Meade's a gem in the Waterford countryside. See Chapter 14.

- ✔ **The Long Valley (Cork):** Belly up to the long bar here to drink pints, munch on giant sandwiches, and shoot the breeze with the friendly regulars. See Chapter 15.

- ✔ **The Bulman (Cork):** This pub has it all — crackling fires, good company, live traditional Irish music, great seafood dishes, and a view of beautiful Kenmare Bay. See Chapter 15.

- ✔ **Dick Mack's (Kerry):** One of Ireland's quaintest pubs, Dick Mack's used to double as a cobbler's shop, and one side of the place still holds the leatherworking tools of the trade. The interior hasn't changed in years, which pleases the many locals who frequent this place. See Chapter 16.

- ✔ **The Poet's Corner (Clare):** A warm, always-humming bar located in the Old Ground Hotel, this place offers some of the best traditional Irish music in Ennis, a town known for its formidable traditional music scene. See Chapter 17.

- ✔ **Crane Bar (Galway):** In a city full of excellent traditional Irish music, this is the place to go for the very best. See Chapter 18.

- ✔ **Nancy's (Donegal):** Cozy and welcoming, Nancy's fulfills all my fantasies of stepping into Middle Earth for an evening at a Shire pub. See Chapter 20.

- ✔ **Crown Liquor Saloon (Antrim):** This is one of the most beautiful pubs in all of Ireland, outfitted with carved wood, brass fittings, and gas lamps. You'll be drooling into your Guinness. See Chapter 22.

The Best Literary Sights

Bring a journal and some nice pens, because you're sure to be inspired by the sights associated with Yeats, Joyce, and the other literary stars of Ireland.

- ✔ **Literary Pub Crawl (Dublin):** You'll fall to the floor laughing on this tour of Dublin's pubs led by two actors who perform excerpts taken from the works of many famous Irish writers. See Chapter 11.

- ✔ **James Joyce Centre (Dublin):** Explore exhibits featuring some of Joyce's possessions, the real people who inspired characters in *Ulysses,* and a library of Joyce's works. See Chapter 11.

- ✔ **Dublin Writers Museum (Dublin):** Biographies, works, personal effects, letters, portraits, and photographs of Ireland's literary luminaries are on display here, along with text about Ireland's literary movements. A terrific audio guide complements the exhibits, relating intriguing facts and presenting snippets of literature and conversations read by actors. See Chapter 11.

- ✔ **Abbey Theater (Dublin):** Founded by writers and literature-lovers W. B. Yeats and Lady Gregory, the Abbey Theater presents some of the finest in Irish drama. There are frequent productions of the works of Sean O'Casey and John Millington Synge, two pillars of the Irish theater. See Chapter 11.

- ✔ **Joyce Tower and Museum (Dublin):** This round tower is the setting for the first scene of *Ulysses;* it features Joyce's walking stick, cigar case, and some correspondence, among other objects. See Chapter 11.

- ✔ **Blasket Centre (Kerry):** The Blasket Islands, located a few miles out from the Dingle Peninsula, were home to a hearty, close-knit community of farmers and fisherfolk until the 1950s. This fascinating heritage center explores all the facets of Blasket Island life, with particular attention paid to the storytelling traditions of the Islanders and the published authors who emerged from this community. See Chapter 16.

- ✔ **Angela's Ashes Walking Tour (Limerick):** Fans of Frank McCourt's beautiful and harrowing tale of growing up poor in Limerick City will want to tour the Limerick sites mentioned in the book. See Chapter 17.

- ✔ **Coole Park (Galway):** These grounds once belonged to Lady Gregory, a writer and literary patron who co-founded the Abbey Theater. Be sure to check out the Autograph Tree, where you find the carved initials of such famous wits and writers as George Bernard Shaw, Oliver St. John Gogarty, Sean O'Casey, and W. B. Yeats. See Chapter 18.

✔ **Thoor Ballylee (W. B. Yeats's Summer Home; Galway):** Yeats's poems "The Winding Stair" and "The Tower" were both inspired by this stone house, which has views of the surrounding fields and forests. The house contains a museum devoted to Yeats's life and work. See Chapter 18.

✔ **Lough Gill Cruise (Sligo):** Yeats wrote poems inspired by this lake (including the well-known "Lake Isle of Innisfree"). You can take in the poet's words as you cruise the lake. See Chapter 19.

✔ **The Verbal Arts Centre (Derry):** Devoted to the spoken and written word, the Verbal Arts Centre presents readings, classes, and performances. Check out the glass sculpture in the lobby, which contains poems and prose written by some of Ireland's top authors. See Chapter 21.

Chapter 2

Digging Deeper into Ireland

· ·

In This Chapter

▶ Taking a short course in Irish history

▶ Discovering the mythology, saints, and literary giants of Ireland

▶ Noting language differences

▶ Eating and drinking your way through Ireland

▶ Getting the lowdown on pubs

▶ Appreciating Irish music

▶ Absorbing books and movies about Ireland

· ·

Sure, you need reviews of hotels, restaurants, and attractions when you travel. But for a rich experience, you also need to know about the history and culture of your destination. This chapter gives you the lowdown on Irish history, language, food and drink, music, sports, and other facets of Irish culture.

History 101: The Main Events

Ireland has one of the most intriguing and complex histories of any nation, stretching back to the prehistoric period, and fraught with invasions, battles, and rebellion.

Invaders welcome

From the beginning, Ireland put out a doormat welcoming invaders, or so it seems. Ireland was first inhabited by Mesolithic hunters and fishermen who appeared in the country around 7500 B.C., most likely hailing from Scotland. They were followed by a wave of Neolithic farmers, also from Scotland, who arrived 4,000 years later, around 3500 B.C. Around 450 B.C., or perhaps even earlier, the Celts arrived from Europe, conquering the earlier settlers and spreading the Gaelic culture and language that still thrives today. Nine hundred years later, in the fifth century A.D., Christian missionaries arrived on the shores of Ireland from various parts of Europe and converted much of the Irish population to Christianity. It was at this time that famed missionary St. Patrick converted thousands of Irish; legend says that he explained the Holy Trinity using a shamrock as a visual aid.

The eighth century saw the graceful longboats of the Norse Vikings landing on several Irish coasts. The Vikings raided and plundered their way through Ireland, setting up coastal bases that evolved into the country's first cities — Dublin, Wexford, Waterford, Cork, and Limerick. After almost three centuries of plundering, the Vikings were routed in 1014 by the armies of high king Brian Boru, who was the first leader to preside over all of Ireland. Upon the defeat of the Vikings, Ireland experienced a period of relative peace.

But that peace only lasted a little more than 150 years. In 1169, Diarmuid MacMurrough, the dethroned king of Leinster (the southeastern portion of Ireland) called on the Anglo-Normans, under the leadership of Strongbow, to help him seize back his kingdom. The Anglo-Normans were Vikings who had settled in Normandy and had control over most of Britain. With their superior military, they had no trouble capturing much of Ireland for themselves. Strongbow's prize for his troubles was the hand of MacMurrough's fair-haired daughter, Aoife, in marriage.

Rebels with a cause

In the 14th and 15th centuries, the Celts (also called the Gaels) rose up against both the British and the Anglo-Norman invaders. They succeeded in containing the British in an area around Dublin known as The Pale, but they had no luck in ridding the island of the powerful Norman overlords. In fact, through intermarriage and the adoption of Irish language and culture, the Normans were becoming as Irish as the Irish themselves. Some of the most popular surnames in Ireland today — Fitzgerald, Burke, Joyce — are actually Norman.

In the 16th century, the British launched a reconquest of Ireland under Henry VIII, who declared himself king of Ireland and forced the Irish chieftains to acknowledge his sovereignty. Though Henry VIII did not introduce British colonists to Ireland, his daughter Mary encouraged colonialism after his death, and her sister, Queen Elizabeth I, sent a steady flow of British settlers into Ireland. Due to Henry VIII's split with the church in Rome, Catholic persecution began in Ireland.

In 1601, Gaelic troops joined with a Spanish army to try to squelch the English army, but the English forces triumphed under Lord Mountjoy, and English law was introduced to much of the island, including Ulster, previously the most Gaelic part of Ireland. Defeated, many of the O'Neills and O'Donnells, the most powerful Gaelic clans in Ulster, fled from Ireland. The English government pronounced the O'Neill and O'Donnell lands forfeit to the crown and sent Protestant English and Scottish settlers to develop farms and towns in the area. Naturally, the Irish Catholic inhabitants of Ulster strongly resented the imposition of these Protestant settlers, and thousands were massacred when the Catholic rebelled in 1641. The 17th-century bitterness between the Protestant settlers and the Catholic natives is one of the roots of the modern Troubles in Northern Ireland.

In 1649, eight years after the Catholic rebellion, the ruthless Puritan English leader Oliver Cromwell arrived in Ireland with the goal of taking the whole of Ireland under English control. Cromwell's army raged through Ireland, butchering thousands, and by 1652, three years later, controlled the country. Cromwell dispossessed every Catholic landowner east of the River Shannon, whether Irish or Old English. Connacht and County Clare, west of the Shannon, were used as a "reservation" for Catholics who had not fled the country. Though Catholics caught a glimpse of hope when Catholic King James II came to the throne, it was a brief peek that ended as the Glorious Revolution brought Protestant William of Orange to the throne. James struck back in Ireland, launching the unsuccessful siege of the Protestant walled city of Derry, during which the inhabitants of Derry slammed the city gates shut and remained inside for 105 days, subsisting on rats and other vermin. In what is arguably the most important battle in Irish history, James was trounced by William at the Battle of the Boyne in 1690, giving Protestant England complete control over Ireland.

Penal Laws were enacted that forbade Gaelic and Old English Catholics alike from owning land, practicing law, holding public office, bearing arms, and even practicing Catholicism (though this last tenet was not strictly enforced). These laws were in effect for almost 100 years. They were finally repealed in 1783 as a result of the combination of unrest in rural areas of the country, the need for Irish Catholic recruits to fight in the American War of Independence, and the liberal philosophies of the European Enlightenment.

The French Revolution in 1789 threw kindling on the fire of rebellious feelings that were already smoldering among the Catholics; and, in 1798, war between Britain and France gave Ireland a window of opportunity for another rebellion. Irishman Wolfe Tone conspired with the French to drive the British out of Ireland, but his rebellion failed, claiming more that 30,000 Irish lives. Captured by British forces, Tone slit his own throat rather than face execution by his enemies.

In 1828, 30 years after Tone's rebellion, Daniel O'Connell ran for a Member of Parliament position, even though, as a Catholic, he would not be able to sit as part of the Parliament. O'Connell was elected by a landslide, and the British Prime Minister, striving to avoid a civil war in Ireland, passed the Catholic Emancipation Act, allowing Catholics to sit as members of Parliament. O'Connell spent his time in Parliament fighting tooth and nail for the rights of Catholics, earning him the nickname "The Great Liberator." O'Connell also strove to dissolve the union between Ireland and Britain. O'Connell's progress was stopped in its tracks when the Great Famine struck in 1845, and O'Connell died in 1847.

The population of Ireland, over eight million in 1841, depended on the potato as their main diet staple. When a fungus killed off potato crops for five successive years, beginning in 1845, the island was thrown into turmoil, as previous healthy children dwindled into wraiths and the dead were left unburied because their families were not able to afford coffins. More than one million people died as a result of starvation and another million abandoned Ireland for the shores of the United States, beginning a stretch of Irish emigration that would keep up until the 1930s. While famine tore through the rest of Ireland, Protestant Ulster began to experience an Industrial Revolution, and Belfast blossomed from a small town into an industrial city. Catholics and Protestants both joined the working class in Belfast, and riots between the two groups, spurred by their rancorous history, were common.

Exhausted by the famine, Ireland didn't see a new leader for almost 30 years, until the 1870s and 1880s, when Charles Stewart Parnell emerged on the scene. Parnell, Ireland's representative to the British Parliament, succeeded in uniting different factions of Irish Nationalists, and began the legislative struggle for home rule (Ireland would have its own parliament while still being part of Britain). Parnell was well on his way to realizing this goal when the news broke in 1890 that he was living with the estranged wife of one of his followers. The Irish Catholic hierarchy turned against him as an adulterer, as did his fellow Nationalist members of Parliament. Parnell never regained his popularity and died in 1891.

In the 1900s, Nationalists reunited under leader John Redmond, who managed to pass a Home Rule bill in 1914. However, Redmond promised that Nationalist Ireland would support the English in World War I. While some of his followers agreed with this plan, others did not and broke away to create the separatist Irish Volunteers. The Volunteers staged Ireland's most famous rebellion: On Easter Monday in 1916, 1,500 freedom fighters, led by Patrick Pearse and James Connolly, seized Dublin's General Post Office. They hoisted the tricolor flag from the roof of the post office and Pearse read the Proclamation of the Irish Republic from the front steps. This rebellion led to swift retaliation by the British, who sailed gunboats up the River Liffey and heavily shelled the city. After six days of battle, the rebels were overwhelmed. Connolly, Pearse, and 13 other leaders of the Rising (as the rebellion was called) were taken to Kilmainham Gaol (jail), tried, and shot. The Irish were outraged at the savage executions, especially that of Connolly, who had been so badly injured in the fighting that he couldn't stand and had to be tied to a chair to face the firing squad. The murdered patriots became martyrs in Ireland, and the Irish commitment to fight for freedom was bolstered.

The Irish flag

Ireland's flag — three thick vertical strips of green, white, and orange — was first used by Irish Nationalists in 1848. The green represents Ireland's Nationalist majority (mostly Catholic), the orange represents the Unionist minority (mostly Protestant), and the white stands for the hoped-for peace between them.

In 1918, two years after the Easter Rising, the Nationalist party of Sinn Fein (pronounced shin fane) won the General Election in Ireland. Rather than taking their seats in the British Parliament, they declared an independent Irish parliament. The British were not pleased with this turn of events, and Ireland plummeted into a civil war for independence, led by Michael Collins. A truce was reached in 1921, followed by the Anglo-Irish Treaty, which gave autonomy to 26 of Ireland's 32 counties. The remaining six counties continued on as part of the United Kingdom and became known as Northern Ireland. Many Irish, eager to finally reach peace, accepted the accord for the Irish Free State, even though it kept parts of Ireland in the British Commonwealth. Others, led by Eamon de Valera, refused to accept the treaty. A civil war broke out in 1922 between the pro-treaty and anti-treaty factions. The pro-treaty side emerged victorious in May 1923. The 26 counties officially cut all ties with Britain when the Republic of Ireland Act was passed in 1948.

There was a nervous peace in Northern Ireland for the first half of the 20th century. However, in the late 1960s, Catholics in Northern Ireland began to campaign against religious discrimination in jobs, politics, and housing. Civil rights meetings spiraled into violence, paving the way for the Irish Republican Army (IRA), a Nationalist paramilitary group that organized several terror attacks. Violence continued on both sides up until the Belfast Agreement (also known as the Good Friday Agreement) of 1998, when the Irish voted to make a fresh start with a new government in Belfast. Unfortunately, the new government was suspended in 2000 because paramilitary groups did not disarm by the deadline. In July 2005, the prospects for a lasting peace were strengthened when the paramilitary PIRA (Provisional Irish Republican Army) announced that it had decommissioned all weapons. Though other paramilitary groups have not yet decommissioned their weapons, the past few years have been peaceful, and hopes are running high that the violent conflict has truly come to an end.

The Celtic Tiger and immigration

As you travel throughout Ireland, you will likely notice that many people in the service industry are emigrants from Eastern Europe (especially Poland). Ireland's economy has been quite strong since the mid-1990s, raising living standards dramatically. Many Eastern European workers are taking advantage of the healthy Irish economy and their EU membership and are coming to Ireland to work for more money than they would make at home. Irish citizens have been reacting to this wave of immigration with attitudes ranging from outright xenophobia to warm acceptance.

Who's Who in Irish Mythology

Some of the folks I describe in this section lived more verifiably real lives than others, but all have entered the mythology to such an extent that you're almost sure to hear them mentioned at some point in your trip.

✔ **Children of Lir:** In this legend, the wicked new wife of King Lir *(leer)* puts a spell on his children to turn them into swans for 900 years. She later regrets her evil deed but can't reverse the spell, so she gives the birds the gift of song. A beautiful sculpture depicting the Children of Lir is the centerpiece of Dublin's Garden of Remembrance, and today it is illegal to kill a swan in Ireland.

✔ **Cuchulainn (coo-*cul*-in):** The famous Celtic warrior of ancient myth, Cuchulainn can grow to such enormous size and strength that he can kill scores of men with one swing of a sword. Many legendary stories are told of his feats. A statue stands in Dublin's General Post Office depicting Cuchulainn in bloody action.

✔ **Queen Medb or Maeve *(mave):*** Cuchulainn's enemy, whom legend credits with stealing the prize bull of Ulster and killing Cuchulainn, among other exploits. Is she real or a myth? See the box "The Mystery of Queen Maeve," in chapter 19.

✔ **Finn MacCool:** An Irish hero immortalized in poems by his son Osian and in many *Fenian ballads,* named after the Fenians (or Fianna), professional fighters whom Finn was said to have led in the third century. Finn and his men defended the country from foreign aggressors and hunted for food; these two activities are the main subjects of the stories about him. He is often portrayed as a giant with supernatural powers and is frequently accompanied by his pet hound, Bran.

✔ **Osian (o-*sheen*):** Finn MacCool's son, a great leader and warrior, as well as a talented poet. The name means "fawn," and legend says that his mother spent part of her life as a deer.

Who's Who among Irish Saints

Getting your Patricks and your Brigids mixed up? Here's a primer on three of Ireland's most important saints:

✔ **St. Brigid:** Known for her compassion and generosity, Brigid is probably the best-known saint in Ireland after Patrick. She founded a convent in Kildare and became an abbess there, holding the same rank as a bishop. Her convent became a monastic city of learning, home to a famous school of metalwork and manuscript illumination. Brigid is renowned for her miracles, especially in the realm of healing. Her feast day is February 1.

✔ **St. Columcille (St. Columba):** This saint's pious nature as a young boy earned him the nickname *Columcille,* which means "dove of the church." Columcille was a busy guy, founding dozens of monasteries, including the monastery in Derry and the monastery on the island of Iona, in Scotland, and converting many of the inhabitants of Northern Scotland to Christianity. A great lover of books and a bard himself, Columcille copied hundreds of manuscripts. His feast day is June 9.

✔ **St. Patrick:** The patron saint of Ireland. Brought to the country as a teenage slave, Patrick later escaped, only to return to Ireland with the goal of converting the Irish to Christianity. Though he was not the first Christian missionary, Patrick was perhaps the most influential. In addition to converting a large percentage of the Irish populace, Patrick succeeded in converting several of the Celtic high kings. His feast day is March 17 (sound familiar?).

Who's Who in Irish Literature

The Irish are fiercely proud of their rich literary tradition, and many writers have places of honor around the country. You can't go to County Sligo without tripping over sights related to poet W. B. Yeats; and repeated references to the novels of James Joyce fill Dublin. The walls of theaters around Ireland resonate with the words of playwrights O'Casey, Shaw, Synge, Beckett, and other Irish wordsmiths.

Contemporary Irish literary luminaries include poet Seamus Heaney; playwrights Brian Friel, Conor McPherson, and Martin McDonough; and writer Roddy Doyle, among many, many others.

Following are some bite-size bios of the literary wonders you're most likely to hear about.

✔ **Samuel Beckett (1906–1989):** Most of playwright and novelist Beckett's work deals with lonely and bewildered people in search of an unknown something. The best-known and most performed of his plays is *Waiting for Godot,* which centers on two men waiting endlessly for the arrival of a mysterious character named Godot.

✔ **Brendan Behan (1923–1964):** Behan's youth was full of run-ins with the law, including a stint with the Irish Republican Army in his teens. The playwright, columnist, and novelist is perhaps most famous for *The Borstal Boy,* a novel based on his experiences in jail and reform school; *The Quare Fellow,* a play that draws on his experiences in prison; and *The Hostage,* a play about the events surrounding an IRA member's execution.

✔ **James Joyce (1882–1941):** Though he moved to Continental Europe at age 22, Joyce's four major works — *Portrait of the Artist as a Young Man, Dubliners, Finnegan's Wake,* and *Ulysses* — are all set in Dublin. Joyce is known for his experimentation with language, and his books are rich in puns, metaphor, and wordplay.

✔ **Sean O'Casey (1880–1964):** This famous playwright shocked theatergoers with controversial plays based on his early, poverty-stricken days and the fight for Irish home rule. Best known are *Juno and the Paycock,* the story of a poor family during the 1916 Rising, and *The Plough and the Stars,* which deals with different perspectives on the 1916 Rising.

- ✓ **George Bernard Shaw (1856–1950):** In his works, Socialist Shaw explored moral and social problems with wit and intellect. His most famous plays include *Pygmalion,* the story of plucky Eliza Doolittle; *Major Barbara,* which centers on a Salvation Army major questioning charity and capitalism; and *St. Joan,* about Joan of Arc.

- ✓ **John Millington Synge (1871–1909):** A noted Abbey Theatre playwright, Synge is best remembered for plays that explore the rural life of western Ireland. *Riders to the Sea* focuses on life in a fishing community on the Aran Islands, where the threat of drowning looms over all residents; in *Shadow of the Glen,* a man fakes his death in order to find out if his wife is cheating on him; and in *Playboy of the Western World,* a man is celebrated as a hero for killing his father.

- ✓ **Oscar Wilde (1854–1900):** Wilde is best known for his plays, including *An Ideal Husband,* a political melodrama, and *The Importance of Being Earnest,* a hilarious comedy of manners.

- ✓ **W. B. Yeats (1865–1939):** Poet and playwright Yeats co-founded Dublin's Abbey Theatre. Many of his poems take the landscapes and mythology of Ireland as their themes, while others riff on the struggle for Irish home rule and on love and romance.

Word to the Wise: The Local Lingo

Sure, English is the main language in use in Ireland, but between slang words and the accent, it can sound like a foreign language at times. Read these handy glossaries so that you don't have to have one of those polite but puzzled smiles on your face while talking with locals.

Getting the lingo

Some of the following terms are slang or just Irish usage, and some are authentic Irish Gaelic:

- ✓ **An Lar:** City center (Gaelic)
- ✓ **Bonnet:** Car hood
- ✓ **Boot:** Car trunk
- ✓ **Bord Fáilte (bord *fal*-cha):** Irish Tourist Board (Gaelic)
- ✓ **Cheers:** "Thanks"
- ✓ **Class:** Great (as in "Lauren is class at playing the tin whistle.")
- ✓ **Craic, crack (*crak*):** Good times, fun (Gaelic)
- ✓ **Creche:** Day care
- ✓ **Deadly, brilliant:** Great, excellent
- ✓ **Dear:** Expensive

The Irish language in contemporary Ireland

Irish Gaelic (usually called "Irish" in Ireland) and English are the official languages of Ireland. Almost the entire population speaks English, and about 95 percent of the population uses English as their primary language. About a million and a half of Ireland's five million residents can speak at least a few words of Irish Gaelic (the language is now taught in all public schools), and about 600,000 people use Gaelic as their first language. Gaelic-speaking areas are called *Gaeltacht* (pronounced *gale*-tokt) and are concentrated in the west of Ireland, though they are found all over the island.

- **Dodgy:** Suspect (as in "I wouldn't eat those clams. They smell dodgy.")
- **Fáilte (pronounced *fal*-cha):** "Welcome" (Gaelic)
- **Fir:** Men (Gaelic, sometimes used on bathroom doors)
- **Footpath:** Sidewalk
- **Garda:** Police officer (plural is gardaí, [*gar*-dee])
- **Go Away (or go [']way):** "Wow!" In the U.S.: "Get out of here!"
- **Gaff:** House
- **Grand:** Great (as in "Would you like some more Guinness?" "Thanks, that'd be grand.")
- **Hash:** Pound sign (on telephone keypads and the like)
- **Lads:** A group of people, regardless of gender (often used to address a group, like "y'all" in the American south)
- **Lift:** Elevator
- **Mna (muh-*nah*):** Women (Gaelic, sometimes used on bathroom doors)
- **Off-license:** Liquor store
- **Petrol:** Gasoline
- **Press:** Cabinet
- **Poitín (pot-*cheen*):** Moonshine, homemade whiskey
- **Ring:** To telephone (as in "I'll ring you later.")
- **Stroke:** Slash (as in "girls/women")
- **Quay *(key)*:** Waterfront, wharf
- **Quid, sterling, or bob:** Pounds, or money

- **Slainte! (*slon*-cha):** Cheers! (Gaelic)
- **Take-away:** Fast food, to go
- **Till:** Cash register
- **Tins:** Canned goods
- **Windscreen:** Windshield

Avoiding misunderstandings

In Ireland (especially Northern Ireland), holding your pointer and middle fingers up in a *V* with your palm facing inward is the same as raising your middle finger to someone. Careful when ordering two pints!

Curses are used rather liberally in Ireland, and you'll probably encounter people saying "shite" as they drop something or "for feck's sake" (the equivalent of "for God's sake") when their favorite football team misses a goal.

The following words and phrases have definitions that are quite different in Ireland than they are in other parts of the world.

- **Cute hoor (pronounced like *whore*):** Boy, does this one have a different meaning than it does in many other countries. In Ireland, *cute* is often used to mean someone who is sly or devious, and a *cute hoor* is a devious person. The phrase is almost always used to describe a man, rather than a woman, and is often used to describe politicians.
- **Fag:** Cigarette.
- **Fanny:** Female genitalia.
- **Flaming:** Drunk.
- **Ride:** Sex or an attractive person. So ask for a lift if you're looking for someone to drive you somewhere.
- **Take the piss out of** (as in, "We were just taking the piss out of him."): Messing with or teasing; another phrase for this is "slagging you."

Irish slang translation: Yer man

If you tour around Ireland for a while, you'll probably hear people referring to *yer man* (as in, "I was talking to *yer man* the other day . . ."). You may well wonder who this incredibly popular person is. Well, he's the fella Americans call *this guy* (for example, "I was talking to *this guy* the other day . . .") and British call "this bloke." You may also hear yer man's feminine counterpart, *yer won*.

Taste of Ireland: Irish Cuisine and Dining

If you think of shepherd's pie, Irish stew, and mashed potatoes when you think of Irish cuisine, you're right. But that's only half the story: In the past few decades, Ireland has seen huge changes in the food scene. A stroll down a row of restaurants is like paging through a book about the world's cuisines. Especially in larger towns and cities, you can find everything from Italian restaurants that would make the Sopranos proud, to Indian restaurants serving fiery curries, to sushi.

Along with these ethnic eateries is a bevy of restaurants creating New Irish cuisine — innovative dishes that showcase the best of Ireland's fresh produce and incorporate international influences. Typical dishes? How about fresh Irish salmon served with wasabi-infused mashed potatoes or local free-range beef with a Thai curry sauce?

If you're in the market for traditional Irish dishes, your best bet is a pub, where you find hearty offerings such as Irish stew, thick vegetable soups, and ploughman's lunches (cheese, pickles, and bread). But even pub grub reflects the influences of the last few decades. The dishes are better than ever, many chefs use as much local produce as possible, and international twists are found in many dishes (who knew that chile jam would go so well with Gubbeen, a West Cork cheese?). And you'd better sit down for what I'm going to say next: Many traditional pubs now squeeze salads and other healthy options onto the menu.

If you want something quick and inexpensive, try a pub or head for one of the loads of small cafes and lunch counters that offer soups and sandwiches. Even more plentiful are *chippers* and *take-aways*, fast-food places where you can get, among other things, traditional fish and chips.

 If you have your heart set on eating at a posh restaurant in one of the larger cities during the summer or on a weekend (or on a summer weekend!), make reservations. For the poshest of the posh restaurants, it's a good idea to make reservations no matter what time of year it is.

See Chapter 24 for my top ten traditional Irish meal and beverage suggestions.

Checking out meal prices

You probably won't have to pay for breakfast, which comes standard with almost every hotel and B&B room and is often quite comprehensive. Lunch typically sets you back around €12 ($19) if you eat in a restaurant or as little as €6 ($9.60) if you have fast food or carry-out, like the ubiquitous fish and chips.

Dinner is more expensive, with entrees ranging from €14 ($22) to €17 ($27) on the low end to €29 ($46) and way up on the high end. After you factor in wine and service, the tab can get rather high. See the introduction for the price scale used in this book.

Many restaurants offer early-bird (usually about 5:30–7:30 p.m.) fixed-price multicourse dinners that are terrific bargains; and several top-of-the-line restaurants offer great fixed-price lunch deals as well. In both cases, the dishes are often the same as those you'll see for much higher prices on the a la carte dinner menu. I include other dining-related money-saving tips in Chapter 5.

Minding your manners: Irish meal times and dining customs

The lowdown on Irish dining habits: You may notice that the Irish, like many Europeans, keep the knife in their right hand and lift food on the fork with the left hand. Table settings are the same, except that a large soup spoon often lies across the top of your place setting.

In Ireland, breakfast begins around 7 a.m. and finishes at 10 or 11 a.m. Lunch goes from noon to about 3 p.m., with 1 to 2 p.m. being the busiest time. Dinner is usually served from about 6 to 10 p.m., sometimes going until 11 p.m. on weekends.

 Your server won't bring the check until you ask for it.

For information on tipping, see Chapter 5.

Deciphering the menu

Here are a few food terms that you may not have run up against before

- ✔ **Aubergines:** Eggplants
- ✔ **Bangers:** Sausages
- ✔ **Barn brack:** A cakelike bread
- ✔ **Boxty:** Potato pancakes filled with meats and vegetables
- ✔ **Champ:** Mashed potatoes with green onions
- ✔ **Chipper:** Fast-food fish-and-chips shop
- ✔ **Chips:** French fries
- ✔ **Colcannon:** Mashed potatoes with cabbage
- ✔ **Coriander:** Cilantro
- ✔ **Courgette:** Zucchini
- ✔ **Crisps:** Potato chips
- ✔ **Fry or fry up:** A traditional Irish fried breakfast
- ✔ **Darne:** A slice of fish (often on the bone)
- ✔ **Dublin coddle:** A thick stew made with sausages, bacon, onions, and potatoes

✔ **Goujons:** Small strips or chunks of chicken, fish, or red meat

✔ **Mange tout:** Snap peas

✔ **Marie Rose sauce:** A ketchup and mayonnaise-based sauce

✔ **Mash:** Mashed potatoes

✔ **Minerals:** Soft drinks

✔ **Ploughman's lunch:** A lunch of cheese, bread, and pickles

✔ **Prawns:** Shrimp

✔ **Rasher:** Bacon (American-style bacon is referred to as crispy or American bacon)

✔ **Rocket:** Arugula (a gourmet salad green)

✔ **Salad:** Aside from its universal meaning, *salad* also indicates a garnish of lettuce and tomato on a sandwich

✔ **Sambo:** Slang for sandwich

✔ **Shepherd's pie:** Ground beef and vegetables topped with mashed potatoes

✔ **Starter:** Appetizer

✔ **Sultanas:** Similar to raisins

✔ **Take-away:** Carry-out or take-out food

Living the Pub Life

Visiting Ireland without stepping foot into a pub would be like going to Egypt and missing the pyramids. Pubs serve as the beating heart of communities around Ireland, offering witty conversation, laughter, fabulous music (often traditional Irish), great pub food, and, of course, drinks. If you want to find out who's dating who, you go to the pub. If you're upset and need a shoulder to cry on, drag yourself to the pub. If you are keen to discuss current politics, existential philosophy, or anything in between, get thee to a pub. And if you want groceries? Well, in the past (and still today in some tiny towns), many pubs had two or even three extra functions on top of providing liquor: serving as grocery stores, post offices, blacksmith shops, undertakers, and so on.

Pubs originated centuries ago, when groups of friends would gather in someone's living room or kitchen to chat and perhaps play some music, dance, and drink some home-brewed liquor. Word of the friendliest places spread, attracting more and more people, and the houses gradually became known as *public houses,* shortened to *pubs.*

There is as wide a variety of pubs as there are folks who drink in them: music pubs; literary pubs (both those that appear in literature and those that writers frequented and still frequent); sports pubs; actors' pubs; even political pubs, where revolutionaries met in secret to plan uprisings. Pub designs also run the gamut. Most familiar are those shiny Victorian dark-wood pubs that show up in cities around the world. But there are also pubs that look like someone's well-loved living room, with tattered, mismatched furniture and dusty books; and, on the other end of the spectrum, modern, streamlined pubs that look an awful lot like clubs.

In many pubs, you may notice small partitioned areas called *snugs.* These small compartments are great places for quiet conversation or to get away from the crowd. But that's not what they were for originally. Until the late 1960s, it was impolite for women to drink in public, so they were confined to the snugs. The barman would pass drinks (only half-pint glasses, of course!) through a small opening.

Figuring out pub hours and drink prices

Pubs can now make their own hours, which means that many are staying open later than they used to. Most pubs are open all day, closing between midnight and 2 a.m.

Wondering what a night in a pub will run you? Ballpark figures are about €4 ($4.80) for a pint in a small town to as much as €5 ($6) in the city. The price for a glass of liquor (called a *short*) ranges from €3 ($3.60) on the low end to €4 ($4.80) for the more expensive areas. Nondrinkers may be shocked to discover that a small bottle of soda costs nearly the same as a pint of Guinness.

Paying attention to pub etiquette

 If you're drinking with a group, think rounds. Everyone (including guests) takes turns buying drinks for the group, even if "the group" is a bunch of people you've just met.

The larger size glass is called a *pint,* and the smaller one (which measures a half-pint) is called a *glass.* If you're ordering hard cider, you may be asked if you want a glass of ice with it. Contrary to what I first thought, this is not a joke and actually makes the drink even more refreshing.

Bartenders do not expect a tip unless they have provided table service. Instead, it is customary to buy the bartender a drink every once in a while.

The Irish version of "cheers" is *slainte* — pronounced *slon*-cha and meaning "health."

If you're hanging out in a traditional music session and someone asks you to perform, they usually really mean it. If you're up for it, recite a poem or sing a song — doesn't matter if it's not Irish.

Finally, if you order a mixed drink (a vodka tonic, for instance), don't be surprised if the barkeep hands you a glass with ice and liquor and a bottle of tonic.

There are worse things than being locked in a pub

Very occasionally, a publican decides to allow patrons to stay in a pub after closing hours. This is called a *lock-in* because the doors are locked and the curtains pulled (and the lights are sometimes dimmed) so that no one else can come in and allegedly so that the gardaí (police) will not think that anyone is in the pub. Locks-ins are great fun and an excellent way to get to know locals, as the wee hours are filled with lively conversation, laughter, and often rollicking traditional Irish music. One of my best nights (mornings?) in Ireland was spent in pub in a tiny Clare town, learning new Irish tunes from several fantastic musicians until about 5 a.m. Lock-ins are much more common in small towns and rural pubs than in big-city pubs.

Savoring the black stuff: Guinness

The pints of Guinness in Ireland taste nothing like Guinness elsewhere. Call it the home-court advantage, or credit the fact that the stuff is as fresh as all get-out in Ireland, but it's a fact that the Guinness you drink in Ireland is a high cut above the Guinness anywhere else.

When Arthur Guinness took over a small brewery in Dublin, he had fantastic foresight. He may not have known then that his brew would account for one of every two pints sold in Ireland or would be sold in more than 150 countries, but he definitely was going for longevity — in 1759, he signed a 9,000-year lease on the brewery's site!

I want to clear up a few misconceptions about Guinness. One misconception is that it has a huge number of calories. Actually, a pint of Guinness has about as many calories as a pint of orange juice — around 260. Another misconception is that Guinness is a particularly heavy drink, an idea that probably comes from the look of it. Really, Guinness is very easy to drink and refreshing — don't let the thick head scare you.

Finally, five words to live by: A good pint takes time. Barkeeps draw the pint about three-quarters and let it sit for about two minutes. Then, by pushing the tap forward so the stout comes out even more slowly than the first draw, they fill the glass the rest of the way (some fill the glass in a three-step process). This slowness isn't cruel taunting; it's how a real pint is pulled and is how you get the best creamy, white head on top. Even when you finally get the pint in your hands, don't drink just yet. Wait until it has settled completely and has turned a deep ruby, almost black. A good test is to take a coin and tap it against the glass, working upward. When the coin makes a heavy thud throughout the glass, rather than a tinny tap, your brew is ready. You can also tell a good pint of Guinness by the circle of foam that it leaves on the inside of the glass with each sip.

Sampling other Irish brews

As hard is it may be to believe, Guinness doesn't have a complete monopoly on Irish beer. Some of the other popular Irish brews are Harp, a light lager that's good for people who aren't into dark beers; Caffrey's, an ale that settles like a stout; Smithwick's, a dark ale; Kilkenny, a red ale with a sweet malty taste and a creamy head like Guinness; Murphy's Amber, a light ale; Murphy's Stout, which is a bit sweeter than Guinness; and Bulmers Cider, a sweet, entirely too drinkable hard cider.

Sipping some Irish whiskey

Monks did a lot for Ireland. They painstakingly crafted the Book of Kells. They protected Irish antiquities in their round towers during invasions. But ask your average man on an Irish street, and he may say that the best thing monks did for Ireland was invent whiskey.

You read that right — monks invented whiskey. In about the sixth century, missionary monks brought the secret of distillation home from the Middle East, forever changing the face of Ireland. Irish whiskey is known all over the world for its smoothness and quality, and it has brought Ireland huge revenues over the centuries. The original Gaelic term for whiskey, *uisce beatha* (*ish*-ka *ba*-ha) means "water of life." Even today, every European country that distills a native spirit refers to theirs as the water of life: *eau de vie* in France, *akvavit* in Scandinavia, *Lebenswasser* in Germany, *agua de la vida* in Spain, and *aqua della vita* in Italy.

Whiskey became more than just a home brew in 1608, when the world's first distillery license was given to Old Bushmills Distillery. Next came John Jameson & Son in 1780 and John Powers & Son in 1791. These licenses blew open the whiskey export trade in Ireland, and the world's love affair with Irish whiskey began. By the end of the 19th century, more than 400 brands were available in America alone.

The money stopped rolling in when Prohibition was introduced in the United States in 1919. Bootleggers began distributing lousy liquor under the respected name of Irish whiskey, destroying its reputation. Meanwhile, Ireland and England were engaged in an economic war and stopped buying each other's products completely. With Irish whiskey out of the

Guinness versus Murphy's

Wondering what the difference is between Guinness and Murphy's Stout? Well, employees at St. James's Gate, where Guinness is brewed, have an idea. According to rumor, a drawing inside the brewery shows a donkey drinking from a trough labeled "Guinness." Behind the donkey is another trough, into which the animal is urinating. This trough, of course, is labeled "Murphy's." I assume Murphy's has its own ideas about its rival.

picture, Scotch jumped in to fill the void. Only recently has Irish whiskey become internationally popular again.

Irish whiskey has a distinctive smoothness, which results from triple-distillation (American whiskey is distilled only once and Scotch, twice).

If you're interested in the distillation of Irish whiskey, three historic and popular distilleries are open for tours: **The Old Bushmills Distillery,** County Antrim (☎ 028-2073-3218); **The Old Jameson Distillery,** Dublin (☎ 01-872-5566); and **The Old Midleton Distillery,** Cork (☎ 021-461-3594).

Sampling poteen

You may have heard of a potent potable called poteen and wondered just what it is. Well, *poteen* (or potcheen or poitín) is unlawfully distilled clear whiskey, banned since 1661. Basically, it's the Irish equivalent of moonshine, originally made from potatoes. Recently, some companies have started to produce a legal poteen (which still contains a huge amount of alcohol), so you may see it around Ireland.

Appreciating Irish Music

This should say something about the importance of music in Ireland: It's the only nation in the world with a musical instrument as a national symbol. The Tara Harp appears on all official documents of the Irish government. You can see the oldest harp in Ireland on display in the Old Library of Trinity College in Dublin (see Chapter 11).

Traditional Irish music (often called *trad*) has been around for centuries and is an integral part of Irish culture, woven into the daily lives of many Irish people. In fact, you'd be hard-pressed to find an Irish person who doesn't know at least a few tunes or songs. Irish traditional music is a living tradition, and new tunes and songs are constantly incorporated into the repertoire, from a snappy new fiddle tune called "Millennium Eve" to a song about the war in Iraq. Trad has been enjoying a huge surge in international popularity since the late 1960s and the 1970s, when traditional groups such as the Clancy Brothers, the Dubliners, and

Turlough O'Carolan

Turlough O'Carolan (1670–1738) is a famous harper and composer (sometimes referred to simply as "Carolan"). After smallpox blinded him in his teens, he learned to play the harp; and for the rest of his years, he traveled throughout Ireland as an itinerant musician and bard, composing tunes for patrons across Ireland. He wrote more than 200 compositions that are still played today, more than 300 years later.

the Wolfe Tones began to tour. The music has become hotter and hotter, with international superstars like Solas, Altan, and the Corrs playing to sold-out audiences all over the world.

The best place to hear Irish music is in a pub. Offerings range from scheduled ballad singers to pick-up traditional instrumental *sessions,* sometimes open to anyone who shows up. Ballad singers sing a range of Irish songs, accompanying themselves on guitar, from upbeat tunes about a night of boisterous drinking to slow songs about the death of an Irish freedom fighter. Instrumental sessions can range from small, planned, miked sessions to giant acoustic sessions open to anyone who wants to play. In instrumental sessions, you often find tin whistles (also called *penny whistles* — thin, recorder-type instruments), wooden Irish flutes, fiddles (the same as violins; just played differently), bodhráns (handheld goatskin drums; pronounced *bow*-rons), mandolins, uilleann pipes (the Irish version of bagpipes; pronounced *ill*-un), concertinas (small accordion-type instruments), and accordions. Other instruments

Starting your Irish music collection

The following six CDs are a great beginning — or addition — to your Irish musical library:

✔ **From the Beginning: The Chieftains 1 to 4 (1999):** Along with several other groups, The Chieftains are responsible for popularizing traditional Irish music. The musicians are top-notch, playing a gorgeous collection of tunes on these four compilation CDs.

✔ **Live in Seattle: Martin Hayes & Dennis Cahill (1999):** Fiddler Martin Hayes and guitar player Dennis Cahill are an unbelievable pair. Hayes is a virtuoso known for his breathtaking improvisations and ornaments on traditional tunes, and Cahill provides the perfect back-up.

✔ **Lake Effect: Liz Carroll (2002):** Chicago-born Liz Carroll is one of my favorite fiddle players. She uses stunning ornamentation and variations in her playing, and composes fabulous new tunes.

✔ **Music at Matt Molloy's (1992):** This CD is as close as you can get to an Irish music session in your living room without inviting a bunch of musicians over. Crack open a can of Guinness and listen to the wild reels, jigs, and songs, all recorded live in Chieftain musician Matt Molloy's Pub in Westport, County Mayo.

✔ **Solas (1996):** This CD features some of the most beautiful and spirited playing of Irish supergroup Solas. Singer Karan Casey's voice is as clear and pure as spring water, giving life to the English and Gaelic songs that pop up between the instrumental tunes.

✔ **The Well-Tempered Bow: Liz and Yvonne Kane (2002):** I swear that I also like musicians who don't play the fiddle and aren't named Liz! That said, this CD, by fiddle-playing sisters from Connemara, contains lovely tunes played with grace and style.

that show up include bones (animal bones used for rhythmic accompaniment), guitars, banjos, harmonicas, bouzuki, and harps.

If you have been turned on to Irish traditional music and want to find sessions near your home, check out the geographic search feature on www.thesession.org.

Background Check: Recommended Books and Movies

Ireland has produced a wealth of wonderful literary figures and has its share of great filmmakers. The books and movies in the following sections should enhance your appreciation and understanding of the island. Also see "Who's Who in Irish Literature," earlier in this chapter.

Fiction

For a look at Dublin in the beginning of the 20th century, wrap your mind around the works of James Joyce, including his famous novels *A Portrait of the Artist As a Young Man, Finnegan's Wake,* and *Ulysses,* and his short story collection, *Dubliners.*

Roddy Doyle offers a funny and sometimes poignant look at contemporary Ireland in his novels, which include *Paddy Clarke Ha Ha Ha, A Star Called Henry,* and the trilogy *The Commitments* (the basis of the movie), *The Snapper,* and *The Van.*

Other novels to check out include:

- *Finbar's Hotel,* edited by Dermot Bolger, is composed of seven intertwining short stories by seven well-known Irish novelists.
- Niall Williams' *Four Letters of Love* is a mystical, poetic, romantic novel set in Galway.
- *Juno and Juliet,* by Julian Gough, is a beautifully written contemporary novel about a pair of twins away for college in Galway.

Autobiography

If you haven't read it yet, pick up *Angela's Ashes,* Frank McCourt's wrenching novel about growing up in poverty in Limerick.

Written by former IRA member Ernie O'Malley, *On Another Man's Wound: A Personal History of Ireland's War of Independence* is a fascinating collection of memoirs about Ireland's fight for independence between 1916 and 1921.

Great Blasket Island, off the coast of the Dingle Peninsula, was home to a small and very traditional Irish community up until the 1950s. This island of storytellers produced several excellent writers. In *Peig: The*

Autobiography of Peig Sayers of the Great Blasket Island, the epony-mous author relates the hardships and joys of life on the island. *Twenty Years A-Growing,* by Maurice O'Sullivan, is a beautifully written, inno-cent book about growing up on Great Blasket.

 McCarthy's Bar: A Journey of Discovery in the West of Ireland, by Pete McCarthy, is a hilarious travelogue about journalist Pete McCarthy's ramblings around Ireland.

Also in the humorous vein, *Round Ireland With a Fridge,* by Tony Hawks, is about . . . well . . . a guy who travels around Ireland with a refrigerator.

Poetry

Poetry is where you hit the jackpot in Ireland. The gorgeous, mystical poems of W. B. Yeats are a wonderful introduction to the mythology, his-tory, and landscapes of Ireland. *Collected Poems: 1909–1962* is the best anthology.

For beautifully spun poems about farming, rural life, and the Irish land-scape, pick up Patrick Kavanagh's *Collected Poems.*

Seamus Heaney's poems about the land are rhythmic and powerful, sounding like music when read aloud. *Opened Ground: Selected Poems 1966–1996* is a great sampler of his poems, and *The Haw Lantern, Death of A Naturalist, The Spirit Level,* and *District and Circle* — all collections — are gems.

History and politics

A Short History of Ireland, by John O'Beirne Ranelagh, gives an overview of Irish history from pre-Christian times to 1998. If you'd like something more comprehensive, pick up the *Oxford History of Ireland* by R. F. Foster. For a look at Irish nationalism, check out *The Green Flag* by Robert Kee.

There are quite a few books out about the political situation in Northern Ireland. Among the best are *We Wrecked The Place,* by Jonathan Stevenson, which features interviews with both Loyalist and Unionist militants, and *The Troubles: Ireland's Ordeal 1966–1996 and the Search for Peace,* by Tim Pat Coogan, a history with a Republican slant.

How the Irish Saved Civilization, by Thomas Cahill, is a lively history of how Irish monks and scribes preserved the great written works of the West when the rest of Europe was immersed in the Dark Ages.

Movies

The Quiet Man (1952) is a version of *The Taming of the Shrew,* set in a small Irish village. John Wayne plays a boxer returning to the village to woo beautiful Maureen O'Hara. In *Ryan's Daughter* (1970), filmed on the Dingle Peninsula, a married woman grapples with her love for a World War I British officer.

On the comedy front, *The Commitments* (1990) is the often-humorous story of a motley crew of working-class Dubliners who form a soul band. You'll laugh through *Waking Ned Devine* (1998), which captures a tiny Irish village turned upside down when one of their own wins the lottery and then promptly dies. *The Boys and Girls of County Clare* (2003) is a funny, quirky, and sweet film about two brothers competing against each other in a traditional Irish music competition. All the great traditional music featured is reason enough to watch the movie.

The Secret of Roan Inish (1996), a magical film that both kids and adults enjoy, centers on a *selkie* — a half-woman–half-seal creature from Celtic mythology — and her impact on an Irish family. In the same magical realism vein, *Into the West* (1992) tells the story of two Irish gypsy boys who travel from the slums of Dublin to the west of Ireland in pursuit of their lost horse.

For a realistic and sweet look at Dublin today, rent *Once* (2006), a modern-day realistic musical (with a gorgeous soundtrack) about two young Dubliners who build a relationship through music.

Quite a few excellent movies have been made about Irish politics. *Michael Collins* (1996) depicts the life of Collins, leader of the Irish Republican Army (IRA), from the Easter Uprising of 1916 to his assassination six years later. *In The Name of the Father* (1993) deals with a man wrongly convicted for an IRA bombing. *The Boxer* (1997) is the story of an ex-IRA man and former boxer building a new life in Belfast. *The Wind That Shakes The Barley* (2006) is an excellent film about two brothers during the Irish War of Independence (from 1921–22) and the subsequent Civil War (from 1922–23).

Chapter 3

Deciding When and Where to Go

In This Chapter
▶ Discovering the Emerald Isle, region by region
▶ Deciding how to spend your time in Ireland
▶ Choosing a time of year to visit
▶ Experiencing Ireland's best festivals and events

*W*ould you rather gaze at the rainbows that show up during the spring in Ireland or enjoy the solitude of the countryside during the winter? Do you want to experience Galway's Arts Festival in July or Cork City's Jazz Festival in October? Should you base yourself in one place and take daytrips or go the nomadic route? This chapter can help you decide when to visit Ireland and gives you tips for planning your itinerary.

Going Everywhere You Want to Be

Should you fly into Shannon or Dublin? Do you want to see the Ring of Kerry or Donegal? Is Northern Ireland worth a visit? The information in this section is a quick primer on the various regions of the island so you can make informed choices about where to spend your precious vacation time. The "Ireland's Regions" map shows the breakdown of the areas I talk about in the following sections.

Experiencing the vibrant Dublin area

People often fly into Dublin airport and set off for the western part of the country, with its dramatic scenery, before their plane even comes to a complete stop. Unless you know there's an honest-to-goodness pot o' gold waiting for you out west, there's no reason to rush away. **Dublin,** with its big-time hotels, restaurants, shops, clubs, pubs, and museums, is a vibrant city with plenty to hold your attention (Chapter 11 covers this city). South of the city, the counties **Wicklow** and **Kildare** (see Chapter 13) offer green hills, loads of outdoor activities, and some of the most beautiful gardens in Ireland. And just north of Dublin are counties **Meath** and **Louth,** which contain magnificent prehistoric ruins (see Chapter 12).

Touring the southeastern counties

The southeastern counties of **Wexford, Waterford, Kilkenny,** and **Tipperary** offer the famous Waterford Crystal Factory, the bustling harbor town of Wexford, the medieval streets and storybook castle of Kilkenny Town, verdant farmland, the historic Rock of Cashel, and more. Sound good? It is — read Chapter 14 to find out more.

Swinging by the southern and southwestern counties

Cork City is a bustling place, with terrific restaurants and a healthy arts scene, plus an array of diverse attractions nearby, including a wildlife park and the Blarney Stone. West Cork County offers quaint towns, including **Kinsale,** the gourmet capital of Ireland, plus stunning cliff, beach, and island scenery.

If the southern counties of Ireland were a high school, **County Kerry** would be the prom queen. It's long been Ireland's hottest tourist spot, offering awe-inspiring vistas of the sea, cliffs, and green mountains (most commonly viewed on a drive around the **Ring of Kerry** or the **Dingle Peninsula**), plus a number of lively towns and a rich offering of Gaelic culture.

Wandering the western counties

The west of Ireland offers the wonderful city of **Galway,** with its great restaurants, excellent pubs (including plenty with traditional Irish music), and hot arts scene. Then there's the incredible scenery of the West, including the beaches and sheer **Cliffs of Moher** in **Clare;** the wild, mountain-filled landscape of **Connemara;** the woods, lakes, and beaches of **Sligo;** and the craggy coastline of **Donegal.**

Rambling through Northern Ireland

When you cross that invisible border between the Republic and Northern Ireland, the first thing you're likely to notice is that you don't notice anything different. The landscape is as green, and the people are as friendly. Highlights are the rolling **Mourne Mountains,** the spectacular **North Antrim** coast, the hopping city of **Belfast,** and the history-rich city of **Derry.**

Scheduling Your Time

You can put together your own custom trip in numerous ways, but the two easiest methods for seeing Ireland on your own are the base-camp approach and the nomadic approach. Check out Chapter 4 for some suggested itineraries.

Settling on the base-camp approach

For this approach, pick two or three cities or towns, and make daytrips out from them. Base yourself in lovely cities like **Kinsale** or **Kenmare** (to explore the South), **Galway** (for the West), **Dublin** (for Dublin City and the areas south and north), and **Belfast** (for the North). If you have only one week, and you've never been to Ireland before, you may want to plant yourself in Dublin for a couple of days and then move out to the West of Ireland.

Many top sights are within an easy drive of these base-camp towns. By staying a couple of nights in the same place, you save the time and hassle of switching hotels every day and worrying about check-in and check-out times.

 Self-catering accommodations (lodgings with kitchens and laundry facilities) are a cost-efficient option that families and groups choosing the base-camp approach may want to consider. For more information, check out Chapter 8.

Opting for the nomadic approach

I recommend touring Ireland with a car and moving from place to place over the course of your vacation. I've laid out this guidebook to introduce areas in a counterclockwise direction from Dublin City. If you take the nomadic approach, plan your itinerary so that you make some sort of circuit, starting and then finishing in the city where you arrive and depart Ireland.

 If you want to see both the East and the West of Ireland and you have limited time, I highly recommend flying into Dublin and out of Shannon, or vice versa. It won't cost you any more than booking a round-trip to and from the same airport, and it's a great time-saver.

 It's sometimes better to forgo seeing a few places entirely than to try to fit too much in. Ireland is a country that invites lingering over meals, spending late nights in the pub, and just parking the car and taking an impromptu ramble.

Revealing the Secrets of the Seasons

This section presents the highlights and drawbacks of the four seasons.

Summer

The most popular and arguably the best time to tour Ireland is the summer.

Summer is great because

✔ Ireland is just plain gorgeous during this time of year. Try to think of your hotel's high-season rates as a cover charge for the great weather. Temperatures often stay comfortably warm and breezy during the day and drop to that perfect light-sweater temperature at night. Don't hold me to this forecast — you'll still get caught in the rain, but it will be a bearable, if not pleasant and refreshing, experience.

✔ Summer is when all attractions are open and offer the longest hours; some attractions (mostly in smaller towns) abbreviate their hours or close completely during the off season.

✔ Daylight lasts seemingly forever (until at least 11 p.m. at the height of summer), giving you extra time for sightseeing.

But keep in mind that

✔ Every major attraction, hotel, and restaurant is likely to be jam-packed. If you'd rather escape crowds, this is not the time to go.

✔ Lodging prices are at their highest during this time.

Fall

Fall is probably the most underrated time to visit Ireland — days are mild, with not too much rain, and daylight lasts until nearly 9 p.m., which is great for marathon sightseeing.

Fall is great because

✔ In late September or early October, hotel prices start to drop. Even some restaurants offer menus with lower prices.

✔ You won't find the overwhelming crowds you do in summer, but there are still enough people traveling the country that the smaller towns don't feel desolate. Plus you're more likely to have the chance to hang out with the Irish folks, because they're back from their summer holidays.

But keep in mind that

✔ Weather can be a little dicey sometimes, with cold temperatures and rain beginning to settle in.

Winter

Although winter is not the ideal time to travel to Ireland, there are a few benefits to going in this harsh season.

Winter is great because

- ✔ Prices are at their lowest all across the country, and you're likely to find the cheapest fares of the year to get to the country.

- ✔ You're liable to have the run of the country. And the landscape is still beautiful — winter doesn't take as hard a toll on Ireland's plants and trees as it does in many areas of North America.

But keep in mind that

- ✔ Ireland is spared snow, for the most part, and the temperature doesn't dip to extreme lows; but the forecast is often cold, rainy, and windy.

- ✔ Lots of places close for the season, including many attractions and some small hotels and B&Bs. If they don't close, attractions often have much shorter hours.

Spring

Spring is a fantastic time to travel in Ireland.

Spring is great because

- ✔ The warmer temperatures, flower-filled scenery, and longer days combine to make wonderful circumstances for touring the country.

- ✔ The locals are fresh from their own break from tourists and are ready to start playing host.

But keep in mind that

- ✔ This is the beginning of the high season, so prices go up starting around March and popular attractions start to get busy (though it's not as crowded as in the summer).

- ✔ The weather's pretty rainy in the spring (though rain showers usually last only part of the day).

- ✔ A few attractions are not open yet, and some still have abbreviated hours.

Walking on Sunshine and Singing in the Rain: Ireland's Climate

Ireland has a pretty moderate climate; it's rare to get a scorching summer day or a bitterly cold winter day. Table 3-1 lists the average temperature of each month.

The key to dressing for Ireland is layers because, as the Irish like to say, you often end up getting all four seasons in one day.

From the true-stereotypes file: It rains often. No matter what time of the year you go, chances are slim that you'll make it back without having an encounter with a shower, so pack a raincoat or umbrella.

Rain falls heavier and more often during certain times of the year — winter especially. Also, certain places on the island see more rain than others. The southwest of the country (Counties Limerick, Clare, and Kerry) tends to get more rain all year round.

Table 3-1	Average Monthly Temperature in Ireland	
Month	**Temp (F)**	**Temp (C)**
January	34–46	1–8
February	35–47	2–8
March	37–51	3–10
April	39–55	4–13
May	43–60	6–15
June	48–65	9–18
July	52–67	11–20
August	51–67	11–19
September	48–63	9–17
October	43–57	6–14
November	39–51	4–10
December	37–47	3–8

Weather and temperature aren't the only factors involved in deciding when to go. The amount of daylight varies greatly from season to season. Ireland is situated at such a high latitude that summer days are blissfully long (sunset as late as 11 p.m.), but winter days are short (sunset as early as 4:30 p.m.). Remember, the more daylight there is, the more sights you get to see.

The best site on the Web for Ireland's weather forecasts is www. ireland.com/weather.

Perusing a Calendar of Festivals and Events

Just about any time you visit Ireland, some sort of event or festival is sure to be going on. About a zillion events are held each year, of all kinds. I've sorted through and picked the highlights. You may notice the absence of January and February on the list below. These two months are the slowest in Ireland in terms of festivals and events.

Dates often fluctuate from year to year, so I generally list roughly the time of the month when the event occurs, rather than the specific dates. For dates, call the event's number or visit its Web site.

Also, check the months before and after the one that you will be in Ireland, as many festivals are on the cusp of two months, and some events (such as the Wicklow Gardens Festival) stretch over several months.

Attention, sports fans: Check out the golf, horse-racing, hiking, and fishing sections in Chapter 9 for events of particular interest to you.

March

The feast day of the patron saint of Ireland is celebrated at the **St. Patrick's Day Dublin Festival** (☎ 01-676-3205; www.stpatricks day.ie), a six-day festival of music, street theater, and fireworks, with a huge parade down O'Connell Street. Usually begins on March 12, with the parade falling on March 17.

Irish dancers from around the world compete in the **World Irish Dancing Championships** (☎ 01-475-2220; www.worldirishdancing. com). Location varies. Late March or Early April.

April

The **Pan-Celtic Festival** (☎ 074-912-1160; www.panceltic.ie) in Letterkenny, County Donegal, celebrates all the Celtic nations and features music, dancing, sports, parades, and more. Early to mid-April.

May

During the **County Wicklow Gardens Festival** (☎ 0404-20-070; www. visitwicklow.ie) many beautiful private gardens and estates open to visitors on select dates. Runs from May through August.

Stand rough side to the world's most famous masters at **The Irish Open** (☎ 0818-719-372). This golf championship attracts the best of the best, and each year, one of the country's top courses plays host. The venue changes from year to year; contact the organizers for more information. Mid- to late May.

Smithwick's Cat Laughs Comedy Festival, in Kilkenny (☎ 056-776-3416; www.thecatlaughs.com), features stand-up comedians from all over the world. Late May or early June.

June

Diversions Temple Bar, in Dublin (☎ 01-677-2255; www.temple-bar. ie), is a free outdoor program offering dance, music, film, theater, visual arts, and more. You can find a guide to the festival online or pick one up at the Temple Bar Information Centre, at 12 East Essex St. June through August.

Classical music by internationally renowned musicians is presented in beautiful buildings and mansions during the **Music Festival in Great Irish Houses,** in Dublin, Wicklow, and Kildare (☎ 01-664-2822; www.musicgreatirishhouses.com). Mid-June.

Bloomsday, in Dublin (☎ 01-878-8547; www.visitdublin.com/bloomsday), commemorates Leopold Bloom, the main character in James Joyce's 900-plus page novel *Ulysses,* which takes place in Dublin on June 16, 1904. Restaurants and pubs do everything to look the part, and there are guided walks of Joyce-related sights. June 16.

Overlapping with the famous Bloomsday celebration, the **Dublin Writers Festival** (☎ 01-222-5455; www.dublinwritersfestival.com) honors writers from all over the world with readings by Irish and visiting writers; a poetry slam; a jazz and poetry night; and events planned specifically for children, including workshops with children's poets and writers. Most of the events are free to the public. Mid-June.

Dublin's **Darklight Film Festival** (☎ 01-670-9017; www.darklight-filmfestival.com) presents creative new films, with a special emphasis on animation. Mid- or late June.

Held in the Curragh, County Kildare, **The Budweiser Irish Derby,** Kildare (☎ 045-441-205; www.curragh.ie) is Ireland's version of the Kentucky Derby. Book tickets as far in advance as possible. Last Sunday in June or first Sunday in July.

July

Galway Arts Festival and Races, Galway City (☎ 091 566-577; www.galwayartsfestival.ie for the arts festival, and ☎ 091-753-870; www.galwayraces.com), is two weeks of terrific music, theater, visual arts, and more. The famous Galway horse races follow the Arts Festival. Second half of July.

The **Lughnasa Fair,** Antrim (☎ 028-9335-1273), is a medieval fair with crafts, entertainment, and costumes, all set inside and on the grounds of the 12th-century Carrickfergus Castle. Last Saturday of July.

Oxegen (www.oxegen.ie), held in County Kildare, is a huge multiday outdoor summer rock festival.

August

The **Kilkenny Arts Festival** (☎ 056-776-3663; www.kilkennyarts.ie) features all sorts of music, films, readings, visual arts, and more. Early to mid-August.

The **Rose of Tralee Festival,** Tralee (☎ 066-712-1322; www.roseof tralee.ie), consists of five days of concerts, entertainment, horse races, and a beauty pageant to pick the new "Rose of Tralee." Late August.

The **Puck Fair** (☎ 066-976-2366; www.puckfair.ie), in Killorglin, is three days of parades, concerts, street entertainment, and general debauchery in the small town of Killorglin. The festivities center on the crowning of "King Puck" — a local goat. August 10 to August 12.

The **Kerrygold Horse Show** (☎ 0818-300-274; www.dublinhorseshow.com), held in Dublin, showcases the best bred Irish horses and features jumping competitions (for the horses), and plenty of balls and celebrations (for the people).

September

The **Lisdoonvarna Matchmaking Festival, Lisdoonvarna** (☎ 065-707-4005; www.matchmakerireland.com), is a huge singles festival, featuring lots of music; dancing; and, of course, matchmaking. Early September to October.

Tickets to the live matches of the **All-Ireland Hurling and Football Finals,** held at Croke Park in Drumcondra, outside Dublin, are virtually impossible to get if you haven't attended all of one county's league games, but the games are televised, and the excitement shouldn't be missed. Get thee to a pub. Mid-September.

Besides eating, events at the **Galway Oyster Festival** (☎ 091-587-992; www.galwayoysterfest.com) include dancing, an oyster-shucking competition, a golf tournament, and a yacht race. Late September through early October.

October

The **Kinsale International Gourmet Festival** (☎ 021-477-3571; www.kinsalerestaurants.com/autumn.php), held in the foodie town of Kinsale, County Cork, features special menus at local restaurants, plus visiting star chefs. Mid-October.

A wide array of films are shown all over Cork City during **Murphy's Cork International Film Festival** (☎ 021-427-1711;

Ireland: Home of Halloween

Many of the traditions that exist around Halloween originated among the Celts thousands of years ago. The Celts marked the beginning of winter on November 1 and they believed that the boundaries between the spirit world and the living world were more permeable than usual at this time. In order to scare off the spirits, many Celts wore masks (the roots of our contemporary tradition of wearing costumes). And in order to satisfy the spirits, many would leave an offering of food by the entrance to their home (the origin of today's treats).

`www.corkfilmfest.org`). You can also find numerous film-related events. Mid-October.

The Guinness Cork Jazz Festival, in Cork City (`www.corkjazzfestival.com`), has an excellent lineup of top jazz musicians. Late October.

Halloween (Samhain) is celebrated with fireworks, bonfires, costumes, and the eating of barnbrack (fruit bread). If you're in the country at the end of October and want to find out where the festivities will occur, just look for the field or lot where kids are stacking up wood scraps. If you're looking for the best party, the people of Derry and the people of Dublin are expert Halloween revelers. October 31.

The popular **Wexford Opera Festival,** Wexford Town (☎ 053-912-2400; `www.wexfordopera.com`), features performances of 18th-, 19th-, and 20th-century operas, plus classical concerts. Late October to early November.

The Belfast Festival at Queen's (☎ 028-9033-4455; `www.belfastfestival.com`) is an all-out arts festival hosted by Queen's University, featuring ballet, dance, film, opera, jazz, and traditional and classical music. Late October and early November.

December

On **St. Stephen's Day,** people all over Ireland have been reviving the old tradition of "Hunting the Wren." In past centuries, groups of boys would chase down and kill a wren, then parade it from house to house while singing songs and collecting money and treats. The money would usually be used to hold a large dance for the whole village. Nowadays, kids and adults, both male and female, travel from house to house with a fake or a caged wren, playing music, singing, and collecting money for charities or community projects. December 26.

Chapter 4

Following an Itinerary: Four Great Options

- -

In This Chapter

▶ Hitting the highlights on a one-week trip

▶ Taking a whirlwind two-week tour

▶ Traveling Ireland with kids

▶ Golfing your way around the country

- -

*I*reland is a jewel box, filled with vibrant cities, charming towns, and stunning landscapes and seascapes. If you're overwhelmed by the bounty of choices and the different routes around the country, the four itineraries in this chapter may help provide some structure.

These itineraries are intended for travelers with a car, but the first three can be followed by bus as long as you keep on top of the schedules.

Seeing Ireland's Highlights in One Week

This tour guides you to many of the Ireland's most popular highlights. If you don't like the idea of switching hotels or B&Bs every night, I recommend skipping some destinations and extending your stay in the places that appeal to you the most. This itinerary takes you through many places that are on the beaten visitor track, so if you'd prefer to visit remote, untouched places, this isn't the route for you.

Day 1: Dublin

Fly into **Dublin** (most flights arrive in the morning). Get settled in your hotel or B&B, and then visit the **Dublin Tourism Centre** if you'd like to scope out some free literature on daytrips, tours, and so on. Head over to **Trinity College** to see the **Book of Kells** and explore the campus. If you like, take the **Historical Walking Tour** that leaves from the front gates of Trinity. Grab a quick lunch, and then catch the **Hop On Hop Off** bus, a bus tour with narration that hits the top sights in Dublin. As the name implies, you can hop off the bus to explore an attraction and then

Suggested Itineraries

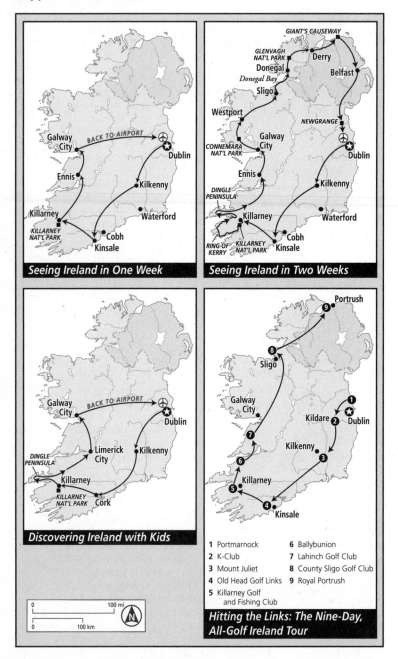

Seeing Ireland in One Week

Galway City — BACK TO AIRPORT — Dublin
Ennis
Kilkenny
Killarney
KILLARNEY NAT'L PARK
Cobh
Kinsale
Waterford

Seeing Ireland in Two Weeks

GIANT'S CAUSEWAY
GLENVAGH NAT'L PARK — Derry
Donegal — Belfast
Donegal Bay
Sligo
Westport
NEWGRANGE
CONNEMARA NAT'L PARK — Galway City
Ennis — Dublin
DINGLE PENINSULA — Kilkenny
Killarney
RING OF KERRY — KILLARNEY NAT'L PARK — Cobh — Kinsale
Waterford

Discovering Ireland with Kids

Galway City — BACK TO AIRPORT — Dublin
DINGLE PENINSULA — Limerick City — Kilkenny
Killarney
KILLARNEY NAT'L PARK — Cork

Hitting the Links: The Nine-Day, All-Golf Ireland Tour

Portrush — 9
8
Sligo
Galway City
Kildare — 2 — Dublin — 1
7
Kilkenny — 3
6
Killarney
5
4
Kinsale

1 Portmarnock
2 K-Club
3 Mount Juliet
4 Old Head Golf Links
5 Killarney Golf and Fishing Club
6 Ballybunion
7 Lahinch Golf Club
8 County Sligo Golf Club
9 Royal Portrush

0 — 100 mi
0 — 100 km

continue your journey on a later bus. Highlights of the bus tour include the **Guinness Brewery,** the **National Museum,** and **St. Stephen's Green.** After your bus tour, have dinner before heading to Oliver St. John Gogarty's Pub for the **Musical Pub Crawl** or to Duke's Bar to begin the **Literary Pub Crawl.** See Chapter 11 for more information on Dublin.

Day 2: Dublin to Kilkenny

Walk off your traditional Irish breakfast by visiting some of the Dublin landmarks you missed yesterday, such as **Merrion Square** or the **Grafton Street** area for shopping. Then pick up your rental car and head south through Wicklow, perhaps stopping to take in beautiful **Powerscourt Gardens** and peaceful **Glendalough.** Make your way to the medieval city of **Kilkenny,** check into your hotel (**Butler House** is a great choice), explore the town if it's still early, and treat yourself to a nice dinner after a long drive. See Chapter 13 for more information on Wicklow and Chapter 14 for more on Kilkenny.

Day 3: Kilkenny to Kinsale

If you didn't get to look around much yesterday, spend the first part of the day visiting the highlights of Kilkenny, including **Kilkenny Castle** and the **Design Centre.** Then head south toward Waterford City to take the tour of the **Waterford Crystal Factory.** After that, drive west along the coast towards Kinsale, stopping at the quaint harbor town of **Cobh.** Definitely plan to be in **Kinsale** for dinner so that you can enjoy one of the town's fabulous restaurants. You can read up on Waterford in Chapter 14; I cover Kinsale in Chapter 15.

Day 4: Kinsale to Killarney

Head off to Killarney in the morning, possibly spending some time on the **Beara Peninsula** along the way. Check into your hotel, and then set out to explore gorgeous **Killarney National Park.** Back in the town of Killarney, you may want to finish your day with a visit to **The Laurels,** where you can always hear someone singing an Irish ballad. For more on County Kerry, including Killarney, turn to Chapter 16.

Day 5: Killarney to Ennis

Get up really early so that you can drive at least part of the **Dingle Peninsula,** County Kerry's lesser-known (and therefore less crowded) driving tour. (Competing with the tour buses that drive the popular Ring of Kerry is not for the faint of heart.) Plan on a late lunch in Dingle Town. Set out toward **Ennis,** stopping in **Adare,** with its thatched-roof cottages, for an early dinner (**The Wild Geese** is excellent) before heading on to **Ennis** to spend the night. Before flopping into bed, check out the traditional music scene in town; **Poet's Corner in the Old Ground Hotel** is always a good bet. For information on Ennis and the rest of County Clare, see Chapter 17.

Day 6: Ennis to Galway City

Right after breakfast, make your way west, and hold onto your hat (it's really windy!) at the **Cliffs of Moher.** Then drive up through the **Burren** to **Galway City,** stopping perhaps for a walking tour of the Burren with **Shane Connolly.** Get into Galway City in time for dinner at one of the city's fabulous restaurants (**Nimmo's** is my favorite) and some excellent traditional Irish music at the **Crane Bar.** Find out more about Galway in Chapter 18.

Day 7: Galway City to Shannon or Dublin

Head back to Dublin or Shannon today. If your flight leaves from Dublin, drive north of the city to see **Newgrange,** a prehistoric burial site, on your way back (I cover Newgrange in Chapter 12). After you check into your hotel, treat yourself to dinner at the **Mermaid Café** or the **Winding Stair,** and then pub-crawl through trendy **Temple Bar.** If you are leaving from **Shannon,** you might explore beautiful **Connemara** during the day (see Chapter 18), and then spend your last night like royalty at **Bunratty Castle** (see Chapter 17).

Touring the Best of Ireland in Two Weeks: A Whirlwind Tour

This tour is for those who want to cram in visits to as many places as possible and don't mind spending significant chunks of time in the car each day. If this doesn't describe you, check out this tour and then cut out a few destinations so that you can spend longer in those destinations that appeal to you.

Discovering the magic of Ireland off the beaten path

Some of the most magical moments of your trip to Ireland may be those times when you turn down that little road toward a tiny farming village or when you happen into a roadside pub, where fires are roaring and fiddles are tuning up for an evening of music, or when you spontaneously decide to take a stroll down to a glimmering lake for a picnic.

This book can help you discover the highlights of the country, but I can't emphasize enough the wonderful rewards that often result from following your instincts in getting off the well-trod path.

For the first ten days, follow the itinerary for a week in Ireland, which I lay out in the preceding section, adding a second day to take in more of Dublin's sights and adding two days between Days 5 and 6 to see the **Ring of Kerry** or the **Dingle Peninsula** — or spend one day on each (I would spend my two extra nights on the Dingle Peninsula). Ignore Day 7, because it outlines the trip back to Dublin or Shannon from Galway.

Day 10: Galway City to Westport

Have a leisurely morning in **Galway City,** and then set out to drive around **Connemara,** visiting **Connemara National Park** and taking the gorgeous **R335 route.** Make your way up to the cute and bustling town of **Westport** in County Mayo for the night. Drop in to **Matt Molloy's** for traditional Irish music. Read up on Connemara in Chapter 18 and Mayo in Chapter 19.

Day 11: Connemara to Sligo

Spend some more time exploring Connemara before meandering up to County **Sligo** today. You many want to book in **Temple House,** arriving early enough to tromp around the grounds before dinner. I cover County Sligo in Chapter 19.

Day 12: Sligo to Derry

Head up through Donegal today, exploring the **peninsula north of Donegal Bay.** End your day by crossing the border into Northern Ireland and staying in **Derry** for the night. **The Merchant's House** and the **Saddler's House** are great places to stay, and you can't go wrong with a meal at **Brown's Bar and Brasserie** or **Spice.** See Chapter 20 for more on Donegal and Chapter 21 for information on Derry.

Day 13: Derry to Belfast

Leave Derry early to head up to Antrim, where stops at **Dunluce Castle, Giant's Causeway,** and the **Carrick-A-Rede Rope Bridge** are musts. Trace the gorgeous coast down to Belfast, where you may want to indulge in a gourmet dinner at **Cayenne,** and then check out the hot club scene. I cover County Antrim, including Belfast, in Chapter 21.

Day 14: Belfast to Dublin

Head back toward Dublin today, stopping at the prehistoric tomb of **Newgrange** before you hit the city (see Chapter 12). Treat yourself to dinner at the **Mermaid Café** or the **Winding Stair** in Dublin and then hit the pubs for your last night in Ireland.

Discovering Ireland with Kids

Ireland is a family-friendly place, and with a little planning, you can have a terrific time with your children. In this itinerary, I pulled together some of the most kid-friendly sights, hotels, and restaurants.

Day 1: Dublin

Fly into **Dublin** (most flights arrive in the morning), and head to your hotel or B&B. Your best option for a hotel is **Jurys Christchurch Inn,** which has family-friendly rates and is within walking distance of most sites and restaurants. Kids will love **Dublinia,** a hands-on museum about Dublin during medieval times. For lunch, head to **Elephant & Castle,** with its great burgers and omelets. In the afternoon, explore **Phoenix Park and Zoo** if it's nice out, or hit the **National Museum.** A fun dinner pick is the **Bad Ass Café.** Turn to Chapter 11 for more information on these and other kid-friendly picks in Dublin.

Day 2: Dublin to Kilkenny

Get rid of excess energy before your car trip with a good walk around Dublin, visiting some of the city's landmarks such as the **Ha'Penny Bridge** and **St. Stephen's Green.** As you make your way to **Kilkenny,** play some good car games, such as "Count the Sheep!", and stop to stroll around **Powerscourt Gardens.** Get your bearings in Kilkenny with a short walk before dinner. You can find more on Kilkenny in Chapter 14.

Day 3: Kilkenny to Cork City

Next stop: **Cork City.** You'll have plenty of time to visit **Blarney Castle** on the way, as well as the exotic animals at **Fota Wildlife Park.** In Cork, **Red Pepper** is a cute spot with a tremendous selection of pizzas. See Chapter 15 for more on Cork.

Day 4: Cork to Killarney

Head out to **Killarney National Park** for lakes, waterfalls, and plenty of scenery to keep young travelers happy. Be sure to visit the **Muckross Traditional Farm.** Back in town, your little princes or princesses will likely enjoy eating at the **Killarney Manor Banquet.** Read up on Killarney and the rest of County Kerry in Chapter 16.

Day 5: Killarney to Limerick City

Stick around County Kerry for an excursion to the **Dingle Peninsula.** Kids (and parents) shouldn't miss a visit with Fungie, Dingle Bay's resident dolphin. After a full day exploring the Dingle Peninsula, head north to spend the night in Limerick City or picture-perfect Adare. See Chapter 17 for more on Limerick City and Adare.

Day 6: Limerick City to Galway City

On the way to **Galway City,** drive through the **Burren.** If your kids are old enough, a walk is a great idea. Get into Galway City early enough for dinner at **Couch Potatas,** an all-baked-potato eatery. Your best bet for a hotel is the **Jurys Galway.** I cover Galway in Chapter 18.

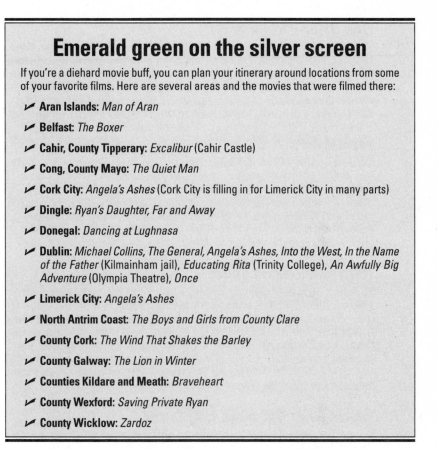

Emerald green on the silver screen

If you're a diehard movie buff, you can plan your itinerary around locations from some of your favorite films. Here are several areas and the movies that were filmed there:

✔ **Aran Islands:** *Man of Aran*

✔ **Belfast:** *The Boxer*

✔ **Cahir, County Tipperary:** *Excalibur* (Cahir Castle)

✔ **Cong, County Mayo:** *The Quiet Man*

✔ **Cork City:** *Angela's Ashes* (Cork City is filling in for Limerick City in many parts)

✔ **Dingle:** *Ryan's Daughter, Far and Away*

✔ **Donegal:** *Dancing at Lughnasa*

✔ **Dublin:** *Michael Collins, The General, Angela's Ashes, Into the West, In the Name of the Father* (Kilmainham jail), *Educating Rita* (Trinity College), *An Awfully Big Adventure* (Olympia Theatre), *Once*

✔ **Limerick City:** *Angela's Ashes*

✔ **North Antrim Coast:** *The Boys and Girls from County Clare*

✔ **County Cork:** *The Wind That Shakes the Barley*

✔ **County Galway:** *The Lion in Winter*

✔ **Counties Kildare and Meath:** *Braveheart*

✔ **County Wexford:** *Saving Private Ryan*

✔ **County Wicklow:** *Zardoz*

Day 7: Galway City to Dublin or Shannon

If you're flying home from Dublin, you'll have to hit the road early. Try to take a walk around Galway before you go, and make a fun stop in the nearby resort and amusement park town of **Salthill.** If you still have the stamina after you reach Dublin, drive a little north of the city to see the ancient burial site of **Newgrange** (see Chapter 12 for more information). By the time you get back to Dublin, the whole family will be tuckered out. If you're leaving from **Shannon,** treat your family to a night at **Bunratty Castle** (see Chapter 17).

Hitting the Links: The Nine-Day, All-Golf Ireland Tour

This ultimate tour for golf-lovers lets you play through nine of the country's best courses.

First hole: Portmarnock

This course was the home of the first Irish Open in 1889 and was renovated and reopened in the early 1990s. It's a natural golf course, incorporating the rugged landscape of the region. It's located 25 minutes from
Dublin's city center, Portmarnock, County Dublin (☎ 01-846-2968;
www.portmarnockgolfclub.ie). Par: 72. Fees: €180 ($288) weekdays,
€215 ($344) weekends. Visitors welcome every day except Wednesday.

Second hole: K Club

Kildare Country Club (K-Club): This 18-hole championship golf course
was designed by Arnold Palmer himself and hosted the Ryder Cup in
2006; you certainly pay for the privilege of golfing here. It's located
27km (17 miles) west of Dublin in Straffan (☎ 01-601-7200. www.kclub.
ie). Par: 72. Fees: €305 to 380 ($488–$608) for 18 holes from May to
September; €195 to 245 ($312–$392) in October; and €130 to €165
($208–$264) from November to April.

Third hole: Mount Juliet

This Jack Nicklaus Signature course was host of the Irish Open from
1993 to 1995. The lakes and waterfalls make a picturesque backdrop to
this course, called the "Augusta of Europe"; it was voted the best inland
course in Ireland. It's located on the N9 Waterford-Dublin Road, Thomastown, County Kilkenny (☎ 056-77-73-000; www.mountjuliet.ie). Par:
72. Fees: From €85 to €155 ($136–$216) Sunday through Thursday; €95
to €190 ($152–$304) Friday and Saturday (lower rates are for off-season
play and guests at the Mount Juliet Estate).

Fourth hole: Old Head Golf Links

Located on a stunning outcrop of land and surrounded by the Atlantic,
the Old Head Links was a cooperative project, built by the top golfers of
the country. It can be challenging, and it is very expensive. It's located in
Kinsale, County Cork (☎ 021-477-8444; www.oldhead.com). Par: 72.
Fees: €295 ($472). Visitors welcome daily.

Fifth hole: Killarney Golf and Fishing Club

Home of the 1991 and 1992 Irish Open Championship, the three courses
here are nestled among the beautiful lakes of Killarney and below the
majestic MacGillycuddy's Reeks Mountains at Mahony's Point, Killarney,
County Kerry (☎ 064-66-31-034; www.killarney-golf.com). Par: 72.
Fees: €90 to €130 ($144–$208) on the Killeen course, €60 to €100
($96–$160) on the Mahony's course, and €30 to €70 ($48–$112) on the
Lackabane. Lower rates are for off-season play. Visitors are welcome
every day and should make reservations ahead of time.

Sixth hole: Ballybunion

This seaside club has two fine 18-hole courses. The newer course was fashioned by the legendary Robert Trent Jones, though the Old Course is the more challenging of the two. It's located on Sandhill Road, Bally-bunion, County Kerry (☎ **068-27-146;** www.ballybuniongolfclub.ie). Par: 71 and 72. Fees: €180 ($288) for the old course and €110 ($176) for the new, or €265 ($424) to play both on the same day. Visitors are welcome on weekdays and most Saturdays, provided you call to book in advance.

Seventh hole: Lahinch Golf Club

High elevations provide amazing views of the sea and valleys below, and local goats are known to cross the fairway. The club has two 18-hole courses; one is a championship course. It's located in Lahinch, County Clare (☎ **065-708-1003;** www.lahinchgolf.com). Par: 72. Fees: €165 ($264) for the Old Course, €55 ($88) for the Castle Course. Visitors are welcome daily, except when there is a tournament.

Eighth hole: County Sligo Golf Club

This difficult course challenges top players, but dabblers have fun playing it too. The course is set between striking Atlantic beaches and the hill of Benbulben. It's located in Rosses Point, County Sligo (☎ **071-917-7134;** www.countysligogolfclub.ie). Par: 71. Fees: €75 ($120) weekdays, €90 ($144) weekends. Fees lower in the low season. Visitors welcome daily.

Ninth hole: Royal Portrush

The two excellent 18-hole courses here offer amazing seaside views of the northern Antrim Coast and of a lush green valley. The club is located on Dunluce Road, Portrush, County Antrim (☎ **028-7082-2311;** www.royalportrushgolfclub.com). Par: 72 and 70. Fees: £120 to £135 ($240–$270) for the Dunluce Course and £35 to £40 ($70–$80) for the Valley Course. Fees are lower for off-season play. Guests are welcome daily on the Dunluce Course except for mornings on Mondays and afternoons on Wednesdays and Fridays. Call for open hours for the Valley Course. Book in advance, especially for the Dunluce Course.

Part II
Planning Your Trip to Ireland

The 5th Wave   By Rich Tennant

"This afternoon I want everyone to go online and research Native American culture, history of the old west, and discount airfares to Ireland for the two weeks I'll be on vacation."

In this part . . .

*B*efore you can start planning your trip to Ireland, you'll want to do some legwork. How much will it cost? What are your options for getting there? What about your choices for getting around? What kinds of accommodations are available? The chapters in this part give you the answers to all these questions and more.

Of course, there's the bottom line. Chapter 5 features information on currency in Ireland, planning your budget, what things cost, and how to save money.

Chapter 6 gives you the lowdown on how to get to Ireland, and Chapter 7 covers the nitty-gritty of getting around the country.

After you figure out how you're getting to Ireland, turn to Chapter 8 for tips on booking accommodations.

Seniors, students, disabled travelers, families, outdoorsy folks, and other travelers should consult Chapter 9 for tips specific to them, and everyone should have a look at Chapter 10 for information on tying up loose ends before you leave.

Chapter 5

Managing Your Money

. . . .

In This Chapter

▶ Budgeting for your trip

▶ Discovering how to save big bucks

▶ Figuring out currency in Ireland and Northern Ireland

▶ Dealing with money issues

▶ Getting some tax back

. . . .

Can you visit Ireland for $5 a day? Maybe in 1965, but not now. How about $40 a day? Perhaps, if you don't mind hostel bunk beds and grocery-store dinners. If you want hotels or B&Bs and restaurant meals, you should figure on spending at least $130 to $175 per person per day — not including a rental car and airfare. Ireland has become much more expensive in the past few years. In fact, even a simple pub dinner may cost you $18 to $25. And you should expect to pay top price in Dublin. But fret not, because this guide — this chapter in particular — gives you lots of money-saving tips, and subsequent chapters offer accommodation and dining selections that won't tap your wallet like a keg of Guinness on St. Patrick's Day. Read on for tips on creating a budget and cutting costs.

Planning Your Budget

Generally speaking, you should factor the following into your budget:

▸ **Airfare:** Airfare to and from Ireland varies depending on where you're flying from, the time of year, and the totally arbitrary whims of the airline gods. On average, airfare from New York to Ireland and back runs about $800. See Chapter 6 for tips on getting the best airfare deals.

▸ **Transportation:** Transportation costs vary depending on whether you're busing or training it or renting a car. Driving — the transportation choice for most tourists — costs around $150 a week for a small car, plus gas, which can be anywhere between double and triple the cost of gas in the U.S. Bus fares can cost anywhere from $2 to $25 per person, depending on your destination. The train is slightly more expensive. See Chapter 7 for more information.

✔ **Lodging:** An average double room runs about $160. Rooms on the low end go for about $120, and those on the high end about $400.

✔ **Meals:** This is one area where it's difficult to save money; even a simple pub lunch can cost about $15. A good per-person allowance for lunch is $15, and for dinner, between $20 and $35. Breakfast is included with most accommodations, so you don't have to figure that into your daily costs.

✔ **Attractions:** A fair amount to budget for sights is $25 per day. Buying a Heritage Card is worth it if you're planning to see a lot of sights (for more information on the Heritage Card, see "Cutting Costs — But Not the Fun," later in this chapter).

✔ **Shopping:** Are you planning to buy clothes, jewelry, Waterford crystal, and antiques or just a few postcards, a snow globe, and some other inexpensive souvenirs? A modest piece of Waterford crystal can set you back $100; a nice Guinness sweatshirt is about $60. Gauge your buying tendencies and factor them in. A perk of buying in Ireland: You can get the value-added tax (VAT) on your purchases refunded (I explain how under "Taking Taxes into Account," later in this chapter).

✔ **Nightlife:** Pubs are the most popular place to spend the evening, and they are as free as the air you breathe, except for all those pints of Guinness (about $6.50).

Table 5-1 offers the average costs of some common items.

Table 5-1	What Things Cost in Ireland
Item	*Cost in U.S. Dollars*
Pint of Guinness	$6.50
Soda in a restaurant	$4
Chocolate bar	$1.50
Double room at an expensive hotel	$400
Double room at a moderate hotel	$192
Double room at a B&B	$160
Lunch for two at most pubs	$35
Dinner for two at an expensive restaurant (with wine)	$150
Walking tour	$18

The ins and outs of tipping

Some restaurants include a service charge (tip) of 10 percent to 15 percent in their bill, while others leave the tip up to you. The service charge is different from the VAT (13.5 percent in the Republic of Ireland and 17.5 percent in Northern Ireland), which is always included. Many restaurants note their service-charge policies on the menu; if you can't figure out whether the service charge has been included, just ask. If no service charge has been added, tip up to 15 percent. If a service charge has been added, but it is less than 15 percent, it is customary to leave a tip that rounds the charge up to 15 percent. Bartenders do not expect a tip for dispensing drinks.

Note: Prices for food and accommodations in Dublin will be slightly higher than the prices given here.

Cutting Costs — But Not the Fun

Worried you won't be able to afford your trip? Well, you can rent *Far and Away,* read *Angela's Ashes,* listen to a Chieftains CD, and just pretend you're in Ireland, but what fun is that? Instead, make your vacation a bargain by cutting a few corners. I scatter various money-saving tips throughout this book, but I also present a list of 21 general money-savers here, organized by category.

✔ **Accommodations:** Cut some corners in the lodging department with these tips.

- **Stay in B&Bs.** I can't emphasize enough how wonderful the bed-and-breakfast experience is. Not only do B&Bs usually cost less than staying in a hotel in the same area, but you also frequently get a friendly insider perspective from the folks running these places.

- **Check out self-catering accommodations.** By renting an apartment or house (called *self-catering accommodations* in this guide) for a week or more, you can save money overall on accommodations (especially if you're traveling with a group) and on food because you can prepare your own meals in the kitchen. (See Chapter 8.)

- **Get out of town.** In many places, hotels just outside the most popular areas can be a great bargain. You may be able to find a great deal just a short cab, bus, car ride, or walk away. And as an extra bonus, hotels that are off the beaten path may even offer free parking.

- **Ask if your kids can stay in your room with you.** Although many accommodations in Ireland charge by the head, some allow kids to stay for free. Even if you have to pay $10 or $15 for a rollaway bed, in the long run you'll save hundreds by not booking two rooms.

- **Skip the fantabulous views.** Rooms with great views are the most expensive rooms in any hotel, but you probably won't be hanging out in your room all day, so why pay the price?

- **Never make a phone call from a hotel.** The marked-up fees that hotels charge are scandalous. Walk to the nearest coin- or card-operated phone for calls in and out of the country, or rent or buy a cellphone.

✔ **Attractions:** Save money as you tour Ireland's sights.

- **Get your hands on a Heritage Card.** A Heritage Card gives you free admission to more than 65 attractions throughout Ireland. You can buy the card at any participating attraction, purchase it over the phone with a Visa or MasterCard (☎ 1-850-600-601 in Ireland, or ☎ 01-647-6000 outside of Ireland), or purchase it on the Internet at www.heritage ireland.com.

- **Pick up those free, coupon-packed visitor pamphlets and magazines.** Detailed maps, feature articles, dining and shopping directories, and discount and freebie coupons give these pocket-size giveaways a good wallop. Especially popular and reliable are *Discover Ireland* and *Ireland Guidebook*. Each tourist office should have an up-to-date magazine with information about the surrounding area. Just ask.

✔ **Food:** Grab your grub for less with these suggestions.

- **Take advantage of free breakfasts.** Most accommodations include a substantial free Irish breakfast, so don't oversleep. If you have a big breakfast and then wait to have a late lunch or early dinner, you'll save the cost of a meal a day. If the breakfast is buffet-style, stash away a piece of fruit for an afternoon snack.

- **Try expensive restaurants at lunch or pre-theater times.** Lunch and early-bird menu prices are usually a fraction of prices during regular dinner hours, and the menu often boasts many of the same specialties. Early-bird fixed-price meals are usually offered between 5:30 p.m. and 7:30 p.m.

- **Look before you tip.** Some restaurants in Ireland add a service fee (gratuity) to the bill. Always check, or you may pay a double tip by mistake (see the sidebar "The ins and outs of tipping," earlier in this chapter).

- **Picnic.** A fancy restaurant may have an indoor waterfall, but can that beat dining near a real waterfall on a warm day? Grab some food from a market or grocery store, and set up camp outside.

✔ **Special prices:** Taking advantage of discounts and group rates can cut your costs substantially.

- **Always ask for discount rates.** Membership in AAA, frequent-flier plans, trade unions, AARP, or other groups may qualify you for savings on car rentals, plane tickets, hotel rooms, and even meals. Students, teachers, youths, and seniors are also often entitled to discounts (see Chapter 9). Ask about discounts; you may be pleasantly surprised.

- **Take advantage of group and family prices.** For travel packages and admission to individual attractions, group rates are a fantastic way to save money, and you don't necessarily have to travel with a busload of other people to get them. Sometimes, a group is as few as three people, so always ask. You and the folks behind you may even be able to form a makeshift group to get the discounted price. Most attractions in Ireland offer significantly reduced family rates for parents and up to four kids. Look for family prices on the rate board at attractions, or just ask.

- **Try a package tour.** For many destinations, you can book airfare, hotel, ground transportation, and even some sightseeing just by making one call to a travel agent or packager for a much lower price than if you put the trip together yourself. (See Chapter 6 for more on package tours.)

✔ **Ground transportation:** Getting around Ireland can be cheaper than you think.

- **Book your rental car at weekly rates, when possible.** Doing so often saves you money over daily rates.

- **Don't rent a gas-guzzler.** Renting a smaller car is cheaper, and you save on gas to boot. For more on car rentals, see Chapter 7.

- **Walk in cities and towns.** You can easily explore all the cities in Ireland and Northern Ireland by foot, even Dublin and Belfast. So save the bus and cab fare and hoof it to save a few extra pounds or euro. As a bonus, you'll get to know your destination more intimately, because you'll be exploring at a slower pace.

✔ **Travel costs:** Getting to Ireland can eat up a large chunk of change, but planning ahead can ease the financial bite.

- **Go in the off season.** Traveling between November and April saves you a lot on your airfare and the cost of accommodations. Christmas week is the exception, when many Irish in other countries come home to visit, and the airlines cash in. (See Chapter 6 for more information on airfares.)

- **Travel midweek.** If you can travel on a Tuesday, Wednesday, or Thursday, you may find cheaper flights to your destination. When you ask about airfares, see if you can get a cheaper rate by flying on a different day.

Making Sense of the Currency in Ireland

The Republic of Ireland uses the euro currency, which is the currency of many countries across Europe. Euro notes come in denominations of €5, €10, €20, €50, €100, €200, and €500. The euro is divided into 100 cents. The coins come in 1¢, 2¢, 5¢, 10¢, 20¢, 50¢, €1, and €2 pieces. The word *euro* is usually used in the singular, so €30 is *30 euro*.

Northern Ireland is part of the United Kingdom, which uses the pound sterling as its currency. Pounds used in Northern Ireland are found in notes of £5, £10, £20, £50, and £100. The pound is divisible by 100 pence (abbreviated as *p*). Coins in circulation are 1p, 2p, 5p, 10p, 20p, 50p, £1, and £2.

The exchange rate fluctuates daily by small amounts, but Tables 5-2 and 5-3 give you an idea of what to expect. For up-to-the-minute currency conversions, visit www.xe.com.

Table 5-2   Republic of Ireland Exchange Rates

Home Currency	Euro
$1 U.S.	€.63 (€1 = $1.60 U.S.)
$1 Canadian	€0.63 (€1 = $1.60 Canadian)
£1 British	€1.28 (€1 = 78p)
$1 Australian	€0.59 (€1 = $1.69 Australian)
$1 New Zealand	€0.47 (€1 = $2.14 New Zealand)

Table 5-3   Northern Ireland Exchange Rates

Home Currency	British Pound
$1 U.S.	50p (£1 = $2 U.S.)
€1 Euro	78p (£1 = € 1.28)
$1 Canadian	£0.49 (£1 = $2.05 Canadian)
$1 Australian	£0.46 (£1 = $2.15 Australian)
$1 New Zealand	£0.37 (£1 = $2.72 New Zealand)

Handling Money

Credit cards, bank cards, and cash are all easy to use in Ireland. The very best way to get cash in Ireland is from ATMs, which are available in all but the tiniest villages. You may want to change $100 or so before departing for Ireland just so you have enough money to tide you over. All the airports have ATMs, though, so you can take out money as soon as you land.

Using ATMs and carrying cash

The easiest and best way to get cash away from home is from an ATM, called a "cash point" in Ireland. The **Cirrus** (☎ 800-622-7747; www.mastercard.com) and **PLUS** (☎ 800-843-7587; www.visa.com) networks span the globe and are all over Ireland; look at the back of your bank card to see which network you're on and then call or check online for ATM locations at your destination. Be sure you know your personal identification number (PIN) before you leave home; almost all Irish ATMs accept four- to six-digit PINs, but the keys sometimes lack letters, so make sure you know your PIN as a number. In addition, be sure to find out your daily withdrawal limit. Also, remember to transfer the money that you think you'll need during your vacation to your checking account, since most Irish ATMs don't let you access your savings account. Finally, keep in mind that many banks impose a fee every time your card is used at a different bank's ATM, and that fee can be higher for international transactions (up to $5 or more) than for domestic ones (where they're rarely more than $2). On top of this, the bank from which you withdraw cash may charge its own fee. Some banks in the U.S. have partner banks in Ireland or the U.K. at which no service charge is assessed (for example, Bank of America in the U.S. is partnered with Barclay's in the U.K.). Check your bank's website or call your bank to find out if this is the case. Otherwise, you can ask your bank for its international withdrawal fees. The best way to beat the system is to take out a lot of cash at each ATM visit, so that you reduce the number of fees over the course of your vacation.

Charging ahead with credit cards

Credit cards are a safe way to carry money. They also provide a convenient record of all your expenses, and they generally offer relatively good exchange rates. You can also withdraw cash advances from your credit cards at banks or ATMs, provided you know your PIN. If you forgot yours, or didn't even know you had one, call the number on the back of your credit card and ask the bank to send it to you. It usually takes five to seven business days, though some banks will provide the number over the phone if you tell them your mother's maiden name or some other personal, identifying information.

Keep in mind that when you use your credit card abroad, many banks now assess a 1 percent to 3 percent "transaction fee" on **all** charges you incur abroad (whether you're using the local currency or your native currency). But credit cards still may be the smart way to go when you factor in such things as exorbitant ATM fees and higher traveler's check exchange rates (and service fees).

Some credit card companies recommend that you notify them of any impending trip abroad so that they don't become suspicious and block your charges when the card is used numerous times in a foreign destination. Even if you don't call your credit card company in advance, you can always call the card's toll-free emergency number if a charge is refused — a good reason to carry the phone number with you. But perhaps the most important lesson here is to carry more than one card with you on your trip; a card may not work for any number of reasons, so having a backup is the smart way to go.

Visa and MasterCard are the most widely accepted credit cards in Ireland, with American Express coming in at a distant second place, and Diner's Club following at a very distant third (you rarely find a B&B that accepts Diner's Club). Discover is accepted very rarely in Ireland.

Some restaurants and hotels put your credit card transaction through in your home currency. This may result in an unfavorable exchange rate, so ask establishments to put your charges through in euro in the Republic of Ireland and pounds in Northern Ireland.

Exchanging money

You get the best exchange rates by using an ATM, though exchanging cash is also easy in Ireland. You can exchange money anywhere you see a Bureau de Change sign, but you get the best rates and the most inexpensive exchange fees at banks. The major banks to look for in Ireland are the **Allied Irish Bank**, the **Bank of Ireland**, **National Irish Bank**, and **Ulster Bank.**

Toting traveler's checks

These days, traveler's checks are less necessary because most towns and cities have 24-hour ATMs that allow you to withdraw cash as needed. However, keep in mind that you will likely be charged an ATM withdrawal fee if the bank is not your own, so if you're withdrawing money every day, you may be better off with traveler's checks — provided that you don't mind showing identification every time you want to cash one. You can cash traveler's checks at the Bureau de Change counter in banks all over Ireland. The vast majority of merchants, restaurants, and lodgings **do not** accept traveler's checks as payment.

You can buy traveler's checks at most banks. They are offered in denominations of $20, $50, $100, $500, and sometimes $1,000. Generally, you'll pay a service charge ranging from 1 percent to 4 percent. The most popular traveler's checks are offered by **American Express** (☎ **800-807-6233** or ☎ 800-221-7282 for card holders — this number accepts collect calls, offers service in several foreign languages, and exempts Amex gold and platinum cardholders from the 1 percent fee.); **Visa** (☎ **800-732-1322**); and **MasterCard** (☎ **800-223-9920)**.

American Express, Thomas Cook, Visa, and **MasterCard** offer **foreign currency traveler's checks,** useful if you're traveling to one country or to the euro zone; they're accepted at locations where dollar checks may not be.

If you choose to carry traveler's checks, be sure to keep a record of their serial numbers separate from the checks themselves in the event that they are stolen or lost. You'll get a refund faster if you know the numbers.

Taking Taxes into Account

All prices for consumer items in Ireland (except books and children's clothing) include a *value-added tax* (VAT) of about 17 percent. Happily, travelers from the U.S. and Canada are entitled to a refund of this tax.

Here's how it works: Many stores have stickers reading "Tax Free for Tourists," indicating that they are part of the Global Refund network (www.globalrefund.com). When you make a purchase in one of these stores, get a refund check, fill it out, and then hand in your completed checks at the VAT-refund counter in the airport (in the departure hall in Dublin and the arrivals hall in Shannon). If you are running late, you can get the checks stamped by customs officials and then send them in to Global Refund. If you forget to get your checks stamped while in Ireland, a notary public or police officer can stamp them for you when you get home. Some stores will give you the VAT refund at the register. In this case, you'll be given papers to mail before you leave the county. You can also get the VAT refunded by stores that aren't part of the Global Refund network; just get a full receipt that shows the shop's name, the address, and the VAT paid, and then get the receipt stamped at the Customs Office when you are leaving Ireland. You can then mail the receipts back to the store where you made the purchase, and it will refund your VAT with a check sent to your home.

Chip and PIN: Cool New Credit Card Machines

If you are paying with a credit card at a restaurant, chances are that a credit card reader will be brought to your table. In the Republic and Northern Ireland, most people have credit cards with an embedded microchip that is activated by the reader when they enter their 4-digit PIN. Most U.S. and Canadian cards do not have a microchip as of this writing, so you must swipe your card, enter the tip (if needed) on the machine, press Enter, and then sign your receipt just like you did back in the good old days.

Dealing with a Lost or Stolen Wallet

Be sure to contact all of your credit card companies the minute you discover your wallet is gone, and file a report at the nearest police precinct. Your credit card company or insurer may require a police report number or record of the loss.

Most credit card companies have an emergency toll-free number to call if your card is lost or stolen; they may be able to wire you a cash advance immediately or deliver an emergency credit card in a day or two. Call the following emergency numbers in Ireland.

- ✔ **American Express:** ☎ 1-336-393-1111 (call collect) in the Republic and Northern Ireland.

- ✔ **Diner's Club:** ☎ 303-799-1504 (call collect) from the Republic of Ireland, or ☎ 0-870-1900-011 in Northern Ireland

- ✔ **MasterCard:** ☎ 1-800-55-7378 in the Republic, or ☎ 0800-96-4767 in Northern Ireland.

- ✔ **Visa:** ☎ 1-800-55-8002 in the Republic, or **0800-89-1725** in Northern Ireland.

If you need emergency cash over the weekend, when all banks and American Express offices are closed, you can have money wired to you via **Western Union** (☎ 800-325-6000; www.westernunion.com).

Identity theft or fraud is a potential complication of losing your wallet, especially if you've lost your driver's license along with your cash and credit cards. Notify the major credit-reporting bureaus immediately; placing a fraud alert on your records may protect you against liability for criminal activity. The three major U.S. credit-reporting agencies are **Equifax** (☎ 800-766-0008; www.equifax.com), **Experian** (☎ 888-397-3742; www.experian.com), and **TransUnion** (☎ 877-322-8228; www.transunion.com).

Finally, if you've lost all forms of photo ID, call your airline and explain the situation; they may allow you to board the plane if you have a copy of your passport or birth certificate and a copy of the police report you filed.

Chapter 6

Getting to Ireland

*B*ecause those jet-packs that we've been promised still haven't materialized, you need to begin your vacation to Ireland with a flight or a ferry crossing. This chapter explores the ins and outs of selecting a flight or a ferry trip. In addition, I cover package and escorted tour options.

Flying to Ireland

The sections here offer tips on winging your way over to the Emerald Isle.

When you book your flight, let the ticket agent know the ages of any children coming along. Some airlines offer child-companion fares and have a special kids' menu upon request. Flight attendants are usually happy to warm up baby food and milk if you ask.

Picking an arrival airport

Your options for major international airports in the Republic of Ireland are **Dublin Airport** (☎ 01-814-1111; www.dublin-airport.com), located 11km (7 miles) outside Dublin on the East Coast of Ireland (via the N1), and **Shannon Airport** (☎ 061-71-2000; www.shannonairport.com), located 24km (15 miles) west of Limerick, on the West Coast (via the N18).

In Northern Ireland, **Belfast International Airport** (☎ 028-9448-4848; www.belfastairport.com) is located 31km (19 miles) west of the city.

Choose your arrival airport based on fares and on the proximity of the airport to the starting point of your itinerary.

If you want to see both the East and the West of Ireland and you have limited time, I highly recommend flying into Dublin and out of Shannon, or vice versa. It won't cost you any more than booking a round-trip to and from the same airport, and it's a great time-saver.

Finding out which airlines fly to Ireland

In addition to Aer Lingus (which is Gaelic for — guess what? — *airline*), a few U.S. airlines fly to Shannon and Dublin airports. Getting fares from more than one airline to compare prices is a good idea.

Here's a list of the major airlines that fly direct to Ireland from North America. Airline destinations change, so check the Web sites below to find the departure and arrival points that are most convenient for you.

- ✔ **Aer Lingus** (☎ 800-474-7424 in the U.S. and Canada, ☎ 0870-876-5000 in the U.K., and ☎ 0818-365-000 in Ireland; www.aerlingus.com): There are direct flights from Boston to Shannon and Dublin; from Chicago to Shannon and Dublin; from New York to Shannon and Dublin; from Orlando to Dublin; from San Francisco to Dublin; from Washington D.C. to Dublin; and from L.A. to Dublin. Flights with layovers are available from several other cities.

- ✔ **Air Canada** (☎ 1-888-247-2262 in the U.S. and Canada; www.aircanada.com): Direct flights from Toronto to Dublin and Shannon.

- ✔ **American Airlines** (☎ 800-433-7300; www.aa.com): Flights out of New York, Newark, Boston, and Chicago to Dublin and/or Shannon (many of these flights make at least one stop).

- ✔ **Continental** (☎ 800-231-0856; www.continental.com): Out of Newark, New Jersey, to Shannon and Dublin.

- ✔ **Delta Air Lines** (☎ 800-221-1212; www.delta.com): Out of Atlanta, New York, and Orlando (one stop) to Shannon and Dublin, and out of L.A. to Dublin (one stop).

Many U.S. airlines fly to England, where you can catch a connecting flight to Ireland (see the list of airlines with flights from England to Ireland later in this section). Some North American travelers take advantage of this option because a flight to England and a connecting flight to Ireland are sometimes cheaper than a direct flight to Ireland.

The major airlines that fly from the United States and Canada to England are:

- ✔ **Air Canada** (☎ 888-247-2262; www.aircanada.ca)

- ✔ **American Airlines** (☎ 800-443-7300; www.aa.com)

- ✔ **British Airways** (☎ 800-AIRWAYS; www.britishairways.com)

- ✔ **Continental Airlines** (☎ 800-231-0856; www.continental.com)

- ✔ **Delta Airlines** (☎ 800-221-1212; www.delta.com)

✔ **Northwest** and **KLM Airlines** (☎ 800-225-2525; www.nwa.com)

✔ **United Airlines** (☎ 800-538-2929; www.united.com)

✔ **Virgin Atlantic** (☎ 800-821-5438; www.virgin-atlantic.com)

Some major airlines that fly direct to Ireland from England are:

✔ **Aer Lingus** (☎ **800-474-7424** in the U.S. and Canada, ☎ 0870-876-5000 in the U.K., and ☎ 0818-365-000 in Ireland; www.aerlingus.com)

✔ **BMI** (☎ **800-788-0555** in the U.K., ☎ 44-1332-64-8181 outside the U.K.; www.flybmi.com)

✔ **British Airways** (☎ **1-800-AIRWAYS** in the U.S. and Canada, ☎ 0844 493-0787 in the U.K., and ☎ 1-890-626-747 in Ireland; www.britishairways.com)

✔ **CityJet** (☎ 01-605-0383 in Ireland and ☎ 0870-142-4343 in the U.K.; www.cityjet.com)

✔ **easyJet** (☎ **0871-244-2377** [call this U.K. number from all areas]); www.easyjet.com)

✔ **Lufthansa** (☎ **800-399-5838** in the U.S., ☎ 0871-945-9747 in the U.K., and ☎ 01-844-5544 in Ireland; www.lufthansa.com)

✔ **Ryanair** (☎ **0818-30-30-30** in Ireland, ☎ 0871-246-0000 in the U.K., ☎ 353-1-249-7791 from elsewhere; www.ryanair.com)

Getting the Best Deal on Your Airfare

Competition among major airlines is unlike that of any other industry. Every airline offers virtually the same product (basically, a coach seat is a coach seat is a . . .), yet prices can vary by hundreds of dollars.

Business travelers who need the flexibility to buy their tickets at the last minute and change their itineraries at a moment's notice — and who want to get home before the weekend — pay (or at least their companies pay) the premium rate, known as the *full fare.* But if you can book your ticket far in advance, stay over Saturday night, and are willing to travel midweek (Tues, Wed, or Thurs), you can qualify for the least expensive price — usually a fraction of the full fare. Obviously, planning ahead pays.

Search the **Internet** for cheap fares. The most popular online travel agencies are **Travelocity.com** (www.travelocity.co.uk), **Expedia.com** (www.expedia.co.uk and www.expedia.ca), and **Orbitz.com.** In the U.K., go to **Travelsupermarket** (☎ 0845-345-5708; www.travelsupermarket.com), a flight search engine that offers flight comparisons for the budget airlines whose seats often end up in bucket-shop sales. Other Web sites for booking airline tickets online include **Cheapflights.com, SmarterTravel.com, Priceline.com,** and **Opodo** (www.opodo.co.uk).

Meta search sites (which find and then direct you to airline and hotel Web sites for booking) include **Sidestep.com** and **Kayak.com** — the latter includes fares for such budget carriers as JetBlue and Spirit as well as the major airlines. **Site59.com** is a great source for last-minute flights and getaways, and UKAIR.com (☎ 1-800-577-2900; www.ukair. com) is known for offering discounted tickets to Ireland on already-scheduled major flights. In addition, most **airlines** offer online-only fares that even their phone agents know nothing about.

Watch local newspapers for **promotional specials** or **fare wars**, when airlines lower prices on their most popular routes. Also keep an eye on price fluctuations and deals at Web sites such as **Airfarewatchdog.com** and **Farecast.com.**

Frequent-flier membership doesn't cost a cent, but membership may entitle you to better seats, faster response to phone inquiries, and prompter service if your luggage is stolen or your flight is canceled or delayed, or if you want to change your seat (especially once you've racked up some miles). And you don't have to fly to earn points; **frequent-flier credit cards** can earn you thousands of miles for doing your everyday shopping. With more than 70 mileage awards programs on the market, consumers have never had more options. Investigate the program details of your favorite airlines before you sink points into any one. Consider which airlines have hubs in the airport nearest you, and, of those carriers, which have the most advantageous alliances, given your most common routes. To play the frequent-flier game to your best advantage, consult the community bulletin boards on **FlyerTalk** (www. flyertalk.com) or go to Randy Petersen's **Inside Flyer** (www.inside flyer.com). Petersen and friends review all the programs in detail and post regular updates on changes in policies and trends.

Getting to Ireland by Ferry

Ferries are not the fastest or cheapest way to get to Ireland, but they're still popular because they can be a more interesting and relaxing way to travel than by air — getting there becomes part of the adventure. Ferry service to Ireland leaves from the U.K. and France and brings you within striking distance of Cork, Dublin, or Belfast. When you arrive, public transportation is available from the ferry terminals to the city. You can bring a car onto all of these ferries.

Note that the Irish Sea can be rough, so you should take a pill or patch if you're prone to seasickness.

For the best fares and availability on all ferries traveling to and from Ireland and Northern Ireland, contact or search on **Direct Ferries** (☎ 0871-222-3312 in the U.K and ☎ 1-800-932-151 in Ireland; www. directferries.ie). **Irish Ferries** (☎ 08705-171717 in the U.K. or ☎ 0818-300-400 in Ireland; www.irishferries.com) travels to Dublin from Holyhead, Wales, and to Rosslare in County Wexford from

Pembroke, Wales, and from Roscoff and Cherbourg, France. **Stena Line** (☎ 08705-83-83-83 in Britain and ☎ 01-204-7777 in Ireland; www.stena line.ie) travels from Holyhead, Wales, to Dun Laoghaire (pronounced dun *leer*-ee) and to Dublin Port; from Fishguard, Wales, to Rosslare; from Fleetwood, England to Larne, Northern Ireland; and from Stranraer, Scotland, to Belfast. **P& O Ferries** (☎ 08716-645-645 in Britain; www. poferries.com) travels from Liverpool to Dublin and from Cairnryan and Troon, Scotland, to Larne, Northern Ireland. **Norfolkline Irish Sea Ferry Service** (☎ 0870-870-1020 in Britain or ☎ 01-819-2999 in Ireland; www.norfolkline.com) travels from Liverpool to Dublin and Belfast.

Joining an Escorted Tour

You may be one of the many people who love escorted tours. The tour company takes care of all the details, and tells you what to expect at each leg of your journey. You know your costs up front and, in the case of the tame ones, you don't get many surprises. Escorted tours can take you to the maximum number of sights in the minimum amount of time with the least amount of hassle.

If you decide to go with an escorted tour, I strongly recommend purchasing travel insurance, especially if the tour operator asks to you pay up front. But don't buy insurance from the tour operator! If the tour operator doesn't fulfill its obligation to provide you with the vacation you paid for, there's no reason to think that they'll fulfill their insurance obligations either. Get travel insurance through an independent agency. (I tell you more about the ins and outs of travel insurance in Chapter 10.)

Depending on your recreational passions, I recommend one of the following tour companies. For companies that run escorted golf tours, see Chapter 2.

✔ **Brian Moore International Tours** (☎ **800-982-2299;** www.bmit. com): Many of these tours take in Ireland's most popular attractions. The nine-day Best of Ireland Tour features voyages to Killarney, Waterford, Dublin, Galway, and the Ring of Kerry and cost $1,199 to $1,529 (airfare not included) at press time.

✔ **CIE Tours International** (☎ **800-243-8687;** www.cietours.com): CIE offers a large selection of tours. The 12-day Irish Classic makes a circuit around the country; it cost $2,048 to $2,498 (airfare not included) at press time.

✔ **Cosmos** (☎ **800-276-1241;** www.cosmosvacations.com). The budget arm of Globus offers a slightly less upscale and less expensive version of Globus trips. As we went to press, the nine-day Irish Explorer tour cost $1,020 to $1,155 (airfare not included).

✔ **Destinations Ireland** (☎ **800-832-1848;** www.destinations-ireland.com) offers at ten-day trip to Ireland for $3,785 to $4,389 (airfare not included). The company also offers an eight-day guided pony trek across Connemara ($2,559–$3,009 without airfare).

✔ **Globus** (☎ **866-755-8581;** www.globusjourneys.com). Globus offers a variety of upscale tours. The seven-day Introduction to Ireland tour cost $1,099 to $1,149 (airfare not included) in 2008.

✔ **Tauck World Discovery** (☎ **800-788-7885;** www.tauck.com) offers deluxe tours of Ireland that house you in the finest hotels in the Emerald Isle. The eight-day A Week In Ireland tour cost $3,360 in 2008 (airfare not included).

For more information on Escorted General-Interest Tours, including questions to ask before booking your trip, see www.frommers.com/planning.

Choosing A Package Tour

In many cases, a package tour that includes airfare, hotel, and transportation to and from the airport costs less than the hotel alone on a tour you book yourself. That's because packages are sold in bulk to tour operators, who resell them to the public. It's kind of like buying your vacation at a buy-in-bulk store — except the tour operator is the one who buys the 1,000-count box of garbage bags and resells them ten at a time at a cost that undercuts the local supermarket.

Package tours can vary widely. Some offer a better class of hotels than others; others provide the same hotels for lower prices. Some book flights on scheduled airlines; others sell charters. In some packages, your choice of accommodations and travel days may be limited. Some let you choose between escorted vacations and independent vacations; others allow you to add on just a few excursions or escorted day trips (also at discounted prices) without booking an entirely escorted tour.

Most package tours in Ireland are of the self-drive, B&B or hotel variety; airfare and a rental car are included, as are vouchers good at some B&Bs. Note that many B&B owners in Ireland are frustrated by the voucher system and choose not to accept vouchers, so your options will be more limited than if you are traveling independently. The length of the car rental and number of vouchers are usually not flexible (most of the package tours cover seven or eight days), but your itinerary is completely up to you.

To find package tours, check out the travel section of your local Sunday newspaper or the ads in the back of national travel magazines such as *Travel + Leisure, National Geographic Traveler,* and *Condé Nast Traveler.* **Liberty Travel** (call ☎ **888-271-1584** to find the store nearest you; www.libertytravel.com) is one of the biggest packagers in the Northeast, and usually boasts a full-page ad in Sunday papers.

Another good source of package deals is the airlines themselves. **Aer Lingus** (☎ 800-495-1632; www.aerpackages.com) offers some excellent air/land packages, as do most major airlines, including **American Airlines Vacations** (☎ 800-321-2121; www.aavacations.com), **Delta Vacations** (☎ 800-654-6559; www.deltavacations.com), **Continental Airlines Vacations** (☎ 800-301-3800; www.covacations.com), and **United Vacations** (☎ 888-854-3899; www.unitedvacations.com). In addition, several big **online travel agencies** — Expedia, Travelocity, Orbitz, Site59, and Lastminute.com — also do a brisk business in packages. If you're unsure about the pedigree of a smaller packager, check with the Better Business Bureau in the city where the company is based, or go online at www.bbb.org. If a packager won't tell you where it's based, don't fly with it.

The following operators offer the best package tours in the business:

✔ **Brendan Worldwide Vacations** (☎ 800-421-8446; www.brendan vacations.com): Brendan's Self-Drive tours included car rental and B&B vouchers for $65 a day (per person) at press time.

✔ **Brian Moore International Tours** (☎ 800-982-2299; www.bmit. com): Brian Moore's Amazing Ireland Tour included car rental and five nights of B&B vouchers for $399 to $449 at press time.

✔ **CIE Tours International** (☎ 800-CIE-TOUR; www.cietours.com): CIE's Go-As-You-Please tours included car rental and six nights of B&B vouchers starting at $51 a day per person at press time.

For more information on Package Tours and for tips on booking your trip, see www.frommers.com/planning.

Chapter 7

Getting around Ireland

● ●

In This Chapter

▶ Renting a car in Ireland

▶ Taking the bus

▶ Traveling by train

● ●

*Y*our choices for transportation around Ireland are trains, buses, or a car. For most trips, I recommend renting a car, because you can get to the less-accessible areas of Ireland (which are, of course, often the most untouched areas in the country), and you can tour at your own pace. In addition, if you are traveling in a group, renting a car can be the most economical option. For those who would rather not drive the winding roads, buses are a great option — they're cheap, run frequently, and have big windows so you can see the country rolling by.

Seeing Ireland by Car

I think the best way to see Ireland is by car. However, I want to mention that driving in Ireland can be harrowing at times, due to the narrow width of some roads (in some cases two-way roads will only be one car-width wide) and the fact that the Irish drive on the left side of the road, which can take some getting used to.

When planning your car trips, check out the handy mileage chart I provide on the tear-out card in the front of this book. Check out www. aaireland.ie (click on "Menu," and then "Route Planning") for route-planning help and specific driving directions. I find that the best driving maps are the **Ordnance Survey Ireland** maps, available at some bookstores or travel shops, online at www.osi.ie, and at ☎ **01-802-5300.**

Booking a rental car

In the off-season (Oct–Mar), you should have little difficulty getting a car on short (or even no) notice. Booking anything during the summer, however, is a different story. To stay on the safe side, book any time from a few weeks to a few months in advance.

Because prices are bound to increase based on demand, the earlier you book your car, the better your chance of getting a deal. Some of the major rental-car companies operating in Ireland are **Auto-Europe, Alamo, Argus, Avis, Budget, Dan Dooley, Hertz, Murray's Europcar,** and **National.** The toll-free numbers and Web sites for these companies are listed in the appendix.

If you fly into Dublin and plan to spend some time there, wait to get a car until you're ready to head out to the countryside. Dublin is relatively walkable, and the bus system in the city is excellent, so you don't need a car — and with the lack of parking, you won't want one. However, if you're planning to leave town straightaway, or if you fly into Shannon airport, getting a car upon arrival is a good idea.

Most rental-car companies allow you to drop cars off at places other than where you picked them up, and most do not charge a drop-off fee (but some do, so be sure to ask). However, some companies don't allow you to pick up a car in the Republic and drop it off in Northern Ireland, or vice versa.

Saving money on your rental

Car rental rates vary even more than airline fares. The price depends on the size of the car, the length of time you keep it, where and when you pick it up and drop it off, where you take it, and a host of other factors. Asking a few key questions may save you hundreds of dollars.

- ✔ Weekend rates may be lower than weekday rates. If you're keeping the car five or more days, a weekly rate may be cheaper than the daily rate. Ask if the rate is the same for pickup Friday morning as it is Thursday night.

- ✔ Some companies may assess a drop-off charge if you don't return the car to the same rental location; others, notably National, don't.

- ✔ Check whether the rate is cheaper if you pick up the car at a location in town rather than at the airport.

- ✔ Find out whether age is an issue. Many car rental companies add on a fee for drivers under 25, while some don't rent to them at all.

- ✔ If you see an advertised price in your local newspaper, be sure to ask for that specific rate, otherwise you may be charged the standard (higher) rate. Don't forget to mention membership in AAA, AARP, and trade unions. These memberships usually entitle you to discounts ranging from 5 percent to 30 percent.

- ✔ Check your frequent-flier accounts. Not only are your favorite (or at least most-used) airlines likely to have sent you discount coupons, but most car rentals add at least 500 miles to your account.

- ✔ As with other aspects of planning your trip, using the Internet can make comparison shopping for a car rental much easier. You can check rates at most of the major agencies' Web sites. Plus, all the

major travel sites — **Travelocity** (www.travelocity.com),
Expedia (www.expedia.com), **Orbitz** (www.orbitz.com), and
Smarter Travel (www.smartertravel.com), for example — have
search engines that can dig up discounted car-rental rates. Just
enter the car size you want, the pickup and return dates, and location, and the server returns a price. You can even make the reservation through any of these sites.

In addition to the standard rental prices, other optional charges apply to
most car rentals (and some not-so-optional charges, such as taxes). The
Collision Damage Waiver (CDW), which requires you to pay for damage
to the car in a collision, is covered by many credit card companies.
Check with your credit card company before you go so you can avoid
paying this hefty fee (as much as $20 a day).

The car rental companies also offer additional *liability insurance* (if you
harm others in an accident), *personal accident insurance* (if you harm
yourself or your passengers), and *personal effects insurance* (if your luggage is stolen from your car). Your insurance policy on your car at home
probably covers most of these unlikely occurrences. However, if your
own insurance doesn't cover you for rentals or if you don't have auto
insurance, definitely consider the additional coverage (ask your car
rental agent for more information). Unless you're toting around the Hope
diamond, and you don't want to leave that in your car trunk anyway, you
can probably skip the personal effects insurance, but driving around
without liability or personal accident coverage is never a good idea.
Even if you're a good driver, other people may not be, and liability
claims can be complicated.

Some companies also offer *refueling packages,* in which you pay for your
initial full tank of gas up front and return the car with an empty gas tank.
The prices can be competitive with local gas prices, but you don't get
credit for any gas remaining in the tank. If you reject this option, you pay
only for the gas you use, but you have to return the car with a full tank
or face high charges for any shortfall. If you usually run late and a fueling
stop may make you miss your plane, you're a perfect candidate for the
fuel-purchase option.

Considering your rental options

You may think you want a larger vehicle, but keep in mind that most
roads are nail-bitingly narrow; winding down a street lined with cars and
filled with oncoming traffic, you'll appreciate driving a minimobile. So
try to get the smallest car you think you'll be comfortable in. Another
thought: Smaller is cheaper.

Unlike the United States, where it's standard for rental cars to have an
automatic transmission, the standard in Ireland is a manual transmission
(stick shift). You can get an automatic — but it will cost you at least 50
percent more than a manual. Prices vary widely, so if you're sure you
want an automatic, shop around for the best deal.

Boots, bonnets, and other brouhaha

To save you confusion about the words and phrases that the Irish have for car-related and driving-related things, here's a list of the most commonly used (and most commonly confused):

✔ **An Lar:** city center

✔ **Bonnet:** Hood

✔ **Boot:** Trunk

✔ **Carpark:** Parking lot

✔ **Dual carriageway:** Divided Highway

✔ **Footpath** or **path:** Sidewalk

✔ **Gear stick:** Stick shift

✔ **Lay-by:** breakdown lane or pullout lane

✔ **Motorways:** Highways

✔ **Petrol:** Gasoline

✔ **Roundabout:** Traffic circle (or a rotary, if you're from New England). These are common, especially entering and leaving cities. Make sure you go left and yield to the right!

✔ **Windscreen:** Windshield

Because the driver's side is on the right side of cars in Ireland, the stick shift is controlled by your left hand, not your right. Sounds wacky and hard to do, but you should get the hang of it in no time.

Paying for a rental car

Some companies require a deposit when you make your reservation, generally on a credit card. If you book by phone, you may be asked for a deposit.

Don't be shocked if the rental company charges you a gas deposit on your card, too. Just be sure to fill the tank before drop-off, and the deposit will be taken off (good thing, because the deposit is always way higher than the actual cost of the gas).

Gas, called *petrol* in Ireland, is costly. The prices that petrol stations advertise may seem decent to U.S. citizens unaware that they're priced per liter, not gallon. Generally you pay twice what you would in the United States. This is another good reason to get a smaller car: better gas mileage.

Getting the scoop on driver's licenses and insurance

If you are from the United States, Canada, the U.K., Australia, New Zealand, or an EU country, all you need to legally drive a car in Ireland is a valid driver's license from your country of residence.

Your personal auto insurance most likely doesn't extend to rental cars in Ireland. If you have a MasterCard Platinum or Gold card in the U.S. or a Visa Gold in Canada, check with your credit card company to find out if they will cover auto insurance in Ireland. You must get a Collision Damage Waiver (CDW) with your rental car (this is usually included in the price quoted). This insurance reduces the renter's financial responsibility in the case of an accident. The car rental companies also offer additional *liability insurance* (if you harm others in an accident), *personal accident insurance* (if you harm yourself or your passengers), and *personal effects insurance* (if your luggage is stolen from your car). Definitely consider the additional coverage of the liability insurance and the personal accident insurance (ask your car rental agent for more information). Unless you're toting around the Hope diamond (and you don't want to leave that in your car trunk anyway), you can probably skip the personal effects insurance.

If you plan on taking the car into Northern Ireland, be sure to inform the rental company, and ask whether additional insurance is required.

Figuring out the rules of the road

Here are some important traffic rules and laws that will help you get around safely and legally.

- ✔ **Speed limits throughout the Republic of Ireland are listed in kilometers per hour, while speed limits in Northern Ireland are in miles per hour.** In the Republic, the speed limit on local and regional roads is 80 kmph, while the speed limit on national roads (indicated by an N in front of a number) is 100 kmph. Standard 80- or 100-kmph signs are indicated only by a black circle with a slash through it (with no numbers). When the speed limit is other than 80 kmph on local and regional roads, and 100 kmph on national roads, there'll be a sign with a red circle with the limit written inside in black. You often see these signs when entering small towns, where you should always reduce speed to 50 kmph. On large motorways (highways), the speed limit is generally 120 kmph. In Northern Ireland, the speed limit on motorways is 70 mph, while the speed limit on other roads is 60 mph, going down to 30 mph in cities and towns.

- ✔ A sign that is a red circle with a red X through the middle means no stopping or parking during posted hours.

- ✔ A flashing yellow light means yield to pedestrian traffic, but proceed with caution if it's clear.

How do I find a place when there's no #&@*$! address!?

Welcome to one of the facts of life in Ireland: Outside of the major cities, American-style street names and addresses simply aren't used. As you leaf through this book, you'll often see the name of a B&B listed with just the town name after it. This is just the way it works. In fact, if you were to write a letter to the place, you'd address it the very same way, with just its name and the town.

I know what you're thinking: "How am I supposed to find any of these places?!" Fear not: It's not as hard as it seems. Often, these places are right on the town's main thoroughfare (such as R236 or the Dublin-Waterford road), and in these cases, if you drive into the town, you can't miss them. Other places are near the town's main street and have signs directing you toward them from the center of town. Of course, there are also several places that are nowhere near the main part of town. In these cases, I include specific directions.

✔ When entering a roundabout (traffic circle), yield to traffic coming from your right.

✔ Seat belts must be worn by drivers and front-seat passengers. If your car has back seat belts, they must be worn as well.

✔ It is illegal to use a cellphone while driving in Ireland.

✔ Drinking and driving is a serious offense and is dealt with harshly. Do not drink and drive under any circumstances.

If you have any further questions about traffic laws, you can call the **National Safety Council** at ☎ **096-25-000,** or visit their Web site at www.nsc.ie.

Driving on the left side of the road

To get an idea of what driving in Ireland is like, simply imagine driving in North America and then turn that image upside down. The steering wheel is on the right side, and the gearshift is on the left (the positions of the gas, clutch, and brake are the same).

In highway traffic, you merge to the right while slower traffic stays on the left. Roundabouts are tricky, and you'll probably pop a few curbs while making sharp lefts, but don't get discouraged. Driving in Ireland just takes practice, practice, practice.

Understanding parking rules and regulations

First, there's no law that prohibits you from parking a car facing into traffic. You will often see cars on one side of the road parked in both directions, which makes it tough to tell if you're going the wrong way on a one-way street. In larger towns, there are some, but not many, parking garages. Street parking is fine, but instead of meters, you often have to buy *parking disks,* which are paper disks that indicate how long you've been in the spot. You can buy disks at machines marked *P* and sometimes at local shops. Purchase a disk and then display it in the window. Residential neighborhoods and some towns require disks but have no parking-disk machines. In those cases, local convenience stores usually sell the disks.

Traveling by Bus

Buses are a pretty great way to see Ireland for a variety of reasons: They make many more stops than trains, you get a great view of the countryside from the huge windows, they're comfortable, and they're pretty inexpensive. On the other hand, you're not free to stop whenever you want, and most buses don't have bathrooms.

Getting to know the major bus companies

Bus Éireann is the country's principal public coach line, with a vast network of routes that web through all the major towns of Ireland and into Northern Ireland. Bus Éireann is pretty much a tool of transportation rather than tourism, so it doesn't always stop right near popular sights. The trick is to get to a town near the attraction that you want to see and then take local transportation from there. Prices, schedules, routes, and other information can be found at Bus Éireann on Store Street, Dublin 1 (☎ 01-836-6111; www.buseireann.ie).

In Northern Ireland, **Ulsterbus** is the area bus service, with routes that include stops at or near the region's attractions. You can call the timetable hot line at ☎ 028-9066-6630, or find information online at www.ulsterbus.co.uk.

Finding bus packages and tours

Bus Éireann offers guided sightseeing tours that cover a number of top attractions. Routes become more limited in the off-season, so call ahead to find out when each tour is offered. The major daytrips out of Dublin are:

- ✔ Glendalough, Wicklow, and Powerscourt Gardens (see Chapter 13)
- ✔ Newgrange and Boyne Valley (see Chapter 12)
- ✔ Kilkenny City and the Nore Valley (see Chapter 14)
- ✔ Waterford Crystal and River Barrow Cruise (see Chapter 14)
- ✔ The Mountains of Mourne (see Chapter 23)

You can also book seasonal trips out from Cork, Galway, and Sligo. For more information, visit www.buseireann.ie or call ☎ 01-836-6111.

Riding the Rails

Ireland has an excellent rail system that connects the major cities of the Republic and Northern Ireland; the "Irish Rail Routes" map shows the system. The advantages of train travel are that it's fast and very comfortable. On the downside, trains are more expensive and travel to fewer destinations than buses, and you have to be ready to jump off with all your luggage, because trains pull into the station and stop for half a second before flying on to the next stop.

Trains between major cities run three to five times daily and are reliable. During low season, you should have no problem buying tickets a half-hour before departure, but during the high season, calling the day before to confirm availability is advisable. For information about destinations, times, and fares, call **Iarnród Éireann** (Irish Rail) at ☎ **1850-366-222** or visit www.irishrail.ie. In Northern Ireland, **NI Railways** information is available at ☎ **028-90-66-66-30** or www.nirailways.co.uk.

Finding train packages and tours

Excellent packages combine train travel to a destination with bus tours that explore non-rail-accessible destinations such as the Burren, Connemara, and the Ring of Kerry. Some of these offerings include hotel accommodations. **Railtours Ireland** (☎ **01-856-0045**; www.railtours.ie), which operates in association with Iarnród Éireann (Irish Rail), is one of the finest tour operators, offering tours that range from half a day to four days.

Bus and rail passes for extended travel

The following bus and rail deals are available through **Bus Éireann** (☎ **1-850-366-222;** go to www.buseireann.ie, then click on "Fares and Tickets," and then "Tourist Travel Passes"). For a flat price, you get a pass allowing you unlimited use of trains and buses.

- ✔ **Irish Explorer Bus & Rail:** Eight days out of fifteen consecutive days combined rail and bus in the Republic of Ireland only (includes Intercity, DART, and Suburban Rail, plus Bus Éireann Expressway and Provincial services and Bus Éireann city services in Cork, Limerick, Galway and Waterford): €210 ($336) adult, €110 ($176) children under 16.

- ✔ **Irish Rover Bus Only:** Good for all Bus Éireann services (including city buses in Cork, Limerick, Galway, and Waterford), plus all Ulsterbus services in Northern Ireland. Three days out of eight consecutive days: €76 ($122) for adults, €44 ($70) for children under 16. Eight days out of fifteen consecutive days: €172 ($275) adult, €94 ($150) children under 16. Fifteen days out of thirty consecutive days: €255 ($408) adults, €138 ($221) children under 16.

Irish Rail Routes

✔ **Emerald Card:** Eight days out of fifteen consecutive days combined rail and bus in the Republic and Northern Ireland (covers Intercity; DART; Suburban Rail; Northern Ireland Railways; Bus Éireann Expressway; Provincial Bus; Ulsterbus Provincial Services; and city buses in Cork, Limerick, Galway, and Waterford): €248 ($397) adult, €124 ($198) children under 16. Fifteen days out of thirty consecutive days: €426 ($682) adult, €213 ($341) children under 16.

✔ **Open Road Pass:** This pass gives unlimited travel on all Bus Éireann buses in the Republic. There are many options for this ticket, from tickets that can be used on three days out of a consecutive six (€49/$78) to tickets that can be used on 15 days out of 30 (€217/$347).

Chapter 8

Booking Your Accommodations

In This Chapter

▶ Exploring your accommodations options

▶ Checking out prices

▶ Getting the best rate

▶ Browsing the Internet for lodging deals

*A*re B&Bs the best value? Where can you find discounts on lodging? How much does a swanky hotel cost? Read on for answers to all your burning accommodations questions.

Knowing Your Options

From grand manor houses to cute and charming B&Bs, Ireland has accommodations for a range of budgets and tastes. Anywhere you stay, you're likely to encounter the warmth and friendliness that are so much a part of Irish culture. People here take a lot of pride in their hospitality.

Two of the best places to find and book hotels and guesthouses online are at www.irelandhotels.com and www.goireland.com. **Gulliver** (☎ 066-979-2030; www.gulliver.ie) also has a tremendous database of lodgings and allows you to reserve with a credit card. The tourist boards of the Republic of Ireland (☎ 1-850-230-330; www.discoverireland.ie) and Northern Ireland (☎ 028-9023-1221; www.discovernorthernireland.com) are also great sources for finding and booking accommodations.

If you're looking for fancy manor houses and castles, check out **Ireland's Blue Book** (☎ 1-800-323-5463 in the U.S., or ☎ 01-676-9914 in Ireland; www.irelands-blue-book.com). For upscale manor houses and guesthouses, including some of the most beautiful and oldest houses in Ireland, contact **Hidden Ireland** (☎ 01-662-7166; www.hidden-ireland.com).

Opting for hotels

Among hotels, the range of accommodations is wide — from castles on down to small family-run lodges. Though you can assume that many of the larger and chain hotels provide fitness equipment, room service, and in-house pubs and restaurants, don't count on these amenities in smaller independent hotels.

The **Irish Hotel Federation's** guide to hotels, manor houses, inns, and castles is a great resource. Contact the Irish Tourist Board for a copy (☎ 1-800-233-6470; www.tourismireland.com) or check it out online at www.irelandhotels.com.

The Irish Tourist Board and the Northern Ireland Tourist Board rank hotels from one to five stars based on the amenities and facilities offered. These ratings give you a rough idea of what you can expect in terms of room service, dataports, and so on, but they don't say much about the character of the places or about the owners and staff.

The following chains have quality hotels in major cities throughout the country. I list them here, starting with the most upscale.

- ✔ **Jurys:** ☎ **01-607-0070;** www.jurys.com (locations in Dublin, Waterford, Cork, Galway, Limerick, and Belfast)
- ✔ **Tower:** ☎ **01-428-2400;** fax 01-428-2411; www.towerhotelgroup. com (locations in Dublin, Waterford, and Derry)
- ✔ **Travelodge:** www.travelodge.ie (locations in Dublin, Waterford, Cork, Limerick, Galway, Derry, and Belfast)

Getting the best room

After you make your reservation, asking one or two questions can go a long way toward making sure you get the best room in the house.

- ✔ Always ask for a corner room. These rooms are usually larger, quieter, and have more windows and light than standard rooms, and they don't always cost more.
- ✔ Ask if the hotel is renovating. If it is, request a room away from the renovation work.
- ✔ Inquire, too, about the location of the restaurants, bars, and discos in the hotel — all sources of annoying noise.

And if you aren't happy with your room when you arrive, talk to the front desk. If they have another room, they should be happy to accommodate you, within reason.

Staying in casual comfort: Choosing B&Bs

Though they're not for everyone, I think that bed-and-breakfasts (B&Bs) are the best lodging option in Ireland. Because they're small, they give you an opportunity to get to know the owners, who much more often than not are friendly and knowledgeable about the area. Another big advantage of choosing a B&B over a hotel is the price. The cost of a double room is usually much lower than at a hotel, averaging between €80 ($52) and €120 ($104).

Keep in mind that some B&Bs don't accept credit cards, so make sure you have enough cash on hand when it's time to check out.

Most B&Bs have between four and ten rooms only, so the better ones fill up quickly during the high season. You should book at least a week in advance of your trip — even sooner if possible.

Some B&B rooms are not *en suite,* meaning that they don't have a private bathroom. If you don't want to share facilities with other guests, make sure you ask for a room with its own bathroom, keeping in mind that you'll probably pay more for privacy.

If you'd like a booklet of the 2,000 or so B&Bs in Ireland, write to or call the **Irish Tourist Board** (☎ 1-850-230-330; www.ireland.ie). For Northern Ireland, ask the **Northern Ireland Tourist Board** (☎ 028-9023-1221; www.discovernorthernireland.com) for the free *Bed & Breakfasts* guide (on the Web site, click on the "Maps & Brochures" link, in the menu on the main page). For upscale B&Bs, including some of the oldest and most beautiful houses in Ireland, contact **Hidden Ireland** (☎ 01-662-7166; www.hidden-ireland.com).

Enjoying self-catering accommodations

Self-catering accommodations are a place for you to drop your bags, settle in, and do things family-style, including cooking your own meals and making your own beds. If you're making the trip with children, this may be a perfect option, both in terms of convenience and cost.

With self-catering, you pay one price, generally for the week. (Some rent for two to three days.) Compared to the amount of money you pay for hotels and B&Bs on a nightly basis, the price is usually a bargain. Plus, food costs decrease when you're buying your own and cooking it yourself.

The drawback is location. Although some self-catering cottages and apartments are in *great* locations, the trouble is that they don't move: Rent one and you're in one place for the whole week; to see the sights around the country, you have to drive to them and then drive "home" again. Of course, this is fine if you intend to spend all your time in one area. But making day trips to sights in far-flung parts of the country may be tough.

The variety of self-catering options is as diverse as types of hotels. You can stay in actual thatched-roof cottages or completely modernized units. All of these accommodations are registered with the tourism authorities and are rated from one to four stars (four being the best).

As with any place to stay, all you have to do is call the tourist board in the area you want to visit, and the staff there will help you with bookings. To get you started, the following organizations deal solely with self-catering accommodations.

- ✔ **Cottages in Ireland** (☎ 0870-236-1630; www.cottagesinireland.com) has properties in gorgeous locations in Northern Ireland.

- ✔ **Irish Cottage Holiday Homes Association** (☎ 01-205-2777; www.irishcottageholidays.com) rents vacation cottages in the Republic of Ireland.

- ✔ **The Irish Landmark Trust** (☎ 01-670-4733; www.irishlandmark.com) restores historic properties to provide some of the coolest self-catering options in Ireland — think staying in a lighthouse keeper's cottage.

- ✔ **Northern Ireland Self-Catering Holidays Association** (☎ 028-9043-6632; www.nischa.com) rents cottages in Northern Ireland.

- ✔ **Rent an Irish Cottage** (☎ 061-41-1109; www.rentacottage.ie) organizes self-catering in cottages all over Ireland.

- ✔ **Self-Catering Ireland** (☎ 053-913-3999; www.selfcatering-ireland.com) is the most comprehensive reservation service, offering three- and four-star self-catering apartments throughout Ireland and Northern Ireland.

- ✔ **Trident Holiday Homes** (☎ 01-201-8440; www.thh.ie) offers a good selection of rentals all over Ireland.

Staying at a hostel

Hostels have a reputation for being the accommodation of choice for the micro-budgeted, and if you have an image in your head of hostels full of young, tireless travelers who don't mind going long stretches without showers or food, you're partly right — though only partly. Today, hostels

Spas!

Ireland has an exploding spa industry. Spas with accommodations are occasionally called "health farms" (which always makes me picture a cow in a bubble bath), and offer all sorts of therapies and treatments in addition to delicious, healthy food. For options, check out **Health Farms of Ireland** (☎ 091-794-959; www.healthfarmsofireland.com).

serve all kinds of independent travelers who cherish flexibility, and many hostels are adding more facilities to accommodate couples and families.

Some Irish hostels offer community kitchens, and many sleep people dorm-style, with anywhere from four to dozens of people per room (some have single-sex dorm rooms while others are co-ed). However, more and more Irish hostels have been adding double and family rooms, and even private single rooms, so you may not need to share a room with other travelers.

Hostels provide a blanket and pillow, and some beds have sheets, but to be safe, bring your own sleep-sack — two twin sheets sewn together.

Because your personal belongings most likely sit at the foot of the bed, you may wonder how safe your luggage will be in a hostel. Theft is not a major problem, but it is something to consider. Many hostels provide security lockers (ask when you reserve if it's important to you), but if not, take some precautions: Make your luggage as difficult to get into as possible by, for instance, stacking bags on top of one another, with the most valuable at the bottom. Also, bring your wallet, passport, and other important personal belongings to bed with you, and under no circumstances leave important documents or money in your room.

As for bathrooms, think of high-school gym restrooms — cold tiles, a row of small sinks and toilets, and shower stalls. You may not love it, but you can get the job done in it.

I can't vouch for every hostel in Ireland, but if there's one undeniable fact, it's that they're cheap. You can get a warm bed in a dorm for under $35. And you meet people from all over the world doing the same thing as you. Sure, you run into your share of hostels that don't exactly disinfect the toilet daily, but on the whole, Irish hostels are the cleanest I've seen anywhere.

Some hostels take reservations. Others are first-come, first-sleep. If you're planning to do a hostel tour of Ireland, you'll really benefit from joining **Hostelling International** (www.hihostels.com) before you depart. Fees are about $28 a year for adults. With a membership card, you get discounts at places affiliated with the group.

To find hostels in the Republic of Ireland, check out **An Óige,** the Irish Youth Hostel Association (☎ **01-830-4555;** fax 01-830-5808; www.anoige.ie). For hostels in Northern Ireland, contact or visit **YHANI** (Youth Hostels Association of Northern Ireland), also called HINI (☎ **028-9032-4733;** fax 028-9031-5889; www.hini.org.uk).

Frolicking at Farmhouse accommodations

For information on staying on a farm, check out the **Irish Farm Holidays Association** (☎ **061-309-955;** www.irishfarmholidays.com).

If you are interested in working on a farm in Ireland, visit the **World-Wide Opportunities on Organic Farms** site (www.wwoof.org).

Seeking out alternatives

If you're looking for something a little different from the usual hotel or B&B, try one of these options:

- ✔ **Caravans (trailers/motorhomes):** For information on renting or buying a caravan or trailer, contact **Irish Caravan & Camping Council** (fax 098-28237; www.camping-ireland.ie).

- ✔ **University housing:** Check with local tourist boards or directly with universities to find out whether they have unused dorm space in campus housing to rent. Cities with large universities include Dublin, Galway, Cork, and Limerick. Housing is usually available only during the summer and Christmas holidays.

Figuring Out Accommodation Prices

To make it easy for you to quickly gauge the price of each lodging in this guide, in Table 8.1, I list the cost of a *double room* for each option — the cost for two people to stay in one room together. The range given typically indicates the lowest price for the room during the low season up to the highest price during the high season. The range also takes into account (no pun intended) the difference in price for a room with a view, a larger room, and so on. If you're traveling alone, count on paying a bit more than half the price listed for a double.

Almost every accommodation I list in the book includes a full Irish breakfast.

Table 8.1	Key to Hotel Dollar Signs	
Dollar Sign(s)	**Price Range**	**What to Expect**
$	Up to $110	Small bed-and-breakfasts often fall into this category, offering cozy rooms and homemade breakfasts. You may miss high-end amenities (usually no pool, restaurant, or the like), but you're sure to appreciate the friendly hosts and hostesses who operate these spots.
$$	$110–$160	B&Bs and hotels both fall into this price range. The more expensive B&Bs are often a bit classier and refined than those in the preceding category, with gourmet breakfasts, prime locations, antiques-filled rooms, and so on. Hotels in this range are usually stylish and offer extras such as hair dryers, irons, and microwaves.

(continued)

Table 8.1 *(continued)*

Dollar Sign(s)	Price Range	What to Expect
$$$	$160–$240	Higher-class still, these accommodations are pretty plush. Think grand manor houses, castles, and top-tier business hotels, boasting perks such as fine linens, hand-carved furniture, antiques, excellent in-house restaurants, and polished service.
$$$$	$240 and up	These top-rated accommodations (most often manors, castles, and luxury hotels) come with luxury amenities such as golf courses, spas, and in-room hot tubs and CD players.

Finding the Best Room Rate at Hotels

The **rack rate** is the maximum rate a hotel charges for a room. It's the rate you get if you walk in off the street and ask for a room for the night. You sometimes see these rates printed on the fire/emergency exit diagrams posted on the back of your door.

Hotels are happy to charge you the rack rate, but you can almost always do better. Perhaps the best way to avoid paying the rack rate is surprisingly simple: Just ask for a cheaper or discounted rate. You may be pleasantly surprised.

In hotels and larger guesthouses, the rate you pay for a room depends on many factors — chief among them being how you make your reservation. A travel agent may be able to negotiate a better price with certain hotels than you can get by yourself. (That's because the hotel often gives the agent a discount in exchange for steering business to that hotel.)

Reserving a room through the hotel's toll-free number may also result in a lower rate than calling the hotel directly. On the other hand, the central reservations number may not know about discount rates at specific locations. For example, local franchises may offer a special group rate for a wedding or family reunion, but they may neglect to tell the central booking line. Your best bet is to call both the local number and the toll-free number, and see which one gives you a better deal.

Room rates (even rack rates) change with the season, as occupancy rates rise and fall. In most of Ireland, hotels charge the highest rate during the high season of June through August and the lowest during the low season of November through March. In Dublin, all bets are off because the city receives a high volume of visitors all year, and most rates don't go down during the winter. See Chapter 3 for more on the seasons in Ireland. Know that even within a given season, room prices are subject to change without notice, so the rates quoted in this book may be different from the actual rate you receive when you make your reservation.

 Be sure to mention membership in AAA, AARP, frequent-flier programs, or any other corporate rewards programs you can think of when you call to book. You never know when an affiliation may be worth a few dollars off your room rate.

See Chapter 6 for information on package tours, which often include air-fare and accommodations sold together for a discounted price.

Surfing the Web for Hotel Deals

Shopping online for hotels is generally done one of two ways: by booking through the hotel's own website or through an independent booking agency (or a fare-service agency such as Priceline). These Internet hotel agencies have multiplied in mind-boggling numbers of late, competing for the business of millions of consumers surfing for accommodations around the world. This competitiveness can be a boon to consumers who have the patience and time to shop and compare the online sites for good deals — but shop they must, for prices can vary considerably from site to site. And keep in mind that hotels at the top of a site's listing may be there for no other reason than that they paid money to get the placement.

In addition to the online travel booking sites **Travelocity, Expedia, Orbitz, Priceline,** and **Hotwire,** you can book hotels through **Hotels. com, Quikbook** (www.quikbook.com), and **Travelaxe** (www.travel axe.net).

HotelChatter.com is a daily webzine offering smart coverage and critiques of hotels worldwide. Go to **TripAdvisor.com** or **HotelShark.com** for helpful independent consumer reviews of hotels and resort properties.

It's a good idea to **get a confirmation number** and **make a printout** of any online booking transaction.

Chapter 9

Catering to Special Travel Needs and Interests

In This Chapter

▶ Sightseeing with your family
▶ Getting tips for mature travelers
▶ Navigating Ireland with disabilities
▶ Taking advantage of being a student
▶ Checking out the gay and lesbian scenes
▶ Finding resources for special interests: hiking, horseback riding, and more

*A*lthough every traveler has different needs, some special cases are common enough that special travel services are set up around the world just for them. In this chapter, I run through some services, give some tips, and note some challenges of travel in Ireland. I also offer resources for travelers with special interests such as genealogy research, golfing, hiking, biking, and fishing.

Traveling with the Brood: Advice for Families

Ireland is a wonderful place to travel with a family; the language, food, and culture is familiar enough to be comforting, while it's different enough to be exciting. As a general rule, children are more than welcome at attractions, accommodations, and restaurants.

You can find good family-oriented vacation advice on the Internet from sites such as the **Family Travel Forum** (www.familytravelforum.com), a comprehensive site that offers customized trip planning; **Family Travel Network** (www.familytravelnetwork.com), an award-winning site that offers travel features, deals, and tips; **Traveling Internationally with Your Kids** (www.travelwithyourkids.com), a comprehensive site offering sound advice for long-distance and international travel with children; and **Family Travel Files** (www.thefamilytravelfiles.com), which offers an online magazine and a directory of off-the-beaten-path tours and tour operators for families.

Most attractions and some public transportation companies in Ireland and Northern Ireland offer reduced fees for children. And most attractions have family group prices (usually for two adults and two or three children) that are a great bargain. Be sure to ask. (See more money-saving tips in Chapter 5.)

Car rental companies provide necessary car seats, and all vehicles have rear seatbelts. The law requires that children always buckle up.

For a small additional fee, you can sometimes add a cot to your room at a hotel, guest house, or B&B so that your child can stay in the same room as you. Check with the concierge or manager.

Throughout this book, I point out kid-friendly accommodations, dining options, and attractions — just look for the Kid Friendly icon.

To find more kid-friendly hotels and B&Bs, go to www.irelandhotels.com, click on "Detailed Search," and specify the child-friendly facilities that you are looking for. Note that a daycare facility in Ireland is called a *creche*.

Making Age Work for You: Advice for Seniors

Mention the fact that you're a senior citizen when you make your travel reservations — many hotels offer discounts for seniors. The **Irish Tourist Board** (☎ 1-850-230-330; www.ireland.ie) publishes a list of discount hotel packages for seniors, called *Golden Holidays/For the Over 55s.*

In Ireland, people over the age of 60 qualify for reduced admission to theaters, museums, and other attractions, as well as discounted fares on public transportation.

Senior discounts will usually be listed under the term "OAP," which means Old Age Pensioner and means that exact same thing that "senior" does in the United States.

Members of **AARP** (formerly known as the American Association of Retired Persons), 601 E St. NW, Washington, DC 20049 (☎ 888-687-2277; www.aarp.org), get discounts on hotels, airfares, and car rentals. AARP offers members a wide range of benefits, including *AARP: The Magazine* and a monthly newsletter. Anyone over 50 can join.

Many reliable agencies and organizations target the 50-plus market. **Elderhostel** (☎ 800-454-5768; www.elderhostel.org) arranges study programs for those ages 55 and older (and a spouse or companion of any age) in the United States and in more than 80 countries around the world. American tour operator **CIE Tours** (☎ **800-CIE-TOUR;** www. cietours.com) gives discounts to seniors on some of its tours.

Recommended publications offering travel resources and discounts for seniors include the quarterly magazine *Travel 50 & Beyond* (www. travel50andbeyond.com); *Travel Unlimited: Uncommon Adventures for the Mature Traveler* (Avalon); *101 Tips for Mature Travelers,* available from Grand Circle Travel (☎ **800-221-2610** or 617-350-7500; www.gct.com); and *Unbelievably Good Deals and Great Adventures That You Absolutely Can't Get Unless You're Over 50* (McGraw-Hill), by Joan Rattner Heilman.

Accessing Ireland: Advice for Travelers with Disabilities

Ireland has accessibility regulations for public areas, though they're not as comprehensive as in the United States. Most sidewalks have ramps, and many accommodations are wheelchair-accessible. Getting around in cities and towns isn't hard, but some of Ireland's attractions are not very accessible. Not every museum has closed captions for video presentations, and not every castle has an entrance ramp. Calling ahead to find out about accessibility at attractions and at B&Bs (many of which aren't wheelchair-friendly) is always a good idea, but you can feel fairly confident that most restaurants and newer hotels are entirely accessible. For further information, the Access Department of the **National Disability Authority,** 24–25 Clyde Rd., Dublin 4 (☎ **01-608-0400**), can connect you with information on wheelchair-friendly attractions, restaurants, and accommodations. For tips on travel in the North, contact **Disability Action** (☎ **028-9029-7880;** www.disabilityaction.org). The Northern Ireland Tourist Board (☎ **028-9023-1221;** www.discover northernireland.com) publishes an *Information Guide to Accessible Accommodation.*

Many travel agencies offer customized tours and itineraries for travelers with disabilities. **The Guided Tour, Inc.** (☎ **215-782-1370;** www.guided tour.com) conducts annual trips to Ireland for developmentally challenged travelers, and **Trips, Inc.: Special Adventures** (☎ **541-686-1013** in the U.S.; tripsinc.com) leads trips to Ireland for travelers with all sorts of disabilities. Also check out **Flying Wheels Travel** (☎ **507-451-5006;** www.flyingwheelstravel.com), **Access-Able Travel Source** (☎ **303-232-2979;** www.access-able.com), and **Accessible Journeys** (☎ **800-846-4537** or 610-521-0339).

Organizations that offer assistance to disabled travelers include **MossRehab** (www.mossresourcenet.org), the **American Foundation for the Blind** (AFB; ☎ **800-232-5463;** www.afb.org), and **SATH (Society** for **Accessible Travel and Hospitality**; ☎ 212-447-7284; www.sath.org). **AirAmbulanceCard.com** is now partnered with SATH and allows you to preselect top-notch hospitals in case of an emergency.

For more information specifically targeted to travelers with disabilities, the community Web site **iCan** (www.icanonline.net/channels/travel/index.cfm) has destination guides and several regular columns on accessible travel. Also check out the quarterly magazine *Emerging Horizons* (www.emerginghorizons.com) and *Open World Magazine,* published by SATH.

Studying Up on Ireland: Advice for Students

With half of its population under 30, Ireland is accustomed to catering to students. Most attractions have student admission prices that are significantly lower than the usual prices, and many transportation companies offer students discounts. Usually you just need to present your university ID card. A few attractions and companies require the presentation of an official student ID card (instead of your regular university ID), so check out the ISE Card (International Student Exchange Card) at www.isecard.com or the ISIC (International Student Identity Card) at www.isiccard.com if you want to make sure you get every last bargain.

In the United States, **STA Travel** (☎ 800-781-4040; www.statravel.com) offers information on all sorts of student travel discounts. In Canada, **Travel CUTS** (☎ 866-246-9762; www.travelcuts.com) does the same.

Also check out youth travel company **USIT** (☎ 01-602-1904 in the Republic of Ireland, ☎ 028-9032-7111 in Northern Ireland; www.usitnow.ie), especially if you are thinking of studying or working in Ireland.

Following the Rainbow: Advice for Gay and Lesbian Travelers

Ireland is becoming more and more gay-friendly. Though some of the smaller towns may still have a negative reaction to homosexuality, the larger towns and cities — especially Dublin, Cork, and Galway — actively support their gay population and make gay visitors feel especially welcome.

Dublin in particular has a pretty thriving gay scene, with hotels, pubs, and clubs geared toward gay men and lesbians. **George,** 89 S. Great George's St. (☎ 01-478-2983), a huge pub and nightclub, is *the* place for gay men to gather.

Your guide to all things gay and lesbian is the *Gay Community News* (www.gcn.ie), a free monthly newspaper devoted to the gay community. The paper is available in gay-oriented venues, especially bookshops, all over Ireland. In Dublin, the city's **Event Guide** (www.eventguide.ie) has several pages listing gay events, organization, clubs, and the like. In addition, **Queer ID** (www.queerid.com) has a great listing of gay events, clubs, and more, mostly in Dublin. Finally, see www.gaydublin.com for information on gay-friendly hotels, pubs, and more in Dublin. **Outhouse,** 105 Capel St., Dublin 1 (☎ 01-873-4932; www.outhouse.ie), offer all sorts of information for gay men and lesbians.

The International Gay and Lesbian Travel Association (IGLTA; ☎ 954-630-1637; www.iglta.org) is the trade association for the gay and lesbian travel industry, and offers an online directory of gay- and lesbian-friendly travel businesses.

Many agencies offer tours and travel itineraries specifically for gay and lesbian travelers. Among them are **Above and Beyond Tours (☎ 800-397-2681;** www.abovebeyondtours.com); **Now, Voyager (☎ 800-255-6951;** www.nowvoyager.com); and **Olivia Cruises & Resorts (☎ 800-631-6277;** www.olivia.com).

Gay.com Travel (☎ 800-929-2268 or 415-644-8044; www.gay.com/travel or www.outandabout.com) is an excellent online successor to the popular *Out & About* print magazine. It provides regularly updated information about gay-owned, gay-oriented, and gay-friendly lodging, dining, sightseeing, nightlife, and shopping establishments in every important destination worldwide.

The following travel guides are available at many bookstores, or you can order them from any online bookseller: *Frommer's Gay & Lesbian Europe,* an excellent travel resource (www.frommers.com); *Spartacus International Gay Guide* (Bruno Gmünder Verlag; www.spartacusworld.com/gayguide) and *Odysseus,* both good, annual English-language guidebooks focused on gay men; and the *Damron* guides (www.damron.com), with separate, annual books for gay men and lesbians.

Exploring Your Special Interests

Whether your tastes run to tracing family history or casting a line for salmon, here are some suggestions for travelers with special interests.

Doing genealogy research

The Ireland Tourist Board publishes a book called *Tracing Your Ancestors in Ireland,* which is available free from any Irish Tourist Board office. The best online sites to begin your search for records pertaining to your Irish ancestors are **Ancestry.com** (www.ancestry.com);

the **Irish National Archives** (www.nationalarchives.ie), which has a database of many of Ireland's records; and **Irish Ancestors** (www.ireland.com/ancestor), where you can begin your search with any information that you currently have (surnames, place of birth, and so on). Most services on the Irish Ancestors Web site require payment.

First-time ancestor-hunters may want to get started by contacting the free genealogy advisory service at the **National Library,** Kildare St., Dublin 2 (☎ 01-603-0200; www.nli.ie). The **Manuscripts Reading Room** at the library has many documents and records. Another terrific resource is the **National Archives,** Bishop Street, Dublin 8 (☎ 01-407-2300; www.nationalarchives.ie). In Northern Ireland, hit the **Public Record Office of Northern Ireland,** 66 Balmoral Ave., Belfast BT9 6NY (☎ 028-9025-5905; www.proni.gov.uk).

Connecting names and counties

Here are just a few popular Irish surnames and the counties or provinces where they originated. Many of these families later spread throughout the island and beyond. Each name has plenty of variations; for instance, Fitzgerald has derivations of Fitzpatrick, Flanagan, Flynn, Fogarty, Foley, and Gaffney.

Ahearne: Clare, Limerick

Butler: Kilkenny

Donoghue: Cork, Kerry

Fitzgerald: Cork, Kerry, Kildare

MacCarthy: Munster

Maguire: Ulster

Martin: Connaught

Murphy: Sligo, Tyrone, Wexford

O'Brien: Clare, Limerick

O'Donnell: Donegal

O'Keeffe: Cork

O'Kelly: Galway

O'Neill: Ulster

O'Sullivan: Tipperary

Power: Waterford, Wicklow

Regan: Dublin, Meath

Ryan: Limerick, Tipperary

Walsh: Dublin, Kilkenny, Leitrim, Waterford, Wicklow

What's in a name? Ages ago, the prefixes of Irish last names signified a great deal. *Mc* or *Fitz* meant "son of," and *O* before a name meant "grandson of" or "from the family of." So the name O'Brien means "ancestors of the Brien family" (in this case, the ancestors of Brian Boru, the most famous of the high kings of Ireland). You also occasionally see a name with a *Ní* prefix (such as Ní Dhomhnaill), but this configuration is, for the most part, archaic. Literally, it means "formerly of," as in Triona Butler Ní Dhomnaill, the name Triona may go by if she were a proud Dhomnaill who married a Butler.

You can also hire someone to research your roots for you. The National Library maintains a list of independent genealogy researchers (go to www.nli.ie and click on "Family History Research," and then "Commissioning Research"). **ENECLANN,** Unit 1b, Trinity College Enterprise Center, Pearse Street, Dublin 2 (☎ **01-671-0338;** www. eneclann.ie), is one of the finest family-research agencies.

See the Fast Facts listings in each chapter for genealogy services specific to that region.

Rambling your way around Ireland by foot

Hiking (usually called *walking* or *hill-walking* in Ireland) is one of the very best ways to soak up the beauty of Ireland, whether you take off on a weeklong trek or go for an afternoon stroll. Check out www.walking. ireland.ie for information on trails, events, festivals, and tour operators. The best way to get information on the various hikes in an area is to visit the local tourist information office (information on the location of the tourist information office is included in the "Fast Facts" section of each chapter).

Failte Ireland, in conjunction with community leaders across the country, has developed a series of looped walks that will make exploring the countryside easy even for casual walkers and hikers. Just drive your car to the start point and follow the well-marked paths, which take you right back where you started. Loops range from casual strolls through open farmland to scenic coastal hikes to more challenging routes along rugged cliffs. There are loops available near most major tourist hotspots (Dublin, Waterford, Killarney, Westport, and Galway, to name a few), so you don't have to go far to get off the beaten path. The brochure "Walking Ireland: A selection of looped walks and walking information" details these loops, as does the Web site www.walking.ireland.ie.

For detailed information on Ireland's long-distance marked trails (many of which are composed of a series of day hikes), visit or contact **Waymarked Ways of Ireland** (☎ **01-860-8800;** www.walkireland.ie). The company puts out a different collection of maps and walking guides for all of the waymarked ways in each province in Ireland. Waymarked Ways' *Selected Day Walks* publication (available as a PDF online) highlights a selection of fabulous day walks all over Ireland. You can usually pick these guidebooks up at the Dublin Tourism Centre and other tourism offices, or order them directly from EastWest Mapping (☎ **053-937-7835;** eastwestmapping.ie).

For information on walking and hiking in Northern Ireland, visit **Northern Ireland's Tourist Board** Web site (www.discovernorthernireland. com), and enter "Walking" in the search bar. The Tourist Board's publication *Walk Northern Ireland* is a great resource, available at the Tourist Board Web site as a PDF and as a hard copy from most major tourist offices in Northern Ireland. Also available at major tourist offices (and in a shortened format online) are detailed guides to all of Northern Ireland's Waymarked Ways.

You can also get a hold of a number of excellent walking guidebooks, including *Walking in Ireland* (Lonely Planet), *Northern Ireland: A Walking Guide* (Collins Press) and *Best Irish Walks* (McGraw-Hill). Good guides are also available from **An Óige,** the Irish Youth Hostel Organization, 61 Mountjoy St., Dublin 1 (☎ **01-830-4555;** www.anoige.ie), and **YHANI,** Northern Ireland's Youth Hostel Association, 22 Donegal Rd., Belfast BT12 5JN (☎ **028-9032-4733**).

A number of companies offer hiking vacation packages; you can find a list at www.walking.ireland.ie. **Hidden Trails** (☎ **888-9-TRAILS;** www.hiddentrails.com) offers weeklong self-guided hiking tours in several regions in Ireland, while **Backroads** (☎ **800-462-2848;** www.backroads.com) offers guided hiking trips. Another option is **Wonderful Ireland** (☎ **087-761-3344;** www.walkinginireland.ie), which arranges tours in several areas of Ireland.

Teeing off on the greenest greens

Golf is the biggest sporting attraction in Ireland. For detailed information on many of Ireland's golf courses, visit www.golfcourse.com. You can find more golfing information at the Golfing Union of Ireland's Web site, www.gui.ie. (For an itinerary of nothing but golf, see Chapter 4.)

Specialty Ireland (☎ **052-70-630;** www.specialtyireland.com) can help you plan and arrange itineraries that include visits to almost any of Ireland's many courses.

Many U.S. companies plan golf packages, including **AtlanticGolf Company** (☎ **800-542-6224** or 203-363-1003; www.atlanticgolf.com); **Golf International** (☎ **800-833-1389** or 212-986-9176; www.golfinternational.com), and **Wide World of Golf** (☎ **800-214-4653** or 831-521-1336; www.wideworldofgolf.com).

Bicycling around Ireland

Stunning scenery, short distances between towns, and many flat roads make Ireland a wonderful place for cycling. **Backroads** (☎ **800-GO-ACTIVE** [☎ 800-462-2848]; www.backroads.com) and **VBT** (☎ **800-245-3868;** www.vbt.com) — both based in the United States — offer package bike vacations that include bikes, gear, luggage transportation, food, and accommodations. **Irish Cycling Safaris** (☎ **01-260-0749;** www.cyclingsafaris.com) plans and outfits trips all over Ireland. **Irish Cycling Tours** (☎ **095-42-276;** www.irishcyclingtours.com) offers both guided and self-guided tours in the West of Ireland. For semi-independent cycling in southeast Ireland (transfer between B&Bs is included, but you will be cycling on your own) contact **Celtic Cycling** (☎ **051-850-228;** www.celticcycling.com).

If you want to create your own itinerary, you can rent a bike from an Irish company that permits one-way rentals. **Eurotrek Raleigh,** Longmile Road, Dublin 12 (☎ **01-465-9659;** www.raleigh.ie), and **Rent-A-Bike Ireland,** 1 Patrick St., Limerick (☎ **061-416-983;** www.irelandrenta bike.com), are two reliable options.

Fishing Ireland's waters

Ireland may be the best place in Europe to cast your line for salmon, sea trout, and brown trout. There are a few exceptions to the dates listed here, but in most cases salmon season is January 1 to September 30, brown-trout season is February 15 to September 30, and sea-trout season is January 1 to September 30. Coarse fishing and sea angling take place all year. Find details about fishing in Ireland from the **Central Fisheries Board** (☎ **01-884-2600;** www.cfb.ie), which also has information about fishing licenses. Check out the **Great Fishing Houses of Ireland** (www.irelandfishing.com) for information on hotels that have private lakes and ponds and offer fishing equipment and guides.

For information on fishing in Northern Ireland, click "Angling," under "View All Activities," on the Northern Ireland Tourist Board Web site (www.discovernorthernireland.com). In Northern Ireland, you must get a rod license and often need a permit: Contact the **Fisheries Conservancy Board** (☎ **028-3833-4666;** www.fcbni.com) to get a license and permit.

Sailing the Irish seas and cruising the Irish rivers

Ireland's clear waters and Gulf Stream winds rival the Caribbean, so if you want to do some sailing, you're in luck. Contact or visit the Web site of the **Irish Sailing Association** (☎ **01-280-0239;** www.sailing.ie), for all sorts of information on sailing in Ireland, including a list of approved teaching schools that rent boats.

For information on renting a boat to cruise the Shannon-Erne Waterways, call ☎ **1-877-298-7205** in the U.S., or ☎ **069-77-686** in Ireland. For information on taking a multiday cruise along the Shannon and Erne waterways, I recommend checking out the Shannon Princess barge at ☎ **087-251-4809** or www.shannonprincess.com.

The charming fishing village of Kinvarra, County Galway, hosts **Cruinniú na mBad** (literally, "Gathering of the Boats") in August. The festival focuses on races among the majestic hooker sailboats that used to carry turf from port to port. Contact the **Galway Tourist Office** for information (☎ **091-53-77-00;** www.irelandwest.ie), or visit www.kinvara.com.

Horseback riding

What could be more romantic than clip-clopping through the Irish countryside on horseback? For a list of horseback-riding outfitters, contact or visit the Web site of the **Association of Irish Riding Establishments,** 11

Moore Park, Newbridge, County Kildare (☎ **045-850-800;** www.aire.ie), in the Republic, or the **British Horse Society** (www.bhs.co.uk), in Northern Ireland. For a selection of horseback-riding vacation outfitters, visit the Web site of **Equestrian Holidays Ireland** at www.ehi.ie.

Spectator sports

Spectator sports are hugely popular in Ireland. Many pubs, especially in larger cities, have the local game on — whether it's football (soccer), Gaelic football, rugby, hurling, or horse racing. Seeing a live sporting event is a quintessential Irish experience.

Horse racing

Steeplechases are run year-round. The flat season (races without hurdles) is from mid-March to early November. The Irish Tourist Board draws up an Irish Racing Calendar every year, and you can visit **Horse Racing Ireland** (www.hri.ie) for information. Here are some of the highlights.

- ✔ **The Dublin Horse Show:** The Horse Show is held during the first or second week in August at the Royal Dublin Society (RDS) Showgrounds, Ballsbridge, Dublin 4. One of the biggest social and sporting events in the country, this show features the best show horses, riders, and jumpers in Ireland and awards the prestigious Aga Khan Trophy. See www.dublinhorseshow.com for more information.

- ✔ **Christmas Horse Racing Festival:** This late-December festival encompasses three days of Thoroughbred racing at Leopardstown Racetrack, in Dublin. Call ☎ **01-289-0500** for information, or visit www.leopardstown.com.

- ✔ **Irish Grand National:** Three days of racing take place at Fairyhouse in County Meath, starting on Easter Sunday. For information, call ☎ **01-825-6167** or visit www.fairyhouseracecourse.ie.

- ✔ **The Budweiser Irish Derby:** Three days of races are held in the Curragh, County Kildare, on the last Sunday in June or the first weekend in July. For information, contact the Curragh Racecourse Office at ☎ **045-441-205** or visit www.curragh.ie.

Greyhound racing

Greyhound racing takes place around the country, usually Monday through Saturday at 8 and 10 p.m. The largest racetracks are the **Shelbourne Park Stadium,** in Dublin, and **Kingdom Greyhound Stadium,** in Tralee. For more information, visit the **Irish Greyhound Board** (www.igb.ie).

Rugby, soccer, hurling, and Gaelic football

These four sports are played throughout the country. *Gaelic football* is a rough-and-tumble sport that combines the best aspects of American football, soccer, and rugby. *Hurling* is a fast-paced and thrilling game akin to field hockey or lacrosse played with a stick called a *hurley stick.* The game is traced to the pre-Christian folk hero Cuchulainn.

Big matches are played in Croke Park in Dublin City (north of O'Connell Street). You can get Gaelic-football and hurling schedule information from the **Gaelic Athletic Association (GAA)** at ☎ **01-836-3222** (www. gaa.ie). You can get schedules and information for soccer from the **Football Association of Ireland,** 80 Merrion Sq., Dublin 2 (☎ **01-8999-500;** www.fai.ie). For rugby schedules and information, go to www. irishrugby.ie or call ☎ **01-647-3800.**

Chapter 10

Taking Care of the Remaining Details

● ●

In This Chapter

▶ Figuring out passports

▶ Looking at travel and health insurance

▶ Keeping in touch with friends and family at home

▶ Bringing the correct electrical adapters

▶ Knowing what to expect regarding airline security

● ●

*N*ow that you're all excited to go to Ireland, here are some final tips on such things as passports, insurance, calling home, and bringing the right electrical adapters.

Getting a Passport

Applying for a U.S. passport

The Web sites listed provide downloadable passport applications as well as the current fees for processing applications. For an up-to-date, country-by-country listing of passport requirements around the world, go to the "International Travel" tab of the U.S. Department of State at **http://travel.state.gov**. *Note:* Children are required to present a passport when entering the United States at airports. More information on obtaining a passport for a minor can be found at http://travel.state.gov.

 Allow plenty of time before your trip to apply for a passport; processing normally takes four to six weeks (three weeks for expedited service) but can take longer during busy periods (especially spring). And keep in mind that if you need a passport in a hurry, you'll pay a higher processing fee.

Applying for other passports

The following list offers more information for citizens of Australia, Canada, New Zealand, and the United Kingdom.

✔ **Australians** can pick up an application from any post office or any branch of Passports Australia, but you must schedule an interview at the passport office to present your application materials. Call the **Australian Passport Information Service** at ☎ **131-232,** or visit the government Web site at www.passports.gov.au.

✔ **Canadians** can pick up applications at travel agencies throughout Canada or from the central **Passport Office,** Department of Foreign Affairs and International Trade, Ottawa, ON K1A 0G3 (☎ **800-567-6868;** www.ppt.gc.ca). *Note:* Canadian children who travel must have their own passport. However, if you hold a valid Canadian passport issued before December 11, 2001, that bears the name of your child, the passport remains valid for you and your child until it expires.

✔ **New Zealanders** can pick up a passport application at any New Zealand Passports Office or download it from their Web site. Contact the **Passports Office** at ☎ **0800-225-050** in New Zealand or 04-474-8100, or log on to www.passports.govt.nz.

✔ **United Kingdom** residents can pick up applications for a standard ten-year passport (five-year passport for children under 16) at passport offices, major post offices, or a travel agency. For information, contact the **United Kingdom Passport Service** (☎ **0870-521-0410;** www.ukpa.gov.uk).

Playing It Safe with Travel and Medical Insurance

The types of insurance travelers are most likely to need are trip-cancellation insurance and medical insurance. The cost of travel insurance varies widely, depending on the cost and length of your trip, your age and health, and the type of trip you're taking. You can get estimates from various providers through **InsureMyTrip.com.** Enter your trip cost and dates, your age, and other information, for prices from more than a dozen companies.

U.K. citizens and their families who make more than one trip abroad per year may find an annual travel insurance policy works out cheaper. Check www.moneysupermarket.com, which compares prices across a wide range of providers for single- and multitrip policies.

Most big travel agencies offer their own insurance and will probably try to sell you their package when you book a holiday. Think before you sign. **Britain's Consumers' Association** recommends that you insist on seeing the policy and reading the fine print before buying travel insurance. **The Association of British Insurers** (☎ **020/7600-3333;** www.abi.org.uk) gives advice by phone and publishes Holiday Insurance, a free guide to policy provisions and prices. You might also shop around for better deals: Try **Columbus Direct** (☎ **0870/033-9988;** www.columbusdirect.net).

Here is my advice on trip-cancellation and medical insurance:

✔ **Trip-cancellation insurance** will help retrieve your money if you have to back out of a trip or depart early, or if your travel supplier goes bankrupt. Trip cancellation traditionally covers such events as sickness, natural disasters, and Department of State advisories. The latest news in trip-cancellation insurance is the availability of **expanded hurricane coverage** and the **"any-reason"** cancellation coverage — which costs more but covers cancellations made for any reason. You won't get back 100 percent of your prepaid trip cost, but you'll be refunded a substantial portion. **TravelSafe** (☎ 888-885-7233; www.travelsafe.com) offers both types of coverage. Expedia also offers any-reason cancellation coverage for its air-hotel packages. For details, contact one of the following recommended insurers: **Access America** (☎ 866-807-3982; www.accessamerica.com); **Travel Guard International** (☎ 800-826-4919; www.travelguard.com); **Travel Insured International** (☎ 800-243-3174; www.travelinsured.com); and **Travelex Insurance Services** (☎ 888-457-4602; www.travelex-insurance.com).

If you're ever hospitalized more than 150 miles from home, **Medjet Assist** (☎ **800-527-7478**; www.medjetassistance.com) will pick you up and fly you to the hospital of your choice in a medically equipped and staffed aircraft 24 hours day, seven days a week. Annual memberships are $225 individual, $350 family; you can also purchase short-term memberships.

Canadians should check with their provincial health plan offices or call **Health Canada** (☎ **866-225-0709**; www.hc-sc.gc.ca) to find out the extent of their coverage and what documentation and receipts they must take home in case they are treated in the United States.

Travelers from the U.K. should carry their European Health Insurance Card (EHIC), which replaced the E111 form as proof of entitlement to free or reduced-cost medical treatment abroad (☎ **0845 606 2030**; www.ehic.org.uk). Note, however, that the EHIC only covers "necessary medical treatment," and for repatriation costs, lost money, baggage, or cancellation, travel insurance from a reputable company should always be sought (www.travel insuranceweb.com).

✔ For travel overseas, you may want to look into **medical insurance.** Most U.S. health plans (including Medicare and Medicaid) do not provide coverage, and the ones that do often require you to pay for services up front and reimburse you only after you return home.

If you require additional medical insurance, try **MEDEX Assistance** (☎ **410-453-6300**; www.medexassist.com) or **Travel Assistance International** (☎ **800-821-2828**; www.travelassistance.com; for general information on services, call the company's **Worldwide Assistance Services, Inc.**, at ☎ 800-777-8710).

Staying Healthy When You Travel

Getting sick will ruin your vacation, so I strongly advise against it (of course, last time I checked, the bugs weren't listening to me any more than they probably listen to you).

For information on purchasing additional medical insurance for your trip, see the previous section.

Talk to your doctor before leaving on a trip if you have a serious and/ or chronic illness. For conditions such as epilepsy, diabetes, or heart problems, wear a **MedicAlert identification tag** (☎ 888-633-4298; www. medicalert.org), which immediately alerts doctors to your condition and gives them access to your records through Medic Alert's 24-hour hotline. Contact the **International Association for Medical Assistance to Travelers (IAMAT)** (☎ 716-754-4883 or, in Canada, ☎ 416-652-0137; www.iamat.org) for tips on travel and health concerns in the countries you're visiting, and lists of local, English-speaking doctors. The United States **Centers for Disease Control and Prevention** (☎ 800-311-3435; www.cdc.gov) provides up-to-date information on health hazards by region or country and offers tips on food safety. The Web site www. tripprep.com, sponsored by a consortium of travel medicine practitioners, may also offer helpful advice on traveling abroad. You can find listings of reliable clinics overseas at the **International Society of Travel Medicine** (www.istm.org).

Calling the Folks Back Home

This section helps you figure out the best ways to stay in touch while you're away from home.

Using a cellphone outside the U.S.

For many, **renting** a phone is a good idea. While you can rent a phone from any number of overseas sites, including kiosks at airports and at car rental agencies, we suggest renting the phone before you leave home. North Americans can rent a phone before they depart from **InTouch USA** (☎ 800-872-7626; www.intouchglobal.com) or **RoadPost** (☎ 888-290-1616 or 905-272-5665; www.roadpost.com). InTouch will also, for free, advise you on whether your existing phone will work overseas; simply call ☎ 703-222-7161 between 9 a.m. and 4 p.m. EST, or go to http://intouchglobal.com/travel.htm. Many people have had positive experiences renting from **Rent A Phone Ireland** (www.rentaphone-ireland.com). You can pick up your rented phone at Dublin or Shannon airports or at a local post office, or the company can mail the phone to the first B&B or hotel that you stay in.

Buying a phone can be economically attractive, as many nations have cheap prepaid phone systems. Once you arrive in Ireland, stop by a local cellphone shop and get the cheapest package; you'll probably pay less than $75 for a phone and a starter calling card. Local calls may be as low as 10¢ per minute, and incoming calls are free on most services in Ireland. The staff at the **Vodafone** store on Grafton Street in Dublin (☎ 01-670-5205) can help you pick out a phone and plan that will suit your needs.

Using pay phones

You can find two types of pay phones in Ireland: coin-operated phones and card-operated phones. Both kinds of phones are spread throughout the country, and you may even see them side by side.

If you use a coin-operated phone, read the directions before you start feeding in coins. Some phones require putting the coins in before you dial; others have you put in the coins after the other party answers. Have change in hand while you're on your call — the phone gives an extremely short warning before disconnecting.

Got no calling card? Got no change? Got no problem. The Irish have phone cards that work the same as those in the United States, similar to a debit card, and you can get one in many shops or at a post office. Phone cards come in varying denominations. What's different about the Irish version is that you use the phone card in its own phone booth, designated by the sign *Cardphone*. When you enter the booth, slide the card in the slot like you would a credit card. There's a screen on the phone that says how many units the card has left. The units decrease while you're on the phone, so you know how much time is left.

Numbers beginning with 800 or 850 within Ireland are called *Freephone numbers* and are toll-free, but calling a toll-free number in the United States from Ireland is not free. In fact, doing so costs the same as a regular overseas call.

Using a U.S. calling card

AT&T, MCI, and Sprint calling cards all operate worldwide, so using any of them in Ireland is no problem (though hotel rooms sometimes block these numbers, so you may need to call via pay phone). Each card has a local access number, which saves you the cost of dialing directly to the United States. When you want to use your card in the Republic of Ireland, just call ☎ 1800-55-0000 for **AT&T,** ☎ 1800-55-1001 for **MCI,** and ☎ 1800-55-2001 for **Sprint.** In Northern Ireland, call ☎ 0500-89-0011 for **AT&T,** ☎ 0800-279-5088 for **MCI,** and ☎ 0800-89-0877 for **Sprint.** The operator will then explain how to make the call.

If you have a calling card with a company other than one of the three I named, contact the company before you go on the trip to see whether it has a local access number in Ireland. Whatever card you have, call the company before you go on your trip to see whether it has a discount plan for calling overseas.

Using Voice over Internet Protocol (VoIP)

If you have Web access while traveling, consider a broadband-based telephone service (in technical terms, **Voice over Internet Protocol,** or **VoIP**) such as Skype (www.skype.com) or Vonage (www.vonage.com), which allow you to make free international calls from your laptop or in a cybercafe. Neither service requires the people you're calling to also have that service (though there are fees if they do not). Check the Web sites for details.

Accessing the Internet Away from Home

Travelers have any number of ways to check their e-mail and access the Internet on the road. Of course, using your own laptop, PDA (personal digital assistant), or electronic organizer with a modem gives you the most flexibility. But even if you don't have a computer with you, you can easily find computer access in Ireland.

Without your own computer

You will have no trouble finding Internet cafes in most towns (even the small ones) in Ireland. I've listed the address and telephone number of an Internet cafe for many of the destinations discussed in the book in the "Fast Facts" sections in each chapter. Tourist Information centers and your hotel information desk or B&B proprietor will almost always be able to help you locate an Internet cafe.

 If you are staying in a hotel that serves business travelers, you will often find a business center with computers. Computer use in business centers is almost always much more expensive than computer use at an Internet cafe.

With your own computer

Many hotels and B&Bs in Ireland now offer wireless access for their guests, usually free of charge. Cafes and some of the larger hotels offer wireless on a pay-as-you-go basis; you open your browser, pay the wireless service by credit card, and then have access to the Internet through the wireless service for the amount of time that you've paid for.

Sending and receiving snail mail in the Republic and Northern Ireland

You do know you'll be hard-pressed to get someone to pick you up at the airport if you don't send home any postcards, right? Post offices in the Republic are called *An Post* (www.letterpost.ie for general information) and are easy to spot: Look for a bright green storefront with the name across it. Ireland's main postal branch, the **General Post Office (GPO),** on O'Connell Street, Dublin 1 (☎ **01-872-6666**), is in the heart of Dublin and is the hub of all mail activity (Mon–Sat 8 a.m.–8 p.m.). Major branches, located in the bigger towns and cities, are usually open Monday through Friday 9 a.m. to 5:30 p.m. and Saturday 9 a.m. to 1 p.m. Minor branches, which are in every small town, are open Monday through Friday 9 a.m. to 1 p.m. and 2 or 2:30 to 5:30 p.m., and Saturday 9 a.m. to 1 p.m. Irish post offices sell phone cards and lottery tickets, and you can even change money at main branches.

From the Republic, mailing an air-mail letter or postcard costs 82p ($1.30). It usually takes mail about a week to get to the United States. If you plan to mail packages, you can save money by sending them economy, or surface, mail.

In Northern Ireland, the post offices and post boxes are bright red. The general hours are the same as those of *An Post.* The cost to send a letter or a postcard is 50p ($1).

If you need mail sent to you while on your trip in Ireland, have the sender address the mail with your name, care of the General Post Office, Restante Office, and the town name (for instance, Joe Smith, c/o General Post Office, Restante Office, Galway, Ireland). Your mail will be held there for you to pick up for 30 days. Only larger post office branches provide this service.

Figuring Out Electricity in Ireland

Electricity in the Republic of Ireland operates on 220 volts with a three-pronged plug, and electricity in Northern Ireland operates on 250 volts. To use American 110-volt appliances, you need a transformer and a three-pronged plug adapter.

Some travel appliances, such as shavers and irons, have a nice feature called *dual voltage* that adapts to the change, but unless your appliance gives a voltage range (such as 110v–220v), don't chance it. Most laptop computers have this feature, but always check with the manufacturer as a precaution. Plug adapters are not hard to find; your local hardware store or even the airport should have what you need. For more information, check out www.walkabouttravelgear.com.

Keeping Up with Airline Security

With the federalization of airport security, security procedures at U.S. airports are more stable and consistent than ever. Generally, you'll be fine if you arrive at the airport **one hour** before a domestic flight and **two hours** before an international flight; if you show up late, tell an airline employee and she'll probably whisk you to the front of the line.

Bring a **current, government-issued photo ID** such as a driver's license or passport. Keep your ID at the ready to show at check-in, the security checkpoint, and sometimes even the gate. (Children under 18 do not need government-issued photo IDs for domestic flights, but they do for international flights to most countries.)

In 2003, the TSA phased out **gate check-in** at all U.S. airports. And **e-tickets** have made paper tickets nearly obsolete. Passengers with e-tickets can beat the ticket-counter lines by using airport **electronic kiosks** or even **online check-in** from your home computer. Online check-in involves logging on to your airlines' Web site, accessing your reservation, and printing out your boarding pass — and the airline may even offer you bonus miles to do so! If you're using a kiosk at the airport, bring the credit card you used to book the ticket or your frequent-flier card. Print out your boarding pass from the kiosk and simply proceed to the security checkpoint with your pass and a photo ID. **Curbside check-in** is also a good way to avoid lines, although a few airlines still ban curbside check-in; call before you go.

Speed up security by **not wearing metal objects** such as big belt buckles. If you've got metallic body parts, a note from your doctor can prevent a long chat with the security screeners. Keep in mind that only **ticketed passengers** are allowed past security, except for folks escorting disabled passengers or children.

Federalization has stabilized **what you can carry on** and **what you can't.** Travelers in the U.S. are allowed one carry-on bag, plus a "personal item" such as a purse, briefcase, or laptop bag. Carry-on hoarders can stuff all sorts of things into a laptop bag; as long as it has a laptop in it, it's still considered a personal item. The Transportation Security Administration (TSA) has issued a list of restricted items; check its Web site (www.tsa.gov/public/index.jsp) for details.

Airport screeners may decide that your checked luggage needs to be searched by hand. You can now purchase luggage locks that allow screeners to open and relock a checked bag if hand-searching is necessary. Look for Travel Sentry certified locks at luggage or travel shops and Brookstone stores (you can buy them online at www.brookstone.com). For more information on the locks, visit www.travelsentry.org.

Part III
Dublin and the East Coast

"Okay, we got one cherry lager with bitters and a pineapple slice, and one honey malt ale with cinnamon and an orange twist. You want these in steins or parfait glasses?"

In this part . . .

Dublin City and the surrounding areas offer attractions that run from quiet mountain towns to hot, trendy clubs. Vibrant Dublin City is home to several excellent museums, an array of fabulous restaurants serving everything from fish and chips to gourmet fusion meals, and a varied and hopping nightlife scene. Just north of the city are Counties Meath and Louth, where you find some of Ireland's most magnificent ancient ruins (see Chapter 12). To the south are Wicklow and Kildare, two counties filled with gardens and estates, mountains, horses (especially in Kildare), and loads of that gorgeous Irish green. You won't want for outdoor activities in these parts. See Chapter 13 for details.

The southeastern counties of Wexford, Waterford, Tipperary, and Kilkenny offer an array of places to see and things to do. Some highlights are driving along the coast and through sweet fishing villages in Wexford; watching Waterford Crystal being created; exploring the Rock of Cashel in Tipperary; and wandering the medieval streets of Kilkenny. See Chapter 14 for more information.

Chapter 11

Dublin

• •

In This Chapter

▶ Arriving in Dublin and finding your way around
▶ Deciding where to stay and where to eat
▶ Discovering Dublin's top attractions
▶ Shopping for the best Irish goods
▶ Hitting the finest of Dublin's 1,000-plus pubs

• •

*W*alking down a street in Dublin filled with hip young things heading for an after-work pub visit, you could be in any cosmopolitan city in the world. Dublin has undergone major changes in the past 15 years or so. The strong software and communications economy (dubbed the Celtic Tiger by locals) pumped money into the city, and the European Economic Community (now the European Union) showered grants on Ireland and on Dublin in particular. Though the Celtic Tiger's roar has died down to a purr, Dublin remains one of Europe's trendiest cities. Dublin's population has gotten younger and much more ethnically diverse, and the 20- and 30-something Dubs are helping create and support vibrant, cutting-edge arts, dining, clubbing, and shopping scenes. Many of the hot restaurants, hotels, pubs, theaters, galleries, and clubs that opened in the '90s and early naughts are still going strong, the streets are bustling, and the city continues to change, though the pace of change has slowed down a bit from the breakneck speed that characterized the late '90s and the first few years of the millennium.

But Dublin is not all new, new, new. Spend a few hours strolling the heart of Dublin, and you start to get a sense of the city's 1,000-year history. Those hip young things are crowding into pubs that natives from two centuries ago would recognize, and walking down cobblestone streets as they talk on their cellphones.

This coexistence of old and new is part of Dublin's appeal. You can explore some of the city's many historical attractions — the Book of Kells, Trinity College, Christ Church Cathedral, and many more — by day, and then sit down to a fusion cuisine meal at a hot restaurant before joining the hordes of glittery pub- and club-crawlers.

Getting to Dublin

Dublin is one of Ireland's two main international gateways, so if you're flying to the country, there's a good chance you'll be touching down here. Dublin is also well connected to the rest of the country by bus, train, and ferry routes.

By plane

Dublin International Airport (☎ **01-814-1111;** www.dublin-airport. com) is 11km (7 miles) north of the city, about a 25- to 45-minute drive from the city center (*An Lar* in Gaelic). Aer Lingus, American Airlines (operated by Aer Lingus), Continental, and Delta fly directly into Dublin from the United States. Aer Lingus, British Midlands, Aer Lingus, CityJet (operated by Air France), Lufthansa, and Ryanair have regular flights from England. See Chapter 6 for more on flights into Ireland.

In the arrivals concourse, you'll find an excellent travel information desk that can help you figure out how to get to your destination, desks for the major car-rental companies listed in Chapter 7, and ATMs.

Taxis are available outside the arrival terminal's main entrance — just look for the signs. The fare to downtown Dublin is about €16 to €30 ($26–$35), and the trip takes 20 to 40 minutes, depending on traffic. You should tip between 10 percent and 15 percent.

AirCoach (☎ **01-844-7118;** www.aircoach.ie) runs 24 hours a day, at 10- to 20-minute intervals (one hour intervals between 12:30 and 4:30 a.m.), from Dublin Airport to various stops in Dublin's city center and south side. The one-way fare is €7 ($11) adults, €1 ($1.60) kids 5 to 12, and free for kids under age 5. **Dublin Bus** (☎ **01-873-4222;** www.dublin bus.ie) has several routes between the airport and the city center; check with the travel information desk in the arrivals concourse to figure out which one to use. If you are looking to catch a bus or train out of Dublin immediately, you can take the **Airlink Express Coach** (☎ **01-873-4222**) to the city bus station or either of the two city train stations. Airlink also stops on O'Connell Street. The Airlink runs every 10 to 20 minutes daily from about 6 a.m. to about 11 p.m. and costs €5 ($8) adults, and €2 ($3.20) children under age 12. Finally, some of the larger hotels offer an airport pickup service for guests.

By ferry

A number of ferry companies have routes to Dublin from harbors in Wales and England. See "Getting to Ireland by Ferry," in Chapter 6, for a listing of ferry companies and the ports that they serve. Ferries dock at **Dublin Ferryport** (☎ **01-855-2222**) or at **Dun Laoghaire** (pronounced dun *leer*-ee) **Ferryport,** less than 13km (8 miles) from Dublin. Public transportation into the city is available from both ports.

By train

Iarnród Éireann (pronounced ee-*arn*-rod *air*-an), or **Irish Rail** (☎ 1-850-366-222; www.irishrail.ie), runs between Dublin and the major towns and cities of Ireland, including Belfast in Northern Ireland. Trains arrive at one of three stations: Connolly Station on Amiens Street (serving trains from the North and Northwest, including Northern Ireland); Heuston Station on Kingsbridge, off St. John's Road (serving trains from the South, Southwest, and West); and Pearse Station on Westland Row, Tara Street (serving trains from the Southeast). The **DART (Dublin Area Rapid Transit)** (☎ 1-850-366-222; www.irishrail.ie) commuter trains connect the city to the suburban towns north (as far as Dundalk) and south of the city (as far as Arklow).

By bus

Ireland's bus system, **Bus Éireann** (☎ 01-836-6111; www.buseireann.ie), runs between Dublin and most cities and towns in the Republic. The city's bus terminal, called **Busaras,** is on Store Street, 3 blocks east of O'Connell Street, north of the river behind the Trading House building.

By car

N1, M1, N2, and N3 lead into Dublin from the North; N4, M4, M7, and N7 lead in from the West, and M11/N11 leads into the city from the South. The M50 is Dublin's beltway, surrounding three sides of the city and linking most major routes into and out of town. Once you get into Dublin, you should return your rental car or leave it in your hotel parking lot, and use your feet, public transportation, and taxis to see the city. If you have to bring a car into the city, there are several car parks available. On the north side of the Liffey, parking choices include a lot off Marlborough Street (at Sean Mac Dermot Street) and one off Jervis Street (at Lower Ormond Quay), among others. There are even more choices on the south side of the Liffey, including one at Trinity Street (off Dame Street), and one on Drury Street (off Stephens Street).

Orienting Yourself in Dublin

The thin ribbon of the River Liffey divides Dublin into north and south sides. On the north side, the main thoroughfare is wide O'Connell Street, which leads up to Parnell Square. Along the river on the south side is hopping Temple Bar, which is filled with pubs, arts venues, and restaurants. Nearby Nassau Street runs along the Trinity College campus and intersects with Grafton Street, a bustling pedestrian street that leads up to St. Stephen's Green, a popular park. See the neighborhood breakdown in this section for more details.

A few words on street names: They have a tendency to change when you least expect it. One minute, you're on Aungiers Street; the next, you're on South Great George's Street. Did you make a turn without knowing it? No, that's just how the streets are in Dublin, so trust your sense of direction.

All Dublin addresses include a digit after the word *Dublin,* as in *General Post Office, O'Connell Street, Dublin 1.* These numbers are postal codes, similar to American zip codes. Most of central Dublin is located within postal codes 1, 2, and 8. Odd numbers are north of the River Liffey, and even numbers are south of it.

Introducing the neighborhoods

Here is a breakdown of Dublin's central city neighborhoods, from trendy Temple Bar to posh Merrion and Fitzwilliam squares.

- ✔ **O'Connell Street Area (north side of the Liffey):** Although this area once thrived as the most fashionable part of the city, it's now something of an aging starlet. However, efforts are being made to restore buildings and generally rejuvenate the locale. Though you'll still find fast-food joints and tacky souvenir shops between stately buildings, such as the **General Post Office** and **Gresham Hotel,** the silvery sky-scraping **Millennium Spire** (affectionately called "the stiletto in the ghetto") is a reminder that things are changing. O'Connell Street's center median is home to impressive statues of noted Irishmen, and at the top of the street, you find the serene **Garden of Remembrance,** the excellent **Dublin City Gallery the Hugh Lane,** and the interesting **Dublin Writers Museum.** A few blocks to the east of O'Connell Street are the famous **Abbey Theatre** and the **James Joyce Centre;** to the west are the bustling shopping streets of Henry, Moore, and Abbey.

- ✔ **Quartier Bloom/The Italian Quarter/Millennium Walk (north side):** You only *thought* you booked your ticket to Ireland. This area of the north side, just over the Millennium Bridge, is Dublin's own Little Italy, featuring Italian wine bars, restaurants, and gelato purveyors in addition to a few new non-Italian restaurants.

- ✔ **Trinity College Area (south side):** Across O'Connell Bridge on the south side of the River Liffey stands **Trinity College,** home to the **Book of Kells.** This sprawling campus of green lawns and Hogwarts-style old buildings sits in the heart of the city and is surrounded by classy bookstores and shops.

- ✔ **Temple Bar (south side):** Tucked into a spot between Trinity and Dublin Castle is the funky and fashionable Temple Bar, where you find pubs, hip shops, restaurants, and arts venues along cobbled alleys. This area is always bustling and hosts a number of excellent weekend markets, including a book market, a fashion market, a furniture market, and an organic food market. In the past few years, the area has been known for a lack of locals and countless rowdy stag and hen (bachelor and bachelorette) parties, but cultural offerings are luring Dubs back to Temple Bar.

- ✔ **Old City–Historical Area (south side):** This historical area boasts narrow streets and ancient buildings, some dating as far back as Viking and medieval times. Some highlights are **Dublin Castle,**

Christ Church Cathedral, St. Patrick's Cathedral, and the **old city walls.** A bit farther on is the **Guinness Storehouse** (described later in this chapter in the "Exploring Dublin" section).

✔ **St. Stephen's Green and Grafton Street (south side):** This area begins at the bottom of the pedestrian Grafton Street, with its many trendy clothing stores and its variety of street performers, and finishes up in St. Stephen's Green — Dublin's favorite park. This pretty part of town has plenty of upscale shops and cafes, and is always teeming with people.

✔ **Merrion and Fitzwilliam squares (south side):** These two square parks are surrounded by some of Dublin's most beautiful Georgian townhouses, each with a distinctive, brightly colored door. Some were once the homes of Dublin's most famous citizens, but today, many of them house professional offices. Some big names from Dublin's past lived on Merrion Square, including the poet W. B. Yeats, Irish nationalist leader Daniel O'Connell, and writer Oscar Wilde.

Finding information after you arrive

Dublin Tourism (☎ 01-605-7700; www.visitdublin.com) runs two walk-in visitor centers around the center of the city and one at the airport. The largest and best visitor center is in the **Church of St. Andrew** on Suffolk Street, Dublin 2, and is open October through May Monday through Saturday 9 a.m. to 5:30 p.m., and Sunday 10:30 to 3 p.m.; June and September Monday through Saturday 9 a.m. to 7 p.m., and Sunday 10:30 a.m. to 3 p.m.; and July and August Monday through Saturday 9 a.m. to 7 p.m., and Sunday 10:30 a.m. to 5:30 p.m. The others are at the **Arrivals Hall,** at the Dublin Airport (daily 8 a.m.–8 p.m.), and at **14 O'Connell St.,** Dublin 1 (Mon–Sat 9 a.m.–5 p.m.).

For information on events once you get to Dublin, pick up a copy of the *InDublin* magazine or the *Event Guide* newspaper, available at the visitors' centers and around Dublin.

Getting Around Dublin

The best way to see Dublin is to lace up a good pair of shoes and hoof it. The center of the city is compact and easily walkable. For attractions that are not within walking distance, take advantage of the excellent bus network. Even if you ignore the rest of this book, heed these words: Don't explore Dublin by car. The slow traffic and confusing streets are a study in frustration, and parking is expensive and out of the way.

Remember that the Irish drive on the left side of the road, so look right first before stepping into the street.

By bus

Dublin Bus, 59 Upper O'Connell St., Dublin 1 (☎ **01-873-4222;** www.
dublinbus.ie), operates double-decker buses, regular buses, and *imps*
(minibuses) throughout Dublin city and its suburbs, with fares under €3
($4.80). The destination and bus number are posted in the windshield;
buses going towards the city center read *An Lar,* which is Irish Gaelic for
"center city." You find bus stops every 2 or 3 blocks, and most bus
routes pass down O'Connell Street, Abbey Street, and Eden Quay on the
north side of the river and down Westmoreland Street, Nassau Street,
and Aston Quay on the south side. Most buses run every 10 to 15 minutes Monday through Saturday from about 6 a.m. to about 11:30 p.m.
and Sunday from around 10 a.m. to about 11:30 p.m. A late-night bus
service runs on a limited route Monday through Thursday from midnight to 2 a.m., and Friday and Saturday from midnight to 4:30 a.m. You
can check out routes and fares online.

Discount one-day, three-day, five-day, and seven-day passes are available
at convenience stores and supermarkets all over the city center, online
at www.dublinbus.ie, and at Dublin Bus headquarters (59 Upper
O'Connell St.). If you don't have a bus pass, the buses accept exact
change only. If you pay more than the required amount, you get a coupon
for a refund that you can redeem at the Dublin Bus headquarters at 59
Upper O'Connell St.

By taxi

To get a taxi in Dublin, go to a taxi rank, where cabs line up along the
street, or hail a cab by sticking out your arm. If the cab's roof light is on,
it means that the cab is unoccupied and ready to pick up passengers. If
possible, take a cab with a meter and a roof sign; unmarked cabs may
overcharge you. Ask for the estimated fare before you begin your journey. There are taxi ranks at large hotels, train stations, the bus station,
the O'Connell Street median near the General Post Office, opposite St.
Stephen's Green shopping center, and near Trinity College on Dame
Street. You can also call a cab; reliable companies include **Castle Cabs**
(☎ **01-802-2222**), **Co-op** (☎ **01-676-6666**), and **VIP Taxis** (☎ **01-478-
3333**).

In Ireland, passengers usually sit up front with the driver, rather than in
the back seat chauffeur-style.

By train

The **DART** commuter train (☎ **1-850-366-222;** www.irishrail.ie) connects the city to suburbs and coastal towns both north (as far as
Balbriggan) and south (as far as Greystones), and is quite a bargain for a
daytrip to a nearby town. The three stops in Dublin's city center are
Connolly Station, Pearse Street Station, and Tara Street Station. It's not
usually worth it to take the DART within the city center, because the
three stops are within such easy walking distance of one another. Most

DART trains runs every 5 to 20 minutes Monday through Saturday from about 6 a.m. to about 11:45 p.m., and from about 9 a.m. to between 6 p.m. and 11 p.m. Sunday (depending on the station). Tickets are on sale in each station and online. See the Cheat Sheet at the beginning of this book for a DART map. The shortest journeys come in at €1.45 ($2.30) each way, with trips to nearby seaside towns costing around €3.60 ($5.80) each way.

By car

If you are completely ignoring my advice and driving in Dublin, remember to avoid parking in bus lanes or along curbs with double yellow lines — these are easy ways to get your tires clamped by parking officials. To park on the streets in Dublin, buy parking discs at one of the black vending machines along the street, and display a disc in the window of your car. See p. 125 for information on parking lots (called *car parks* here).

By Luas (tram)

Luas (☎ 1-800-300-604; www.luas.ie) is Dublin's sleek, shiny tram system. You probably won't need it if you are spending time in the center of the city, which is easily walkable. However, check out the map if you are traveling outside of the city center. It is also useful for moving between Connolly and Heuston stations. One-way fares run between €1.50 (€2.40) and €2.20 ($3.50) depending on your destination.

Spending the Night in Dublin

There's no denying it: Dublin is a hip and cosmopolitan city, and a hip and cosmopolitan city breeds trendy (and expensive) hotels. If you're looking for luxury, Dublin offers an embarrassment of riches. If that trust fund hasn't turned up yet, your accommodation options are more limited, because central Dublin lacks the cozy, inexpensive B&Bs found in abundance across the rest of Ireland. But fear not: This section includes accommodation options ranging from deals for budget travelers to extravagant hotels, where penthouse accommodations cost €1,000 or more. See Chapter 8 for more tips and information on finding and booking various types of accommodations.

 Unlike accommodations in the rest of the country, some Dublin hotels don't significantly lower prices during the off-season (Oct–Apr). However, many lodgings offer weekend or midweek packages, so ask.

Some of the accommodations listed here have free or discounted parking, and all include breakfast in their prices unless otherwise noted.

Dublin Accommodations and Dining

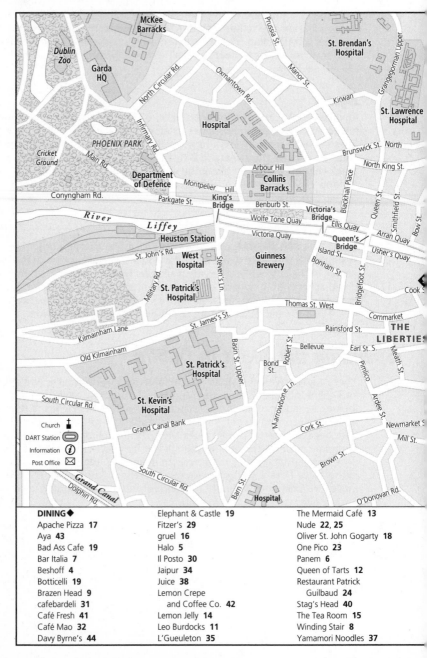

DINING ◆

Apache Pizza **17**	Elephant & Castle **19**	The Mermaid Café **13**
Aya **43**	Fitzer's **29**	Nude **22, 25**
Bad Ass Cafe **19**	gruel **16**	Oliver St. John Gogarty **18**
Bar Italia **7**	Halo **5**	One Pico **23**
Beshoff **4**	Il Posto **30**	Panem **6**
Botticelli **19**	Jaipur **34**	Queen of Tarts **12**
Brazen Head **9**	Juice **38**	Restaurant Patrick
cafebardeli **31**	Lemon Crepe	Guilbaud **24**
Café Fresh **41**	and Coffee Co. **42**	Stag's Head **40**
Café Mao **32**	Lemon Jelly **14**	The Tea Room **15**
Davy Byrne's **44**	Leo Burdocks **11**	Winding Stair **8**
	L'Gueuleton **35**	Yamamori Noodles **37**

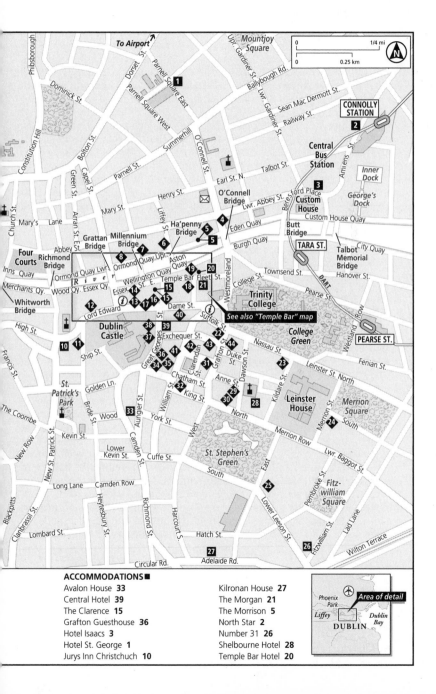

ACCOMMODATIONS ■

Avalon House **33**
Central Hotel **39**
The Clarence **15**
Grafton Guesthouse **36**
Hotel Isaacs **3**
Hotel St. George **1**
Jurys Inn Christchuch **10**

Kilronan House **27**
The Morgan **21**
The Morrison **5**
North Star **2**
Number 31 **26**
Shelbourne Hotel **28**
Temple Bar Hotel **20**

Ariel House
$$–$$$$ Ballsbridge, Dublin 4

Sure, it's located in a leafy residential area that's about a 20-minute walk from the center of the city (or a super-quick ride on the DART), but this romantic hotel is worth any tradeoff in convenience. Rooms in the 1850s house are high-ceilinged, spacious, and gorgeously furnished with Victorian and Georgian antiques and period-style wallpaper and fabrics. Picture velvet drapes, canopy beds (in many of the rooms), and lovely framed prints and portraits. Don't come expecting museum quality surroundings, however; furnishings have a well-worn quality that you may expect in a rich Irish great-aunt's house. The drawing room is elegant and welcoming — you may be inspired to take out your quill pen and write some postcards in front of the crackling fire. If e-mail is more your style, take advantage of the free wireless Internet connection. Ariel House's beauty is more than skin deep; the staff are some of the friendliest and most knowledgeable in Dublin, making this hotel, like Kilronan House (reviewed later in this section), one of the best choices for first-time Dublin visitors.

*52 Lansdowne Rd. ☎ **01-688-5512.** Fax: 01-688-5845.* www.ariel-house.net. *DART: Lansdowne Road. Rates: €89–€190 ($142–$304). MC, V.*

Avalon House
$ Old City, Dublin 2

This funky hostel, which plays host to a mix of travelers from teens to young families to older groups of friends, is legendary among backpackers for its friendliness, clean rooms, and sense of community. The atmosphere of the hostel can be summed up in the fact that you can rent an acoustic guitar at the front desk with a €20 ($32) deposit. Avalon House offers singles, twins, quads, and dorm-style rooms, some with private bathrooms and some without. Rooms are pretty cramped and get a zero on the décor scale (they're pretty sparse), but that probably won't matter, because you can chill out in the self-catering kitchen or in the airy Avalon Café, which offers hot drinks and pastries and often hosts free live entertainment (***Note to performers:*** If you agree to put on a show, your stay is free). Be aware that the halls here are often filled with chatter and laughter until the wee hours of the morning, and as with any hostel, you never know if you'll be sharing a dorm room with early-to-bed early-to-rise travelers or those whose bedtime falls around 4 a.m. The young staff can tell you about the hottest and hippest places in Dublin, and can arrange all sorts of excursions and tours.

*See map p. 130. 55 Aungier St. ☎ **1-800-AVALON** or 01-475-0001. Fax: 01-475-0303.* www.avalon-house.ie. *DART: Tara Street Station. Bus: 16, 16A, 19, or 22. Rates: €60–€78 ($96–$125) double. MC, V.*

The Clarence
$$$$ Temple Bar, Dublin 2

This high-class hotel has a lot to offer, including a terrific location at the doorstep of the lively Temple Bar area, an elegant modern look, and superior service. It's even touched by fame: The hotel is partly owned by Bono and The Edge of the Irish rock band U2. You may not want to leave your enormous bed (featuring Egyptian linens), where you can bliss out to CDs on the room's stereo. Décor is simple and chic, and each room is decorated in one of the hotel's five signature colors: crimson, royal blue, amethyst, gold, or chocolate. The classy Octagon bar, the wonderful Tea Room restaurant (reviewed later in this chapter), and the full-service Therapy Spa are downstairs. The Clarence is the Jackie O of the city's top hotels — just plain classy.

See map p. 130. 6–8 Wellington Quay. ☎ *01-407-0810. Fax: 01-407-0820.* www.the clarence.ie. *DART: Tara Street Station. Bus: 26, 66, 66A, 66B, 66D, 67, 67A. Valet parking. Rates: €370–€760 ($592–$1216) double. Breakfast not included. AE, DC, MC, V.*

Grafton Guesthouse
$$$ Old City, Dublin 2

This guesthouse is an incredible value, offering exceptionally neat, cute rooms at ridiculously low prices (for Dublin, anyway). Rooms (which range from tiny to average) are simply decorated with kitschy touches, such as wallpaper with bright flowers and mod lamp, and there is free Wi-Fi for those who can't live without their Internet. The kicker is that this place is in a central location, on hip Great George's Street, right near Grafton Street and Trinity College. Service is a little rushed but still friendly. Start your day with the traditional full Irish breakfast, or try the vegetarian version, complete with nonmeat sausages. Try to get a room on one of the upper floors if possible, as some of the rooms on the lower floor can be noisy.

See map p. 130. 26–27 S. Great George's St. ☎ *01-679-2041. Fax: 01-677-9715.* www. graftonguesthouse.com. *DART: Tara Street Station. Bus: 16A Rates: €115–€145 ($184–$232) double. AE, MC, V.*

Jurys Inn Christchurch
$$$ Old City (near Temple Bar), Dublin 8

You can't beat Jurys for value if you're traveling as a family: This hotel group is one of the few in Ireland that doesn't charge extra if more than two people share a room. Rooms here are rather uninspiring standard hotel fare, with modern wood furnishings and white-tiled bathrooms. However, any lack of character is compensated for by the friendly and helpful staff and the hotel's central location at the top of Dame Street, right near Christ Church Cathedral and Dublin Castle (ask for a room with a view of the cathedral). There is a restaurant and a casual cafe downstairs, and the hotel can arrange babysitting services.

See map p. 130. Christ Church Place. ☎ *800-44-UTELL from the U.S., or 01-454-0000. Fax: 01-454-0012.* www.jurysinns.com. *DART: Tara Street Station. Bus: 49, 50, 51B, 54A, 56A, 65, 77, 77A, 78A. Rates: €112–€215 ($179–$344) for up to 3 adults or 2 adults and 2 children. Breakfast not included (full Irish breakfast €12/$19). AE, DC, MC, V.*

Kilronan House
$$$ St. Stephen's Green, Dublin 2

This small family-run hotel, with only 15 rooms, is one of the best places to stay if this is your first visit to Dublin. Terry Masterson, the hotel's friendly proprietor, makes a point to sit down with each guest to help plan an itinerary and to field questions about the city. Located on a quiet street within a ten-minute walk of St. Stephen's Green, the Georgian townhouse features many original details, such as beautiful ceiling molding, large bay windows, Waterford chandeliers, and hardwood floors in the public areas. The spacious bedrooms are modern, brightly painted, and filled with natural light — ask for one with a skylight. An excellent full Irish breakfast is served in the elegant dining room.

See map p. 130. 70 Adelaide Rd. ☎ **01-475-5266.** *Fax: 01-478-2841.* www.dublinn. com/kilronan.htm. *DART: Pearse Street Bus: 14, 15A, 15B, 44, 44N, 48A, 48N. Rates: €110–€170 ($176–$272) double. AE, MC, V.*

The Morgan
$$$ Temple Bar, Dublin 2

You know those people whose houses are the opposite of cluttered? Well, you can pretend you're in one of them in the Morgan's soothing bedrooms, which feature the whitest of bed linens, beechwood furnishings, and abstract paintings. The staff is well aware that simplicity and luxury are not mutually exclusive; they do their best to cater to your every need, whether you are ordering a drink in the stylish bar, choosing music from the CD collection, or setting up an on-site massage appointment.

See map p. 130. 10 Fleet St. ☎ **01-643-7000.** *Fax: 01-643-7060.* www.themorgan. com. *Bus: 7B, 7D, 11, 14A, 16, 16A, 46, 46A, 46B, 46C, 46D, 51N, 58X, 67N, 69N, 116, 121, 122, 150, 746. Rates: €120–€160 ($192–$256) double. AE, DC, MC, V.*

The Morrison
$$$$ North Liffey, Dublin 1

This top-notch hotel, in league with the Clarence, is a utopia for those who love modern, minimalist style. Public spaces are a visually pleasing mix of high ceilings, stone floors, and modern art. The elegant, uncluttered bedrooms are decorated in cream, black, and cocoa, and are filled with amenities, including a state-of-the-art sound system. A recent expansion has added rooms with all sorts of additional features including sunken tubs with leather headrests and footrest. If all this doesn't sound relaxing enough, consider a treatment at the hotel's new spa. Service throughout the hotel is pampering and flawless. Halo, the hotel's stylishly rustic restaurant (reviewed later in this chapter), serves fabulous food made with fresh Irish ingredients. Though the Morrison is located on the less-happening north side of the Liffey, it is within easy walking distance of Temple Bar, Dublin Castle, and many other top attractions.

See map p. 130. Ormond Quay (in front of the Millennium Bridge). ☎ **01-887-2400.** *Fax: 01-874-4039.* www.morrisonhotel.ie. *DART: Connolly Station. Rates: €145– €355 ($232–$568) double. AE, DC, MC, V.*

Mt. Herbert Hotel
$$–$$$ Ballsbridge, Dublin 4

Family pride may play a part in the excellent maintenance of this hotel: John Loughran, the director, grew up here when his parents were in charge, and he seems to take pleasure in providing guests with a comfortable stay. Located in a residential section of Dublin, only a short DART ride away from the heart of the city, Mt. Herbert offers sleek, slightly Asian-influenced public areas that retain some of their original architectural features. Bedrooms are contemporary and bright, with pine wall units and tomato-colored carpeting. Service is friendly and helpful.

Herbert Rd. ☎ *01-668-4321. Fax: 01-660-7077.* www.mountherberthotel.ie. *DART: Lansdowne Road. Rates: €89–€129 ($142–$206). MC, V.*

Number 31
$$$–$$$$ St. Stephen's Green, Dublin 2

Designed by Sam Stephenson, one of Ireland's most famous modern architects, this guesthouse is tucked away behind a vined wall on a peaceful little lane about a ten-minute walk from St. Stephen's Green. The style inside is a marriage of modern design and country chic. The spacious rooms have intentionally weathered white-wood country furniture and cozy quilts, plus little modern surprises such as a burnished gray mirrored wall or a sunken bathtub created with turquoise mosaic tiles. After sitting in the glass-walled conservatory, munching on fresh-made granola and delightful hot breakfast dishes (I loved the eggs with salmon), and chatting with Deirdre and Noel Comer, your warm hosts, you may want to move in permanently. Be sure to say hi to Homer, the resident Golden Labrador.

See map p. 130. 31 Lower Leeson Close, Lower Leeson Street. ☎ *01-676-5011.* www. number31.ie. *Bus: 70X, 92. Rates: €150–€320 ($240–$512) double. AE, DC, MC, V.*

Shelbourne Hotel
$$$$ St. Stephen's Green, Dublin 2

Fingers were crossed when this grande dame of Dublin was taken over by the Marriott chain and closed for a renovation. Happily, the Shelbourne's stately character is still intact. Rooms are large and traditionally furnished, and now boast all sorts of luxury amenities, including 300-thread count sheets and LCD flat-screen TVs. Peek into Room 121, where history was made when the Irish constitution was drafted here in 1922.

See map p. 130. 27 St. Stephen's Green. ☎ *01-663-4500. Fax: 01-661-6006.* www. marriott.com. *Bus: 10, 10A, 11, 11A, 140. Rates: €285–€475 ($456–$760). AE, DC, MC, V.*

Temple Bar Hotel
$$$–$$$$ Temple Bar, Dublin 2

This hotel has everything: a terrific location in the heart of Temple Bar, a welcoming and helpful staff, Wi-Fi, an airy Art Deco lobby, and a pleasant restaurant serving light fare under the glow of skylights. In fact, the only drawback to the hotel is the small size of the bedrooms, which feature mahogany furniture, deep green and burgundy colors, and firm double beds. Ask for a room away from the street if you're a light sleeper.

See map p. 130. Fleet Street. ☎ *01-677-3333. Fax: 01-677-3088.* www.templebar hotel.com. *DART: Tara Street Station. Bus to Fleet Street: 7B, 7D, 11, 14A, 16, 16A, 46, 46A, 46B, 46C, 46D, 51N, 58X, 67N, 69N, 116, 121, 122, 150, 746. Rates: €176–€232 ($282–$371) double. AE, DC, MC, V.*

Runner-up hotels

Azalea Lodge

$$ You'd be hard-pressed to find kinder hosts than Bernadette and Padraig Sweeney, who greet you with tea and cookies and do everything within their power to make your visit one to remember. Rooms are large and clean, and though the B&B is outside of the city center, there is a bus right across the street that will get you into Dublin's heart in about 15 minutes. *67 Upper Drumcondra Rd.* ☎ *1-837-0300. Fax: 1-8370300.* www.azalea lodge.com.

ABC Guesthouse

$ **North Dublin, Dublin 9**   This guesthouse, located north of the city center, gets rave reviews for its kind and helpful hosts, and its great value. *57 Upper Drumcondra Rd.* ☎ *01-836-7417.* www.abchousedublin.com.

Central Hotel

$$$ **Old City, Dublin 2**   This hotel is very accurately named, located just a stone's throw from Grafton Street, Temple Bar, and Trinity College. Bedrooms are spacious and bright, and public rooms have a Victorian look. *See map p. 130. 1–5 Exchequer St.* ☎ *800-780-1234 in the U.S. or 01-679-7302. Fax: 01-679-7303.* www.centralhoteldublin.ie.

Hotel Isaacs

$$–$$$ **O'Connell Street Area, Dublin 1**   This moderately priced hotel is right across the street from the Bus Éireann station, close to Dublin's main shopping area and a mere five-minute walk from the city center. The building is a restored wine warehouse, and much of the original brickwork is still visible, giving it a lot of character. Rooms are modern and tastefully furnished. Il Vignardo, an Italian restaurant, is downstairs. *See map p. 130. Store Street.* ☎ *01-813-4700. Fax: 01-836-5390.* www.isaacs.ie.

Hotel St. George

$$$ **O'Connell Street Area, Dublin 1**   One in a row of classic Georgian townhouses, the Hotel St. George sits at the top of O'Connell Street on the north side of the Liffey, a nice location if you're planning to visit the Abbey, Peacock, or Gate theaters; the Writers Museum; the Hugh Lane Gallery; or the James Joyce Centre. The bustling shopping area around Henry Street is also close by. The rooms are large and grand, with high ceilings and antiques, and the staff is friendly and helpful. *See map p. 130. 7 Parnell Sq.* ☎ *01-874-5611. Fax: 01-874-5582.* www.hotel-st-george.ie.

North Star

$$$ **O'Connell Street Area, Dublin 1**   This family-owned hotel is right near the Connolly rail and DART station on the north side of the River Liffey, close to the financial-services district. The large, clean, reasonably priced rooms make this a great place to stay if you have business in the area — and even if you don't. *See map p. 130. Amien Street.* ☎ *01-836-3136. Fax: 01-836-3561.* www.regencyhotels.com.

Dining in Dublin

You can't swing a cat in Dublin (not that you'd want to) without hitting a pleasant place to eat. The city is chock-full of great restaurants for all budgets and tastes. The trend now in Dublin (as in the rest of the country) is towards creative dishes made with the freshest Irish products (think Irish free-range chicken served with a sauce made from local heirloom tomatoes). Being a diverse city, Ireland's capital is also home to eateries that offer cuisines from across the globe. Looking for Indian or Mediterranean? You've got it. Or is it French, Tex-Mex, or Creole that's tempting your taste buds? No problem. And, of course, there are Dublin's myriad pubs, many of which offer tasty Irish fare — stew, sandwiches, shepherd's pie — for low prices.

You don't usually need reservations to dine out in Dublin, especially during the off-season or during the week. However, if you plan on dining somewhere posh and popular, phone ahead a couple of days, especially on weekends or during the summer. I indicate when reservations are necessary in the following listings.

Dublin diners tend to dress in smart casual clothes when going out to a fancy restaurant. At all but the most chi-chi places, even a nice pair of jeans is fine.

Lunch on the move: quick, delicious, inexpensive options

Need to grab a bite between attractions? Hit **O'Brien's Irish Sandwich Bar,** which offers prepackaged sandwiches, beverages, and salads; or **Nude,** which sells delicious pasta, salads, sandwiches, and other quick bites made with organic ingredients. You find branches of O'Brien's all over town; some of the most popular locations are 23 Dawson St., 34B Grafton St., and St. Stephen's Green Shopping Centre. The two Nudes in Dublin are at 38 Upper Baggot St. and 21 Suffolk St. Meals from Nude tend to taste best when eaten on the cricket *pitch* (field) or in the garden at Trinity College (walk straight through the Trinity gate, walk past the Old Library, and make a right at the pretty little garden with benches). On the north side of the Liffey, **Panem,** Ha'penny Bridge House, 21 Ormond Quay Lower (☎ 01-872-8510), is a popular spot for a lunch of soup or pasta of the day. The baked goods are a big draw, and the coffee and hot chocolate are delicious. Kid-friendly **Apache Pizza,** 58 Dame St., at Eustace Street (☎ 01-677-8888) is a perfect stop for some quick chow

Temple Bar

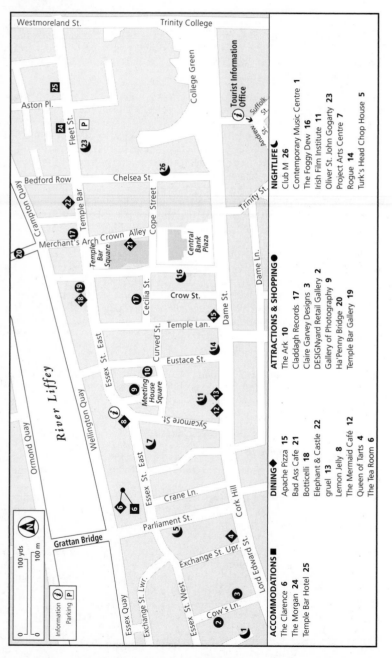

Westmoreland St.

Trinity College

College Green

Aston Pl. **25**

24

Fleet St. **P**

23

Tourist Information Office (i)

Suffolk St.

Andrew St.

Bedford Row

Chelsea St.

26

Crampton Quay

22

Temple Bar

Merchant's Arch **17**

Cope Street

Central Bank Plaza

Crown Alley **21**

20

Temple Bar Square

Trinity St.

Dame Ln.

16

18 19

Crow St.

Cecilia St. **17**

Temple Lan.

15

Dame St.

Essex St. East

Curved St.

14

Eustace St.

10 Meeting House Square

9

11 13

12

(i)

8

Sycamore St.

Wellington Quay

7

River Liffey

Ormond Quay

Essex St. East

Crane Ln.

6 6

Parliament St.

Cork Hill

5

Exchange St. Upr.

4

Grattan Bridge

Exchange St. Lwr.

Lord Edward St.

100 yds

100 m

Essex Quay

Essex St. West

Cow's Ln.

2 **3**

1

0

0

N

Information (i) Parking **P**

NIGHTLIFE♪

Club M **26**
Contemporary Music Centre **1**
The Foggy Dew **16**
Irish Film Institute **11**
Oliver St. John Gogarty **23**
Project Arts Centre **7**
Rogue **14**
Turk's Head Chop House **5**

ATTRACTIONS & SHOPPING●

The Ark **10**
Claddagh Records **17**
Claire Garvey Designs **3**
DESIGNyard Retail Gallery **2**
Gallery of Photography **9**
Ha'Penny Bridge **20**
Temple Bar Gallery **19**

DINING♦

Apache Pizza **15**
Bad Ass Cafe **21**
Botticelli **18**
Elephant & Castle **22**
gruel **13**
Lemon Jelly **8**
The Mermaid Café **12**
Queen of Tarts **4**
The Tea Room **6**

ACCOMMODATIONS■

The Clarence **6**
The Morgan **24**
Temple Bar Hotel **25**

or a postbar bite. You can get pizza by the pie or slice, or try a famous Totem Roll: pizza ingredients stuffed into a hoagie bun and baked. The new **cafebardeli,** in the former location of Bewley's Oriental Café, on 12 South Great Georges St. (☎ **01-677-1646**), serves up simple, inexpensive fare in sumptuous surroundings of stained glass, dark wood, marble tables, and crystal chandeliers.

Finally, I can't think of a better sightseeing pick-me-up than a freshly made crepe folded around banana slices and Nutella. Follow the crowds to the incredibly popular **Lemon Crepe & Coffee Co.,** 68 South William St., Dublin 2 (☎. **01-672-9044**). **Lemon Jelly,** 10–11 Essex St. (☎ **01-677-6297**), in Temple Bar, is another spot where you can satisfy your crepe cravings.

Pub grub
Pubs are a great place to get a good, relatively cheap lunch or dinner. Most serve real stick-to-the-ribs Irish options, such as stew or shepherd's pie, along with a few lighter options such as salads and sandwiches. Some of your best bets for good food are:

- ✔ **Brazen Head,** 20 Lower Bridge St. Dublin 8 (☎ **01-679-5186**)

- ✔ **Davy Byrne's,** 21 Duke St., Dublin 2 (☎ **01-677-5217**)

- ✔ **Oliver St. John Gogarty,** 58 Fleet St., Temple Bar, Dublin 2 (☎ **01-671-1822**)

- ✔ **Stag's Head,** 1 Dame Ct. (off Dame Street), Dublin 2 (☎ **01-671-3701**)

Dublin's Top Restaurants A to Z

Keep an eye out for the reopening of **Café Mao,** 2–3 Chatham St. (☎ **01-670-4899**). At press time, this excellent Asian fusion restaurant was closed due to a fire, but is planning to reopen.

Aya
$$–$$$$ Grafton Street Area, Dublin 2   JAPANESE

This place bears a striking resemblance to my idea of heaven, with an endless parade of sushi and other Japanese treats traveling before your eyes, courtesy of a refrigerated conveyor belt. Here's how it works: You take a seat at the conveyor belt, and grab whatever looks good. The five different colors of the plates correspond to different prices, and your server calculates your bill based on the number and colors of the plates that you stack up. The restaurant offers a number of deals, including the popular *55 Time* special (Sun–Wed and Fri from 5 p.m. on), which allows you to eat all you can from the conveyor belt in 55 minutes for €25 ($40; drink and miso soup included). Prices are also slashed half an hour before closing — to €1.25 ($2) per plate Sunday through Thursday, and €1.75 ($2.80) on

Friday and Saturday. I particularly recommend the eel sushi, the shrimp tempura maki rolls, the edamame (steamed soybeans), and the rich caramel-and-banana dessert. The modern décor is simple and chic, but it probably won't matter, because you'll be hypnotized by the conveyor belt. The restaurant also offers fine pan-Asian sit-down meals such as a chile-and-lemon beef udon dish.

See map p. 130. 49–52 Clarendon St. ☎ *01-677-1544. DART: Tara St. Bus: 16A, 10, 11, 11a, 11b, 46a, 46b. Main courses (including a conveyor-belt meal): €10–€26 ($16–$42). AE, DC, MC, V. Open: Mon–Fri 12:30–10 p.m., Sat 12:30–11 p.m., Sun 1–9:30 p.m.*

Bad Ass Cafe
$$–$$$ Temple Bar, Dublin 2 AMERICAN

No, you don't have to be tough to come here (the name refers to the restaurant's donkey mascot), but you do have to be hungry. This Dublin institution occupies an old warehouse and has a fun, casual, airy look and feel, with cash shuttles that whisk your money across the room to the cashier, bright colors, and windows looking out onto the teeming streets of Temple Bar. Some of the best pizza in the city is served here, including the delicious *Kitchensinkio,* which sports every topping you can think of. Pastas, burgers, and other basic dishes round out the menu, and the salads are fresh and delicious. The whole menu is kid-friendly, especially the bottom portion, which lists the sundaes and other desserts.

See map p. 130. 9–11 Crown Alley. ☎ *01-671-2596.* www.badasscafe.com. *DART: Tara Street Station. Bus to Fleet Street: 7B, 7D, 11, 14A, 14B. Main courses: €9–€19 ($14–$30). AE, MC, V. Open: Daily 8 a.m.–11 p.m.*

Bar Italia
$$$ Millennium Walkway/Bloom's Lane ITALIAN

This isn't the place for a romantic dinner; the restaurant is so noisy with chatter and laughter that your companion may mistake your sweet nothings for "Please pass the peas." However, the buzz doesn't distract diners from digging into such delicious classic southern Italian dishes as delicate gnocchi in marinara sauce and an out-of-this-world bruschetta with garlic, tomatoes, and basil. The setting is classy, with white walls, candles, and light wood, and the service is good. Most dishes are at the lower end of the price range listed below.

See map p. 130. Bloom's Lane/Millennium Walkway. ☎ *01-874-1000. Reservations recommended. Main courses: €13–€28 ($21–$45). AE, DC, MC, V. Open: Mon–Thurs 8 a.m.–10:30 p.m., Fri 8–11 p.m., Sat 9–11 p.m., Sun 11–9 p.m.*

Beshoff
$ O'Connell Street area, Dublin 2 FISH AND CHIPS

If there were an Olympic category for best *chipper* (fish-and-chips shop), and I were the judge, Beshoff would get the gold. The fish here is as fresh as can be, its juices sealed in by a fried golden-brown crust; the *chips* (fries) are cut fresh each day and are thick and deliciously dense. If you like salt and vinegar to begin with, you'll love how they complement fish and chips, so ask for them. If you feel the same way about fish that my friend Shannon does — "If it comes from the sea, let it be" — take heart and order the chicken option. Beshoff's rival is **Leo Burdocks,** at 2 Werburgh St., Dublin 8 (☎ **01-454-0306**). I think Beshoff is better, but let me know your vote.

See map p. 130. 6 Upper O'Connell St. ☎ 01-872-4400. DART: Tara Street Station. Bus: 1, 2, 3, 121, 122, 123. Main courses: €5–€7 ($8–$11). No credit cards. Open: Mon–Sat 9 a.m.–10 p.m., Sun 1:15 a.m.–9 p.m.

Botticelli
$$–$$$ Temple Bar, Dublin 2   ITALIAN/PIZZA

This restaurant, run by Italians, serves food for people who know and love their Italian cuisine. It's frequented by groups of locals, making it hard to get into on weekends, but the gnocchi, huge variety of pizzas, and tiramisu make it worth the wait. The interior is casual, with warm lighting and blue tablecloths. Save room for the delicious gelato served up at the storefront next door, run by the same folks. Come here for a casual Italian meal if you are in the Temple Bar area; if you're looking for something more formal, try Il Posto (reviewed later in this section) or Bar Italia (reviewed earlier in the section).

See map p. 130. 2 Temple Bar Rd. ☎ 01-672-7289. DART: Tara Street Station. Bus to Fleet Street: 7B, 7D, 11, 46, 46A, 46B, 63, 150. Main courses: €12–€27 ($19–$43). AE, DC, MC, V. Open: Daily 12:30 p.m. to midnight.

Café Fresh
$ Trinity Area, Dublin 2   VEGETARIAN

Fennel, spinach, and goat-cheese lasagna; pumpkin, butternut, and rosemary soup; Sri Lankan butterbean and vegetable curry — the tasty dishes at this inexpensive vegetarian cafe will satisfy even the omnivores in your group. Housed in a refurbished 18th-century mansion that now accommodates an upscale shopping center, Café Fresh is one of Dublin's top choices for a casual lunch. The kitchen works to accommodate people with various food allergies.

Little Italy in Dublin

Two for the price of one! You buy a ticket to Ireland and get a free trip to a mini Italy. Quartier Bloom/Millennium Walkway, right over the Millennium footbridge on the north side of the Liffey, has recently become home to authentic Italian wine bars, Italian restaurants (see the review of Bar Italia earlier in this chapter), a cafe serving panini (Caffé Cagliostro; ☎ 01-888-0834), and a gelato spot. There is even a hip little piazza and a contemporary Roman arch. Check out the mural near the center of Bloom's Lane, a riff on da Vinci's Last Supper in which Jesus and his apostles are replaced by people plucked randomly from Dublin's sidewalks (Jesus is an Indian student at Trinity College).

See map p. 130. Unit 25 I Powerscourt Townhouse Centre, top floor. ☎ *01-671-9669.*
*DART: Tara Street Station. Bus: 10, 10A, 11, 11A, 14D, 15A. Main courses: €4–€11
($6.40–$18). MC, V. Open: Mon–Fri 10 a.m.–6 p.m., Sat 9 a.m.–6 p.m.*

Café Mao
$$–$$$ Grafton Street Area, Dublin 2 ASIAN FUSION

Take a seat outside or in the airy interior of this excellent restaurant, and
settle down for a long, casual meal, and some great people-watching. The
menu roams Asia and is full of flavorful dishes, including tender salmon with
sweet sauce and vegetables, Malaysian chicken curry, and the popular sweet
potato-and-pumpkin curry served on jasmine rice. Don't miss the superb
pumpkin spring rolls, served with a sweet and zingy plum sauce.

See map p. 130. 2–3 Chatham Row. ☎ *01-670-4899. Bus: 7, 10, 11, 11A, 11B, 46A, 46B.
Main courses: €10–€19 ($16–$30). AE, MC, V. Open: Mon–Wed noon to 10 p.m.,
Thurs–Sat noon to 11 p.m., Sun 2–9 p.m.*

Elephant & Castle
$$–$$$ Temple Bar, Dublin 2 AMERICAN

Locals and visitors alike pile into this immensely popular, buzzing joint in
the heart of Temple Bar, which serves exceptional burgers, salads, omelets,
and other American diner fare. Burger-slingers around the world should
cross their fingers that Elephant & Castle doesn't open a branch in their
town, because these juicy, flavorful burgers are some of the best I've ever
tasted. Garlic-philes must try the garlic burger, with roasted garlic cloves,
garlic butter, and aioli; another winner is the burger with horseradish, black
pepper, and sour cream. Or go for a tasty omelet or a fresh, generous salad.
And don't miss the beverage list, which offers everything from elderflower
soda to fresh limeade. This warm, relaxed restaurant, with its wood booths
and funky paintings and photos (my favorite is a painting of a sign shop,
reading "Advertise with SIGNS. We make them."), is the perfect place to
watch the crowds of people who parade down Temple Bar.

See map p. 130. 18 Temple Bar St. ☎ *01-679-3121. DART: Tara Street Station. Bus: 7B,
7D, 11, 14A, 16, 16A, 46, 46A, 46B, 46C, 46D, 51N, 58X, 67N, 69N, 116, 121, 122, 150, 746.
Main courses: €12–€23 ($19–$37). AE, DC, MC, V. Open: Mon–Fri 8 a.m.–11:30 p.m.,
Sat and Sun 10:30 a.m.–11:30 p.m.*

Fitzer's
$$$$ St. Stephen's Green Area, Dublin 2 NEW IRISH/WORLD

Owned by the Fitzpatricks of Dublin, a family that began as fruit and vegetable merchants in the city, Fitzer's cafes use some of the freshest produce
around. From creative and filling salads to innovative pasta dishes to lamb
tandoori, Fitzer's menu features a variety of delicious, simply prepared
dishes from around the world. The surroundings are casual and airy, the
atmosphere is classy without being unapproachable, and the staff is
friendly. Fitzer's is a chain, though each of the three locations has a different menu and prices. The one located on Dawson Street, just blocks

from Grafton Street, is the one I recommend. Just for the record, though, the other locations are the Millennium Wing of the National Gallery, Merrion Sq., Dublin 2 (☎ **01-670-6577**), and 42 Temple Bar Sq., Dublin 2 (☎ **01-679-0440**).

See map p. 130. 51 Dawson St. ☎ *01-677-1155. DART: Tara Street Station. Bus: 33X, 74, 128, 140, 142B. Main courses: €20–€30 ($32–$48). AE, DC, MC, V. Open: Daily noon to 11 p.m.*

gruel
$$ Dublin 2 NEW IRISH/WORLD

"Please sir, may I have some more?" I'm sure the friendly staff at gruel would happily accommodate little Oliver Twist's appeal, though after seeing the gigantic portions here he may reconsider his request. Every city should have a place like gruel — a bright, casual restaurant that serves inexpensive, hearty, creative dishes. Groups of friends and couples chat over fresh salads, homemade soups, and main courses that change daily but may include the likes of vegetable tagine served with couscous and mint yogurt, and bangers and mash with onion jam. As you wait for your food, check out the art exhibits on one wall, the posters for upcoming concerts on another wall, and the funky pink fireplace graced with Campbell's Tomato Soup cans.

See map p. 130. 68a Dame St. ☎ *01-670-7119. DART: Tara Street Station. Bus: 49, 56A, 77, 77A, 123. Main courses: €14–€16 ($22–$26). No credit cards. Open: Daily 8 a.m.–10 p.m., Sun 10:30 a.m.–9 p.m.*

Halo
$$$$ North Liffey, Dublin 1 NEW IRISH

This newly restyled rustic cathedral of a restaurant is one of the most popular places to try fresh New Irish cuisine. Settle into the airy room, and dig into creative dishes prepared with Irish ingredients (often organic). Stars of the menu include a short-rib cooked for two, and spinach and ricotta tortellini topped with garlic cream and crushed pumpkin seeds.

See map p. 130. Ormond Quay (in the Hotel Morrison in front of the Millennium Bridge). ☎ *01-887-2400. Reservations recommended. DART: Connolly Station. Bus: 68, 69, 69X. Main courses: €28–€32 ($45–$51). AE, DC, MC, V. Open: Mon–Fri 7–10:30 a.m. and 7–10:30 p.m., Sat–Sun 8 a.m.–noon and 7–10:30 p.m.*

Il Posto
$$$–$$$$ Dublin 2 ITALIAN

Everything about this place is warm, inviting, and elegant, from the friendly service to the orange-and-cream paintings on the wall to the candles on each table. The delicious and filling food, served in giant portions, just adds to the general feeling of ease and comfort. The menu features many creatively put-together "nouveau" Italian dishes, such as the duo of duck breast and lamb's liver with braised balsamic lentils and walnuts, served with a red-wine-and-cinnamon poached pear and a toffee jus. The seafood dishes, including pan-fried Dover sole with pine nuts, coriander, and lemon butter sauce, are especially delicious. The early-bird set menu, served from 5:30 to 7 p.m. daily, is a good deal.

See map p. 130. 10 St. Stephen's Green. ☎ *01-679-4769. Reservations recommended. Main courses: €18–€29 ($29–$46). AE, DC, MC, V. Open: Mon–Fri noon to 2 p.m. and 5:30–11 p.m., Sat noon to 2:30 p.m. and 5:30–11 p.m., Sun 5:30–11 p.m.*

Jaipur
$$$ Grafton Street Area, Dublin 2   INDIAN

You know you're in for a delicious Indian meal as soon as you take a bite of the complimentary airy pappadum, which are served with a trio of sauces: sweet pineapple chutney, tangy cilantro sauce, and a spicy red sauce. The atmosphere is refined and romantic, with exotic fresh flowers on each table and candlelight casting a golden glow on the faces of the couples and small groups of friends dining here. The menu is filled with great options, from traditional Indian favorites such as Chicken Tikka Masala to more unusual choices such as Nalli Gosht — tender roast lamb in a hot broth with the chef's special spices. Be sure to order the Pulao Rice — fluffy, spiced basmati rice — to complement your main dish.

See map p. 130. 41 South Great George's St. ☎ *01-677-0999. Reservations recommended. DART: Tara Street Station. Bus: 16A. Main courses: €12–€21 ($19–$34). AE, DC, MC, V. Open: Daily 5 p.m. to midnight.*

Juice
$$–$$$ Old City, Dublin 2   GLOBAL/VEGETARIAN

Juice is a casual, friendly little slice of health-conscious California in the heart of Dublin. Small groups of friends and solo diners drop in to chat, flip through the newspaper, or write in their journals over generous portions of vegetarian and vegan dishes that take their inspiration from cuisines all over the planet. You find everything from miso soup to spicy bean burgers to crepelike pancakes served with organic maple syrup shot through with mango puree. And as the name not-very-subtly suggests, you also find all kinds of juices, which are so fresh, they taste like you just inserted a straw directly into the fruit or vegetable. High ceilings, curved walls, a metal panel covered with Christmas lights, and candy-colored glass flower vases and votive holders give this place a warm, funky air that invites lingering, especially on a cool, rainy day (not that Dublin has any of those).

See map p. 130. 73–83 S. Great George's St. ☎ *01-475-7856. DART: Tara Street Station. Bus: 16A. Main courses: €13–€16 ($21–$26). AE, DC, MC, V. Open: Daily 11 a.m.–11 p.m.*

L'Gueuleton
$$$–$$$$ Old City, Dublin 2   NEW IRISH/FRENCH

This restaurant boasts an inspired menu, polite service, and a casually elegant atmosphere that hums with conversation and laughter. Choosing a single dish from the inventive offerings can be difficult. The menu changes often, but dishes on a recent night included Asian braised pork belly with wilted greens and pear-and-watercress salad; duck with potatoes, sweetened chicory and green peppercorns; and Bayonne ham with watermelon, arugula, and feta cheese. Everything is prepared with an eye to preserving the character and flavor of the ingredients; I was especially happy that the vegetables were not cooked into submission. The atmosphere is a happy marriage of stylish and casual; groups of friends pull up mismatched chairs to tables adorned with tea lights and small bowls filled with cracked pepper and sea salt, and there is a cute garden in the back for warm-weather dining. A kind of strange thing: They don't serve any soda.

See p. 130. 1 Fade St. (right off of S. Great George's Street). ☎ *01-675-3708. Bus: 16A. Main courses: €16–€27 ($26–$43). MC, V. Open: Mon–Sat 12:30–3 p.m. and 6–10 p.m.*

The Mermaid Café
$$$$ Dublin 2   NEW IRISH

This is one of my favorite restaurants in Dublin, because it serves innovative dishes made with some of the freshest, most flavorful ingredients around. The menu changes seasonally, offering the likes of Irish Angus rib-eye steak with sage-and-mustard mashed potatoes and garlicky beans; yellowfin tuna with plum tomatoes, capers, mint, and wasabi mayonnaise; and a salad of asparagus and quail eggs with shaved parmesan and greens. The crowd is always buzzy and chic; businesspeople descend on the restaurant at lunch, while dinner sees more couples and small groups. The surroundings are cozy and modern, featuring contemporary art, white wood walls, high-backed pine chairs, and solid pine tables. Save room for the unbelievable desserts, including pecan pie served with maple ice cream. The two- and three-course lunch deals are excellent.

See map p. 130. 70 Dame St. ☎ *01-670-8236. Reservations recommended. DART: Tara Street Station. Bus: Bus: 68, 69, 69X. Main courses: €20–€33 ($32–$53). MC, V. Open: Mon–Sat 12:30–2:30 p.m. and 6–11 p.m., Sun noon to 3:30 p.m. and 6–9 p.m.*

One Pico
$$$$ Grafton Street Area, Dublin 2   CONTINENTAL-NEW IRISH

This is my number-one pick for sealing a business deal in Dublin. A classy crowd (including quite a few businesspeople) fills this elegant restaurant, decorated with browns and golds, to sample star chef Eamonn O'Reilly's creations. Like the chefs at the **Tea Room, Halo,** the **Winding Stair,** and **Mermaid Café** (all reviewed in this section), O'Reilly creates adventurous dishes with fresh Irish produce, though his menu seems to have more of a French influence than the menus at those four restaurants. The menu changes often, featuring such delights as a starter of seared rare tuna with black sesame seeds, coriander (cilantro) puree, and red onion crème fraiche, served alongside a fennel, pear, and cucumber salad, and an Irish Angus beef filet with artichoke puree, boiled asparagus, Pomme Anna (thinly sliced potatoes layered with butter), and cabernet sauvignon sauce. Whatever you do, be sure to try the desserts; Cookies & Cream, a haute re-creation of some of the world's most beloved cookies, was one of my recent favorites. The prix-fixe lunch and pretheater deals are excellent, at €25 ($40) for a two-course lunch and €40 ($64) for a three-course pretheater dinner.

See map p. 130. 5–6 Molesworth Place, Schoolhouse Lane. ☎ 01-676-0300. Reservations recommended. DART: Pearse. Bus: 10, 11A, 11B, 13, or 20B. Main courses: €30–€40 ($48–$64). AE, DC, MC, V. Open: Mon–Sat 12:30–2:15 p.m. and 6:15–9:30 p.m.

Queen of Tarts
$ Dublin 2   BAKERY/CAFE

If I lived near this bakery and cafe, I'd weigh about 900 pounds, and that would be tragic, because then I may not be able to fit through the door to sample more of their incredible desserts. Savory lunch tarts (such as a goat cheese, tomato, olive, and pesto combo), salads, sandwiches, and toothsome homemade soups attended by a thick slice of brown bread are served in a cheerful, casual yellow room. But the excellent lunch fare is just the opening act for the glorious desserts, including a tangy blackberry-and-apple crumble offset by sweet cream that I could eat every day.

See map p. 130. 4 Corkhill (part of Dame Street across from Dublin Castle). ☎ 01-670-7499. DART: Tara Street Station. Bus: 49, 56A, 77, 77A, 123. Main courses and baked goods: €3.50–€11 ($5.60–$18). No credit cards. Open: Mon–Fri 7:30 a.m.–7 p.m., Sat–Sun 9 a.m.–7 p.m.

Restaurant Patrick Guilbaud
$$$$ Dublin 2   FRENCH

Some of the finest cuisine in Dublin is served in this bright, cream-colored room, which sports abstract paintings. Dishes combine fresh Irish and French ingredients with French cooking techniques and pure creativity for some real stunners, such as the caramelized veal sweetbread glazed with licorice sauce and parsnip sauce, and served with a lemon confit; and the roast black sole with Moroccan lemon and curd. Desserts are appropriately complex and impressive; a recent menu listed a plate of five different cold and hot dark-chocolate confections. The €50 ($80) three-course lunch is a great deal (relatively speaking of course).

See map p. 130. In the Merrion Hotel, 21 Upper Merrion St. ☎ 01-676-4192. Reservations required. DART: Westland Row. Bus: 48A. Main courses: €48–€56 ($77–$90); lobster is more. AE, DC, MC, V. Open: Tues–Sat 12:30–2 p.m. and 7–10 p.m.

The Tea Room
$$$$ Temple Bar, Dublin 2   NEW IRISH

This is *the* place in Dublin to try out New Irish cuisine, which uses Ireland's bounty of fresh ingredients in imaginative dishes. Expect intriguing options such as the roast rack of Wicklow lamb marinated in Indian spices and preserved lemon, and served with a mixture of natural lamb juices and curry oil. Housed in the fabulous Clarence Hotel (reviewed earlier in this chapter), the Tea Room has an airy feel, with soaring ceilings, large windows and blond wood. The new slightly-less-fancy €39 ($62) market menu is served all during dinner from Sunday through Thursday and from 7 to 8 p.m. Friday and Saturday night.

See map p. 130. In the Clarence Hotel, 6–8 Wellington Quay. ☎ *01-407-0820. Reservations required. DART: Tara Street Station. Bus: 51, 51B, 68, 68A, 69X, 78A, 79, 90, 210. Dinner (prix-fixe only): €39 ($62) for 3-course "market menu," €55 ($88) for 3-course "signature menu." AE, DC, MC, V. Open: Daily 7 a.m.–11 a.m. (7:30 a.m.–11:30 a.m. Sat–Sun), Mon–Sat 12:30–2:30 p.m. and 7–10:30 p.m., Sun 7–9:30 p.m.*

Winding Stair
$$$$ Dublin 2   NEW IRISH

The Winding Stair is the best new restaurant in Dublin, giving you the best of both worlds: traditional Irish ingredients presented with impeccable modern cooking skills. The chefs are obsessed with finding the top sources for their local ingredients, from the Irish Aberdeen beef (which is accompanied by sticky onions, garlic butter, and homemade French fries) to the fromage heaven that greets you on the Irish Cheese Board. And don't miss the desserts, especially the unbelievable sticky pear and ginger cake. The setting is casual and airy, with views over the Liffey River through ceiling-high windows. You may find yourself elbow-to-elbow with your fellow patrons, but with the good spirits, laughter, and transcendent food you should hardly mind.

See map p. 130. 40 Ormond Quay (near the Ha'penny Bridge). ☎ *01-872-7320. DART: Tara Street Station. Bus: 68, 69, 69X. Main courses: €20–€25 ($32–$40). AE, MC, V. Open: Mon–Sat 12:30–3:30 p.m. and 6–10:30 p.m., Sun 12:30–3:30 p.m. and 6–9:30 p.m.*

Yamamori Noodles
$$$ Old City, Dublin 2   NOODLES/JAPANESE

If you're craving Japanese noodle dishes and soups and a boisterous atmosphere, Yamamori is your place. In a large, simply furnished space decorated with white lanterns and a glass panel sandwiching delicate cherry-blossom-shaped lights, groups of friends talk and laugh over super-fresh sushi, bowls of delectable ramen big enough to drown in, and other Japanese dishes, such as wok-fried noodles; rare tuna loin served with a trio of soba, rice, and green tea noodles; and various teriyaki plates. Try the sushi hand rolls — cones of delicate seaweed wrapped around warm vinegary rice and the fresh filling of your choice.

See map p. 130. 71–72 S. Great George's St. ☎ *01-475-5001. DART: Tara Street Station. Bus: 16A. Main courses: €15–€21 ($24–$34). AE, MC, V. Open: Sun–Wed 12:15–11 p.m., Thurs–Sat 12:15–11:30 p.m.*

Exploring Dublin

Dublin is packed with things to see and do. An exploration of the city is like a journey through history as you discover medieval churches, Viking ruins, an 18th-century college campus, and museums containing artifacts such as 3,000-year-old Celtic gold jewelry. Modern Dublin is

Dublin Attractions

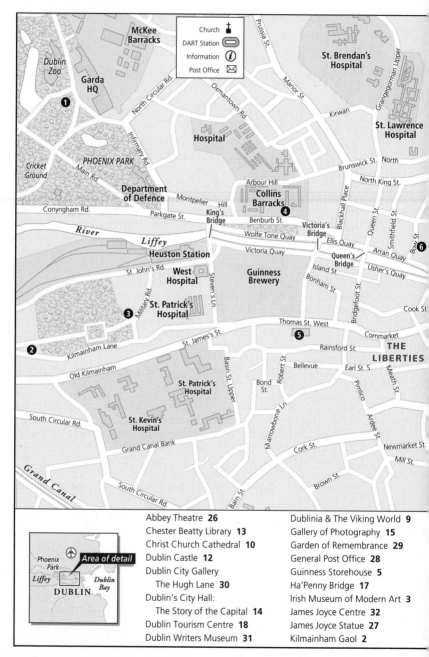

	Church ✝
	DART Station ⬭
	Information ⓘ
	Post Office ✉

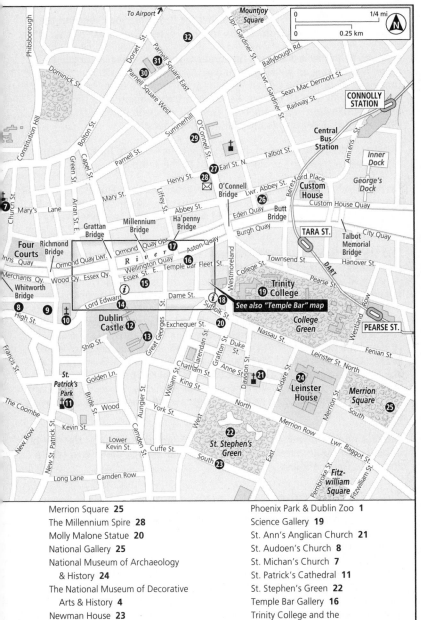

evident in sights ranging from a recent portrait of U2 singer Bono in the National Gallery to a slew of über-trendy shops.

As you explore Dublin, keep an eye out for brass plaques laid into the ground with passages from James Joyce's *Ulysses* that relate to that site.

If you're in Dublin for a short time, one of the best ways to take in as many attractions as possible is to use the Hop On Hop Off tour bus. The bus visits 23 of Dublin's most popular attractions, and as the name indicates, you can hop off the bus to see an attraction and then pick up another bus when you're finished. See the review in "Seeing Dublin by Guided Tour," later in this chapter, for more details.

Dublin is relatively compact, but it still makes sense to look at a map and plan to see attractions in the same area in the same day.

No need to break the bank sightseeing; all the parks in Dublin are free, as are many other attractions listed here. You can also get combined tickets to some attractions, which could save a few euro (see reviews for further information).

The Dublin Pass offers a terrific deal. You pay a flat price and get free admission to tons of Dublin and Dublin-area attractions, plus discounts on several tours and at some restaurants, shops, and entertainment venues. The pass even includes a free ride from Dublin Airport to the center of Dublin City on Aircoach. The one-day pass is €29 ($46) adults and €17 ($27) for kids younger than 16; a two-day pass is €49 ($78) adults and €29 ($46) kids younger than 16; a three-day pass is €59 ($94) adults and €34 ($54) kids under age 16; and a six-day pass is €89 ($142) adults and €44 ($70) kids under age 16. The pass is available at any Dublin tourism office (☎ **01-605-7700**), including the office at the arrivals concourse at Dublin Airport, or at www.dublinpass.com. If you know that you're going to do a lot of sightseeing, the Dublin Pass may be perfect for you.

Families should be aware that most attractions in Dublin and the rest of Ireland offer family rates — low flat rates that usually cover two adults and up to four children.

The top attractions

Chester Beatty Library
Dublin 2

The Chester Beatty Library is one of those gems that often gets overlooked in favor of the more flashy attractions of Dublin. But this extensive collection of books, artwork, manuscripts, and religious objects from around the world is worth at least a few hours of precious vacation time. On the first floor, you find an exhibit called Arts of the Book, an awe-inspiring and diverse collection of ancient books, from Egyptian Books of the Dead to medieval illuminated manuscripts Narrated videos of craftspeople at work are found throughout the gallery, illuminating crafts such as bookbinding, papermaking, and printmaking. The second floor is dedicated to books and objects from many of the world's religious traditions. A beautifully created audiovisual explores religious practices and belief systems around the world. The treasures on this floor are numerous, including a Hindu cosmological painting from 18th-century Nepal; a standing Tibetan Buddha; and some of the earliest New Testament and Gospel texts, including the Gospel of St. John, written on Greek papyrus, circa 150 to 200. If you are spiritually satiated but physically hungry, the Silk Road Café is excellent.

See map p. 148. Dublin Castle. ☎ 01-407-0750. www.cbl.ie. *Bus: 13, 16, 19, 123. Admission: Free. Open: May–Sept Mon–Fri 10 a.m.–5 p.m., Sat 11 a.m.–5 p.m., and Sun 1–5 p.m.; Oct–Apr Tues–Fri 10 a.m.–5 p.m., Sat 11 a.m.–5 p.m., and Sun 1–5 p.m. Suggested visit: 1½–2 hours.*

Christ Church Cathedral
Dublin 8

Christ Church Cathedral, an Anglican/Episcopal church, has existed in various forms in this spot for almost a thousand years. The Vikings built a simple wood church at this location in 1038. In the 1180s, the original foundation was expanded into a cruciform, and the Romanesque cathedral was built in stone. The church you see today is the result of restoration and rebuilding on the 1180s building during the 1870s. The cathedral provides an informative self-guided tour brochure when you enter, or you can call to make reservations for a guided tour. Don't let all the soaring architecture and intricate stonework above you distract you from the beautiful 13th-century tile floor. On your way to the Peace Chapel of Saint Laud, check out the mummified rat and cat found in a pipe of the organ in the late 1860s. Also take time to see the tomb of Strongbow, the Viking leader who captured Dublin in 1170. Your ticket covers admission to the medieval crypt, which houses the cathedral's Treasury. Visitors are welcome at services; just call ahead for times. Choral services (Wed and Thurs at 6 p.m., Sat at 5 p.m., and Sun at 11 a.m. and 3:30 p.m.) are especially beautiful. Note that admission is reduced if you visit Dublinia (reviewed later in this section) first.

See map p. 148. Christ Church Place. ☎ 01-677-8099. www.cccdub.ie. *DART: Tara Street Station. Bus: 49, 50, 65, 77. Admission: €6 ($9.60) adults, €4 ($6.40) students and seniors, free for children accompanied by a parent. Open: June–Aug daily 9 a.m.–6 p.m. (last admission at 5:30 p.m., and access is limited during services); Sept–May daily 9:45 a.m.–5 p.m. Suggested visit: 45 minutes.*

Dublin Castle
Dublin 2

This is not your typical storybook castle. Originally, it was built in the 13th century, but many additions were made over the following 800 years. Today, the castle looks like an encyclopedia of European architectural styles, from the 13th-century Norman Record Tower to the Church of the Holy Trinity, designed in 1814 in Gothic style. The castle now hosts official state functions, such as the president's inauguration, and the clock tower is home to the excellent Chester Beatty Library (reviewed earlier in this section). Guided tours (listed as 50 minutes long, but often extended) take you through many of the impressively furnished State Apartments, including the Drawing Room, which features a breathtaking Waterford Crystal chandelier; the Throne Room, where Queen Victoria ordered servants to lop several inches off the legs of the throne so that her feet wouldn't dangle as she spoke to her subjects; and Patrick's Hall, which boasts the banners of the Knights of St. Patrick and historical ceiling paintings. You'll end up in the moat, gazing at the original city and castle walls. Art and history lovers alike should appreciate the tour, which focuses on both the aesthetics of the castle and its history. It would be ideal to read the "History 101" section in Chapter 2 before your tour if you need to brush up on your Irish history. Don't miss the Church of the Holy Trinity, with its beautiful carved oak panels and stained-glass windows. Note the statue of Justice in the courtyard. See how she faces away from the city? Cynical Dubliners will tell you that was intentional. During state occasions, the State Apartments may be closed.

See map p. 148. Cork Hill, off Dame Street. ☎ **01-645-8813.** www.dublin castle.ie. *Bus: 49, 56A, 77, 77A, 123. Admission: €4.50 ($7.20) adult, €3.50 ($5.60) students and seniors, €2 ($3.20) under 12. Visits are by guided tour only. Open: Mon–Fri 10 a.m.–5 p.m., Sat–Sun 2–4:45 p.m. Suggested visit: 1 hour.*

Guinness Storehouse
Dublin 8

Though the actual Guinness Brewery is closed to the public, the Guinness Storehouse will fill you in on everything you've ever wanted to know about "black gold." This temple to Guinness is housed in a 1904 building that was used for the fermentation process — when yeast is added to beer. The core of the building is a seven-level, pint-shaped structure that could hold approximately 14.3 million pints of Guinness. The Storehouse explores every facet of Ireland's favorite beverage, from the ingredients that go into each batch to the company's advertising campaigns to the role of Guinness in Irish culture. Though there is a sense of unabashed propaganda to the whole attraction, the exhibits are beautifully done in a cool, modern design. There is a lot to see, but you'll definitely want to make time for the ingredients exhibit, which features a veritable beach of barley and a waterfall of Irish water; the intriguing audiovisual journey through the Guinness brewing process; the tasting laboratory (where you get to sample several different brews); and the fun display of Guinness advertisements through the years. And don't bypass the "Start the Brew" section on the first floor, where 100 lucky visitors per week get to press a button that initiates the brewing process at the actual Brew House. The top-floor Gravity Bar is (literally) the Storehouse's crowning glory, offering 360-degree views of Dublin through floor-to-ceiling glass walls, and dispensing a free pint of black stuff to every visitor over the age of 18.

See map p. 148. St. James's Gate. ☎ **01-408-4800.** www.guinness-store house.com. *Bus: 51B, 51C, 78A, 123. Admission: €14 ($22) adults, €10 ($16) seniors and students 18 and over, €8 ($13) students under 18, €5 ($8) children 6–12, free for children under 6. Price includes a free pint of stout or a soda. Open: July–Aug daily 9:30 a.m.–7 p.m., Sept–June daily 9:30 a.m.–5 p.m. Suggested visit: 2½ hours.*

Exploring Temple Bar

In the 1970s, artists of all kinds began setting up shop in Temple Bar, and the area, which had hitherto been in decline, became a hotbed for cutting-edge visual and performing arts. Though the 1980s were rough for Temple Bar, the area rallied during the economic boom of the early 1990s. The result of this boom money is that Temple Bar is now both bohemian *and* upscale, much like Manhattan's SoHo — you can get a gorgeous one-of-a-kind handmade dress, but it certainly won't be a bargain.

Temple Bar is especially fun to visit when the Food Market, Book Market, Craft & Furniture Market, and Cow's Lane Fashion & Design Market are taking place (see the "This little traveler went to market" sidebar in the "Shopping in Dublin" section, later in this chapter).

Check out a few of my favorite spots in Temple Bar (shown in the "Temple Bar" map).

✔ The **Gallery of Photography,** Meeting House Square (☎ **01-671-4654**), has a great permanent exhibit of early-20th-century Irish photography and also puts on excellent temporary exhibits by contemporary Irish and international photographers.

✔ **The Irish Film Institute,** 6 Eustace St. (☎ **01-679-5744**), is one of the hippest places in Dublin, showing a terrific selection of old and independent films. The cute cafe there serves the best nachos in Dublin. During the summer, they project films on an outdoor screen in Meetinghouse Square on Saturday nights.

✔ **Temple Bar Gallery,** 5–9 Temple Bar (☎ **01-671-0073**), exhibits new works by up-and-coming artists.

✔ **Project Arts Centre,** 39 East Essex St. (☎ **01-881-9613**), presents new and often avant-garde art exhibits, theater, and dance.

Drop into the **Temple Bar Information Centre,** 12 East Essex St. (☎ **01-677-2255;** www.visit-templebar.com) for all sorts of information on Temple Bar, including the lowdown on the area's many free outdoor events. The information center is open June through September Monday to Friday 9 a.m. to 5:30 p.m., Saturday 10 a.m. to 6 p.m., and Sunday noon to 3 p.m.

The Ha'Penny Bridge
Dublin 1 and 2

This famous footbridge has connected the north side of the river directly to Temple Bar since 1816. Its name comes from the half-penny toll that it once cost to cross the bridge. (The poet W. B. Yeats and others were not fans of the toll and walked down to O'Connell Bridge to avoid it.) You can't miss the bridge — it's bright white and arches high over the River Liffey, and at night, it's festooned with cheerful lights. The bridge offers views up and down the River Liffey. If you want a view of the Ha'Penny Bridge stretching over the Liffey, walk to the Millennium Bridge, a shimmery little wisp of a bridge directly west of the Ha'Penny. You'll find a peaceful board-walk along the north side of the river.

See map p. 138 and 148. Over the River Liffey between O'Connell and Millennium bridges, across from Liffey Street Lower on the north side. Suggested visit: 5 minutes.

Kilmainham Gaol
Dublin 8

From the 1780s to the 1920s, many Irish rebels against the British crown were imprisoned at Kilmainham Gaol (pronounced *jail*), some for years and others only for the short period before they met the firing squad. Used as the set for the 1993 Daniel Day Lewis film *In the Name of the Father,* the jail has been restored and offers excellent tours, plus intriguing exhibits about the political history of Ireland and the fascinating history of the jail. Peering into the dank cells, you can practically see the figures of the famous patriots who were imprisoned here, among them Charles Stewart Parnell, Joseph Plunkett, and James Connolly. A short audiovisual about the jail and Irish political history is shown in the chapel where Plunkett was allowed to marry Grace Gifford just hours before being shot for his part in the 1916 Rising. Perhaps the most haunting part of the tour is the visit to the stark courtyard where firing squads executed many of the rebels from the 1916 Rising, including Connolly, who was so badly injured during the fighting that he couldn't stand up by himself and had to be strapped into a chair to be shot.

See map p. 148. Inchicore Road, Kilmainham. ☎ 01-453-5984. Bus: 51B, 78A, 79, 79A. Admission: €5.30 ($8.50) adult, €3.70 ($5.90) seniors, €2.10 ($3.40) students and children. Open: Apr–Sept daily 9:30 a.m.–6 p.m. (last admission 5 p.m.), Oct–Mar Mon–Sat 9:30 a.m.–5:30 p.m. (last admission 4 p.m.), Sun 10 a.m.–6 p.m. (last admission 5 p.m.). Tours leave every hour on the hour. Suggested visit: 2 hours.

Merrion Square
Dublin 2

This is my favorite of Dublin's parks. Thick with old trees and brilliant, splashy flowers during the warm months, Merrion Square's park is filled with little nooks and paths that make it seem many times larger than it is. Take one path, and you're walking in a lush, dense forest filled with bird-song; make a turn, and there's a sun-dappled field with school kids kicking around a soccer ball; turn again, and you're greeted by a couple picnick-ing on a bench in a formal garden area. Lining the square are textbook Georgian row houses, characterized by their brightly painted doors, elegant brass door knockers, and *fanlights* — half-moon-shaped windows over the doors. Around the square are plaques that identify the former homes of poet W. B. Yeats (no. 82), playwright Oscar Wilde (no. 1), and Catholic liberator Daniel O'Connell (no. 58). On Sundays, some of the city's top artists hang their works for sale from the rails surrounding the square.

See map p. 148. Merrion Square takes up the block directly behind the National Gallery. Take Nassau Street on the south side of Trinity College and continue east for a few blocks until it becomes Merrion Square North. DART: Pearse Street Station and head south on Westland Row and Merrion Street Lower. Bus: 4, 5, 7, 7A, 44,45,49x. Admission: Free. Open: Daylight hours. Suggested visit: 20 minutes.

The National Gallery
Dublin 2

This fine collection of Western European art (mostly paintings) from the Middle Ages through the 20th century is often overlooked by visitors planning their itineraries in Dublin, which is a shame, because the collection is varied and interesting. The museum has an extensive collection of Irish works from the 18th century through today and boasts 17th-century treasures such as Caravaggio's *The Taking of Christ,* Vermeer's *Lady Writing a Letter,* and Rembrandt's *Rest on a Flight Into Egypt.* A gem of the museum is a large room (no. 21) devoted to the works of the Yeats family, with a focus on the mystical, vivid paintings of Jack Yeats (brother of W. B.). The star of the Portrait Gallery just may be a recent portrait of U2 singer Bono, by Louis le Brocquy. The minimalist cafe is a great spot to rest your museum-weary feet and indulge in a cup of sweet hot chocolate. If you're in the museum on Saturday or Sunday, take advantage of the free guided tours.

See map p. 148. Merrion Square West. ☎ 01-661-5133. DART: Pearse Street Station and head south on Westland Row and Merrion Street Lower. Bus: 5, 7, 7A, 44, 45, 49X, 77X. Admission: Free, although special exhibits may have a cost. Open: Mon–Wed and Fri–Sat 9:30 a.m.–5:30 p.m., Thurs 9:30 a.m.–8:30 p.m., Sun noon to 5:30 p.m. Free guided tours available Sat 3 p.m., Sun on the hour 2–4 p.m. Suggested visit: 1½ hours.

National Museum of Archaeology & History
Dublin 2

This grand museum, featuring a huge rotunda and beautiful mosaics, is home to many of Ireland's most dazzling and important artifacts from 7000 B.C. through the medieval period. The stars of the museum's collection are in The Treasury, where you find the gorgeous Tara Brooch and Ardagh Chalice, plus masterpieces of craftsmanship from Ireland's Iron Age; and in Ireland's Gold, where elegant gold ornaments dating from 7000 to 2000 B.C. are displayed. The ancient gold torque necklaces are especially stunning. The other exhibits, including Prehistoric Ireland, The Road to Independence (featuring uniforms and other objects from the nationalist struggle of the early 20th century), Viking Ireland, Medieval Ireland, and the somewhat-out-of-place Ancient Egypt also boast interesting and beautifully presented objects. Be sure to check out the well-preserved human bodies from the Iron Age unearthed in 2003.

See map p. 148. Kildare and Merrion streets. ☎ 01-677-7444. DART: Pearse Street. Bus: 7, 7A, 10, 11, 13. Admission: Free. Open: Tues–Sat 10 a.m.–5 p.m., Sun 2–5 p.m. Guided tours available. Suggested visit: 2 hours.

St. Patrick's Cathedral
Dublin 8

St. Patrick's Cathedral, the national cathedral of the Church of Ireland, derives its name from the belief that in the fifth century, St. Patrick baptized converts to Christianity in a well that once existed on this land. Though there have been churches on this spot since the fifth century, the glorious church that stands today was built in the early 13th century, with restorations to the west tower in 1370 and the addition of a spire in 1749. Volunteers provide an informative map pamphlet that guides you through the church, explaining the highlights of the interior. You can visit the moving memorial of author and social critic Jonathan Swift, who served as the dean of the cathedral and is buried next to his beloved friend Stella; and pay your respects to the monument of Turlough O'Carolan (1670–1738), one of Ireland's finest and most prolific harpers and bards, who composed many tunes that are still played by Irish musicians today. Don't miss the choir, which is adorned with colorful medieval banners and helmets. Beautiful matins (Sept–June Mon–Fri 9:40 a.m.) and evensongs (Mon–Fri 5:45 p.m. and Sun 3:15 p.m.) are sung here. Your ticket includes admission to Living Stones, an exhibit that uses objects to explore the cathedral's place in history and in the world today.

See map p. 148. Patrick's Close. ☎ 01-475-4817. www.stpatrickscathedral. ie. *DART: Tara Street Station. Bus: 49, 49A, 49X, 54A, 54N. Admission: €5.50 ($8.80) adults, €4.20 ($6.70) students and seniors, services free. Mar–Oct Mon–Sat 9 a.m.–6 p.m., Sun 9–11 a.m., 12:45–3 p.m., and 4:15–6 p.m.; Nov–Feb Mon–Fri 9 a.m.–6 p.m., Sat 9 a.m.–5 p.m., Sun 10–11 a.m. and 12:45–3 p.m. Suggested visit: 45 minutes.*

St. Stephen's Green and Newman House
Dublin 2

Sitting in this beautiful, centrally located park on a sunny Saturday, you'll probably see about half of Dublin's population promenading by, pushing strollers, lugging shopping bags, munching on sandwiches, and so on. The 11 hectare (27-acre) park encompasses several different landscapes, from a large duck pond shaded by the trailing leaves of a weeping willow to formally laid-out flower gardens to open green spaces that beg you to settle down for a picnic. During the summer months, you can enjoy the frequent lunchtime concerts. Newman House, on the south side of the green, was once home to the Catholic University of Ireland. You can take a guided tour of the house, which is filled with some gorgeous examples of Georgian furniture and interior design, including the finest in 18th-century plasterwork.

See map p. 148. St. Stephen's Green takes up the block at the top of Grafton Street; Newman House is located at 85–86 St. Stephen's Green, between Harcourt Street and Earlsfort Terrace. Take Grafton Street away from Trinity College. ☎ 01-716-7422. DART: Tara Street Station. Bus: 10, 11, 13, 14, 14A, 15A, 15B. Admission: Green is free; Newman House is €5 ($8) adults, €4 ($6.40) students and seniors. Open: Green in daylight hours; Newman House tours run on the hour June–Aug Tues–Fri at 2–5 p.m., tours at 2, 3, and 5 p.m.; open to groups only Sept–May. Suggested visit: About 1 hour.

Trinity College and the Book of Kells
Dublin 2

Trinity College, founded in 1592 by Elizabeth I, looks like the ideal of an impressive, refined, old-world college, with Georgian stone buildings and perfectly manicured green lawns. The campus sits in the middle of the busy city, but within its gates, everything is composed and quiet. As you enter the main gate, look to your left to see the cross-denominational Christian chapel. Directly opposite, on your right, is the college exam hall. If you're passing through during exam time, you may see students sprinting from chapel to exam hall, having just offered up a prayer for a good mark. On your left, next to the chapel, is the dining hall. As you wander the cobbled paths around Trinity, you can imagine the days when former students Oscar Wilde, Samuel Beckett, Jonathan Swift, and Bram Stoker (a great athlete at Trinity) pounded the same pavement on their way to class. During nice weather, students lounge on the well-kept greens or on benches for picnics or studying. There is nothing finer than taking a picnic lunch (try fish and chips from Beshoff, reviewed earlier in this chapter, in the "Dining in Dublin" section) to Trinity's little hidden garden or cricket and rugby pitch (walk past the Old Library, and make a right at the pretty little garden with benches).

The jewel in Trinity College's crown is the **Book of Kells** along with its attending exhibit, housed in the Old Library. This manuscript of the four gospels of the Bible was painstakingly crafted by monks around A.D. 800. The gospels are written in ornate Latin script, and the book is filled with stunning, vivid illustrations, including intricate Celtic knots and fantastical animals. The engaging exhibit that leads to the Book of Kells (and three other ancient Irish religious texts) explains the historical context in which the books were created and reveals the techniques used in the creation of the books. You get to see only one page of the Book of Kells on each visit (they turn a page each day).

You may be tempted to turn around and leave the exhibit after you've seen the Book of Kells. Don't. Instead, go upstairs to the Long Room, which has gallery bookcases filled with Trinity's oldest books and is lined with marble busts of dead white men (I mean that in the most affectionate way), from Shakespeare to Swift. This room, used as a model for the Hogwarts dining hall in the Harry Potter movies, also boasts the oldest known harp in Ireland, made of oak and willow.

Finally, if you're a science lover, check out the new Science Gallery (see description on p. 162 while you're on the Trinity campus.

See map p. 148. Main entrance on College Street at the eastern end of Dame Street. Walk 2 blocks south of the River Liffey from O'Connell Street Bridge; entrance is on your left. Walk through the front entrance arch, and follow signs to the Old Library and Treasury. ☎ **01-896-1000** *for Trinity College information, or* **01-896-166** *for Book of Kells information. DART: Tara Street Station. Bus: 1, 2, 3, 25, 25a, 26, 27x, 44, 44c, 48a, 49x, 50x, 66, 66a, 67, 67a, 77. Admission: College grounds is free; Old Library and Book of Kells is* €8 ($13) *adults;* €7 ($11) *students, children 12–17, and seniors 60 and over; free for children under 12. Open: May–Sept Mon–Sat 9:30 a.m.– 5 p.m., Sun*

9:30 a.m.–4:30 p.m.; Oct–Apr Mon–Sat 9:30 a.m.– 5 p.m., Sun noon 4:30 p.m. Closed for 10 days during Christmas holiday. Suggested visit: 2½ hours.

More cool things to see and do

The following sections list other great attractions in Dublin, including churches, museums, and historic buildings.

More landmarks and historic buildings

✔ **General Post Office:** The bullet holes scarring the pillars of the General Post Office (GPO) testify to the violent battle between Irish patriots (also called Republicans) and English forces during the Easter Rising of 1916. The Republicans commandeered the building, and leader Pádraig Pearse read the Proclamation of the Irish Republic from the front steps. The patriots held their ground for a week before shelling from the British forces drove them to surrender. Thirteen of the Republican leaders were executed shortly thereafter, and the interior of the post office was burned to the ground. Rebuilt in 1929, this is now Dublin's main post office. Inside, an evocative series of paintings depicting the 1916 Rising — a visual history lesson — used to grace the walls. The paintings have been taken down for cleaning and the post office staff is not sure if they will be rehung or if they will be moved to a new location. However, you will still find a statue of the ancient mythic Irish hero Cuchulainn, dedicated to those who died during the Rising.

Location: North of the River Liffey, halfway up the left side of O'Connell Street, Dublin 1 (see map p. 148). ☎ **01-705-8600.** Admission: Free. Open: Monday through Saturday from 8 a.m. to 8 p.m. Suggested visit: Ten minutes.

✔ **Glasnevin Cemetery:** This primarily Catholic cemetery, founded in 1832, is the final resting place of many famous Irish citizens, including political heroes Michael Collins and Charles Stewart Parnell and playwright Brendan Behan. There are many stunning Celtic crosses throughout the cemetery. There's a heritage map that lists who is buried where (pick one up at the visitor center), and the guided walking tour is filled with interesting information that gives a face to many parts of Irish history.

Location: Finglas Road (see map p. 165). ☎ **01-830-1133.** www. glasnevin-cemetery.ie. Bus: 19, 19A, or 13 (from O'Connell Street to Harts Corner, a five-minute walk from the cemetery) or 40, 40A, 40B, or 40C (from Parnell Street to the main cemetery entrance). Admission: Free entry and tours. Open: Daily from 8 a.m. to 5:30 p.m. Tours meet at the main entrance of the cemetery at 2:30 p.m. on Wednesday and Friday. Suggested visit: An hour or two.

✔ **James Joyce Statue:** This statue pays homage to the wiry, bespectacled man whose inspired words have become the essence of Dublin in the "auld times."

Location: Halfway up O'Connell Street, just at the top of Earl Street North, Dublin 1 (see map p. 148). Suggested visit: A few seconds, unless you decide to recite a sentence or two from *Finnegan's Wake,* which could take a month.

✔ **The Millennium Spire:** This 120m (394-ft.) high spike of stainless steel is meant to represent 21st-century Dublin. The spire replaces Nelson's Pillar, which was erected during the British occupation of Ireland.

Location: O'Connell Street, Dublin 1 (in front of the main post office; see map p. 148). Suggested visit: Time enough to gaze up in vertiginous awe and snap a photo.

✔ **Molly Malone Statue:** Sing along, now: "In Dublin's fair city, where the girls are so pretty, there once was a girl named sweet Molly Malone . . ." Inspired by the traditional song "Cockles and Mussels," this statue is a tribute to the fictional Molly Malone, who represents all the women who hawked their wares on Dublin's busy streets in the past. Affectionately known as "The Tart with the Cart," Molly welcomes shoppers at the head of Grafton Street.

Location: Corner of Nassau and Grafton streets (see map p. 148). Suggested visit: About 30 seconds, unless you take time to sing the whole song.

More museums

✔ **Dublinia & Viking World:** Try on some chain mail, rummage through the apothecary's drawers to find a cure for what ails you, and sniff through the spice merchant's wares at the Medieval Fayre, one of several exhibits at Dublinia, a hands-on museum that illustrates life in medieval Dublin from 1170 to 1540. Though the wall text is comprehensive and geared to adults, kids older than 4 or 5 should enjoy the activities and the walk-through scenes. Kids and adults alike will likely be intrigued by the medieval artifacts found during excavations in Dublin. A recently opened exhibit on the top floor explores the life and history of the Vikings through objects and text. Be warned that the museum is a bit tattered around the edges (parts are missing from some exhibits and so on), and that overlapping audio explanations can make the experience a loud one.

Location: St. Michael's Hill, High Street (next to Christ Church; see map p. 148). ☎ 01-679-4611. www.dublinia.ie. Bus: 49, 50, 65, 77. Admission: €6.25 ($10) adults, €5.25 ($8.40) students, €5 ($8) seniors, €3.75 ($6) children 5 and over, free for children under 5. Open: April through September daily 10 a.m. to 5 p.m. (last admission is 4:15 p.m.), October through March Monday to Friday 11 a.m. to 4 p.m. (last admission 3:15 p.m.), Sunday 10 a.m. to 4 p.m. (last admission at 3:15 p.m.). Suggested visit: One and a half hours.

✔ **Dublin City Gallery The Hugh Lane:** Travelers who enjoy contemporary and modern art should pay a visit to this recently renovated and expanded museum. The museum features an interesting and varied collection, including many works by Irish artists. Some of my favorite pieces are *Eve of Saint Agnes,* a stained glass masterpiece with more shades of blue than I thought possible, Renoir's *Les Parapluies,* and paintings by Jack B. Yeats and Louis le Brocquy. Check to see if the museum is hosting any temporary exhibits, and don't miss Francis Bacon's studio, which has been reconstructed on-site in the museum.

Location: Parnell Square North (see map p. 148). ☎ 01-222-5550. www.hughlane.ie. Bus: 3, 10, 11, 13, 16, 19, 46A, 123. Luas: Abbey Street. Admission: Free (suggested donation €2/$3.20). Open: Tuesday through Thursday 10 a.m. to 6 p.m., Friday and Saturday 10 a.m. to 5 p.m., and Sunday 11 a.m. to 5 p.m. Suggested visit: Forty-five minutes.

✔ **Dublin's City Hall: The Story of the Capital:** Located in Dublin's beautiful city hall, this exhibit gives a good overview of Dublin history through audiovisuals, text, and objects. Even if you decide not to go to the exhibit, the rotunda, featuring frescoes representing the early history of Dublin, is worth a peek.

Location: Dame Street near Dublin Castle (see map p. 148). ☎ 01-222-2204. Bus: 56A, 77, 77A, 123. Admission: €4 ($6.40) adults, €2 ($3.20) seniors and students, €1.50 ($2.40) children. Open: Monday to Saturday from 10 a.m. to 5:15 p.m., Sunday from 2 p.m. to 5 p.m. Suggested visit: Forty-five minutes.

✔ **Dublin Writers Museum:** Who said to U.S. Customs officials: "I have nothing to declare — except my genius?" That would be witty Oscar Wilde. Wilde's life and literature are presented at this museum, along with the biographies, works, personal effects, letters, and portraits and photographs of Ireland's literary luminaries from ancient times through the 20th century. Exhaustive and interesting text on the walls relates the biographies of the writers and explains Ireland's literary movements. If you're lacking time, you can just read the two- or three-line summary posted at the bottom of the text panel. The audio tour gives brief descriptions of the writers and includes snippets of text read by actors and music appropriate to the display that you're looking at (don't be cowed by the listening device; it takes everyone a few minutes to master it). Lectures, actors portraying writers, readings, and children's programs are on offer (call for details). You can contemplate the words of the literary giants over a snack in the tranquil Zen Garden or have a complete meal at the museum's restaurant (see Chapter 1), which was recently named the best restaurant in Dublin by the hip magazine *The Dubliner.* Kids under 14 or so will probably be bored at this museum. If you'd like to hear the words of the great writers spoken by an Irish actor, get tickets at the museum for The Writers Entertain, a one-man performance. Shows start at 1:10 p.m. every day during July and August.

Location: 18 Parnell Sq. N., Dublin 1 (see map p. 148). ☎ 01-872-2077. DART: Connolly Station. Bus: 10, 11, 11A, 11B, 13, 16, 16A, 19,

19A, 121, 122. Admission: €7.25 ($12) adult, €6.10 ($9.80) students and seniors, €4.55 ($7.30) children under 12. Open: June to August, Monday through Friday from 10 a.m. to 6 p.m., Saturday from 10 a.m. to 5 p.m., and Sunday from 11 a.m. to 5 p.m.; September to May, Monday through Saturday from 10 a.m. to 5 p.m., Sunday from 11 a.m. to 5 p.m. Suggested visit: Two hours if you want to read all the text, 45 minutes if you want to zip through.

✔ **Irish Museum of Modern Art:** Sitting grandly at the end of a tree-lined lane, this is one of Ireland's most magnificent 17th-century buildings, built in 1680 as a hospital for injured soldiers. The building is so impressive that when it was finished, many lobbied to use it as the campus for Trinity College. Be sure to check out the Baroque chapel, with its wood carvings and stained glass. The permanent collection includes an exciting array of Irish and international works, and the museum hosts frequent temporary exhibitions.

Location: Military Road, Kilmainham, Dublin 8 (see map p. 148). ☎ **01-612-9900.** www.modernart.ie. Bus: 26, 51, 79, 123. Admission: Free. Open: Tuesday and Thursday through Saturday from 10 a.m. to 5:30 p.m., Wednesday from 10:30 a.m. to 5:30 p.m., Sunday from noon to 5:30 p.m. Suggested visit: One hour.

✔ **James Joyce Centre:** "The supreme question about a work of art is out of how deep a life does it spring?" writes James Joyce in *Ulysses.* Joyce fans can begin to plumb the depths of the writer's life at this museum, which features a recreation of Joyce's bedroom, the original door from Joyce's Dublin home, portraits of the Joyce family, interactive displays about each of the writer's books, and a comprehensive library and archives. Walking tours of Joyce's Dublin are offered Tuesday, Thursday, and Saturday at 11 a.m. and 2 p.m. (€10/$16 adults; €8/$13 students and seniors). Though I enjoy many of the displays, this museum often leaves me wanting more — more exhibits, more depth in the exhibits, and more ways to know about Joyce's life and works.

Location: 35 N. Great George's St., Dublin 1 (see map p. 148). ☎ **01-878-8547.** www.jamesjoyce.ie. Bus: 123. Admission: €5 ($8) adults, €4 ($6.40) seniors, students, and children under 10. Open: Tuesday through Saturday from 10 a.m. to 5 p.m. Suggested visit: One hour.

✔ **The National Museum of Decorative Arts and History (Collins Barracks):** This well-designed museum, housed in 18th-century army barracks, exhibits some of Ireland's finest decorative objects. Galleries are organized by theme — Scientific Instruments, Irish Period Furniture, Irish Silver, and so on — and feature engaging descriptions of the history of the various items. My favorite exhibit is the Curator's Choice, which comprises 25 diverse objects chosen by the museum's curators because of the intriguing stories that they tell. Fashion buffs won't want to miss "The Way We Wore," an exhibit displaying Irish fashions over the past 250 years.

Location: Collins Barracks, Benburb Street, Dublin 7 (see map
p. 148). ☎ 01-677-7444. www.museum.ie. DART: Connolly Station.
Bus: 25, 25A, 66, 67, 90. Admission: Free. Open: Tuesday through
Saturday from 10 a.m. to 5 p.m., Sunday from 2 to 5 p.m. Suggested
visit: Two hours.

✔ **Old Jameson Distillery:** Take an interesting guided tour through
part of Jameson's now-unused Bow Street distillery. You can watch
a short film about Irish whiskey and follow the life of this spirit
from raw materials through distillation to finished product. The
tour finishes off with a blind whiskey tasting for a lucky handful of
volunteers and a dram of Jameson's for all other visitors of legal
age. On the bottom floor of the distillery, keep an eye out for
Smithy the cat, who kept the distillery mouse-free. The Distillery
store sells all kinds of Jameson whiskeys and whiskey products,
including some addictive whiskey fudge.

Location: Bow Street, Dublin 7 (see map p. 148). ☎ 01-807-2355.
DART: Connolly Street. Luas: Smithfield. Admission: €13 ($20)
adults, €9 ($14) students and seniors, €6 ($9.60) children. Open:
Daily from 9:30 a.m. to 6 p.m. (last tour at 5:30 p.m.). Suggested
visit: Forty-five minutes.

✔ **Science Gallery:** Trinity College's new Science Gallery hosts
intriguing exhibits that blur the line between art and science. A
recent exhibit about light featured offerings from a life-size playable
Pong game projected on an old building from to an interactive
artist's rendition of the Northern Lights.

Location: Pearse Street (at the back of Trinity College), Dublin 2
(see map p. 148). ☎ 01-896-4091. DART: Tara Street Station. Bus: 1,
2, 3, 25, 25a, 26, 27x, 44, 44c, 48a, 49x, 50x, 66, 66a, 67, 67a, 77.
Admission: Free. Open: Tues–Sun noon to 6 p.m.

More parks (And a zoo!)

✔ **Garden of Remembrance:** This small, peaceful park is dedicated to
the men and women who died in pursuit of Irish freedom from
British rule during the 1916 uprising. Near the entrance is a still
reflecting pool with a mosaic at its bottom depicting broken
weapons — symbols of peace. Farther back, the large statue near
the fountain portrays the myth of the Children of Lir, who were
turned into swans by their selfish and cruel stepmother. The park's
location is significant — it is where several leaders of the 1916
Easter rebellion were held overnight before being taken to
Kilmainham Gaol and put to death.

Location: The north end of Parnell Square at the top of O'Connell
Street, Dublin 1 (see map p. 148). Open: Daily during daylight
hours. Admission: Free. Suggested visit: Fifteen minutes.

✔ **Phoenix Park and Dublin Zoo:** This is Europe's largest enclosed
city park — five times the size of London's Hyde Park. You can
drive through it, but if the weather's nice, don't pass up the chance

to walk, because Phoenix Park is more than just a green spot for picnic lunches: Enclosed within it are the homes of Ireland's president and the U.S. ambassador. The Zoological Gardens is the world's third-oldest zoo and houses a wide variety of animals, from lions to red pandas. Other sights include the Papal Cross, where Pope John Paul II said Mass to a million Irish in 1979, and Ashton Castle, a 17th-century tower house that's now the visitors' center. Originally a deer park, the area is still home to many deer.

Location: Park Gate, Conyngham Road; Phoenix Park Visitor Centre, Dublin 8 (see map p. 148). Visitor Centre ☎ **01-677-0095;** Zoological Park ☎ **01-677-1425.** To the Park: Bus 37, 38, or 39 to Ashtown Cross Gate. To the Zoo: Bus 10, 10A, 25, 26, or 66. Admission: Free to park; to zoo €15 ($23) adults, €12 ($19) students, €10 ($16) kids under 16, free for kids under 3. The park is open all day every day. The zoo is open Monday through Saturday from 9:30 a.m. to 6 p.m., Sunday from 10:30 a.m. to 6 p.m. Closes at sunset in winter. Last admission is one hour before closing. Suggested visit: Two and a half hours.

More cathedrals and churches

✔ **St. Ann's Anglican Church:** In this church, the writer of the creepy novel *Dracula,* Bram Stoker, married Florence Balcombe, witty playwright and Oscar Wilde's first love. Wolfe Tone, the famous rebel, was also married here. Highlights are the gorgeous stained-glass windows and ornate plasterwork.

Location: Dawson Street, Dublin 2 (see map p. 148). ☎ **01-676-7727.** www.stannschurch.ie. DART: Tara Street Station. Bus: 10, 11A, 11B, 13, 20B. Admission: Free. Open: Monday through Friday 10 a.m. to 4 p.m. Suggested visit: Thirty minutes.

✔ **St. Audoen's Church:** There are actually two churches of the same name off of Cook Street, but you're looking for the smaller and older of the two. St. Audoen's is situated right next to the only remaining gate of the Old City, which was built in 1214. The only surviving medieval church in Dublin, St. Audoen's features a doorway from 1190; a 13th-century nave; and three of the oldest church bells in Ireland, cast in 1423. A nicely done exhibit explains the history of the church, and tour guides who take you through the church itself really know their stuff.

Location: Cornmarket (off High Street; see map p. 148). ☎ **01-677-0088.** Admission: Free. Open: June through October daily from 9:30 a.m. to 5:30 p.m. (last entry and tour at 4:45 p.m.). Suggested visit: Forty minutes.

✔ **St. Michan's Church:** Unless you plan to make your next vacation a tour of the ancient pyramids, this may be your best chance to see actual mummies. It's hard to believe, but the combination of cool temperatures, dry air, and methane gas at this location preserves bodies, and the vaults below the church contain the remains of such people as Henry and John Sheares, leaders of the Rebellion of 1798, and a crusader. The church itself is also worth a look, boasting an organ believed to have been played by Handel, and detailed wood carvings of instruments above the choir area. Call before going, as the church can occasionally be closed without notice.

Location: Church Street, Dublin 7 (see map p. 148). ☎ 01-872-4154. DART: Tara Street Station. Bus: 34, 70, or 80. Admission: €4 ($6.40) adults, €3.50 ($5.60) seniors and students, €3 ($4.80) children under 12. Open: March 17 through October, Monday through Friday from 10 a.m. to 12:45 p.m. and from 2 to 4:45 p.m., and Saturday from 10 a.m. to 12:45 p.m. November through March 16, Monday through Friday from 12:30 to 3:30 p.m. and Saturday from 10 a.m. to 12:45 p.m.. Suggested visit: Thirty minutes.

Green on green: Dublin's top golfing spots

Check out Chapter 4 for a countrywide golf itinerary, or enjoy these courses near Dublin. Try to reserve your tee time at least one day in advance.

✔ **Portmarnock:** This links course has been home to several major championships. It's a natural golf course, incorporating the rugged landscape of the region rather than being purpose-built.

Location: Portmarnock, County Dublin (see map p. 165). ☎ 01-846-2968. www.portmarnockgolfclub.ie. Par: 72. Fees: €180 ($288) weekdays, €215 ($344) weekends. Visitors welcome every day except Wednesday.

✔ **Royal Dublin:** Situated on manmade North Bull Island in Dublin Bay, only 6.4km (4 miles) from the center of Dublin, this is a championship course that has offered exciting play amid great scenery for more than 100 years. The links are located along the seaside.

Location: North Bull Island, Doillymount, Dublin 3 (see map p. 165). ☎ 01-833-6346. www.theroyaldublingolfclub.com. Par: 72. Fees: €170 ($272) every day. Visitors welcome every day except Wednesday.

✔ **St. Margaret's:** One of the hosts of the Irish Open, this is a relatively new, challenging, and exciting inland course of the highest standard, with an infamously difficult finishing hole.

Location: Stephubble, St. Margaret's, County Dublin (see map p. 165). ☎ 01-864-0400. www.stmargaretsgolf.com. Par: 73. Fees: €50 ($80) Monday, €60 ($96) Tuesday through Thursday, and €80 ($128) Friday through Sunday. There is an early-bird special of €35 ($56) if you play before 9:30 a.m. or after 4:30 p.m. Monday to Friday. Visitors welcome daily.

Attractions around County Dublin

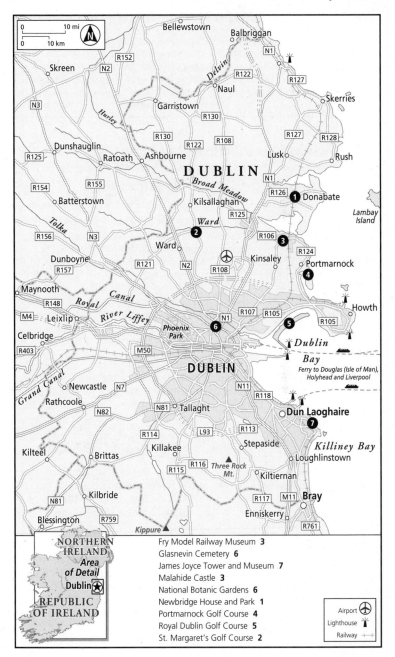

NORTHERN IRELAND
Area of Detail
Dublin ⭐
REPUBLIC OF IRELAND

Fry Model Railway Museum **3**
Glasnevin Cemetery **6**
James Joyce Tower and Museum **7**
Malahide Castle **3**
National Botanic Gardens **6**
Newbridge House and Park **1**
Portmarnock Golf Course **4**
Royal Dublin Golf Course **5**
St. Margaret's Golf Course **2**

Airport ⊕
Lighthouse 🗼
Railway ┼┼┼

DART out of town

I love the DART train (see p. 128). It's inexpensive, runs very frequently, and takes you through the pretty countryside surrounding Dublin. In the mood for a little seaside jaunt? Spend a handful of euro and end up in the charming town of Greystones. Want to have a look at Ireland's finest racing horses? Hop on the DART and head out to Kildare. See Chapters 12 and 13 for more about the areas surrounding Dublin City.

Attractions a little out of town

Dublin Bus (☎ 01-873-4222) runs two great tours that cover the outlying areas of Dublin. The *North Coast and Castle Tour* travels north and covers the fishing villages of Dublin Bay, the coastline, and Malahide Castle. It leaves at 10 a.m. and 2 p.m. daily. The *South Coast & Gardens Tour* covers the port towns of Dun Laoghaire and beautiful Dalkey, Killiney Bay, Powerscourt Gardens, and the Wicklow Mountains. It leaves at 11 a.m. daily. Tours depart from 59 Upper O'Connell St., Dublin 1. Prices for both are €25 ($40) adult, €12 ($19) children 5 to 14, free for children under 5. Call for reservations.

Wild Wicklow Tours (p. 203) and Mary Gibbons tours (p. 192) are excellent ways to see Wicklow and Meath, respectively.

Check the "Attractions Around County Dublin" map for the location of these sights.

✔ **James Joyce Tower and Museum:** This tower was made famous in the first scene of *Ulysses,* in which Joyce has his main character, Stephen Dedalus, stay here with the character Buck Mulligan. Located on a rocky beach in the quaint town of Sandycove, the tower was built, along with 11 others, in 1804 as protection against a possible invasion by Napoleon. Joyce actually did stay in the tower with his friend Oliver St. John Gogarty (who inspired the fictional Mulligan) at the start of the century, and now the place is officially known as Joyce Tower. It houses such Joycean effects as letters, a walking stick, and a cigar case. Lovers of Joyce and *Ulysses* will have a great time here; less enthusiastic fans may be disappointed by the small size of the exhibit and may want to stick to the James Joyce Centre (reviewed in "More cool things to see and do," earlier in this chapter).

Location: Sandycove (see map p. 165). ☎ 01-280-9265. DART: Sandycove Station. Bus: 8. Admission: €7.25 ($12) adults, €6.10 ($9.80) students and seniors, €4.55 ($7.30) children under 12. Open: April through September Monday through Saturday from 10 a.m. to 1 p.m. and from 2 p.m. to 5 p.m., Sunday from 2 to 6 p.m. Other times by arrangement. Suggested visit: One hour.

✔ **Malahide Castle:** This castle was witness to the longevity of one of Ireland's great and wealthy families, the Talbots, who resided here from 1185 to 1973. The architecture of the house is varied, and period furniture adorns the rooms. There's a large collection of Irish portraits, many from the National Gallery. The Great Hall chronicles the Talbots with portraits of family members. One tragic legend tells of the morning of the Battle of the Boyne in 1690, when 14 members of the family shared a last meal; by the end of the battle, all had been killed. The grounds are spectacular; be sure to check out the Botanic Gardens. Kids will have a great time at the Fry Model Railway Museum (see the next review), located on the castle grounds.

Location: Malahide (see map p. 165). ☎ **01-846-2184.** Irish Rail: Malahide Station from Connolly Station. Bus: 42. Admission: €7.25 ($12) adults, €6.10 ($9.80) seniors and students, €4.55 ($7.30) children under 12; combined tickets available with Fry Model Railway Museum (see next review). Open: April through September, Monday through Saturday from 10 a.m. to 5 p.m., Sunday from 10 a.m. to 6 p.m.; October through March, Monday through Friday from 10 a.m. to 5 p.m., Sunday from 11 a.m. to 5 p.m. Suggested visit: One and a half hours.

✔ **Fry Model Railway Museum:** Located on the grounds of Malahide Castle (see the previous review), the Fry Model Railway Museum will entertain kids of all ages. This unique collection of handmade trains spans the history of train travel in Ireland and runs over an area covering over 230 sq. m (2,500 sq. ft.), with stations, bridges, trams, buses, and a mini representation of the River Liffey. The collection was assembled by railway engineer Cyril Fry during the 1920s and 1930s.

Location: Malahide Castle (see map p. 165). ☎ **01-846-3779.** Irish Rail: Malahide Station from Connolly Station. Bus: 42. Admission: €7.25 ($12) adults, €6.10 ($9.80) seniors and students, €4.55 ($7.30) children under 12; combined tickets available for castle and museum. Open: April through September, Monday through Tuesday and Thursday and Saturday 10 a.m. to 1 p.m. and 2 p.m. to 5 p.m., Sunday from 1 to 5 p.m. Suggested visit: One hour.

✔ **National Botanic Gardens:** With a huge plant collection (more than 20,000 species) this is a must for anyone who has a green thumb (or aspires to have one). Highlights include a rose garden, an alpine area, and an arboretum. The huge greenhouses (called *glass houses* in Ireland) shelter tropical plants and other exotic species.

Location: Glasnevin, Dublin 9 (see map p. 165). ☎ **01-837-7596.** Bus: 13, 19, 134. Admission: Free. Open: Mid-February through mid-November daily 9 a.m. to 6 p.m.; mid-November through mid-February daily 9 a.m. to 4:30 p.m. Suggested visit: Forty-five minutes.

✔ **Newbridge House and Park:** Walking around Dublin, you see plenty of examples of Georgian exteriors, but here's your chance to see a fine Georgian interior. Each gorgeous room in the manor house features original furniture and objects. The extensive park grounds are home to a kid-friendly animal farm.

Location: Donabate (see map p. 165). ☎ **01-843-6534.** Irish Rail: Donabate Station from Connolly Station. Bus: 33B. Admission: House €7 ($11) adults, €6 ($9.60) seniors and students, €3.50 ($5.60) children under 12. Farm €3.80 ($6.10) adults, €2.80 ($4.50) student and seniors, €2.50 ($4) children under 12. Open: April through September, Tuesday through Saturday from 10 a.m. to 1 p.m. and 2 p.m. to 5 p.m., Sunday from noon to 6 p.m.; October through March, Saturday and Sunday from noon to 5 p.m. Suggested visit: One and a half hours.

Seeing Dublin by guided tour

If you want something more independent than the guided tours listed below, check out one of the Dublin Tourism Board's many self-guided tours of the city. Examples include the **Georgian Trail,** which covers five 18th-century squares, surrounded by period homes; the **Viking and Medieval Trail,** concentrating on the medieval area of Dublin; and the **In the Steps of Ulysses** route, which follows the steps of Joyce's famous character. Maps and guides are available at the **Dublin Tourism Board** on Suffolk Street, and online at www.visitdublin.com (enter "self-guided tours" in the search feature). Tours are also available from the tourism board as iWalks, free podcasts for your iPod. Download by visiting www.visitdublin.com (enter "Podcasts" in the search feature). Give yourself an afternoon for each tour.

Dublin Literary Pub Crawl

Literature has never been more fun! Two excellent Irish actors perform humorous tidbits by Dublin's best-known writers as they guide you to pubs of literary fame and other interesting stops. You'll be laughing hysterically by the end of the tour — and not just because of the numerous pints you've consumed. Yes, there will be a quiz at the end (with prizes), so pay attention. If you haven't gotten your tickets at the tourist office on Suffolk Street, you should arrive at the Duke Pub at least half an hour before the tour begins to ensure a spot. For small groups who want more literature and less libations, a new Literary Walk (without the pubs) is being offered by advance reservation (call ☎ **01-87-263-0270**).

Tours leave from Duke Pub, at 9 Duke St., off Grafton. Purchase tickets at the tourist office on Suffolk Street (☎ 01-670-5602). www.dublinpubcrawl.com. *Price: €12 ($19) adults, €10 ($16) students. Tours run Apr–Oct every evening at 7:30 p.m., plus Sun at noon; Nov–Mar Thurs–Sun at 7:30 p.m., Sun noon. The crawl lasts just over 2 hours.*

Historical Walking Tours of Dublin

Walk this way for an interesting historical look at the city and at Ireland at large. On the Original Tour, nicknamed the "Seminar on the Street," Trinity history students and graduates give a relatively in-depth account of Irish history as they guide you to some of the city's most famous sites, including Trinity, the Old Parliament House, Dublin Castle, City Hall, Christ Church, and Temple Bar. This tour is likely to thrill history buffs and anyone interested in the details of Irish history, but it may bore anyone looking for short anecdotes. During the summer, the company adds several special tours, including Piety, Penance & Potatoes, a sexual history of Ireland; The Gorgeous Mask, a look at architecture and society; and A Terrible Beauty, a tour focusing on the birth of the Irish state (1916–1923).

Leaves from the front gate of Trinity College on College Street, Dublin. Information: ☎ *01-878-0227.* www.historicalinsights.ie. *Price: €12 ($19) adults, €10 ($16) students, seniors, and children. Original Tours: May–Sept daily at 11 a.m. and 3 p.m.; Apr and Oct daily at 11 a.m.; Nov–Mar Fri–Sun at 11 a.m. Special tours: May–Sept daily (call to see which days and at what time each special tour runs).*

Hop On Hop Off Bus Tours

I highly recommend this tour, which is perfect if you want some guidance but also want the freedom to take as much time as you want checking out the sights. Pretty much every attraction the city has to offer is at one of the bus stops, and there's commentary throughout. The tour takes one and a quarter hours if you just ride the bus straight through, but your bus ticket is valid for 24 hours and you can (and should!), as the name says, hop on and hop off, stretching the tour out to a whole day. Some attractions offer discounts for people taking this tour.

All tours leave from Dublin Bus, 59 Upper O'Connell St., Dublin 1, but you can join the tour at any stop. ☎ *01-873-4222.* www.dublinbus.ie. *Price: €15 ($24) adults, €13 ($21) students and seniors, €6 ($9.60) children under 14. Bus runs daily 9:30 a.m.–6:30 p.m. (A bus stops at each stop every 10 minutes from 9:30 a.m.–3 p.m., every 15 minutes from 3–5:30 p.m., and every 30 minutes from 5–6:30 p.m.)*

Traditional Irish Musical Pub Crawl

This pub crawl is a fabulous experience for anyone even remotely interested in Irish music. Two excellent musicians guide you from pub to pub, regaling you with Irish tunes and songs; cracking many a joke; and filling you in on the instruments used in Irish music, the history of the music, and the various types of tunes and songs. The musicians who present this tour care deeply about Irish music and create an experience that is as authentic as possible. Get thee to the Temple Bar Information Centre (12 E. Essex St.), the phone, or the Internet to order tickets, or show up early at the pub to assure yourself of a spot on the tour.

Tours leave from Oliver St. John Gogarty's Pub in Temple Bar (corner of Fleet and Anglesea streets). ☎ *01-475-3313.* www.discoverdublin.ie. *Price: €12 ($19) adults, €10 ($16) students and seniors. Tours take place Apr–Oct daily 7:30 p.m.; Nov–Mar Thurs–Sat at 7:30 p.m. Arrive early or book ahead.*

Viking Splash Tours

Two things make this 75-minute tour stand out from the competition: First, you're riding around in a World War II amphibious vehicle (called a *duck*) that at one point leaves the normal tourist trail to sail along the Grand Canal. Second, the Viking theme doesn't just color the historical information related along the tour; all riders are given Viking helmets and encouraged to roar at "rival" tour groups. Kids, I promise, will not be bored.

Half of the tours leave from Bull Alley beside the gardens of St. Patrick's Cathedral, around the corner from the tour's ticket office and gift store at 64–65 Patrick St, Dublin 8. The other half of the tours leave from St. Stephen's Green. ☎ 01-707-6000. www.vikingsplash.com. Price: €20 ($32) adult, €18 ($29) students and seniors, €10 ($16) children under 13 (higher prices apply June–Aug). Runs daily every 1½ hours 10 a.m.–5 p.m. Call if you wish to take a tour Nov–Mar, as times will vary.

Suggested one-, two-, and three-day sightseeing itineraries

If you just have **one day** and really want to pack the sightseeing in, I recommend taking the **Hop On Hop Off Bus Tour** (see the preceding section with that title) so that you can see as many attractions as possible in the most efficient way.

Take in **Trinity College** and the **Book of Kells** (see the listing in the "The top attractions" section, earlier in the chapter) first, and then wander around the excellent shopping areas of Grafton Street and Nassau Street.

Grab lunch at **Beshoff** (see the previous "Dublin's Top Restaurants A to Z") or **Nude** (covered in the earlier "Lunch on the move" section), and picnic in **Merrion Square** or **St. Stephen's Green** (see "The top attractions"). In the afternoon, visit the nearby **National Museum** and **National Gallery** (both in the preceding "The top attractions" section).

Treat yourself to a delicious dinner at the **Winding Stair** (listed in "Dublin's Top Restaurants A to Z," earlier in the chapter) before meeting up with the **Traditional Irish Musical Pub Crawl,** outlined in the previous "Seeing Dublin by guided tour" section. If you're still craving more traditional music after the pub crawl, end your day at the **Cobblestone** (see the "Traditional Irish music venues" section, later in the chapter).

If you have **two days,** follow the itinerary for day one. On the morning of the second day, take the **Historical Walking Tour** (see the earlier "Seeing Dublin by guided tour" section). Then head over to the **Chester Beatty Library** (in the preceding "The top attractions" section) to gaze at the gorgeous books and art housed within.

Eat lunch in one of the pubs recommended in the "Pub grub" section and then head out to see **St. Patrick's Cathedral, Dublin Castle,** and the **Guinness Storehouse** (all outlined in the "The top attractions" section). Drop into the **Queen of Tarts** (see the listing in "Dublin's Top Restaurants A to Z") for an afternoon treat on your way back to Temple Bar.

Stroll the Grafton Street area, and have dinner at **L'Gueuleton** (listed in the "Dublin's Top Restaurants A to Z" section) before joining up with the **Literary Pub Crawl** (outlined in the "Seeing Dublin by guided tour" section).

If you have **three days,** follow the itineraries for days one and two. On your third day, after breakfast, make your way to the north side of the River Liffey, and walk up O'Connell Street., stopping to take pictures of the monuments lining the street and picking up a few pieces of fruit on Moore Street.

Get your fill of literary Dublin with a visit to the **James Joyce Centre** and the **Dublin Writers Museum,** which has a great little cafe for lunch. (Both are listed in the "More museums" section.)

After lunch, head over the **Ha'Penny Bridge** to take the guided tour of **Dublin Castle** (both described in "The top attractions"), then walk over to Temple Bar to leisurely explore the shops, galleries, and pubs. You may want to indulge in dinner at the **Tea Room** (listed in the "Dublin's Top Restaurants A to Z" section) before heading off to see a show at the famous **Abbey Theatre,** described in the upcoming "Checking out Dublin's excellent theater scene" section.

Shopping in Dublin

Dublin is the shopping capital of Ireland. Within the city limits, you can easily find all sorts of famous Irish items, including Donegal tweed, Waterford Crystal, Belleek china, and Claddagh rings. The nearby map locates the shopping meccas.

Locating the best shopping areas

There are three main shopping areas in Dublin. The first, on the north side of the River Liffey, is the **Henry Street–Mary Street area,** off O'Connell Street. You can find reasonably priced goods, especially clothing, at the malls and stores in this area. **Moore Street,** just off the main shopping drag, offers a daily open-air market with plenty of the freshest (and cheapest) fruits and vegetables in the city. This is where you'll hear the perfected lilt of the vendors hawking their wares — a Dublin attraction in its own right.

The **Grafton Street area** (including Duke, Dawson, Nassua, Wicklow, and other nearby streets) on the south side of the River Liffey offers a variety of shopping options. Bustling Grafton Street itself is lined with trendy big-name clothing stores and is home to **Brown Thomas,** Ireland's ultrafashionable department store. The side streets off Grafton are home to upscale and funky boutiques and stores. Nearby Nassau Street is the place to find the best in Irish crafts, from sweaters to crystal.

Dublin Shopping

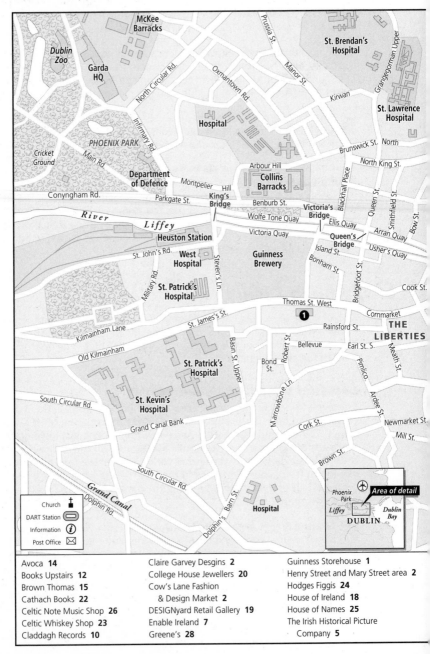

Avoca **14**
Books Upstairs **12**
Brown Thomas **15**
Cathach Books **22**
Celtic Note Music Shop **26**
Celtic Whiskey Shop **23**
Claddagh Records **10**

Claire Garvey Desgins **2**
College House Jewellers **20**
Cow's Lane Fashion
  & Design Market **2**
DESIGNyard Retail Gallery **19**
Enable Ireland **7**
Greene's **28**

Guinness Storehouse **1**
Henry Street and Mary Street area **2**
Hodges Figgis **24**
House of Ireland **18**
House of Names **25**
The Irish Historical Picture
  Company **5**

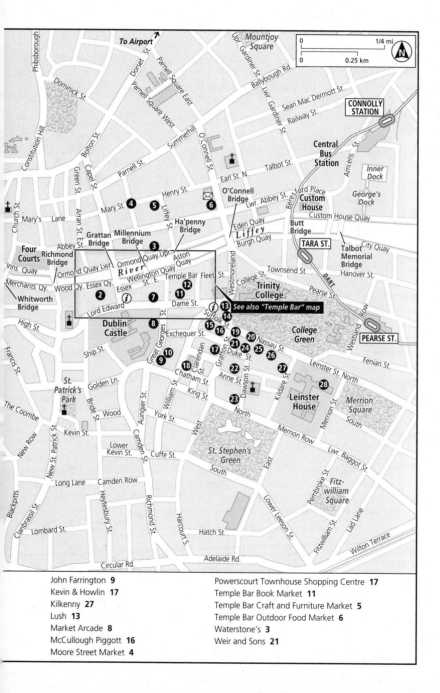

John Farrington **9**
Kevin & Howlin **17**
Kilkenny **27**
Lush **13**
Market Arcade **8**
McCullough Piggott **16**
Moore Street Market **4**

Powerscourt Townhouse Shopping Centre **17**
Temple Bar Book Market **11**
Temple Bar Craft and Furniture Market **5**
Temple Bar Outdoor Food Market **6**
Waterstone's **3**
Weir and Sons **21**

If you're looking for the funkiest fashions, jewelry, art, and music, head to the **Temple Bar area.** The hottest new places to shop in these parts are on Cow's Lane.

Teenagers: You may want to drag your parents to the **Market Arcade,** on South Great George's Street, between Exchequer Street and Fade Street, for music, fun clothes, a grungy coffee shop, and stalls selling jewelry and ephemera such as a sign that says, "Tired of being harassed by your parents?"

If your idea of shopping consists mostly of pampering yourself, the **Powerscourt Townhouse Shopping Centre,** 59 S. William St., Dublin 2 (☎ 01-679-4144), is for you. This restored Georgian townhouse is home to a variety of shops, ranging from clothes boutiques to antiques stores.

Finally, Dubliners are in love with the new **Dundrum Town Centre** (www.dundrum.ie), a sprawling mall outside of the city. You can get there by bus nos. 17, 44, 44C, 48A, 48N, or 75, and by Luas to Balally.

Finding Ireland's best wares

Ireland is known the world over for its handmade products and fine craftsmanship, and Dublin, as Ireland's commercial center, is a one-stop source for the best of Irish products.

Antiques

Dublin offers two main areas of concentration for antiques dealers: **Francis Street** (between Thomas Street West and the Coombe) and **Dawson** and **Molesworth streets** (between St. Stephen's Green and Trinity College). The following places are some of your best bets for quality and value.

Also see Cathach Books in the next section and John Farrington in the Crafts and Jewelry section.

 ✔ **The Irish Historical Picture Company,** 5 Lower Ormond Quay, Dublin 1 (☎ 01-872-0144), is a vast treasure trove of photographs documenting the life of Ireland since the invention of the camera in every region and theme you can imagine.

Books

Like any section of a city that surrounds a college campus, there are loads of good bookstores near Trinity College. You can find works of Irish writers here that may be hard to find at home.

 ✔ **Books Upstairs,** 36 College Green and Dame Street, across from the Trinity College front entrance, Dublin 2 (☎ 01-679-6687), has a comprehensive collection of Irish fiction and nonfiction, a sizable gay and lesbian selection, and some fiction bargains.

- ✓ **Cathach Books,** 10 Duke St., off Grafton Street, Dublin 2 (☎ **01-671-8676**), sells rare editions of Irish literature, plus old maps of Ireland.

- ✓ **Greene's,** 16 Clare St., Dublin 2 (☎ **01-676-2554**), was mentioned in Joyce's *Ulysses* and boasts a huge Irish literature section and a giant secondhand selection.

- ✓ **Hodges Figgis,** 56–58 Dawson St., Dublin 2 (☎ **01-677-4754**), is Ireland's top independent bookstore, offering a wide selection of books. There's a nice cafe on the first floor.

- ✓ **Waterstone's,** Jervis Centre, Mary Street, Dublin 1 (☎ **01-679-1415**), is pretty much the Barnes & Noble of the Emerald Isle.

Clothes

You don't have to go all the way to the Aran Islands or Donegal for authentic Irish knitwear. Here are some Dublin shops where you can find the real deal, plus a few places for less traditional items.

- ✓ **Avoca,** 11–13 Suffolk St. (☎ **01-677-4215**), sells the Irish-designed and -made Anthology line of clothes, with all the vivid colors and funky lace, beads, and ribbons that a 20- or 30-something girl could want, plus it offers all sorts of household goods and clothes for hip babies (such as a onesie that says *It girl*).

- ✓ **Claire Garvey Designs,** 6 Cow's Lane, Dublin 2 (☎ **01-671-7287**), is where fairy queens would buy their clothes. Garvey creates shimmery, sheer pieces, many with lace-up bodices and beads. Looking like a goddess doesn't come cheap, though.

- ✓ **Enable Ireland,** South Great George's Street, Dublin 2 (next to Juice; ☎ **01-478-2763**), sells used clothes from silver vinyl pants to girls' flowery dresses. All profits go to Enable Ireland, which helps people with disabilities lead independent lives.

- ✓ **Kevin & Howlin,** 31 Nassau St., Dublin 2 (☎ **01-677-0257**), sells authentic hand-woven tweed jackets and hats for men and women.

Crafts and jewelry

If you're in the market for Irish crafts and jewelry, point yourself in the direction of Nassau Street, on the edge of Trinity College, which is lined with shops selling Irish items. Also see "Souvenirs and gifts," later in this chapter.

- ✓ **Brown Thomas,** 88–95 Grafton St., Dublin 2 (☎ **01-605-6666**), stocks Irish fashion and giftware.

- ✓ **College House Jewellers,** 44 Nassau St., Dublin 2 (☎ **01-677-7597**), stocks gorgeous Celtic-style jewelry and has a comprehensive collection of Claddagh jewelry, from classic to modern.

This little traveler went to market

One of the best ways to experience Dublin is to hit the markets. Here are some of the best.

✔ **Cow's Lane Fashion & Design Market**, Cow's Lane, Old City, Temple Bar, is a heaven for those who love hip, handmade clothing and jewelry. Every Saturday from 10 a.m. to 5:30 p.m.

✔ **Moore Street Market**, Moore Street, is a bustling market full of vendors selling fresh vegetables, fruits, and flowers. Many vendors still hawk their wares in a lilting, singsong voice reminiscent of the Molly Malones of the past. Monday through Saturday from 9 a.m. to 5 p.m.

✔ **Temple Bar Book Market**, Temple Bar Square, is a smallish outdoor used-book market. Grab some lunch at the outdoor food market, and browse through the offerings. Every Saturday and Sunday 10 a.m. to 5:30 p.m.

✔ **Temple Bar Craft and Furniture Market**, Meeting House Square, showcases original crafts and furniture from Irish and international designers and artists. Every Sunday from noon to 6 p.m.

✔ **Temple Bar Outdoor Food Market**, Meetinghouse Square in Temple Bar, with entrances on East Essex and Eustace streets, Dublin 2 is an orgy of Irish gourmet and organic food, including delicacies such as Chez Emily's chocolates, artisanal breads and cheeses, and gorgeous produce. Every Saturday from 10 a.m. to 5 p.m.

✔ **DESIGNyard Retail Gallery,** 48–49 Nassau St., Dublin 2, along Temple Bar's main thoroughfare (☎ 01-670-9371), stocks exquisite and generally affordable contemporary Irish-designed jewelry, textiles, glass, sculpture, and earthenware.

✔ **John Farrington,** 32 Drury St., Dublin 2 (☎ 01-679-1899), is a good bet for vintage jewelry, from Georgian silver earrings to Victorian lockets.

✔ **Weir and Sons,** 96 Grafton St., at Wicklow Street, Dublin 2 (☎ 01-677-9678), sells fine jewelry, Waterford Crystal, silver, leather, and watches in elegant showcases.

Irish music and musical instruments

If you fell in love with the sounds of the traditional session you heard at the pub last night, head to one of these stores to pick up a CD, or even a tin whistle or *bodhrán* (*bow*-rahn; a goatskin drum) of your very own.

✔ **Celtic Note Music Shop,** 12 Nassau St., Dublin 2 (☎ 01-670-4157), is a great place to find any type of Irish music, from traditional to contemporary rock. Prices here are slightly lower than at Claddagh Records. They occasionally host free midday in-store concerts by hot traditional Irish bands.

✔ **Claddagh Records,** 2 Cecilia St., Temple Bar (☎ 01-677-0262), sells the best traditional Irish and world-music CDs. The staff here is exceedingly knowledgeable, so this is the place to go if you're not sure what you're looking for.

✔ **McCullough Piggott,** 11 S. William St., Dublin 2 (☎ 01-677-3138), sells all sorts of instruments and the tutorial books and CDs that help you play them.

Souvenirs and gifts

Also see the recommendations in "Crafts and jewelry," earlier in this chapter.

✔ **Celtic Whiskey Shop,** 27–28 Dawson St., Dublin 2 (☎ 01-675-9744), sells everything from the best-known brands of whiskey, such as Bushmills, to rare bottlings from distilleries that have closed their doors. They host tastings in the store each day to whet your palate.

✔ **Guinness Storehouse,** St. James's Gate, Dublin 8 (☎ 01-408-4800; www.guinness-storehouse.com), stocks all things Guinness, from posters and slippers to clocks and candles.

✔ **House of Ireland,** 37 Nassau St., at the corner of Dawson Street, Dublin 2 (☎ 01-671-1111), is one-stop shopping for authentic Irish goods such as Waterford Crystal, china, hand-knit Aran sweaters, and more.

✔ **House of Names,** 26 Nassau St. (☎ 01-679-7287), creates and sells wall shields and plaques; clothing; and jewelry with the crest, coat of arms, and motto of most European family names. Here's hoping you have one of those cool dragons on your coat of arms.

✔ **Kilkenny,** 5–6 Nassau St. (☎ 01-677-7066), boasts original Irish designs, including glass, knitwear, jewelry, and a large selection of gorgeous pottery.

✔ **Lush,** 166 Grafton St., near the entrance to Trinity College (☎ 01-677-0392), is not particularly Irish, but when your giftees open their packages of colorful homemade soaps, bubble baths, shampoos, and more, they won't care. All the items here look good enough to eat, and you probably *could* eat them, because they're all made with as many natural ingredients as possible. And who can resist a store that hacks individual slices of soap off huge slabs?

Hitting the Pubs and Enjoying Dublin's Nightlife

James Joyce put it best in *Ulysses:* "Good puzzle would be cross Dublin without passing a pub." With more than 1,000 pubs in the city (the "Dublin Nightlife" map helps locate them), there's something to suit

Dublin Nightlife

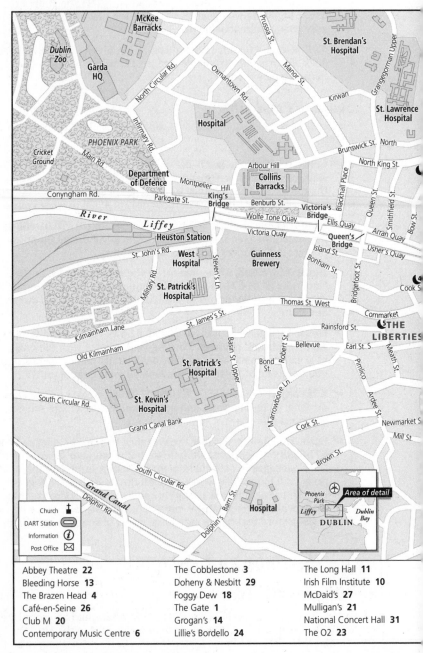

Abbey Theatre **22**	The Cobblestone **3**	The Long Hall **11**
Bleeding Horse **13**	Doheny & Nesbitt **29**	Irish Film Institute **10**
The Brazen Head **4**	Foggy Dew **18**	McDaid's **27**
Café-en-Seine **26**	The Gate **1**	Mulligan's **21**
Club M **20**	Grogan's **14**	National Concert Hall **31**
Contemporary Music Centre **6**	Lillie's Bordello **24**	The O2 **23**

O'Donoghues **28**
Oliver St. John Gogarty **19**
The Peacock **22**
Project Arts Centre **9**
Renards **25**

Ri-Rá **16**
Rogue **17**
Scholar's **7**
The Stag's Head **15**
Toner's **30**

Turk's Head Chop House **8**
UCG Multiplez **2**
Vicar Stret **5**
Whelan's Pub **12**

everyone, whether your taste runs to Victorian pubs with globe lights and polished mahogany bars or to local watering holes with worn couches and clocks that read the wrong time.

Hitting the pubs

The Brazen Head
Dublin 8

The Brazen Head claims to be the oldest pub in Dublin. That may or may not be true, but certainly many a pint has been pulled here since its opening in 1661 (an older pub, from 1198, stood on this site before the "new" pub was built). The unusual name comes from a story about a bold woman who was so curious during one of the country's many rebellions that she stuck her head out of the window — only to have it chopped off! Though it's a bit touristy, it's a beautiful pub, lit by lanterns. There's music every night beginning at 9:30 p.m.

20 Lower Bridge St. ☎ *01-677-9549. Bus: 78A, 79, 90.*

Doheny & Nesbitt
Dublin 2

A poster-child of Victorian pubs, "Nesbitt's" boasts *snugs* (cozy compartments), dark wood, and bartenders full of wisdom. The clientele is heavy on lawyers, economists, and politicians.

5 Lower Baggott St. ☎ *01-676-2945. Bus: 10, 11, 11A.*

Grogan's
Dublin 2

This small, unpretentious pub is filled with artists, writers, and assorted characters. The walls are covered with works by local artists. You're sure to meet some interesting folks here.

15 S. William St. ☎ *01-677-9320. Bus: 16, 16A, 19, 19A, 65, 65B, 83, 112.*

Café-en-Seine: The anti-pub?

Though it's called a pub, **Café-en-Seine**, 40 Dawson St., Dublin 2 (☎ 01-677-4567), looks like it was flown over intact from 19th-century Paris. This incredibly popular spot has a gorgeous Art Deco interior, with a glass atrium, brass chandeliers, murals, and large mirrors. You can get light bites, pastries, and coffees by day and wine, beer, and cocktails by night. The crowd can be a bit snooty, making for excellent people-watching.

The Long Hall
Dublin 2

Rumored to have the longest bar in the city, The Long Hall is a gorgeous, ornate specimen of a pub. There's a vast array of antique clocks, Victorian lamps, a mahogany bar, and plenty of snugs to get lost in. It backs up to Dublin Castle, so stop in on your way.

51 S. Great George's St. ☎ *01-475-1590. Bus: 50, 50A, 54, 56, 77.*

McDaid's
Dublin 2

Attention, writers and literature-lovers: This was bad-boy playwright Brendan Behan's favorite watering hole, and the pub is still known as the place to go for the latest on literary news in Dublin.

3 Harry St., off Grafton Street. ☎ *01-679-4395. Bus: 10, 11, 13B, 14, 14A, 15, 15A, 15B, 15C.*

Mulligan's
Dublin 2

This is an authentic old Dublin pub and favorite watering hole for the journalists of the nearby *Irish Times* newspaper. JFK drank here as a young European correspondent for the Hearst newspapers in 1945 and again when he visited as president. It's mentioned in *Ulysses,* and locals say it serves one of the best pints of Guinness in town.

8 Poolbeg St. (off south quays near O'Connell Bridge). ☎ *01-677-5582. Bus: 5, 7, 7A, 7X, 8.*

Scholar's
Dublin 8

The spacious bar at Scholar's, a restored all-boys National School, has a giant screen that offers a perfect view from any seat of the latest football (read: soccer), rugby, hurling, or Gaelic football matches.

Donovan's Lane, off Clanbrassil Street, below St. Patrick's Cathedral. ☎ *01-453-2000. Bus: 49, 49a, 49x, 54a, 54n.*

The Stag's Head
Dublin 2

The Stag's Head is a Victorian classic, with gleaming rich auburn wood, frosted globe lamps, and stained-glass windows. It's popular with Trinity students, journalists, and theater folk. Try to score a seat in the small, opulent room on the right in the rear. And stick around if you get hungry — the food here is terrific.

1 Dame Ct. (look for the mosaic stag head inlaid into the sidewalk on Dame Street pointing the way). ☎ *01-679-3701. Bus: 21A, 50, 50A, 78, 78A, 78B.*

Toner's
Dublin 2

This is a great, old, authentic Dublin pub with a high *craic* (fun) factor. You'll find everyone from older folks enjoying a drink to boisterous rugby fans celebrating their team's victory.

139 Lower Baggott St. ☎ *01-676-3090. Bus: 10.*

Pulling an all-nighter: Late-night bars

Still up for some partying after last call? I recommend the following extended-hours pubs, plus Café-en-Seine (see the box earlier in this chapter).

- ✔ **Bleeding Horse,** 24–25 Camden St., Dublin 2 (☎ 01-475-2705).

- ✔ **The Foggy Dew,** 1 Upper Fownes St., Temple Bar, Dublin 2 (☎ 01-677-9328).

- ✔ **Turk's Head Chop House,** Parliament Street, Temple Bar, Dublin 2 (☎ 01-679-9701).

- ✔ **Whelan's Pub,** 25 Wexford St., Dublin 2 (☎ 01-478-0766).

Taking in some music

Dublin has a hot music scene, featuring everything from jazz to rock to traditional Irish music.

Traditional Irish music venues

In addition to visiting the pubs below, I suggest the **Traditional Irish Music Pub Crawl** (listed in "Seeing Dublin by guided tour," earlier in this chapter). Also, see The Brazen Head (reviewed earlier in this chapter).

- ✔ The **Cobblestone,** 77 North King St., at Red Cow Lane (☎ 01-872-1799), a dark pub filled with instruments and photographs of traditional Irish musicians, hosts a lively, mostly Irish crowd and friendly sessions each night, with some exceptional musicians. No fuss, no show, no hip location — just the best traditional Irish music in Dublin. This is the real thing.

- ✔ **O'Donoghues,** 15 Merrion Row, Dublin 2 (☎ 01-676-2807), mostly hosts traditional Irish ballad singers. The dark pub is a bit touristy, but you'll also find a good many locals enjoying themselves.

✔ **Oliver St. John Gogarty,** 58 Fleet St., Temple Bar, Dublin 2 (☎ **01-671-1822**), is a popular pub named for surgeon, wit, and writer Oliver St. John Gogarty, who was the model for Buck Mulligan, a flip character in *Ulysses.* The interior screams Irish pub, with its décor of old books and bottles and portraits of traditional Irish music greats. The pub is always packed with travelers from all over the world, and you find live Irish music seven nights a week starting at 9 p.m., plus Saturdays at 4:30 p.m. and Sundays from noon to 2 p.m. Check out the great lunch buffet.

Rock, jazz, and other music venues

Dublin is by no means all jigs and reels all the time. The hopping live-music scene encompasses rock, jazz, country, folk, blues, classical, and more. The venues listed here consistently offer fantastic concerts.

✔ **The Contemporary Music Centre,** 19 Fishamble St., Temple Bar, Dublin 8 (☎ **01-673-1922;** www.cmc.ie) brings the very best new music from Irish composers.

✔ **The National Concert Hall,** Earlsfort Terrace, Dublin 2 (☎ **01-417-0000;** www.nch.ie), is Dublin's best venue for classical music performances.

✔ **The O₂,** Eastlink Bridge, North Wall Quay (☎ **818-719-391;** www.thepoint.ie), is Dublin's gorgeous new top venue for internationally known rock and folk acts, seating up to 6,000 people in arena seating.

✔ **Vicar Street,** 58–59 Thomas St., Dublin 8 (☎ **01-454-5533;** www.vicarstreet.com), is a small concert venue with seating. It hosts excellent (and often well-known) rock, jazz, folk, and traditional music.

✔ **Whelan's,** 25 Wexford St., Dublin 2 (☎ **01-478-0766**), has a cozy wooden interior; a nice atmosphere; and a great lineup of well-known rock, folk, and traditional musicians.

Clubbing your way through Dublin

As in most European capitals, clubbing is taken seriously in Dublin, and dress is pretty important, especially at the trendiest, most popular clubs — don't be surprised it you're turned away because you're wearing jeans or sneakers. Often, there are cover charges (usually between €5/$8 and €25/$40), and you may need to show an ID. Clubs usually open just when buses stop running (about 11:30 p.m.), so expect to take a cab back to your hotel.

Here are some of the best clubs in Dublin.

- ✔ **Club M,** Blooms Hotel, Angelsea Street (☎ **01-671-5274**), packs 'em in Tuesday through Sunday for sweaty, all-night DJ dance parties. This place has a reputation as a pickup joint.

- ✔ **Lillie's Bordello,** Adam Court off Grafton Street (☎ **01-679-9204**), is still one of the hottest Dublin clubs after ten years, with a lipstick-red interior and the members-only (you can pay to be a member) "Library" room.

- ✔ **Renards,** 35–37 S. Frederick St. (☎ **01-677-5876**), pulls in celebrities and locals alike with three floors of bars, dancing, and frequent live jazz.

- ✔ **Ri-Rá,** 1 Exchequer St. (☎ **01-671-1220**), fills up every night with dancers getting down to funk, jazz, and other grooves.

- ✔ **Rogue,** 64 Dame St. (☎ **01-675-3971**) is a hot, newly renovated spot for house and techno.

Checking out Dublin's excellent theater scene

Dubliners have long held theater in high reverence, and the city has a thriving theater scene that encompasses everything from the plays of Synge to new multimedia projects.

Ireland's most famous playhouse, the **Abbey Theatre,** 26 Lower Abbey St., Dublin 1 (☎ **01-878-7222;** www.abbeytheatre.ie), is best known for staging superb productions of works by some of Ireland's best-loved playwrights, including Sean O'Casey and J. M. Synge. The Abbey's sister theater, **The Peacock,** 26 Lower Abbey St., Dublin 1 (☎ **01-878-7222;** www.abbeytheatre.ie), boasts excellent productions of new plays. The **Gate,** 1 Cavendish Row, Dublin 1 (☎ **01-874-4045;** www.gate-theatre.ie), does a beautiful job with European, Irish, and American classics and new plays. The theater is particularly lauded for its productions of Samuel Beckett's work. **Project Arts Centre,** 39 E. Essex St., Dublin 2 (☎ **01-881-9613**), is the place to go for new and experimental theater. Call the theaters or check the *Irish Times* newspaper for details about shows.

Going to the movies

Or, as the Irish say, "the cinema." There are lots of places to catch a flick in Dublin. **UCG Multiplex,** midway down Parnell Street in Parnell Center, Dublin 1 (☎ **01-872-8444**), is a streamlined and very modern multiplex, with 12 screens showing the latest commercial movies. The **Irish Film Institute (IFI),** 6 Eustace St., Temple Bar, Dublin 2 (☎ **01-679-5744**), shows up-and-coming Irish independent cinema, European exclusives, and classics. A place for true film buffs, the IFI is as hip as it gets. There is a cafe, a lively bar, and a book and video/DVD shop on the premises (note that Irish videos and DVDs come in a different format than in the U.S., and most American VCRs and DVD players can't play them).

Fast Facts: Dublin

Area Code

The area code for Dublin city and county is **01**. Dial the area code only if you're calling Dublin from outside the city. If you're calling from outside the country, you can drop the 0.

Currency Exchange

Currency exchange is indicated by the sign BUREAU DE CHANGE. You can exchange money at travel agencies, hotels, and some post offices, but the best rates are to be found at banks.

Dentists

The American Embassy, 42 Elgin Rd., Ballsbridge, Dublin 4 (☎ 01-668-8777), can provide you a list of dentists.

Doctors

Usually, your hotel or B&B is able to get you an appointment with its house doctor. The American Embassy, 42 Elgin Rd., Ballsbridge, Dublin 4 (☎ 01-668-8777), can provide you a list of doctors. Also see "Hospitals."

Embassies and Consulates

United States, 42 Elgin Rd., Ballsbridge, Dublin 4 (☎ 01-668-8777); Canada, 65 St. Stephen's Green, Dublin 2 (☎ 01-234-4024); United Kingdom, 31 Merrion Rd., Dublin 4 (☎ 01-205-3700); Australia, Fitzwilton House, Wilton Terrace, Dublin 2 (☎ 01-664-5300).

Emergencies

Dial ☎ **999** for police, fire, or ambulance.

Hospitals

The two best hospitals for emergency care in Dublin are St. Vincent's Hospital, Elm Park, Dublin 4 (☎ 01-221-4000), on the south side of the city; and Beaumont Hospital, Beaumont Road, Dublin 9 (☎ 01-809-3000), on the north side.

Information

Dublin Tourism (☎ 01-605-7700; www.visitdublin.com) runs three walk-in visitor centers around the center of the city. The largest and best is on Suffolk Street, Dublin 2. The others are in the arrivals concourse at the Dublin airport; at Exclusively Irish, and at 14 O'Connell Street, Dublin 1.

The trendy Temple Bar district has its own information Web site at www.temple-bar.ie. Some good Web sites for Dublin include www.visitdublin.com and www.softguides.com/dublin.

Internet

Dublin has a number of Internet cafes, including Central Cyber Cafe, 6 Grafton St., Dublin 2 (☎ 01-677-8298), opposite Weir and Sons Jewelers.

Maps

Good maps are available at the Dublin Tourism Centre, Suffolk Street, and online through the Tourism Centre's Web site at www.visitdublin.com, type "maps" in the search feature.

Newspapers/Magazines

The major newspaper in Ireland is the *Irish Times* (www.ireland.com). The best events listings are found in *In Dublin* and *Event Guide* (www.eventguide.ie and www.hotpress.com). *Where: Dublin* is geared to travelers and features restaurant, shopping, and entertainment information.

Pharmacies

Hamilton, Long & Co., 5 O'Connell St., Dublin 1 (☎ 01-874-8456), is a central pharmacy with extended hours.

Police

Dial ☎ **999** in case of emergencies. You can contact the police headquarters at Phoenix Park, Dublin 8 (☎ 01-666-0000). Police in Ireland are known as Garda or Gardai (*Gard*-ee) or the Guards.

Post Office

The General Post Office (GPO) is located on O'Connell Street, Dublin 1 (☎ 01-705-7600). Its hours are Monday through Saturday 8 a.m. to 8 p.m. Branch offices, called *An Post* and noted with green storefront awnings, are generally open Monday through Saturday from 9 a.m. to 6 p.m.

Safety

Late-night crime is not uncommon, so don't walk back to your hotel alone after pub closing time (11:30 p.m. for some pubs); get a taxi. Be especially careful around O'Connell Street and its side streets after the pubs close.

Smoking

Smoking is not permitted in most public buildings, and is banned in restaurants and bars. Most hotels and some B&Bs offer smoking rooms. Currently, about one-third of Irish adults are smokers, though this number is on the decline.

Taxis

To get a taxi in Dublin, go to a taxi rank or hail a cab by sticking out your arm. If you need to call a cab, try Castle Cabs (☎ 01-802-2222), Co-op (☎ 01-676-6666), and VIP Taxis (☎ 01-478-3333).

Weather

Phone ☎ 1550-365-247 for weather information.

Chapter 12

Easy Trips North of Dublin: Counties Meath and Louth

ollectively, Counties Meath and Louth are known as the ancient land of the Celts. They're the country's hot spots for visiting prehistoric and mythical sites, including ancient sacred burial mounds, areas where the old Irish high kings held court, and Celtic high crosses.

County Meath has some of the most important ancient religious and political attractions in Ireland — the prehistoric tombs of **Newgrange** and **Knowth,** and the **Hill of Tara,** long the seat of Irish kings. The heart of the area is the River Boyne, home of the famous Battle of the Boyne, in which Protestant William of Orange defeated Catholic King James II, changing the course of Irish history. This region has been fought over by the country's many invaders, and all of those invaders, from the Normans to the English, have left their mark here. The history-rich towns of **Kells, Slane,** and **Trim** (with minor attractions including Slane Castle and Trim Castle) are the best places to stay in Meath. My favorite town in the area, Carlingford, in Louth, is not far from the major attractions).

What **County Louth** lacks in big tourist attractions it makes up for in history and in the charm of small towns such as **Carlingford, Dundalk,** and **Drogheda** (pronounced *dragh*-da). These towns are the stomping grounds of legends such as Cuchulainn (pronounced coo-*cul*-in), Queen Maeve, and the great warrior Finn MacCool (see Chapter 2 for more information on these mythical characters). The most beautiful area of Louth is the far northern area, encompassing the **Cooley Mountains** and **Peninsula,** and the delightful heritage town of Carlingford, which overlooks the Irish Sea.

You can easily take day trips from Dublin to both counties, which you may well think of as one destination because they're so complementary. But I encourage you to set up camp for a night, especially in Carlingford.

Counties Meath and Louth

ATTRACTIONS
Carlingford Adventure
   Centre 1
Causey Farm 10
Cooley Peninsula 2
Hill of Tara 7
Knowth 5
Monasterboice 4
Newgrange Farm 7
Newgrange 5
Old Mellifont
   Abbey 5
Táin Trail 2
Táin Way 2

ACCOMMODATIONS
Ballymascanlon House Hotel 3
Bellinter House 11
Best Western Boyne Valley Hotel
   and Country Club 6
Shalom Bed and Breakfast 1
Station House Hotel 8
Tigh Catháin 9

DINING
Ghan House 1
Kingfisher Bistro 1
Monk's 5

SHOPPING
Crystal Antiques 1

NIGHTLIFE
McManus' 3
P.J.'s (O'Hare's) 1

Getting To and Around Meath and Louth

Most visitors to Louth and Meath arrive by car, often on a daytrip from
Dublin. Take the M1 north toward Dundalk and follow the signs for most
of the major towns and attractions mentioned in this chapter. To get to
the Cooley Peninsula from Dundalk, take the R173, which loops to the
town of Newry.

Irish Rail (☎ 1-850-366-222; www.irishrail.ie) has stops in the
County Louth towns of Drogheda and Dundalk from Dublin.

Bus Éireann (☎ 01-836-6111; www.buseireann.ie) has year-round routes to Navan, Kells, Slane, Drogheda, Dundalk, Carlingford, and other smaller towns throughout the area.

Mary Gibbons organizes an excellent bus tour of Meath from Dublin (see "Exploring Meath and Louth: The Top Attractions," later in this chapter, for details).

Spending the Night in Meath and Louth

In addition to its cooking school and restaurant, the Ghan House, in Carlingford (see "Cooking up a storm") offers charming, spacious accommodations. For locations, see the "Counties Meath and Louth" map.

Ballymascanlon House Hotel
$$$$ Dundalk, County Louth

You can't beat staying in an authentic Victorian mansion with tons of amenities. This house retains an old-world ambience, and the spacious rooms are tastefully decorated with antiques and Victorian touches. This is a great place for sporty folks — there's an 18-hole course on the grounds, and a leisure center boasts a pool, a gym, a Jacuzzi, tennis courts, and more. An elegant restaurant serves lunch and dinner, and 24-hour room service is available. Don't miss the 4,000-year-old Proleek dolmen on the property.

At the end of the M1, take the second exit off the second roundabout for Carlingford. The hotel is approximately 400 meters down the road, on the left-hand side. ☎ *042-935-8200. Fax: 042-937-1598.* www.ballymascanlon.com. *Rates: €370 ($592) double. AE, DC, MC, V.*

Bellinter House
$$$$ Navan, County Meath

Let's see . . . What would a typical day at the grand Bellinter House be like? You could sleep late in your room, featuring lovely Georgian details, and then head down to the well-appointed breakfast room. Perhaps read for a while in one of the lounges, which marry traditional Georgian elements with hip modern design. Then walk the extensive grounds of the property, heading to either the indoor or outdoor infinity pools (the outdoor option overlooks a herd of horses munching in a field). You wouldn't want to forget your appointment at the spa, which offers a complete menu of treatments, from head massages to full body wraps. Then will it be cocktails, an excellent dinner of fresh Irish produce, a dip in the hot tub, or watching a video on your large, flat-screen TV? In short, this is a luxurious destination perfect for those looking for relaxation.

Off the road to Kilmessan, near Navan. ☎ *046-903-0900.* www.bellinter house.com. *Rates: €200–€320 ($320–$512). AE, DC, MC, V.*

Best Western Boyne Valley Hotel and Country Club
$$$ Drogheda, County Louth

Though it's in Louth, this hotel is a great starting point for touring the sites of Newgrange, Knowth, and Mellifont Abbey (all located in nearby Meath). Beautiful gardens and woodlands surround the elegant house and make for a pleasant stroll or a great view from the large atrium. All rooms are spacious and have been smartly refurbished. Amenities include a pool and a spa. The fish dishes that are served in the restaurant are as fresh as it gets; they're caught in the Boyne River.

Stameen, Dublin Road, Drogheda. ☎ *041-983-7737. Fax: 041-983-9188.* www.boyne-valley-hotel.ie. *Rates: €140–€170 ($224–$272) double. AE, DC, MC, V.*

Shalom Bed and Breakfast
$$ Carlingford, County Louth

Shalom means "peace" (among other things) in Hebrew, and that's just what you'll find here. This B&B is located across the road from the shores of sparkling Carlingford Lough, which is rimmed by the Mourne Mountains. Conveniently, the bustling town of Carlingford is an easy five-minute walk from the house. Rooms are simple and spacious, painted with bright colors and featuring contemporary fabrics and little touches such as Japanese lanterns and chocolate bars on the in-room tea trays. Friendly owners Kevin and Jackie Woods know the area inside and out and make every effort to help you plan your visit. Self-catering apartments are available.

Upon entering Carlingford on R173, make a right turn just past the Four Seasons Hotel. ☎ *042-937-3151.* www.jackiewoods.com. *Rates: €90 ($144). No credit cards.*

Station House Hotel
$$$$ Kilmessan, County Meath

Located in a rural setting near the Hill of Tara, this unique hotel was once a railway junction building and uses the old ticket office, luggage room, platforms, engine sheds, and signal box for various hotel functions. Beautifully furnished rooms, warm colors, and an interesting theme make this hotel a standout.

From Dublin city, take the N3 until the R125, and then follow the signposts for Kilmessan. ☎ *046-902-5239. Fax: 046-90-2-5588.* www.thestationhouse hotel.com. *Rates: €240 ($384) double. AE, DC, MC, V.*

Tigh Catháin
$$ Trim, County Meath

This Tudor-style country cottage offers three luxuriously large bedrooms decorated in a sweet country style with floral prints and embroidered white linens. But you won't be spending much time in your room if the weather's nice, because the cottage also boasts pretty gardens and a grassy backyard. Owner Marie Keane knows the area well and will make you feel right at home.

Longwood Road (R160), about 1km (⅔ mile) outside Trim. ☎ *046-943-1996.* www. tighcathaintrim.com. *Rates: €84 ($134). No credit cards. Closed Nov–Jan.*

Dining Locally in Meath and Louth

Locations are indicated on the "Counties Meath and Louth" map. If you are touring the Newgrange and Knowth, the cafeteria at the visitor center is a good place for lunch.

Kingfisher Bistro
$$$ Carlingford, County Louth   NEW IRISH

How does Thai-spiced pork with sticky rice, curry oil, sweet soy, and Asian salad sound? Or are you more intrigued by the roast duck breast with celeriac mash, fried onions, and star anis jus? The Kingfisher creatively combines the best of Irish produce with influences from around the world. The intimate dining room manages another balancing act, pulling off modern and rustic at the same time, with pine floors, Edward Hopper–style paintings, and glass candleholders. With friendly service and a relaxed atmosphere, you may spend hours lingering over your dinner.

McGees Court, Carlingford. ☎ *042-937-3716. Main courses: €17–€29 ($27–$46). MC, V. Open: Mon–Fri 6:30–9:30 p.m., Sat 6:30–11 p.m., and Sun 6–8:30 p.m.*

Monk's
$$ Drogheda, County Louth   ECLECTIC

This bright, casual, modern cafe, located by a river, is the place to go for a filling, delicious breakfast or lunch. Settle at one of the tables (on one of the couches, if you're lucky) to peruse the huge menu, encompassing breakfast dishes, panini, sandwiches, fajitas, pastas, salads, and more. Choices run from the Cajun chicken Caesar salad (the most popular dish) to smoked salmon and avocado tossed in lemon-and-basil butter and served over salad greens.

North Quay. ☎ *041-984-5630. Main courses: €8–€13 ($13–$21). AE, DC, MC, V. Open: Daily 9 a.m.–6 p.m.*

Cooking up a storm

Ghan House (☎ 042-937-3682; www.ghanhouse.com), a grand Georgian house, offers all sorts of cooking classes and demonstrations. There is an excellent restaurant on the premises (the fish dishes are especially popular), and the house also offers luxurious guest rooms (€190/$304 for a double).

Exploring Meath and Louth: The Top Attractions

The knowledgeable Mary Gibbons narrates superb bus tours of Meath, which include visits to Newgrange and the Hill of Tara, and a drive along the beautiful and historical Boyne River and through the village of Slane. For information and reservations, call **Newgrange Tours** at ☎ **01-283-9973,** or visit www.newgrangetours.com. Tours cost €35 ($56) for adults, €30 ($48) for students and older children, and €20 ($32) for younger children. Tours last about seven hours, and leave Monday through Saturday from Dublin (there are pick-ups between 9:30 and 10:30 a.m. at several Dublin hotels).

Newgrange and Knowth (via Brú na Bóinne Visitor Centre)
Donore, County Meath

The Brú na Bóinne Visitor Centre provides access to the wondrous prehistoric passage-tombs of Newgrange and Knowth. Newgrange is a huge, impressively intact round mound — 200,000 tons of earth and stone covering a magnificent and well-preserved 5,000-year-old burial chamber. Take a walk around the tomb to see the ancient stone carvings — spirals, diamonds, and other designs. No one knows what these carvings symbolize, but there are numerous theories, from the conjecture that they are mathematic symbols to the theory that they may have been produced under the effects of hallucinogenic drugs. Over the entrance stone to Newgrange is an opening that allows light to slowly creep into the burial chamber during the five days surrounding the winter solstice, filling the room with a warm, golden glow for about 15 minutes. You enter the tomb through a low arch and make your way Indiana Jones–style down the long and narrow stone passage to the cool, dark central burial chamber, where you see more stone carvings and may be party to a very special surprise (no hints; you have to go see for yourself).

Knowth is a tomb of similar size to Newgrange, used from the Stone Age through the 1400s. The main tomb is attended by many smaller satellite tombs, and the stones surrounding the tomb sport beautiful designs. You can't enter the chambers at Knowth, though you can gaze down the long entry passageway. Be sure to take the opportunity to climb on top of the tomb to see the Boyne Valley laid out before you.

If you have to choose between Newgrange and Knowth, I recommend Newgrange — there's more to see, and you can actually enter the chambers. But if you can, see both.

You can only access Newgrange and Knowth through the visitor center; purchase tickets there and take the minibus shuttle to the sites. If you have extra time, check out the offerings in the visitor center, which include interpretive displays about the society that created the tombs, as well as an audiovisual that provides an interesting introduction to the tombs. Arrive early to ensure a ticket — this is a very popular site, and tickets are limited. Also, be aware that the last shuttle bus for the tombs leaves one and three-quarter hours before the visitor center closes.

Off N51, Donore, east of Slane. Off N1 from Drogheda or N2 from Slane. ☎ *041-988-0300. Admission: Exhibit €2.90 ($4.60) adults, €2.10 ($3.40) seniors, €1.60 ($2.60) children and students; Newgrange €5.80 ($9.30) adults, €4.10 ($6.60) seniors, €2.90 ($4.60) children and students; Knowth €4.50 ($7.20) adults, €2.90 ($4.60) seniors, €1.60 ($2.60) children and students. Open: June to mid-Sept daily 9 a.m.–7 p.m.; May and last half of Sept daily 9 a.m.–6:30 p.m.; Mar–Apr and Oct daily 9:30 a.m.–5:30 p.m.; Nov–Feb daily 9:30 a.m.–5 p.m. Knowth is only open May–Oct. Last shuttle bus leaves 1¾ hours before the visitor center closes. Restricted access for people with disabilities. Suggested visit: 4 hours.*

Other Cool Things to See and Do

✔ **Biking all or part of the Táin Trail Cycling Route:** This cycling route, 589km (365 miles) long in total, goes past some major historical sights in Louth, including castles, ruins, Celtic crosses, and areas associated with the ancient Irish epic of the Cattle-Raid of Cooley. For more information, call the **Dundalk Tourist Office** (☎ 042-933-5484).

✔ **Carlingford Adventure Centre:** This place offers the staff, equipment, and instructions for great outdoor activities. Among the many options are windsurfing, kayaking, and sailing on Carlingford Lough, and trekking and rock-climbing in the Cooley Mountains.

Location: Thosel Street, Carlingford, County Louth. ☎ 042-937-3100. www.carlingfordadventure.com. Open: Year-round.

✔ **Causey Farm:** Want to get your hands dirty while having some old-fashioned Irish fun? The Causey Farm gives you the opportunity to make your own brown bread, munch on scones, cut up some turf in a bog, learn some set dancing and Irish drumming, see a sheepdog demonstration, have a traditional dinner, and end the day with a traditional music session *Note:* The experience runs only for groups, so it is essential that you call in advance to find out when a group is coming and then join with them. Bring lunch if you don't want to buy it at the farm. Dinner is included during the long-day program.

Location: Fordstown, Navan, County Meath. ☎ 046-943-4135. www.causeyexperience.com. Causey Farm is located midway between the towns of Kells and Athboy in County Meath, between the N51 and the N52. Cost: Call for exact pricing for different programs. To give you a general idea, the long program (about six hours) is €40 ($64) per adult and €20 ($32) per child. Open: Call in advance to find out days and times. Suggested visit: All day.

✔ **Driving the Cooley Peninsula, Louth:** This peninsula offers a gorgeous scenic drive with impressive views of the Irish Sea and Carlingford Lough (pronounced lock). At one point, the road actually passes through the mountainside. The peninsula is the mythic home of legendary heroes, namely Cuchulainn and Finn MacCool. Dotted along the drive are *dolmen* (Neolithic tombs), forests, mountains, rivers, ruins, and quaint fishing villages. The largest village, Carlingford, is a good place to stop for a stretch or a night. Walk around the ruins of King John's Castle (especially impressive in the evening), and stroll along Carlingford Lough, a natural fjord from the Ice Age that separates the Republic and Northern Ireland in this area.

Location: Outside Dundalk, County Louth. By car: R173 loops around the Peninsula, off N1 outside Dundalk. Suggested visit: three hours.

✔ **Hill of Tara:** The hill of Tara is known as the royal seat of the Irish high kings, who presided over a lively national assembly held every three years to pass laws and resolve disputes. The last assembly was held in A.D. 560, and it is said that 242 kings were crowned on the hill. This site takes some imagination to enjoy, because the only remnants of this pre-Christian political center are mounds and depressions where buildings once stood, plus a few old building stones. A late–Stone Age passage tomb also exists on the site. Take advantage of a guided tour (available on request, so just ask) and the audiovisual in the visitor center to get a better feel for the site. There are dazzling views from the hill.

Location: South of Navan off the main Dublin road (N3), County Meath. ☎ **046-90-25-903** May through mid-September, or ☎ **041-988-0300** mid-September through April. From Dublin, take the N3 toward Navan, and look for signs beginning about 15km (9 miles) before reaching Navan. Near the village of Kilmessan. Admission: €2.10 ($3.40) adults, €1.30 ($2.10) seniors, €1.10 ($1.80) students and children. Open: Mid-May to mid-September daily 10 a.m. to 6 p.m. Last admission 45 minutes before closing. Suggested visit: Forty-five minutes.

✔ **Monasterboice:** Two remarkable tenth-century decorated High Crosses keep a solemn watch over the ruins of a sixth-century monastery and a graveyard. High Crosses combine Celtic and Christian symbols and designs and were often decorated with biblical scenes so that they could be used as teaching tools to help the illiterate to better understand the bible. The first cross that you encounter, known as Muiredach's Cross, depicts the Last Judgment and many Old Testament scenes (check out the interpretive panel opposite the Cross). The other cross (sometimes called the West Cross) is one of the largest in Ireland. The remains of a round tower and church ruins are other highlights.

Location: Off the main Dublin road (M1) near Collon, County Louth. By car: M1 from Dublin. Admission: Free. Open: Daylight hours. Suggested visit: Thirty minutes.

✔ **Newgrange Farm:** This is your average Irish working-farm turned tourist attraction. The friendly Redhouse family gives a tour of the farm, livestock, garden, and 17th-century buildings. You may get to hold a baby chick, watch a threshing machine in action, see a horse get a new pair of shoes, pet a donkey, and more. This attraction is definitely one for the kids, but adults can enjoy themselves as well and may learn a few pointers for the garden at home. If you can, try to be here for the Sheep Race (the jockeys are teddy bears), held every Sunday afternoon. Try to book your visit as far in advance as possible.

Location: Off N51, Slane, County Meath. ☎ **041-982-4119.** www. newgrangefarm.com. Admission: €8 ($13) per person, €6 ($9.60) per person in a family. Open: Easter through September daily 10 a.m. to 5 p.m. Suggested visit: One and a half hours.

✔ **Old Mellifont Abbey:** Founded by St. Malachy in 1142, Mellifont was the first Cistercian monastery in Ireland. This historic house of worship was suppressed by Henry VIII, then became a pigsty (literally), and later was the headquarters for William III during the Battle of the Boyne. The site is a peaceful and tranquil place. The unique octagonal *lavabo* (a washing trough for religious ceremonies) remains intact, along with several of the abbey's arches, all set along the River Mattock. The visitor center contains examples of masonry from the Middle Ages. You can visit the site for free at any time.

Location: Tullyallen, Drogheda, County Louth. ☎ **041-982-6459** May through September. Tour prices: €2.10 ($3.40) adults, €1.30 ($2.10) seniors, €1.10 ($1.80) students and children. Tours: May through September daily 10 a.m. to 5:15 p.m. Suggested visit: One hour.

✔ **Walking the Táin Way:** This 40km (25 mile) walking route encircles the Cooley Peninsula, offering stunning mountain and sea views, sites of mythological importance, and medieval buildings. You'll climb through mountains, skirt the water, and hike through forests. Most people take two days for this walk. For more information, contact the Dundalk Tourist Office at ☎ **042-933-5484.**

Shopping

Crystal Antiques, on Dundalk Street, in Carlingford (☎ **087-127-8482**), sells all sorts of interesting and relatively inexpensive objects, from old spice jars to magic lanterns.

Hitting the Pubs

The "Counties Meath and Louth" map shows the locations of the following pubs.

McManus'
Dundalk, County Louth

This family-run establishment is like three pubs in one. The Music Bar usually hosts traditional music sessions on Mondays, Tuesdays and Fridays, and spontaneous sessions are not uncommon at other times. On cold days, make your way to the back Kitchen Bar, an intimate room with brick interior and a warm cast-iron stove. The Secret Beer Garden's outdoor seating area has coal and turf fires burning year-round, as well as the occasional barbecue.

Seatown Place (near St. Patrick's Church off the main road). ☎ **042-933-1632.**

P.J.'s (also known as O'Hare's)
Carlingford, County Louth

As part-grocery, part-pub, O'Hare's is a dying breed of places that combine a local watering hole with a neighborhood convenience store. But this popular place brings in the tourists for another unique attraction: the leprechaun in a glass case. (Judge its authenticity for yourself.) The pub also features traditional music on Tuesdays. The pub grub is good, but you've gotta try the house specialty — oysters. Simply scrumptious. This is Irish folk-rock band The Corrs' favorite Louth pub.

Located on the Tholsel Street (the main street) in Carlingford. ☎ **042-937-3106.**

Fast Facts: Counties Meath and Louth

Area Codes
042 and **046** for Meath; **042** and **041** for Louth.

Emergencies/Police
Dial ☎ **999** for all emergencies.

Genealogical Resources
In Meath, contact the Meath Heritage Centre, Castle Street, Trim (☎ 046-943-6633; www.meathroots.com). For information about Louth, contact the Louth County Archives Service, Old Gaol, Ardee Road, Dundalk (☎ 042-933-9387; www.louthcoco.ie).

Hospitals
Louth County Hospital is on Dublin Road in Dundalk (☎ 042-933-4701).

Information
For visitor information in Drogheda, go to the tourist office on Mayorality Street (☎ 041-983-7070; www.drogheda.ie). For visitor information in Dundalk, go to the tourist office at Jocelyn Street (☎ 042-933-5484; www.discoverireland.ie/eastcoast.aspx), open year-round. In Carlingford, the Tourist Information Center is in the Old Dispensary in town (☎ 042-937-3033; www.carlingford.ie).

Internet Access
WEBintegra is at 27 West St., in Drogheda (☎ 041-980-3200).

Post Office
Clanbrassil Street, Dundalk, Louth (☎ 042-932-5200).

Chapter 13

Easy Trips South of Dublin: Counties Wicklow and Kildare

. . . .

In This Chapter

▶ Wandering through some of Ireland's most beautiful gardens

▶ Hiking the Wicklow Mountains

▶ Making a pilgrimage to the home of Irish racing

. . . .

*I*mmediately south of bustling Dublin, you find the beginnings of all that famous Irish green. County Wicklow's people trim all that lush greenery into beautiful gardens (many with gorgeous manor houses crowning the properties), and hike through the verdant hills and valleys in the delightful Wicklow Mountains. County Kildare's citizens tend to feed their greenery to the horses — the county is home to dozens upon dozens of horse farms, as well as many racetracks, including Ireland's best, the Curragh.

County Wicklow

County Wicklow is known as "The Garden of Ireland," and it's easy to see why. The county begins just barely out of Dublin's limits, and almost immediately the cityscape gives way to rural roads and delightful hill and coastal scenery. Wicklow's eastern coast is studded with resort areas and harbor towns, where you can have a fine seafood dinner (**Greystones,** a peaceful little hamlet, is my favorite of these towns). Then, there are the famed gardens and manor houses of the area, including the must-see Powerscourt Gardens. Inland, the velvety valleys and wooded glens of the Wicklow Mountains beckon. To really get a feel for the area, take a walk on a stretch of the **Wicklow Way,** a signposted walking path that follows forest trails, sheep paths, and county roads from just outside Dublin all the way to Clonegal (a total of about 130km/80 miles), passing through

Counties Wicklow and Kildare

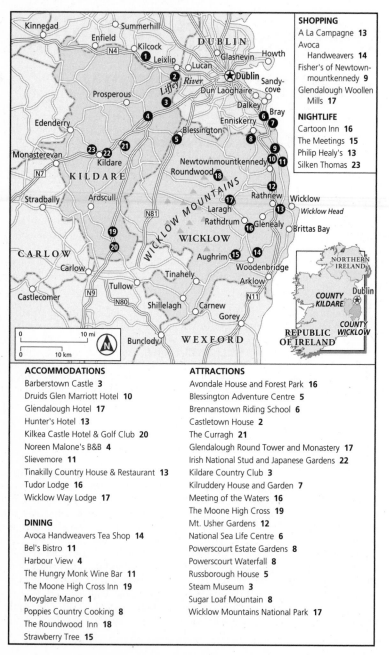

SHOPPING
A La Campagne **13**
Avoca
Handweavers **14**
Fisher's of Newtown-
mountkennedy **9**
Glendalough Woollen
Mills **17**

NIGHTLIFE
Cartoon Inn **16**
The Meetings **15**
Philip Healy's **13**
Silken Thomas **23**

ACCOMMODATIONS
Barberstown Castle **3**
Druids Glen Marriott Hotel **10**
Glendalough Hotel **17**
Hunter's Hotel **13**
Kilkea Castle Hotel & Golf Club **20**
Noreen Malone's B&B **4**
Slievemore **11**
Tinakilly Country House & Restaurant **13**
Tudor Lodge **16**
Wicklow Way Lodge **17**

DINING
Avoca Handweavers Tea Shop **14**
Bel's Bistro **11**
Harbour View **4**
The Hungry Monk Wine Bar **11**
The Moone High Cross Inn **19**
Moyglare Manor **1**
Poppies Country Cooking **8**
The Roundwood Inn **18**
Strawberry Tree **15**

ATTRACTIONS
Avondale House and Forest Park **16**
Blessington Adventure Centre **5**
Brennanstown Riding School **6**
Castletown House **2**
The Curragh **21**
Glendalough Round Tower and Monastery **17**
Irish National Stud and Japanese Gardens **22**
Kildare Country Club **3**
Kilruddery House and Garden **7**
Meeting of the Waters **16**
The Moone High Cross **19**
Mt. Usher Gardens **12**
National Sea Life Centre **6**
Powerscourt Estate Gardens **8**
Powerscourt Waterfall **8**
Russborough House **5**
Steam Museum **3**
Sugar Loaf Mountain **8**
Wicklow Mountains National Park **17**

quaint villages along the way. If you want to stay right in the mountains, the towns of **Roundwood** and **Laragh** are great choices.

Getting to and around County Wicklow

If you're arriving by car, take the N11 (which becomes M11 periodically) south from Dublin toward Arklow. You can turn off along this route to reach most major towns and attractions. The **Irish Rail's** Dublin– (Connolly Station) Rosslare Harbour train line (☎ **01-836-6222;** www.irishrail. ie) has stations in Bray, Greystones, Wicklow, Rathdrum, and Arklow. Dublin Area Rapid Transit (DART) extends as far as Greystones. **Dublin Bus** (☎ **01-873-4222;** www.dublinbus.ie) runs from City Centre to Dun Laoghaire and the Bray DART station. **Bus Éireann** (☎ **01-836-6111;** www.buseireann.ie) travels year-round between Bray, Wicklow, Arklow, Rathdrum, and Avoca.

Spending the night in County Wicklow

Druids Glen Marriott Hotel
$$$ **Newtownmountkennedy**

This hotel, beautifully situated between the Irish Sea and the Wicklow Mountains, has the distinction of being the first Marriott hotel in Ireland. The rooms are larger than most, and the hotel has every amenity you can think of, plus a few you probably wouldn't, such as a whirlpool, solarium, and steam room in the pool area and an award-winning steak restaurant on-site. If you're a golfer, you'll appreciate the location — on the 160 hectare (400-acre) Druid's Glen Golf Resort.

From Dublin, take the N11 national route toward Wexford. Turn off toward Newtownmountkennedy and follow the signs to Druids Glen. ☎ *1-800-228-9290 in the U.S. and Canada, or* ☎ *01-287-0800. Fax: 01-287-0801.* www.marriott hotels.com. *Rates: €170–€220 ($272–$352) double. AE, DC, MC, V.*

Glendalough Hotel
$$$ **Glendalough**

Occupying a woody area overlooking the ruins of the monastery complex at Glendalough, this 1800s hotel is the perfect launching point for an exploration of Glendalough and the Wicklow Mountains National Park. The public rooms are beautifully furnished with antiques. The good-size, pastel bedrooms are nothing to write home about, but you'll probably be exploring the area the whole day anyway. The traditional Irish dishes served in the dining room are excellent and fresh, and the Glendalough Tavern has some of the best pub food you'll find in a hotel, including a wonderful lamb stew. Check the Web site for special offers and discounts, which run often.

On the 755. Take the R755 off the N11. ☎ *0404-45-135. Fax: 0404-45-142.* www. glendaloughhotel.com. *Rates: €118–€184 ($189–$294) double. AE, DC, MC, V. Closed: Dec–Jan.*

Hunter's Hotel
$$$ Rathnew

This family-run hotel is one of Ireland's oldest coaching inns, offering views of breathtaking gardens and nearby mountains. Rooms are huge, with attractive art and warm lighting. Irish dishes, such as Wicklow lamb with fresh vegetables from the hotel's gardens, are served in the restaurant. Blazing fires and antique furniture add to the charm.

Newrath Bridge. Take the N11 from Dublin, and take a left in Ashford village by the bridge and opposite Ashford House pub. Hunter's is 2km (1½ miles) from Ashford. ☎ *0404-40-106. Fax: 0404-40-338.* www.hunters.ie. *Rates: €190 ($304) double (see Web site for specials). MC, V.*

Slievemore
$$$ Greystones

You could spend all day gazing at Greystone's pretty harbor from Slievemore, an impeccable, whitewashed B&B run by a pleasant couple. Rooms are bright, spacious, and sweet, with sparkling-clean bathrooms. A delicious and filling breakfast is served in the back conservatory, where you can watch robins flit by as you munch your bacon. It's an easy walk to Slievemore from the DART station, so you don't even need a car to enjoy this darling seaside town and this excellent B&B.

The Harbour. Follow signs south out of Bray to Greystones village. ☎ *01-287-4724.* www.slievemorehouse.com. *Rates: €150 ($240) double. No credit cards.*

Tinakilly Country House and Restaurant
$$$$ Rathnew

This country-house hotel brings together everything you've heard about the grandeur and friendliness of Ireland. Staying here may strain your budget, but when your every whim is being catered to, and you're relaxing in your charming room, you'll be happy you splurged. The hotel is an impressive Victorian mansion filled with antiques and nautical memorabilia. Most of the elegant rooms have four-poster or canopy beds and overlook the mountains, the Irish Sea, or carefully tended gardens. The cherry on top is Brunel, a wonderful restaurant serving fixed-price dinners (€65/$53) featuring modern cuisine and the freshest ingredients.

Take the R750 off the main Dublin-Wexford Road. ☎ *0404-69-274, or 800-525-4800 from the U.S. Fax: 0404-67-806.* www.tinakilly.ie. *Rates: €130–€250 ($208–$400) double. AE, MC, V.*

Tudor Lodge
$ Laragh

This B&B boasts simple, tidy, spacious rooms; a cozy living room; and a patio and terrace that offer views of the surrounding green hills. With a central location in the Wicklow Mountains, the house is a convenient spot to hang your hat while exploring the area.

☎ *0404-45-554.* www.tudorlodgeireland.com. *Rates: €80 ($128) double. MC, V.*

Wicklow Way Lodge
$$ Laragh

Your hosts here, Marilyn and Seamus, have to be responsible for at least a few thousand of Ireland's famous hundred thousand welcomes. Come here for incredibly friendly hosts, a scrumptious breakfast (the porridge is legendary), and spacious, soothing, sparkling-clean rooms. The location of the B&B, in the Wicklow Mountains, is both lovely and central.

From Laragh, turn left at the sign for St. John's Church. ☎ *01-281-8489.* www.wicklowwaylodge.com. *Rates: €90–€100 ($144–$160). MC, V.*

Dining locally in County Wicklow

In addition to the choices below, see Tinakilly Country House and Restaurant, and Glendalough Hotel in the previous section.

Avoca Handweavers Tea Shop
$ Avoca ECLECTIC

If you thought this little eatery was just a decent place to get some tea and baked goods while blowing your budget on Avoca's beautiful woven items, think again. Located in the back of the shop, this cheerful cafe serves some divine lunch choices, from salads, soups, and sandwiches to main courses such as smoked trout and honey-glazed ham. The low lunch prices make it easy to justify buying that extra woolen throw.

☎ *0402-35105. Main courses: €10–€15 ($16–$24). MC, V. Open: Daily May–Sept 9 a.m.–6 p.m.; Oct–Apr 9:30 a.m.–5:30 p.m.*

Bel's Bistro
$–$$$ Greystones ECLECTIC

Local families and groups of friends fill this casual, modern spot for lunches, leisurely after-work drinks and snacks, and dinners. This is the kind of menu that you don't have to think too hard about — no tomato foams or tapenades; just simple, well-prepared food such as burgers, blackened-chicken pasta, fish and chips, and Thai chicken curry, along with a great wine list. I'm a big fan of the mushroom tart with leek-and-garlic sauce. The bright interior is stylishly decorated with high-backed pine chairs and small contemporary paintings, but the patio out front is the place to be on a nice day.

Church Road. ☎ *01-201-6990. Main courses: €8–€25 ($13–$40). MC, V. Open: Tues–Sat 9:30 a.m.–10 p.m., Sun 10 a.m.–10 p.m.*

The Hungry Monk Wine Bar
$$–$$$$ Greystones   ECLECTIC

Excellent wines, glowing candles, dark wood furnishings, and simple hearty food are the catalysts for the convivial atmosphere at this place. Clink your wineglasses over plates of simply prepared fish, stew, or perhaps the excellent Monk Burger, a thick hunk of hamburger cooked with herbs and topped with gherkins. Keep your eyes peeled for the various works of art with monks as their subject. Groups may want to reserve early in order to snag the large, candelabra-lit table. If you feel like a more formal meal, head upstairs to the Hungry Monk's fancier restaurant, where steaks are a favorite.

Church Road. ☎ *01-287-5759. Reservations recommended. Main courses: Restaurant €20–€28 ($32–$45); wine bar €15–€21 ($24–$34). MC, V. Open: Restaurant Tues–Sat 6:30–11 p.m., Sun 12:30–8 p.m.; wine bar Mon–Sat 5–11 p.m., Sun 4–9 p.m.*

The Roundwood Inn
$$–$$$ Roundwood   SEAFOOD/IRISH/ECLECTIC

Forget about greasy fish and chips; the Roundwood Inn offers seafood that will knock your socks off, including a platter of salmon, oysters, lobster, and shrimp. In addition, you'll find beautifully prepared Irish and Continental dishes, from a succulent steak to Irish stew. If you want a cheaper meal or a bite to tide you over between meals, check out the terrific pub grub in the bar. The inn was built in the 18th century and is furnished with dark wood and an open fireplace. Service could be friendlier, but the food makes up for that.

Main Street. Out of Bray, take the R755 to Roundwood. ☎ *01-281-8107. Reservations recommended for dinner. Main courses: €17–€30 ($27–$38). AE, MC, V. Open: Pub daily noon to 9 p.m.; restaurant Fri–Sat 7:30–9 p.m., Sun 1–4 p.m.*

Poppies Country Cooking
$$ Enniskerry   CAFÉ

The name says it all. This is simple country cooking at its best, with such tasty options as vegetable quiche, a leek and brie cheese tart, and the amazing beef and Guinness pie.

The Square. ☎ *01-282-8869. Main courses: €5–€11 ($8–$18). MC, V. Open: Summer daily 8:30 a.m.–7 p.m.; winter 8:30 a.m.–6 p.m.*

Strawberry Tree
$$$$ Aughrim   NEW IRISH

Everybody is talking about this restaurant, which was one of the first in Ireland to use wild and organic ingredients exclusively. The menu changes all the time, and dishes are flavorful and unfussy. Recently, offerings included a beef filet with beetroot and balsamic jus, and luscious tarragon pasta with wild mushrooms. The room is formal and elegant.

The BrookLodge & Wells Spa, Macreddin Village (take the R753 to Aughrim and follow the signs). ☎ *0402-364-44. Prix-fixe dinner €65 ($104). AE, MC, V. Open: Daily 7–9:30 p.m.*

Exploring County Wicklow

Here are some of the best ways to enjoy the emerald landscape of County Wicklow.

Organized tours

Because Wicklow is so close to Dublin, a number of operators offer bus tours, and others take advantage of the area's beauty to offer such interesting options as horseback tours.

Bus Éireann (☎ **01-836-6111;** www.buseireann.ie) offers day tours of the Wicklow area from Dublin. The **Glendalough and Powerscourt Gardens Tour** (€33/$56 adults, €27/$43 students and seniors, €23/$37 children, not including attraction admission) runs from mid-March through November, covering the south coast of Dublin, the Wicklow Mountains, Powerscourt, Roundwood, Laragh, and Glendalough. Tours leave from Busaras, on Store Street, at 10 a.m. daily.

The **Wild Wicklow Tour** (☎ **01-280-1899;** www.DiscoverDublin.ie), which uses a small Mercedes coach that goes where the big and bulky buses can't, packs in many of the highlights of Wicklow. First, you visit the beautiful seaside town of Dalkey, home to Bono, Enya, and many of Ireland's other rich and famous; then move on to Avoca Handweavers, which sells colorful woolen items and funky clothing, as well as delicious lunches. Next, you hit Wicklow's top attraction, the enchanting sixth-century monastic settlement of Glendalough, before stopping for a pub lunch. Your day ends with a visit to Sally Gap, which has stunning views of the surrounding mountains, and Lough Tay, a quietly magnificent mountain lake. I particularly recommend this tour because the guides are friendly, fun, and informative, and allow you time to explore a bit on your own. The full-day tour leaves from the Dublin tourist office and picks up passengers at various hotels around Dublin (tell them where you're staying, and they'll tell you the closest pickup point). Prices are €28 ($44) adults, and €25 ($40) student or child. The same company also runs a half-day **Wild Powerscourt Tour,** touring the famous gardens. Advance reservations are required.

The top attractions

Glendalough Round Tower and Monastery
Glendalough

This secluded, leafy site, centered on two peaceful lakes, has been a sacred one since the sixth century, when St. Kevin founded a monastery here. The area flourished as a community of learning for almost 900 years, with the sounds of theories and ideas bouncing off the majestic trees and stone buildings. The entire complex was sacked by Anglo-Norman invaders in the 14th century, and most of the buildings were destroyed. However, you can still explore many ruins around the Upper and Lower lakes, including the remnants of a seventh- to ninth-century cathedral; a graveyard full of beautifully designed Celtic crosses; and the highlight, a stunningly preserved 31m (103-ft.) round tower capped with a belfry. Drop into the well-done visitor center to get a sense of the context of this site. I highly recommend the peaceful walk from the Lower Lake to the less-visited Upper Lake.

Glendalough. ☎ *0404-45-325. Take N11 to R755 from Dublin, R752 to R755 from Wicklow. Admission: €2.90 ($4.70) adults, €2.10 ($3.40) seniors, €1.30 ($2.10) children and students. Open: Mid-Oct to mid-Mar daily 9:30 a.m.–5 p.m.; mid-Mar to mid-Oct daily 9:30 a.m.–6 p.m. Last admission 45 minutes before closing. Suggested visit: 1½ hours.*

Mt. Usher Gardens
Ashford

More than 5,000 species of plants from all over the world populate these informal gardens, located along the River Vartry. These 8 hectares (20 acres), which started as a humble potato patch in 1860, have blossomed into a wild ocean of flowers, trees, meadows, and waterfalls, with small suspension bridges crossing the river, and birds and wildlife flitting above and through the exotic greenery. The spot where a mini suspension bridge spans a little waterfall just may be one of the most romantic spots in Ireland. Also on the premises are a tearoom and a courtyard filled with shops.

Off the main Dublin-Wicklow Road (N11); look for the signs. ☎ *0404-40-205. Admission: €7 ($11) adults, €6 ($9.60) seniors and students, €3 ($4.80) children 5–12. Open: Mar 10–Oct daily 10:30 a.m.–6 p.m. (last entry 5 p.m.). Suggested visit: 1½ hours.*

National Sea Life Centre
Bray

This highly interactive aquarium follows the route of a river from its origin to its ocean destination, bringing you face to face with thousands of seawater and freshwater creatures along the way. Kids will have a ball following an adventure trail with puzzles and games, using touch screens, picking up ocean dwellers at the touch tank, and hanging out at the new shark nursery. It's worth planning your visit around the feedings, talks, and demonstrations by the aquarium's staff.

Strand Road on the boardwalk. ☎ *01-286-6939.* www.sealifeeurope.ie. *DART: The center is a 10-minute walk from the Bray Station. Admission: €11 ($18) adults, €9.95 ($16) seniors and students, €7.90 ($13) children 3–15. Open: Daily 10 a.m.–6 p.m. (last admission 5 p.m.). Suggested visit: 2 hours.*

Powerscourt Estate Gardens
Enniskerry

These gardens are the finest in Wicklow County, which is saying a lot, because the county is known for its abundance of exceptionally beautiful gardens. First laid out from 1745 to 1767, the gardens were redesigned in Victorian style from 1843 to 1875. The gardens have many different facets, among them a wooded glen graced with a stone round tower that was modeled on Lord Powerscourt's dining-room pepper pot, a magical moss-covered grotto, a formal Italianate area with a circular pond and fountain presided over by sculptures of winged horses, and a walled garden where blazing roses cling to the stone. Don't miss the moving pet cemetery, with sweet monuments to various pets owned by the Powerscourt family, from faithful dogs to a particularly prolific dairy cow. I recommend following the route around the entire estate, which should take you a good hour to two hours. Skip the tour of the house; it's not very interesting. Powerscourt Waterfall is down the road (see "Other cool things to see and do," later in this chapter).

Off the main Dublin-Wicklow Road (N11). By car: Take the N11 out of Dublin (it becomes the new motorway M11), and follow signs for the garden. By bus: 44 from Dublin to Enniskerry, or Alpine Coach (☎ 01-286-2547) from the Bray DART station to the gardens. ☎ 01-204-6000. Admission: Garden €8 ($13) adults, €7 ($11) students and seniors, €5 ($8) children under 16, free for children under 5. Open: House and gardens daily 9:30 a.m.–5:30 p.m. (gardens close at dusk in winter). Suggested visit: 2–3 hours.

Wicklow Mountains National Park
Glendalough

This park, covering nearly 20,000 hectares (50,000 acres), encompasses forest, hills, and large mountain bogs, and protects such wildlife as the rare peregrine falcon. The park centers on beautiful Glendalough (reviewed earlier in this section) and includes Glendalough Valley and the Glendalough Wood Nature Reserve. An information office (open daily at the Upper Lake during the summer and on weekends from about September through about June) offers information on hiking in the park, including route descriptions and maps, and organizes free nature walks (call or check the Web site for the schedule). A tough stretch of the Wicklow Way (described in the next section, "Outdoor activities"), runs through the park. In May and October, the park hosts two-day walking festivals. The best maps of trails are available from Harvey Maps in England (☎ 01786-841202; www.harveymaps.co.uk).

Take the N11 to R755 from Dublin; the R752 to R755 from Wicklow. The Information Point is located by Upper Lake, R756 off R755. ☎ 0404-45-425 or 0404-45-656. www.wicklownationalpark.ie. Park open all day every day. Suggested visit: 1–3 hours.

Outdoor activities

Also see the description of Wicklow Mountains National Park (earlier in this chapter) and Sugar Loaf Mountain (in the next section, "Other cool things to see and do").

- ✔ **Blessington Adventure Centre:** This company offers canoeing, kayaking, sailing, and windsurfing on the sparkling Blessington Lakes. It also runs horseback rides.

  Location: Adventure Centre Pier, Blessington (off N81). ☎ **045-86-5092.** Prices vary. Open: Daily 10 a.m. to 5 p.m.

- ✔ **Brennanstown Riding School:** Everyone from beginners to advanced riders can take advantage of the indoor and outdoor riding facilities here. The best option is a ride or pony-trek through the scenic Wicklow countryside.

  Location: Brennanstown Riding School, Hollbrook, Kilmacanogue, near Bray. ☎ **01-286-3778.** Take the DART to Bray. Prices vary, depending on activity.

- ✔ **Hiking the Cliff Trail between Bray to Greystones:** This 8km (5-mile) path (which is relatively flat and easy) snakes along some gorgeous cliffs. Allow about two hours for your hike. The route begins (or ends, depending on your point of view) by the harbor in Greystones. In Bray, the trailhead appears on the left as you follow the promenade and climb up Bray head.

- ✔ **The Wicklow Way:** This 122km (76-mile) trail extends from Marlay Park in County Dublin to Clonegal in County Carlow, running through forests, over hills, around bogs and farms, along country roads and old stone walls, and through charming villages high in the Wicklow Mountains. You can walk the whole trail in five or six days, staying in towns along the way, or just drop in for a day hike. The walk from the Deerpark parking lot near the River Dargle to Luggala is a gorgeous day-hike option, as are the hikes between the

The ideal picnic spot

Just beyond Avondale House is the famed **Meeting of the Waters,** where the Avonmore and Avonbeg rivers come together. This spot is so beautiful, it inspired Thomas Moore to write: "There is not in the wide world a valley so sweet / as the vale in whose bosom the bright waters meet." Pack some fruit, bread, and cheese and head to this spot, 5km (3 miles) south of Rathdrum heading toward Arklow on the R752 (which becomes the R755 as you leave Rathdrum).

towns of Tinahely, Shillelagh, and Clonegal. You can get information on hikes at Wicklow Mountains National Park (described in the previous section) or any Wicklow tourist office. Check out the Wicklow Trail Sheets, available at Wicklow tourist offices, for shorter hikes.

A daily Bus Éireann bus runs from Dublin and Waterford to Bunclody near the County Carlow end of the trail, and local buses run from Dublin to Marlay Park.

Other cool things to see and do

✔ **Avondale House and Forest Park:** Built in 1779 and set in a lush forest valley, this house was the birthplace and home of one of Ireland's great leaders, Charles Stewart Parnell (1846–1891), who fought for Irish home rule and for land reform. The Georgian house has been restored beautifully and features original furniture and a museum illustrating Parnell's life and career. The grounds are lovely, and you're free to explore along a number of well-marked nature trails, including a pretty 5½km (3½-mile) walk along the river. Avondale is a center of Irish forestry, and its grounds have served as a model of forest preservation for the country.

Location: Rathdrum. ☎ 0404-46-111. Take N11 to R752 to Rathdrum crossroads, and follow signs to the house. Admission to the house is €6 ($9.60) adults, €5 ($8) seniors and children under 12. Admission: Free. Open: Mid-March to April and September to October Tuesday to Sunday 11 a.m. to 6 p.m.; May through August daily 11 a.m. to 6 p.m. (last admission to house 5 p.m. at all times). Suggested visit: One and a half hours.

✔ **Killruddery House and Garden:** Killruddery is the oldest surviving formal garden in Ireland, laid out in the 1680s in the French style of the time. Highlights are the outdoor theater, exotic shrubs, orangerie featuring Italian statues, and pond. The gardens are certainly the draw here, but the grand Elizabethan-revival house is also worth a visit. The house has been in the family of the Earls of Meath since 1618 and features a stunning conservatory.

Location: Off the main Dublin-Wicklow Road (N11), Killruddery. ☎ 0404-46024. Admission: House and garden €10 ($16) adults, €8 ($13) seniors and students, €3 ($4.80) children; garden only €6 ($9.60) adults, €5 ($8) seniors and students, €2 ($3.20) children. Open: House May to June and September daily 1 to 5 p.m.; garden May through September daily 1 to 5 p.m., and April weekends 1 to 5 p.m. Suggested visit: One and a half hours.

✔ **Powerscourt Waterfall:** This pretty waterfall, located in a leafy glen, is Ireland's highest. On a nice day, get some ice cream, and enjoy the view. Don't expect solitude; there are usually a handful of visitors here at any given time.

Location: Off the main Dublin-Wicklow Road (N11), Eniskerry.
☎ 01-204-6000. Admission: €5 ($8) adults, €4.50 ($7.20) students,
€3.50 ($5.60) children. Open: May through August daily 9:30 a.m. to
7 p.m.; March, April, September and October 10:30 a.m. to 5:30
p.m.; November through February 10:30 a.m. to 4:30 p.m.

✔ **Russborough House:** This house, built in the mid-1700s in the
Palladian style, is home to the world-famous Beit Collection of
paintings, which includes pieces by Gainsborough, Reynolds,
Rubens, and Guardi. The furnishings of the house — including tapestries, silver, bronzes, porcelain, and ornate furniture — are also
works of art. Visits are by guided tour only. The grounds are open
for exploration, and there is a restaurant, a shop, a hedge maze,
and a children's playground.

Location: Off N81, Blessington. ☎ 045-86-5239. From Dublin, take
the N7 to Naas, and pick up the R410. The house is located where
the R410 meets the N81. Admission: €10 ($16) adults, €8 ($13)
seniors and students, €5 ($8) children under 12. Open: April
and October Sunday and bank holidays 10:30 a.m. to 6 p.m.; May
through September daily 10:30 a.m. to 6 p.m. (last admission
5 p.m. throughout the year). Suggested visit: One hour.

✔ **Sugar Loaf Mountain:** There are spectacular views from the top of
Sugar Loaf Mountain. The climb is pretty easy, and you can get to
the top in under an hour. You'll be happy you did — on a clear day,
you can see all the way to Wales!

Location: Near Kilmacanogue. Take R755 off N11.

Shopping in County Wicklow

Wicklow is known for pottery and knitwear. The **County Tourism Office
in Wicklow,** at Kilmantin House in the town of Wicklow (☎ 0404-66-058)
puts out a publication called the *Crafts Trail,* with a full list of pottery,
crafts, and knitwear locations throughout the county.

In Wicklow Town, **A La Campagne,** Main Street (☎ 0404-61-388), offers
unique items, including gifts, kitchenware, pottery, and glass; plenty of
artsy objects, such as candles and holders; and Irish country pottery.
The owner, Stephen Falvin, is often on hand to help pick out a gift or
advise on choices. **Avoca Handweaver,** Avoca Village (☎ 0402-35-105),
is the oldest handweaving mill in Ireland (dating to 1723) and sells colorful knitwear, including tweed and knit clothing and blankets; beautiful
trendy/bohemian clothing; and a wide range of fine Irish crafts. There is
also an outlet store in Kilmacanogue, near Bray (☎ 01-286-7466). Located
in a converted schoolhouse, **Fisher's of Newtownmountkennedy,** in the
big pink building on R765, off N11, Newtownmountkennedy (☎ 01-281-
9404), has tons of men's and women's clothes and accessories, both
elegant and country-casual, plus cool items such as hip flasks and pool
cues. **Glendalough Woollen Mills,** in Laragh, on the R755 (☎ 0404-

45-156), is housed in an old farmhouse and sells Irish handcrafts including pottery, glass, jewelry, and handknits.

Hitting the Pubs

Cartoon Inn
Rathdrum

Make sure you don't snort Guinness through your nose as you laugh at the cartoons on the wall of this pub, many of which were drawn by famous cartoonists. Ireland's annual Cartoon Festival is held in Rathdrum in early summer. You can get lunch here too.

28 Main St. ☎ *0404-46-774.*

The Meetings
Vale of Avoca

Nestled in the beautiful Vale of Avoca, The Meetings is a Tudor-style pub that's popular with visitors to Wicklow. You can get good pub grub all day and listen to traditional music on weekend nights. Plus, when the weather's warm, you can sit outside on the patio and take in the view. It's clearly geared to tourists, but that's not necessarily a bad thing. After all, how many pubs provide a Bureau de Change and a crafts shop?

☎ *0402-35-226.*

Philip Healy's
Wicklow

This unpretentious spot is where locals meet for a leisurely drink and chat. The high ceilings make it feel open and airy, but the pub has plenty of nooks to settle into if you want to have a quiet conversation.

Main Street. ☎ *0404-67-380.*

Fast Facts: County Wicklow

Area Codes

County Wicklow's area codes (or city codes) are **01, 0404, 0402**, and **045**.

Emergencies/Police

Dial ☎ **999** for all emergencies.

Information

For visitor information and help reserving accommodations, go to the tourist office in Fitzwilliam Square, Wicklow (☎ 0404-20-100; www.wicklow.ie), open year-round. They can also provide reservation services.

Hospital

The main hospital is in Wicklow (☎ 0404-67-108).

County Kildare

Welcome to horse country. A land of gentle hills and open grasslands, County Kildare is home to hundreds of stud farms. And, of course, one needs a place to race all these fine horses, so the county boasts three large racetracks, including the Curragh, where the Irish Derby is held each year.

Getting to and around County Kildare

By car, take the N7 from Dublin or Limerick to get to Kildare, or take N4 to Celbridge and then use R403. **Irish Rail** (☎ 1-850-366-222; www. irishrail.ie) has daily service to Kildare town, and **Bus Éireann** (☎ 01-836-6111; www.buseireann.com) services Kildare, Straffan, Newbridge, and other towns throughout the area.

Spending the night in County Kildare

Barberstown Castle
$$$$ Straffan

This lavish hotel is made up of several different parts: a 13th-century castle keep, a 16th-century building, a Georgian country house, and a 20th-century addition. Rooms are elegant, with antiques and reproductions and sumptuous fabrics, and afternoon tea is available in the sitting room.

From Dublin, take the N7 to Kill, where you turn for Straffan; from the west, take N4 to Maynooth, where you turn for Straffan. ☎ *01-628-8157. Fax: 01-627-7027.* www.barberstowncastle.ie. *Rates: €240–€280 ($384–$448). AE, DC, MC, V. Closed: Jan.*

Kilkea Castle Hotel and Golf Club
$$$$ Castledermot

Keep an eye out for the 11th earl of Kildare, who is said to haunt this medieval castle, built around 1180. The décor here evokes the Middle Ages, with medieval banners and coats of armor, but the luxurious bedrooms, with chandeliers and dark wood furnishings, top anything that King Arthur and his compatriots would be used to. You can amuse yourself all day on the grounds here, which include an 18-hole golf course, an indoor pool, fishing, tennis, archery, and other sporty pursuits.

☎ *0503-45-156. Fax: 0503-45-187.* www.kilkeacastlehotel.com. *Rates: €256 ($410) double. AE, DC, MC, V.*

Noreen Malone's B&B
$$ Naas

This is the kind of B&B you'd love to move into. Noreen Malone's comfortable house is a welcome departure from the sometimes-impersonal nature of hotels. The exquisitely manicured lawn hints at the clean and nicely decorated rooms and dining area. The town of Naas is just a five-minute walk away, and the price of this lovely stay-over can't be beat.

Sallins Road. Take the N7 from Dublin to Naas. ☎ **045-89-7598.** *Rates: €80–€95 ($128–$152) double. No credit cards.*

Dining locally in County Kildare

Also see "Hitting the pubs," later in this chapter.

Harbour View
$$–$$$ **Naas IRISH**

The food here is home-cooked, wholesome, delicious, and served in hearty portions. Don't let the nondescript exterior fool you; one foot in the door, and you'll know you're in for a meal that will keep you going all day long or satisfy you after a day spent exploring.

Limerick Road. Take the N7 from Dublin to Naas. ☎ **045-87-9145.** *Main courses: €12–€22 ($19–$35). AE, DC, MC, V. Open: Daily 7 a.m.–9 p.m.*

The Moone High Cross Inn
$$ **Moone PUB GRUB**

Take a seat and enjoy the friendly atmosphere at this authentic pub, which serves shrimp, salmon, duck, steak, shepherd's pie, and other simple, delicious, well-prepared dishes. Be sure to check out the décor, consisting of old photographs and all sorts of local curios.

Bolton Hill; 7½km (5 miles) south of Ballytore. ☎ **059-862-4112.** *Main courses: €10–€23 ($16–$37). MC, V. Serves food Daily 10 a.m.–8 p.m.*

Moyglare Manor
$$$$ **Maynooth FRENCH**

Dinner in this formal and romantic dining room is a long and luxurious experience; don't plan anything else for the evening if you dine here. The cuisine is classic French and uses as many fresh local ingredients as possible, with such dishes as pork stuffed with herbs, plaice in champagne sauce, and the very popular crab croquettes. The fresh vegetables served alongside the meal are fresh from the manor's garden. Service is terrific.

29km (18 miles) west of Dublin on the N4. ☎ **01-628-6351.** *Reservations recommended. Prix-fixe dinner €60 ($72). AE, DC, MC, V. Open: Daily 7–9 p.m.*

Exploring County Kildare

This section lists the top sights in County Kildare, from historic homes to Ireland's most famous racetrack.

The top attractions

Castletown House
Celbridge

This stately house was built in the early part of the 18th century for William Connolly, the then Speaker of the Irish House of Commons. Its grandeur is staggering, and it remains a standout in Irish architecture. The mansion was built in the Palladian style, a Renaissance style meant to copy the classicism of ancient Rome. The interior is decorated with Georgian furnishings, and the main hall and staircase are covered with intricate plasterwork. Run by the state and open to the public, the house is worth the drive — about 16km (10 miles) northeast of Naas. Access is by guided tour only.

From Dublin, take the N4 west, picking up the R403 several miles out of the city. Located on the R403 just before you reach the village of Celbridge. By bus: 67 and 67A from Dublin. ☎ *01-628-8252. Admission: Required guided tours €4.50 ($7.20) adults, €3.50 ($5.60) seniors, students, and children. Open: Mid-Mar to Nov Tues–Sun 10 a.m.–5 p.m. Call in Dec, as the house is sometimes still open. Suggested visit: 1½ hours.*

The Curragh
Newbridge

This racetrack, the country's best-known, is often referred to as the Churchill Downs of Ireland. You can catch a race here at least one Saturday a month from March to October. In late June, the Curragh is host to the famous Irish Derby.

On the Dublin-Limerick Road. Take the N7 from Dublin or Naas. By train: Daily service into Curragh. Bus Éireann (☎ 01-836-6111) offers a round-trip bus from Dublin. ☎ *045-44-1205.* www.curragh.ie. *Admission: €15 ($24) for most races, €25–€50 ($40–$80) for the Derby. Call ahead for upcoming dates. Races usually begin at or around 2 p.m.*

Irish National Stud and Japanese Gardens
Tully

One of the foremost horse breeding grounds in the country, the National Stud is consistently ranked as one of Ireland's top-20 tourist attractions. You can see the majestic horses being groomed and exercised, and during spring, you can ooh and aah over the mares with their foals. Check out the Horse Museum, with exhibits on racing, hunting, and show jumping, plus the skeleton of the famed horse Arkle, who won several racing victories in the 1960s.

On the same grounds are the striking Japanese Gardens, which boast bonsai, bamboo, and cherry trees. The gardens portray the journey of life, starting with birth and ending at eternity, which is represented by a Zen rock garden.

Take N7 from Dublin or Naas. By train: Daily service into Kildare Railway Station. ☎ ***045-52-1617.*** *Admission: €11 ($18) adults, €8 ($13) seniors and students, €6 ($9.60) under 16. Open: Mid-Feb to Dec daily 9:30 a.m.–6 p.m. Suggested visit: 3 hours.*

More cool things to see and do

✔ **Kildare Country Club (K-Club):** This 18-hole championship golf course was designed by Arnold Palmer and hosted the Ryder Cup in 2006; you certainly pay for the privilege of golfing here.

Location: 27km (17 miles) west of Dublin in Straffan. ☎ **01-601-7200.** www.kclub.ie. Par: 72. Fees: €305 to €380 ($488–$608) for 18 holes from May to September; €195 to €245 ($312–$392) in October; and €130 to €165 ($208–$264) from November to April.

✔ **The Moone High Cross:** This 1,200-year-old high stone cross boasts beautiful carvings of Celtic designs, as well as biblical scenes.

Location: Moone. On the southern edge of Moone village, signposted off N9.

✔ **Steam Museum:** Anyone with an interest in steam locomotion will enjoy this museum, housed in a restored church. The collection of 18th-century locomotive engines includes Richard Trevithick's Third Model of 1797, the oldest surviving self-propelled machine in existence. Another room contains stationary engines from the Industrial Age. You can find plenty of steam-locomotion literature in the shop. If it's nice out, check out the 18th-century walled garden.

Location: Off the Dublin-Limerick Road (N7), Lodge Park, Straffan, near Celbridge. By car: Take the N7 from Dublin or Naas. By train: Daily service into Kildare Railway Station. ☎ **01-627-3155** in summer; ☎ **01-628-8412** in winter. Admission: €7.50 ($12) adults, €5 ($8) seniors, students, and children. Open: June through August Wednesday to Sunday 2 to 6 p.m., May and September open by arrangement only. Suggested visit: Two hours.

Hitting the pubs

Also see the Moone High Cross Inn, reviewed in "Dining locally in County Kildare," earlier in this chapter.

Silken Thomas
Kildare

Silken Thomas is an entertainment complex with three bars (including a warm and welcoming thatched-roof, oak-beamed pub and a glistening Victorian-style hangout), a restaurant, and a state-of-the art club. Fortify yourself with some of Silken Thomas's delicious pub grub, including steaks, sandwiches, and soups. The pub's name comes from a member of the Fitzgerald family known for wearing luxurious clothing and being accompanied by standard-bearers carrying silken banners.

The Square. ☎ *045-52-2232.*

Fast Facts: County Kildare

Area Codes

Kildare's area codes (or city codes) are **01, 045, 053,** and **0507.**

Emergencies/Police

Dial ☎ **999** for all emergencies.

Genealogical Resources

Get in touch with the Kildare Library (☎ 045-431-109).

Hospital

Naas General Hospital (☎ 045-897-221) is in Craddockstown, Naas.

Information

The tourist office is at 38 Main St., in Naas (☎ 045-898-888).

Internet

Tech Store, Unit 2, Fagans Lane, Maynooth (☎ 01-629-1020) offers Internet access.

Chapter 14

The Southeast: Counties Wexford, Waterford, Tipperary, and Kilkenny

In This Chapter

▶ Traveling back in time at the Irish National Heritage Park
▶ Discovering the wonders of the Hook Peninsula
▶ Touring the Waterford Crystal Factory
▶ Visiting Ireland's version of The Rock (the Rock of Cashel, that is)
▶ Exploring medieval streets and buildings in Kilkenny

*W*exford, Waterford, Tipperary, and Kilkenny are among Ireland's Southeast counties, and are often referred to as the sunny Southeast because they generally enjoy more sunshine than the rest of the country. This area is not full of Ireland's greatest hits; instead, the region offers many lesser-known but just as intriguing attractions and activities — such as strolling through tiny fishing villages in Wexford, watching the famous Waterford Crystal being created in Waterford, wandering the medieval streets of Kilkenny, or exploring the Rock of Cashel in Tipperary, to name a few.

County Wexford

County Wexford is one of the unsung treasures of Ireland, offering myriad peaceful beaches, rolling hills, winding rivers, great traditional music, and, in my opinion, some of the friendliest people in all of Ireland. If you're looking for don't-miss attractions, you may find Wexford disappointing, but if you're interested in wandering along beaches and down the streets of fishing villages, chatting with locals, hearing excellent impromptu Irish music, and visiting a number of very well-done museums, such as the Irish National Heritage Park, you're in for a treat.

The Southeast

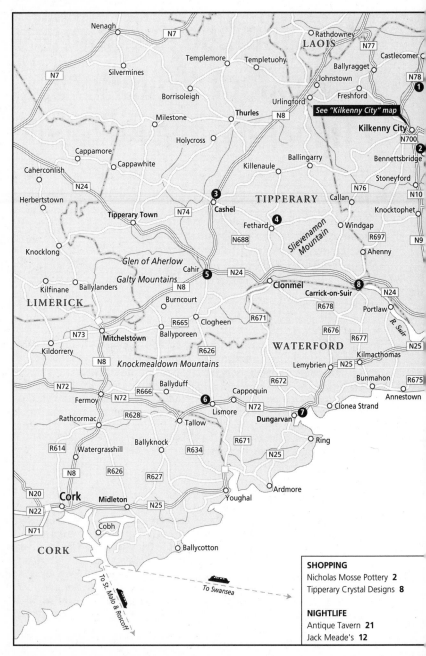

SHOPPING
Nicholas Mosse Pottery **2**
Tipperary Crystal Designs **8**

NIGHTLIFE
Antique Tavern **21**
Jack Meade's **12**

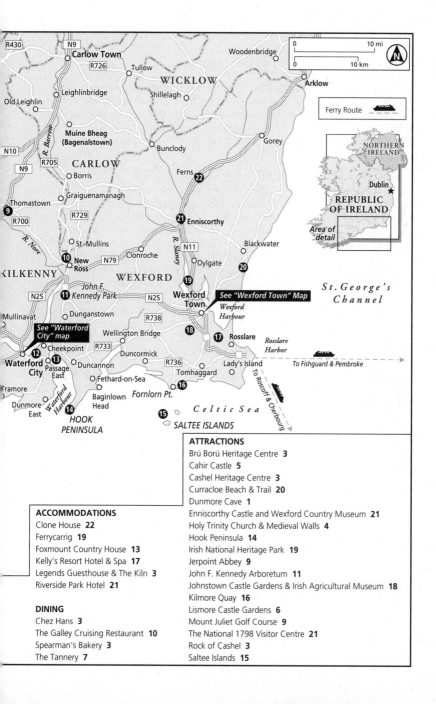

ATTRACTIONS
Brú Ború Heritage Centre **3**
Cahir Castle **5**
Cashel Heritage Centre **3**
Curracloe Beach & Trail **20**
Dunmore Cave **1**
Enniscorthy Castle and Wexford Country Museum **21**
Holy Trinity Church & Medieval Walls **4**
Hook Peninsula **14**
Irish National Heritage Park **19**
Jerpoint Abbey **9**
John F. Kennedy Arboretum **11**
Johnstown Castle Gardens & Irish Agricultural Museum **18**
Kilmore Quay **16**
Lismore Castle Gardens **6**
Mount Juliet Golf Course **9**
The National 1798 Visitor Centre **21**
Rock of Cashel **3**
Saltee Islands **15**

ACCOMMODATIONS
Clone House **22**
Ferrycarrig **19**
Foxmount Country House **13**
Kelly's Resort Hotel & Spa **17**
Legends Guesthouse & The Kiln **3**
Riverside Park Hotel **21**

DINING
Chez Hans **3**
The Galley Cruising Restaurant **10**
Spearman's Bakery **3**
The Tannery **7**

The county's largest town is Wexford Town (see the map of the same name), a sweet and pretty harbor town that attracts Ireland's yuppies for weekend trips (lots of chi-chi clothing stores stand amidst the main street's cute bakeries and pubs). Along with Enniscorthy, Wexford Town is a great base for exploring the county.

County Wexford was the heartbeat of the 1798 rebellion, when Irish rebels took a brave stand against the strong arm of the Brits, and it was at Vinegar Hill, near Enniscorthy, where 20,000 rebels were massacred by English cannons, effectively ending that rebellion. As a result, you may encounter a ferocious pride in Irish freedom in these parts.

Getting to and around County Wexford

If you're driving from Dublin, take the N11 (which becomes M11 periodically) or the N80 south to Enniscorthy and Wexford Town; from Wexford Town, take the N25 west to New Ross. Most attractions are along the route between Wexford Town and New Ross. A fast and cost-effective shortcut across Waterford Harbour between Passage East, which is about 16km (10 miles) east of Waterford City, and Ballyhack, about 32km (20 miles) southwest of Wexford Town, is provided by **Passenger East Car Ferry** (☎ 051-38-2480). The ferry runs April to September Monday through Saturday from 7 a.m. to 10 p.m., Sunday from 9:30 a.m. to 10 p.m.; October to March Monday to Saturday from 7 a.m. to 8 p.m., Sunday from 9:30 a.m. to 8 p.m. Fares are €8 ($13) one-way and €12 ($19) round-trip for a car and passengers, €1.50 ($2.40) one-way and €2 ($3.20) round-trip for walk-ons. Bicycles are permitted for €3 ($4.80) round-trip and €2 ($3.20) one-way.

The Dublin (Connolly Station)– Rosslare Harbour line of **Irish Rail** (☎ 1-850-366-222; www.irishrail.ie) has stations in Rosslare, Wexford, and Enniscorthy. **Bus Éireann** (☎ 01-836-6111; www.buseireann.ie) travels year-round to Wexford, Enniscorthy, Rosslare, New Ross, and other towns throughout the area.

Ferries connect Britain and Rosslare Harbour, which is 19km (20 miles) south of Wexford Town. **Stena Line** (☎ 01-204-7777; www.stenaline.ie) has passenger and car ferries from Fishguard, Wales, to Rosslare Harbour Ferryport. **Irish Ferries** (☎ 0818-300-400; www.irishferries.ie) has service from Pembroke, in Wales, and from Roscoff and Cherbourg, in France, to Rosslare.

Walking is the best way to get around County Wexford's towns. Even the largest town, Wexford, is easily walkable.

Spending the night in County Wexford

Clone House
$$ Enniscorthy

This 250-year-old farmhouse, set in the picturesque countryside, feels like a quiet getaway spot, so it's almost a surprise to realize that it's also close

Wexford Town

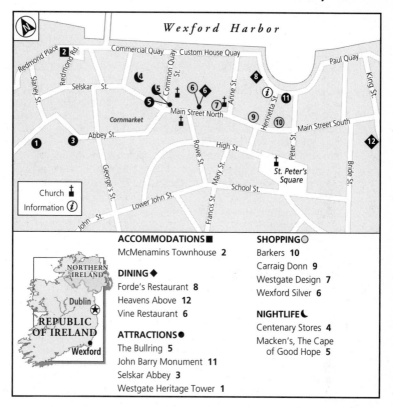

Wexford Harbor

Commercial Quay — Custom House Quay — Paul Quay

Redmond Place **2**
Redmond Rd.
Slaney St.
Selskar St.
Common Quay St.
Anne St.
King St.

6 6
5
7
8
(i) **11**
9 **10**

Main Street North
Cornmarket
Main Street South

1 **3** Abbey St.
George's St.
Rowe St.
Mary St.
High St.
Peter St.
Bride St.
12

St. Peter's Square

Francis St.
School St.

Lower John St.
John St.

Church ✝
Information (i)

NORTHERN IRELAND
Dublin ✪
REPUBLIC OF IRELAND
Wexford ●

ACCOMMODATIONS ■
McMenamins Townhouse **2**

DINING ◆
Forde's Restaurant **8**
Heavens Above **12**
Vine Restaurant **6**

ATTRACTIONS ●
The Bullring **5**
John Barry Monument **11**
Selskar Abbey **3**
Westgate Heritage Tower **1**

SHOPPING ○
Barkers **10**
Carraig Donn **9**
Westgate Design **7**
Wexford Silver **6**

NIGHTLIFE ☾
Centenary Stores **4**
Macken's, The Cape of Good Hope **5**

to golf, beaches, and area attractions. Rooms are furnished with antiques. The best things about this place are the comfy beds and Mrs. Breen, the lovely woman who runs the house. She is wonderfully knowledgeable about the area and is glad to help you decide where to go and what to see.

Ferns, off the N11 between Enniscorthy and Gorey. ☎ **053-936-6113**. *Fax: 054-66-225. Rates: €90 ($144) double. No credit cards. Closed Nov–Apr.*

Ferrycarrig
$$$–$$$$ **Ferrycarrig**

This hotel has a stunning location, perched over the River Slaney estuary. The rooms are stylish and modern, the facilities (including a health club, indoor pool, two waterside restaurants, and a terrific new spa) are unbeatable, and the staff is friendly and warm. Plus, there's not a bad view in the house.

Ferrycarrig Bridge. Take N11 from Wexford toward Enniscorthy. ☎ *053-912-0999. Fax: 053-912-0982.* www.ferrycarrighotel.ie. *Rates: €130–€245 ($208–$392) double. AE, DC, MC, V.*

Kelly's Resort Hotel & Spa
$$–$$$$ Rosslare

Situated along an 8km (5-mile) stretch of sandy beach, this family-run hotel is truly a resort accommodation. You'll be spoiled by the gorgeous spa (overlooking the beach and offering all sorts of different treatments), two pools, indoor and outdoor tennis courts, the sauna, and a gym. Be warned that you may feel more like you're in the Caribbean than the Emerald Isle as you sip cocktails on the beach. Rooms are simple, bright, and clean; the resort restaurant serves great fare; and nighttime entertainment is on offer. Rates include all three meals daily. The resort isn't far from the ferry terminal.

Take N25 about 16km (10 miles) south from Wexford Town to Rosslare. ☎ *053-913-2114. Fax: 053-913-2222.* www.kellys.ie. *Rates: €99–€245 ($158–$392) double. AE, MC, V.*

McMenamin's Townhouse
$$ Wexford Town

You'll feel at home immediately at this welcoming Victorian B&B, run by sweet and charming Kay and Seamus McMenamin, who offer what just may be Ireland's best breakfast. The good-size bedrooms are furnished eclectically, with some antiques and some modern touches. The linens are scented with lavender, and the beds are so comfortable that you'd be tempted to sleep in each morning if it weren't for the scent of Kay's gourmet breakfast wafting up the stairs. A former restaurant owner and chef, Kay treats her guests to an array of breakfast choices, from fresh-caught fish to light-as-a-cloud pancakes dusted with sugar. Sides, such as homemade marmalade made with whiskey, oranges, and brown sugar and thick, tangy homemade yogurt, accompany your breakfast. The B&B is in Wexford Town, about a five-minute walk from the bus and train station, so it's perfect for those without a car.

3 Auburn Terrace. Off Redmond Road in Wexford Town. ☎ *053-914-6442. Fax: 053-914-6442. Rates: €100 ($160) double. MC, V.*

Riverside Park Hotel
$$$ Enniscorthy

Built in 1998, the Riverside Park Hotel is situated on the banks of the River Suir. The hotel's beautiful brick-and-glass wall and round tower are difficult to miss as you're coming into or leaving town. Rooms are simple and warm, with great views. Sporty folks will be in heaven here — the hotel offers a fully-equipped gym and a swimming pool on the premises, and reduced greens fees on area courses.

The Promenade. On the N11 just outside Enniscorthy. ☎ *053-92-37800. Fax: 054-923-7900.* www.riversideparkhotel.com. *Rates: €180–€190 ($288–$304) double. AE, DC, MC, V.*

Dining locally in County Wexford

Heavens Above, located above The Sky and The Ground (see p. 226) is another superb restaurant.

Forde's Restaurant
$$$$ Wexford Town   NEW IRISH

This inventive restaurant took Wexford Town by storm, placing in the top 100 restaurants in Ireland. The quiet room looks as though it were decorated by hip royalty, with dramatic wine-colored walls, standing cast-iron candle holders, ivory candles, and mirrors. The hip/dramatic theme extends to the menu, which offers local meats and produce with interesting modern twists, such as a potato side dish folded into a spring-roll wrapper. Menu standouts include salmon wrapped in seaweed with white wine sauce, crab beignets, chicken cakes with ginger and garlic, and a steak filet with a brie fritter. Service is attentive and unobtrusive.

Crescent Quay. ☎ *053-912-3832. Main courses: €20–€29 ($32–$46). MC, V. Reservations recommended. Open: Daily 6–9:45 p.m.*

The Galley Cruising Restaurant
$$–$$$$ New Ross   IRISH

Picture this: You're cruising along a glassy river, taking in the picturesque shoreline. You wander in from the outdoor deck to sit down to a beautifully prepared five-course meal featuring fresh local produce. What could be more relaxing? Lunch and tea cruises last two hours; dinner cruises between two and three hours. You have two or three options for each course, with the emphasis on Continental favorites such as chicken stuffed with cheese and served in a white wine sauce or salmon bathed in hollandaise. Dress is casual.

New Ross Quay. West on N25 from Wexford. ☎ *051-42-1723.* www.river cruises.ie. *Cost of cruise: €25 ($40) lunch, €12 ($19) afternoon tea, €40 ($64) dinner. MC, V. Reservations required. Cruises depart June–Aug daily at 12:30 p.m. (lunch), 3 p.m. (afternoon tea), and 6:30 or 7 p.m. (dinner). Cruises may go out in Apr or May if there is enough interest. Call and ask. You can also pay just for the cruise if you don't wish to eat. Without food, prices are €12 ($19) lunch, €10 ($16) tea, and €20 ($32) dinner.*

Vine Restaurant
$$ Wexford Town   THAI

This Thai restaurant came up again and again when I asked people in Wexford about their favorite place to eat. You can chow down on all sorts of Thai specialties in a beautiful high-ceilinged room with funky décor. You can't go wrong with any of the dishes flavored with Thai herbs and spices; the duck with tamarind is particularly delicious.

109 N. Main St. ☎ 053-912-2388. €16–€22 ($26–$35). DC, MC, V. Tues–Sun 6:30–10:30 p.m.

Exploring County Wexford

John Bayley, who has a degree in local history, leads excellent one-and-a-half-hour walking tours of Wexford Town. Tours usually leave from the White's Hotel, on Abbey St., Monday through Friday at 11 a.m. (but you should call ☎ 053-912-3111 to confirm), and cost €5 ($8) adults and €3 ($4.80) seniors and students.

See also the review of the Galley Cruising Restaurant in the previous section; you can opt just to take the cruise and skip the meal.

The top attractions

Enniscorthy Castle, a Norman Castle built in the beginning of the 13th century, is closed for renovations right now but should be open in 2010 (call the Enniscorthy Tourist Information Centre for information: ☎ 053-923-4699).

Driving the Hook Peninsula

There's so much to see on this small foot of land in southwest County Wexford that it's worth spending the afternoon driving and walking parts of the lovely 201km (125-mile) Slí Charman (Wexford's Coastal Pathway). Highlights include the richly ornamented ruins of **Tintern Abbey** (☎ 051-56-2650; daily mid-June to Sept), near Saltmills, with its walled gardens, fortified bridge, and maze of ancient paths; **Ballyhack Castle** (☎ 051-38-9468; Apr–Sept), with displays on the Crusades; **Slade Castle,** an amazing fortress ruin near the **Hook Lighthouse** (☎ 051-39-7055; year-round), one of the oldest lighthouses in Europe; **Duncannon Fort** (☎ 051-38-9454; June–Sept), built to fend off attacks from the Spanish Armada; and the magnificent ruins of **Dunbrody Abbey** (3km/4 miles beyond Duncannon; May through mid-Sept). All of the sites listed here have minimal admissions fees, usually about €1.50 to €3 ($2.40–$4.80) per adult.

Tintern Abbey, Ballyhack, and Duncannon are off R733. To get to Hook Head, go south toward Fethard on R734 from New Ross. Park in Fethard, and walk the coastal path to Slade Castle, the Lighthouse, and even on to Duncannon. Suggested visit: Varies, depending on the distance you go, but give it at least 3–4 hours.

Irish National Heritage Park
Ferrycarrig

Set on 14 hectares (36 acres), this intriguing living-history park traces the region's history from its earliest Stone Age settlements through the Celtic, Viking, and Norman periods. The 16 historical sites feature re-creations of castles, boats, homes, and the landscape during each period, bringing the past off the pages of books and into three dimensions. Exhibits are hands-on, making this a great place for kids.

Off Dublin-Wexford Road (N11). A few miles west of Wexford off the N11 at Ferrycarrig. ☎ *053-912-0733. Admission: €8 ($13) adults, €6.50 ($10) students and seniors, €4.50 ($7.20) children ages 13–16, €4 ($6.40) children ages 4–12. Open: Daily 9:30 a.m.–6:30 p.m. (last admission 5 p.m.); time subject to changes in the off season. Suggested visit: About 2 hours.*

John F. Kennedy Arboretum
New Ross

Plant-lovers will enjoy meandering down self-guided trails through gardens featuring more than 4,500 species of trees and exotic shrubs from five continents.

Off Duncannon Road (R733). ☎ *051-38-8171. Admission: €2.90 ($4.60) adults, €2.10 ($3.40) seniors, €1.30 ($210) students and children. Open: May–Aug daily 10 a.m.–8 p.m., Sept and Apr daily 10 a.m.–6:30 p.m., Oct–Mar daily 10 a.m.–5 p.m. (last admission 45 minutes before closing). Suggested visit: 1½ hours.*

Johnstown Castle Gardens and
Irish Agricultural Museum
Wexford Town

The fairytale gardens here offer 20 hectares (50 acres) of trees and flowers, plus lakes, hothouses, and ornamental structures. On the grounds is a museum focusing on the important role of farming in Wexford's history, with exhibits on farm transport, dairy farming, and farmhouse furniture, and a comprehensive look at the potato and the Famine. A highlight is the exhibit depicting the typical Irish kitchen in 1800, 1900, and 1950.

Johnstown Castle Estate, Bridgetown Road, off Wexford-Rosslare Road (N25). A couple miles east of Wexford off the R733. ☎ *053-917-1200. Garden admission (only charged Apr–Oct): €6 ($9.60) per car. Museum admission: €6 ($9.60) adults, 5 ($8) seniors, €4 ($6.40) students and children. Gardens open: Daily 9 a.m.–5 p.m. Museum open: Apr–Nov Mon–Fri 9 a.m.–5 p.m., Sat and Sun 11 a.m.–5 p.m.; Dec–Mar Mon–Fri 9 a.m.–5 p.m. Suggested visit: 2 hours.*

Kilmore Quay and the Saltee Islands

This is a picture-postcard fishing village with a row of whitewashed thatched cottages. You can arrange for an angling trip (contact Dick Hayes, of Enterprise, at ☎ 053-912-9704); visit **Kehoe's Pub** (☎ 053-912-9830), the center of Kilmore Quay's social life and a museum of fascinating marine artifacts discovered on various dives; and (if the weather is right) take a trip to the **Saltee Islands,** Ireland's largest bird sanctuary. To arrange a trip around the islands, call Dick Hayes at ☎ 053-912-9704.

On R739, 22km (14 miles) south of Rosslare.

Selskar Abbey
Wexford Town

The story behind this ruined abbey is oddly romantic: Our tale begins when Alexander de la Roche left his fiancée behind to join the Crusades. Hearing that he had been killed, his fiancée became a nun. However, de la Roche was very much alive and was so grieved at the state of affairs upon his return that he joined an Augustinian order, and founded and endowed the abbey at Selskar. If only they'd had cellphones! It is said that Henry II did penance at the abbey for having Thomas à Becket beheaded. Near the abbey are the ruins of a Church of Ireland church from the 1800s. When the congregation at this church merged with a nearby congregation, the church roof was removed so that no rent would be required on the building.

Westgate Street. You are free to roam around the site when the gates are unlocked. If gates are locked, let someone at the Westgate Heritage Center know, and they will open them for you. Suggested visit: 30 minutes.

Wexford Wildfowl Reserve
Wexford Town

This national nature reserve, located in amusingly named North Slob, draws many species of ducks, swans, and other waterfowl. About 10,000 Greenland white-fronted geese call the area home during the winter. Blinds and an observation tower are set up for birders, and the reserve has a visitor center with an audiovisual show and exhibits.

North Slob just 4.8km (3 miles) east of Wexford Town. ☎ 053-912-3129. Admission: Free. Open: Daily 9 a.m.–5 p.m. Suggested visit: 1–1½ hours.

More cool things to see and do

- ✔ **The Bullring:** The first declaration of an Irish Republic was made here in 1798, and a statue memorializes the men who fought for Irish independence at that time. The name of the area comes from the bloody sport of bull-baiting that took place here in the 17th century. There is a weekly outdoor market here on Friday mornings.

  Location: Off Quay Street, Wexford Town. Suggested visit: A few minutes.

- ✔ **Curracloe Beach and a Cycling Trip:** This beach is where the opening scenes of *Saving Private Ryan* were filmed. It is home to many migratory birds and is a popular swimming destination during the summer. A nature trail leads you through the sand dunes here. From Wexford, the road up through Curracloe to Blackwater makes an excellent day-long bike trip. Visit **Hayes Cycle Shop,** 108 S. Main St. (☎ 053-912-2462), to rent a bike and get directions.

Location: The beach is 11km (7 miles) northeast of Wexford Town on the R742. Suggested visit: A couple hours to swim or a full day if you bike here.

✔ **John Barry Monument:** "Who's John Barry?" you ask. No less than the father of the American Navy! Barry bravely went to the colonies and signed up for the Revolutionary War to fight against the British. He was captain of the famous ship the *Lexington* and, in 1797, was appointed by George Washington as commander-in-chief of the brand-spanking-new U.S. Navy.

Location: Crescent Quay, Wexford Town. Suggested visit: Enough time to give him a salute and snap a photo.

✔ **The National 1798 Visitor Centre:** The story of the United Irishmen's first rebellion against the British is told in multimedia pomp at this small but interesting museum. The museum engages visitors with objects, an audiovisual presentation, and interactive computer programs. If it's nice outside, this is a great place for a picnic.

Location: Mill Park Road, Enniscorthy. ☎ 053-923-7596. www.iol.ie/~98com. On the N30 and N11 next to Vinegar Hill. Admission: €6 ($9.60) adults, €3.50 ($5.60) students, seniors, and children. Open: April through September Monday through Friday from 9:30 a.m. to 5 p.m., Saturday and Sunday from 1 to 5 p.m.; October through March Monday through Friday 9:30 a.m. to 4 p.m. Suggested visit: One hour.

✔ **Westgate Heritage Tower:** Before exploring Wexford Town, you may want to stop by this heritage center, housed in one of the five original gate towers along the Viking city walls. A well-done film, *In Selskar's Shadow,* relates the rich history of Wexford Town, and a gallery on the first floor sells beautiful handcrafted gifts made by Wexford artisans. Craftspeople work in the tower, and you may be able to visit their workshops.

Location: Westgate Street, Wexford Town. ☎ 053-914-6506. Ticket to film: €3 ($3.60) adults, €1.50 ($1.80) students. Opening hours change from week to week, so call for current information. Suggested visit: 45 minutes.

Shopping in County Wexford

Barkers, 36–40 S. Main St., Wexford Town (☎ 053-912-3159), sells Waterford Crystal, china, and local and international crafts. Far from the Aran Islands, **Carraig Donn,** 3 S. Main St., Wexford Town (☎ 053-912-3651), nonetheless specializes in authentic Aran knitwear — sweaters mostly, but also accessories such as scarves and hats. **Westgate Design,** 22 N. Main St., Wexford Town (☎ 053-912-3787), offers a large selection of Irish crafts, from wool clothing to pottery to jewelry. A family of silver- and goldsmiths run **Wexford Silver,** 115 N. Main St., Wexford Town (☎ 053-912-1933), which sells finely crafted pieces that make perfect gifts or keepsakes. Also see Westgate Heritage Tower, in the previous section.

Hitting the pubs in County Wexford

Antique Tavern
Enniscorthy

A black-and-white Tudor-style exterior makes this place easy to find. Inside, the dark and cozy pub is full of antiques (hence the name). Check out the famous memorabilia that lines the walls, from weapons used during the 1798 Rebellion to farm equipment. Try for a spot on the outdoor balcony when the weather's pleasant.

14 Slaney St. ☎ *053-923-3428.*

Centenary Stores
Wexford Town

This Victorian-style pub serves excellent bar food and hosts entertainment almost every evening.

Charlotte St. (between Main St. and the Quay). ☎ *053-912 4424.*

Macken's, The Cape of Good Hope
Wexford Town

As you venture into Wexford's famous Bullring area, you're sure to do a double-take when you see Macken's: The awning over the entrance advertises a bar, undertaker, and grocery. And it's no joke — you can have a pint, pick up a loaf of bread, and make funeral arrangements in one convenient stop! Irish rebels made Macken's a popular meeting place over the centuries, and mementos from their struggles line the walls. Definitely a place like no other.

The Bullring. ☎ *053-912-2949.*

The Sky and the Ground
Wexford Town

This simply decorated, homey pub, which was the winner of Les Routiers' Traditional Irish Music Pub of the Year award in 2003, is the hot spot for Wexford's traditional music scene. Take a seat, nurse a pint, listen to great trad, and chat with the locals — you'll feel like you were born and raised in Wexford.

112 S. Main St. ☎ *053-912-1273.*

Fast Facts: County Wexford

Area Codes

County Wexford's area codes (or city codes) are **051, 053, 054,** and **055.**

Emergencies/Police

Dial ☎ **999** for all emergencies.

Genealogical Resources

Contact the Genealogy Centre, Yola Farmstead, Tagoat, County Wexford (☎ 053-923-2610; http://homepage. eircom.net/~yolawexford).

Hospital

Wexford General Hospital is on New Town Road, Wexford (☎ 053-914-2233).

Information

For visitor information, go to the tourist office at Crescent Quay, Wexford (☎ 053-912-3111; open year-round). It can also provide reservation services. Seasonal offices (open Apr–Sept) are in Enniscorthy, at the Castle Museum (☎ 054-923-4699), and Rosslare, at the Harbour Terminal Building (☎ 053-913-3232). Another great source is the Web site www.wexford tourism.com.

Post Office

The main post office is on Anne Street, Wexford (☎ 053-912-2587).

Visiting County Waterford and Waterford City

Waterford City is the oldest town in Ireland, founded by Viking invaders in the ninth century. It's a cute town to explore, but aside from the Waterford Treasures museum and the historic area surrounding Reginald's Tower, there isn't a whole lot to see in the city (the Waterford Crystal Factory is outside the city).

The main reasons to come to this county are to take the superb tour of the Waterford Crystal Factory and to ramble around the county's lovely coastal villages and ethereal inland mountains.

Getting to and around Waterford City

If you're driving, take N25 from Cork and the south, N24 from the west, N19 from Kilkenny and points north, the N11 to the N30 to the N25 from Dublin, or N25 from Wexford. Lismore is off the N72. A fast and cost-effective route across Waterford Harbour, between Passage East, County Waterford (16km/10 miles east of Waterford), and Ballyhack, County Wexford (32km/20 miles west of Wexford), is provided by **Passenger East Car Ferry** (☎ 051-38-2480). See "Getting to and around County Wexford," near the beginning of this chapter, for more details.

Irish Rail (☎ 1-850-366-222; www.irishrail.ie) serves Waterford at Plunkett Station, next to the Ignatius Rice Bridge. **Bus Éireann** (☎ 01-836-6111; www.buseireann.ie) travels year-round to Waterford, Lismore, and other major towns in County Waterford. In Waterford City, buses arrive at Plunkett Station, next to the Ignatius Rice Bridge.

Waterford City

Waterford is an easily walkable city. Stroll up the Quays toward Reginald's Tower, take a right, and you're in the heart of town. You need a car to get out to the Waterford Crystal Factory, though, unless you take a taxi; you can catch at Plunkett Station on the Quay (call **Rapid Cabs** at ☎ **051-85-8585** if you need one to pick you up). The fare should be around €10 ($16). If you're parking your car here, buy parking disks at local shops near the block you're parking on or at the tourist office. Hotels in the city center generally have their own parking areas.

Spending the night in County Waterford

Days Hotel Waterford
$$ **Waterford City**

This large hotel overlooking the River Suir is one of the oldest in Waterford, but it has been updated to provide every modern comfort. It's run like a tight ship by the Treacy family but has a friendly, jovial atmosphere. Bedrooms are spacious and bright, and two in-house restaurants are reliable places to get a good meal.

1 The Quay. Take The Quay to the foot of the Ignatius Rice Bridge. ☎ *051-87-7222. Fax: 051-87-7229.* www.dayshotelwaterford.com. *Rates: €89–€149 ($142–$238) double. AE, DC, MC, V.*

Dooley's Hotel
$$$ Waterford City

This family-run hotel offers bright, generic hotel rooms right in the center of Waterford City. Service is top-notch. The hotel's pub serves tasty, budget-friendly meals, and the Continental cuisine at the hotel's New Ship restaurant is filling and well-prepared.

The Quay, near the clock tower. ☎ *051-87-3531. Fax: 051-87-0262.* www.dooleys-hotel.ie. *Rates: €110–€160 ($176–$256) double. AE, DC, MC, V.*

Foxmount Country House
$$ Passage East

This 17th-century B&B is only 15 minutes away from Waterford City, but you'll feel as though you're in the middle of nowhere — in a good way. The imposing ivy-covered house sits on a large stretch of stunningly landscaped grounds with grand trees, flowers, and a paddock where four horses and a donkey reside. The house is located on a working dairy farm, so you may catch a glimpse of a herd of cows. Want to relax? Head out to the peaceful herb garden at the back of the house. Looking to stretch your legs? Ramble down one of the dirt roads, past emerald pastures. Rooms have beautiful views and are spacious and elegantly furnished with antiques, and the large bathrooms feature comfortable tubs. Cordial hostess Margaret Kent serves a bang-up breakfast; I especially enjoyed the porridge with honey, brown sugar, and exceptionally fresh cream, and the tasty scrambled eggs. Head down the road for a pint at Jack Meade's pub (reviewed in "Hitting the pubs in County Waterford," later in this section), which looks as if it was transplanted from Middle Earth.

Passage East Road. Take Dunmore East Road from Waterford City for 6km (3½ miles) until you reach a fork where you see a garage. Take the left fork toward Passage East, and keep right at the next junction. Turn right just before Jack Meade's pub, beside the bridge. ☎ *051-87-4308. Fax: 051-87-4906.* www.foxmountcountry house.com. *Rates: €130 ($208) double. No credit cards.*

Waterford Castle Hotel & Golf Club
$$$$ Balinakill

Staying in this castle is like living a fairytale. Located on a private island in the River Suir (accessible only by the castle's car ferry), only 3.2km (2 miles) from Waterford City, the Norman castle and its Elizabethan-style wings are filled with tapestries, large stone fireplaces, antiques, and oak-paneled walls. All of the richly decorated rooms have stunning views. The staff is warm and friendly, and golf lovers will appreciate having a course right in their backyard.

The Island. ☎ *051-87-8203. Fax: 051-87-9316.* www.waterfordcastle.com. *Rates: €335–€380 ($536–$608) double. AE, MC, V.*

Dining locally in County Waterford

In addition to the places I list in this section, you can combine your dinner with a river cruise aboard The **Galley Cruising Restaurant.** Although you catch the boat on the River Barrow in New Ross, County Wexford (see the review in "Dining locally in County Wexford," earlier in this chapter), the trip takes you down to the River Suir and through County Waterford.

Bodega
$$ Waterford City   NEW IRISH

A Spanish wine bar vibe defines this new Waterford restaurant, which is decorated with patio stone, warm amber lighting, built-in wooden wine racks, and strings of lanterns and Christmas lights. The sounds of jazz and Latin music are just audible against the buzz of laughter and clinking glasses. The menu focuses on casual New Irish cuisine, including the excellent lamb burger with mint crème fraiche, the superb mussels with french fries, and the succulent duck served with berries and red wine sauce. The raspberry sabayon, with crushed berries, mascarpone cheese, raspberry sorbet, and crunchy anisette cookies, has to be one of the best desserts in Ireland.

54 John St. ☎ *051-844-177. Main courses: €16–€27 ($26–$43). AE, MC, V. Open: Mon–Wed noon to 5 p.m. and 5:30–10 p.m., Thurs–Sat noon to 5 p.m. and 5:30–10:30 p.m.*

Café Goa
$$ Waterford City   INDIAN

This is a great place to people-watch in Waterford, with a cross-section of the city, from families to club-going friends, passing through. The look here is casual, with abstract paintings in red, black, and gold, and bistro tables and chairs. The restaurant does a top-notch job with the Indian classics, from a mild but delicious tikka masala to the toothsome aloo gobi (a chick pea and potato dish) to the outstanding shrimp bhuna, with tomato, garlic, ginger, and spices.

36 The Quay. ☎ *051-304-970. Main courses: €13–€21 ($21–$34). MC, V. Open: Daily 5–11 p.m.*

Jade Palace
$$–$$$$ **Waterford City   CHINESE**

Jade Palace offers authentic, mouthwatering Cantonese and Szechuan in downtown Waterford. This is the kind of place where you tell the manager what you think you'd like, let him decide for you, and then stuff yourself silly. The steamed fish with ginger is excellent, and the early-bird menu, served from 5 to 7 p.m. every night (€17/$20), is quite a bargain. If you are not ravenously hungry, you may want to get some pub food downstairs.

3 The Mall, next to Reginald's Tower in the city center. ☎ *051-85-5611. Main courses: €13–€28 ($21–$45). AE, MC, V. Open: Mon–Fri 12:30–2:30 p.m. and 5–11 p.m., Sat 5–11:30 p.m., Sun 12:30–10:30 p.m.*

The Tannery
$$$–$$$$ **Dungarvan   NEW EUROPEAN**

This stylish, contemporary restaurant was an operating tannery until 1995. The kitchen is wide open so that patrons can watch innovative chef Paul Flynn in action. Flynn adds unique twists to whatever dish he's cooking, such as roast rump of lamb with spiced carrot, tomato, and chickpea risotto or hot smoked duck served with spiced lentil sauce, chili, pineapple, and buttered cabbage. The interior is minimalist — white dishes on unadorned light-wood tables. The early-bird dinner (€30/$32), served Tuesday through Friday from 6 to 7:30 p.m., is a great deal.

10 Quay St. From Waterford or Cork, take the N25 to Dungarvan. ☎ *058-45-420. www.tannery.ie. Main courses: €23–€30 ($37–$48). AE, DC, MC, V. Open: Tues–Thurs and Sat 6–9:30 p.m., Fri 12:30–2:30 p.m. and 6–9:30 p.m., Sun 12:30–3 p.m. and (July and Aug only) 6:30–9 p.m.*

Exploring County Waterford: The top attractions

Waterford Tourist Services' award-winning **Walking Tours of Historic Waterford** (☎ 051-87-3711) leave year-round daily from the Waterford Treasures Museum at 11:45 a.m. and 1:45 p.m. and from the Granville Hotel, on Meagher Quay, at noon and 2 p.m. Cost is €7 ($11).

For self-guided hikes and walks, visit Waterford City's tourist office (see "Fast Facts: County Waterford," at the end of this section) to pick up route maps.

Lismore Castle Gardens
Lismore

The two gardens here (upper and lower) are wonderfully varied, with riotously bright blossoms, apple trees, and a kaleidoscope of roses, all set against the backdrop of a still-occupied 12th-century castle. Because this

---

By Hook or by Crooke

Waterford is the only city in Ireland that was spared Oliver Cromwell's brutal and bloody 1649 attack, though not through lack of effort. He attempted to invade Waterford from two routes, through Hook Head and Crooke Village — neither of which is a direct or easy way to enter Waterford. Both attempts failed. This event was the genesis of the phrase "by hook or by crook" — when one resorts to unconventional and extreme tactics to get something done.

---

is an inhabited castle, you can't tour the inside (however, if you've come into some money, you can stay in the castle when the duke is not in residence). The magical yew tree walk in the lower garden is where Edmund Spenser is said to have written the *Faerie Queen*. Be sure to budget enough time to see the upper garden, which is bigger than the lower garden and boasts a thriving vegetable plot. This is a lovely place for a picnic.

Lismore. ☎ *058-54-424. Admission: €6 ($7.20) adults, €3 ($3.60) kids 16 and under. Open: Apr–May and Sept–Oct daily 1:45–4:45 p.m., and St Patrick's Day–September 30 11 a.m.–4:45 p.m. Suggested visit: 1½ hours.*

Reginald's Tower
Waterford City

Restored to its medieval appearance and furnished with appropriate medieval artifacts, this small but significant landmark in the heart of Waterford City is worth the three-story climb to the top. The tower was built by a Viking governor in 1003 and is Ireland's oldest standing building in continuous use. It has been used in many different capacities — as a mint, a fortress, a prison, and an air-raid shelter. It is said that Norman leader Strongbow married Celtic Aoife (Eva) here, beginning a bond between the Norman invaders and the native Irish. Guided tours are available on request.

The Quay. ☎ *051-30-4220. Admission: €2.10 ($3.40) adults, €1.30 ($2.10) seniors, €1.10 ($1.80) students and children. Open: Easter–May and Oct 10 a.m.–5 p.m., June–Sept 10 a.m.–6 p.m., Nov–Easter Wed–Sun 10 a.m.–5 p.m. Suggested visit: 1 hour.*

South East Coastal Drive

This well-marked drive takes you along the coast through the beautiful seaside towns of Tramore, Dunmore, and Passage East. Along the way, you encounter meandering rivers and tiny fishing villages. If you'd like to bike this route, rent a bike from May to September from **Altitudes Bike Store,**

Ballybricken Green, Waterford (☎ **051-87-0356**). The route, about 80km (50 miles), begins as you cross the bridge from Youghal on the N25 and ends in Tramore.

The end points of the route are Youghal and Tramore. Out of Youghal, take the N25; out of Tramore, take the R675.

The Vee Drive

This winding 18km (11-mile) drive leads you through the lush Knockmealdown Mountains up to a stunning viewpoint of the farmland laid out like a quilt below and the glowing Galtee Mountains beckoning in the distance. The Vee Gap viewpoint, at the highest point of the drive, opens onto a variety of walking trails. Look for the parking lot and a sign mapping out the trails.

The endpoints of the signposted Vee drive are Lismore and Clogheen. From Lismore, take the R668 or the R669 (hook up to the R669 via the N72). From Clogheen, take the R668.

Waterford Crystal Factory
Kilbarry

What makes crystal shine brighter than regular glass? It's a lead oxite called *litharge*. You'll be able to spout off this fact and many more after a fascinating tour of the Waterford Crystal Factory, where you can watch the factory's craftspeople as they go about their daily work. You'll be shown every step of the meticulous process that goes into the creation of world-renowned Waterford Crystal, from the blowing of the molten glass to the engraving, which is done using a rotating copper wheel. You also get the opportunity to ask questions and get up close to the action as a master craftsperson cuts or engraves a piece. Talk about a stressful job: The Waterford Crystal Factory has a six-step screening process for every piece that's made, and the glass blowers and craftspeople get paid only for perfect pieces. About 45 percent of pieces are destroyed for minor flaws, and only perfect pieces of crystal make it out of the factory, which is why you'll never see Waterford seconds. Along the tour, you have a chance to see some unique crystal pieces, including hefty sports trophies. Don't leave your camera in the car: you are welcome to take pictures on the tour. After the tour, stop in the Waterford Crystal Gallery to stock up; pieces cost about the same here as they do in most stores, so the main attraction is the vast selection.

From Waterford, take the main road to Cork (N25); the factory is 8km (5 miles) outside town on the right. ☎ 051-33-2500. Tours: €10 ($16) adults, €7.50 ($12) seniors, €7 ($11) students, free for kids under 12. Open: Mar–Oct tours daily 8:30 a.m.–4 p.m., showroom daily 8:30 a.m.–6 p.m.; Nov–Feb tours Mon–Fri 9 a.m.–3:15 p.m., showroom daily 9 a.m.–5 p.m. Suggested visit: 2 hours.

Waterford Treasures Museum
Waterford City

This exceedingly well-done museum, housed in a gorgeously restored granary, presents artifacts that illustrate the history of Waterford from the arrival of the Vikings almost 1,000 years ago up to the present. High-tech interactive audiovisuals, including a ride on a Viking ship, are engaging and entertaining, and the objects here are true treasures, from the sword of King Edward IV to a variety of crystal items.

Merchant's Quay. ☎ *051-30-4500. Admission: €4 ($6.40) adults, €3 ($4.80) seniors and students, €2 ($3.20) children 5–16, free for children under 5. Open: June–Aug daily 9:30 a.m.–9 p.m., Apr–May and Sept daily 9:30 a.m.–6 p.m., Oct–Mar daily 10 a.m.–5 p.m. Suggested visit: 2–3 hours.*

Shopping in Waterford City

In addition to the choices listed here, you may want to pay a visit to the **Waterford Crystal Factory** store (reviewed in the previous section). At 150 years old, **Kelly's,** 75–76 The Quay, Waterford City (☎ **051-87-3557**), is one of the oldest businesses in town, selling crafts, linens, Aran sweaters, Waterford Crystal, and Belleek pottery.

Hitting the pubs in County Waterford

Jack Meade's
Ballycanavan

This cozy, low-ceilinged pub with crackling fireplaces is located under a stone bridge a few miles out of town and is well worth the drive. Locals tell stories in the bar, and the pub serves great food. During the summer, point yourself in the direction of the banner reading "BBQ," where you'll find excellent steaks, garlicky mushrooms, and other treats, all cheerfully served at picnic tables.

Checkpoint Road, Halfway House. ☎ *051-85-0950.*

The Munster Bar
Waterford City

The Munster (also known as Fitzgerald's) is superbly decorated with Waterford Crystal, antique mirrors, and wood walls taken from the old Waterford toll bridge. This place is a favorite with Waterford locals.

Bailey's New Street. ☎ *051-87-4656.*

T. & H. Doolan's
Waterford City

The oldest tavern in Waterford, Doolan's has long been considered one of the best establishments in the area. The black-and-white 18th-century pub opens onto a pedestrian street in the center of town and has excellent traditional music sessions most nights, plus warm fires, delicious pub grub, warm welcomes, and a cheerful crowd. Oh, and the stout is perfect as well. What does the T. & H. stand for? That's for you to find out.

32 George's St. ☎ *051-84-1504.*

Fast Facts: County Waterford

Area Codes

County Waterford's area codes (or city codes) are **051, 052,** and **058.**

Emergencies/Police

Dial ☎ **999** for all emergencies.

Genealogical Resources

Contact the Waterford Heritage Genealogical Centre, Jenkins Lane (St. Patrick's Church), Waterford (☎ 051-87-6123).

Hospital

Waterford Regional Hospital is on Dunmore Road, Waterford (☎ 051-848-000).

Information

For visitor information, go to the tourist office at 41 The Quay (☎ 051-87-5788), open Monday to Saturday from August through May, and daily July and August.

Internet Access

Voyager Internet Cafe, 85 The Quay (☎ 051-84-3843), has Internet access and printing capabilities.

Post Office

The main post office is at 100 The Quay, Waterford City (☎ 051-317-312).

Roaming in County Tipperary

County Tipperary and its towns are certainly not bustling in any way whatsoever, but that's what makes this place so special: It's the fantasy of a quiet, rolling, green Ireland come true. Because there are a limited number of attractions, one or two days should suffice here, unless you're looking for a long getaway retreat.

Quite a long way to Tipperary

While you're moseying around and hitting the pubs, you're likely to hear the song "It's a Long Way to Tipperary," a happy yet plaintive tune about an Irishman in England missing his home. The song was actually composed by Englishman Jack Judge — a man who'd never been to Ireland in his life! He chose the town's name for his song simply because it rhymed well. The song is perhaps best known by Americans as the tune that the cast of *The Mary Tyler Moore Show* sang as they left the station for the last time.

Getting to and around County Tipperary

If you're coming by car, take the N8 from Cork or Dublin (via N7) to Cashel and Cahir. Take the N24 from Limerick or Waterford to Tipperary and Cahir. **Irish Rail** (☎ 1850-366-222; www.irishrail.ie) serves Tipperary, Cahir, and Carrick-on-Suir; and **Bus Éireann** (☎ 01-836-6111; www.buseireann.ie) travels year-round to Tipperary, Cahir, Cashel, and Carrick-on-Suir, as well as other major towns in County Tipperary.

Spending the night in County Tipperary

Legends Guesthouse and the Kiln
$$ **Cashel**

This small, comfortable guesthouse looks out onto the Rock of Cashel and offers simple, good-size rooms and bathrooms. Your hosts, John and Grazielle Quinlan, are welcoming and can help you plan your days in the area. The real draw, though, is the restaurant, the Kiln, which serves modern European dishes that sparkle with flavor. After dinner, you can waddle upstairs to your bedroom.

Near the junction of R660 and the N8, traveling in the direction of Holycross. ☎ *062-61292.* www.legendsguesthouse.com. *Rates: €70–€128 ($112–$204). AE, MC, V.*

Dining locally in County Tipperary

Also see Legends Guesthouse and the Kiln, in the previous section.

Chez Hans
$$$$ **Cashel FRENCH**

This is French cuisine at its finest, and it is served in a gorgeous Gothic structure that began life as a chapel. From the black-and-white uniformed waitstaff to the artistic presentation of the dishes, everything is professional and elegant. The portions are generous, and the famous Cashel blue cheese finds its way into many dishes. All the dishes are top-notch, especially the seafood offerings, such as seafood cassoulet and fresh mussels in a chive sauce.

Moore Lane. (Just look for the giant rock; the restaurant is located below it.) ☎ *062-61-177. Reservations required. Main courses: €30–€40 ($48–$64). MC, V. Open: Tues–Sat 6–9:30 p.m. (closed for 2 weeks in Jan).*

Spearman's Bakery
$$ **Cashel CAFE**

If everyone could drop into Spearman's once in a while for a pot of tea and a slice of cake, we might come that much closer to world peace. The décor here is simple, but who's focusing on the tablecloths when there are such wonderful homemade sandwiches, paninis, and pastries to focus on? I especially recommend the light-as-air pavlova.

97 Main St. ☎ *061-61-143. Main courses: €4–€8 ($6.40–$13). Open: Mon–Fri 9–5:45 p.m., Sat 9 a.m.–5 p.m.*

Exploring County Tipperary: The top attractions

The **Cashel Heritage Centre** (☎ 062-62-511) has a model of the city of Cashel in 1640, accompanied by an audio tape describing what you are seeing. Entrance is free and the center is open June through September daily 9:30 a.m. to 5:30 p.m., and October through May Monday to Saturday 9:30 a.m. to 5:30 p.m.

The Rock of Cashel
Cashel

The word "rock" doesn't really do justice to this giant limestone outcropping crowned with spectacular medieval ruins.

The Rock of Cashel was the seat of the kings of Munster from about A.D. 360 to 1101 and was probably also a center of Druidic worship at this time. Legend places St. Patrick in Cashel in about A.D. 432 for his famous explanation of the Holy Trinity. He is said to have shown the pagans a shamrock to illustrate the relationship of the Father, Son, and Holy Ghost. Legend also has it that this is the place where St. Patrick converted the local king, King Aenghus, and baptized him. In the 11th century, Ireland's most important high king, Brian Boru, was crowned king of Ireland here (which explains the presence of the Brú Ború Heritage Centre nearby — see the next listing).

At the summit of the rock, you can explore the shell of the 13th-century St. Patrick's Cathedral, which was gutted in a fire set by Cromwell's troops. You can also visit the 28m-high (92-ft.) round tower, which is well-preserved. Don't miss the Romanesque Cormacs Chapel, located on a dramatic outcrop, which is decorated with carved beasts and human figures. The unique St. Patrick's Cross (a replica — the original is in the museum) has the carved figure of St. Patrick on one side and Jesus on the other. The roofless cathedral is the largest building on the Rock; it was never restored after Cromwell's men set fire to it (along with the villagers hiding inside). An interpretive center, housed in the beautifully restored Vicar's Choral, has great views for photos, contains stone carvings and silver religious artifacts, and offers a 15-minute audiovisual display. I highly recommend joining one of the tours, which really helps you to envision the life of the buildings.

Take N8 from Dublin or N74 east from Tipperary to Cashel. ☎ *062-61-437. Admission: €5.30 ($8.50) adults, €3.70 ($5.90) seniors, €2.10 ($3.40) children and students. Open: Mid-Mar to early June and mid-Sept to mid-Oct daily 9 a.m.–5:30 p.m.; early June to mid-Sept daily 9 a.m.–7 p.m.; mid-Oct to mid-Mar 9 a.m.–4:30 p.m. Suggested visit: 1½ hours.*

Brú Ború Heritage Centre & Theatre
Cashel

Located next to the Rock of Cashel, the Heritage Centre's central attraction is its theater, which resonates with the sounds of well-played traditional Irish music on most nights. An exhibit relates the intriguing history of Irish music (the connection between this place and Brian Ború is that Ború was a harper). In addition to the theater and exhibit (€5/$8 adults, €3/$4.80 children under 12) there is a restaurant and a comprehensive computerized genealogical research center. If you come for the music, you may also want to book for the well-done four-course dinner (prices listed below).

Take N8 from Dublin or N74 east from Tipperary to the Rock of Cashel. ☎ *062-61-122. Admission: Free to center; evening performances €20 ($22) adults, €10 ($16) kids under 12; performances with dinner €50 ($80) adults, €25 ($40) kids under 12. Open: Mid-June to Aug Mon–Sat 9 a.m.–11:30 p.m., shows Tues–Sat at 9 p.m.; Sept to mid-June Mon–Fri 9 a.m.–5 p.m. Suggested visit: 30 minutes if you're not seeing a show, a few hours if you are.*

Cahir Castle
Cahir

This was a defensive castle from the 13th to 15th centuries and is one of Ireland's largest and best preserved castles. It sits on an island in the middle of the River Suir. The walls and towers are in excellent condition, and the interior is fully restored. The 20-minute audiovisual presentation is interesting and covers the history of the castle and of the region's other historic sites. Engaging guided tours of the castle grounds are available (the tour does not enter the castle, so be sure to see the inside of the castle either before or after your tour). Attention, movie buffs: The castle was used as the set for John Boorman's film *Excalibur*.

Off the N8 from Cashel or Cork or the N24 from Tipperary. ☎ *052-41-011. Admission: €2.90 ($4.60) adults, €2.10 ($3.40) seniors, €1.30 ($2.10) students and children. Open: Mid-Mar to mid-June and mid-Sept to mid-Oct daily 9:30 a.m.–5:30 p.m.; mid-June to mid-Sept daily 9 a.m.–7:30 p.m.; mid-Oct to mid-Mar daily 9:30 a.m.–4:30 p.m. (last admission 45 minutes before closing). Suggested visit: 1 hour.*

Holy Trinity Church and Medieval Walls
Fethard

Sitting along the River Clashawley, the small town of Fethard (population: under 1,000) claims the most complete circuit of medieval town walls in Ireland. Enter the walled inner city at the cast-iron gateway on Abbey Street, which opens into the pretty churchyard of Holy Trinity. The views of the heather-strewn valley are best from the top of one of the towers, and the castlelike church itself is a fine example of medieval construction.

Take the small road connecting Cashel and Windgap east from Cashel, or go north off the N24 to Fethard. No telephone. Admission: Free. Open: No official hours, but the

Abbey Street gate of the town wall is often locked. During normal business hours, you can get a key from Whytes grocery store, just a few doors down on Main Street. And, if the church is closed and you want to enter, you can get a key from Dr. Stoke's office at the eastern end of Main Street. Suggested visit: 1 hour.

Shopping in County Tipperary

A band of rebel craftsmen left Waterford Crystal in 1988 to start **Tipperary Crystal Designs,** Carrick-on-Suir (☎ **051-64-0543**), where they produce top-quality items, just as they did under their former label. These folks are so good that they're the only Irish crystal producer to supply prestigious Tiffany & Co. The shop is located off N24, next to the Dovehill Castle.

Fast Facts: County Tipperary

Area Codes

County Tipperary's area codes (or city codes) are **051, 052, 062,** and **067.**

Emergencies/Police

Dial ☎ **999** for all emergencies.

Genealogy Resources

Contact the Brú Ború Heritage Centre, Rock of Cashel (☎ 062-61-122; fax: 062-62-700),

or the Tipperary Family History Research Centre, Excel Heritage Centre, Mitchell Street, Tipperary Town (☎ 062-80-555).

Information

A Tourist Office is open year-round at Cashel Heritage Centre, on Main Street (☎ 062-62-511).

County Kilkenny

Polish up your old armor and rev up your trusty steed; Kilkenny City in County Kilkenny is one of the best-preserved medieval towns in Ireland, anchored by the majestic 12th-century Kilkenny Castle. The compact city (see the "Kilkenny City" map) overflows with tourists during the high season, but you can always get a breath of fresh air in the Kilkenny countryside. Save some space in your luggage, because Kilkenny County is one of the craft capitals of Ireland, with stores selling everything from one-of-a-kind gold bracelets to richly colored pottery.

Getting to County Kilkenny

By car, take the N9 or N78 south from Dublin and points north and east; the N9/N10 north from Waterford or Wexford; the N8 and N76 from Cork and the southwest; and the N7 or N77 from Limerick and the west. **Irish Rail** (☎ **1-850-366-222;** www.irishrail.ie) serves Kilkenny City and Thomastown. **Bus Éireann** (☎ **01-836-6111;** www.buseireann.ie) travels year-round to Kilkenny City and other towns in County Kilkenny.

Kilkenny City

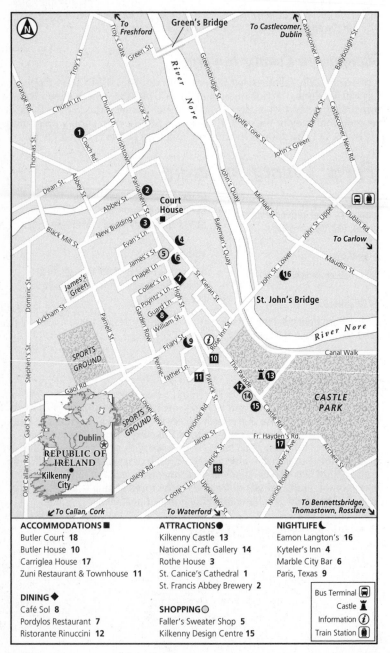

ACCOMMODATIONS ■
Butler Court **18**
Butler House **10**
Carriglea House **17**
Zuni Restaurant & Townhouse **11**

DINING ◆
Café Sol **8**
Pordylos Restaurant **7**
Ristorante Rinuccini **12**

ATTRACTIONS ●
Kilkenny Castle **13**
National Craft Gallery **14**
Rothe House **3**
St. Canice's Cathedral **1**
St. Francis Abbey Brewery **2**

SHOPPING ○
Faller's Sweater Shop **5**
Kilkenny Design Centre **15**

NIGHTLIFE ☾
Eamon Langton's **16**
Kyteler's Inn **4**
Marble City Bar **6**
Paris, Texas **9**

Bus Terminal 🚌
Castle ♜
Information ⓘ
Train Station 🚉

Bus Éireann (☎ 01-836-6111; www.buseireann.ie) also has a tour bus out of Dublin covering Kilkenny City and the Nore Valley. It leaves Busaras, on Store Street (off O'Connell St.) at 9:30 a.m. and returns at 7 p.m. on Fridays from mid-June through mid-September.

Spending the night in County Kilkenny

Butler Court
$$ Kilkenny City

I have a whole stack of accolades for Yvonne and John Dalton, who are hailed as some of the most helpful and genial hosts in Ireland. The Daltons can help you plan your itinerary in Kilkenny City (the center of the medieval town is a ten-minute walk away from the guesthouse) and the surrounding area. Rooms are modern, comfortable, and cheerful, and the continental breakfast (which you'll find in the room) makes a nice break from the usual Irish fry-up.

Patrick Street. ☎ **056-77-61-178.** *Fax: 056-77-90-767. Rates: €130 ($208) double (rates can be lower in the off season). MC, V.*

Carriglea House
$ Kilkenny City

This B&B has everything: It's a 5-minute walk from Kilkenny Castle and the center of town, has one of the nicest and most helpful proprietors this side of the Atlantic, and is a beautiful house. Bedrooms are comfortable, airy, and homey, and furnished with antiques. Owner Josephine O'Reilly greets you with tea and cookies in the lovely sitting room. The breakfast is one to write home about, with the usual offerings, plus homemade scones, omelets, and pancakes with maple syrup.

1 Archers Ave. ☎ **056-776-1629.** www.iol.ie/~archers. *Rates: €66–€75 ($106–$120). Closed Nov–Feb.*

Butler House
$$$ Kilkenny City

Not many places could pull off modern abstract artwork alongside Georgian-era designs on plastered ceilings, but ivy-covered Butler House does it with style. Built in the 1770s as part of the Kilkenny Castle Estate, Butler House effortlessly blends the traditional elements of the building with contemporary design. Rooms are spacious, soothing, and airy; each is decorated uniquely, and many feature cream and deep orange colors. Bathrooms are sparkling and up-to-date. Try to book a room overlooking the formal courtyard gardens, with a view of the castle, which is lit up at night. The thoughtful and friendly staff will happily recommend an area restaurant or attraction to suit you. The excellent location puts you right next to the castle and Kilkenny Design Centre, and a short walk from most other Kilkenny City attractions.

16 St. Patrick St. ☎ *056-77-65-707. Fax: 056-77-65-626.* www.butler.ie. *Rates: €120–€225 ($192–$360) double. AE, DC, MC, V.*

Zuni Restaurant & Townhouse
$$–$$$ Kilkenny

If you're overdosed on ornate, cluttered Victorian bedrooms, rush yourself to Zuni for an antidote of clean, Asian-inspired minimalist décor. The 13 guest rooms here are simply furnished in black, white, and deep red, with beds that make you want to sleep late. The location is fabulous — less than a five-minute walk to Kilkenny's main thoroughfare. The hotel's sleek restaurant, one of the hottest eateries in Kilkenny, serves lively dishes from all over the world, from tempura to Moroccan lamb. The friendly, helpful staff goes above and beyond to make your stay pleasant — when I left my globetrotting stuffed elephant in one of the rooms, they sent it out to me in Dublin the very next day.

26 Patrick St. ☎ *056-77-23-999. Fax: 056-77-56-400.* www.zuni.ie. *Rates: €100–€170 ($160–$270) double. AE, MC, V.*

Dining locally in County Kilkenny

Also see Zuni Restaurant & Townhouse in the previous section (the Zuni Restaurant is one of the best restaurants in the city) and Kyteler's Inn in "Hitting the pubs in County Kilkenny," later in this chapter.

Café Sol
$–$$$$ Kilkenny City INTERNATIONAL/MEDITERRANEAN

This bright, cheerful, casual spot serves homemade food all day, starting with hearty and scrumptious soups, salads, and sandwiches for lunch, and segueing into a dinner menu containing such innovative dishes as a delicious roasted organic goose with stuffing.

6 William St. ☎ *056-77-64-987. Main courses: €16–€29 ($26–$46). MC, V. Open: Mon–Sat 11:30 a.m.–10 p.m., Sun noon to 9 p.m.*

Pordylos Restaurant
$$$ Kilkenny City INTERNATIONAL

A concierge at a Kilkenny hotel told me that two of the hotel's guests loved Pordylos so much that they ate dinner there all eight nights of their stay. And I believe it. Warm and romantic, with wood-beamed ceilings, 16th-century stone walls, and hanging plants, Pordylos invites long, lingering meals and rambling conversation. You can discourse over dishes that draw from cuisines all over the world, such as plump mussels bathed in a lemongrass, coconut, and green curry brew; tagliatelli pasta with blackened Cajun chicken, bacon, and a spicy tomato-and-basil cream sauce; and vanilla risotto with spinach, butternut squash, green peas, and citrus crème fraiche.

Butterslip Lane. ☎ **056-77-70-660.** *Reservations recommended. Main courses: €20–€27 ($32–$43). AE, MC, V. Mon–Sat 5–10:30 p.m., Sun 5–9:30 p.m.*

Ristorante Rinuccini
$$$–$$$$ Kilkenny City   ITALIAN

Two large Renaissance portraits dominate this restaurant's romantically-lit dining room. Italianate mirrors, alabaster fixtures, and wooden wine racks add to the ambience. Service is formal, and guests dress up. The Italian fare is fresh and full of flavor, and the homemade pasta puts dried pasta to shame. The menu runs from traditional pasta dishes to fish and meat offerings such as calf's liver in a cream sauce with brandy. I recommend the baked bruschetta (served hot); the well-spiced, generous meatballs; and the Tortelloni al Pomodoro: crescent-shaped pasta stuffed with ricotta cheese and spinach, served with a chopped tomato, basil, garlic, and white wine sauce.

*1 The Parade, opposite Kilkenny Castle. ☎ **056-77-61-575.** Reservations required. Main courses: €19–€30 ($30–$48). AE, DC, MC, V. Open: Mon–Sat noon–2:30 p.m. and 5:30–10 p.m., Sun noon–3 p.m. and 5:30–9:30 p.m.*

Exploring County Kilkenny

Pat Tynan leads walking tours through the medieval streets of Kilkenny, relating the history of the area and some local lore. A highlight is a little visit to one of the city's old jail cells. This is a great way to get a sense of the layout of Kilkenny City and a grasp of this region's history. Tours leave from the Kilkenny Tourist Office, located in the Tourist Information Shee Alms House in Rose Street. Departure times are mid-March through October Monday through Saturday at 10:30 a.m., 12:15 p.m., 3 p.m., and 4:30 p.m.; Sunday at 11:15 a.m. and 12:30 p.m. Pat will set up tours November through mid-March if you contact him in advance. Tours cost €6 ($9.60) for adults, €5.50 ($8.80) students and seniors. Call ☎ **087-265-1745** to reserve your spot.

The best attractions

If you're lucky enough to be in Kilkenny on a Tuesday, swing by the market on The Parade leading up to Kilkenny Castle. Sausages, smoked fish, fresh vegetables, baked goods, and other treats are all there for the buying, and the grounds at Kilkenny Castle are perfect for picnicking.

Also see the **Kilkenny Design Centre,** in "Shopping in County Kilkenny," later in this chapter.

Dunmore Cave
Ballyfoyle

An underground river formed these large limestone caverns, which contain some of the most beautiful formations in Ireland. The cave was the site of a Viking massacre in A.D. 928, and Viking artifacts are on display. Guided tours lead you down into the earth and across catwalks that traverse the caverns.

Castlecomer Road (N78) in Ballyfoyle (not Dunmore Village, as the name may imply), 11km (7 miles) north of Kilkenny. ☎ 056-77-67-726. Admission: €2.90 ($4.60) adults, €2.50 ($4) seniors, €1.30 ($2.10) students and children. Open: Mid-Mar to mid-June and mid-Sept to Oct daily 9:30 a.m.–5 p.m.; mid-June to mid-Sept daily 9:30 a.m.–6:30 p.m.; Nov–Dec Sat–Sun and bank holidays 10 a.m.–4:30 p.m. (last admission 45 minutes before closing time). Inaccessible for wheelchairs. Suggested visit: About 1 hour.

Kilkenny Castle
Kilkenny City

This 12th-century medieval castle, which was remodeled in Victorian times, cuts quite the storybook-castle profile and is the principal attraction in the town of Kilkenny. Surrounded by 20 hectares (50 acres) of grounds, including rolling parklands, a riverside walk, and formal gardens, the castle was home to the distinguished Butler family from the late 14th century to the mid-20th century. Guided tours of the castle take you through restored rooms, where you learn a bit about the Butler dynasty as you admire the period furnishings (rooms are decorated as they were in the 1830s). A highlight of the tours is a visit to the 45m-long (150-ft) Long Gallery, which houses portraits of the Butler family and has a beam ceiling gorgeously decorated with painted Celtic knots. The castle's Butler Gallery hosts modern art exhibits. Tours fill up fast, so get to the castle early to sign up for one. And be sure to stop by the play area if you have kids.

The Parade. ☎ 056-77-21-450. Admission: €5.30 ($8.50) adults, €3.70 ($5.90) seniors, €2.10 ($3.40) students and children. Open: Apr–May daily 10:30 a.m.–5 p.m., June–Aug daily 9:30 a.m.–7 p.m., Sept daily 10 a.m.–6:30 p.m., Oct–Mar daily 10:30 a.m.–12:45 p.m. and 2–5 p.m. Suggested visit: 1½ hours.

Jerpoint Abbey
Thomastown

This Cistercian abbey is considered one of the best-preserved monastic ruins in the country. It houses Celtic crosses and unique stone carvings of knights and dragons. There's a ton to see as you tiptoe through the graveyard and 15th-century cloister grounds. The small visitors' center provides information about the history of the carvings and abbey. I highly recommend taking a tour if possible.

Off the Waterford Road (N9). ☎ 056-77-24-623. Admission: €2.90 ($4.60) adults, €2.10 ($3.40) seniors, €1.30 ($2.10) children. Open: Mar–May and mid-Sept to Oct daily 10 a.m.–5 p.m., June to mid-Sept daily 9:30 a.m.–6:30 p.m., Nov daily 10 a.m.–4 p.m. (last admission is 1 hour before closing time). Closed: Dec–Feb except for prearranged groups. Suggested visit: 1 hour.

St. Canice's Cathedral
Kilkenny

This 13th-century church has a beautiful Gothic interior, restored after Cromwell stabled his horses here and destroyed many of the windows, tombs, and monuments in 1650. Check out the four colors of marble used on the floor (green from Connemara, red from Cork, gray from Tyrone, and black from Kilkenny) and the sculpted knight-and-lady effigies on the memorials that pepper the cathedral. The round tower on this site was built around A.D. 849, and you can climb the 167 steps that lead to the top of the tower; it's worth some huffing and puffing for the phenomenal views.

Off St. Canice's Place and Coach Road. ☎ *056-77-64-971. Admission to cathedral: €4 ($6.40) adults, €3 ($4.80) seniors and students, children under 12 free. Admission to round tower: €3 ($4.80) adults, €2.50 ($4) students and children 12 and over (children under 12 are not permitted to climb the tower). Open: May and Sept Mon–Sat 10 a.m.–1 p.m. and 2–5 p.m., Sun 2–6 p.m.; June–Aug Mon–Sat 10 a.m.–6 p.m., Sun 2–6 p.m.; Oct–Mar Mon–Sat 10 a.m.–1 p.m. and 2–4 p.m., Sun 2–4 p.m. Suggested visit: 45 minutes.*

More cool stuff to see and do

✔ **Mount Juliet Golf Course:** Mount Juliet was host of the Irish Open from 1993 to 1995. The lakes and waterfalls make a picturesque backdrop to this course, called the Augusta of Europe and voted the best inland course in Ireland.

Location: On the Waterford-Dublin Road (N9), Thomastown, County Kilkenny. ☎ 056-77-73-000. Par: 72. Fees: From €90 to €155 ($144–$248) Sunday through Thursday, €100 to €190 ($160–$304) Friday and Saturday.

✔ **National Craft Gallery:** If you enjoy innovative crafts and design, pay a visit to this gallery, where changing themed exhibitions (from glass to metalwork) showcase the best new creations from Irish and international artists.

Location: Castle Yard (across from Kilkenny Castle), Kilkenny, County Kilkenny. ☎ 056-77-61-804. www.ccoi.ie. Admission: Free. Open: Monday through Saturday from 10 a.m. to 6 p.m. (plus Sun 11 a.m.–6 p.m. Apr–Dec). Suggested visit: One-half hour.

✔ **Rothe House:** This example of a middle-class home circa 1594 includes an exhibit of clothing from that period and Kilkenny artifacts. Also on site is a genealogical research center and a recently-opened medieval garden.

Location: Parliament Street, Kilkenny, County Kilkenny. ☎ 056-77-22-893. Admission: €5 ($3.60) adults, €4 ($2.40) seniors and students, €4 ($1.20) children under 16. Open: April through October Monday through Saturday from 10:30 a.m. to 5 p.m. and Sunday from

3 to 5 p.m.; November through March Monday through Saturday from 10:30 to 4:30 p.m. Suggested visit: Forty-five minutes.

✔ **St. Francis Abbey Brewery:** This brewery produces **Smithwick's,** a thick red ale, and — of all things — Budweiser.

Location: Parliament Street, Kilkenny, County Kilkenny. ☎ 056-77-21-014. Free admission. Open (video screenings and tastings): June to August Monday through Friday at 3 p.m.

Shopping in County Kilkenny

County Kilkenny is a center for crafts and design, and the town of Bennettsbridge (6km/4 miles south of Kilkenny City on the R700) is a focal point. Here and in surrounding locations, you find the workshops of potters, woodworkers, glassblowers, and other craftspeople. If this interests you, be sure to pick up the *Kilkenny Craft Trail* brochure from the tourist office, which will give you details for and directions to a number of workshops.

One of the most popular workshops you'll find in Bennettsbridge is **Nicholas Mosse Pottery** (☎ 056-77-27-505; www.nicholasmosse.com). Expert potter Mosse uses the River Nore to produce the electricity to fire his pots, and each piece is hand-thrown. The earthenware clay pottery, sold as individual pieces or in sets, is hand-painted with charming country themes such as flowers, fruits and vegetables, and farm animals. The shop also sells Nicholas Mosse glassware and linens, plus furniture, jewelry, and other items from some of Ireland's best craftspeople. Be sure to check out the seconds (slightly imperfect works) upstairs for good deals.

In Kilkenny Town, **Faller's Sweater Shop,** 75 High St. (☎ 056-77-70-599), stocks all sorts of tasteful knitwear, from fishermen sweaters to cloaks. And ladies and gentlemen, hold on to your credit cards, because **Kilkenny Design Centre,** Castle Yard, Kilkenny (☎ 056-77-22-118), stocks a large selection of Ireland's best handcrafted items, including pottery, linen, jewelry, glassware, clothing, fine art, and leatherwork. Be sure to visit the many craft workshops in the converted stables behind the Design Centre, where you can watch craftspeople at work as you browse.

Hitting the pubs in County Kilkenny

Eamon Langton's
Kilkenny City

This place is a deserved four-time winner of the National Pub of the Year award. It has all the hallmarks of a classic Victorian pub, from a beautiful fireplace to globe lamps. Check out the garden area in back if the weather permits.

69 John St. ☎ *056-77-65-133.*

Kyteler's Inn
Kilkenny City

This 650-year-old coaching inn is named for Dame Alice Kyteler, who ran the place in the 17th century. Kyteler, who buried four husbands, was accused of witchcraft. She fled to England, but her maid was not so lucky — she was burned at the stake. The cozy upstairs bar buzzes with conversation and live music. Downstairs, enjoy some good pub grub in a medieval cellar featuring the original stone walls and columns. You may be graced by the presence of Ms. Kyteler herself — she's rumored to haunt the place, so make sure she doesn't slip anything into your stew.

27 St. Kieran's St. ☎ *056-772-1064.*

Marble City Bar
Kilkenny City

Even if you don't stop for a drink at this friendly, welcoming pub, check out the gorgeous facade of wrought iron, brass, and carved wood, all lit by gas lamps.

66 High St. ☎ *056-77-61-143.*

Paris, Texas
Kilkenny City

Round up your friends, and head on down to this spacious saloon straight out of the American West. This place is always hopping and often hosts excellent traditional Irish music.

92 High St. ☎ *056-77-61-822.*

Fast Facts: County Kilkenny

Area Codes

County Kilkenny's area codes (or city codes) are **056** and **051.**

Emergencies/Police

Dial ☎ **999** for all emergencies.

Genealogy Resources

Contact the Kilkenny Archaeological Society, 16 Parliament St., Rothe House (☎ 056-77-22-893).

Information

The Tourist Information Office is located in the Shee Alms House, Rose Street (☎ 056-77-94-130).

Internet

You can access the Internet at WEB-Talk, Rose Inn Street, Kilkenny (http://www.geocities.com/webtalk1/).

Post Office

The Kilkenny Post Office is at 73 High St., Kilkenny (☎ 056-776-2327).

Part IV
Counties Cork and Kerry

The 5th Wave   By Rich Tennant

"Let me ask you a question. Are you planning to kiss the Blarney Stone, or ask for its hand in marriage?"

In this part . . .

Cork City (Chapter 15) is a happening big city with the soul of a small town. It has a nice selection of restaurants, an interesting arts scene, proximity to many attractions, and some very friendly locals.

The south and southwest counties certainly have their share of natural beauty, with the gorgeous beaches, seascapes, and hills of West Cork (Chapter 15), the peaceful woodlands and lakes of Killarney National Park (Chapter 16), and the stunning mountains, cliffs, beaches, and sea views of the popular Ring of Kerry and Dingle Peninsula (both in Chapter 16).

Chapter 15

County Cork

County Cork (see the nearby map) occupies the eastern half of Southern Ireland and encompasses the country's second-largest city (Cork City); one of its most beautiful golf courses (at the Old Head of Kinsale); a host of historical sights; and, bar none, the most famous rock on the island: the Blarney Stone. Pucker up!

Many travelers breeze into Cork City, look around, stop at Blarney Castle on the way out for a quick smooch, and then head right for Killarney. Big mistake. The stretch of coast from the lovely seaside town of Kinsale to the tip of the Beara Peninsula is just too beautiful to pass up. More and more people are finding out about West Cork's unspoiled beauty, so come now before the real crowds start showing up. East Cork is a gentle land that boasts several wonderful guesthouses; the pretty harbor town of Cobh; and some great attractions, including Fota Wildlife Park. Stick around a while.

Cork City and East County Cork

The first thing you notice about Corkonians is that they have a fierce pride in their city, which they have nicknamed "The People's Republic of Cork." And they should be proud of Cork; it manages to have a small-town, friendly feel while offering many things that a large city should, including a lively arts scene and quite a few great restaurants. That said, there aren't a whole lot of attractions in the city itself, and Cork City is better used as an urban base for visiting the surrounding areas than as multiday destination in itself (you can take in the highlights of the city in a day). East County Cork is home to popular attractions such as the Blarney Stone and Castle and Fota Wildlife Park, and the sweet seaside town of Cobh.

County Cork

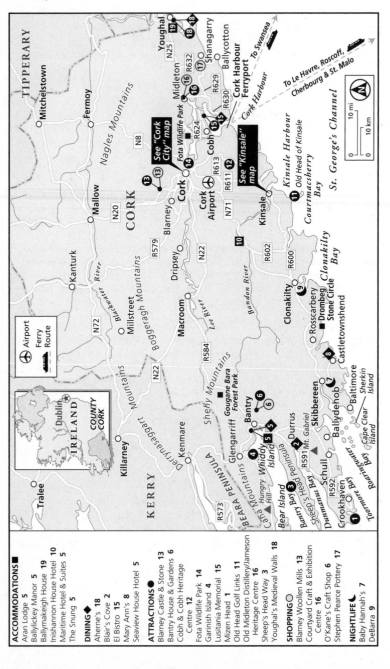

ACCOMMODATIONS ■
Aran Lodge **5**
Ballyickey Manor **5**
Ballymakeigh House **19**
Inishannon House Hotel **10**
Maritime Hotel & Suites **5**
The Snung **5**

DINING ◆
Aherne's **18**
Blair's Cove **2**
El Bistro **15**
Mary Ann's **8**
Seaview House Hotel **5**

ATTRACTIONS ●
Blarney Castle & Stone **13**
Bantry House & Gardens **6**
Cobh & Cobh Heritage
 Centre **12**
Fota Wildlife Park **14**
Garinish Island **4**
Lusitania Memorial **15**
Mizen Head **1**
Old Head Golf Links **11**
Old Midleton Distillery/Jameson
 Heritage Centre **16**
Sheep's Head Way **3**
Youghal's Medieval Walls **18**

SHOPPING ○
Blarney Woollen Mills **13**
Courtyard Craft & Exhibition
 Centre **16**
O'Kane's Craft Shop **6**
Stephen Pearce Pottery **17**

NIGHTLIFE ◗
Baby Hannah's **7**
DeBarra **9**

Cork City

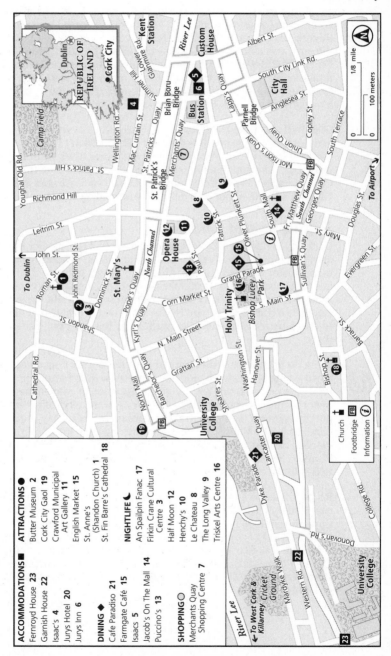

ACCOMMODATIONS ■
Fernroyd House **23**
Garnish House **22**
Isaac's **4**
Jurys Hotel **20**
Jurys Inn **6**

DINING ◆
Cafe Paradiso **21**
Farmgate Café **15**
Isaacs **5**
Jacob's On The Mall **14**
Puccino's **13**

SHOPPING ○
Merchants Quay
Shopping Centre **7**

ATTRACTIONS ●
Butter Museum **2**
Cork City Gaol **19**
Crawford Municipal
Art Gallery **11**
English Market **15**
St. Anne's
(Shandon Church) **1**
St. Fin Barre's Cathedral **18**

NIGHTLIFE ◖
An Spailpin Fanac **17**
Firkin Crane Cultural
Centre **3**
Half Moon **12**
Henchy's **10**
Le Chateau **8**
The Long Valley **9**
Triskel Arts Centre **16**

Church ■† Footbridge FB Information ⓘ

Getting to Cork City and East County Cork

To get to **Cork City** by car, take the N25 west from Waterford, the N20 south from Limerick, or the N22 east from Kilkenny. The towns of east County Cork are located off the N25. If you're coming to Cork City from the east, you can save lots of time by taking the **Carrigaloe-Glenbrook Ferry** (☎ 021-481-1485) between Cobh on the east side of the bay and Ringaskiddy (16km/10 miles south of Cork) on the west side. The scenic trip takes only about five minutes and runs year-round, 7:15 a.m. to 12:05 a.m. daily. The cost is €6 ($9.60) round-trip or €4 ($6.40) one-way.

Irish Rail (☎ 1850-366-222; www.irishrail.ie) serves Cork City, Fota, and Cobh regularly; and **Bus Éireann** (☎ 01-836-6111; www.buseireann.ie) serves Cork City, Cobh, Youghal, and other cities throughout County Cork daily. The main bus depot in Cork City is located at the **Travel Centre,** Parnell Place, Cork, and the rail station is located at **Lower Glanmire Road,** about a 20-minute walk northeast of the city center.

Getting around Cork City

Cork City is best seen by foot, because most of the smaller roads and alleys are open exclusively to pedestrian traffic. In addition, the city can be confusing to find your way around in by car, because the city's River Lee forks and winds, and creates two sets of *quays* (wharves or piers). Although roads are not as narrow as in most towns, the one-way streets can be frustrating when you're carried across a bridge you didn't mean to cross, or you see where you want to go but can't quite seem to get there.

If you do have a car, either park at your hotel if it's convenient or park when you get downtown, and see the city by foot. Parking in Cork City runs on a disc system. You can purchase discs at convenience stores all over the city. Or you can make use of one of the city's eight multistory parking garages (some central ones are on Lavitt's Quay (near Paul Lane) or North Main Street (near Bachelor's Quay), and off Grand Parade). **St. Patrick's Street** is the city's hub for shopping, and **Oliver Plunkett Street** is the main place for a Cork City pub-crawl. If you need a taxi in town, call **Taxi Co-Op** (☎ 021-427-2222).

It's best to have a car for getting to and from attractions and towns in east County Cork. All the major car-rental companies have offices at Cork Airport (see p. 457 for car-rental contact information). **Bus Éireann** (☎ 01-836-6111) operates local service around Cork City to neighboring towns such as Blarney, Cobh, and Fota. Most buses leave from the Parnell Place Bus Station. If you need a taxi in the outlying towns, call **Castle Cabs** (☎ 021-438-2222) in Blarney and **Harbour Cabs** (☎ 021-481-4444) in Cobh.

Spending the night in Cork City and East County Cork

Ballymakeigh House
$$$ Killeagh

This is one of my favorite accommodations in all of Ireland. A quiet, casual, beautifully managed farmhouse, it's the kind of place that makes you feel that all is right with the world, especially as you gaze at the blue dusk settling on the dairy cows in the field. The soothing, comfortable bedrooms feature knotty-pine furniture, luxurious comforters, and well-chosen, eclectic art — my room had a painting of the tropics and a large photograph of the Golden Gate Bridge. And then there's the food. Oh, wow. Your warm and friendly hostess, Margaret Browne, happens to be a professional gourmet cook. Her breakfasts are delicious, and if you book before 5 p.m., she will create a glorious six-course dinner for you, using the freshest of local ingredients, including flowers from around her property. Don't miss the dinner — it may turn out to be the best meal of your whole trip. This is a fantastic place for couples looking for a romantic escape.

Killeagh. The house is 9.5km (6 miles) west of Youghal off the N25; look for the signs. ☎ *024-95-184. Fax: 024-95-523. Rates: €120–€130 ($192–$208) double. MC, V.*

Fernroyd House
$$ Cork City

This recently opened B&B just may give Garnish House (see below) some serious competition. Located on a quiet street about a ten-minute walk from the center of the city, Fernroyd House offers rooms that are simplicity itself, with pretty white quilts on the bed and bright little reading lamps. Hosts Avril and Tony Lyons couldn't be more helpful and welcoming, and their breakfasts (with many choices, including Avril's homemade scones) will get you right out of bed in the morning.

4 Donovan O'Rossa Rd. ☎ *021-427-1460.* www.fernroydhouse.com. *Rates: €85 ($136) double. MC, V.*

Garnish House
$$–$$$ Cork City

This townhouse B&B is the best in the city. The large rooms are sweet, soothing, and stylish, boasting brightly painted walls, beds that are an ocean of white sheets and blankets, a bowl filled with fresh fruit, and another bowl with flowers floating in it. Breakfasts are legendary — you'd need a full year of mornings to sample every single treat that friendly hostess Hansi Lucey offers, and I'm willing to bet that you'll make multiple trips to the buffet. The B&B is about a 20-minute walk from the heart of Cork City. Check out the beautiful wood-framed photos of Ireland that decorate the house.

Western Road. ☎ *021-427-5111. Fax: 021-427-3872.* www.garnish.ie. *Rates: €90–€140 ($144–$224) double. AE, DC, MC, V.*

Isaac's
$$$–$$$$ Cork City

A great location, a fabulous restaurant, and a courtyard garden featuring a beautiful waterfall are the highlights of this comfortable hotel. The rooms are large and comfortable, and the two- and three-bedroom apartments are an excellent deal if you're traveling with several people.

48 MacCurtain St. ☎ **021-450-0011.** *Fax: 021-450-6355.* www.isaacs.ie. *Rates: €135–€145 ($216–$232) double. AE, MC, V.*

Jurys Hotel
$$$–$$$$ Cork City

As at all the jewels in the Jurys Hotel crown, the service here is professional and efficient; and the rooms, refurbished in 2006, are modern and attractive, with dark woods, quality fabrics, and luxury amenities such as LCD TVs, air-conditioning (quite rare in Ireland), pillow-top beds, and down duvets. As at most Jurys Hotels, the clientele are often business-people. The enclosed grounds, featuring a walking path and pool, the new spa, and a fully equipped gym make this hotel a standout.

Western Road. Take Lancaster Quay from the city center; it becomes Western Road. ☎ **021-425-2700.** *Fax: 021-27-4477.* www.jurysdoyle.com. *Rates: €129–€249 ($206–$398) double. AE, DC, MC, V.*

Jurys Inn
$$–$$$ Cork City

The service is good, and the modern rooms are comfortable, but there's nothing exceptional about Jurys Inn — except the low price and the excellent location, within a few minutes of the city center. A flat rate for up to three adults or two adults and two children in a room makes this a good deal for traveling families. Ask for a room away from the street if you're a light sleeper.

Anderson's Quay between the Custom House and bus station at the mouth of the north channel. ☎ **021-494-3000.** *Fax: 021-427-6144.* www.jurysinns.com. *Rates: €94–€139 ($150–$222) up to 3 adults or family of 4. Breakfast is not included in all room rates. AE, DC, MC, V.*

Dining in Cork City and East County Cork

Aherne's
$$$$ Youghal   SEAFOOD

This port-town restaurant has a reputation for serving the freshest and tastiest seafood in this part of the country. New Englanders may never order cod back home again after having it at Aherne's. The seafood chowder is unmatched as well. If you're really hungry, go for the award-winning fish and shellfish platter. Aherne's also has a luxurious hotel. If you don't want to shell out (pun intended) for the restaurant, the pub food, ranging from lamb burgers to fresh fish platters, is also a great choice.

163 N. Main St. Take the main road to Waterford (N25), then turn off onto Main Street. ☎ *024-92-424. Main courses: €28–€38 ($45–$61), set 5-course menu €45 ($72). AE, DC, MC, V. Open: Bar food daily noon to 10 p.m., restaurant daily 6–10 p.m.*

Café Paradiso
$$$$ Cork City   VEGETARIAN

Before you even sit down, you feel the vibe. This bright and electric restaurant is filled with books and toys and a certain . . . energy. Then there's the food: a vegetarian's nirvana with an eclectic and fresh menu offering dishes such as feta, pistachio, and couscous cakes with sweet-and-hot-pepper relish, sweet-spiced kale, coriander yogurt, and chickpeas with fresh chili and tomato; artichoke and sheep's cheese mezzaluna with sage butter and broad beans; and vegetable sushi with pickled ginger, wasabi, and a dipping sauce, served with eggplant and cauliflower tempura. For dessert, try the honey-roasted peaches with lavender ice cream and pistachio biscotti. Is your mouth watering yet? After you dine, you can purchase the *Café Paradiso Cookbook* and try out the recipes at home.

16 Lancaster Quay. Just beyond Wood Street, down the south channel of the river, across the street from Jurys Hotel. ☎ *021-427-7939. Main courses: €24–€25 ($38–$40). AE, MC, V. Open: Tues–Sat noon to 3 p.m. and 6:30–10:30 p.m.*

El Bistro
$–$$ Cobh   CAFE

Looking for a cute place to pop into as you explore Cobh? Check out El Bistro, a bright spot that's always buzzing with families and groups of friends. Food is simple and delicious, from pasta to open-faced sandwiches. I highly recommend the Thai chicken curry.

4 East Beach St. ☎ *021-481-6935. Main courses: €7–€12 ($11–$19). No credit cards. Open: Daily 8:30 a.m.–6 p.m.*

Farmgate Café
$$ Cork City   IRISH

This casual little cafe is located on an indoor balcony overlooking the bustling English Market (reviewed in the following section, "The top attractions"). It serves up excellent, rib-sticking traditional Irish food, made with fresh local ingredients from the market below. This is the place to try tripe and drisheen (blood sausages), specialties specific to County Cork. The Irish stew is wonderful, as are the lighter dishes, such as quiches and sandwiches. This is a great place to get a taste of Cork food, and to get a taste of Corkonians themselves, as locals frequent the place.

English Market. ☎ *021-427-8134. Main courses: €11–€15 ($18–$24). MC, V. Open: Mon–Sat 9 a.m.–5 p.m.*

Isaacs
$$$–$$$$ Cork City   INTERNATIONAL/PIZZA

An informal restaurant that's trendy but doesn't act like it, Isaacs is an amalgam of contemporary and traditional — much like Cork City itself. Located in a converted Victorian warehouse with a vaulted ceiling, Isaacs has redbrick walls adorned with local art pieces, as well as a chatty evening crowd. The international cuisine, from salads to burgers to pizzas, is reliably delicious.

48 MacCurtain St. Above the north channel; take a right off of St. Patrick's Hill. ☎ *021-450-3805. Main courses: €17–€30 ($27–$48). AE, DC, MC, V. Open: Mon–Sat 12:15–2:30 p.m. and 6–10 p.m., Sun 6–8:45 p.m.*

Jacob's on the Mall
$$$–$$$$ Cork City   INTERNATIONAL

From the crisp vegetable-and-duck confit spring roll to the penne pasta with basil pesto, bacon, leeks, peas, and pine nuts, this restaurant creates simple yet sophisticated dishes that let each fresh, flavorful ingredient shine. The chef takes advantage of seasonal local produce, so choosing a dish that's in season (such as wild salmon from mid-June through July) is an excellent idea. The restaurant is located in the former Turkish baths, giving it a chic and airy feel.

30A South Mall. ☎ *021-425-1530. Main courses: €17–€32 ($27–$51). AE, MC, V. Open: Mon–Sat 12:30–2:30 p.m. and 6:30–10 p.m.*

Puccino's
$–$$ Cork City   CAFE

It was a dark and stormy day. I had just wandered all over the city, and was craving some banoffee pie (that wonderful symphony of bananas and toffee on a crumbled cookie crust). And lo and behold, I discovered this casual cafe, home to not only an excellent banoffee pie, but other luscious light dishes including salads, pizzas, baked potatoes, pastas, and soups. The cafe also offers a tapas menu featuring such tasty bites as roasted peppers with feta, garlic mussels, and spicy chorizo. The atmosphere is relaxed, with small groups of friends chatting at the burnished copper tables, and newspaper-readers relaxing on the comfy couches.

9 Paul St. ☎ *021-436-6001. Main courses: €8–€12 ($13–$19). MC, V. Open: Mon–Wed 9 a.m.–6 p.m., Thurs–Sat 9 a.m.–9 p.m., Sun 10 a.m.–6 p.m.*

Exploring Cork City and East County Cork

Bus Éireann (☎ 01-836-6111) offers half-day tours of Cork City and Blarney (where you have an option of staying and taking another bus later) on an open-top bus. Tours leave from and arrive at Parnell Place in Cork City. They depart daily from June through September at 10:30 a.m. and return at 1:30 p.m. Prices are €11 ($17) for adults, €9 ($14) for students and seniors, and €7.20 ($12) for children.

The **Cork City Hop On/Hop Off Bus Tour** (☎ 021-430-9090) is an open-topped bus with a route that goes to most of Cork City's major sights. You can get on and off the bus at your leisure, joining the next bus after you have finished exploring each stop. The bus runs every 45 minutes (and every 30 minutes in July and Aug) from 9:30 a.m. to 5 p.m., from the end of March through the end of October. You can board at any of the stops, though the "official" starting place is on Grand Parade, across from the Tourist Office. Prices are €13 ($21) adults, €11 ($18) students and seniors, and €5 ($8) children.

Cork Historic Walking Tours (☎ 085-100-7300; www.walkcork.ie) offers great walking tours that tell the story of Cork City. Currently, tours leave from Emmet Place (beside the Opera House) Monday through Friday at 10 a.m. (history of the city from its founding to the present), 2 p.m. (history of the city from 606 to 1690) and 4 p.m. (history of the modern city [1690 to the present day]). Tours cost €10 ($16) for adults and €5 ($8) for seniors, students, and children. Call to confirm times and meeting place, as they change each year.

The top attractions

Blarney Castle and Stone
Blarney

To kiss or not to kiss, that is the question. Yes, it's touristy, but there is a satisfaction that comes from kissing a hunk of rock that's famous across the world, and there is a fun camaraderie with your fellow smoochers as you wait in line. The Blarney Stone, located at the top of the ruins of a 15th-century castle (after a fair amount of climbing up narrow, twisting stairways), allegedly imparts eloquence, or *the gift of gab,* to those daring enough to contort upside down from the parapet walk and kiss it. It's a real feat to lean back into nothing and tip your head to kiss the smooth rock — it may even be a little frightening to people afraid of heights (or germs). It's customary to tip the guy who holds your legs, and you may want to give it over *before* he holds you over the faraway courtyard. Blarney is one of the most fortified castles in Ireland — its walls are 5.5m (18 ft.) thick in some parts. You can climb through the ruins of the castle, exploring various rooms (including the "murder holes") along the way. Don't leave Blarney without seeing the castle grounds, with their pretty gardens. If you have no intention of puckering up and have explored (or will explore) other castle ruins, a trip out here is probably not worth the time.

Off the N20 north of Cork City, heading toward Limerick. ☎ 021-438-5252. *By bus: You can catch a Bus Éireann round trip to the castle from the bus station in Cork, at Parnell Place. Admission: €10 ($16) adults, €8 ($13) students and seniors, €3.50 ($5.60) children 8–14. Open: June–Aug Mon–Sat 9 a.m.–7 p.m., Sun 9:30 a.m.–5:30 p.m.; May and Sept Mon–Sat 9 a.m.–6:30 p.m., Sun 9:30 a.m.–5:30 p.m.; Oct–Apr Mon–Sat 9 a.m. to dusk, Sun 9:30 a.m. to dusk. Not accessible by wheelchair. Suggested visit: 2 hours.*

Cobh and Cobh Heritage Centre
Cobh

Cobh (pronounced *cove*) is a lovely seaside town, and a ramble by the harbor and through the streets, with their vividly colored buildings, is a great way to spend a morning or afternoon.

Cobh Harbor was the main point of departure for thousands of starving Irish on their way to the United States during the Great Famine and for convicts being sent to Australia. It was also the last port of call for the ill-fated *Titanic* and *Lusitania*. The heritage center, located in a beautiful restored railway station, uses objects, dioramas, text, and sound to relate the stories of these ships and their connections with Cobh. The highlight is the life-size replica of the inside of a ship full of convicts. You can almost feel the waves battering the hull. This whole exhibit will be particularly interesting to those whose relatives emigrated through Cobh.

If you want to know more about Cobh's maritime history, book yourself onto one of Michael Martin's superb **Titanic Trail Walking Tours** (☎ 021-481-5211), which will take you to locations connected to the doomed ship as well as sites linked with the three million emigrants who left from Cobh. Tours leave from the Commodore Hotel, in Cobh, at 11 a.m. daily from June through August (call for times during the rest of the year). Tours cost €9.50 ($15) for adults and €4.75 ($7.60) for children under age 12.

Heritage Centre: Cobh Railway Station. ☎ *021-481-3591. Admission: €7.10 ($11) adults, €6 ($9.60) seniors and students, €4 ($6.40) children. Open: May–Oct daily 9:30 a.m.–6 p.m. (last admission 5 p.m.), Nov–Apr daily 9:30 a.m.–5 p.m. (last admission 4 p.m.). Suggested visit: 1 hour.*

Crawford Art Gallery
Cork City

Recently renovated and expanded, the Crawford Art Gallery displays a broad array of art, and hosts interesting and varied temporary exhibits. Highlights of the museum include an extensive collection of classical Greek and Roman sculpture casts, and many 19th- and early-20th-century Irish works, including some gems by Jack B. Yeats.

Emmet Place. ☎ *021-490-7855. Admission: Free. Open: Mon–Sat 10 a.m.–5 p.m.*

English Market
Cork City

This pretty, old-world, stone-floored food market, dating from 1786, is one of the best in Ireland. The market was damaged by fire in 1980, but it has been beautifully renovated, featuring the original cast-iron fountain, columns, and railings. All sorts of meat, vegetables, fruits, sweets, breads, and prepared foods are sold here, and the market is famous for its alley full of sparkling fresh fish. Of the many stalls, locals recommend Arbutus and the Alternative Bread Co. for bread, Kay O'Connell's Fish Stall for fish,

On the Pig's Back for sausages and meats, and O'Reilly's for Cork specialties such as tripe and drisheen. This is the perfect place to get the makings of a picnic, and Bishop Lucey Park, a little green park at Grand Parade, is a great spot to enjoy your meal. If the weather gods are not cooperating with your picnic plans, the Farmgate Café (reviewed in the previous section, "Dining in Cork City and East County Cork") is the next-best thing.

Between Grand Parade and Princes Street. Entrances on Patrick Street, Grand Parade, Oliver Plunkett Street, and Princes Street. Open: Mon–Sat 9 a.m.–5 p.m. Suggested visit: 45 minutes.

Fota Wildlife Park
Carrigtwohill

This place is not Irish in the least, but it's a fascinating attraction, where more than 70 species of exotic wildlife roam relatively freely (except the cheetahs — for both your safety and theirs). Giraffes nibble on leaves, peacocks strut their stuff, zebras nuzzle one another, and maras (guinea-pig-type animals from Argentina) bounce along everywhere. Highlights are the families of monkeys, who love to hoot and show off their amazing acrobatics on rope "vines." Panels with text explain where the animals came from and how they live, always with an eye to conservation (the park does a lot of breeding for conservation), and excellent talks are offered each day. If you can, try to catch the Cheetah Run, during which the park's cheetahs run with incredible speed to catch their dinner. An open-air train circles the park, but you'll see more by walking. Admission to the wildlife park also includes free admission to the Fota Arboretum, with its collection of temperate and subtropical plants and trees.

Cork Harbour. 16km (10 miles) from Cork City toward Cobh off the N25. ☎ **021-81-2678.** *Admission: €13 ($21) adults, €8.50 ($14) students, seniors, and children under 16. Open: Mon–Sat 10 a.m.–6 p.m. (last admission 5 p.m.), Sun 11 a.m.–5 p.m. (last admission 4 p.m.) Suggested visit: 2 hours.*

This is no blarney: The origins of blarney

Wondering just where the old "gift of gab" lore stems from? Well, we've all heard some blarney in our lives, but the person who did it best (and first) was the charismatic Lord of Blarney, Cormac McDermot McCarthy. When Queen Elizabeth asked all Irish lords to effectively sign over their land to the crown, McCarthy was determined not to. For every demand the queen made, he responded with eloquent letters that claimed undying loyalty and dripped with flattery, although he had no intention of giving in to her demands. After receiving yet another crafty letter, the queen, exasperated, proclaimed, "This is all Blarney. What he says, he rarely means." So today, anyone who uses a lot of eloquence and empty phrases and playfully deceives or exaggerates is said to be talking *blarney.*

St. Anne's (Shandon Church)
Cork City

Until 1986, when they were repaired, each of the four clock faces on the tower of St. Ann Shandon, on Church Street, gave a different time, earning it the nickname "The Four-Faced Liar." You can climb the bell tower for the city's best view. And there's an added attraction: You get to ring the church bells yourself with the help of some tune cards. The church has a small display of old books (including an Irish-language bible) on the left as you enter. Visitors are welcome to come to Sunday services (Anglican) at 9 and 10 a.m.

Church Street. ☎ *021-450-5906. Admission: €6 ($9.60) adults, €5 ($8) seniors and students. Open: Easter–Nov Mon–Sat 10 a.m.–4:30 p.m.; Nov–Easter 10 a.m.–3 p.m. Suggested visit: 20 minutes.*

St. Fin Barre's Cathedral
Cork City

This cathedral was built on the site of a monastery and university created by St. Fin Barre, Cork City's founder, around A.D. 650. Interesting highlights of the *cruciform* (cross-shaped) cathedral include the one-of-a-kind underground church organ, zodiac symbols on the stained glass, and gilded ceilings. You'll get more out of your visit to this French Gothic–style Protestant cathedral if you take the short informative tour.

Dean Street. ☎ *021-496-3387. Admission: €3 ($4.80) adults, €1.50 ($2.40) students and children. Open: Apr–Sept 30 Mon–Sat 10 a.m.–5:20 p.m., Sun 1–5 p.m.; Oct–Mar Mon–Sat 10 a.m.–12:45 p.m. and 2–5 p.m. Suggested visit: 30 minutes.*

Other cool things to see and do

✔ **Butter Museum:** You'll never look at a package of Kerrygold (or Land O'Lakes) the same way after you visit this museum, which traces the history of butter-making and the butter trade (Cork had a booming butter market until the early 20th century) from ancient times to today. The exhibit comprises audiovisuals, wall text, and butter-related artifacts. If you're one of those people who enjoy museums on quirky subjects (I am one of those people), you will probably like this place; if not, you will likely be bored.

Location: O'Connell Square, Shandon, Cork City. ☎ 021-430-0600. Admission: €3.50 ($5.60) for adults, €2.50 ($4) for seniors and students, €1.50 ($2.40) children. Open: July and August daily 10 a.m. to 6 p.m. March to June and September and October daily from 10 a.m. to 5 p.m. Suggested visit: One hour.

✔ **Cork City Gaol:** The history of Cork's City's old jail, operational from 1824 to 1923, is brought to life with wax figures, recreations of the cells, and an audio tape telling the stories of the jail and its prisoners.

Location: Convent Avenue, in the Sunday's Well neighborhood of Cork City. ☎ **021-430-5022**. Admission: €7.50 ($12) for adults, €6.50 ($10) for students and seniors, €4 ($6.40) for children. Open: March through October 9:30 a.m. to 6 p.m., and November through February 10 a.m. to 5 p.m. Suggested visit: One hour.

✔ *Lusitania* **Memorial:** This is an impressive and sobering memorial to the 1,195 people who died aboard the *Lusitania* when it was hit by a German torpedo off the Irish coast in 1915. The sinking of the boat was one of the events that prompted the U.S. to enter into World War I.

Location: Cobh Harbour, on the square right by the water. Suggested visit: A couple of minutes.

✔ **Old Midleton Distillery/Jameson Heritage Centre:** Journey through the history of Irish whiskey. You'll see an interesting audio-visual presentation and parts of this restored 18th-century distillery, including the largest pot still in the world, able to hold an intoxicating 30,000 gallons. The modern distillery here (entrance is not permitted) is the largest in Ireland, producing many different whiskies, including Jameson and Tullamore Dew. At the end of the tour, you get to sample some of the smoothest whiskey ever made. The souvenir shop sells everything from shot glasses to bottles of the Water of Life.

Location: Distillery Road, off Main Street, Midleton. Off the N25, east of Cork City and west from Youghal. ☎ **021-461-3594**. Admission: €13 ($20) adults, €9 ($14) seniors and students over age 18, €6 ($9.60) children and students under age 18. Open: March through October daily 10 a.m. to 5 p.m., from November through February tours are conducted daily at 11:30 a.m. and 1, 2:30 and 4 p.m. Suggested visit: One and a quarter hours.

✔ **Youghal (Medieval Walls):** This lovely little port town is worth a stop to get out, stretch your legs, and see what Dublin may have looked like if it hadn't become the capital of the country. Like Dublin, Youghal (pronounced *yawl*) was settled by the Vikings and later fortified by the Normans, who built a wall around the city, half of which still stands. As you make your way from the main Water Gate along the old wall, you see several towers (originally built close enough to allow guards to shout to one another) and the main arched gate, called Cromwell's Arch because it's believed that Oliver Cromwell ended his bloody English campaign here. Don't miss the restored Clock Gate (formerly Trinity Gate) at the southern entrance to the town, once an execution site and prison. The guided tours of the walls and town are excellent.

You may want to top off your stop in Youghal with a trip to the town's long, sandy stretch of beach, located right past the town center.

Location: Youghal Heritage Center, Market Square (☎ 024-20170). It's on the N25 east of Midleton. Tours: €7 ($11) adults, €4 ($6.40) students. Open: June through September daily from 9:30 a.m. to 5:30 p.m. (call for opening hours or for guided-tour information from Oct–May, as they vary). Suggested visit: Two hours.

Shopping in Cork City and East County Cork

Cork is a diverse city for shopping. From the highbrow stores on Patrick's Street to the eclectic mix of small retail shops along Oliver Plunkett Street, you can find everything from designer clothing and linen to gourmet cheeses and homemade crafts. The **Merchants Quay Shopping Centre,** home to 40 shops and the upscale department stores Roches and Marks & Spencer, is on Patrick's Street. For all sorts of tasty edibles see the English Market, reviewed in "The top attractions," earlier in this chapter.

The **Blarney Woollen Mills,** near Blarney Castle, off the N20, Blarney (☎ 021-451-6111), is the original in a string of famous stores, which sell everything from crystal to tweed to, of course, sweaters. **Stephen Pearce Pottery,** on the R629, Shanagarry (☎ 021-464-6807), is the place to go for the popular and unique handmade white-and-terra-cotta earthenware that you see all over. The **Courtyard Craft & Exhibition Centre,** in Midleton (☎ 021-463-4644) sells Irish-made pottery, stained glass, linens, and many other crafts.

Nightlife and pubs

The **Triskel Arts Centre,** Tobin Street (off Main Street; ☎ 021-427-2022; www.triskelart.com), offers theater, contemporary and traditional Irish music, opera, and readings. The **Firkin Crane Cultural Center,** John Redmond Street (☎ 021-450-7487), presents all sorts of shows and dance concerts. Opera, dance, and concerts make up the schedule at the **Cork Opera House,** Emmet Place (☎ 021-427-0022). **The Half Moon,** in the Cork Opera House, Emmet Place (☎ 021-427-0022), stages blues, jazz, and pop bands, plus experimental theater and music.

After the shows let out, try one of the following.

An Spailpin Fanac

Open fireplaces, plenty of brickwork, and traditional music Sunday through Thursday make An Spailpin one of the best pubs in town. It's also one of the oldest pubs in Cork and is located opposite the Beamish Brewery, which should give you a good idea what you should order.

28 S. Main St. ☎ 021-427-7949.

Henchy's

A *snug* (a separate room where women were once relegated to drink), a mahogany bar, polished brass, and stained glass characterize this elegant classic pub.

40 Saint Luke's St. ☎ **021-450-7833.**

Le Chateau

Centrally located in the heart of Cork and built more than 200 years ago, this labyrinthine Victorian-decorated pub with an inexplicably French name is one of the oldest and most-favored places in town. City memorabilia is featured prominently in the many sections and snugs. The Irish coffee is legendary.

93 Patrick St. ☎ **021-427-0370.**

 ### The Long Valley

This wonderful watering hole is one of the most popular in Cork, known for excellent (and giant) sandwiches and great conversation. A long bar stretches the length of the room, and historic photos line the walls.

10 Wintrop St., at the corner of Oliver Plunkett St. across from the General Post Office. ☎ **021-427-2144.**

Fast Facts: Cork City and East County Cork

Area Codes

Cork City and East County Cork's area codes (or city codes) are **021, 022,** and **024.**

Emergencies/Police

Dial ☎ **999** for all emergencies.

Genealogy Resources

Mallow Heritage Centre, 27–28 Bank Place, Mallow (☎ 022-50-302).

Hospital

Cork University Hospital is in Wilton, in Cork City (☎ 021-454-6400).

Information

For visitor information, go to the Cork Tourist Office, 42 Grand Parade (near Oliver Plunkett St.), Cork (☎ 021-425-5100).

Internet

You can check e-mail and surf at Wired to the World, 28 North Main St. (☎ 021-453-0383).

Post Office

The General Post Office in Cork is on Oliver Plunkett Street (☎ 021-485-1042).

Kinsale and West County Cork

You can feast on some of the finest cuisine in Ireland (especially seafood) in the charming and popular port city of **Kinsale,** which is known as the Gourmet Capital of Ireland. Between meals, wander the winding streets, browse through some terrific little shops, and stroll around the sheltered harbor.

Past Kinsale, **West County Cork** looks like a magazine advertisement for Ireland, with fishing villages, cozy pubs (many with excellent music), and awe-inspiring cliffs and craggy coastline. If you are looking for Ireland without the crowds, this is one of the places (along with parts of County Donegal and Mayo, and much of the North) that I would recommend. In fact, due to its proximity to many other gorgeous (but more well-known) parts of the West, this would be my first choice for an off-the-beaten-path adventure. Be aware, however, that there is less tourism infrastructure in West Cork than in most parts of Ireland because there has not been as much demand for attractions, restaurants, and hotels . . . yet.

Getting to Kinsale and West County Cork

To get to Kinsale by car, take the R600 south from Cork or the R605 south from Inishannon. The N71 links Cork to most of the major towns in west County Cork. **Bus Éireann** (☎ **01-836-6111**) travels year-round to Kinsale, Bantry, and other major towns in West County Cork.

Bus Éireann also runs a tour along the source of the river Lee to the scenic towns of Bantry and Schull, where you depart for a cruise to craggy Cape Clear Island, a stunningly rugged island with a population of about 120 (most of whom speak Irish as a first language), loads of birds and sea life, and several ancient sites (including at 5,000-year-old passage tomb). Tours are offered on Saturdays from late June to late September and leave Parnell Place in Cork City at 9:30 a.m., returning at 9:45 p.m. The price is €26 ($42) adults, €23 ($36) seniors and students, and €17 ($27) children.

Easy Tours Cork (☎ **021-454-5328;** www.easytourscork.com) offers two tours of West Cork. The first tour takes you to Kinsale and several charming small towns before returning to Cork via the lovely coastal route. The second tour takes you first to a peaceful lakeside spot that was once home to a sixth-century monastery, before bringing you to the pretty little town of Glengariff, where you'll have the option of sailing to Garinish Island (see p. 275). Both tours run about eight hours, leaving from the Cork City Tourist Office, 42 Grand Parade (near Oliver Plunkett St.). Tours run from May through September. The first tour leaves at 9:30 a.m. Tuesdays and Friday, while the second tour leaves at 9:30 a.m. on Wednesdays and Saturdays. Tours are €30 ($48) for adults, €28 ($45) for students and seniors, and €15 ($24) for children.

Kinsale

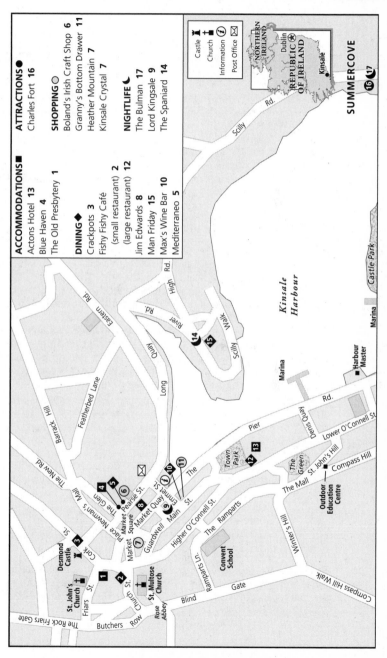

ACCOMMODATIONS ■
Actons Hotel **13**
Blue Haven **4**
The Old Presbytery **1**

DINING ◆
Crackpots **3**
Fishy Fishy Café
 (small restaurant) **2**
 (large restaurant) **12**
Jim Edwards **8**
Man Friday **15**
Max's Wine Bar **10**
Mediterraneo **5**

ATTRACTIONS ●
Charles Fort **16**

SHOPPING ○
Boland's Irish Craft Shop **6**
Granny's Bottom Drawer **11**
Heather Mountain **7**
Kinsale Crystal **7**

NIGHTLIFE ☾
The Bulman **17**
Lord Kinsale **9**
The Spaniard **14**

Castle 🏰
Church ✝
Information ⓘ
Post Office ✉

NORTHERN IRELAND
REPUBLIC OF IRELAND
Dublin ✴
Kinsale ●

SUMMERCOVE

Spending the night in Kinsale and West County Cork

Actons Hotel
$$–$$$$ **Kinsale**

Three-story Actons Hotel has exceptional amenities, including an indoor heated pool, a gym, a sauna, a steam room, an outdoor hot tub, a Jacuzzi, a children's pool, a solarium, and spa treatments. The modern rooms boast giant beds. Pay the extra cash for a sea view overlooking Kinsale's beautiful harbor and yachting marina — it's worth it. The outdoor breakfast is another nice feature.

Pier Road. From the direction of West Cork (Clonakilty), take the N71 to R605. ☎ **021-477-9900.** *Fax: 021-477-2231.* www.actonshotelkinsale.com. *Rates: €79–€179 ($126–$286) double (during the high season, rates are usually €129/$206 per double during the week and €179/$286 per double on weekends). MC, V.*

Aran Lodge
$$ **Ballylickey (outside of Bantry)**

Cross your fingers for clear weather, because the views of the surrounding hills and valleys from this simple B&B are delightful. This place feels like a real family home; Joe and Deirdre O'Connell's four kids laugh and play outside, and the cozy rooms are furnished in a down-to-earth country style. Deirdre caters to all tastes and appetites at breakfast, offering everything from a full Irish fried breakfast to pancakes to vegetarian options such as quiche. Families will appreciate the large grounds (great for running around), the friendly O'Connell kids, and the laid-back atmosphere. The picnic tables outside are a great place for dinner or lunch. The O'Connells will happily pack a picnic for you, or you can pick up gourmet supplies at Manning's Emporium (see p. 270).

Ballylickey. About 4km (2½ miles) outside of Bantry on the Glengarriff Road (N71). ☎ **027-50-378.** www.aran-lodge.com. *Rates: €80 ($128). DC, MC, V.*

Ballylickey Manor
$$$ **Ballylickey (outside of Bantry)**

"Peace" is the word that comes mind at this manor house, where old trees arch over the gorgeous landscaped grounds. You can choose to stay either in a room in the manor house or in a small cottage with a bedroom, giant sitting room, and bathroom. Both the rooms and the cottages are serene, airy, and uncluttered, and are furnished with elegant furniture and fabrics. Service is professional and gracious, if slightly detached.

Bantry Bay. From Bantry Town, go 4.8km (3 miles) north on the N71 toward Glengarriff. Ballylickey Manor is on the left, facing the water. ☎ **027-50-071.** *Fax: 027-50-124.* www.ballylickeymanorhouse.com. *Rates: €100–€150 ($160–$240) double. AE, DC, MC, V. Closed: Nov–Apr.*

Blue Haven
$$$–$$$$ **Kinsale**

There's nothing fishy about this award-winning small hotel, located on the site of Kinsale's old fish market, near the heart of town. The tasteful rooms are bright and elegant, featuring local crafts, beautiful wood furniture, and modern touches such as plasma TVs. The staff is friendly and welcoming, and the restaurant is terrific.

3–4 Pearse St. Pearse Street becomes Long Quay at the harbor. ☎ **021-477-2209.** *Fax: 021-477-4268.* www.bluehavenkinsale.com. *Rates:* €120–€205 *($192–$328) double. AE, DC, MC, V.*

Innishannon House Hotel
$$$$ **Innishannon**

Innishannon House boasts of being "the most romantic hotel in Ireland." Although the romance pretty much depends on you, the top-shelf wine cellar, fine dining, woodland walks, river's-edge locale, rose garden, and rooms with Irish country-house décor undoubtedly help things along. Boating and private salmon and trout fishing are available.

Take the N71 west from Cork and east from Clonakilty to Innishannon. ☎ **021-477-5121.** *Fax: 021-477-5121.* www.innishannon-hotel.ie. *Rates:* €160 *($256) double. AE, DC, MC, V.*

Maritime Hotel and Suites
$$$ **Bantry**

It was inevitable. As Bantry becomes part of more and more peoples' travel itineraries, the town was bound to invest in a modern luxury hotel. Located right on the harbor in downtown Bantry, this new hotel is all about amenities, with everything from a large pool to a Jacuzzi to flat-screen TVs in each room. Rooms are spacious and contemporary, decorated with shades of garnet and brown. The staff is friendly, helpful, and attentive.

The Square, on Bantry Harbor. ☎ **027-54-700.** *Fax: 027-54-701.* www.the maritime.ie. *Rates:* €130–€160 *($208–$256). AE, MC, V.*

The Old Presbytery
$$$–$$$$ **Kinsale**

The uncluttered rooms here are the picture of casual comfort, unvarnished farmhouse-chic furniture, large windows, and beds that are a mass of embroidered white pillows and blankets. Just to make sure you're totally relaxed, many of the rooms have claw-foot tubs or Jacuzzis (just ask when you book). The staff is warm and friendly, and the guesthouse has a perfect location within a few minutes of the heart of town yet away from the tour-bus hustle and bustle.

43 Cork St. ☎ **021-477-2027.** *Fax: 021-477-2166.* www.oldpres.com. *Rates:* €110–€170 *($176–$272). MC, V. Closed: Dec–Feb 14.*

Rivermount House Bed and Breakfast
$$ Kinsale

If you've reached your limit of floral bedspreads and antique furniture, I have just the place for you. Rivermount, located about a ten-minute drive from downtown Kinsale, has a gorgeous super-modern decor in tones of silver, black, gold, and deep purple. Bedrooms have luxurious textured wallpaper and feature contemporary paintings and sculpture, while the light-filled public rooms overlook a quilt of fields below. Service is kind, and the breakfasts are excellent (try the pancakes with real maple syrup).

Barrell's Cross (signposted off the R600). ☎ **021-477-8033.** *Fax: 021-477-8225. www.rivermount.com. Rates: €90 ($144) double. No credit cards. Closed Nov 1–Feb 14.*

Dining locally in Kinsale and West County Cork

For a dream picnic, check out the dazzling selection of local cheese, sausages, and more at **Manning's Emporium,** in Ballylickey, on the Glengarriff Road about 3km (1.9 miles) outside of Bantry (on the way to Glengarriff).

Blair's Cove
$$$$ Darrus CONTINENTAL

For starters, let's talk about the starters — a host of delicious options, arranged buffet-style for you to pick and choose among. Then the main-course options arrive, mostly fish and meat, all cooked to perfection. Expect options such as duck with plum sauce and rib-eye steak with béarnaise sauce. And finally, the piano becomes a dessert tray, with a vast array of to-die-for sweet delectables. The Cove is on the water and has an open terrace for summer dining. During the off season, you can have a romantic meal in the candlelit stone barn.

Barley Road, 1.6km (1 mile) from Durrus, on the road to Barleycove. ☎ **027-61-127.** *Reservations recommended. Full dinner €58 ($93), buffet and dessert €48 ($86). MC, V. Open: Mar 17–Oct 31 daily 7–9 p.m., plus Sun 1–3 p.m.*

Crackpots
$$$–$$$$ Kinsale NEW IRISH/SEAFOOD

Fresh ingredients are expertly prepared at this warm, candlelit restaurant. Perhaps roasted chicken with a parsley stuffing on cauliflower puree with spring onion sauce whets your appetite? Or maybe you're more intrigued by the baked hake with crispy shrimp and chorizo on creamed leeks with a red pepper and watercress sauce? Chandeliers, beautiful paintings, antique mirrors, gorgeous crockery, and the golden glow of candlelight create a setting that is elegant and artsy without being at all stuffy. Wondering about the name? There is a gallery upstairs where you can purchase paintings and dishes like the ones you just ate from.

3 Cork St. ☎ *021-477-2847. Reservations recommended. Main courses: €17–€28 ($27–$45). AE, MC, V. Open: Mon–Thurs 6:30–10 p.m., Fri and Sat 1–3 p.m. and 6–10:30 p.m., Sun 1–3 p.m. and 6–10 p.m.*

Fishy Fishy Café
$$$–$$$$ Kinsale SEAFOOD

Looking for the freshest seafood in town? Fishy Fishy has become so popular for their sparkling fresh seafood and fish that they recently opened a new 150-seat restaurant on O'Connell Street. At both locations, the chef handpicks the best of the day's catch each morning and then serves it up in classy but simple dishes that let the flavor of the fish shine. The open-face crab sandwich and the chowder are excellent, but I recommend going for it and polishing off the seafood platter, a banquet of smoked and fresh salmon, mussels, oysters, crab, and langoustines. Don't miss the chickpea spread served with the bread. The secret is out, and they don't take reservations, so come early or late to avoid the crowds. The large new restaurant is on O'Connell Street, though I prefer the original because it has a great fish counter that's fun to browse.

Two locations: Smaller restaurant on Guardwell, next to St. Multoge Church; large restaurant on O'Connell Street. ☎ *021-477-4453 for the smaller restaurant and* ☎ *021-4700-415 for the larger restaurant. Main dishes: €16–€25 ($26–$40). No credit cards. Small restaurant Tues–Sat noon to 3:45 p.m.; large restaurant May–Oct Tues–Fri noon to 9 p.m., Sat–Mon noon to 4:30 p.m., Nov–Apr daily noon to 4:30 p.m.*

Jim Edwards
$$$–$$$$ Kinsale PUB GRUB-SEAFOOD

This cozy bar, with polished wood and nautical décor, serves up mouth-watering, uncomplicated dishes such as rack of lamb, seafood chowder, mussels with garlic crumbs, steaks, and possibly the best crab claws with garlic butter in all of Ireland. There's a popular candlelit restaurant upstairs, but I recommend hanging out in the bar with a pint and some of this superior pub grub.

Market Quay off Emmet Place. ☎ *021-477-2541. Main courses: €16–€27 ($26–$43). AE, MC, V. Open: The pub serves food daily noon to 9:45 p.m.*

Man Friday
$$$$ Kinsale CONTINENTAL-SEAFOOD

Maybe it's the lantern-style lamps casting a warm glow on the wood-and-stone interior, or maybe it's the cozy banquettes, but something makes you want to linger over dinner at this buzzing, romantic restaurant. Maybe it's just that you want to keep eating the fresh, skillfully prepared dishes. The black sole, cooked on the bone, melts in your mouth, and the steak *au poivre* is juicy and full of flavor. You'll be licking the shells if you order the mussels stuffed with buttered breadcrumbs and garlic for starters. But then you'd be missing out on the deep-fried brie with plum and port sauce.

On the Scilly Road. ☎ **021-477-2260.** *Main courses: €21–€32 ($34–$51). AE, MC, V. Open: Mon–Sat 6:30–10:15 p.m.*

Mary Ann's
$$$–$$$$ Castletownshend SEAFOOD

Although this place is a traditional 150-year-old pub, Mary Ann's doesn't serve up the old pub-grub standards. Located in the pleasant small town of Castletownshend, this (along with the Fishy Fishy Café mentioned earlier) is known as *the* place to go for top-notch seafood in West. Popular dishes include fillet of sole with Mornay sauce glaze, scallops meunière, and deep-fried prawns. Also delicious and popular are the local West Cork cheeses. If the weather is nice, you may want to have your meal out on the garden patio.

Castletownshend. Take the N71 to Skibbereen and go 8.1km (5 miles) south on the Castletownshend Road (R596). ☎ **028-36-146.** *Main courses: €14–€29 ($22–$46). MC, V. Open: Daily 12:30–2 p.m. and 6–9 p.m.*

Max's Wine Bar
$$$$ Kinsale SEAFOOD/NEW IRISH

A meal in this small townhouse restaurant, located in the heart of Kinsale, is one of the best gourmet dining experiences you'll have in the area — as a columnist in the *Irish Independent* wrote, "No visit to Kinsale is complete without a visit to Max's." The menu changes all the time, featuring such dishes as heavenly scallops poached in vermouth and cream and an unforgettable rack of lamb with red wine and rosemary sauce. Seafood is definitely the restaurant's strongest point — they serve at least six different catches of the day, and their "symphony of oysters," an array of oysters prepared in different styles, is fantastic.

Main Street. ☎ **021-477-2443.** *Main courses: €19–€29 ($30–$46). MC, V. Open: Mon–Sat 12:30–3 p.m. and 6:30–10 p.m., Sun 1–3 p.m. and 6:30–10 p.m. Closed: Dec–Feb.*

Mediterraneo
$$–$$$$ Kinsale

Blues and whites, plus small paintings of Italy, set the scene in one of my favorite Italian restaurants in all of Ireland (though top honors still go to Ristorante Rinuccini [see p. 243]). They've got all the classics down to a science, from penne *all'arrabiata,* with tomato, garlic, and fresh chilies, to tagliatelle with chicken and mushrooms. But the menu doesn't stop there. The restaurant also aces more daring dishes such as risotto with fresh mussels, fresh asparagus, and saffron sauce. Service here is gracious in a way that my grandfather (a career waiter at the Algonquin Hotel in New York) would have appreciated.

7 Pearse St., ☎ **021-477-3844.** *Main courses: €12–€26 ($19–$42). AE, MC, V. Open: Mon–Fri 6–11 p.m., Sat–Sun 5–11 p.m.*

Seaview House Hotel
$$$$ **Ballylickey**

Clear your schedule for the night, because you'll want to linger over dinner here, either in the gracious, antiques-filled dining room or in the airy conservatory, both with views over Bantry Bay. The menu changes every night, making use of the finest local ingredients in hearty dishes such as lamb with rosemary and Dover sole with lemon butter. The wine list is extensive, and the desserts are excellent (don't miss the strawberry meringue roulade).

Ballylickey. About 4km (2.5 miles) outside of Bantry, on the Glengarriff Road (N71). ☎ *027-50-073. Prix-fixe dinner: €35 ($56) 2 courses, €40 ($64) 3 courses, €45 ($72) 31 courses and dessert. AE, MC, V. Open: Daily 6:45–9:30 p.m.*

The Snug
$–$$$$ **Bantry** **IRISH/PUB FOOD**

You know that place at home that you go to for dinner when you just want something good in a comfortable setting? This is Bantry's version of that restaurant. Aptly named, the Snug is a cozy and relaxing joint, with warm wood-paneled walls decorated with antique signs, stained glass, tree branches, and a turn-of-the-century bicycle. The food is comfortable too, with options such as roast stuffed chicken, burgers, and tagliatelle bolognaise. If they're in season, go for the strawberries and cream for dessert. The staff is fantastic, and the bartender has tons of stories.

The Square, By the Bantry Habour. ☎ *027-50-057. Main courses: €4–€23 ($6.40–$37). AE, MC, V. Open: Mon–Sat 10:30–9 p.m., Sun 12:30–9 p.m.*

Exploring Kinsale and West County Cork: The top attractions

See p. 266 for information on bus companies that conduct tours of Kinsale and other parts of West Cork leaving from Cork City.

The **Old Head Golf Links** (☎ **021-477-8444;** www.oldhead.com) is a challenging course located on a stunning outcrop of land surrounded by the Atlantic Ocean, just south of Kinsale. Par is 72, and greens fees are €295 ($472) for 18 holes.

Mizen Head, the Beara Peninsula, and the Sheep's Head Peninsula offer great biking. You can rent a bike from **Roycroft's Stores** (☎ **028-21-235**) in Skibbereen, or from **Nigel's Bicycle Shop** in Bantry (☎ **027-52-657**).

If you'd like to get out on the water in Kinsale on a *ketch* (a small sailboat), contact **Shearwater Cruises** (☎ **023-496-10**). If you'd prefer touring the harbor on a larger boat, contact **Kinsale Harbour Cruises** (☎ **086-250-5456**).

To get a sense of Kinsale history from an excellent tour guide, take **Herlihy's Guided Tour** (☎ 021-477-2873), which leaves from the tourist office at 11:15 a.m. daily. The walk costs €7 ($11) for adults, €1 ($1.60) for children.

In the mood for a creepy, funny adventure? Try the **Kinsale Ghost Tour** (☎ 087-855-5043) which leaves from the tourist office Monday through Friday at 9 p.m.

Bantry House and Gardens
Bantry

If I had to choose to visit only one of Ireland's many great houses, Bantry House, built for the earls of Bantry in 1750, would be my pick. This sumptuously furnished house is unique in that there are no velvet ropes guarding the rooms; you are free to wander through the house at will with a written guide that identifies the origins and history of each work of art, decoration, or piece of furniture. There are many treasures within the house, including several tapestries created to celebrate Marie Antoinette's wedding; *The Fruit Market,* a massive painting by Snyders and Rubens; and a rosewood grand piano in the 18m (60-ft.) long library. Set aside time to explore the vast grounds and gardens, which offer stunning views of Bantry Bay below. The most magnificent panorama of the house, gardens, and bay is afforded by climbing the steep stairs in the garden behind the house. You can recover from your climb with a cup of tea and a piece of cake at the tearoom. If you have fallen in love with Bantry House, you may want to consider staying here for a few nights. B&B rates run from €200 to €300 ($320–$480) per night.

On N71, between Glengarriff and Skibbereen, on the western outskirts of Bantry Town. ☎ **027-50-047.** www.bantryhouse.ie. *Admission to the house, gardens, and armada centre €10 ($16) adults, €8 ($13) seniors and students, free for kids under 14; admission to gardens only €5 ($8) adults, free for children under 14. Open: Mid-Mar to Oct daily 10 a.m.–6 p.m. Suggested visit: 2 hours.*

Charles Fort
Kinsale

Military history buffs and view-lovers will both be pleased here. One of Ireland's largest forts, Charles Fort is a star-shaped fortification constructed in the late 17th-century. There is a small museum, but the highlight is wandering through the rooms of the fort and along the ramparts, where you are afforded superb views of Kinsale's harbor. To get here, you can take the Scilly Walk, a path that curves along the harbor and through woodlands from Kinsale, offering beautiful views of the water. James Fort (1602) is across the river.

Summer Cove. Scilly Road or coastal walk (signposted and called Salmon Walk from Kinsale) starts at Perryville House, on Pearse Street. ☎ **021-477-2263.** *Admission: €3.70 ($5.90) adults, €2.60 ($4.20) seniors, €1.30 ($2.10) students and children. Open: Mid-Mar to Oct daily 10 a.m.–6 p.m., Nov to mid-Mar daily 10 a.m.–5 p.m. (last* *admission 45 minutes before closing). Restricted wheelchair access due to uneven terrain. Suggested visit: About 1 hour.*

Driving, biking, or hiking the Beara Peninsula

When you get home, don't forget to tell your friends that the Beara peninsula was terribly ugly and boring. That way, the peninsula will remain the wild and unspoiled place that it is now, with many ruins (both ancient and more recent), magnificent seascapes, and sweeping hills. If you want a peninsula drive like those on the Ring of Kerry or the Dingle peninsula, but with fewer crowds, the Beara is for you. Be aware that the Beara peninsula has much less tourist infrastructure than the other two peninsulas (fewer restaurants, hotels, and built-up attractions). The drive around the peninsula (begin your loop around the peninsula either at Kenmare [take R571] or at Glengariff [take R572], making sure to take the cut-off leading to Healy Pass from either Adrigole or Lauragh) takes a whole day, if you do it at a leisurely pace. A stop in the cute town of Ahillies is a great way to break up your journey. Beara Tourism (www.bearatourism.com) provides all the information you need to plan a hike or bicycle trip on the peninsula.

Garinish Island (Ilnacullin Island)

This little island is an amazing sight — an Italian garden of rare trees, vivid flowers, and shrubs set along walkways and pools, all sitting out in the sea on an uninhabited 18-hectare (37-acre) island. Before the owner brought over hundreds of tons of topsoil to grow the exotic plants, the island was bare rock. Half the fun is the short journey getting there on one of the small ferries that serve the island (keep an eye out for basking seals!)

The Blue Pool Ferry (☎ 027-63-333) leaves from the harbor in Glengarriff every half-hour or so and takes 15 minutes to reach the island. Round-trip is €10 ($16) adults, €8 ($13) students, €5 ($8) children under 12. ☎ 027-63-040. Admission: €3.70 ($5.90) adults, €2.60 ($4.20) seniors, €1.30 ($2.10) children and students. Open: May and Sept Mon–Sat 10 a.m.–5:30 p.m., Sun noon–5:30 p.m.; June Mon–Sat 10 a.m.–5:30 p.m., Sun 11 a.m.–5:30 p.m.; July–Aug Mon–Sat 9:30–5:30 p.m., Sun 11–5:30 p.m.; Apr Mon–Sat 10 a.m.–5:30 p.m., Sun 1–5:30 p.m.; Mar and Oct Mon–Sat 10 a.m.–4:30 p.m., Sun 1–5 p.m. Closed: Nov–Feb. Suggested visit: 1½ hours, including ferry trip.

Mizen Head

The Visitor Centre and the Fog Signal Station on the very tip of this point are exciting additions to an already popular spot, where you get priceless views of the wild Atlantic waves and the jagged rocks of Ireland's south-western-most point. You can traverse the famous suspension bridge over craggy cliffs and sea, and climb to the top of Mizen Head. The lightkeeper's house and engine room have been converted into a museum about light-keepers and the flora and fauna of Mizen Head; the video about light-keeping is interesting, but the museum itself is a little down at the heels. Set down as far as you can go on the Bantry Peninsula, Mizen Head seems a little out of the way, but the drive from the east is gorgeous, all beautiful beaches and green hills.

Mizen Head. From Skibbereen, the drive is about an hour. Take the N71 to the R592 in Ballydehob to the R591 in Toomore, and follow the signs for Mizen Head. (You don't really know you're on the R591. You begin seeing signs for Mizen back in Skibbereen, and you basically just follow the signs to get there.) ☎ **028-35-115** *or 028-35-591. Admission: €6 ($9.60) adults, €4.50 ($7.20) students and seniors, €3.50 ($5.60) children under 12, free for children under 5. Open: June–Sept daily 10 a.m.–6 p.m., mid-Mar to May and Oct daily 10:30 a.m.–5 p.m., Nov to mid-Mar Sat–Sun 11 a.m.–4 p.m. Suggested visit: 45 minutes.*

Visiting the West Cork Islands

In addition to the must-see Garinish Island (described above), West Cork has several other islands that are worth a visit. Rugged **Cape Clear Island** offers cliffs, bogland, and lakes, and is home to about 120 year-round residents (most of whom speak Irish as a first language). This is arguably the best place to go birding in Ireland, and you may also spot sea life including whales and dolphins. To get to Cape Clear Island, contact **Cape Clear Island Ferry Service** (☎ **086-346-5110**), which sails from Baltimore Harbour. Though **Dursey Island** is striking in its own right, with a craggy landscape, great birding, and gorgeous seascapes, getting there is half the fun. You'll take an old **cable car** (☎ **027-73017**) from the tip of the Beara Peninsula (the end of R572) over the sea to the island (don't worry about plunging into the waters below — the car is licensed to hold a cow).

Walking the Sheep's Head Way

This 89km (55-mile) route was voted the best walk in Ireland by *Country Walking Magazine.* The marked route makes a loop out of the town of Bantry, traveling through vast moorland and along craggy cliffs. Most hikers take four days to complete the entire hike. Of course, you can hike smaller sections of the route. For more information on the Sheep's Head Way, contact the Waymarked Ways of Ireland (☎ **01-860-8823;** www.walkireland.ie) or the Cork Guide (☎ **021-4894049;** www.cork-guide.ie). To purchase a detailed map of the Sheep's Head Way, contact EastWest Mapping (☎ **053-937-7835;** http://eastwestmapping.ie).

Shopping

Boland's Irish Craft Shop, Pearse Street, Kinsale (☎ **021-477-2161**), offers a variety of items including Irish pottery, jewelry, crafts, and clothing. **Granny's Bottom Drawer,** 53 Main St., Kinsale (☎ **021-477-4839**), sells traditional linen and lace: pillowcases, placemats, tablecloths, and more, all handweaved with delicate care. **Heather Mountain,** 15 Market St., Kinsale (☎ **021-477-3384**), sells a good selection of Aran sweaters and other Irish-made clothing. **Kinsale Crystal,** Market Street (☎ **021-477-4493**), sells faceted crystal pieces that positively glow. **O'Kane's Craft Shop,** Glengarriff Road, Bantry (☎ **027-50-003**), offers the best of everything: pottery by Nicholas Mosse and Stephen Pearse; glass by Jerpoint Glass Studio; silver jewelry by Linda Uhleman; plus candles, leatherwork, baskets, and more.

If you can, try to make it to Bantry for the weekly **Friday market,** which takes place in the town square from about 9 a.m. to about 5 p.m. You will find absolutely everything here, from rugs to roosters. On my last visit, I purchased an old Guinness sign, homemade goat cheese, and some fresh vegetables.

Hitting the pubs

Baby Hannah's

This is the place to go for traditional music in Skibbereen, and locals say they pull the best pint in town.

42 Bridge St., Skibbereen. ☎ **023-22783.**

 ### The Bulman

This pub offers a stunning view of Kinsale Harbor, excellent seafood dishes, a warm stone interior, crackling fires, and great traditional Irish music on most nights. What more could you want?

On Scilly Road, on the way to Charles Fort from Kinsale. ☎ **021-477-2131.**

 ### De Barra

From top to bottom and inside and out, everything about this lovely traditional pub is authentic. The décor is hand-painted signs and old-fashioned whiskey jars, and the music is terrific, ranging from traditional Irish to the latest heavy metal from West Cork (really!).

55 Pearse St., Clonakilty. ☎ **023-33-381.**

Lord Kingsale

A classic black-and-white-exterior pub, Lord Kingsale is a romantic little spot, with small snug areas, and live music almost every night of the week during the summer (weekends and Mon, during the winter). Delicious home-cooked food is served all day long, and a comfortable, lived-in atmosphere draws a pleasant, subdued crowd.

4 Main St., Kinsale. ☎ **021-477-2371.**

 ### The Spaniard

The best part of the Spaniard is the outdoor seating that overlooks the harbor. Inside are cozy turf and log fires and traditional, jazz, folk, and blues music. This fisherman-theme pub is built over the ruins of a castle and named in honor of Don Juan del Aquila, commander of the Spanish fleet and ally to the Irish during the Battle of Kinsale in 1601.

Scilly Road. ☎ **021-477-3303.**

Fast Facts: Kinsale and West County Cork

Area Codes

Kinsale and West County Cork's area codes (or city codes) are **021, 027,** and **028.**

Emergencies/Police

Dial ☎ **999** for all emergencies.

Information

The tourist office in Kinsale, on Pier Road (☎ 021-477-2234; www.kinsale.ie), is open March through November. In Skibbereen, there is a tourist office at North Street (☎ 028-21-766) that's open year-round. In Bantry, the tourist office is on top of the town square in the Old Courthouse (☎ 027-50-229).

Internet

Finishing Services Internet Bureau, 71 Main St., Kinsale (☎ 021-477-3571), offers Internet access.

Chapter 16

County Kerry

County Kerry is not nicknamed *The Kingdom* for nothing. The county encompasses some of the most famous and stunning natural sights in Ireland, including the Ring of Kerry, the Dingle Peninsula, and Killarney National Park. You'll find sea cliffs, rolling green hills, charming seaside villages, and aquamarine lakes. This area has long been one of the centers of Gaelic culture — many people speak Gaelic as their first language here, and the traditional Irish music and crafts scenes are thriving. Sound like a place you'd like to go? A lot of other people think so, too, making County Kerry one of the most-visited areas in Ireland. During the summer, the town of Killarney (and to a lesser extent Kenmare) swarms with visitors. If this is not your thing, my advice is to plan your vacation for the spring or fall — or, even better, take some turns off the well-trodden tourist trails. I provide some off-the-beaten-track options in this chapter, such as a mountain drive on the Dingle Peninsula and a hidden farmhouse off the Ring of Kerry.

The brochure *Kerry Gems,* which you can pick up at any Tourist Information office, has many excellent suggestions for exploring this region.

Killarney and Killarney National Park

Killarney National Park is a must-see in this area — a gorgeous park with velvety valleys and deep blue lakes. Killarney Town itself doesn't have a ton of attractions, but it makes an excellent base for visiting the park and for beginning or ending your tour of the Ring of Kerry. The town swarms with visitors in the summer, meaning that you can get everything you need, but you'll need to wait in line with everyone else visiting the area.

County Kerry

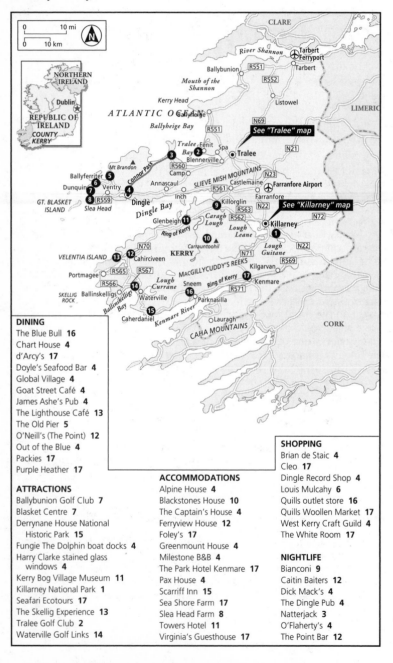

DINING
The Blue Bull **16**
Chart House **4**
d'Arcy's **17**
Doyle's Seafood Bar **4**
Global Village **4**
Goat Street Café **4**
James Ashe's Pub **4**
The Lighthouse Café **13**
The Old Pier **5**
O'Neill's (The Point) **12**
Out of the Blue **4**
Packies **17**
Purple Heather **17**

ATTRACTIONS
Ballybunion Golf Club **7**
Blasket Centre **7**
Derrynane House National
    Historic Park **15**
Fungie The Dolphin boat docks **4**
Harry Clarke stained glass
    windows **4**
Kerry Bog Village Museum **11**
Killarney National Park **1**
Seafari Ecotours **17**
The Skellig Experience **13**
Tralee Golf Club **2**
Waterville Golf Links **14**

ACCOMMODATIONS
Alpine House **4**
Blackstones House **10**
The Captain's House **4**
Ferryview House **12**
Foley's **17**
Greenmount House **4**
Milestone B&B **4**
The Park Hotel Kenmare **17**
Pax House **4**
Scarriff Inn **15**
Sea Shore Farm **17**
Slea Head Farm **8**
Towers Hotel **11**
Virginia's Guesthouse **17**

SHOPPING
Brian de Staic **4**
Cleo **17**
Dingle Record Shop **4**
Louis Mulcahy **6**
Quills outlet store **16**
Quills Woollen Market **17**
West Kerry Craft Guild **4**
The White Room **17**

NIGHTLIFE
Bianconi **9**
Caitin Baiters **12**
Dick Mack's **4**
The Dingle Pub **4**
Natterjack **3**
O'Flaherty's **4**
The Point Bar **12**

Getting to Killarney

To get to Killarney by car, take the N21 southwest from Limerick or the N22 northwest from Cork. From the Ring of Kerry and West Cork, take the N70. To get to Tralee from Killarney, take the N22 north. To continue on to Dingle, take the N86 from Tralee. The tip of the Dingle Peninsula can be driven via the R559, beginning and ending in Dingle. **Irish Rail** (☎ 1-850-366-222; www.irishrail.ie) serves Killarney from Dublin, Limerick, Cork, Galway, and smaller towns on those routes. Trains arrive daily at the Killarney Railway Station, Railway Road, off East Avenue Road. **Bus Éireann** (☎ 01-836-6111; www.buseireann.ie) comes into Killarney from all over Ireland. The bus depot is next to the train station.

Getting around Killarney

This compact town is entirely walkable. The **Tourist Trail** takes you past the highlights of the town: Just follow the signs, or get a pamphlet about the trail at the tourist office (see "Fast Facts: Killarney," later in this chapter, for the address). If you have a rental car with you, I recommend just parking it at your hotel until you're ready for a daytrip to Killarney National Park. Most accommodations offer free parking for guests, but there's also street parking and parking lots. During the day you need to display a parking disc in your car; discs are available at shops and hotels. There's no bus service within the town, but you can get a taxi at the taxi rank on College Square. For taxi pick-up, call **Dero's Taxi Service** (☎ 064-66-31-251) or **O'Connell Taxi** (☎ 064-66-31-654). For information on getting around Killarney National Park, see "Exploring Killarney National Park," later in this chapter.

Spending the night in Killarney

In addition to the options listed below, you may also like to check out **The Ross,** Town Centre (☎ 064-35-555), a swanky new hotel in the center of Killarney.

Aghadoe Heights
$$$$ Killarney

Located far from the crowds of Killarney Town, Aghadoe Heights is all about hip luxury. Rooms are meant to be hideaways, with freestanding tubs, plasma screen TVs, cushy beds, Frette linens, and stunning views of Killarney's lakes and mountains. And then there is the spa, which recently won Best Resort Spa of the Year, and offers all sorts of treatments in slick surroundings (check out the Zen relaxation suite). Service is friendly and helpful.

Lakes of Killarney (off N22). ☎ *064-31-766. Fax: 064-31-345. Rates: €250–€500 ($400–$800). AE, MC, V.*

Killarney

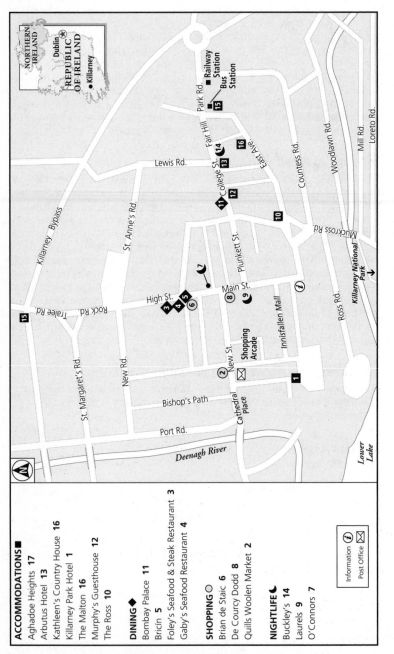

NORTHERN IRELAND

Dublin ✪

REPUBLIC OF IRELAND

● Killarney

Park Rd.

■ Railway Station

Bus Station

15

Fair Hill

Lewis Rd.

14 ☽

16

13

East Ave.

College St.

12

17

10

Woodlawn Rd.

Countess Rd.

Mill Rd.

Loreto Rd.

St. Anne's Rd.

Killarney Bypass

Plunkett St.

7 ☽

Muckross Rd.

Killarney National Park →

High St.

3 **4** **5** **6**

Main St.

8 **9** ☽

i

Ross Rd.

Rock Rd.

Tralee Rd.

15

St. Margaret's Rd.

New Rd.

New St.

2

Shopping Arcade

⊠

Cathedral Place

Innisfallen Mall

1

Bishop's Path

Port Rd.

Deenagh River

Lower Lake

ACCOMMODATIONS ■
Aghadoe Heights **17**
Arbutus Hotel **13**
Kathleen's Country House **16**
Killarney Park Hotel **1**
The Malton **16**
Murphy's Guesthouse **12**
The Ross **10**

DINING ◆
Bombay Palace **11**
Bricín **5**
Foley's Seafood & Steak Restaurant **3**
Gaby's Seafood Restaurant **4**

SHOPPING ○
Brian de Staic **6**
De Courcy Dodd **8**
Quills Woolen Market **2**

NIGHTLIFE ☽
Buckley's **14**
Laurels **9**
O'Connors **7**

Information *i*
Post Office ⊠

Arbutus Hotel
$$$–$$$$ **Killarney**

This hotel in the center of town has a traditional Irish feel to it, with cozy chairs arranged around a turf fire in the lobby. Rooms (especially those on the second floor) are large and tastefully furnished with beautiful fabrics and furniture. The downstairs Buckley's Pub has an oak-paneled bar, and local opinion says that the bartenders there pull the best pints of Guinness in town. Good traditional music fills the air nightly. The Arbutus is a family-run hotel (three generations of the Buckley family have pitched in since the hotel was opened), and the entire staff is friendly and willing to help with anything.

College Street. From Main Street, turn onto Plunkett Street (it only goes one way). Plunkett becomes College, and the hotel is at the roundabout where College meets Lewis Road. ☎ **064-66-31-037.** *Fax: 064-34-033.* www.arbutuskillarney.com. *Rates: €135–€160 ($216–$256) double. AE, DC, MC, V.*

Friar's Glen
$$–$$$ **Killarney**

Everything at this bed and breakfast is about comfort, from the peat fire that blazes in the lovely sitting room to the soothing guest rooms. Mary Fuller welcomes you to her grand country home with tea and cookies, and will happily sit down with you to help plan your visit to Killarney National Park. The house is located right in the park, with the entrance to Muckross House and Gardens (see p. 288) less than a five-minute drive away. Rooms are large, decorated with light yellow walls, watercolors, and windows looking out on the surrounding mountains. Breakfasts are exceptional; be sure to try the banana "fritters," which are actually more like delicate crepes.

Mangerton Rd. Coming from Killarney Town, turn left a Molly Darcy's Pub. ☎ **064-37-500.** *Fax: 064-66-37-388.* www.friarsglen.ie. *Rates: €100–€120 ($160–$192). MC, V.*

Kathleen's Country House
$$$ **Killarney**

This B&B and Friar's Glen are the top choices for those who are country mice rather than city mice. Kathleen's is located about 1.6km (1 mile) out of Killarney, on large grounds filled with gardens. The bright, recently renovated rooms are furnished with antique furniture and original contemporary art. Kathleen herself is warm, friendly, and always willing to help.

Madam's Height, Tralee Road (N22). ☎ **064-66-32-810.** *Fax: 064-32-340. €110–€130 ($176–$208) double. AE, MC, V. Closed: Mid-Nov to Feb.*

Killarney Park Hotel
$$$$ **Killarney**

Every inch of this luxurious hotel is a study in old-world elegance. This is the place for people who want comfort, class, and refinement. The

Victorian-style lobby has plush couches and armchairs surrounding open fires, and there's a fully stocked library where you can plan out your day over a cup of tea. The Garden Bar maintains the country-house style, with wood everywhere and strategically placed fireplaces and snugs, and breakfast is served in a vaulted dining room complete with large oil portraits and plush, high-backed chairs. Guest rooms are spacious and tastefully furnished with antiques and attractive fabrics. This hotel is definitely worth a splurge. Kids are welcome, and a few family rooms are available.

Kenmare Place, between the railway station and the cineplex. ☎ *064-66-35-555. Fax: 064-35-266.* www.killarneyparkhotel.ie. *Rates:* €270–€400 ($432–$640) *double. AE, DC, MC, V.*

The Malton
$$$$ Killarney

This hotel has true manor-house style. The Victorian décor in the public rooms is polished and ornate, with detailed plasterwork, chandeliers, and inviting fireplaces. The rooms are large and traditionally furnished, and overlook the hotel's lush, gorgeously landscaped 8-hectare (20-acre) grounds. The hotel has an abundance of amenities, including a leisure center with pool and Jacuzzi, a cocktail bar, 24-hour room service, and a new full-service spa. You'll feel completely isolated from the world, even though the hotel's just a short walk from the center of town.

Railway Road, off East Avenue Road between the railway station and the tourist office. ☎ *064-66-38-000.* www.themalton.com. *Rates:* €280 ($448) *double. AE, DC, MC, V.*

Murphy's Guesthouse
$$ Killarney

The rooms here, though clean and large, are pretty generic. But you're not paying for top-of-the-line interior design here; you're paying for a superb location. The hotel is in the heart of town and is conveniently located right above an excellent pub; so at the end of the night, after a few pints and some traditional music, you can crawl upstairs to your bed. Service is helpful and professional.

18 College St. Go through the roundabout and down College Street. ☎ *064-66-31-294. Fax: 064-31-294.* www.murphysbar.com. *Rates:* €90–€110 ($144–$176) *double. Breakfast not included. AE, DC, MC, V.*

Dining in Killarney

Bombay Palace
$$ Killarney INDIAN

After feasting on farmhouse cheeses, baby greens, and other gastronomic staples at sleek "New Irish" establishments, you may just be ready for a change of pace. Bombay Palace reminds me of my favorite reliable Indian restaurant back home — warm lighting, comfy tapestried chairs, friendly service, and all the usual favorites: chicken biryani, aloo gobi (cauliflower and potatoes), warm and fragrant garlic naan, and a sweet mango lassi to wash it all down.

10 College St. ☎ 064-37-755. Rates: €10–€13 ($16–$21). AE, MC, V. Open: Daily 5–11 p.m.

Bricín
$$$$ Killarney IRISH

If you're hankering for some hearty, well-made Irish food, you'll definitely want to try this cozy place, with dark wood furniture, raspberry walls, and stained glass windows. The restaurant specializes in *boxty,* traditional Irish potato pancakes filled with the meat or vegetable filling of your choice. Other options are delicious versions of such tried-and-true Irish restaurant dishes as lamb with rosemary, and beef medallions with pepper sauce.

26 High St. ☎ 064-66-34-902. Main courses: €19–€28 ($30–$45). MC, V. Open: Tues–Sat noon–3 6–9:30. Closed: Late Jan–Feb.

Foley's Seafood & Steak Restaurant
$$$–$$$$ Killarney SEAFOOD-IRISH

The elegant black-and-white exterior of Foley's is a good indicator of the classy interior. Though it's primarily a seafood restaurant, the meat dishes are very good too. The menu changes all the time, but look for the duck or pheasant and the steak with garlic butter. Foley's also serves several excellent vegetarian dishes. Whatever you choose, be sure to take advantage of the homemade brown bread. The wine list here boasts more than 200 selections.

23 High St. ☎ 064-66-31-217. Main courses: €16–€32 ($26–$51). AE, DC, MC, V. Open: Daily 12:30–3 p.m. and 5–11 p.m.

Gaby's Seafood Restaurant
$$$$ Killarney SEAFOOD

The finest seafood in Killarney is served here. Gaby's is well known for its lobster dishes, but the Kerry shellfish platter takes the cake (or maybe the crab cake?), with prawns, mussels, lobster, scallops, and oysters. The rustic brickwork and wooden floors make for pleasant surroundings. Gaby's diverse wine list complements the excellent food well. You're practically guaranteed a great meal — in fact, you may be so satisfied that you won't mind what it costs you.

27 High St. ☎ 064-66-32-519. Main courses: €25–€50 ($40–$80). AE, DC, MC, V. Open: Mon–Sat 6–10 p.m.

Exploring Killarney

Killarney Town is a fine place to sleep and eat while absorbing the majestic beauty of nearby Killarney National Park, but be forewarned: The town is thronged with visitors. There are a few interesting attractions in Killarney Town, including St. Mary's Cathedral on Cathedral Place, off Port Road and St. Mary's Church on Church Place, across from the tourist office, but mostly you find good restaurants, lodgings, pubs, and an assortment of shops selling souvenirs of the leprechaun-sitting-on-a-horseshoe-holding-a-shamrock variety.

The **Killarney Tourist Trail** takes you to the highlights, keeping you on track through a series of signposts. The tour begins at the Killarney of the Welcomes Tourist Office at the Town Centre Car Park on Beech Road (☎ 064-31-633) and takes about two hours, if you walk at a leisurely pace.

Exploring Killarney National Park

Killarney National Park is a place of sapphire lakes studded with grass-covered islands, heather-blanketed mountains towering above bogs, lush forests filled with rhododendron, and paths leading through rocky gaps threaded with ribbons of stream. A well-defined (but occasionally dippy and curvy) road winds through part of the park past the three main lakes, but much of the land is accessible only by hiking, biking, horseback-riding, or riding in a horse-drawn jaunting car. If you decide to drive along the road, make time to stop at the various viewpoints, and park your car to take some short walks into the park. Without stopping, the drive takes just over an hour, but you should give it at least half a day, because there's so much to see. Biking, hiking, boating, or taking a jaunting car are the best options for exploring the park (see "Exploring the park by foot, bicycle, or horseback," below). The main entrance and visitor center is at **Muckross House** (☎ 064-66-31-440; www.muckross-house.ie), where you can find maps and guides detailing hikes and other activities in the park. I definitely recommend stopping here to get your bearings and plan your day out. Admission to the park is free, and the park is open during daylight hours.

Gap of Dunloe

This breathtaking valley is bound on either side by craggy glacial rocks and soaring cliffs and passes streams and lakes of a deep blue. The gap is accessible only by horse-and-cart, by foot, on horseback, or by bicycle (see the following section, "Exploring the park by foot, bicycle, or horse-back," for more information). The best time to take the journey is during the off-season, when a quiet peace descends on an area that can be over-crowded during July and August. If you are visiting during the high season, I recommend either going as early or as late in the day as possible.

Ladies View

Ladies View looks out on an exhilarating panorama of the surrounding mountains and the three lakes. How did it get its name? In the 1800s, Queen

Killarney National Park

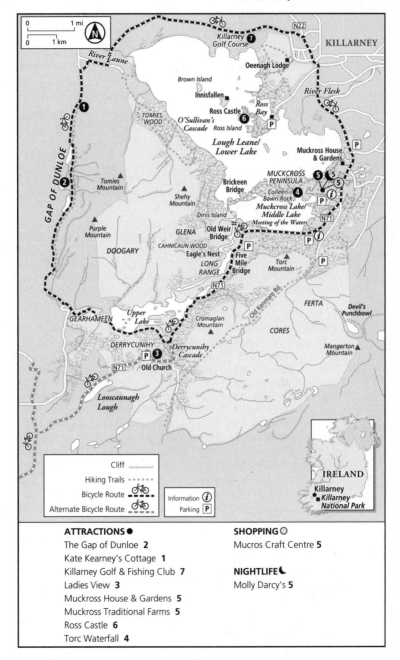

Cliff

Hiking Trails

Bicycle Route

Alternate Bicycle Route

Information

Parking

IRELAND

Killarney
*Killarney
National Park*

ATTRACTIONS ●
The Gap of Dunloe **2**
Kate Kearney's Cottage **1**
Killarney Golf & Fishing Club **7**
Ladies View **3**
Muckross House & Gardens **5**
Muckross Traditional Farms **5**
Ross Castle **6**
Torc Waterfall **4**

SHOPPING ○
Mucros Craft Centre **5**

NIGHTLIFE ☾
Molly Darcy's **5**

Victoria of England made a trip to Killarney and took her entourage through what is now the National Park. The queen's ladies-in-waiting were particularly thrilled with the view from this spot.

Off N71, near the Upper Lake.

Muckross House and Gardens

This Victorian mansion is one of Ireland's finest stately manors. The décor and furnishings of the upper part of the home illustrate the lifestyle of the mid–19th-century gentry, while the basement surroundings give you an idea of the harsher environment that the domestic servants endured. A craft center here houses artisans working at traditional crafts such as weaving, bookbinding, and pottery making. The beautiful gardens are known for their rhododendrons and azaleas, and their recently restored Edwardian greenhouses; and the grand lawns are enough to make any suburban homeowner drool with jealousy. Unfortunately, there is restricted accessibility for the disabled.

Take Kenmare Road (N71) out of Killarney. ☎ *064-66-31-440.* www.muckross-house.ie. *Admission: Muckross House and Gardens alone are €5.75 ($9.20) adults, €4.50 ($7.20) seniors, €2.35 ($3.80) children and students. Combined ticket for house, gardens, and traditional farms (see the next review) are €10 ($16) adults, €8 ($13) seniors, €5 ($8) children and students. Open: July–Aug 9 a.m.–7 p.m., Sept–June 9 a.m.–5:30 p.m. Last admission 1 hour before closing. Suggested visit: 1½ hours.*

Muckross Traditional Farms

Turn off your cellphone, forget that you stayed in a hotel with electric lighting last night, and immerse yourself in the world of 19th-century rural Ireland. Farms of three sizes (small, medium, and large) occupy the pretty grounds and are populated by folks in period dress who go about their daily tasks: milking cows, cutting hay, gathering eggs from the chickens, harvesting potatoes, baking bread, and so on. You also find a carpenter's workshop, a saddler's workshop, and a blacksmith's forge, all in operation. You are invited to step inside the farmhouses to enjoy home baking in front of the turf fires, to join the farmers in their tasks, and to watch the craftsmen at work. And of course, you are welcome to ask the farmers and workers any questions you may have.

Take Kenmare Road (N71) out of Killarney. ☎ *064-66-31-440.* www.muckross-house.ie. *Admission: Farm admission alone is €6.50 ($10) adults, €5 ($8) seniors, €3 ($4.80) children and students. Combination tickets for traditional farms with the house and gardens also available (see the previous review). Open: June–Sept daily 10 a.m.–6 p.m.; May daily 1–6 p.m.; Mar–Apr and Oct Sat–Sun 1–6 p.m. Suggested visit: 1–2 hours.*

Ross Castle

This fortified castle was built by the O'Donoghue chieftains, probably during the 15th century, and was the last stronghold in the province of Munster to surrender to Cromwell in 1652. What remains today is a huge tower house, surrounded by a wall with four smaller towers at each corner — clearly, fortification was a priority. Inside the tower is an admirable collection of furniture from the 16th and 17th centuries. The castle sits on a peninsula projecting into Lough Leane, Killarney's largest lake. The M.V. *Pride of the Lakes* (see "Joining an organized tour," later in this chapter) and other boats leave to explore the lake from the castle. The boat tour to Innisfallen Island, where you can see monastery ruins, is particularly magnificent. You can also take a pretty lakeside walk between Killarney Town and the castle.

Ross Road. ☎ 064-35-851. Head south from town on Ross Road. Admission: €5.30 ($8.50) adults, €3.70 ($5.90) seniors, €2.10 ($3.40) children and students. Open: Mid-Mar to May and Sept to mid-Oct daily 9:30 a.m.–5:30 p.m., June–Aug daily 9 a.m.–6:30 p.m., mid-Oct to mid-Nov daily 9:30 a.m.–4:30 p.m. Suggested visit: 1 hour.

Torc Waterfall

This crashing waterfall is just off N71, near Muckross House and Gardens. You can see the waterfall after a short walk on the lower path, but climb the stone stairs for an even better view of the falls and the surrounding mountains.

Take the lower path from Muckross House.

Exploring the park by foot, bicycle, or horseback

If you're looking to explore on your own, pick up **Simple Pocket Maps for Walkers and Cyclists in Killarney,** at the Killarney of the Welcomes office or the Killarney tourist office at Town Hall (see "Fast Facts: Killarney," later in this chapter). These concise color maps guide you into some of the area's delightful hidden scenery.

✔ **By foot:** There are several signposted trails in the park, including the 2.4km (1.5-mile) Blue Pool Nature trail, which winds through woodlands and past a small lake; the Old Boat House Nature Trail, which travels half a mile near Muckross Lake; the 2.4km (1.5-mile) Mossy Woods Nature Trail, which takes you through woods along low cliffs; and the 4.8km (3-mile) Arthur Young's Walk, which takes you through forest and along the Muckross Peninsula.

My favorite hike involves getting a boat from the Old Boathouse across Muckross Lake to Dinas Cottage (a cute tearoom with beautiful views), and then hiking back along the Muckross Peninsula until you join up with the Arthur Young Trail. This hike should take most people about 2 hours. The visitor center at Muckross House can provide maps of the trails.

✔ **By bicycle:** Killarney National Park is a cyclist's paradise, with many marked bike trails. Biking through the Gap of Dunloe is a breathtaking experience (in both senses of the word). You can rent a bicycle at the **Bike Shop and Outdoor Store Killarney,** Bishops Lane, off New Street in Killarney Town (☎ 064-66-31-282).

✔ **By horseback:** You take a guided one- two- or three-hour ride through the park with **Killarney Riding Stables,** N72, Ballydowney (☎ 064-31-686). The company also offers multiday horseback adventures that travel the Iveragh Peninsula (home to the Ring of Kerry). **Muckross Riding Stables,** Mangerton Road, Muckross (☎ 064-32-238), also leads horse treks through the national park.

Joining an organized tour

If you want to add some structure to your explorations, check out the organized tours in the following list.

✔ **Dero's Killarney National Park Tours:** These two tours are terrific, though touristy, ways to see the spectacular Kerry Mountains up close and personal. **Killarney Highlights** is a three-hour bus tour that takes you to all the highlights of Killarney National Park, including Ross Castle, Muckross House and Gardens, Torc Waterfall, Aghadoe, and the Gap of Dunloe. The five-and-a-half-hour **Gap of Dunloe** tour takes you by bus to Kate Kearney's Cottage, a craft shop that was once an inn run by famed local beauty Kate Kearney. From there, you can either take a horse cart or hike through the breathtaking Gap of Dunloe. Once you've emerged on the other side of the gap, you will take a boat down a river to Ross Castle, where the bus will meet you for your journey back to Killarney Town.

Where and when: May to September daily at 2:30 p.m. (call to confirm). Killarney Highlights tours depart from Dero's Tours office at 22 Main St., Killarney at 2:30 p.m.; The Gap of Dunloe tours leave from the tour office daily at 10:30 a.m. Information: ☎ 064-66-31-251. Price: Killarney Highlights €18 ($29); Gap of Dunloe tour €50 ($80) with the horse cart ride, €30 ($48) without the horse cart ride.

✔ **Jaunting-Car Tour:** These horse-drawn buggies are as much a part of Killarney as the lakes and mountains. The drivers will take you through the town or as far as the Gap of Dunloe, and they go into Killarney National Park as far as Muckross House and Torc Waterfall. The drivers are characters, and pretty persuasive — even if you had no intention of taking one, you could find yourself bouncing in the back of a buggy with a blanket snug around your legs. This adventure is best undertaken in the off season or towards the end of the day, when the Gap of Dunloe is quieter and, thus, much more magical.

Where and when: You can find jaunting cars all over town — or, rather, they'll find you. If you want to book in advance, contact **Tangney Tours** at ☎ 064-66-33-358, though you won't have a problem finding a car in town on a moment's notice. Price: It's not as though the carts have cab meters, so ask the tourist office or your hotel what to expect. The going rate for a one-hour tour is about

€25 ($40) per person (up to four people can be taken in one car). To be on the safe side, have the driver quote a price before heading out.

✔ **M.V.** *Lily of Killarney* **Waterbus Tour:** This tour leaves from Ross Castle and takes you around Lough Leane, Killarney's largest lake, in a luxurious passenger cruiser.

Where and when: Tours leave from the pier at Ross Castle, from March to October (call for times). ☎ **064-66-31-633** or **087-253-5895.** Price: €10 ($16) adults, €5 ($8) children.

If you get a yen to do the golf thing while you're in the midst of all this green, visit the **Killarney Golf and Fishing Club.** This course is nestled among the beautiful Lakes of Killarney and below the majestic Macgillycuddy's Reeks Mountains. It's on Mahony's Point, Killarney (☎ **064-66-31-034;** www.killarney-golf.com). The greens fees are €120 ($192) to €130 ($208) on the Killeen course, €90 to €100 ($144–$160) on the Mahony's course, and €60 to €70 ($96–$112) on the Lackbane course. Visitors are welcome every day and should make reservations ahead of time.

Shopping in Killarney

Avoca Handweavers, Molls Gap (in Killarney National Park off the N71; ☎ **064-66-34-720**), has a huge selection of sweaters and tweeds for men and women. You also find unique pottery, jewelry, and crafts, as well as plenty of souvenirs. The handcrafted jewelry at Brian de Staic, 18 High St. (☎ **064-33-822**), ranks among the most respected in Ireland, and focuses on Celtic designs. **De Courcy Dodd,** 68 New St. (☎ **064-31-351**) sells antiques of all kinds, for everyone from serious collectors to hobbyists. **Mucros Craft Centre,** Muckross House (☎ **064-66-31-440**), features all sorts of Irish crafts. If you're in the market for sweaters and handknits, **Quills Woollen Market,** 3 New St. (☎ **064-66-32-277**), is the place for you. From cardigans to pullovers, you find the finest Irish knitwear here.

Hitting the pubs

Buckley's
Killarney

Locals say this pub pulls the best pint of Guinness in town. The interior is oak-paneled, and turf fires burn, making it cozy and welcoming. As the story goes, publican Tim Buckley spent some time in New York but, in the 1920s, returned to Ireland because he deeply missed his hometown. He created this pub to combine all the great things he missed about Ireland while in the United States; maybe that's why it exudes such Irish comfort. Pub grub is served all day, and you can find traditional music frequently during the summer.

College Street. ☎ *064-66-31-037.*

Laurels
Killarney

If you stick around until the music begins at 9 p.m., you'll understand why Con O'Leary's place has been dubbed "The Singing Pub." Irish ballad singers perform here every night, making for a convivial, jovial atmosphere. *Main Street.* ☎ *064-66-31-149.*

Molly Darcy's
Killarney

This cozy, traditional pub with stone walls, a beamed ceiling, and a thatched roof is the perfect place to hunker down with a pint. *Muckross Road. In the Muckross Hotel complex across from Muckross House.* ☎ *064-66-23-400.*

O'Connors
Killarney

Wood from floor to ceiling, stools and tables low to the floor, and beautiful stained glass characterize this friendly pub, which has been run by the O'Connor family for three generations. Good soup and sandwiches are served all day. *7 High St.* ☎ *064-66-30-200.*

Fast Facts: Killarney

Area Code
Most numbers have the area code **064** followed by the numbers **66**.

Emergencies/Police
Dial ☎ **999** for all emergencies.

Genealogical Resources
You best bet is to contact the Kerry County Libraries (☎ 066-712-1200).

Hospital
Killarney Community Hospital is on St. Margaret's Road (☎ 064-66-31-076).

Information
For visitor information, go to Killarney of the Welcomes Tourist Office, on Beech Road

(☎ 064-66-31-633), open year-round. A great resource is the free publication *Kerry Gems*, which includes useful information such as maps, events, and entertainment. It's available at most hotels and guesthouses in town.

Internet Access
Check out the funky Rí-Rá Internet Café on Plunkett Street (☎ 064-38-729). For free access, head to Killarney Library, on Rock Road (☎ 064-32-655).

Post Office
The Killarney Post Office (☎ 064-31-461) is on New Street.

Getting the hang of Gaelic football

County Kerry is known for its excellent Gaelic football and rugby teams. If you are interested in seeing a match, check out the schedules on www.gaa.com and www.irishrudby.ie, or call the tourist office in Killarney (☎ 064-66-31-633).

The Ring of Kerry and the Iveragh Peninsula

The Ring of Kerry, a 176km (110-mile) circuit around the Iveragh Peninsula, is one of the most popular routes in Ireland. And there are good reasons for its renown: The winding route provides thrilling, dramatic views of the sea and the high inland mountains, and passes through a succession of charming villages, each with its own unique points of interest.

See the Cheat Sheet at the front of this book for a map of the Ring of Kerry.

Getting to and around the Ring of Kerry

By car, take the N70 south from Tralee or the N71 southwest from Killarney. A car is the best way to get to the Ring of Kerry and the best way to see it all. **Bus Éireann** (☎ 01-836-6111) has limited service from Killarney to Cahersiveen, Waterville, Kenmare, and a few other towns on the Ring.

Railtours Ireland (☎ 01-856-0045; www.railtoursireland.com) runs a one-day tour that leaves from Dublin. You'll take a train to Killarney and then board a bus for your tour of the Ring of Kerry. Tours cost €109 ($174) and leave daily at 7 a.m., returning at 9:15 p.m. You can also explore the area on **Bus Éireann Ring of Kerry Day Tour** (☎ 021-450-8188; www.buseireann.ie). Unfortunately, the buses don't stop very often, but you still get the incredible views. Tours leave from the Cork Bus Station at 10 a.m. and return at 9:30 p.m. They operate May through September on Mondays, Wednesdays, Fridays, and Sundays (call to confirm the schedule), and cost €26 ($42) for adults, €23 ($37) for seniors and students, and €17 ($27) for children.

The Ring of Kerry is short enough to drive in a single day, but there are lots of things to see and do throughout the peninsula, and there are many places to spend the night, so I recommend taking two days for the drive. See "Exploring the Iveragh Peninsula and the Ring of Kerry," below, for information on how to drive the Ring.

Spending the night on the Iveragh Peninsula and the Ring of Kerry

Blackstones House
$ Glencar

You may feel as though you're staying in a friend's house at this cozy farmhouse B&B, located in the mountains next to a rushing river. There are no locks on the bedroom doors, and guests can snuggle up with a book and a pot of tea in the family living room or hang out with one of the dogs while sitting at the picnic table in front of the house. Rooms are modern and have a ski-lodge feel to them, with knotty-pine furniture and original watercolors. All rooms have spectacular views of the swift river that runs through the property (fishing equipment is available at the house), backed by rounded mountains. Hiking opportunities abound, and there are several golf courses nearby, though the isolated location won't suit you if pub-crawling is a priority. Your hosts, Padraig and Breda Breen, are sweet, friendly, and helpful. Evening meals are available on request.

Outside Glencar, off the Killorglin Road. ☎ *066-976-0164. Fax: 066-976-0164. Rates: €70 ($112) double. MC, V. Closed: Nov–Mar (although they will take guests during the off-season, if you call in advance).*

Ferryview House
$$ Caherciveen

If you're taking your time exploring the Ring of Kerry, Ferryview is a comfortable, homey spot for a rest. Mary Guirey and her dog Misty welcome you to the house, which is situated on a picturesque mini-peninsula just minutes away from the ferry to lovely Valentia Island. Rooms are airy and bright, with flower prints and colorful fabrics. Make time to walk to O'Neill's which serves up seafood that was swimming its way through the deep earlier that day.

Renard's Point, Caherciveen (right near the Valentia Island car ferry). ☎ *066-94-72052. Rates: €56–€76 ($90–$122) double. No credit cards.*

Foley's
$$ Kenmare

This small B&B has everything: location, food, music, drink, and comfort, all for a reasonable price. Set in the heart of Kenmare, Foley's is located within walking distance of golf, horseback riding, and fishing. The downstairs pub is cozy and welcoming, and has excellent traditional Irish music most nights during the summer. Rooms are of the standard hotel variety, with floral bedspreads and pine furnishings.

Henry Street, where the N70 and N71 meet. ☎ *064-42-162.* www.foleys kenmare.com. *Rates: €78–€98 ($125–$157) double. MC, V.*

The Park Hotel Kenmare
$$$$ **Kenmare**

This grand hotel is beautifully situated, with lawns running down to Kenmare Bay and gorgeous views of the Caha Mountains in the distance. And that's just the outside. The interior is all luxury, all the time, with open fireplaces, high ceilings, rich upholstery, and stunning antiques. The spacious rooms are decorated with sumptuous fabrics and Victorian or Georgian furnishings, and some even boast canopy or four-poster beds. Service is warm and welcoming. The hotel's restaurant serves excellent modern Irish cuisine, and the fabulous spa, named one of Conde Nast's top 25 spas in the world, offers a range of treatments and movement classes. If you're so relaxed after your massage that you can't possibly think of going out, take in a classic movie in the hotel's own 12-seat cinema.

On the R569 in Kenmare, past the golf club. ☎ **064-41-200.** *Fax: 064-41-402.* www.parkkenmare.com. *Rates: €182–€249 ($291–$398). AE, DC, MC, V. Closed: Nov 27–Dec 22 and Jan. Open weekends only in Nov, Feb, and early Mar.*

Scarriff Inn
$$ **Caherdaniel**

You get a fantastic view of Derrynane Harbor from this family-run inn, located on the Ring of Kerry and offering a perfect place to rest your weary head after a long day of sightseeing. Whether it's fishing, diving, sailing, or plain relaxation you're looking for, this is a fine spot to set up camp. A seafood restaurant offers full meals or just nibblers, and there is a bar.

Caherdaniel (take the N70 to get there). ☎ **066-947-5132.** *Fax: 066-947-5425.* www.caherdaniel.net. *Rates: €90–€100 ($144–$160) double. MC, V. Closed: Mid-Oct to mid-Mar.*

Sea Shore Farm
$$$ **Kenmare**

The selling point of this spacious farmhouse is the unbelievable view of the luminous Bay of Kenmare and the mountains of the Beara Peninsula beyond, visible through the large windows and sliding doors in most rooms. The style of the spacious, uncluttered rooms is sort of a country twist on standard modern hotel décor, with flowery quilts and antique-style furniture. The house is a five- or ten-minute drive from the town of Kenmare, but it feels much more secluded, especially when you ramble down to the empty seashore. Hosts Mary Patricia and Owen O'Sullivan are friendly, helpful, and full of tips about the area.

Tubrid (right outside Kenmare). ☎ **064-41-270.** *Fax: 064-41-270. From Kenmare, take the N71, make a left on N70, and then take another left turn at the sign for Sea Shore Farm. Rates: €100–€130 ($160–$208). MC, V. Closed: Mid-Nov to Feb.*

Towers Hotel
$$$ Glenbeigh

This elegant hotel is a great place to spend the night after the first leg of your drive around the Ring. Sandy beaches and lofty mountains are just a short walk away, and fishing and golfing are nearby. Rooms feature warm lighting, contemporary furniture, and high ceilings. The hotel's classy restaurant creates superb seafood dishes, and the traditional pub draws locals, so even if you just go in for a bite, you get to see a real slice of this part of Kerry.

Glenbeigh. Right off the N70, between Killarney and Cahirciveen. ☎ *066-976-8212. Fax: 066-976-8260. Rates: €100–€150 ($160–$240) double. AE, MC, V. Closed: Oct–Mar.*

Virginia's Guesthouse
$$–$$$ Kenmare

Located right in the center of charming Kenmare, this B&B has some of the kindest owners in these parts. Neil and Noreen Harrington consistently go the extra mile for guests, helping with everything from planning your itinerary in Kerry to finding the best lunch spot. Breakfast is divine, with such interesting options as melted blue cheese over pears, served with crispy (American-style) bacon. The culinary adventure continues at Mulcahy's, the terrific restaurant located under the guesthouse. Rooms are bright, spotless, and simply furnished in blue and beige. Ask for a room away from the street if you are sensitive to noise.

Henry Street. ☎ *064-41-021. Fax: 064-42-415.* www.virginias-kenmare.com. *Rates: €70–€120 ($112–$192). MC, V.*

Dining in Kenmare and along the Ring

The Blue Bull
$$–$$$$ Sneem SEAFOOD-IRISH

This roadside pub, decorated with old black-and-white prints of Kerry, is known throughout the county for its fresh seafood, so you can't go wrong with the seafood platter. It also serves steaks, hearty soups, and other classic Irish fare, including a delectable Irish stew. Stick around after dinner for some Irish music on Tuesdays and Thursdays.

South Square. On the Ring of Kerry, 24km (15 miles) west of Kenmare. ☎ *064-45-382. Main courses: €10–€30 ($16–$48). AE, DC, MC, V. Open: Bar food daily 11 a.m.–6 p.m.; restaurant menu daily 6–9:30 p.m.*

d'Arcy's
$$$$ Kenmare IRISH

Get ready for real gourmet Irish food, prepared with fresh ingredients by a talented chef. Highlights are oysters (served in many different guises), baked sea trout in puff pastry with smoked salmon, and loin of Kerry lamb with eggplant, tomato, and garlic. The kitchen is happy to accommodate vegetarians. The dining room has a big, open fireplace.

Main Street. ☎ *064-41-589. Reservations recommended. Main courses: €20–€29 ($32–$46). AE, MC, V. Open: May–Sept Tues–Sun noon to 10 p.m., Oct–Apr Thurs–Sun 6–10 p.m. Closed: Jan to mid-Feb.*

The Lighthouse Café
$–$$$ Valentia Island   IRISH

The indoor area of this cafe is a cute place to sit on a rainy day, but wish hard for a sunny day if you really want to enjoy this place. Pick a table outside and soak in the views of green cliffs running down to the sea below. The menu is not extensive, but the food is fantastic, especially the thick seafood chowder, studded with mussels, smoked haddock, fresh cod, and vegetables. Be sure to try a salad, as the cafe grows many of its vegetables and edible flowers in organic gardens on-site.

Dohilla, Valentia Island (follow signs from Knightstown). ☎ *066-947-6304. €6–€18 ($9.60–$29). No credit cards. Open: June–Aug noon to 6 p.m.*

O'Neill's (The Point)
$$$$ Cahirciveen   SEAFOOD

At first glance, this might look like your everyday, cozy pub, with model boats, bottles of liquor and jars on shelves lining the walls, and stone floors. But after you settle in, you'll likely note the delicious smells wafting from the kitchen. Toothsome seafood dishes are the specialty — from smoked salmon to crab claws tossed with olive oil, garlic, and chile peppers. O'Neill's owns its own fleet of fishing boats, so you can be sure that your dish was just swimming (or scuttling, in the case of the crabs) that morning. My favorite dish is the hot and cold seafood selection, a sampler plate offering pan-fried hake, deep-fried squid, crab, shrimp, fresh salmon, and smoked salmon.

Renard Point, right near the ferry to Valentia Island. ☎ *066-947-2165. Main courses: €20–€24 ($32–$38). No credit cards. Open: Mon–Sat noon–2 p.m., daily 5:30–9:30 p.m. Weekends only Oct–Apr.*

Packies
$$$–$$$$ Kenmare   IRISH/NEW IRISH

This hip, cheerful restaurant, with stone walls displaying contemporary local art, serves up delectable dishes that range from traditional Irish to internationally influenced fare. The simple crab claws in garlic butter will have you licking your fingers, and more-adventurous dishes, such as plaice with orange, lime, and cilantro, may have you licking your plate.

Henry Street. ☎ *064-41-508. Reservations recommended. Main courses: €15–€35 ($24–$56). MC, V. Open: Apr–Dec Mon–Sat 6–10 p.m. Closed Jan–Mar.*

Purple Heather
$–$$$ Kenmare   HAUTE PUB

Here's something different: hearty, delicious pub grub with a haute-cuisine edge. This centrally located eatery is perfect for a light meal or snack and is guaranteed not to be ordinary. Tasty seafood salads, vegetarian omelets, soups, and platters piled high with farmhouse cheese are just some of the offerings.

Henry Street. ☎ *064-41-016. Main courses: €9–€22 ($14–$35). No credit cards. Open: Mon–Sat 11 a.m.–7 p.m.*

Exploring the Iveragh Peninsula and the Ring of Kerry

In addition to taking in the glorious views the Ring of Kerry offers around every bend, history and natural history buffs should enjoy the sights in these sections.

The top attractions

The draw of the Ring of Kerry and the Iveragh Peninsula is the breathtaking mountain, cliff, and coastal scenery, best seen by driving or biking, with frequent stops for hikes and walks. I highly recommend driving the Ring yourself if you don't mind a lot of twists and turns and the occasional monster tour bus hogging the road.

The Ring is usually driven counterclockwise, beginning in Killarney or Killorglin and going around to Kenmare. During the peak tourist season, you'll encounter a good number of other drivers along this route. So if you want to avoid the crowds, begin in Kenmare and go clockwise — that way, you'll be going against the traffic. Another way to beat the tour buses is to hit the road before they do — buses leave Killarney and Killorglin at 9 or 10 a.m.

If you don't think you're up for driving yourself around the Ring, check out the **Bus Éireann Ring of Kerry Day Tour** (☎ **01-836-6111**) or the **Railtours Ireland Ring of Kerry Tour** (see "Getting to and around the Ring of Kerry," earlier in this chapter).

If you take the standard counterclockwise route and start in **Killorglin,** known as the gateway to the Ring, the next town you come to is **Glenbeigh,** which is partially surrounded by mountains. At **Rossbeigh,** you first catch sight of the Atlantic. You'll hit the town of **Cahirciveen** before arriving at **Portmagee,** a pretty fishing harbor where you cross the bridge to **Valentia Island.** You'll find interesting sights on the island, including tetrapod footprints left more than 350 million years ago, the Skellig Experience (see the review below), and a recently reopened slate quarry. This is the place to depart for a boat tour of the Skellig rocks, which rise like cathedrals from the Atlantics. I also highly recommend taking the Bray Head hike to an overlook of the Skelligs. To get to Bray Head, start at the Skellig Experience (see p. 300), then continue on R565 until it hits a T, then make a left and park in the small parking lot at the beginning of the hike. **Ballinskelligs** is a *Gaeltacht,* or Irish-speaking area, that has an Irish college where children can attend summer classes to learn the language. If the weather is good, you may be able to see the Skelligs from here.

Waterville, the next town on the Ring, is known as a fishing resort but has plenty of other sporting attractions to divert you from the drive. In beautiful **Caherdaniel,** you can see the home of Daniel "The Liberator" O'Connell, and nearby **Castlecove** is loaded with sandy beaches. The lovely village of **Sneem,** filled with vividly colored buildings, has mountain and river scenery and is a haven of peace and quiet. **Parknasilla** benefits from the Gulf Stream and has a (comparably) warm climate and even subtropical plants. Finally, the Ring of Kerry ends in the charming, picturesque town of **Kenmare,** where you'll enjoy fine hotels, restaurants, shopping, and pubs.

Now, some insider advice: Yes, the Ring is spectacular, but it is only a small part of the Iveragh Peninsula. I highly recommend taking some of the local interior roads through the mountains and hills that make up the center of the peninsula, particularly in the area around gorgeous Caragh Lake. It's amazing how untouched this area is. Instead of tour buses, you may encounter a farmer leading his herd of cows down the road to a different pasture. And you'll certainly encounter incredible mountain scenery. All you need is a good driving map.

Derrynane House National Historic Park
Caherdaniel

This home was where early-19th-century political figure Daniel O'Connell, often called "The Liberator," lived for most of his life. O'Connell was a lawyer and politician who fought for the repeal of anti-Catholic laws, and for the separation of Ireland from Great Britain. O'Connell's former home is now a museum displaying many personal artifacts; don't miss the interesting 25-minute video on his life. The house sits on gorgeous grounds along the coast and boasts extensive gardens.

Right off the Ring, in Caherdaniel. You see a sign 1.6km (1 mile) north of Caherdaniel for parking. ☎ *066-9475-113. Admission: €2.90 ($4.60) adults, €2.10 ($3.40) seniors, €1.30 ($2.10) students and children. Open: Nov–Mar Sat–Sun 1–5 p.m., Apr and Oct Wed–Sun 10:30–5 p.m.; May–Sept daily 10:30 a.m.–6 p.m. Last admission 45 minutes before closing. Suggested visit: About 1 hour.*

Seafari Ecotours

A two-hour cruise aboard this boat, which holds up to 150 people and has both covered and uncovered areas, is the best way to get up close and personal with the many gray seals that call this area home. The cruise is also a great way to see the castles, ruins, and megalithic monuments that line the shores of the bay. Captain Ross is both hilarious and knowledgeable, providing interesting commentary on local geology and history, and expertly spotting the dolphins, sea otters, and water birds that often frequent the bay along with the seals. If you'd prefer to cruise with a smaller group of travelers, a smaller cruise (☎ **087-259-2209;** www.kenmareanglingand sightseeing.com) explores the bay with just ten passengers.

Leaves from Kenmare Pier (next to the Kenmare suspension bridge), Kenmare. ☎ *064-42-059.* www.seafariireland.com. *Price: €20 ($32) adults, €18 ($28) for students above 18 students, €15 ($24) students 12–18, €13 ($20) children under 12. Frequent departures daily May–Oct; call for information on departures in the low season.*

The Skellig Experience
Valentia Island

The two Skellig rock islands, Skellig Michael and Little Skellig, jut steeply out of the sea about 14km (8 miles) from the Iveragh Peninsula. This heritage center, located on beautiful Valentia Island, has excellent exhibits and audiovisuals explaining the natural and human history of the Skelligs. You find out about the lives and work of the early Christian monks who created their monastery on Skellig Michael, discover the history of the Skellig lighthouse and its keepers, and find out about the intriguing bird and plant life of the Skelligs. The highlight of the visit is the two-hour cruise around the islands. Note that the water is often very choppy, so if you left your sea legs at the hotel, you can visit the Skelligs virtually through a 15-minute audiovisual tour. If you'd like a chance to climb on the Skelligs, check out the Skellig Michael boat trip, reviewed below.

Skellig Heritage Centre. Take the R565 to Portmagee and Valentia Island. The Heritage Centre is just across the bridge from Portmagee as soon as you cross over onto Valentia Island. ☎ *066-947-6306. Admission: Exhibit and movie €5 ($8) adults, €4 ($6.40) seniors and students, €3 ($4.80) children under 12; exhibit, movie, and cruise €28 ($45) adults; €25 ($40) seniors and students; €15 ($24) children under 12. Open: July–Aug daily 10 a.m–7 p.m.; May, June, and Sept daily 10 a.m.–6 p.m.; Mar–Apr and Oct–Nov Mon–Fri 10 a.m.–5 p.m. (call to confirm during these months). Closed: Dec–Mar. Suggested visit: 2 hours.*

Skellig Michael Boat Trip and Exploration

This fabulous adventure begins with a 45-minute boat ride to the larger of the Skellig Islands, Skellig Michael. Once there, you can ascend the steep steps that lead up to the monastery, which was founded in the sixth or seventh century and flourished until the 12th or 13th century. Among the ruins of the monastery complex, you'll find a church, a number of small beehive-style huts, and two oratories. The thousands of nesting gannets on Little Skellig and the many puffins on nearby Puffin Island are quite a sight.

Most trips depart from Portmagee and takes about 45 minutes. Price: Currently about €40 ($64) per person. Ferries usually run only in the high season (Apr–Sept) and depart between 9 a.m. and noon. For a trip from Portmagee, contact Des Lavelle

(☎ 066-947-6124) or Ken and Joe Roddy (☎ 087-120-9924). Suggested visit: At least 4 hours for the entire experience.

Other cool things to see and do

✔ **Kerry Bog Village Museum:** This collection of thatched-roof cottages illustrates life in Kerry in the 1800s. It has a blacksmith's forge and house, a stable, a dairy house, a laborer's house, a turf-cutter's house, a thatcher's house, and a tradesman's house. Plenty of freshly cut turf is lying about. Dug out from bogs, turf was once the main fuel for heating houses. Inside the dwellings are authentic furnishings from across County Kerry.

Location: Ring of Kerry Road (N70), Glenbeigh. ☎ 066-976-9184. Follow signs from the village of Glenbeigh. Admission: €4 ($6.40) adults, €2 ($3.20) students, €1.25 ($2) children. Open: Daily from 8:30 a.m. to 6 p.m. (closes at sunset Nov–Feb). Suggested visit: One and a half to two hours.

✔ **Walking the Kerry Way:** This long-distance hike of 202km (125 miles) leaves from and returns to Killarney and includes a circuit of the Iveragh Peninsula.

Pick up maps at a tourist office in Killarney or Kenmare (see "Fast Facts: The Iveragh Peninsula and the Ring of Kerry," later in this chapter).

✔ **Waterville Golf Links:** If you're craving some golf, visit Waterville — golf course to the stars. It's scenic, overlooking the Atlantic, and it's where Sean Connery plays when he's in Ireland. Call to reserve a tee time as far ahead as possible.

Location: Newrath, Waterville. ☎ 066-947-4102. Par: 71. Fees: €150 ($240).

Shopping

Plenty of small crafts shops dot the Ring of Kerry, but the best shopping is in the town of Kenmare. You find a variety of specialty shops and souvenir stores and plenty of what the town is known for — Kenmare lace.

Cleo, 2 Shelbourne St., Kenmare (☎ 064-41-410), sells stylish women's clothes and is noted for its colorful tweed and linen items. The **White Room,** Main Street, Kenmare (☎ 064-34-447), stocks a fine collection of tablecloths, sheets, nightgowns, and more made with linen and the famed Kenmare lace. **Quills Woolen Market,** corner of Market and Main streets, Kenmare (☎ 064-32-277), has a fine selection of Irish crafts such as Aran sweaters, Donegal tweeds, and Irish linen. If you're a bargain-hunter, check out the **Quills outlet store** (☎ 064-32-277) at South Square in Sneem, which is about 20km (12 miles) from Kenmare along the Ring of Kerry.

Hitting the pubs

Bianconi
Killorglin

Bianconi offers good Irish lunches, including smoked salmon and oysters. There's a piano player most evenings, and you can count on a friendly welcome from the staff.

Right on the N70, near where it meets the N72. ☎ *066-976-1146.*

Caitin Baiters
Cahirciveen

This thatched-roof pub is as authentic as they get, and inside, you enjoy hearty food and a well-pulled pint, both at reasonable prices. Some nights (it's hit-or-miss), there are music sessions.

Kells Bay. From the town's main street, follow the turnoff to Kells Bay; it's on that little road. ☎ *066-947-7614.*

The Point Bar
Cahirciveen

If the weather's good, this is the place to be. Sitting outside on the patio, sipping a pint and looking out at the water, is simply idyllic. The bar also serves plenty of good, fresh seafood dishes during the high season from 12:30 to 3 p.m. Monday through Saturday, and 5:30 to 10 p.m. daily.

On the road to Renard Point (off the Ring road), just a minute or 2 from the N70. ☎ *066-947-2165.*

Fast Facts: The Iveragh Peninsula and the Ring of Kerry

Area Codes

Most numbers on the Ring of Kerry have the area codes **064** or **066**.

Emergencies/Police

Dial ☎ **999** for all emergencies.

Hospital

Kenmare Community Hospital can be reached at ☎ 064-41-088.

Information

For visitor information, go to the Kenmare Tourist Office at The Square (☎ 064-41-233).

Internet

You can access the Internet at Kenmare Library (☎ 064-41-416).

The Puck Fair

For three days during the second week of August, Killorglin explodes into a fiesta of music, drinking, storytelling, and general merrymaking during the Puck Fair. A billy goat is crowned King Puck, and the ribbon-bedecked goat presides over the festivities from a high pedestal. The origins of this celebration stretch far back — it is thought to have originated as a pagan festival in honor of Lugh, the Celtic sun god. When I asked a Killorglin gent whether he had taken part in the festivities for all three days, he replied "Aye, and three nights."

Tralee and the Dingle Peninsula

Don't tell the Irish Tourism Board, but I think that the Dingle Peninsula is even more beautiful than the Iveragh Peninsula and the Ring of Kerry. While the Ring is dramatic, the Dingle Peninsula has a gentler beauty (though, like the Iveragh Peninsula, it also boasts awe-inspiring views of wave-pounded cliffs) and is less clogged with visitors. Long sandy beaches, hills of a thousand different stunning shades of green divided into a patchwork by old stone walls and hedges, extraordinary pre-Christian ruins, craggy cliffs, and a large *Gaeltacht* (Irish-speaking area) — what more could you want? I also have a special place in my heart for the sweet and funky town of Dingle (also known as An Daingean, the town's Irish name), with its many shops, restaurants, and galleries, and its beautiful views of Dingle Harbor. The town is a busy place in July and August, but it still manages to retain its friendly, artsy, small-town character.

You may want to begin your exploration of the Dingle Peninsula (just north of the Ring of Kerry) in **Tralee,** the little town known as the *Gateway to Kerry.* Tralee is the capital town of County Kerry; it's a pleasant place to stay overnight, but there is not a lot to see or do in the town. However, it is home of the world-famous **Rose of Tralee Pageant,** the highlight of the annual Festival of Kerry. The festival lasts for five days at the end of August and includes concerts, street entertainment, and horse races leading up to the beauty and talent contest that names the Rose (call the festival office at ☎ 066-712-1322, or visit www.rose oftralee.ie for more information).

If you are traveling without a car, **Deros Tours** (☎ 064-31-251; www.derostours.com) runs a bus tour that takes you from Killarney along the rugged Dingle coastline, past many of the prehistoric highlights of the peninsula. See p. 310 for more information on tours of the Dingle Peninsula.

Tralee

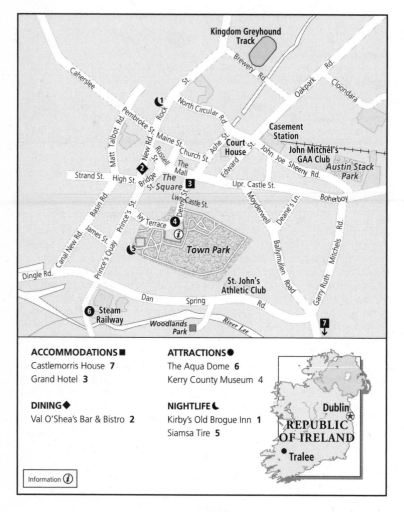

Kingdom Greyhound Track

Caherslee

Brewery Rd.

Oakpark Rd.

Cloondara

North Circular Rd.

St.

Rock St.

Pembroke St.

Matt Talbot Rd.

New Rd.

Maine St.

Church St.

Russell St.

Ashe St.

Court House

Edward St.

Casement Station

John Joe Sheehy Rd.

John Mitchel's GAA Club

Austin Stack Park

Strand St.

High St.

The Mall

The Square

Bridge St.

Basin Rd.

Upr. Castle St.

Lwr. Castle St.

Moydewell

Deane's Ln.

Boherboy

Canal New Rd.

James St.

Prince's St.

Prince's Quay

Ivy Terrace

Denny St.

Town Park

Ballymullen Road

Garry Ruth

Mitchels Rd.

Dingle Rd.

Dan Spring Rd.

St. John's Athletic Club

River Lee

Steam Railway

Woodlands Park

ACCOMMODATIONS ■
Castlemorris House **7**
Grand Hotel **3**

DINING ◆
Val O'Shea's Bar & Bistro **2**

ATTRACTIONS ●
The Aqua Dome **6**
Kerry County Museum **4**

NIGHTLIFE ☾
Kirby's Old Brogue Inn **1**
Siamsa Tire **5**

REPUBLIC OF IRELAND
Dublin ⭐
● Tralee

Information ⓘ

Getting to and around Tralee and the Dingle Peninsula

If you're coming by car from Dublin, follow signs for N7 south to Limerick, and then get on the N21 or N69 (Coast Road) to Tralee. From the Ring of Kerry and points south, take N70 to Tralee. From Killarney, Cork, and the east, take N22. Trains and buses to Tralee arrive at the station on John Joe Sheehy Road (call ☎ **01-836-6111** for bus information; ☎ **1-850-366-222** for train information).

Bus Éireann also provides service to Dingle Town daily; the depot is on Upper Main Street.

Spending the night in Tralee and on the Dingle Peninsula

Alpine House
$$ **Dingle Town/An Daingean**

People rave about this guesthouse. The sizable, bright rooms offer all sorts of perks, such as tea- and coffeemaking facilities, hair dryers, direct-dial phones, and central heating (sure beats huddling next to a radiator on chilly days!). Plus you have use of a roomy guest lounge and can enjoy the hospitality of Paul O'Shea. The heart of Dingle Town is just a two-minute walk away, and the views of Dingle Bay are splendid.

Mail Road. ☎ *066-915-1250. Fax: 066-915-1966.* www.alpineguesthouse.com. *Off the main road (N86). Rates: €70–€110 ($112–$176) double. AE, MC, V.*

The Captain's House
$$ **Dingle Town**

I grew up in a turn-of-the-century house, with rooms of all different sizes, and my stay in this late-19th-century former sea captain's house, with its nooks and crannies, reminded me of my childhood home. The bedrooms are cozy, with warm lighting and lovely quilts, and there is an enchanting garden outside. Your hosts, Mary and Jim Milhench, have decorated the living rooms (you have three to choose from) with antiques, interesting nautical objects (Jim is a Master Mariner), and souvenirs from their world travels. The effect is at once homey and elegant. Breakfasts, served in the conservatory, are an experience in themselves, as Mary offers everything from fresh smoked kippers to homemade scones to eggs with local salmon. The house has a fantastic location on a quiet side street right near the heart of Dingle Town.

The Mall. ☎ *066-915-1531. Fax: 066-915-1079. Rates: €90–€100 ($144–$160) double. AE, MC, V. Closed: Dec–Mar.*

Castlemorris House
$$ **Tralee**

A 1790s manor house accommodation at these rates? Nope, you're not dreaming. Rooms here are clean and large, furnished with reproduction antique furniture, but it's the hosts that really make the place. Tony and Ciara Fields are more than willing to help with plans, directions, and anything else that you might need. The breakfasts are excellent, and the location is superb: a ten-minute walk from downtown Tralee and perfect for launching your visit to the Dingle Peninsula.

Tralee (off the N86). ☎ *066-718-0060.* www.castlemorrishouse.com. *Rates: €80–€90 ($128–$144). MC, V.*

Grand Hotel
$$$ Tralee

This hotel is a winner in all categories. The staff is warm and helpful, and the public rooms have that great old world hotel look, with lots of mahogany and ornate plasterwork. Rooms are comfortable and up-to-date. The hotel restaurant, Samuels, is a destination in itself, serving fresh, well-prepared dishes. End your night in the lovely bar, where you will likely find a convivial mix of locals and visitors.

Denny Street. ☎ **066-712-1499.** *Fax: 066-712-2877. Rates: €100–€130 ($160–$208). AE, MC, V.*

Greenmount House
$$–$$$$ Dingle

Beware: The views of Dingle Bay and Dingle Town from this modern lodging may cause you to delay your day's plans in favor of lingering over breakfast or relaxing in the sitting room. Though the house doesn't have many rooms, it feels more like a small hotel than a B&B, with spacious rooms (those in the bungalow building have sitting areas and balconies), large bathrooms, upscale modern furniture, and extremely comfortable beds. Service is kind and professional, but if you're looking for a lot of warmth and helpful hints from your hosts, you may be better off at Milestone House or Alpine House. Breakfast is amazing in both scope and quality — be sure to try some of the mouthwatering cheeses from the buffet. The main streets of Dingle Town are about a 10- or 15-minute walk away.

John Street. ☎ **066-915-1414.** *Fax: 066-915-1974.* www.greenmount-house.com. *Rates: €80–€170 ($128–$272). MC, V.*

Milestone B&B
$$ Dingle Town

It's hard to do anything but gush about the Milestone, which is located about a 15-minute walk from Dingle Town. The rooms are simple, impeccably clean, and bright, furnished with IKEA-style furniture; the views of Dingle Bay are dazzling; and the breakfasts are excellent. But what sets this B&B apart from the pack are your hosts, Michael and Barbara Carroll. The Carrolls love the Dingle Peninsula, and they know it inside and out (despite having moved here only about five years ago). Happily, they make it their mission to share their knowledge with their guests, spending at least 20 minutes helping visitors to plan an itinerary that suits their needs. If this is your first time in Dingle, definitely book a room here.

Milltown (1km [½ mile] outside of Dingle on the R559). ☎ **066-915-1831.** www.iol.ie/~milstone. *Rates: €80–€90 ($128–$144). No credit cards.*

Pax House
$$$ **Dingle Town**

The first thing that you notice about this place is the view — it's spectacular. Overlooking the water, with mountains in the distance, Pax House will tempt you to just lounge around on the comfortable balcony all day. Inside, everything's meticulously decorated, and the rooms are gorgeous. A gourmet breakfast welcomes you in the morning.

Upper John Street. ☎ *066-915-1518. Fax: 066-915-2461.* www.pax-house.com. *Rates: €120 ($192) double. MC, V. Closed: Dec–Feb.*

Slea Head Farm
$ **Dunquin**

Located on a working farm, this cozy B&B is situated in a rural area between Ventry and Dunquin. The panoramas surrounding the house are pure, gorgeous Ireland: cows and sheep grazing on emerald-green grass, a maze of old stone walls creeping up a gentle hill, and a ruined stone house next door. And the finest views are reserved for travelers whose bedroom windows look out onto the nearby sea and the famed Blasket Islands. Rooms are cozy and cute, with homey touches such as stuffed animals perched on the furniture. The Irish-speaking family who runs the B&B is warm and welcoming.

On road between Ventry and Dunquin. ☎ *066-915-6120.* www.sleaheadfarm.com. *Rates: €70 ($112). MC, V. Closed: Nov–Mar.*

Dining locally in Tralee and on the Dingle Peninsula

Visiting a place right on the water pretty much promises you'll find plenty of good seafood, and the restaurants on the Dingle Peninsula won't fail you. From elegant to simple, the dishes in these parts are delicious.

Chart House
$$$$ **Dingle Town** **NEW IRISH**

This place is like the restaurant equivalent of a spa treatment, with everything from the country décor to the warm service conspiring to create a relaxing atmosphere. The freshest of Irish ingredients are used in the inventive dishes, which on my last visit included such gems as herb-crusted skate with a leek and parmesan risotto, served with aged balsamic vinegar; and a seared filet of Kerry beef with dauphinoise potatoes, caramelized shallots, and port wine jus. The room is inviting, with stone walls, stained glass windows, and pine tables set with a blue-and-orange runner and mismatched pottery. It would be a shame to leave this restaurant without ordering their warm sticky toffee pudding.

The Mail Road. ☎ *066-915-2255. Reservations recommended. Main courses: €24–€30 ($38–$48). MC, V. Open: May–Sept daily 6:30–10 p.m.; Oct–Dec and Feb–Apr Sun–Thurs 6:30–10 p.m.*

Doyle's Seafood Bar
$$$$ **Dingle Town** SEAFOOD

If you're looking for lobster, look no further — Doyle's won't disappoint. Here, when you have lobster, you pick it out of a tank in the bar. Or you can go for some variety with the popular seafood platter, a plate brimming with sole, lobster, salmon, oysters, and crab claws. The menu depends on the fresh seafood caught daily by local fishermen, so although you can't always depend on a certain dish, you can be sure whatever you get will be fresh. The dining room is cozy, with plenty of brick and stone — you may feel like you're eating in someone's wide-open kitchen.

4 John St. ☎ *066-915-1174. Reservations recommended. Main courses: €20–€30 ($32–$48). MC, V. Open: Mon–Sat 6–9 p.m. Closed: Mid-Nov to mid-Feb.*

Global Village
$$$$ **Dingle Town** NEW IRISH/SEAFOOD

Families, groups of friends, and couples all love this relaxed restaurant. The walls are a sunshine yellow, graced with contemporary oil paintings, and (more importantly) the food is terrific. The chef is creative in preparing fresh, local ingredients. On my last visit, I had braised beef cheeks with horseradish mashed potatoes and red wine jus, and my dad had pan-friend mackerel in an oatmeal crust with a warm potato, butter bean, and orange salad. Check out the early-bird specials, which include two or three courses at a great price.

Upper Main St. ☎ *066-915-2325. Main courses: €22–€29 ($35–$46). AE, MC, V. Open: June–Aug daily 5:30–10 p.m.; Sept–May daily 6–9:30 p.m.*

Unbeatable ice cream & amazing pastries

I would consider moving to Dingle Town just for **Murphy's Ice Cream,** Strand Street, Dingle (☎ **066-915-2644**). The Murphy brothers opened their store in 2000 with a quest to create the perfect ice cream, and I'd say they're well on their way to attaining their goal. The smooth ice cream is made with top-quality ingredients: Kerry cream and milk (thank those cows the next time you drive past them), and the best natural flavorings, such as Madagascar and Organic Mexican Vanilla in the vanilla ice cream, real Champagne and peaches in the Bellini sorbet, Jamaican rum in the rum raisin, and so on. You may want to go for one of the distinctly Irish flavors, such as Irish-cream ice cream, black-currant-and-Guinness sorbet, or brown-bread ice cream. After intense menu research, the delicious, caramel-tinged honeycomb ice cream has emerged as my favorite.

O'Curnain's Bakery (☎ **066-915-1583**), located in the courtyard next to Dick Mack's Pub on Green St., sells divine pastries. Their fresh cream and apple pastry is perfection.

Goat Street Café
$$ Dingle Town   Café/Vegetarian

This bright little cafe draws its influences from around the world, with offerings such as a potato tortilla with grilled chorizo and sweet red pepper jam, and a Thai green curry served with Basmati rice. Friends chat and laugh over long lunches and dinners, and the service couldn't be nicer. Vegetarians will be thrilled with the non-meat choices.

Main St. ☎ 066-915-2770. Main courses: €11–€13 ($18–$21). AE, MC, V. Open: Mon–Wed 10 a.m.–5 p.m., Thurs–Sat 10–5 p.m. and 6–9 p.m., and Sun 11–3 p.m.

James Ashe's Pub
$$$$ Dingle Town   GOURMET PUB FOOD/SEAFOOD

The scene: A traditional pub, with dark wood tables and chairs and warm golden lighting. The supporting players: The friendly manager and helpful staff. The stars: A menu featuring terrific and creative seafood dishes along with Irish pub standards such as beef-and-Guinness stew. Standouts include "tempura of today's catch" served with remoulade; steamed Thai mussels with chile, cilantro, garlic, ginger, lemongrass, and coconut; and an out-of-this-world seafood chowder.

Lower Main Street. ☎ 066-915-0989. Reservations recommended. Main courses: €20–€30 ($32–$48). MC, V. Serving food: Mon–Sat noon to 3 p.m. and 6–9 p.m.

The Old Pier
$$$–$$$$ Ballydavid

For me, there's something about eating seafood with a view of the sea that makes it taste even better, so I find the Old Pier's view of Smerwick Harbour very satisfying. Though the meat dishes are excellent, it's the seafood dishes — featuring locally caught fish and shellfish — that keep bringing people back. Choices range from monkfish, brill, and salmon with prawn sauce to black sole served in a butter, lemon, and parsley sauce.

Located north of Ballydavid on the R559. ☎ 066-915-5242. Main courses: €16–€30 ($26–$48). MC, V. Open: Wed–Mon 6–7:30 p.m. Closed: Mid-Nov to Feb.

Out of the Blue
$$$$ Dingle Town   SEAFOOD

The official name of this place is Out of the Blue Fresh Fish Seafood Only Restaurant, because it serves only dishes that once swam or crawled through the nearby briny deep (though it also offered a vegetarian plate while I was there). A little pompous, maybe, but Out of the Blue is allowed to be egotistical, because it serves the best seafood in Dingle Town. The chalkboard menu changes daily depending on the catches of the day. Preparations, such as skate (ray wings) with caper butter and haddock on tomato sauce, are relatively simple and allow the flavor of the fish to sparkle. The garlic crab claws are unbelievable. The restaurant itself has a Mediterranean feel, with simple pine tables; bright blue, yellow, and red walls and ceiling; and oil paintings of fish and the sea gracing the walls. Lunch here is much less expensive than dinner.

Waterside. ☎ *066-915-0811. Reservations recommended for dinner; not accepted for lunch. Main courses: €23–€34 ($37–$54) dinner. MC, V. Open: Fri–Mon 12:30–3 p.m., Thurs–Tues 12:30–3 p.m. Closed: Nov–Mar 17.*

Exploring Tralee and the Dingle Peninsula

If you are interested in a boating trip on Dingle Bay, contact Dingle Marine Eco Tours, located at The Pier in Dingle Town. Book in advance at ☎ 066-915-1344.

A dazzling tour of the Dingle Peninsula

Like the Ring of Kerry, the big attraction of the Dingle Peninsula is driving, biking, or hiking your way around, taking in all the scenery as well as the many prehistoric ruins. I recommend starting in **Castlemaine** and taking the coastal road (R561 or R559) toward Dingle Town. Along the way, you may want to pay a visit to **Inch Beach,** a long sandy beach with the Atlantic waves on one side and curvy, sea-grass-covered dunes on the other. It's a strange sight to stand on the dunes looking at the vast Atlantic in one direction and grazing cows and sheep in the other. Move on toward **Dingle Town,** which is a great place to spend a night or two before driving the Slea Head Tour.

From Dingle Town, take the gorgeous 48km (33-mile) **Slea Head Tour,** a round-trip circuit that takes you along the south coast, past miles and miles of small patchwork fields, up the west end of the peninsula and then back to Dingle Town. You may want to make your first stop at pretty **Ventry Beach,** before visiting the remains of **Dunbeg Fort,** created in 800 B.C. Right near Dunbeg Fort, look out for signs indicating the location of **beehive huts** (known as clocháin in Irish), small stone structures that are thought to date from around 1000 B.C. The highlight of the route is **Slea Head,** which features towering cliffs with incredible views of the Atlantic ocean and the **Blasket Islands** (described later in this section), sandy beaches (be aware the waters are not safe for swimming), and several trail heads. Visit the village of **Dún Chaoin** (Dunquin), the heart of the Dingle *Gaeltacht* (Irish-speaking area), with its striking views of the Blasket Islands, before checking out the **Blasket Centre** and possibly taking a boat trip to Great Blasket Island. You may want to have lunch at Tig Áine and then move on to visit **Clogher Strand,** a small beach with beautiful stones that look like they're decorated with maps from some undiscovered land (the beach is located off the second turn after the Louis Mulcahy pottery shop). Next stop: **Gallarus Oratory,** an astoundingly intact seventh-century Christian church built without any sort of mortar. Adventurers will want to depart from the Slea Head Drive at Feothanagh, driving east (and up) on narrow mountain roads through **Conor Pass,** where you have a thrilling panoramic view of the entire peninsula, plus views of several peaceful glacial lakes, and then down to

The Sleeping Giant?

As you tour the Dingle Peninsula on the Slea Head Drive, keep an eye out for an island that looks like a giant taking a snooze on his back. From most parts of the peninsula he looks like he is slumbering peacefully. However, on other parts of the peninsula it appears that he has a dagger embedded in his neck. In those parts, he is known as The Murdered Bishop rather than the Sleeping Giant.

the picture-postcard fishing villages of **Cloghane** and **Brandon.** From there, you can drive east past unspoiled sandy beaches, cute fishing villages, and farmland. *Note:* Only confident drivers should attempt the Conor Pass route, as it's winding and steep.

This route will take you a whole day. I recommend staying in Dingle Town or west of Dingle Town on the nights before and after your drive or bike ride.

If you are visiting Dingle Peninsula without a car (and even if you have a car) **Sciuird Tours Bus and Walking Tour** (☎ 066-915-1606) offers a great three- or four-hour expert-led bus tour along the Slea Head drive, with stops to enjoy the scenery and to explore four or five monuments from the Stone Age to the Middle Ages (including Gallarus Oratory). You'll do some light walking. Tours leave daily at 10:30 a.m. and/or 2 p.m., as long as at least six people have booked (14 is the maximum). Tours are €20 ($32) per person. Call for information on departure location; pick-up is often available from Dingle Town accommodations. If you want to take a personalized guided tour, contact **Denis Ryan** (☎ 086-325-2996; www.dingletours.com), who takes travelers out to explore the peninsula in his cab. Tours start at €20 ($32) per person.

The Slea Head route is superb for biking. You can rent bikes from **Foxy John's,** Main Street, Dingle (☎ 066-915-1316).

The Dingle Peninsula is also a wonderful place for hiking. See "Hiking," later in this section.

The Aqua Dome
Tralee

If your kids don't think they've been on vacation if they haven't gotten a chance to submerge themselves in water, this indoor water park is the place to go. Kids can splash around in the kiddie pools, fly down sky-high slides, and battle raging rapids — all under one roof. Meanwhile, adults can relax in the sauna dome, which has two saunas, a steam room, a cool pool, and a sun bed. The main pool is for the whole family, and next door is an over-16-only health suite (which is really just a spot with hot tubs and saunas). If you or your kids get sick of the water, there's also a minigolf course, remote-controlled trucks and boats, and a giant trampoline.

Dingle Road (next to the steam railway heading out of town). ☎ *066-712-8899. Admission: €12 ($19) adults, €10 ($16) children, and free for children under 2. Open: July–Aug daily 10 a.m.–10 p.m.; Sept–June Mon–Fri 10 a.m.–10 p.m., Sat–Sun 10 a.m.–8 p.m. Suggested visit: As long as you like!*

Blasket Centre (1onad an Bhlascaoid Mhoir)
Dunquin

This heritage center, on the tip of the Dingle Peninsula, celebrates the Blasket Islands, which lie a few miles from the mainland. Great Blasket, the largest of the islands, was home to a Gaelic-speaking community until the 1950s. Photographs, a video presentation, and other exhibits illustrate the lives of the Blasket Islanders, who farmed and fished for sustenance and have a rich storytelling and musical tradition. Much of the museum focuses on the literary achievements of the Blasket Islanders — several autobiographies and collections of Blasket Island tales were published with great success. The exhibits, while very well done, are heavy on text, so younger children may be bored. There are incredible views of the islands through the large windows in the center. If you are interested in visiting the Blasket Islands, see the information in the next review.

Village of Dunquin (right off the R559). ☎ *066-915-6444. Admission: €3.70 ($5.90) adults, €2.60 ($4.20) seniors, €1.30 ($2.10) children and students. Open: Easter–June daily 10 a.m.–6 p.m.; July–Aug daily 10 a.m.–7 p.m.; Sept–Oct daily 10 a.m.–6 p.m. Last admission is 45 minutes before closing time. Closed: Nov–Easter. Suggested visit: 1½ hours.*

Blasket Islands

Intrigued by what you've seen and heard at the Blasket Centre? There's only one thing to do: Book a trip to peaceful Great Blasket Island, where you can walk amongst the ruins of the village, hike the "green roads" (roads that have been reclaimed by grass), and watch seals (and sometimes dolphins, porpoises, shark, and whales) from the white sand beach.

The Blasket Island Ferry departs from Dunquin Harbour. ☎ *066-915-6422. Ferries depart daily Apr–Sept 30 starting at 10:30 a.m. Reservations recommended. Tickets: €30 ($48) adults, €15 ($24) children under 12.*

Corn Maze

Every year, a different maze is created in this 2.4-hectare (6-acre) field of corn. Your mission (if you choose to accept it) is to actually make your way through this labyrinth. Last year the maze theme was Harry Potter; this year it is Fungie the Dingle Dolphin. Leave yourself at least an hour.

Upper Main St. ☎ *087-610-9563. €6 ($9.60), under 5 free. Mid-July to Aug daily 11–6 p.m. (closed on rainy days).*

Harry Clarke stained glass windows at Díseart
Dingle

This Irish Cultural Centre contains a treasure of Irish art — six magnificent stained glass windows created by master stained glass artist Harry Clarke in 1922. The windows depict scenes from the Bible, with glowing colors and tremendous detail, especially in the animated faces of the subjects. An audio tour gives you the details on the history of Clarke and the windows, and explains the scene portrayed in each window. On your way in or out of Díseart, check to see if the center is holding any of their frequent cultural events.

Off Green Street, behind St. Mary's Church. ☎ *066-915-2476. Admission: €3.50 ($5.60). Open: Daily 9 a.m.–5 p.m.*

Fungie the Dolphin
Dingle

Dingle's most famous resident, Fungie the Dolphin, is a friendly, playful dolphin who has been hanging out around the waters of Dingle Bay since 1984. He's not in captivity, so theoretically, he could take off for bluer waters at any time, but he's stuck around for more than two decades, so odds are good that he's in Dingle to stay. Fungie seems to love playing with humans, and if you take boat tour to see him (there are separate trips for swimmers and nonswimmers), you will likely be treated to a display of arcing jumps and up-close encounters as Fungie swims alongside the boat. Plus you'll have wonderful views of serene Dingle Bay. If you're up for it, I recommend going whole-hog and renting a wetsuit and snorkel gear so that you can play with Fungie in the water. Floating peacefully in the blue water of Dingle Bay and seeing this winsome creature eye-to-eye are worth the initial shock of climbing into the cool water.

The Pier. ☎ *066-915-2626 for boat trips;* ☎ *066-915-1967 for wetsuit hire and swimming trips. Call to pick up a wetsuit and make reservations* **the day before** *for swimming trips. Cost: Boat trip €16 ($26) adults, €8 ($13) children 2–12, and free for children under 2; swimming trip €25 ($40); wetsuit €25 ($40) adults, €15 ($24) children under 12. You can buy tickets for the boat ride at a kiosk at the pier. Call for times and to reserve a spot.*

Kerry County Museum
Tralee

Kerry's history, starting 7,000 years ago, unfolds before you at this well-done heritage center. Exhibits cover everything from myths and legends of the county to local music to Gaelic football. The highlight just may be the theme-park-style ride that takes you through a life-size exhibit of Tralee of the Middle Ages, enhanced with sounds and even smells of the time.

Ashe Memorial Hall, Denny Street. ☎ *066-712-7777. Admission: €8 ($13) adults, €6.50 ($10) students, €5 ($8) children. Open: May–Oct daily 9:30 a.m.–5:30 p.m.; Nov–Apr Tues–Sat 9:30 a.m.–5 p.m. Suggested visit: 1½–2 hours.*

More outdoor activities

Try some of these activities to get you out into the bracing Dingle air.

✔ **Golfing:** On Sandhill Road, you find **Ballybunion Golf Club** (☎ 068-27-146; www.ballybuniongolfclub.ie), a seaside club with two excellent 18-hole, par-71 courses. The newer course was fashioned by the legendary Robert Trent Jones, though the Old Course is the more challenging of the two. Greens fees are €180 ($288) for the old course and €110 ($176) for the new, or €265 ($424) to play both on the same day. Visitors are welcome, provided you call to book in advance. The par-71 **Tralee Golf Club,** located at West Barrow, Ardfert, in Tralee (☎ 066-713-6379; www.traleegolf club.com), is the original European Arnold Palmer–designed course. This course is set against an amazing backdrop, boxed in by river, the sea, and the crumbling castles of Ardfert. Greens fees are €180 ($288). Visitors are welcome from May to October every day except Sunday. Visitors are not permitted on Wednesdays in June, July, and August. You must book in advance either over the phone or on the website.

✔ **Hiking:** The Dingle Way leaves from Tralee and makes a 153km (95-mile) circuit of the peninsula. The trail winds through beaches and farmland and along cliffs. For day-hikers, there is a beautiful stretch between Dunquin and Ballyferriter, and another going northeast out of Féohanagh. Get your hands on the *Dingle Way Map Guide* (available at tourist offices and shops in the area) before you begin the trail.

Another hiking trail, the Pilgrim's Route (48km/30 miles), meanders through the fields of the peninsula, connecting many of the peninsula's interesting early Christian sites. The ascent to Mount Brandon's summit, located at the end of the Route, is difficult but spectacular. Pick up a Pilgrim's Route map (available at tourist offices and shops in the area) before you begin the trail.

✔ **Horseback riding:** Mountain and beach rides are available through **Dingle Horse Riding** (☎ 066-915-2199; www.dinglehorseriding.com), located a mile outside of Dingle Town.

Shopping

Dingle Town is home to many artists, making it a fabulous place to buy contemporary fine art as well as crafts. In addition, there are some great pottery shops along roadsides throughout the Dingle Peninsula; just drop in when you come across them.

Brian de Staic, Green Street, Dingle (☎ 066-915-1298), offers unique handcrafted gold jewelry. Many of his pieces incorporate Celtic designs. **West Kerry Craft Gallery,** Main Street (☎ 066-915-2976), features works by an assortment of wonderful Dingle craftspeople. **Dingle**

Record Shop, Green Street (across from St. Mary's Church; ☎ 087-298-4550), is a great place to buy traditional music recordings. Out on the peninsula, well-known craftsman **Louis Mulcahy** (☎ 066-915-6229) creates lustrous pieces of pottery. Mulcahy's workshop is located about 4km (2.5 miles) west of Ballyferriter.

Hitting the pubs

The Dingle Peninsula, and Dingle Town in particular, is a great place for music. Drop into most any pub during the summer, and you'll hear tin whistles, fiddles, pipes, and other instruments going strong.

Dick Mack's
Dingle Town

Undoubtedly one of Ireland's quaintest pubs, Dick Mack's retains an aura of times gone by — years ago, pubs often doubled as providers of other essential services; this one doubled as a cobbler's shop, and one side of the place still holds the leatherworking tools of the late owner. There is a great little snug at the end of the bar side and an authentic back room that once served as the kitchen. Apparently, when Tom Cruise and Nicole Kidman stayed in Dingle while filming *Far and Away,* they fell in love with the place. Many other stars have stopped in for a pint — there's even a little walk of fame outside.

Green Street. ☎ *066-915-1960.*

The Dingle Pub
Dingle Town

Facing the harbor and easily distinguished by the green-and-white shamrock outside, this place is just what it sounds like: the pub that represents Dingle. The inside of the pub is much like Dingle itself: It seems as though nothing's changed in generations, and you can relax in the laid-back atmosphere. Stop in for a pint and a talk with the locals.

Main Street, at the harbor. ☎ *066-915-1370.*

Irish folk theater

Siamsa Tíre: The National Folk Theatre of Ireland, Town Park, Tralee (☎ 066-712-3055; www.siamsatire.com), performs theater that celebrates the rich dance, music, and folklore traditions of Ireland.

Past performances have included beautiful theatrical and musical retellings of the Irish myths of the Children of Lir and Oisín's Return to Tír na nÓg (the land of eternal youth), a production about the people of the Blasket Islands, and a show celebrating life on a small Irish farm a century ago.

Kirby's Old Brogue Inn
Tralee

This bright-yellow alehouse has dubbed itself "your landmark in Tralee." Given the great atmosphere and food, it probably will be. Its quaint exterior gives way to a wonderful old pub inside, where you'll hear traditional Irish music and jazz in the summers, and where you can nosh on glorified pub grub all day — steaks and seafood barside are quite a treat.

Rock Street. ☎ *066-712-3357.*

Natterjack
Castlegregory

This old pub, which concentrates more on great traditional music and food than on the latest trend in décor, is a perfect place to stop in for a bite and a refreshing pint after the drive to the north end of the peninsula. The pub offers a children's menu and a beer garden in summertime.

The West End. ☎ *066-713-9491.*

O'Flaherty's
Dingle Town

You can count on the music in O'Flaherty's to be good — the owner frequently performs. Check out the posters and clippings that line the walls to get a real feel for Dingle Town. Everything about this place screams *authentic,* and the locals who frequent it often chat in Irish Gaelic. It's big and open, and because of the stone-flagged floor, it doesn't exactly get cozy until it gets full.

Bridge Street. ☎ *066-915-1983.*

Fast Facts: Tralee and Dingle Peninsula

Area Code

The main area code for Tralee and Dingle is **066**.

Emergencies/Police

Dial ☎ **999** for all emergencies.

Hospital

In Tralee, the Tralee General Hospital is on Killarney Road (N22) (☎ 066-714-9800). In Dingle, the Dingle District Hospital is on Upper Main Street (☎ 066-915-1455).

Information

For visitor information in Tralee, go to the Tralee Tourist Office at Ashe Memorial Hall, Denny Street, Tralee (☎ 066-712-1288), which is open year-round. The Dingle Tourist Office is on Strand Street, Dingle (☎ 066-915-1188).

Internet

Dingle Internet Cafe, Lower Main Street, Dingle (☎ 066-9155-2478), has Internet access and printing capabilities.

Part V
The West and the Northwest

The 5th Wave   By Rich Tennant

In this part . . .

You can't beat the West and Northwest for their sheer diversity of landscapes. In Clare (Chapter 17), take in the steep Cliffs of Moher, plummeting down to the sea; the rocky moonscape of the Burren, studded with a rainbow of wildflowers; and the county's sandy beaches. Up in County Galway (Chapter 18), explore the wild lakes, bogs, mountains, and beaches of Connemara, and gaze out at peaceful Galway Bay. Mayo (Chapter 19) offers gorgeous heather-covered islands, beaches, and a continuation of the Connemara landscape of bogs, cliffs, and mountains, while travelers to Sligo (Chapter 19) will find lakes, beaches, and woodlands, many connected in some way with poet W.B. Yeats. If you want to get way off the well-trodden track, head up to wild, sparsely populated County Donegal (Chapter 20) and explore the craggy coastline, towering cliffs, sandy beaches, and impressive mountains of the region.

And I haven't even mentioned the cities and towns in these parts. Westport in County Mayo (Chapter 19) is one of the most charming, bustling, and picturesque towns in Ireland. Sligo Town (Chapter 19), a friendly town with a healthy arts scene, is an ideal base for exploring sights associated with Yeats. Limerick (Chapter 17) has shed its image of dilapidation, and offers some excellent historic sights, restaurants, and pubs, while Ennis is a small town with winding medieval streets and a fair share of traditional Irish music. And Galway City (Chapter 18) may turn out to be your favorite city in Ireland, with its beautiful location on the shores of Galway Bay and Lough Corrib, its tremendous selection of excellent restaurants, and its thriving pubs and traditional Irish music scenes.

Chapter 17

Counties Limerick and Clare

Sure, **County Clare** is famous for the sheer, breathtaking Cliffs of Moher. But this county is no one-trick pony. In the north, you'll find the rocky moonscape of The Burren, with its diversity of plant species poking up through cracks in the rocks (where else can you find Arctic and tropical plants flowering side by side?). In the south are long sandy stretches of beach backed by rolling green hills. And throughout the county are charming towns and villages whose pubs ring to the rafters with some of the best traditional music in all of Ireland.

Many people know **County Limerick** through Frank McCourt's *Angela's Ashes,* in which Limerick City is depicted as a sodden and sullen place. Yes, it rains in Limerick (as it does all over the West of Ireland), but you may be surprised at the new restaurants, shops, and attractions that are popping up all over the city. Though it's still not a destination city, it is worth a stop if you are interested in any of the attractions in the area, including **Adare,** a sweet little village of thatched-roof cottages with some excellent restaurants.

County Limerick: Limerick City and Adare

County Limerick has never exactly been the tourist hub of the country, but many visitors to Ireland pass through at some point. Those who have read Frank McCourt's *Angela's Ashes* often picture **Limerick City** as a town wracked with poverty, unemployment, alcoholism, and rain — lots of rain. "Out in the Atlantic Ocean," McCourt writes, "great sheets of

Counties Limerick and Clare

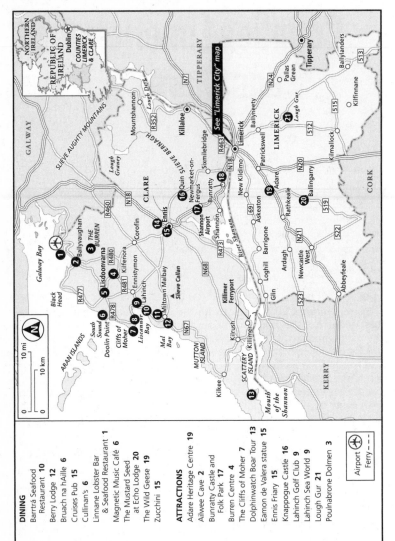

ACCOMMODATIONS
Adare Manor Hotel & Golf Resort **19**
Ballyvara House **6**
Berry Lodge **12**
Bunratty Castle Hotel **18**
Carrabawn House **19**
Dromoland Castle **17**
Drumcreehy House **2**
Dunraven Arms Hotel **19**
Grey Gables **15**
Roadford House **6**
Shamrock Inn Hotel **9**

SHOPPING
Belleek Shop **15**
Burren Perfumery **3**
The Burren Smokehouse **5**
Custy's Traditional Music Shop **15**
George Stacpoole Antiques **19**
The Rock Shop **8**
Traditional Music Shop **6**

NIGHTLIHFE
Cois na hAbhna **14**
Durty Nelly's **18**
glór **15**
McGann's **6**
Monk's Pub **2**
O'Briens **11**
O'Connor's **6**
The Poet's Corner **15**

DINING
Barrtrá Seafood Restaurant **10**
Berry Lodge **12**
Bruach na hAille **6**
Cruises Pub **15**
Cullinan's **6**
Linnane Lobster Bar & Seafood Restaurant **1**
Magnetic Music Café **6**
The Mustard Seed at Echo Lodge **20**
The Wild Geese **19**
Zucchini **15**

ATTRACTIONS
Adare Heritage Centre **19**
Ailwee Cave **2**
Bunratty Castle and Folk Park **17**
Burren Centre **4**
The Cliffs of Moher **7**
Dolphinwatch Boar Tour **13**
Eamon de Valera statue **15**
Ennis Friary **15**
Knappogue Castle **16**
Lahinch Golf Club **9**
Lahinch Sea World **9**
Lough Gur **21**
Poulnabrone Dolmen **3**

Limerick City

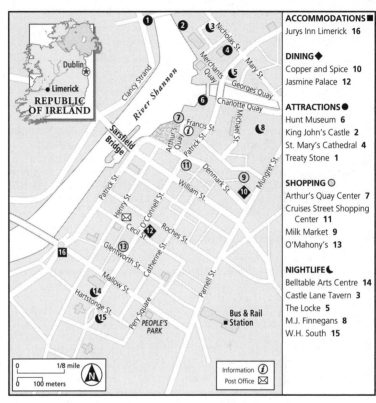

ACCOMMODATIONS ■
Jurys Inn Limerick **16**

DINING ◆
Copper and Spice **10**
Jasmine Palace **12**

ATTRACTIONS ●
Hunt Museum **6**
King John's Castle **2**
St. Mary's Cathedral **4**
Treaty Stone **1**

SHOPPING ○
Arthur's Quay Center **7**
Cruises Street Shopping
    Center **11**
Milk Market **9**
O'Mahony's **13**

NIGHTLIFE ☾
Belltable Arts Centre **14**
Castle Lane Tavern **3**
The Locke **5**
M.J. Finnegans **8**
W.H. South **15**

rain gathered to drift slowly up the River Shannon and settle forever in Limerick. . . . The rain drove us to the church — our refuge, our strength, our only dry place. . . . Limerick gained a reputation for piety, but we knew it was only the rain."

The whole west of Ireland does get its fair share of rain, but you'll be surprised to see how different in all other respects the Limerick of today is from the Limerick McCourt remembers from his youth. In recent years, the city has been pulling itself up from near dilapidation and is becoming a bustling place with a crop of great restaurants and good shopping, plus an excellent museum and several historic sights. Some places in the city still fit McCourt's description, but these are becoming fewer and fewer, as funky cafes open up in previously boarded-up buildings, and so on. A stroll along the River Shannon offers a striking vista of the city, and the imposing sight of **King John's Castle** is never far from view. Limerick City still isn't a destination city, like Dublin, Cork, Belfast, and Galway are, but it is worth a stop if you are in the area and are interested in any of the attractions listed in this section.

With its main street of thatched-roof cottages sporting window boxes full of flowers, narrow streets, and ruined ivy-covered churches, the pretty little town of **Adare** looks like a set for a movie about old Ireland. The town is clearly geared for tourism, and you find no lack of fellow travelers enjoying the little shops, excellent restaurants, and handful of historic sights. You don't need more than a day at most to explore.

Getting to County Limerick

Shannon International Airport (☎ 061-71-2000; www.shannonairport. com), located on the N19, off the N18, south of Ennis and 24km (15 miles) west of Limerick City, receives direct flights from North America, Europe, and Britain (see Chapter 6 for more information), as well as flights from within Ireland. Rental-car company desks are located at Shannon Airport's Arrivals Hall. All the major car-rental companies listed in Chapter 7 are represented there. **Bus Éireann** (☎ 01-836-6111; www.buseireann.ie) offers service from Shannon to the Limerick Bus and Rail Station and other destinations.

Getting to and around Limerick City

If you're coming by car, Limerick City can be reached by the N20 from Cork, N21 from Tralee, N24 from Tipperary, N7 from Dublin, or N18 from Ennis and Galway.

Irish Rail (☎ 1-850-366-222; www.irishrail.ie) services Limerick City from Dublin, Cork, Killarney, and other cities throughout Ireland. Trains arrive at Colbert Station, Parnell Street, and Limerick. **Bus Éireann** (☎ 01-836-6111; www.buseireann.ie) has daily service to Limerick City (Colbert Station, Parnell St.) and most towns in County Limerick.

Limerick City is best seen on foot. Park near King John's Castle (for free!), and hoof it from sight to sight. (Parking elsewhere in Limerick City requires discs that can be purchased at local shops.) A car is your best way of getting to the major attractions throughout the county, though Limerick has local bus service that covers the city's suburbs — running from Colbert Station on Parnell Street — and Bus Éireann has service to other parts of the county. You can also catch a cab at Colbert Station (the train and bus station) or call **Top Cabs** (☎ 061-41-7417).

Getting to and around Adare

By car, take N21 southwest from Limerick City. **Bus Éireann** (☎ 01-836-6111) runs through Adare. The town itself is completely walkable.

Spending the night in Limerick City and Adare

In addition to food, the Mustard Seed at Echo Lodge (see p. 325) also offers splendid, antiques-furnished rooms.

Adare Manor Hotel and Golf Resort
$$$$ Adare

If nothing but the very best will do, this is the place for you. This tremendous castlelike manor house is one of the most beautiful properties in Ireland. There is nothing subtle about it — the structure was designed to reflect a variety of Irish and English homes admired by the first owners, the Lord and Lady Dunraven. It is an amalgam of styles, with turrets, 52 chimneys, and stone gargoyles gracing its exterior. The public rooms are breathtaking, especially the giant hall inspired by the Hall of Mirrors at Versailles. Opulent fabrics, hand-carved woodwork and stone, and gorgeous views of a river characterize the private rooms. And I haven't even mentioned the 226-hectare (840-acre) grounds. The perfectly groomed emerald grounds boast a Robert Trent Jones–designed golf course (home to the Irish Open in 2007, 2008, and 2009), a trout-filled river, formal French gardens, sweeping parklands, and majestic trees. A spa on the premises provides all sorts of relaxing treatments.

Off the N21. ☎ **061-60-5200** *or 1-800-462-3273 in the U.S.* www.adaremanor.ie. *Rates: €250–€500 ($400–$800). AE, MC, V.*

Carrabawn House
$$ Adare

Attention to detail and warm hospitality are the cornerstones of this luxurious guesthouse. It's not a thatched-roof cottage, but it is a comfortable, roomy house that you're sure to feel welcome in. It's right on Adare's main road, putting all of County Limerick's attractions within easy reach. Rooms are simply and tastefully decorated and are fully equipped with conveniences: television, phone, hair dryer, and a tea and coffeemaker. Be sure to check out the award-winning gardens.

Killarney Road (N21). ☎ **061-39-6067.** *Fax: 061-39-6067.* www.carrabawnhouse adare.com. *Rates: €70–€90 ($112–$144) double. MC, V.*

Dunraven Arms Hotel
$$$ Adare

Other hotels are going to seem like roughing it after you stay in the luxurious Dunraven Arms, built in 1792 and across the street from the well-preserved thatched cottages of little Adare. The charm of the village is carried into the hotel, where rooms are decorated with antique furniture. Modern-day does seep into some parts, though: There is a pool, a steam room, and a gym for guests' use, and many of the rooms have Wi-Fi access. Service can run from cool to welcoming and friendly.

Main Street (N21). ☎ **061-60-5900.** *Fax: 061-39-6541.* www.dunravenhotel.com. *Rates: €100–€280 ($160–$448) double. AE, MC, V.*

Jurys Inn Limerick
$$ Limerick City

This hotel is your standard, comfortable place to stay, and though the rooms are rather nondescript, the location is great — in the heart of the city. Best of all, though, kids stay free. This is one of the few places in Ireland that charges a flat room rate for up to three adults or two adults and two children, so if there are more than two of you, it's a great value. There is an informal restaurant and a pub on the premises, and a nearby public parking lot is convenient for those with a car.

Lower Mallow Street. In the city center, just over the Shannon Bridge (N18). ☎ **061-20-7000.** www.jurysinns.com. *Rates: €60–€89 ($96–$142) double. AE, DC, MC, V.*

Dining locally in Limerick City and Adare

Copper and Spice
$$ Limerick City   INDIAN AND THAI

This cool, modern restaurant does a bang-up job with both Thai and Indian standards and novel twists on these dishes, such as the monkfish curry with tandoori-roasted eggplant, tomatoes, and onions. The chef uses spices boldly to complement the flavors of the meat, fish, or vegetables. Large abstract paintings with fiery colors hang on the wall, small teardrop-shaped lamps dangle from the ceiling, and hammered-copper glasses and pitchers grace the tables. There are a number of excellent vegetarian options here, including the okra with crunchy spiced onions. The €25 ($40) three-course meal is quite a deal.

2 Cornmarket Row. ☎ **061-31-3620.** *Main courses: €12–€16 ($19–$26). AE, MC, V. Open: Tues–Sun 5–10:30 p.m.*

The Irish coffee of champions

Every year, the best Irish coffeemakers duke it out for the title of Champion of Champions. The Championship takes place in Foynes, in County Limerick, during a three-day festival complete with a smattering of festivities, including music and dancing. See www.irishcoffeefestival.com for more information.

In case you want to practice to compete, here's the basic recipe:

1. Warm a stem glass.

2. Add two teaspoons of sugar and a splash of whiskey.

3. Fill almost to the top with hot black coffee, and stir well.

4. Pour lightly whipped cream on top.

Jasmine Palace
$$–$$$ Limerick City   CHINESE

This place is widely acknowledged as the best spot for Chinese food in the Limerick area, with a menu that ranges from standard North American/European Chinese dishes, such as General Tso's chicken, to an excellent roast duck Cantonese-style. Not only is the food fantastic, but the crisp table linens and warm lighting also make for a nice atmosphere. A word to the wise: If you're really hungry, get some soup as a starter, because service can be slow.

O'Connell Mall, O'Connell Street (between Cecil and Roaches streets in the city center). ☎ 061-41-2484. Main courses: €11–€23 ($18–$37). AE, DC, MC, V. Open: Mon–Sat 12:30–11 p.m., Sun 12:30–10:30 p.m.

The Mustard Seed at Echo Lodge
$$$$ Ballingarry   NEW IRISH

The surroundings are gorgeous enough to distract your attention, but even endless gardens, a splashing fountain, and a beautiful country manor can't take away the impact of the food at the Mustard Seed. You'll spend a bit more than at many other places mentioned in this book, but you'll get a true gourmet meal in return. Organic vegetables (from the restaurant's own garden), fruits, and cheeses, combined with local meats and fish, are the foundation of the adventurous dishes. The menu changes all the time. Recently, some of the gems included pan-fried filets of sea bass with caramelized endive, onion veloute, and an avocado and sweet corn salsa; and the imaginative breast of Barbary duck on a bed of buttered greens, served with lime and vanilla mashed potatoes and chocolate oil. The atmosphere is calm and gracious. Early in the week a special two-course early bird menu is available from 7 to 8 p.m.

Newcastlewest Road, Echo Lodge. From Limerick City, take the N21 southwest to Adare, and then the R519 south to Ballingarry. ☎ 069-68-508. Reservations recommended. Main courses: €63 ($101) prix-fixe. AE, MC, V. Open: Daily 7–9:30 p.m. Closed: Usually Sun–Mon in winter (call to check).

The Wild Geese
$$$$ Adare   NEW IRISH

Just to give you an idea of the kind of restaurant this is, when the gracious server came around with the bread basket, in addition to the usual white and wheat rolls, we were offered banana rolls, which turned out to be excellent. The chef here is not afraid to use his locally sourced ingredients with a sense of fun and daring. The menu changes, but expect main courses such as a breast of corn-fed chicken stuffed with brie and sun-dried tomatoes, wrapped in pancetta and served with a wild-mushroom risotto, and appetizers such as the onion-and-parmesan tartlet studded with raisins. The interior is simple and candlelit, and the mood is convivial. An early-bird menu, served Sunday to Friday from 6:30 to 7:30 p.m., is a terrific deal at €35 ($56) for three courses.

Rose Cottage, Main Street. ☎ **061-39-6451**. *Reservations recommended. Main courses: 2-course fixed-price dinner €30 ($48) for all main courses. AE, DC, MC, V. Open: May–Sept Tues–Sun 6:30–10 p.m., Sun 6–9 p.m.; Oct–Apr Tues–Sat 6:30–10 p.m.*

Exploring Limerick City and Adare

Limerick City has enough interesting sights to make a full day of sightseeing. Adare really only has one major attraction — the Heritage Centre — but it's a lovely place to wander for a few hours.

Joining an organized tour

The popular two-hour *Angela's Ashes* **Walking Tour** covers many sights mentioned in Frank McCourt's book. Tours leave daily at 2:30 p.m. from the tourist office at Arthur's Quay. Book by calling ☎ **061-32-7108** or 087-635-3648. Tours cost €10 ($16).

Join experienced tour guides for an informative and interesting 90-minute **historical walking tour,** covering many of Limerick's most interesting historical sights. Tours leave from the tourist office on Arthur's Quay daily at 11 a.m. Price is €10 ($16) per person. You can book at ☎ **061-31-7522,** or just show up.

If you'd rather see the town on your own, pick up the well-done Tourist Trail walking-tour map at the visitor center.

If you are interested in a longer cruise on the Shannon, check out the seven-day barge cruises offered on the *Shannon Princess* (☎ **087-251-4809;** www.shannonprincess.com). You will visit several different towns and cities while sleeping and eating (gourmet meals) on the barge.

Seeing the top attractions

Adare Heritage Centre
Adare

This museum does a nice job of presenting the tumultuous history of Adare through displays, text, and audiovisuals. The highlight is the model of Adare during the Middle Ages; various areas light up in sync with a 20-minute narration. A 20-minute video also presents the town as it is today, which is interesting, but I suggest you spend the time seeing the real thing instead. The Heritage Centre is also the starting point for tours of Adare Castle, a handsome example of a medieval fortified castle (€6/$9.60 adults, €5/$8 students, children over 10, and seniors). Stop into the craft and knitwear shops on the premises, and pop into the cafe for some fresh-baked bread. Books are available if you want to know more about the area, and there is a tourist information desk on-site. This place should give you a sense of what else you want to see in and around town.

Main Street. ☎ **061-39-6666**. *Admission: €5 ($8) adults, €3.50 ($5.60) seniors, students, and children over 10, children under 10 free. Open: Feb–Oct daily 9 a.m.–5:30 p.m.; Nov–Jan daily 10 a.m.–5 p.m. Suggested visit: 1 hour.*

Hunt Museum
Limerick City

Located in Limerick's beautifully refurbished Custom House, this museum's art collection was generously donated by the Hunt family and includes many world-class pieces that occasionally go out on loan to international exhibitions. The range of art is extremely wide, with Picasso and da Vinci sculptures; medieval paintings, jewelry, and crystal; ancient Egyptian, Greek, and Roman pieces; and a great deal of Irish art and artifacts from as far back as prehistoric times. Highlights include a gold cross once owned by Mary Queen of Scots, and a menu designed by Picasso. The fabulous shop in the lobby sells classy souvenirs, and the museum restaurant serves light meals.

The Custom House, Rutland Street (next to Arthur's Quay, on the River Shannon). ☎ *061-31-2833. Admission: €7.75 ($12) adults, €6.25 ($10) students and seniors, €4 ($6.40) children. Open: Mon–Sat 10 a.m.–5 p.m., Sun 2–5 p.m. Suggested visit: 1 1/2–2 hours.*

King John's Castle
Limerick City

This impressive fortress, on the banks of the River Shannon, was the brainchild of King John, who commissioned it in 1210, and whose name will forever be linked with it in the public mind (even though its real name is Limerick Castle). Clearly a place built to keep people out rather than hold court or host lavish parties, this castle is one of the finest examples of a fortified Norman structure in Ireland. Fierce war defenses sit in the courtyard (how often do you get to manhandle a real battering ram?), and you can get a great view of the city from the corner towers. The interior has been completely restored. To get a complete understanding of the castle's function over the centuries, check out the interpretive center. Models, displays, and graphics combine to explain the past, and the show *The Story of Limerick* explains the turbulent history of this city in an interesting way.

Nicholas Street (east of the Thomond Bridge, at the corner of Nicholas and Castle streets). ☎ *061-41-1201. Admission: €8.35 ($13) adults, €6.25 ($10) seniors and students, €4.95 ($7.90) children. Open: Mar, Apr and Oct daily 9:30 a.m.–5 p.m. (last admission at 4 p.m.); May–Sept daily 9:30 a.m.–5:30 p.m. (last admission at 4:30 p.m.); Nov–Feb daily 10 a.m.–4:30 p.m. (last admission at 3:30 p.m.). Suggested visit: 1½ hours.*

Lough Gur
Southeast of Limerick City

Burial mounds, a wedge tomb, a dwelling built between 500 and 1000 A.D., a 4,000-year-old stone circle (the largest in Ireland), and other treasures surround a glittering lake at this rich archeological site, which was continuously inhabited from prehistoric to late medieval times. An interpretive center, housed in authentic-looking Stone Age huts right on the location of the original settlement, features models of unearthed tools, weapons, and pottery, plus audiovisual displays and text about different aspects of the site. There are regular walking tours of the area, but I recommend exploring on your own with a map from the visitor center.

Lough Gur. 11km (7 miles) southeast of Limerick City, off R512. ☎ **061-36-1511.** *Admission: Museum €5 ($8) adults; €3 ($4.80) seniors, students, and children. Open: Park year-round; visitor center May–Sept daily 10 a.m.–6 p.m. (last admission 5:30 p.m.). Suggested visit: 45 minutes.*

More cool things to see and do

✔ **St. Mary's Cathedral:** Built in the 12th century, this is the oldest building in Limerick City. The rounded Romanesque doorway is a remnant of the original church. Inside are many beautiful 15th-century carvings in black oak. Mass is said daily.

Location: Bridge Street, 1 block south of King John's Castle on Nicholas Street, Limerick. ☎ **061-31-0293.** Donation: €2 ($3.20). Open June to September, Monday through Saturday from 9 a.m. to 5 p.m.; October to May, Monday through Saturday from 9 a.m. to 1 p.m. Suggested visit: 45 minutes.

✔ **Treaty Stone:** This noble slab of limestone is reportedly where the Treaty of Limerick was signed in 1691, ending the bloody Siege of Limerick, led by Protestant William of Orange, who defeated Catholic King James II.

Location: Across the Thomand Bridge, facing King John's Castle across the Shannon, Limerick. Suggested visit: A few minutes.

Shopping

Limerick, like nearly all of Ireland's major cities, is a hub of shopping for the surrounding region. The main city thoroughfares, **O'Connell Street** and **William Street,** are lined with small shops and department stores. You won't find a load of places that sell souvenirs; the shopping here is vast and varied, but it mainly suits the needs of the people who live here.

Limerick City has two major shopping areas — one old and one new. The **Milk Market** (corner of Wickham and Ellen streets) is a restored medieval marketplace. Bordered by the original city walls, this quaint area offers country produce and arts and crafts on Saturdays. From Monday to Saturday, stalls and open-fronted shops make up the market, selling all sorts of products, including secondhand clothes and books. Most of city's real shopping gets done at the **Arthur's Quay Centre,** a modern mall in the heart of town. Inside this open, multistoried mall are 30 stores and places to eat. Locals also shop at **Cruises Street Shopping Center,** a complex of more than 50 retail outlets. **O'Mahony's,** 120 O'Connell St., Limerick (☎ **061-41-8155**), has a great selection of books, maps, and stationery. You can catch up on your Joyce or write friends back home in style.

In **Adare,** on the main street, Michelina and George Stacpoole sell sophisticated, brightly colored knitwear; great old Irish prints and postcards; old and rare books; and a vast selection of antiques in **George Stacpoole Antiques** (☎ **061-39-6409;** www.stacpooleantiques.com).

A day at the races

Horse-racing is extremely popular in Ireland. You can get in on the action in Limerick at the **Limerick Racecourse** (☎ 061-32-0000), or visit www.hri.ie to see the racing schedules for the whole country. If the horses aren't fast enough, check out greyhound racing at the **Limerick Track** (☎ 061-31-6788), or see www.igb.ie for greyhound-racing schedules for all of Ireland.

Hitting the pubs

Before a night out, you may want to catch a film, play, or concert at **Belltable Arts Centre** (☎ 061-31-5871; www.belltable.ie). Just call or check the site to see what's going on when you're in town.

Castle Lane Tavern
Limerick City

This beautiful tavern's décor (a medieval re-creation, in sort of a Disney way) is so detailed and authentic-looking, you may be tempted to summon the barmaid with a hearty "Beer, wench!" — but I don't recommend it. I do suggest you grab a drink and maybe some soup or a sandwich and settle into one of the comfortable sunken benches or stools. The tavern is right next to King John's Castle and just down a cobbled alleyway. The whole area gives the pleasant feeling of being in a time warp.

Nicholas Street (next to St. John's Castle). ☎ **061-31-8044.**

The Locke
Limerick City

Dating back to 1724, The Locke is one of Limerick City's oldest and best pubs, and it has a great location, too. It sits right on the bank of the river, amid some of the city's oldest landmarks: the Old Custom House (now the Hunt Museum) and the Old Court House. When weather permits, there's seating across the street on the quay. Inside, you can warm up at the open fires and listen to traditional music every Sunday, Tuesday, and Wednesday night. Hot, home-cooked food is available.

3 George's Quay. ☎ **061-41-3733.**

M. J. Finnegans
Annacotty

Beautifully decorated in an old-world style, this pub combines elegance with homey comforts. Inside, you'll be surrounded by brickwork, wood, stone, and almost distracting vintage décor. If you're hungry, you're in luck; the food is above the usual pub-grub standards, and steaks and seafood are a specialty. There's seating outside when the weather permits. Finnegans is just outside Annacotty on the main Dublin Road.

Dublin Road. Take the N7 east from Limerick City. ☎ 061-33-7338.

W. H. South
Limerick City

Made famous by Frank McCourt's *Angela's Ashes,* this pub still basks in the fame bestowed by the Pulitzer Prize–winning author. The walls bear newspaper accounts of the local uproar that occurred when the book was published (many Limerick natives objected to the negative light it cast on their city). Of course, there are also those who consider McCourt the local boy who made good. Star element aside, South's is a gorgeous pub — all wood, marble bar, and snugs, and always buzzing with people. During the day, hot and delicious lunches are served; the soup is consistently good.

The Crescent, O'Connell Street (right near the Jesuit church). ☎ 061-31-8850.

Fast Facts: County Limerick

Area Codes
County Limerick's area code is **061.**

Emergencies/Police
Dial ☎ **999** for all emergencies.

Hospital
St. John's Hospital (☎ 061-46-2222) is on St. John's Square, Limerick.

Information
For visitor information in Limerick City, go to the tourist center at Arthur's Quay, Limerick (☎ 061-31-7522). In Adare, visit the Adare Heritage Centre, on Main Street (☎ 061-39-6666).

Post Office
The General Post Office is on Post Office Lane, off Cecil Street, Limerick (☎ 061-21-2055).

County Clare

County Clare sometimes gets lost somewhere between the dazzle of Counties Galway and Kerry, but people who skip this county are missing out on some of Ireland's finest scenery and several interesting historic (and prehistoric) attractions. They are also missing out on great little towns and villages that are less heavily visited than those in Counties Galway and Kerry. In the north, The Burren is a strange and breathtaking sea of cracked rocks that is home to several archeological sights and an incredible range of plant life, including species that normally thrive only in Arctic or tropical climates. To the south, there are the famed sheer Cliffs of Moher, and a stretch of long sandy beaches backed by gently rolling farmland. Main attractions include two completely restored and furnished castles from the Middle Ages, and a sprinkling of ancient sights. Clare doesn't have any large cities, but it's dotted with quaint towns and villages, such as Doolin, Lahinch, and Milltown Malbay, that boast terrific traditional music (Doolin in particular). **Ennis,** the main town in the county, is one of my favorite towns in Ireland. Its medieval streets are bustling and lively with a mix of locals and visitors, and there is excellent traditional music every night.

Getting to and around County Clare

Shannon International Airport (☎ 061-71-2000; www.shannonairport. com), located on the N19, off the N18, about 24km (15 miles) south from County Clare's main town of Ennis and 24km (15 miles) west of Limerick, welcomes direct flights from North America, England, and other locations in Ireland. See Chapter 6 for more information on the airport.

If you're coming by car, take the N18 north from Limerick or south from Galway to Ennis. Rental-car company desks at Shannon airport's Arrivals Hall represent all the major car-rental companies listed in Chapter 7.

Shannon Ferries (☎ 065-905-3124; www.shannonferries.com) runs a car ferry connecting Tarbert, County Kerry, with Killimer, County Clare, bypassing Limerick. It runs April to September Monday to Saturday from 7 a.m. to about 9 p.m., and Sunday from about 9 a.m. to about 9:30 p.m. From October to March, it runs Monday to Saturday from 7 a.m. to about 7:30 p.m., and Sunday from about 9:30 a.m. to about 7:30 p.m. It costs €17 ($27) one-way, €28 ($45) round-trip for a car with passengers. Ferries leave Killimer and Tarbert every hour between the times indicated above.

Irish Rail (☎ 1-850-366-222; www.irishrail.ie) serves Ennis at the Ennis Rail Station on Station Road. All routes run through Limerick. **Bus Éireann** (☎ 01-836-6111; www.buseireann.ie) travels year-round to Ennis, Ballyvaughan, Doolin, Kilkee, and most towns in County Clare.

Spending the night in County Clare

Ballyvara House
$$ Doolin

This guesthouse seems to have everything. Location? Yup. The house is situated in the countryside (say hello to the resident ponies) and is half a mile from the delightful little village of Doolin, known for its traditional music, and just a ten-minute drive from The Burren. Good food? Check. The breakfast menu includes such treats as crepes and omelets, and the house chef prepares interesting and delicious dinners. Helpful hosts? You got it. Becky and John Flanagan know the area and can help you figure out the best itinerary. Rooms are spacious, sparkling clean, and bright, and bathrooms feature spa or Jacuzzi tubs.

Off the R479 to Doolin Village. ☎ **065-707-4467.** *Fax:* **065-707-4868.** www.bally varahouse.ie. *Rates: €140–€150 ($224–$240). MC, V.*

Berry Lodge
$$ **Annagh, Miltown Malbay**

This is a must-stay for any serious gourmet. Originally a well-known cooking school, this 17th-century country house near the sea now offers surprisingly inexpensive accommodation as well. The rooms are simple and colorfully decorated, but the real draw of the place is the food, grown and caught locally. You'll definitely want to have dinner, and you may want to consider taking one of the cooking classes — special weekend rates combine rooms with classes. Views of farmlands and sea are spectacular.

From Kerry, take the car ferry from Tarbert to Killimer. Take the N67 into Quilty village; take the third turn right, and then take the first right into Berry Lodge. ☎ **065-708-7022.** *Fax:* 065-708-7011. www.berrylodge.com. *Rates: €84–€90 ($134–$144) double. AE, MC, V.*

Bunratty Castle Hotel
$$$ **Bunratty**

This bright-yellow Georgian hotel is in the center of Bunratty village, with the famed pub Durty Nelly's and the castle (home of the celebrated medieval banquets) just across the street. Rooms are tastefully decorated with dark woods and floral bedspreads, and have every convenience, including air conditioning — pretty rare in Ireland. Everyone is friendly and willing to help. County Clare's top sights are only a short drive away.

On the Shannon/Limerick road (N18). ☎ **061-47-8700.** *Fax:* 061-36-4891. www. bunrattycastlehotel.com. *Rates: €99–€170 ($158–$272) double. AE, MC, V.*

Dromoland Castle
$$$ **Newmarket-on-Fergus**

If you have ever had fantasies of living in a castle, this place is calling your name. The 19th-century building (built to replace the original 16th-century structure) has all the round and square towers and crenellations that fairy-tales have embedded in the collective Western subconscious. Public spaces and rooms are magnificently decked out with crystal chandeliers, portraits, and oak paneling, and rooms are luxuriously furnished. Ask for a room in the main wing, as rooms in the newer wings, though still beautiful, feel more like standard hotel rooms than castle suites. The hotel and picturesque grounds have everything that modern royalty could require, including a spa, an excellent golf course, fishing, boating, gardens, restaurants, and a gracious and helpful staff. Dromoland is located near Shannon Airport, making it the perfect first or last night's stop in Ireland.

Located on R458 (signposted off of N18). ☎ **061-36-8144.** *Fax: 061-36-3355.* www.dromoland.ie. *Rates: €150–€225 ($240–$360). AE, DC, MC, V.*

Drumcreehy House
$$ Ballyvaughan

Drumcreehy is a fantastic choice for travelers who wish to explore The Burren. The wide selection of delicious breakfast offerings, served in a cheerful dining room, will fuel you for a day of hiking. After you've returned from your explorations of the rocky landscape, chill out in your bright and spacious room, furnished with pine furniture, or over tea in the antiques-furnished sitting room. Your hosts, Bernadette and Armin, can advise you on everything from where to dine in the area to how to experience The Burren.

Outside of Ballyvaughan on the N67. ☎ **065-707-7377.** *Fax: 065-707-7379.* www.drumcreehyhouse.com. *Rates: €80–€100 ($128–$160). MC, V.*

Grey Gables
$ Ennis

This is a terrific B&B for those who want to be near the hustle and bustle of Ennis without being in the middle of it. Located a ten-minute walk from the city center, Grey Gables offers impeccably tidy, bright rooms; a warm welcome; and great breakfasts.

Station Road. ☎ **065-682-4487.** www.bed-n-breakfast-ireland.com. *Rates: €70 ($112). MC, V.*

Old Ground Hotel
$$$$ Ennis

This busy hotel is located right in the middle of Ennis, so you can just pop up from a rollicking night of traditional music in the fabulous hotel pub (see "Hitting the pubs," later in this chapter) or a dinner in the excellent Town Hall restaurant, and fall into your exceptionally comfortable bed, with its fluffy white duvet. All the rooms are comfortable, but it is worth asking for one of the new rooms, which have a more stylish, up-to-date look.

O'Connell Street. ☎ **065-682-8127.** www.flynnhotels.ie. *Rates: €150–€170 ($240–$272). AE, DC, MC, V.*

Roadford House
$ Doolin

Doolin is known for its traditional music, and you'll find two of the famed music pubs just down the road from this guesthouse. Rooms are large, airy, and simply furnished with pine furnishings, and windows overlook the rolling farmland. Breakfast is exceptional, which makes sense given that the couple who run the guesthouse also run an excellent restaurant on-site.

Doolin. ☎ **065-707-5050.** www.roadfordrestaurant.com. *Rates: €70 ($112). MC, V.*

Shamrock Inn Hotel
$$$$ **Lahinch**

This little hotel, located in the heart of the pretty seaside resort town of Lahinch, is pleasant and charming. Rooms are attractively decorated, with pastels and colorful bedspreads, and have TVs, hair dryers, and tea- and coffeemakers. The restaurant is cozy, relaxing, and popular with locals, offering a variety of home-cooked dishes. Food is served in the pub during the day, and at night, good Irish music often fills the room.

Main Street. ☎ **065-708-1700.** *Fax: 065-708-1029.* www.shamrockinn.ie. *Rates: €150 ($240) double. AE, MC, V.*

Dining locally in County Clare

Berry Lodge, reviewed in the previous section, is one of the best restaurants in all of Clare. **Monk's Pub,** in Ballyvaughan (reviewed in the section "Nightlife in County Clare," near the end of this chapter), serves great seafood. Newcomer **Roadford Restaurant** (reviewed earlier in the chapter) is a winner in Doolin.

Barrtrá Seafood Restaurant
$$$ **Lahinch SEAFOOD**

This small and homey restaurant is down a wee farm road, overlooking Liscannor Bay. The friendly staff serves some of the freshest fish and shellfish on the west coast, all prepared with simple and innovative sauces, spices, or herbs that highlight the taste of the fish, such as the delicious cod with orange and ginger. The wine list is extensive, and the desserts, such as the pear and almond tart, are delicious.

Off the N67. Go 3.2km (2 miles) south of Lahinch on the Lahinch/Miltown Malbay coast road (N67) until you see the small road to the restaurant. ☎ **065-708-1280.** *Reservations required. Main courses: €18–€32 ($29–$51). AE, MC, V. Open: July–Aug daily 6–9:30 p.m.; May–June and Sept–Oct Wed–Sat 6–9:30 p.m. (call to ask for off-season hours).*

Bruach na hAille
$$ **Doolin SEAFOOD & NEW IRISH**

This cottagelike restaurant offers a simple, delicious menu. Local, incredibly fresh seafood is the highlight, and it's prepared creatively. Don't miss the grilled Doolin lobster, if it's available. Non–fish lovers have options too, including the tasty duck breast marinated in sesame oil, soy sauce, fresh ginger, and cinnamon.

Drive through Doolin, north along the coast road (R479) 1.6km (1 mile). ☎ **065-707-4120.** *Main courses: €13–€23 ($21–$37). DC, MC, V. Open: June–Sept daily 10 a.m.–9:30 p.m. (call to ask for hours during the off-season).*

Cullinan's
$$$ **Doolin** **SEAFOOD & NEW IRISH**

The chefs at Cullinan's use fresh local ingredients to create beautiful, creative, and delectable dishes such as oven-roasted filet of Clare lamb loin served with spiced couscous and garlic aioli, or plump pan-seared scallops with baby spinach fondue, a chorizo disk, and a balsamic and black pepper reduction. The excellent food is complemented by the setting: an airy, elegant white room with two walls of windows looking out onto green fields.

Doolin (on the R479). ☎ **065-707-4183.** *Reservations recommended. Main courses: €22–€29 ($35–$46). MC, V. Open: Easter–Oct Thurs–Tues 6–9 p.m.*

Cruises Pub
$$ **Ennis** **IRISH**

The staff at this cozy, authentic pub is the living embodiment of Irish hospitality, and it serves up a wide range of well-done dishes, from superb lamb stew to excellent pizzas and calzones to salmon with lemon-dill sauce, plus a selection of vegetarian dishes. The interior is dim and traditional, with beautiful carved wood; open fireplaces; tin signs on the wall; and shelves filled with old and weathered miscellany, from jugs and bottles to books. There's top-quality traditional Irish music most nights.

Abbey Street. ☎ **065-684-1800.** *Main courses: €11–€20 ($18–$32). AE, DC, MC, V. Open for food: Mon–Fri 3–9 p.m., Sat–Sun 12:30–9 p.m. (pub open until midnight on weekdays and 1:30 a.m. on weekends).*

Linnane's Lobster Bar & Seafood Restaurant
$$–$$$$ **New Quay** **SEAFOOD**

Seafood lovers, you have found your mecca. A simple restaurant with a view of the water, Linnane's serves up first-rate fresh seafood dishes. The menu changes depending on what's fresh, but expect such unfussy seafood dishes as fresh lobster, garlic clams, raw local oysters, and a smoked trout salad.

New Quay (near Ballyvaughan). ☎ **065-707-8120.** *Main courses: €11–€33 ($18–$53). Open: May–Oct daily noon to 9 p.m.; Oct–Apr Thurs and Sun noon to 8 p.m., Fri–Sat noon to 9 p.m.*

Magnetic Music Café
$ **Doolin** **CAFE**

Stop into this adorable cafe for a snack or a light lunch (perhaps the Mediterranean Medley, a platter of meats, cheeses, and Mediterranean vegetables). Inside you'll be surrounded by the sounds of Irish music (the cafe sells all sort of traditional Irish music CDs), while outside in the garden you may chance upon the cafe's golden lab, Molly.

Fisherstreet, Doolin. ☎ **065-707-4988.** *Main courses: €7–€8 ($11–$13). Open: 10 a.m.–7 p.m. (closed Mon–Tues from Sept–Nov and Mar–Apr, and may close earlier during the winter months).*

Zucchini
$$$–$$$$ Ennis NEW IRISH

This terrific new restaurant features dishes that are inventive and interesting without being frilly or eccentric. All are made with the best local ingredients. Stars of the menu include the roast crispy half duck with vegetable confit and black-cherry-and-Kirsch sauce, and medallions of pork steak with a caramelized-apple-and-Calvados cream sauce. There are also great vegetarian and fish options, such as the braised filet of John Dory in Champagne and sorrel cream. The restaurant has a feeling of warmth and casual elegance, with candles and a single rose in a modern vase gracing each table. Service is exceptional.

7 High St. ☎ **065-684-0011.** *Reservations recommended. €17–€30 ($27–$48). MC, V. Open: Daily 5–9 p.m. (from Oct–June, the restaurant sometimes closes Sun–Mon; call in advance).*

Exploring County Clare

Several bus companies run tours of The Burren, the Cliffs of Moher, and other attractions in Clare out of Galway City. For details on the various tours, call or visit the Galway Tourist Office (also known as Ireland West Tourism or Aras Fáilte) on Forster Street, just off Eyre Square, Galway City (☎ **091-53-77-00;** www.irelandwest.ie). **Healy Tours** (☎ **091-77-0066;** www.healytours.ie) is the current favorite for touring the area; tours depart from the Galway tourist office daily during the summer and a few times a week during the off-season (call for schedules).

The top attractions

Aillwee Cave
The Burren

A guide takes you down into this vast cave, where you see ancient stalagmites and stalactites, cross bridges that span frighteningly deep chasms, and get wet standing near the crashing underground waterfall. You'll also be taken into the eerie hibernation chamber of the brown bear that inhabited this area 10,000 years ago. Back above ground, you can shop for minerals and fossils, watch as cheese is being made in the on-site dairy (an odd attraction at a cave, but an interesting one nonetheless), and have a light snack in the tearoom.

Off the R480, south of Ballyvaughan. ☎ **065-707-7036.** *Admission: €15 ($24) adult, €13 ($21) seniors and students, €8 ($13) children. Open: July–Aug daily 10 a.m.–6:30 p.m.; Sept –June daily 10 a.m.–5:30 p.m. Suggested visit: 1 hour.*

Bunratty Castle and Folk Park
Bunratty

This formidable castle, built in 1425 and pillaged many times, is one of Ireland's biggest attractions. It's one of the most authentic medieval castles in the country, and great care has been taken to ensure that the interior is as it was in the 15th century, with furnishings and tapestries that reflect the era. Great halls and tiny stairways characterize the castle, and the dungeon is quite eerie. On the castle grounds is the Bunratty Folk Park, an excellent re-creation of a 19th-century Irish village. You can poke your head into farmhouses, a blacksmith's forge, and a watermill, and go down a typical village street that has it all: post office, school, pawn shop, doctor's house, printers, hardware shop, and a real pub where you can stop in for a bite and a drink. At night, Bunratty Castle hosts huge medieval banquets (see the nearby sidebar "Feasting at a castle!").

On the N18, north of Limerick. The short exit ramp off the N18 takes you to the entrance of the castle. ☎ **061-36-0788.** *Admission: €13 ($21) adults, €8.95 ($14) students, €7.50 ($12) seniors, €6.50 ($10) children. Admission is a flat €8 ($13) if you are also coming to the banquet. Open: Castle daily 9 a.m.–4 p.m. (last admission at 4 p.m.). Folk park June–Aug daily 9 a.m.–6 p.m. (last admission at 5:15 p.m.); Apr–May and Sept–Oct daily 9 a.m.–5:30 p.m. (last admission at 4:15 p.m.); Nov–Mar daily 9:30–5:30 p.m. (last admission at 4:15 p.m.). Suggested visit: At least 2 hours.*

The Burren
Northwest County Clare

Don't miss this awesome phenomenon — a vast expanse of cracked limestone, as far as the eye can see, that's home to a variety of unique plants and animals. The name *Burren* comes from the Irish *bhoireann,* for "a rocky place," and the "rocky" designation is totally accurate. You find expansive fields of broken stone, interrupted every so often by a small river or pond. Because the limestone covers a maze of underground caves, water seeps up through cracks in the rock, supporting a wide and spectacular variety of flowers and plants, including species that usually thrive only in the Arctic or Mediterranean. Lizards, badgers, frogs, and numerous birds call The Burren home. In addition, 26 species of butterflies have been seen here, including one that's indigenous to the area: the lovely Burren Green. Despite the lack of soil, humans lived in the area from the Neolithic period through medieval times, leaving behind a variety of structures from dolmens (burial monuments) to ancient cooking sites to churches. Though there is much to be enamored with at ground level, don't forget to look up at the glorious views of Clare and Galway Bay.

The best way to explore The Burren is by walking. You can either set off on foot or bicycle on part (or all) of the 42km (26-mile) Burren Way, which leads from Ballyvaughan to the Cliffs of Moher (you can get an information sheet on the trail from any tourist office in the area), or join a guided tour. I recommend the latter choice, as the terrain is rough and a guide can help you to truly understand the history, geology, and biology of this amazing place. The hands-down best guided tours are those by **Shane Connolly** (☎ **065-707-7168**; call ahead to book and find out details), a scholar of

The Burren who covers the history, folklore, animal and plant life, and geology of the area. The Burren is at its most colorful, with tons of wildflowers, in May and June, but you'll find a variety of flora year-round. You may want to begin your exploration of The Burren at The Burren Centre (see the next review). It is worth packing a pair of hiking shoes with ankle support for your visit to The Burren.

Burren Centre
Kilfenora

This excellent center presents a fascinating and clear introduction to the natural and social history of The Burren through audiovisuals and exhibits. I recommend visiting if you're planning to explore the area.

Kilfenora. ☎ 065-708-8030. Admission: €6 ($9.60) adults, €5 ($8) seniors and students, 4 ($4.80) children under 16, free for children under 6. Open: July–Aug 9:30 a.m.–6 p.m. mid-Mar to May and Sept–Nov 10 a.m.–5 p.m. (last admission 30 minutes before closing time).

The Cliffs of Moher

Spectacular doesn't begin to describe the view from these breathtaking sheer cliffs. At places, they rise more than 213m (700 ft.) above the crashing Atlantic and stretch for miles in both directions. On the highest cliff is O'Brien's Tower, which was built in the 1800s as a viewing point for tourists. From the tower, you can see the Clare coast, the Aran Islands, and, on a clear day, mountains as far away as Kerry and Connemara. When it's sunny, the cliffs take on a purple hue (hence, the Purple Cliffs of Moher, of story and song), and when the wind and rain blow in, it can be a bit harrowing up there. The cliffs can be very touristy during the high season, so be prepared for Irish fiddlers in the parking lot and so on. If you are looking for cliffs that are almost as spectacular but don't draw as many visitors, head up to the towering cliffs of Slieve League (p. 394).

A flashy new visitor center has just opened at the Cliffs with a permanent interpretative exhibit called the Atlantic Edge. The exhibit is relatively small, featuring a 3-D movie that makes you feel as if you're soaring over the Cliffs, pictures of and quotations from people associated with this area, and some interactive pieces dealing with the science of the Cliffs. The €4 ($6.40) for adult admission price is a little steep for such a small display, so I would only go if you know that you usually enjoy this type of exhibit.

One of the best ways to appreciate the grandeur of the Cliffs of Moher is to see them from the ocean. **Cliffs of Moher Cruises (☎ 065-707-5949;** www.cliffs-of-moher-cruises.com) makes one-hour trips to the Cliffs daily between April 1 and October 31 (weather-permitting). During the summer months, book ahead of time to ensure a spot on the boat.

Off the R478, on the Atlantic coast. Take the R487 northwest from Lahinch or southwest from Lisdoonvarna. ☎ 061-36-0788. Open: Cliffs are always accessible; visitor center Nov–Feb 9 a.m.–5 p.m.; Mar and Oct 9 a.m.–6 p.m.; Apr 9 a.m.–6:30 p.m.; May 9 a.m.–7 p.m.; June 8:30 a.m.–7:30 p.m.; July and Aug 8:30 a.m.–8:30 p.m.; Sept 8:30 a.m.–6:30 p.m. Suggested visit: 1 hour.

Painting The Burren

The **Burren Painting Centre**, Lisdoonvarna (☎ 065-707-4208; www.burrenpainting centre.com) offers courses in painting. Every day, a different painting location around The Burren or the Atlantic coast is chosen, and expert tutors provide feedback and instruction. Courses can last anywhere from a day to nine days, and you can stay at the center or attend on a daily basis.

Knappogue Castle
Quinn

This imposing 15th-century castle has seen its share of history. Built by the McNamaras, it was the pride of the tribe, which dominated the area for 1,000 years. But the stronghold had its troubles. In the 1700s, Cromwell's troops occupied the castle for ten years; and during the War of Independence in the 1920s, revolutionary forces camped within its walls. The castle has been extraordinarily refurbished, and the interior is over-flowing with 15th-century antiques and period furnishings. This castle also hosts a medieval banquet.

Just off the Ennis-Killmury road (R469) southeast from Ennis. ☎ *061-36-0788. Admission: €7.35 ($12) adults; €3.50 ($5.60) seniors, students, and children. Open: Apr–Oct daily 9:30 a.m.–5:30 p.m. (last admission 4:30 p.m.). Suggested visit: 1 hour.*

Poulnabrone Dolmen
The Burren

This structure is an ancient burial monument dating back about 6,000 years. More people photograph this landmark than almost any other in Ireland. Don't be embarrassed about standing under the humongous stone and pre-tending you're holding it up — many, many people have done the same.

The Burren. Off R480, south from Ballyvaughan.

More cool things to see and do

✔ **Lahinch Golf Club:** High elevations at this club provide amazing views of sea and valley. Watch your ball — local goats are known to cross the fairway. There are two 18-hole courses here: the Old Course and the Castle Course.

Location: Lahinch Golf Club, Lahinch, County Clare (☎ 065-708-1003). Par: Old course 71, Castle Course 70. Fees: Old Course €165 ($264), Castle Course €55 ($88). Visitors are welcome daily, except when there is a tournament.

✔ **Dolphinwatch Boat Tour:** This fun and informative two-hour boat trip takes you out among a resident group of friendly bottleneck dolphins. The boat is equipped with a hydrophone, so you can listen to dolphins communicate underwater.

Location: The trip leaves from the port village of Carrigaholt daily April through the end of September, weather permitting. You must book ahead for July and August trips (☎ 065-905-8156); to book in other months, call the morning of the trip. Tickets: €24 ($38) adults, €12 ($19) children age 16 and under; €3 ($4.80) children age 3 and under.

✔ **Eamon de Valera Statue:** Eamon de Valera, Irish freedom fighter, president, and prime minister, is honored with a bronze statue in Ennis. De Valera was born in New York; his American citizenship kept him from facing the firing squad after his part in the Easter Rising of 1916. Find out more about Irish history in Chapter 2.

Location: Ennis town park, off Gort Road (R352). Suggested visit: A few minutes.

✔ **Ennis Friary:** This 13th-century Franciscan abbey was a well-known seat of learning in medieval times, home to more than 1,000 friars and students. Though the building fell to ruin after it was abandoned in the 1692, parts of it have been restored, and you will find beautiful statues, bas-reliefs, tombs, and carvings.

Location: Abbey Street. ☎ 065-682-9100. Admission: €1.60 ($2.60) adults, €1.10 ($1.80) seniors, €1 ($1.60) children. Open: April to mid-September daily 10 a.m. to 6 p.m., mid-September to October 10 a.m. to 5 p.m. Suggested visit: One hour.

✔ **Lahinch Sea World:** This fascinating Atlantic aquarium will entertain all ages. You come face to face with creatures from the Irish coast, such as sharks, lobsters, rays, and Conger eels. Kids love the touch pool, where they can feel starfish, anemones, and other underwater life, and the regular feeding sessions draw crowds. Want a chance to swim like the fishes? Lahinch Sea World also has a huge indoor heated pool, Jacuzzi, sauna, and kiddie pool. The souvenir shop is well stocked, and the cafe serves light meals and snacks.

Location: The Promenade. West of Ennistymon, on the N67, Lahinch. ☎ 065-708-1900. Admission: Aquarium only €9 ($14) adult, €8 ($13) seniors and students, €7 ($11) children under age 16, €5 ($8) children ages 2 to 4. Open: June through September Monday through Friday 10 a.m. to 6:30 p.m., October through May 10 a.m. to 5 p.m. Suggested visit: Two hours.

Shopping

Belleek Shop, 36 Abbey St., Ennis (☎ 065-686-7891), is the best store in the area for Waterford Crystal; Irish tweed; and, of course, Belleek pottery — that thin white pottery decorated with shamrocks. They have top-notch customer service. The oldest perfumery in Ireland, **Burren Perfumery,** Carron (☎ 065-708-9102), uses local flora to create unique fragrances. To get there, take the R480 to the Carron turnoff; the shop is located just north of town. **The Burren Smokehouse,** Lisdoonvarna (☎ 065-707-4432), is a gourmet store selling the finest smoked Irish

Atlantic salmon, trout, mackerel, and eel. You can watch the process of smoking at the visitor center. **Craft Showcase Kilkee,** O'Connell Street, Kilkee ☎ 065-905-6880), sells crafts from ceramics and sheepskin rugs to Celtic jewelry and baskets. The store is on the main Kilkee-Kilrush Road, on the right from Kilkee city center. **The Rock Shop,** in Liscannor, near the Cliffs of Moher (☎ 065-708-1930) displays and sells minerals and fossils. The **Traditional Music Shop,** Doolin (☎ 065-7074-407), is one of the best shops in the area for Irish instruments (such as an authentic tin whistle), plus a large variety of Irish music on CD and cassette — a little traveling music for the rental car! Another terrific traditional music shop is **Custy's Traditional Music Shop,** 2 Francis St., Ennis (☎ 065-682-1727).

Nightlife in County Clare

If you've ever wanted to try Irish set dancing (a partnered form of dance that resembles American square dancing), get yourself over to **Cois na hAbhna,** Gort Road (☎ 065-682-4276), on a Wednesday night. Classes run between 9 p.m. and midnight. Call to confirm, as times and venue may change.

Ennis's fabulous performing arts complex **glór,** Friar's Walk, Ennis (☎ 065-684-3103; www.glor.ie), offers music, theater, dance, and visual arts. This place books many of the finest traditional Irish music legends, so be sure to find out which musicians are performing while you're around.

In Doolin, check out **Magnetic Music** (☎ 065-707-4988; www.magnetic-music.com) for terrific traditional Irish music concerts.

Feasting at a castle

Bunratty and Knappogue castles both stage fun (albeit touristy) **medieval banquets,** complete with a feast of food and lively entertainment.

Both castles feature a delicious feast (eaten with your hands, of course) and period music and song (including harp and fiddle music and medieval choral singing), and both are presided over by the "earl," who will fill you in on the history of the castle. Generally, people seem to prefer the Knappogue banquet, which feels slightly less touristy.

The Corn Barn in Bunratty Folk Park hosts **Traditional Irish Nights,** which aim to replicate a night of celebration in old Ireland. You'll dine on Irish stew, brown bread, and apple pie with cream, and then listen to live foot-tapping Irish music.

Reservations are required for all of these events; call ☎ 061-36-0788. The Bunratty banquet costs €58 ($93) per adult, the Knappogue banquet costs €55 ($88) per adult, and the Traditional Irish Night costs €48 ($77) per adult. Children ages 12 and under get discounted rates.

Hitting the pubs

Also see the excellent **Cruises,** in "Where to dine in County Clare," earlier in this chapter.

Durty Nelly's
Bunratty

Since 1620, this world-famous tavern has been a thirst-quencher for everyone from the guards who once protected Bunratty Castle to the tourists who explore it today. The interior looks like it hasn't changed over the centuries, with sawdust-strewn floors, low lighting from lanterns, and traditional music sessions that commence at any time in any room of the pub. There's seating outside for nice days, and a pretty good restaurant is upstairs.

Next to Bunratty Castle. Take N18 north from Limerick. ☎ **061-36-4861.**

McGann's
Doolin

This Doolin pub has excellent traditional Irish music and well-pulled pints of Guinness, and is often less packed than O'Connor's (reviewed later in this section).

Lisdoonvarna Road. ☎ **065-707-4133.**

Monk's Pub
Ballyvaughan

Peat fires burn and rustic furnishings invite you to take a seat at this pub. It's right on the water, and good pub grub is served all day (the seafood chowder is unbelievable). Music fills the air on many nights.

Main Street. ☎ **065-707-7059.**

O'Briens
Miltown Malbay

This is the cutest pub in all of Ireland. It is just larger than a walk-incloset — room enough for one bench, two bar stools, a 4-foot bar, and a single Guinness tap (don't worry — the pints are full-size). Joe Murray runs the place and keeps things shipshape.

Main Street. No phone.

O'Connor's
Doolin

This is one of the premier spots in the country for traditional sessions, and fans travel from all over to hear them. The same family has run this combination pub and market for more than 150 years. The pub sits amid a row of thatched fisherman cottages and really comes to life at night. If this proves too packed (it seems everyone knows about O'Connor's), head up to McGann's (reviewed earlier in this section).

Off the N67, west of Lisdoonvarna. ☎ **065-707-4168.**

The Poet's Corner
Doolin

This welcoming pub, in the Old Ground Hotel, plays host to locals and visitors alike. The Irish music sessions here (Thurs–Sun) are a force to be reckoned with.

O' Connell Street. ☎ **065-682-8127.**

Fast Facts: County Clare

Area Codes
County Clare's area codes (or city codes) are **061** and **065.**

Emergencies/Police
Dial ☎ **999** for all emergencies.

Genealogy Resources
Contact the Clare Heritage Centre, Church Street, Corofin (☎ 065-683-7955).

Hospital
Ennis Hospital is on Galway Road (☎ 065-682-4464).

Information
For visitor information, go to the Ennis Tourist Office Arthur's Row, off O'Connell Square, Ennis (☎ 065-682-8366); open year-round.

Post Office
A General Post Office is on Bank Place, Ennis (☎ 065-686-6540).

Chapter 18

County Galway: Galway City, the Aran Islands, and Connemara

· ·

In This Chapter

▶ Hearing some great traditional Irish music in Galway City

▶ Dining in the best restaurants in the West

▶ Visiting the peaceful Aran Islands, bastions of tradition

▶ Exploring the vast boglands, mountains, and coastlines of Connemara
  (and meeting some sweet Connemara ponies!)

· ·

County Galway is a winning combination of the fun and bustle of Galway City with its great music, pubs, restaurants, and shops; the wild and breathtaking mountain-and-bog landscape of Connemara; the peaceful Aran Islands; picturesque small towns; and one of the largest Gaeltachts (Irish-speaking regions) in the country.

Galway City

Buzzing Galway City serves as a gateway to the rest of the county. It's a fabulous city to explore, with a youthful university population; constant street entertainment; a robust arts scene; loads of traditional Irish music; and a great variety of both trendy and traditional places to eat, sleep, drink, and shop. One gets the sense that the city caters to visitors and locals equally — they certainly don't roll up the sidewalk when the visitors go home. The city also has a gorgeous location, set on peaceful Galway Bay, which is home to a number of swans, and the River Corrib, a favored fishing location. The only thing that Galway City doesn't have is major sights within the city; there are places to visit, but there aren't any must-see attractions. The medieval center of the city is so tiny that you'll know your way around in no time.

County Galway

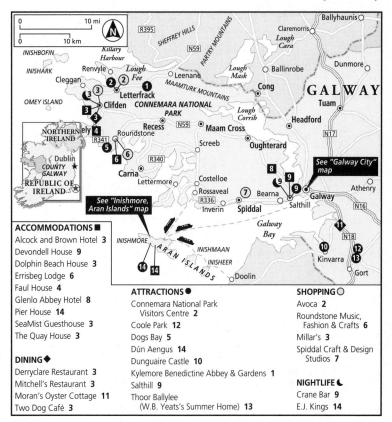

ACCOMMODATIONS ■
Alcock and Brown Hotel **3**
Devondell House **9**
Dolphin Beach House **3**
Errisbeg Lodge **6**
Faul House **4**
Glenlo Abbey Hotel **8**
Pier House **14**
SeaMist Guesthouse **3**
The Quay House **3**

DINING ◆
Derryclare Restaurant **3**
Mitchell's Restaurant **3**
Moran's Oyster Cottage **11**
Two Dog Café **3**

ATTRACTIONS ●
Connemara National Park
   Visitors Centre **2**
Coole Park **12**
Dogs Bay **5**
Dún Aengus **14**
Dunguaire Castle **10**
Kylemore Benedictine Abbey & Gardens **1**
Salthill **9**
Thoor Ballylee
   (W.B. Yeats's Summer Home) **13**

SHOPPING ○
Avoca **2**
Roundstone Music,
   Fashion & Crafts **6**
Millar's **3**
Spiddal Craft & Design
   Studios **7**

NIGHTLIFE ☾
Crane Bar **9**
E.J. Kings **14**

I would spend just one day exploring Galway City itself, but it is a great place to base yourself for daytrips to Connemara, the Aran Islands, The Burren, and other County Galway and County Clare attractions.

Getting to and around Galway City

Aer Lingus (☎ **0818-365-000;** www.aerlingus.com) has daily service from Dublin into Galway Airport, in Carnmore (☎ **091-75-5569;** www.galwayairport.com). The best way to get into town from the airport is by taxi, which should cost about €16 ($26).

If you're driving to Galway City, take the N4 and N6 from Dublin, or the N17 from Sligo. If you'd like to rent a car in Galway, try **Budget** (☎ **091-566-376**), on Eyre Square.

Irish Rail (☎ **1-850-366-222;** www.irishrail.ie) pulls into Ceannt Station, near Eyre Square, in the center of Galway, from Dublin and other

Galway City

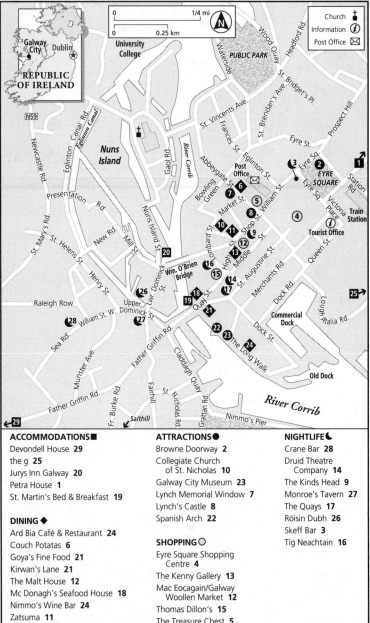

ACCOMMODATIONS■
Devondell House **29**
the g **25**
Jurys Inn Galway **20**
Petra House **1**
St. Martin's Bed & Breakfast **19**

DINING◆
Ard Bia Café & Restaurant **24**
Couch Potatas **6**
Goya's Fine Food **21**
Kirwan's Lane **21**
The Malt House **12**
Mc Donagh's Seafood House **18**
Nimmo's Wine Bar **24**
Zatsuma **11**

ATTRACTIONS●
Browne Doorway **2**
Collegiate Church
    of St. Nicholas **10**
Galway City Museum **23**
Lynch Memorial Window **7**
Lynch's Castle **8**
Spanish Arch **22**

SHOPPING○
Eyre Square Shopping
    Centre **4**
The Kenny Gallery **13**
Mac Eocagain/Galway
    Woollen Market **12**
Thomas Dillon's **15**
The Treasure Chest **5**

NIGHTLIFE☾
Crane Bar **28**
Druid Theatre
    Company **14**
The Kinds Head **9**
Monroe's Tavern **27**
The Quays **17**
Róisin Dubh **26**
Skeff Bar **3**
Tíg Neachtain **16**

points. **Bus Éireann** (☎ **01-836-6111;** www.buseireann.ie) also travels to Ceannt Station. The private coach service **CityLink** (☎ **1-890-28-08-08;** www.citylink.ie) travels between Galway and Dublin. The rail trip takes about two and a half hours and the bus trip takes three and a half.

Galway City is best seen on foot. The town is compact, and the heart is pedestrian-only, so a car wouldn't do you much good. If you do take a car into the city, know that parking in Galway City requires discs that you can purchase at local shops. Galway has a great local bus service that covers the city's suburbs, running from the city center (many routes start at Roches Store on Eyre St. near Eyre Square) out to Salthill and the coastal towns. Contact **Galway City Direct Bus Company** (☎ **091-860-814;** www.citydirectgalway.com) for schedules and fares. You can pick up a taxi on Eyre Square or by calling a taxi company such as **Abby Taxi** (☎ **091-533-333**) or **Cara Cabs** (☎ **091-563-939**).

Anchored by **Eyre Square** (*Eyre* is pronounced *air*), the city's picturesque main streets stretch down to the harbor.

Spending the night in Galway City

Devondell House
$$ Galway City

Berna Kelly should run a school for aspiring B&B hosts and hostesses. Warm and welcoming, she greets every guest with a tea tray filled with home-baked treats and is happy to help you plan your days in Galway and the surrounding area. Her home is cozy and sparkling clean, and rooms are homey and comfortable, with patchwork quilts and crisp Irish linens. You may not want to make any sightseeing plans for the morning because Berna's incredible breakfast, which is served at two tables so that you can chat with your fellow guests, invites lingering. The options are endless, from delicious stewed pears, plums, rhubarb, and other fruits to a comprehensive cheese plate to fruit smoothies. And that's just the preamble to the main course! The house is about a 20-minute walk from the heart of Galway City and is within walking distance of the seafront.

47 Devon Park, Lower Salthill. ☎ **091-528-306.** *Rates: €90 ($144) double. No credit cards. Closed: Nov–Feb.*

the g
$$$$ Galway City

Okay, you already know that this has to be a hip hotel, because the name of the place is in lowercase letters. "But just how hip is it?" you ask. Well, you enter the dramatic black-glass lobby to find a wall-length aquarium filled with Connemara seahorses and a huge neon sign reading: "This must be the place". And indeed it is. Dreamt up by couture hat designer Philip Treacy (Camilla Parker Bowles is just one of his famous clients), the hotel is luxurious and theatrical, like the set of a glamorous avant-garde film. Treacy blends ultramodern design elements, such as movie scenes

projected silently on the wall of the Grand Salon, with unexpected baroque
and natural touches (many inspired by the coast of Connemara). The effect
is dazzling. Set aside time to spend in all of the public rooms, from the
Grand Salon, with its impossibly high ceilings, glass-and-silver sphere installation, and tables filled with Swarovski crystal bits; to the Blue Room, which
has rich purple and amber velvet couches and chairs. The spa offers all
sorts of treatments and is another beauty, with a flock of origami fabric
cranes gliding over the hot tub, which is lit in green. The bedrooms are simpler than the rest of the hotel, decorated in cool whites and creams, with a
space-age-style lamp that looks like it could cook breakfast for you and a
bed that feels like a cloud. Service is exceptional. Though the rack rates are
ridiculous, the hotel often has special offers available on its Web site.

Wellpark. ☎ **091-865-200.** *Fax: 091-865-203.* www.theghotel.ie. *Rates:* €450–
€2,500 ($720–$4,000) double. AE, DC, MC, V.

Glenlo Abbey Hotel
$$$$ **Galway City**

Located about 3.2km (2 miles) outside Galway, this 1740s manor house is
the picture of gracious living. The hotel is surrounded by peaceful
grounds, including its own 9-hole golf course, and the interior is furnished
with luxurious fabrics, antiques, and hand-carved furniture. The spacious
guestrooms boast Georgian furnishings, marble bathrooms, and pastoral
views. Check out the Pullman Restaurant, which serves meals in two
retired *Orient Express* cars.

Bushypark. ☎ **091-526-666.** *Fax: 091-527-800.* www.glenlo.com. *Rates:* €189–€880
($302–$1408) double. AE, MC, V.

Jurys Inn Galway
$$$ **Galway City**

Location, location, location. This hotel, part of the excellent Jurys chain,
is situated in a terrific spot, right on the edge of the hopping heart of the
city, near pretty Lough Corrib (the lake that separates the city center from
the surrounding areas). Rooms are of the standard hotel variety, with pine
furnishings and warm colors. A restaurant downstairs serves full meals,
and the hotel's pub is a jovial place to chat over a drink (and perhaps listen
to some live music). If you are a light sleeper, ask for a room away from
the main street.

Quay Street. ☎ **091-566-444.** *Fax: 091-568-415.* www.jurysinns.com. *Rates:*
€94–€149 ($150–$238) double. AE, DC, MC, V.

Petra House
$$–$$$ **Galway City**

This is a great place to stay if you want to be close to the buzz of the city
but not in the middle of it. The city center is an easy ten-minute walk and
there is parking for those who have a car. Owners Joan and Frank Maher
are perfect B&B hosts — friendly and helpful without being intrusive.

Rooms are simple and spotless, with pine furnishings and colorful bed-spreads, and breakfast is excellent, offering many vegetarian options, fresh fruit salad, home-baked brown bread, and lots of other treats.

29 College Rd. ☎ **091-566-580.** *Fax: 091-566-580. Rates: €80–€100 ($128–$160) double. AE, MC, V.*

St. Martin's Bed and Breakfast
$ Galway City

Who could pass up a bed and breakfast where you are greeted at breakfast by a plump Corgi named Tubbs? Tubbs and your kind hostess Mary will give you a warm welcome and help you plan your Galway visit. If stylish room décor is important to you, try Devondell or Petra House instead (it's comfortable and cozy, but pretty Plain Jane here); if a central location is what you're seeking, this is your place. St. Martin's is located on a quiet street that's less than a five-minute walk from the hustle and bustle of downtown Galway.

2 Nuns Island. ☎ **091-568-286.** *Rates: €70 ($112) double. No credit cards.*

Dining in Galway City
You can find a great meal in any of the restaurants listed in this section. But if you're in the mood for something sweet, try **Goyas Fine Food,** 2–3 Kirwan's Lane (☎ **091-567-010**), which offers up incredible cakes and tarts, along with generous mugs of tea, coffee, and hot chocolate, in an airy, sky-blue-ceilinged cafe. Try the orange Madeira, or the fudge cake, or the baked cheesecake, or . . .

Ard Bia Café & Restaurant
$–$$$ Galway City   CAFE AND NEW IRISH

This place has two different personalities. At lunch artsy types fill the bright and casual restaurant, chatting over giant pots of tea and tasty dishes such as a pear, walnut, and mixed leaf salad with blue cheese dressing, or a toasted sandwich with chorizo, gubeen (a Cork cheese), and onion marmalade. At dinner things get a bit more sophisticated as the restaurant serves up inventive New Irish dishes such as Irish beef filet with a root vegetable and thyme gratin, stout-braised shallots, and Port jus; or pan-fried Monkfish with fondant potatoes, cider-braised leeks, and lemon-roasted fennel.

Long Walk, through the Spanish Arch. ☎ **091-539-897.** *Main courses: Cafe €5–€12 ($8–$19); restaurant €18–€29 ($29–$46). MC, V. Open: Cafe Mon–Sat 10 a.m.–3:30 p.m., Sun noon to 3:30 p.m.; restaurant Wed–Sat 6:30–10:30 p.m.*

Couch Potatas
$ Galway City   BAKED POTATOES

This casual baked-potato joint is constantly bustling with chatty 20- and 30-somethings. Sit down at one of the wood tables in the white-walled, wood-ceilinged restaurant, and select your spud. There is something to please everyone (as long as you like potatoes), from the Venice By Night, a potato filled with tuna, corn, peppers, tomato sauce, onions, mushrooms and mozzarella cheese, to the Nora Barnacle, a potato stuffed with strips of chicken breast and served with a creamy garlic sauce. There are a few non-potato appetizers and salads if you are feeling starched out. Be sure to check out the paintings of spuds as famous movie characters (the intrepid-looking Batman potato is my favorite) while you wait for your order. The casual atmosphere and fun meal choices make this a great place for families.

40 Upper Abbeygate St. ☎ 091-561-664. Main courses: €9–€10 ($14–$16). No credit cards. Open: Mon–Sat noon to 9:30 p.m., Sun 12:30–10 p.m.

Kirwan's Lane
$$$–$$$$ Galway City   CONTINENTAL-NEW IRISH

Not only do I recommend this upscale, candlelit restaurant, but so does the entire group who sat next to me: They couldn't stop raving about the food and proclaimed their meal the best they had eaten in Ireland. The décor on the lower floor is modern and Scandinavian-looking, while the upper floor is painted with vivid reds and yellows. Dishes use the freshest of ingredients, and a few successfully borrow Indian, African, and Asian spices, condiments, and cooking techniques, such as the sautéed tiger prawns with Madras-scented cream, broccoli, and mushrooms, served with sweet chile rice. Other dishes are straight-up New Irish; I recommend the melt-in-your-mouth Connemara lamb with braised garlic potatoes and a rosemary jus. The several vegetarian dishes are very classy, including such treats as a spicy chickpea, cauliflower, and date tagine with wild Tunisian-style pilaf rice. Finish up with the heavenly French-chocolate cake served with pistachio ice cream if it's on the menu.

Kirwan's Lane (the small lane next to McDonagh's Restaurant, off Quay St.). ☎ 091-568-266. Reservations recommended. Main courses: €18–€28 ($29–$45). AE, DC, MC, V. Open: Daily 6–10 p.m., and Mon–Sat 12:30–2:30 p.m.

Zatsuma
$ Galway City   CREPES

Crepes are an ideal walking food, and Galway an ideal walking city, so this new creperie is a welcome addition to the city. The scrumptious crepes run the gamut from savory (try the Tantalizing Tikka, with chicken, bell peppers, spring onions, a cheese mix, and Dijon mustard) to the sweet (just try to resist the Bananarama, with sliced banana, melted chocolate and homemade banana ice cream). Take your crepe on the go or sit at one of the cafe tables outside. Yum.

27 Shop St. ☎ 091-895-877. Main courses: €6–€7 ($9.60–$11). No credit cards. Open: Daily 10 a.m. to late.

The Malt House
$$$–$$$$ Galway City   CONTINENTAL/NEW IRISH

This Galway institution has just undergone a massive overhaul. Gone are the carpets and other trappings of Old World Continental dining. In their place is an airy modern restaurant with a relaxed feel. The mission of the Malt House is to serve locally sourced, in-season dishes, and the chef and owner have worked hard to find the best producers in the region. These local ingredients are highlighted in dishes such as the Galway Bay mussels (served with either garlic and white wine or Asian style), and the spiced lamb tagine with couscous and mint tzatziki.

High Street. ☎ **091-567-866.** *Main courses: €20–€30 ($32–$48). AE, DC, MC. V. Open: Mon–Sat noon to 3 p.m., daily 5:30–10 p.m.*

McDonagh's Seafood House
$–$$$ Galway City   SEAFOOD

Fish doesn't get fresher or better than at this popular place, where rope ladders twist across the ceiling and murals of old fish markets in Galway decorate the walls. The McDonaghs, who've been at it for four generations, have had plenty of practice in the trade. The day's catch is personally inspected and chosen before it comes in the door. In the restaurant, you can decide exactly how you'd like your fish cooked, whether it's salmon, trout, sole, or one of many other options. Shrimp and lobsters come the way the sea made them: in the shell. If you're looking for something simple and quick, stop by the top-notch fish-and-chips shop in the front of the restaurant, grab a bench outside, and watch the world pass by as you dig into your moist and delicious cutlet of fish. If you are curious about curry chips (French fries with curry sauce) this is the place to try them.

22 Quay St. (beside Jurys Inn, near the Spanish Arch). ☎ **091-56-5001.** *Main courses: €13–€25 ($21–$40); fish and chips €6–€7 ($9.60–$11). AE, DC, MC, V. Open: Restaurant Mon–Sat 5–11 p.m.; fish-and-chips counter Mon–Sat noon to midnight, Sun 5–11 p.m.*

Nimmo's Wine Bar
$$$ Galway City   NEW IRISH

This atmospheric restaurant serves some of the best food in Ireland. Though I've never had dinner at an eccentric sea captain's home, I imagine that it would be a lot like dining at Nimmo's. Located on the fast-flowing River Corrib, Nimmo's is cozy and romantic, with worn wooden floors and plaster walls, weathered glass bottles and nautical objects, faded black-and-white photographs of ships, and brightly colored candles gracing the tables. The menu uses fresh, local ingredients and complements them with inventive preparations, spicing, and sauces inspired by cuisines all over the world. The dishes change all the time, but if it's on the menu, try the salmon and brill with a veil of creamy Thai curry sauce, served with perfectly steamed vegetables. I also loved the goat cheese in phyllo with sweet chile-and-lime dressing.

Long Walk, through the Spanish Arch. ☎ *091-561-114. Reservations recommended. Main courses: €17–€26 ($27–$42). MC, V. Open: Tues–Sun 6–10:30 p.m.*

Exploring Galway City: The top attractions

Galway doesn't have any don't-leave-Ireland-without-seeing-it attractions; it's more of a place to wander around, enjoy the excellent street performers who flock to the city in the summer, shop a little, and take advantage of the fabulous restaurant and nightlife scenes. It is also an excellent place to base yourself for explorations of Connemara, The Burren (see Chapter 17), and the Aran Islands.

The compact heart of Galway is a pedestrian area that begins west of Eyre Square. The main street here starts as William Street at Eyre Square and then changes names many times before hitting the River Corrib.

If you'd like to take a walking tour of Galway City's sights, check out **Galway Tours** (☎ 086-402-1819). If you are looking for a darker perspective on the city, try **Galway Gore** (☎ 093-43611). All tours depart from the tourist information office on Foster Street, just off Eyre Square (call for times and prices, as they change each season).

Here are some attractions that you may want to look out for as you wander the city.

Browne Doorway

Looking pretty odd at the head of Eyre Square, the Browne Doorway is a towering stone archway that's connected to nothing. Dating from 1627, the doorway comes from an old mansion on Lower Abbeygate Street, and it has the coats of arms of the families Browne and Lynch, two of the original fourteen families who founded Galway City.

Located on the northwest side of Eyre Square.

Cruising Lough Corrib

Want to get away from the buzz of the city? **Celtic Boat Safaris** offers a 90-minute guided cruise along vast, scenic Lough Corrib in a traditional West of Ireland lake boat. You'll pass peaceful uninhabited islands, see all sorts of birds, and get a real sense of the geography and history of the area. If you're feeling more adventurous, you may want to take the company's one- or two-day journeys. The one-day journey takes you to charming Cong village, where you'll pick up a mountain bike and tour the surrounding forest, home to caves and old castles. The two-day journey adds a scenic hike and a stop on beautiful Inchagoil Island, where you'll find the ruins of a fifth-century church. **Corrib Ferries** (see "Exploring Connemara," later in this chapter) offers similar cruises on standard boats, leaving from Cong and Oughterard.

Cruises depart from Woodquay, behind Court House and the Town Hall Theatre. ☎ *087-981-1579. Tickets: 90-minute cruise €10 ($16) adults, €5 ($8) children under 18. Reserve in advance.*

Searching for Galway's mermaids

Mermaids show up frequently in Irish folklore, often representing something alluring but dangerous. According to legend, if you happen to see a mermaid sitting on a rock, it means bad luck is coming your way. So don't stare out at the rocks too long!

You can look as long as you like at the mermaid depictions around town, though. Galway supposedly has more representations of mermaids than any other place in Ireland. Check out the mermaids in the window of the Collegiate Church of St. Nicholas, in the center of town.

Collegiate Church of St. Nicholas

Columbus is rumored to have prayed in this well-preserved medieval church, built in 1320, before setting sail for the New World. You'll find beautiful stone carvings, gargoyles, and the tomb of a Crusader here.

Lombard Street. ☎ **091-564-648.** *Admission: Free. Apr–Nov 9 a.m.–7 p.m.; Dec–Mar 9 a.m. to sunset.*

Eyre Square

This giant grassy square has recently been restored and is a hangout for locals and travelers alike. There is nothing particularly special about the square itself, though Eamon O'Doherty's modern sculpture of an old sailing ship is spectacular.

Galway City Museum

It's a rainy day and you want to hang out somewhere dry. Spend an hour or so in the Galway City Museum, which has several nice exhibits on the history of the area. Be sure to check out the model of a Galway hooker boat on the ground floor.

Spanish Arch. ☎ **091-532-460.** *Admission: Free. Open: Daily 10 a.m.–7 p.m.*

Lynch's Castle (now AIB Bank)

If this isn't the first castle you've seen in Ireland, you may expect something . . . well, larger. This 14th-century home of the legendary Lynch family was restored and now houses a bank, though you can still marvel at the coats of arms and the Spanish-style stonework on the exterior.

Upper Abbeygate Street (between Shop and Market streets).

Lynch Memorial Window

James Lynch FitzStephen, unyielding magistrate and mayor of Galway, earned his place in dictionaries when he condemned and executed his own son (convicted of murder) in 1493 as a demonstration that the law does not bend even under family ties. That's where we get the word *lynch*. The Lynch Memorial Window commemorates this event and is set into a wall just above an ornate Gothic doorway on Market Street.

Market Street (1 block northwest of Eyre Square).

Salthill

This fun little resort strip is Ireland's closest thing to the United States' Coney Island in its heyday. It makes for a fun day with the family. Walk along the boardwalk, eat fast food, play arcade games, and visit the Leisureland amusement park.

Take the R336 west from Galway for about 3km (2 miles).

Spanish Arch

The Spanish Arch was built in 1584 to protect ships from looting. It earns its name from the Spanish galleons that used to dock under its protection.

Between Wolfe Tone Bridge and the Long Walk, at the mouth of the River Corrib.

Taking short side trips from Galway City

Coole Park
Gort

The house and grounds here were once home to Lady Gregory — writer, friend of many an Irish luminary, and cofounder of Dublin's Abbey Theatre. The grounds are now a park, with red deer, red squirrels, and badgers, among others animals. There are beautiful nature trails, a lake, and lush gardens. One of the most interesting parts of the park is the *Autograph Tree*, which bears the carved initials of such famous people as George Bernard Shaw; Oliver St. John Gogarty; Sean O'Casey; and W. B. Yeats, Lady Gregory's friend and partner in the Abbey. In the restored courtyard you'll find a visitor center, which shows two interesting presentations on the history of Coole Park. An on-site restaurant serves filling main courses and great desserts.

Take the N6 out of Galway to the N18; north of Gort, follow the signs. ☎ 091-63-1804. Admission: Free. Open: Park year-round; visitor center Mar 22–May and Sept daily 10 a.m.–5 p.m., June–Aug daily 10 a.m.–6 p.m. Suggested visit: 1–2 hours.

The swans of the River Corrib

The waters of Lough Corrib, the largest lake in the Republic of Ireland, run through the River Corrib to join the sea at the edge of Galway City. Go down to the pier, near the Spanish Arch, to see the huge flock of mute swans who make their home here.

Dunguaire Castle
Kinvarra

How better to tell the story of a castle's rich history than to show it? Each floor of Dunguaire (dun-*gware*) Castle reflects a different and very colorful time in its history. It's been perfectly restored, and the interior is one of the finest in its class, with furnishings that mirror the time. According to legend, the castle was built on the site of the Palace of Guaire, sixth-century king of Connaught, and that's where the name comes from. Later, it was owned by Oliver St. John Gogarty, poet, surgeon, and satirical model for Buck Mulligan, one the characters of James Joyce's *Ulysses*. Although born in Dublin, Gogarty lived mostly in Connemara. The view of Connemara and Galway Bay from the top of the battlements is awe-inspiring. The castle is also the setting for excellent medieval-style banquets (book in advance).

From Galway City, take the N6 to N18; turn right on the N67 and follow it to Kinvarra. ☎ *061-360-788. Admission: €5.50 ($8.80) adults; €3.15 ($5) seniors, children, and students. Open: Mid-Apr to Sept daily 9:30 a.m.–5 p.m. (last admission at 4:30 p.m.). Suggested visit: 1½ hours.*

Thoor Ballylee (W. B. Yeats's Summer Home)
Gort

This stone tower was poet W. B. Yeats's summer home. Yeats wrote many works here, including "The Winding Stair" and "The Tower," both inspired by this building. The view from the battlements takes in Galway's lush fields and forests. An audiovisual tour and museum are dedicated to Yeats's life and work, and the tower has been restored to look just like it did when the poet lived there in the 1920s. The gardens and a picnic area make for a gorgeous lunch stop when the weather's nice.

Off the Limerick-Galway road (N18) in Gort. ☎ *091-63-1436. Admission: €6 ($9.60) adults, €5.50 ($8.80) seniors and students, €2.50 ($4) children. Open: June–Sept Mon–Sat 9:30 a.m.–5 p.m. Suggested visit: 1½ hours.*

Shopping in Galway City

Galway City is home to lot of shops, and you're bound to find items to suit your taste as you stroll around the heart of the city. **Eyre Square Shopping Centre,** lined by old stone walls, has more than 50 shops and an antiques market under one glass roof. A great item to buy in Galway is a Claddagh ring — you know, the ones with two hands clasping a heart below a crown. The design originated in the Galway area, and you find numerous stores selling these rings. **Thomas Dillon's,** 1 Quay St., near the Spanish Arch (☎ **091-566-365**), claims to be the original maker and is worth a stop for its small homemade Claddagh museum (a little rough around the edges but interesting all the same), even if you aren't in the market for a ring.

MacEocagain/Galway Woollen Market, 21 High St. (☎ 091-56-2491), specializes in Aran handknits and other knitwear, linen, lace, sheepskins, and jewelry. **Kennys Bookshop and Galleries,** a Galway institution, has closed the bookstore portion of its offerings (though it still does a brisk business online at www.kennys.ie), and has expanded its outstanding gallery of art, antiquarian maps, and prints. The store is now called **The Kenny Gallery,** High Street (☎ 091-56-4760). **The Treasure Chest,** 31–33 William St. (☎ 091-563-862), has just about every Irish gift item you could want under one roof — Waterford Crystal, Royal Tara china, Belleek china, Claddagh rings, Aran knitwear, linen, and more.

Enjoying Galway City nightlife

Galway has some excellent theater and live music that you can take in before hitting one of the pubs listed in this section. **Róisín Dubh,** Dominick Street (☎ 091-586-540; www.roisindubh.net) books spectacular bands and singers, from traditional Irish musicians to singer-songwriters to alternative country bands to jazz groups to rock groups. The **Druid Theatre Company,** Flood St. (☎ 091-568-660; www.druid theatre.com), presents inventive performances of 20th-century and new Irish and European plays.

For information on what's going on in pubs, clubs, theaters, and more, pick up a free copy of *XPOSED Weekly Entertainment Guide* (available around town and online at www.irelandxposed.com). This is the best place to figure out which of Galway's several clubs are hot at the moment.

Crane Bar

This is arguably the best place in Galway City for traditional Irish music. Casual sessions take place every night with some of the best musicians in town. The décor is nothing special, but it won't matter once you get carried along on the current of jigs and reels.

2 Sea Rd., Salthill (less than a mile out of Galway City). ☎ 091-587-419.

The Kings Head

The Middle Ages live on in The Kings Head, with original medieval fireplaces and windows. It's all or nothing here, and every bit of the place looks the part of a pub from the 1500s. There's history galore associated with this place, and a chat with the barkeep will reveal some of its stories. This isn't a cramped, elbow-room pub, either: It's spread over three floors, and has a rock or pop band, or a DJ, every night. Take your picture sitting on the throne next to the downstairs fireplace and enjoy some of the great pub grub or pizza.

15 High St. ☎ 091-56-6630. www.thekingshead.ie.

The Claddagh ring

Claddagh rings feature two hands holding a heart, which is topped by a crown. The hands symbolize friendship, the crown symbolizes loyalty, and the heart represents love.

According to tradition, the wearer wears the ring on the ring finger of the left hand with the crown pointing toward the fingertips to show he or she is in love or married. If, on the other hand, the heart is pointing toward the fingertips the wearer is said to be unattached. Traditionally, the ring serves as an engagement or wedding ring.

The name comes from Claddagh, the oldest fishing village in Ireland, located on the west bank of the Corrib Estuary right across from Galway City. In Gaelic, *An Cladach* means "flat, stony shore."

Monroe's Tavern

Feeling footloose? Monroe's regularly packs the place every Tuesday night (after 9:30 p.m.) for set dancing — a partnered form of Irish dance that resembles American square dancing. And every night features live traditional Irish music — whirling reels keeping a fast, sweaty pace as onlookers shout out in a frenzy of good *craic* (fun). And the crowd isn't all tour-bus shutterbugs; the tavern is most popular with locals. Set in an old house with low ceilings and timber floors, it may seem large for a pub, but it needs the room so that you can get your jig on. During the day, you should stop in for a bite: Monroe's actually has excellent pub food.

Dominick Street. ☎ **091-58-3397.**

The Quays

No trip to Galway is complete without a stop at this lively pub, a city institution since the 1600s. The stone interior was once the inside of a medieval French church and boasts beautiful details such as stained glass and carved wood. Good music, sometimes of the traditional Irish ilk, is on tap every night. The pub grub is quite tasty.

Quay Street and Chapel Lane. ☎ **091-56-8347.**

Skeff Bar

This pub is a good place for conversation. It incorporates all different kinds of décor: Some parts look like an upper-class drawing room, with elegant couches, coffee tables, and Persian rugs; other parts are distinctly Irish pub, with low stools or tall booths. Fireplaces, intricate ceiling work, and stained glass give the place a posh feel. Staircases throughout lead to more bars upstairs. The American food (burgers, chicken fingers, and so on) is good, and there's often a DJ on weekends.

Eyre Square. ☎ **091-56-3173.**

Tíg Neachtain

This is the real deal. This cozy pub, in a building that dates from the Middle Ages, is filled with old snugs that have seen infinite pints of Guinness and been party to countless late-night conversations. There is music here most nights, ranging from traditional Irish to Cajun to jazz and blues.

17 Cross St. ☎ **091-568-820.**

The Aran Islands

The Aran Islands — Inishmore, Inishmaan, and Inisheer — are havens of traditional Irish culture: Islanders speak Irish Gaelic as a first language, and many still don traditional Aran sweaters with their jeans. The islands have a moody kind of beauty — they are flat and rocky, with small human-made farms divided by stone walls, and cliffs plunging into the sea below. Visitors arrive at Inishmore, the largest and most developed of islands, by the boatload during the summer. **Dún Aengus,** a prehistoric stone fort, is the main attraction on the island. Visitors can get around by bicycle or by using the minibuses and horse-and-pony carts that meet you at the ferry pier. Those craving a bit more solitude should visit Inishmaan, the second-largest island, which also has several prehistoric ruins; or Inisheer, the smallest of the islands, which is filled with farms and, from June to August, meadows of wildflowers; it also has several sandy beaches.

If you are going to come to the Aran Islands, I highly recommend spending the night. The true personality of the islands (and the islanders) seems to emerge only after the day-trippers have gone back to the mainland.

For more information on the islands, check out www.visitaran islands.com.

Getting to and around the Aran Islands

The most common way to get to the Arans is by ferry. **Aran Island Ferries** (☎ **091-56-8903;** www.aranislandferries.com), located at the Galway Tourist Office off Eyre Square, operates ferries that depart from Rossaveal Pier in Connemara (the bus trip from Galway to Rossaveal is included in the price). Prices are €25 ($40) for adults, €20 ($32) for seniors and students, and €13 ($21) for children. The ferries call at each of the islands, with the most popular (and busiest) port being Kilronan, on Inishmore. Aran Islands Ferries travels between Inisheer and Inishmaan; if you want to travel between other combinations of islands, you need to travel back to Rossaveal first. If you'd rather fly, **Aer Arann Islands** (☎ **091-59-3034;** www.aerarannislands.ie) takes off from Connemara airport, about 29km (18 miles) west of Galway City (a bus from the city is available to the airport; just ask when you book), and flies to all three islands; its most popular flights land in Kilronan, on Inishmore. The ten-minute flight is the shortest scheduled flight in the world. Prices are currently around €45 ($72) round-trip for adults, €37 ($59) for students, and €25 ($40) round-trip for children.

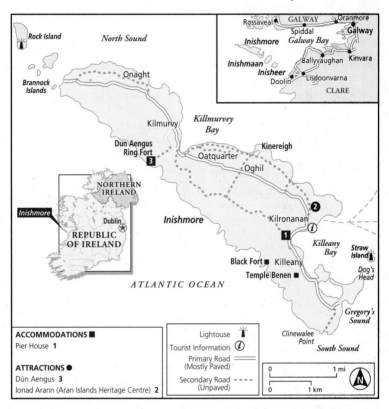

Inishmore, Aran Islands

ACCOMMODATIONS ■
Pier House **1**

ATTRACTIONS ●
Dún Aengus **3**
Ionad Arann (Aran Islands Heritage Centre) **2**

Lightouse
Tourist Information *(i)*
Primary Road (Mostly Paved)
Secondary Road (Unpaved)

You can't bring your car to the Arans, and there are no car rentals, so when you reach the islands, you have a couple of choices: You can rent a bike at **Aran Bike Hire** at Frenchman's Beach in Kilronan (☎ 099-61-132), which is what I recommend, or you can hire a driver and minibus or a bumpy horse and cart (there will be a bunch waiting when you arrive at the islands).

You can also tour the Arans by foot. Walking-tour maps are available at the **tourist office** in Kilronan (☎ 099-61-263). Each route takes a couple of hours.

Spending the night on the Aran Islands

Each island has several B&Bs; for information, contact the Galway Tourist Office at ☎ 091-53-77-00. In addition to Pier House (listed below), other favorites are **Man of Aran,** on Inishmore (☎ 099-61-0301), and **Radharc An Chlair,** on Inisheer (☎ 099-75019).

Pier House
$$$ Lower Kilronan, Inishmore

On a small island, you're pretty much guaranteed a view of the water from anywhere, but from a room in the Pier House, you get that and more. It's only feet from the harbor; sandy beaches, pubs, and restaurants are all a short walk away; and the ocean breeze makes its way into your room's open window at night. Rooms are quite nice, and it's obvious that great care goes into ensuring a guest's comfort. Plus it's a great value for the price.

☎ *099-61-416. Fax: 099-61-122.* www.galway.net/pages/pierhouse. *Rates: €90–€120 ($144–$192). MC, V. Closed: Nov–Feb.*

Exploring the Aran Islands

The Arans are attractions in and of themselves. Rent a bike (my top recommendation), flag a pony cart or minivan, or lace up your sneakers, and then poke around these beautiful islands. The heritage center, **Ionad Arann,** Kilronan, Inishmore (☎ **099-61-355**), is a good place to begin your visit to the islands. The center offers exhibits and a film investigating the culture, history, and geography of the islands. Admission is €4 ($6.40) for adults, €2.50 ($4) for students, and €2 ($3.20) for seniors and children. It's open daily April, May, September, and October from 11 a.m. to 5 p.m., and June through August 10 a.m. to 7 p.m.

Dún Aengus
Kilmurvey, Inishmore

This well-preserved immense prehistoric stone fort stretches over 4.4 hectares (11 acres) and is set on a sheer cliff overlooking the Atlantic Ocean. The fort is composed of three dry-stone walls, set one inside the other. The former use of the fort is still unknown. Views of Connemara, Galway Bay, and the Burren are superb from the innermost wall. Be sure to enter the area through the visitor center.

7km (4½ miles) west of Kilronan. ☎ *099-61-008. Admission: €2.10 ($3.40) adults, €1.30 ($2.10) seniors, €1.10 ($1.80) children and students. Open: June–Sept daily 9 a.m.–7 p.m.; Oct and Apr daily 9 a.m.–6 p.m.; Nov 10 a.m.–4 p.m.*

The origins of the Aran sweater

Aran sweaters may be one of Ireland's biggest exports today, but they came from humble beginnings. Originally, the almost-waterproof wool sweaters were knit by the women of the Aran Islands to ensure that the islands' fishermen stayed warm and dry (the waterproofing comes from natural oils from the sheep's skin, which remain on the wool). The various stitches on the sweater signify different ideas and objects, from a "honeycomb" stitch that symbolizes abundance to a "tree of life" stitch that represents the stages of life.

Shopping

If you've held out long enough, now's your chance to buy an authentic, often-copied-but-never-reproduced, hand-knit fisherman's sweater on the Aran Islands. Numerous shops sell these sweaters.

Connemara

The area west of Galway City, known as Connemara, offers some of the most stunning and varied scenery in Ireland. It's a wild and untamed place of still glacial lakes, stands of evergreens, 12 towering mountains (called the Twelve Bens or Twelve Pins), endless quiet boglands, beaches, and granite moorlands. In addition, it is home to Killary Harbor, a dazzling fjord that reflects mirror-images of the surrounding mountains. A large part of Connemara is a *Gaeltacht* — an area where you may hear Irish Gaelic being spoken. You also may encounter the rugged little Connemara ponies, the only purebred horses native to Ireland. There are only a few towns of any size in this region. The roughly 1,100-person town of **Clifden** is the unofficial capital of Connemara. Nestled in a valley at the foot of the Twelve Bens mountain range, the town's lively center and excellent location make it a popular base for visitors, who throng the town streets in the summer. A slightly quieter option is **Roundstone,** a bustling and charming little fishing village.

Getting to and around Connemara

The best way to see Connemara is by driving or biking. Take either N59, the inland route (you'll see signs for the road on Galway City's ring road), or R340 and R341, the coastal routes.

Bus Éireann (☎ 011-836-6111; www.buseireann.ie) serves Clifden and other towns in Connemara.

Spending the night in Connemara

Alcock and Brown Hotel
$$–$$$ Clifden

This large hotel is named after John Alcock and Arthur Brown, who, in 1919, landed in a Clifden bog after completing the first nonstop transatlantic flight. Set right in the center of Clifden, the hotel is now a great liftoff location for touring the spectacular landscape of Connemara. Rooms are of the typical large hotel variety — clean, spacious, and bright but lacking in any real character. The bar, which often hosts traditional Irish music and dance, is a lively and cozy place to relax after a day of sightseeing, and the hotel's restaurant serves fantastic seafood and meat dishes.

The square in the center of town. ☎ *095-21-206. Fax: 095-21-842.* www.alcockand brown-hotel.com. *Rates: €120–€170 ($192–$272) double. AE, DC, MC, V.*

Dolphin Beach House
$$$ Clifden

This is a stylish, restful place to base yourself. The 19th-century house has been well restored, and the spacious bedrooms have soaring ceilings, heated floors, antique furnishings, and pristine bed linens. Large windows bring the outside in and take full advantage of the spellbinding views. It all combines for a feeling of homespun luxury, with the beach just a stone's throw away. Meals are fashioned from ingredients grown on the estate or purchased locally. Dinner is available for €40 ($64). Sisters Sinead and Clodagh Foyle are friendly, knowledgeable hosts (the Foyle family own several hotels in the area — see also the Quay House, below). Sinead is an avid hiker and a great resource to those wishing to explore the majestic Connemara countryside.

Lower Sky Road, about 5km (3 miles) outside the center of Clifden. ☎ **095-21-204.** *Fax: 095-22-935.* www.dolphinbeachhouse.com. *Rates: €130–€180 ($208–$288) double. MC, V.*

Errisbeg Lodge
$$$ Roundstone

This peaceful B&B has views of the Errisbeg Mountains and the Atlantic Ocean, both of which are close at hand. Nature-lovers take note: The B&B has a vast amount of land (as proprietors Jack and Shirley King like to say, "We have a national park in our backyard"). You can wander through the wildflower garden, encountering the Kings' sweet Connemara ponies and donkey; stroll and shell-hunt on the nearby smooth, sandy beaches (Dogs Bay is especially beautiful); and climb Errisbeg Mountain for panoramic views of the area. Rooms are simple and airy, with pine furnishings, king-sized beds, and colorful comforters. The Kings are incredibly friendly and enthusiastic about sharing this beautiful location with their guests. Kids will love running around the grounds and playing with the ponies.

Ballyconneely-Roundstone Road (R341). West of Roundstone 1.5km (1 mile), opposite Gurteen Beach. ☎ **095-35-807.** www.errisbeglodge.com. *Rates: €85–€110 ($136–$176) double. No credit cards. Closed: Nov to mid-Mar.*

Faul House
$$ Ballyconneely

About half of the Faul House's guests are return visitors, which makes complete sense given the warmth and friendliness of owners Kathleen and Michael Conneely. Kathleen and Michael are a compendium of Connemara knowledge (Michael grew up on this land), and are genuinely happy to help visitors develop an itinerary that suits their individual needs and interests. The house is located on a peaceful country lane and has miles of land, where you'll find the Conneely's donkeys and sweet Connemara ponies. You'll definitely want to make time to explore the property, visit the animals, and walk down to the sea. The house has a gentle, welcoming feel about it, with a turf fire burning in the living room and bedrooms that are simple and airy, decorated with hand-painted watercolors and sporting king-sized beds. Breakfast is fantastic, particularly the scrambled eggs blanketed with fresh smoked salmon.

Ballyconneelly Road (2km/1.25 miles southwest of Clifden) ☎ **095-21-239.** *Fax: 095-21-988.* www.faulhouse.com. *Rates:* €*70–*€*80 ($112–$128) double. No credit cards. Closed: Nov–Mar 15.*

SeaMist Guesthouse
$$ **Clifden**

This place has a serene and homey feel that you may not expect in the middle of the bustling town of Clifden. The bedrooms are furnished in a modern country style, with a chic combination of burgundies, creams, and golds, and you'll find original art and interesting furnishings throughout the house. Plan extra time in the morning to linger over the excellent breakfasts (including such treats as pancakes and scrambled eggs with feta cheese) in the glass-walled conservatory.

Seaview Street. ☎ **095-21441.** *Rates:* €*80–*€*120 ($128–$192) double. MC, V. Closed: Weekdays Nov–Feb.*

The Quay House
$$$$ **Clifden**

The décor here is certainly not your run-of-the-mill prints of Ireland and Victorian-reproduction tables. Owners Paddy and Julia Foyle have furnished this grand restored harbormaster's house with bold, artistic choices, including zebra, tiger, and other animal skins; dramatic paintings in gilded frames; and glass chandeliers. One wall of the airy conservatory breakfast room is decorated with the lids of silver serving platters. Bedrooms are spacious and individually furnished, running from ornate Victorian-style quarters to rooms that look like they belong in a chic hunting lodge in Africa. Birders many want to ask for the Bird Room, featuring several stuffed parrots. Seven suites have balconies and small kitchens. Paddy and Julia have a deep knowledge of the area and are always happy to advise visitors on outdoor activities, dining, drives, and so on. The house is located a ten-minute walk from the town of Clifden.

Beach Road. ☎ **095-21-369.** *Fax: 095-21-608.* www.thequayhouse.com. *Rates:* €*150–*€*180 ($240–$288) double. MC, V. Closed: Mid-Nov to mid-Mar.*

Dining locally in Connemara
Browns, located in the Alcock & Brown Hotel (reviewed earlier in this chapter), has a good Irish menu.

Derryclare Restaurant
Clifden $$–$$$ **SEAFOOD-IRISH**

Warm and cozy is the name of the game here. Candles in cast-iron holders cast a golden glow on the dark, shiny wood tables and benches, and weathered signs decorate the walls. The restaurant buzzes with conversation and laughter from a convivial crowd that runs from couples to large families. Dishes are made with the freshest ingredients, simply prepared and boasting some inspired sauces and spices. My tagliatelle with olive oil, cherry tomatoes, and herbs was delicious, and the couple next to me was enjoying their braised Connemara lamb shank *au jus.* Enjoy vegetables, such as buttery creamed carrots and perfectly steamed broccoli, with your meal.

Market Street. ☎ **095-21-440.** *Main courses: €14–€24 ($22–$38). MC, V. Open: Daily noon to 10 p.m.*

Mitchell's Restaurant
$$$ Clifden   SEAFOOD/IRISH

Seafood is the staple of this stylish restaurant. Expect dishes such as baked filet of salmon with parsley mashed potatoes and creamed leeks, and pan-fried brill with sun-dried tomato champ (mashed potatoes) and chive sauce. Steaks and stews (including a luscious Connemara lamb stew) are also on offer, and noteworthy lighter meals, including pastas, quiche, and salads, are served during the day. The interior juxtaposes contemporary sleekness with ornate and rustic touches — contemporary paintings hang right next to an elaborately carved altar.

Market Street, in the center of town. ☎ **095-21-867.** *Main courses: €17–€27 ($27–$43). AE, MC, V. Open: Mid-Mar to Nov noon to 10 p.m. (last orders at 9:30 p.m.).*

Moran's Oyster Cottage
$$$ Kilcolgan   SEAFOOD

This is possibly the best place in Ireland for oysters. Moran's has been run by the same family for six generations and is dedicated to serving the very best oysters along with a well-pulled pint. If you are not a friend of the bivalve, there are other options on the menu, from chile-spiced prawns to baked salmon. All of these treats are served overlooking the weir, which is frequented by swans.

The Weir, Kilcolgan. On the N6, outside the village of Clarenbridge. ☎ **091-796-113.** *Main courses: €16–40 ($26–$64). AE, MC, V. Open: Daily noon to 10 p.m.*

Two Dog Café
$ Clifden

This cute, casual, bright cafe serves up teas and coffees, plus enticing wraps and panini, including a Chinese duck wrap with hoisin sauce, plum sauce, cucumbers, and spring onions. I believe it is illegal to leave the premises without sampling something from the selection of homemade cakes, cookies, and scones (and if not, it should be). The cafe has comprehensive Internet service upstairs.

1 Church Hill. ☎ **095-22-186.** *Main courses: €7–€8 ($11–$13). No credit cards. Open: Mon–Sat 10 a.m.–5 p.m.*

Exploring Connemara

If you are carless, you can choose among several guided bus tours of Connemara. I suggest hitting Galway City's tourist office (see "Fast Facts: County Galway," at the end of this chapter), either in person or virtually, to figure out which one suits you. **Bus Éireann's** (☎ **01-836-6111;** www.buseireann.ie) **Connemara Bus Tour** includes a stop at Kylemore Abbey, but the tour focuses on the beautiful mountain and coastal scenery and the stunning views of Killary Fjord. The bus leaves Galway Bus Station, in Eyre Square, at 10 a.m. daily, May 4 through September 27, and returns at 5:50 p.m. It costs €23 ($36) adults, €16 ($26) students and seniors, and €12 ($19) for children.

Corrib Ferries (☎ **092-46-029;** www.corribcruises.com) offers round-trip cruises on lovely Lough Corrib, Ireland's largest lake. You cruise from Oughterard, in County Galway, to Cong Village, in County Mayo, where you can gaze upon the exterior of the beautiful 13th-century Ashford Castle. Along the way, you stop on Inchagoill Island for a guided tour of the fifth-century ruins there. The cruise options range from a one-hour cruise to a five-and-a-half-hour cruise. If you have the time, go for the longer cruise, which gives you ample time to explore quaint Cong village. Also see Celtic Boat Safaris (see "Cruising Lough Corrib" in the Galway City section, earlier in this chapter), which does similar trips out of Galway City.

Connemara Walking Center, the Island House, Market Street, Clifden (☎ **095-21-379**), offers a number of well-done guided walks of Connemara. Call for a schedule and prices (closed in winter). Hikers should also consider a visit to Connemara National Park (see below).

Bicycling is a great way to explore this area; you can rent bikes from **John Mannion,** Bridge Street, Clifden (☎ **095-211-60**). The following routes also make good driving tours.

Tour 1: The N59 out of Clifden connects up with R344, which in turn connects again with N59 as you reenter Clifden, making a loop that takes you past shimmering lakes and bays and along the Twelve Bens — twelve mountains that stand like proud sentries in the wild landscape. You'll also travel through the moody boglands around Connemara National Park, and catch a glimpse of Kylemore Abbey (reviewed below) perched above a lake. You many want to stop to visit the Abbey and Gardens. If you are driving, allow about two to three hours for the tour.

Tour 2: Use the N59 south out of Clifden to get to the R341, which will trace the coastline and hook up with the R344 to take you back to the N59 into Clifden. If you are going counterclockwise from Clifden, you will pass the site where the first transatlantic flight landed in a bog (the pilots didn't realize that the soft green grass covered soggy land). Stop at Dogs Bay (see earlier in this chapter) and Gorteen Bay, two pristine beaches (both signposted off R341, at the most southerly point). You may want to get lunch or a snack in the cute fishing village of

Roundstone before joining up with R344, which will take you through some subtly beautiful bogland.

Tour 3: The Sky Road, signposted out of Clifden, is aptly named. I felt like I was flying as the road climbed higher and higher over farmland and sea cliffs.

Finally, there are several **pony trekking** outfitters in Connemara, and **Errislannan Manor** (☎ 095-21-134) is one of the finest, offering guided rides across Connemara's moors and coastland. To get there, take the Ballyconneely Road out of Clifden. The Errislannan Manor is signposted on the road about 3.2km (2 miles) outside of Clifden. Rates are €35 ($56) per hour; call to arrange times (closed Sun).

Connemara National Park and Visitor Centre
Letterfrack

Some of most beautiful scenery in Connemara is contained in this 2,000-hectare (5,000-acre) park. Vast bogland cloaks this area, and four of the mountains in the impressive Twelve Bens range are within its boundaries, including Benbaun, the highest of the 12, which reaches 720m (2,400 ft.). There are 4,000-year-old prehistoric structures, flowers that grow only here (look for the carnivorous sundew), and a contained herd of sturdy Connemara ponies. The clearly marked trails take you up through the boglands, revealing beautiful panoramas of the sea and the undulating hills. This is the kind of beauty that many find to be subtle rather than striking — the bogland reveals its splendor to those who walk slowly and look carefully. There are three loop walks within the park (easy, moderate, and hard), making it a good stop for a group of varying abilities — you can all meet up for tea in the Visitor Centre when you're done. Those who take the challenging Diamond loop will be rewarded with splendid views of the land and sea. The Visitor Centre (on the N59) has fascinating exhibits on the history of the area and on all things bog-related, and an audiovisual show on the park, and organizes nature trail walks (call in advance to see when they're being offered). I recommend wearing sturdy shoes and socks that you don't mind getting dirty (bogland is quite soggy).

Off the Clifden-Westport road (N59). ☎ *095-41-054 or 095-41-006. Free Admission. Open: Park year-round; Visitor Centre June–Aug 9:30 a.m.–6:30 p.m.; Mar–May and Sept–Oct 10 a.m.–5:30 p.m. Suggested visit: Several hours.*

Dogs Bay
Roundstone

You will certainly see dogs taking their owners for walks on this perfect crescent of a beach. You will also find lovely shells and some of the finest and softest white sand in Ireland here.

Off R341, west of Roundstone village. Suggested visit: 45 minutes.

Kylemore Benedictine Abbey & Gardens
Kylemore

Sitting in a stunning setting at the base of the mountains and on the shores of a lake, this abbey looks like a storybook castle — and it is, in a way. An English tycoon had the gorgeous neo-Gothic building constructed for his adored wife and sold it to the duke and duchess of Manchester upon her death. Several owners later, a group of nuns escaping the horrors of World War I in Belgium took up residence and converted it into an abbey. Today, the nuns also run a girls' boarding school here (though the school is being phased out; the current students will be the last to graduate from the school here, in 2010). You can visit the striking main hall and reception rooms, and walk along the lake to the restored neo-Gothic chapel. The star of the abbey is the magnificent walled Victorian garden, which slopes up on either side like an open book and contains an astounding assortment of vegetables, fruits, and flowers. Have a look inside the greenhouse, a restored version of one in a series of connecting greenhouses that origi- nally stood in the garden (in Victorian times, the lady of the house and her friends were treated to the unique pleasure of eating a fresh banana in the dead of winter — quite an unusual delicacy at that time). The Abbey is also known for its pottery; you can watch it being created and can pur- chase some in the craft shop.

On the Clifden-Westport road (N59), east of Letterfrack. ☎ **095-41-146.** www. kylemoreabbey.com. *Admission: €12 ($19) adults, €8.50 ($14) seniors, €7.50 ($12) students. Open: Abbey Mar–Nov 9 a.m.–5:30 p.m., Dec–Feb 10 a.m.–4 p.m.; gardens Easter–Oct daily 10 a.m.–4:30 p.m. Suggested visit: About 1½ hours.*

Shopping in Connemara

Owner Malachy Kearns and his staff at **Roundstone Music Craft & Fashion** in **Roundstone** (off Route 59; ☎ **095-35-808;** www.bodhran. com) make and sell a large and high-quality selection of *bodhráns* (Irish drums). Malachy Kearns is something of a celebrity: He made the drums for the *Riverdance* ensemble and is even featured on an Irish postage stamp. **The Spiddal Craft and Design Studios,** Spiddal (☎ **091-553-376**), houses craftspeople who make and sell a variety of crafts, from musical instruments to candles. **Millar's,** on Main Street, Clifden (☎ **095-21-038**), sells beautiful trendy handmade clothing, tweeds, and interesting jew- elry and knickknacks. **Avoca,** in Letterfrack (☎ **095-41-058**), sells all sorts of beautiful Irish crafts, furnishings, and clothing.

Hitting the pubs

E. J. Kings
Clifden

Almost anyone who's been to Clifden is familiar with E. J. Kings, because when you go, you can't forget it. Always humming, Kings has many floors, and in the high season, music fills the air. Seafood is the feature of the fantastic pub-food menu, but there's also good traditional fare. When it's cold, a welcoming fire warms the pub, and in nice weather, the outdoor patio is the hottest spot. The atmosphere in Kings is relaxed, and you're sure to get a warm welcome from the chatty staff.

The Square. ☎ **095-21-330.**

Fast Facts: County Galway

Area Codes

County Galway's area codes (or city codes) are **091**, **095**, and **099**.

Emergencies/Police

Dial ☎ **999** for all emergencies.

Genealogy Resources

Contact the Galway Family History Society West, in Shantalla (☎ 091-860-464).

Hospital

University College Hospital is on Newcastle Road, Galway (☎ 091-52-42-22).

Information

For visitor information and reservation services for Galway City and the whole of County Galway, go to the Galway Tourist Office (also known as Ireland West Tourism or Aras Fáilte), on Forster Street (on Eyre Square), Galway City (☎ 091-53-77-00; www.irelandwest.ie); open year-round.

Internet

NetAccess, in Galway, at Olde Malte Arcade, off High Street (☎ 091-395-725), has high-speed Internet access

Post Office

Galway Post Office is on Eglinton Street, Galway City (☎ 091-53-4727).

Chapter 19

Counties Mayo and Sligo

. . . .

In This Chapter

▶ Imagining the past at the megalithic ruins at Carrowmore
▶ Exploring Yeats' beloved countryside
▶ Watching falcons fly (and petting an owl)
▶ Driving through lovely mountain, coastal, and bogland scenery

. . . .

*L*ike Donegal, sparsely populated **Mayo** is one of the unsung beauties of Ireland, boasting stunning mountains and coastlines, a glassy fjord, and pretty green fields. A drive, walk, or bike through parts of the county could be one of the highlights of your trip. **Westport,** a charming little town that's popular with Irish and international travelers alike, is a great place to base yourself.

In general, **Sligo** has a gentler look than Mayo, with rolling farmland punctuated by pretty beaches, meadows, and mountains. This is the county that W.B. Yeats so loved, and many of his poems are based on places in the area. You will find no shortage of Yeats-related sights here. **Sligo Town** is in the throes of a renaissance right now, with new restaurants and shops popping up by the month.

Both counties are known for their remarkable megalithic and Neolithic sights, including Carrowmore, in Sligo, and Ceide Fields in Mayo.

Getting to and around Counties Mayo and Sligo

If you're driving from Dublin, take the N4 to Sligo Town or the N5 to Castlebar and Westport in County Mayo. From Galway, take the N17 to meet the N5 in County Mayo or straight to Sligo. From Donegal, go south on the N15 to Sligo. **Irish Rail** (☎ 1-850-366-222; www.irishrail.ie) serves Sligo Town (at Lord Edward Street), Collooney, Ballymote, and Boyle in County Sligo. In County Mayo, the rail service serves Westport, Foxford, Ballina, and Castlebar. **Bus Éireann** (☎ 01-836-6111; www.buseireann.ie) travels year-round to Sligo, Strandhill, Drumcliffe, and other major towns in County Sligo, and to Westport, Cong, Ballina, and other towns in County Mayo. Bus Éireann also has local service between Sligo and Rosses Point in July and August.

Counties Mayo and Sligo

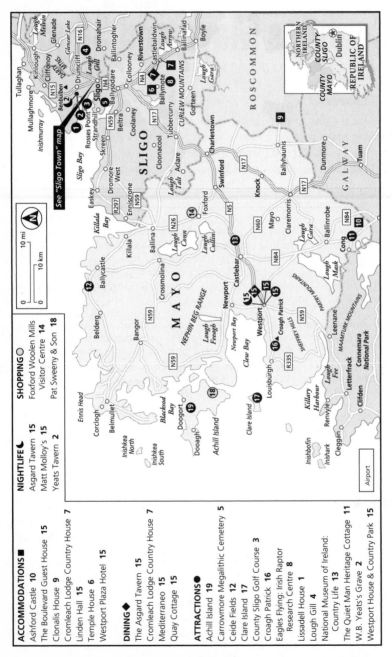

ACCOMMODATIONS ■
Ashford Castle **10**
The Boulevard Guest House **15**
Clonalis House **9**
Cromleach Lodge Country House **7**
Linden Hall **15**
Temple House **6**
Westport Plaza Hotel **15**

DINING ◆
The Asgard Tavern **15**
Cromleach Lodge Country House **7**
Mediterraneo **15**
Quay Cottage **15**

ATTRACTIONS ●
Achill Island **19**
Carrowmore Megalithic Cemetery **5**
Ceide Fields **12**
Clare Island **17**
County Sligo Golf Course **3**
Croagh Patrick **16**
Eagles Flying: Irish Raptor
   Research Centre **8**
Lissadell House **1**
Lough Gill **4**
National Museum of Ireland:
   Country Life **13**
The Quiet Man Heritage Cottage **11**
W.B. Yeats's Grave **2**
Westport House & Country Park **15**

NIGHTLIFE ◖
Asgard Tavern **15**
Matt Molloy's **15**
Yeats Tavern **2**

SHOPPING ○
Foxford Woolen Mills
   Visitor Centre **14**
Pat Sweeny & Son **18**

Aer Lingus (☎ 0818-365-000; www.aerlingus.com) has daily flights into both Sligo airport, in Strandhill (☎ 071-916-8280; www.sligo airport.com), and Knock airport, in Charlestown, County Mayo (☎ 094-936-8100; www.knockairport.com).

Taxis in Sligo Town line up on Quay Street. Call **Ace Cabs** (☎ 071-914-4444) if you need to be picked up.

Spending the Night

Check out the "Sligo Town" map for locations of accommodations there.

Ashford Castle
$$$$ Cong, County Mayo

Okay, time for a quiz: What do Fred Astaire, Joan Baez, and Jerry Springer have in common? If you answered that they've all stayed at luxurious Ashford Castle, you are correct. Perched on the banks of sapphire Lough Corrib and surrounded by 140 hectares (350 acres) of woodlands and gardens, this place feels like a resort, with golf, fishing, tennis, horseback riding, spa treatments, and many other offerings (including an on-site school of falconry). The castle is a mélange of architectural styles: The original building dates from 1228, with a French chateau–style addition added in the 18th century and two Victorian wings added in the 19th century. The interior is sumptuously decked out with carved oak paneling, crystal chandeliers, gorgeous oil paintings hanging in gilt frames, and lush fabrics. The spacious, bright bedrooms are less extravagant than the public rooms but are still beautifully furnished, with designer fabrics and lovely furniture. Two restaurants serve gourmet menus in opulent period surroundings.

Take the R346 to Cross, and turn left at the church, going towards Cong. Ashford Castle is on the left side of the road before you reach the village of Cong. ☎ *094-954-6003, or 800-346-7007 within the U.S. Fax: 094-954-6260.* www.ashford.ie. *Rates: €380–€452 ($608–$723) double. AE, DC, MC, V.*

The Boulevard Guest House
$$ Westport, County Mayo

Could this place be more pleasant? My favorite B&B in Westport, the Boulevard is located right near the center of town. Each of the homey, bright, uncluttered rooms is artistically decorated in different shades of one color (I really like the green room) and graced with a framed picture that complement the hues. White country-style furniture rounds out the look. You are invited to spend time in the simple and pretty common areas, including a delightful little courtyard where you may have a chance to chat with Sadie Moran, your kind and friendly host.

South Mall. ☎ *098-25-138.* www.boulevard-guesthouse.com. *Rates: €90 ($144) double. No credit cards.*

Sligo Town

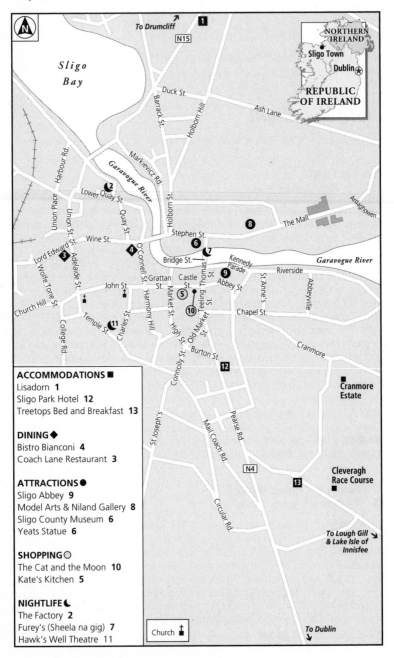

To Drumcliff

N15

Sligo Bay

NORTHERN IRELAND
Sligo Town
Dublin
REPUBLIC OF IRELAND

Duck St.

Ash Lane

Barrack St.

Holborn Hill

Harbour Rd.

Markievicz Rd.

Garavogue River

Lower Quay St.

Union Place

Union St.

Quay St.

Holborn St.

Stephen St.

The Mall

Ardaghowen

Wine St.

Lord Edward St.

Adelaide St.

O'Connell St.

Bridge St.

Kennedy Parade

Garavogue River

Riverside

Wolfe Tone St.

John St.

Grattan St.

Castle St.

Market St.

Teeling St.

Abbey St.

St. Anne's

Abbeyville

Church Hill

Harmony Hill

High St.

Old Market St.

Chapel St.

Temple St.

Charles St.

Burton St.

Cranmore

College Rd.

Connolly St.

St. Joseph's

Pearse Rd.

Mail Coach Rd.

Cranmore Estate

N4

Cleveragh Race Course

Circular Rd.

To Lough Gill & Lake Isle of Innisfee

Church

To Dublin

ACCOMMODATIONS ■
Lisadorn **1**
Sligo Park Hotel **12**
Treetops Bed and Breakfast **13**

DINING ◆
Bistro Bianconi **4**
Coach Lane Restaurant **3**

ATTRACTIONS ●
Sligo Abbey **9**
Model Arts & Niland Gallery **8**
Sligo County Museum **6**
Yeats Statue **6**

SHOPPING ○
The Cat and the Moon **10**
Kate's Kitchen **5**

NIGHTLIFE ☾
The Factory **2**
Furey's (Sheela na gig) **7**
Hawk's Well Theatre **11**

Clonalis House
$$$$ **Castlrea, County Roscommon**

Just over the County Mayo border is the Victorian Italianate mansion and ancestral home of the O'Conors of Connacht, descendants of Ireland's high kings. If you're an O'Conor (or O'Connor) yourself, you'll find the library and historical heirlooms of particular interest (don't miss famous Irish bard Turlough Carolan's harp). O'Conor or not, you will likely enjoy the four-poster beds, beautiful estate grounds, and nearby woods. The caretaker, Pyers O'Conor-Nash, will gladly chat over whiskey by the fireplace about his family's history or the area attractions. The expansive grounds are heaven for kids who like to run and explore, and the house dinner is excellent.

Take the N60 west from Castlerea or east from Ballyhaunis. ☎ **094-962-0014.** www.clonalis.com. *Rates: € 190–€ 220 ($304–$352) double. MC, V. Closed: Oct to mid-Apr.*

Cromleach Lodge Country House
$$$$ **Castlebaldwin, County Sligo**

A real hideaway, this modern inn overlooks large Lough Arrow and is surrounded by gentle countryside. This is a place for slow rambles around the hills, and leisurely afternoons spent enjoying views of the lake and its little islands from the glass-walled sun porch. The spacious rooms are furnished in a country style with Victorian touches. The lauded restaurant serves local seafood and may very well provide the most memorable meal of your trip.

Take the N4 south from Sligo town toward Boyle to Castlebaldwin. ☎ **071-916-5-155.** *Fax: 071-91-65-455.* www.cromleach.com. *Rates: € 150–€ 400 ($240–$640) double. AE, DC, MC, V.*

Linden Hall
$$ **Westport, County Mayo**

This B&B, which is a five-minute walk from the heart of Westport, offers clean, simple, bright rooms with comfortable beds. Your hosts, Maria and Stephen Breen, are friendly and fun, and know the area well. Ask for a room overlooking the wild garden in back.

Altamount Street. ☎ **098-27-005.** www.lindenhallwestport.com. *Rates: € 75–€ 95 ($120–$152) double. No credit cards.*

Lisadorn
$ **Sligo Town, County Sligo**

This stately home is at the end of a flower-lined drive; a perfect welcome to a lovely guesthouse. Rooms are large and beautifully furnished, and the place offers amazing hospitality and comfort for the cost. Lisadorn has a great location, only five minutes from town and ten minutes from the seaside and beaches at Rosses Point.

Donegal Road. From the center of town, take the N15 north. ☎ **071-91-43-417.** *Fax: 071-91-46-418. Rates: €64–€70 ($102–$112) double. No credit cards.*

Sligo Park Hotel
$$$$ Sligo Town, County Sligo

This large (by Ireland standards) contemporary hotel is like a small town, with a restaurant, pub, gym, indoor pool, and tennis courts on-site. Rooms — tastefully decorated with earth tones — are comfortable, bright, and clean.

Pearse Road (N4). ☎ **071-919-0400.** *Fax: 071-916-9556.* www.sligoparkhotel. com. *Rates: €89–€150 ($142–$240) double. AE, DC, MC, V.*

Temple House
$$$$ Ballymote, County Sligo

I am trying to figure out if there is any possible way that I could be related to the Percevals, who have lived on these breathtaking 400 hectares (1,000 acres) of land since 1665. If I was, say, a second-cousin twice-removed, perhaps I could return regularly to their expansive 1825 manor and again experience the kind of warmth that makes one feel like a member of the family. The splendor of the grounds and the house alone would make this one of the finest places to stay in Ireland, but it is the feeling that you are an honored guest of your hosts, Roderick and Helena Perceval, and their family (including the past generations, who look out from portraits and photographs throughout the house) that draws me so strongly to the place. A perfect day at Temple House: Wake up in your canopy bed in your vast room (most are bigger than my entire Brooklyn apartment was), surrounded by rich brocade draperies, gilt mirrors, gleaming mahogany furnishings, and family heirlooms. Head down to breakfast in the grand dining room, and then take a stroll with Fudge, Tara, and Treacle (the house dogs) around the gorgeous property, checking out the ruins of a 12th-century Knights Templar castle, rowing a boat on the lake (and perhaps trying your luck with the giant pike), and wandering miles of forest trails. Finish your day with a delicious three-course dinner (available on request), served at the immense table in the dining room (€45/$72); gatherings have the feel of a dinner party.

Ballymote. Signposted from the N17, near Ballinacarrow. ☎ **071-918-3329.** *Fax: 071-918-3808.* www.templehouse.ie. *Rates: €160–€190 ($256–$304) double. MC, V.*

Treetops Bed and Breakfast
$$ Sligo Town, County Sligo

Artsy folks will want to make extra time to look around this terrific bed and breakfast, where original contemporary Irish paintings, drawings, and sculpture grace the walls and surfaces. Your hosts couldn't be kinder and more helpful, and they cook your Irish breakfast to perfection. The contemporary rooms are spotless and cozy. You get the best of both worlds in the location: you're about a ten-minute walk from downtown Sligo on a quiet, peaceful road.

Cleveragh Road (off Pearse Road [R287]). ☎ **071-916-2301.** www.sligobandb.com. *Rates: €76 ($122). AE, MC, V.*

Westport Plaza Hotel
$$$ Westport, County Mayo

Rooms at this luxurious hotel are spacious and plush, with incredibly comfortable beds, and every bathroom features a Jacuzzi tub. The restaurant does a beautiful job with fresh ingredients, offering creative dishes such as the recent pan-fried halibut filet with a fennel-and-Pernod coulis. The new spa promises to soothe away any traveling stress.

Castlebar Street. ☎ **098-51-166.** *Fax: 098-51-133.* www.westportplazahotel.ie. *Rates: €130–230 ($208–$368). AE, MC, V.*

Dining Locally

Cromleach Lodge (reviewed in the previous section) offers a wonderful New Irish menu in a dining room with views of the surrounding countryside. In Westport, the **Westport Plaza Hotel** (also reviewed in the previous section) is a terrific place for a night out.

The Asgard Tavern
$$–$$$ Westport, County Mayo   IRISH/STEAKS/SEAFOOD

This nautical-themed restaurant is right on the water and serves award-winning food. Filling and hearty fare, including stews and pasta dishes, is served all day downstairs in the relaxing pub. Dinner is served upstairs, in a tasteful, candlelit dining room. The dinner menu is varied, including creatively prepared steaks and seafood.

The Quay. Drive west out of Westport and take the Coast Road 1.6km (1 mile). ☎ **098-25-319.** *Main courses: €15–€22 ($24–$35). AE, DC, MC, V. Open: Daily noon to 9:30 p.m.*

Bistro Bianconi
$$–$$$$ Sligo Town, County Sligo   ITALIAN-PIZZA

The menu at this large, bustling Italian restaurant includes no fewer than six pages full of different kinds of pizza, from a Cajun chicken pizza with sliced peppers and smoked bacon to the Michelangelo, with mozzarella, caramelized onions, pepperoni, goat cheese, and basil pesto. And that's just the pizza. The bistro also offers steak, chicken, and a wide selection of pastas. Families and groups of friends fill the restaurant, which is decorated in trattoria style, with Roman busts, mosaics, and columns.

44 O'Connell St. ☎ **071-914-1744.** *Main courses: €12–€29 (most in the mid teens) ($19–$46). AE, DC, MC, V. Open: Mon–Sat 12:30–11 p.m.*

Coach Lane Restaurant
$$$ **Sligo Town, County Sligo NEW IRISH**

Imagine a farmhouse, with brick and stone walls and broad wooden beams. Now imagine that your hippest friend has just moved in, decorating the place with just the right quantity of stylish touches like white pillar candles, vases of wildflowers, gilt mirrors, and garnet silk curtains. That's Coach Lane, which serves a varied New Irish menu featuring such creative dishes as grilled filet mignon and Cajun shrimp served with a shot of Guinness and a sauce of mustard and crème fraiche, plus Italian-influenced dishes such as linguini with clams in a white wine and garlic sauce. Specials include many fresh fish dishes. Ask for a table on the recently added top floor, which has pretty views of the town below.

1–2 Lord Edward St. ☎ *071-916-2417. Main courses: €18–€26 ($29–$42). AE, DC, MC, V. Open: Mon–Sat 3–10 p.m., Sun 3:30–10 p.m.*

Mediterraneo
$$ **Westport, County Mayo ITALIAN**

Aah, Florence. A fresco of a compass beckons you to a table in this Italian restaurant, where low-hanging lamps cast a golden glow on honey-colored walls and sculpted arches, and jazz music is audible under the hum of talk and laughter. You'll find all sorts of Italian dishes on the menu, from saltimbocca to Spaghetti Mediterraneo — pasta adorned with octopus, calamari, shrimp, and mussels in a garlic, tomato, and chile sauce. Specials often include a variety of fish dishes.

1 Brewery Lane (off Bridge St.). ☎ *098-26-730. Main courses €13–€27 ($21–$43). AE, MC, V. Open: Daily 6–10 p.m.*

Quay Cottage
$$$ **Westport, County Mayo SEAFOOD**

This little restaurant overlooks the harbor, and the three warm and cozy rooms are appropriately decked out with nautical treasures. The menu focuses on simple preparations of seafood that was most likely swimming that morning. Specials change depending on what's fresh, but you're likely to find salmon, John Dory, turbot, sole, scallops, oysters, and mussels. Vegetarians and non–seafood eaters are well cared for with options such as a Thai vegetable stir-fry and a sirloin steak.

On Westport Harbour at the entrance to Westport, just before the gates of the Westport House. ☎ *098-26-412. Reservations recommended. Main courses: €18–€28 ($29–$45). AE, MC, V. Open: Daily noon to 4 p.m. and 6–9:30 p.m.; Sept–May Tues–Sat 6–10 p.m.*

Exploring Mayo and Sligo

If you are a Yeats fan without a car, luck is on your side, because **Discover Sligo Tours** (☎ 071-914-7488) offers excellent narrated bus tours of the Sligo area and of sights associated with Yeats.

The top attractions

Achill Island
County Mayo

At 22km (13 miles) long and 19km (12 miles) wide, Achill is Ireland's largest offshore island. The island has stunning coastal and cliff scenery, which is best seen by taking the twisty Atlantic Drive (signposted off the bridge that connects the mainland to the island). Golfing, fishing, and scuba diving are popular activities on and around the island. Hikers and walkers will be in paradise here, tromping along the sandy beaches or hill trails. For more information about Achill Island, contact Achill Tourism at ☎ **098-47-353** or www.achilltourism.com. If you'd like to spend the night on the island, The Bervie (☎ **098-43-114;** www.bervieachill.com), a guesthouse on the sea, gets rave reviews.

Carrowmore Megalithic Cemetery
Carrowmore, County Sligo

You may imagine that you hear the whispers and see the ritual fires of generations past as you tour this ancient group of *passage tombs* (burial mounds with entrance passageways) and *dolmen* (tombs composed of one rock lying flat across other standing rocks), which are spread out over a great grassy field ringed by mountains. This is the largest collection of megalithic tombs in Ireland, and some of the oldest tombs in the country are found here, including one that's estimated to be more than 7,000 years old. The Carrowmore area is only a small portion of a vast local group of such tombs; look at the bumps at the tops of the surrounding mountains to locate other tombs. Definitely take the free guided tour; the exceptionally knowledgeable guides bring the site to life, painting a picture of the activities that may have taken place here thousands of years ago, and discussing various theories surrounding the creation and use of these tombs. A restored cottage houses exhibits and information related to the site.

Located off the R292, going west out of Sligo Town. ☎ *071-916-1534. Admission: €2.10 ($3.40) adults, €1.30 ($2.10) seniors, €1.10 ($1.80) children and students. Open: Mid-Mar to Nov daily 10 a.m.–6 p.m. (last admission 5 p.m.). Suggested visit: 1½ hours.*

Ceide Fields
Ballycastle, County Mayo

This is the world's most extensive Stone Age monument, with a dwelling area, grazing grounds, planting fields, and megalithic tombs from 5,000 years ago. Tools and pottery have been uncovered and are on display in the interpretive center, where films and exhibits do a nice job of explaining the history of the area and the lives of the people who lived here. Although a bog now covers most of the fields (and you can admire the bog's wild plants and flowers), portions have been cut out to show where the fields were partitioned by stone walls for growing food and grazing animals. The fields back up to some of the most captivating cliffs and rock formations in the country.

Take the R314 coastal road north from Ballina, 8.1km (5 miles) west of Ballycastle.
☎ *096-43-325. Admission: €3.70 ($5.90) adult, €2.60 ($4.20) seniors, €1.30 ($2.10)*
children and students. Open: Mid-Mar to May and Oct–Nov daily 10 a.m.–5 p.m.;
June–Sept daily 10 a.m.–6 p.m. Suggested visit: 1 hour.

Clare Island
Clew Bay, County Mayo

This island is a sanctuary, with a pretty sandy beach, two large hills, and
miles of walking trails. History buffs will be delighted to find a 12th-century
Cistersian abbey, the ruins of a castle that belonged to 1600s pirate queen
Grace O'Malley, and a 19th-century Napoleonic signal tower.

The Pirate Queen ferry (☎ 098-28-288) runs several times daily (weather permitting)
from Roonagh Quay. Follow signs from Louisburgh, off the R335. Tickets: Round-trip
€15 ($24) adults, €12 ($19) students and children 12–16, €8 ($13) children 5–12 years,
free for children under 5. Call for sailing times. Suggested visit: A few hours.

Croagh Patrick
Murrisk, County Mayo

According to legend, St. Patrick achieved divine inspiration on this pyra-
mid-shaped mountain after praying and fasting for 40 days — although I
don't suggest staying up there that long, no matter how beautiful the view.
On the last Sunday of July, more than 25,000 devout Catholics climb the
762m (2,500-ft.) mountain (some barefoot) in honor of their patron saint.
There are stunning views of Mayo and Clew Bay from the mountaintop.
The climb takes two to three hours and is tough work but not impossible.
(If you can make it to the saddle, a flat stretch about 610m/2,000 ft. up,

---

The mystery of Queen Maeve

Legend has it that the great Celtic warrior Queen Maeve (first century A.D.) ordered
her followers to bring her body to Sligo and bury her standing up and facing down her
enemies to the north. She is said to stand within a tomb atop Knocknarea Mountain,
one of the impressive ring of mountains that surround Carrowmore (see the description of Carrowmore above). The unmistakable loaf-shaped outline of the passage tomb
can be seen from almost every location in Sligo. Some say Queen Maeve was a mythic
goddess, some say she was a very real and ruthless Celtic queen. Archaeologists
speculate that the Knocknarea tomb contains much older megalithic remains. But still,
the tomb remains undisturbed in respect for the legend of Maeve, and thus far, there
are no plans to excavate it. In Sligo there is a custom of adding a stone to the tomb,
ostensibly to "keep away the fairies," though many say the custom may have originated as a way to make sure that Maeve stays put in her resting place. You can hike
up to the tomb in about 45 minutes; park at the base of the mountain, accessible off
R292, southwest of Sligo Town. You'll need good shoes, as there is a bit of a scramble
towards the top.

you'll be rewarded with spectacular panoramic views and still avoid the most difficult part of the climb.) A visitor center on the Pilgrim's trail in Murrisk sells crafts and mementos and offers information on the mountain, a restaurant, and hot showers.

Between Louisburgh and Westport, off the R395. Admission: Free. Open: Daylight hours. Suggested visit: A few hours.

Drive around Lough Gill
Drumcliffe, County Sligo

Serene, azure Lough Gill makes many appearances in Yeats's poems. You may be inspired to jot down a few lines of poetry yourself as you make the 42km (26-mile) drive around this gorgeous lake, stopping to ramble along the nature trails and gaze at the island of Innisfree, made famous in Yeats's poem "The Lake Isle of Innisfree." On the north side of the lake drive, you may want to stop to take a guided tour of the beautiful 17th-century Parke's Castle. The lakeside Hazelwood Sculpture Trail is a splendid walk, passing by a number of large wood sculptures. Take along some food for the ducks and swans.

Go south from Sligo Town 1.6km (1 mile). Take Stephen Street in Sligo Town, which turns into N16; turn right onto R286, and follow the signs. Suggested visit: 1½ hours or more, depending on how often you stop.

Eagles Flying: Irish Raptor Research Centre
Ballymote, County Sligo

If having a flying falcon's wing graze your hair isn't an amazing experience, I don't know what is. The highlights of this beautiful sanctuary for birds of prey are the daily hour-long free-flying demonstrations (at 11 a.m. and 3 p.m.), when falconers fly eagles, hawks, owls, and falcons over your head as they explain the behaviors and characteristics of each bird. You'll get a chance to pet an owl during the demonstration, and you can wander the grounds before or after the show, getting another look at the birds or petting and feeding some of the other animals, including ferrets, donkeys, chicks, a pig, and a friendly hedgehog.

Portinch, Ballymote (follow directions for Temple House [p. 374], and then turn left at the gate of Temple House). ☎ *071-918-9310. Admission: €9 ($14) adults, €8 ($13) students, €5.50 ($8.80) children 3–16; free for children under 3. Open: Good Friday–Nov 7 10:30 a.m.–12:30 p.m. and 2:30–4:30 p.m. (demonstrations daily during these months at 11 a.m. and 3 p.m.) Suggested visit: 1½ hours.*

Lissadell House
Drumcliffe, County Sligo

W. B. Yeats called Lissadell House "that old Georgian mansion," which is quite the understatement. This grand square stone house was owned by the Gore-Booth family, friends of Yeats. One of the Gore-Booth daughters was Countess Markievicz (she married a Polish count), who took part in the Easter Rising of 1916; she was the first woman elected to the British House of Commons and the first woman cabinet member in the Irish Dáil. Her sister, Eva, was a poet. Highlights of the house include a grand marble staircase; paintings and engravings by Countess Markievicz, John Butler Yeats (father to William and Jack), and Percy French; and a collection of Regency books. The restored upper walled garden (a kitchen garden) is a treat. Parts of the property will be undergoing restoration over the next few years, though this shouldn't affect visitors.

Off the N15, between Sligo and Donegal. ☎ *071-916-3150. Admission: Guided tours of the house are €6 ($9.60) adult, €3 ($4.80) children; garden €5 ($8). Open: Daily 10:30 a.m.–6 p.m. (last tour begins at 5 p.m.). Suggested visit: 2 hours.*

Lough Gill Cruise (The Rose of Innisfree)
Lough Gill, County Sligo

Relax on *The Rose of Innisfree* as you cruise Loch Gill and view the isle of Innisfree, made famous in the eponymous poem by W.B. Yeats. Snacks and drinks are on offer, and Yeats' poetry is recited live.

Cruises leave from Parke's Castle, located 11km (7 miles) from Sligo Town, on R286. ☎ *071-916-4266. Price: €15 ($24) adults, €7.50 ($12) children. Call for a schedule and to make reservations.*

Model Arts and Niland Gallery
Sligo Town, County Sligo

The Yeats family legacy is a cornerstone of this excellent museum, which features many paintings by Jack Yeats and his father, John Yeats, in addition to the works of many other 20th-century Irish artists. The gallery also puts on popular temporary shows by contemporary Irish and international artists, and offers a jam-packed schedule of gallery talks, music, film, and live comedy. The gallery is undergoing a massive renovation as we go to press but should be open starting in the spring of 2009.

The Mall. ☎ *071-914-1405.* www.modelart.ie. *Admission: Free. Open: Tues–Sat 10 a.m.–5:30 p.m., Sun 11 a.m.–4 p.m. Suggested visit: About 1½ hours.*

National Museum of Ireland: Country Life
Castlebar, County Mayo

Surrounded by pretty gardens, this museum features well-crafted, interesting exhibits on life in rural Ireland from 1850 to 1950. You'll find artifacts, such as spinning wheels and clothing, alongside video footage of country traditions. The museum works hard to make sure that visitors come away with a real sense of the people behind the objects. This place is definitely worth a stop if you are interested in the history and culture of rural Ireland.

Off the N5, in Turlough village, 8km (5 miles) east of Castlebar, County Mayo. ☎ *094-90-3751.* www.museum.ie. *Admission: Free. Open: Tues–Sat 10 a.m.–5 p.m. and Sun 2–5 p.m.*

Sligo-style spa treatment & a Mayo massage

Getting into a bathtub filled with warm water and seaweed may not be the first thing that you think of when you picture a relaxing bath, but that may be because you haven't experienced the moisturizing and calming properties of a hot bath strewn with fresh Irish seaweed. The **Celtic Seaweed Baths**, in Strandhill, right outside of Sligo Town (☎ 071-916-8686), offers private seaweed baths plus massages and facials.

In Westport, **Westport Leisure Park,** off James Street (☎ 098-29-160), has great massage deals, at €50 ($80) for an hour.

Sligo Abbey
Sligo Town, County Sligo

This is the city's only surviving medieval building, constructed in the mid-13th century for Dominican monks. Inside are carvings and tomb sculptures. The highlight is the superbly carved high altar from the 15th century, the only one of its kind in a monastic church in Ireland. The abbey burned down in 1414 and was damaged again in the 1641 Rebellion. According to local legend, worshippers saved the abbey's silver bell from thieves by putting it in Lough Gill; it was retrieved later and is back in the abbey. Some say that those free from sin can hear its toll. The abbey is always cool inside, even in warm weather, so you may want to grab a jacket.

Abbey Street, 1 block south of Kennedy Parade in the center of Sligo Town. ☎ *071-91-46-406. Admission: €2.10 ($3.40) adult, €1.30 ($2.10) seniors, €1.10 ($1.80) children and students. Open: Mid-Mar to Oct 10 a.m.–6 p.m.; Nov–Dec 15 Fri–Sun 9:30 a.m.–4:30 p.m. (last admission 45 minutes before closing). Suggested visit: 45 minutes.*

Westport House & Country Park
Westport, County Mayo

Fans of Georgian architecture will appreciate this limestone house, which sits at the head of Clew Bay. For many years, the house belonged to the Browne family, descendents of 16th-century pirate queen Grace O'Malley. It's a grand residence, featuring beautiful original furnishings and architectural details from the late 18th and 19th centuries. You'll find high ceilings, an extraordinary white marble staircase, portraits of the Brownes, and a dining room full of antiques, including Irish silver and Waterford crystal. The extensive grounds are (somewhat incongruously) a kid's paradise, offering log flume rides, swan pedal boats, two giant slides, an animal and bird park, and more.

Two splendid drives

In County Sligo, hook up with the N17, south of Sligo Town, and take it in the direction of Ballinacarrow. After you've gone through Ballinacarrow, look out for the sign for Temple House. At the sign, make a right in the direction of Killoran, taking the road through the unspoiled Ox Mountains (keep following signs pointing towards Ladies' Brae). The road will open onto a panoramic view of patchwork fields rippling down to Sligo Bay, with the distinctive Ben Bulben Mountain rising at the far end of the bay. Take a left when you reach N59, and then a right onto the Coast Road, following signs for Aughris Head. Your destination is Maggie Maye's Beach Bar, at Aughris Strand, where you can have a pint on an unspoiled rocky beach with gorgeous views of Ben Bulben and Knocknarea (see "The mystery of Queen Maeve" box, above). To get back to the main roads, leave the Coast Road for N59, which is much simpler to follow.

The following scenic route takes you from County Mayo to Connemara. Take the R335 out of Westport. You'll drive past Clew Bay, studded with tiny grass-green islands, and the bottom of the pyramid-shaped Croagh Patrick (described above). Continue through the steep and windswept bogland of Doolough Pass, and along glassy Killary Fjord, which reflects the surrounding mountains. You may want to stop at powerful Aasleagh Falls. From here, you can either continue on into Connemara on N59 or retrace the route back to Westport.

In the city center. ☎ **098-25-430.** *Admission: House, gardens, and attractions €21 ($34) adult, €20 ($32) students, €12 ($19) seniors, and €17 ($26) children; house and gardens only €12 ($18) adults, €9 ($14) seniors and students, and €6.50 ($10) children. Open: All attractions open Mar 22–Mar 30 daily 11:30 a.m.–5:30 p.m.; May Sun 11:30–5:30 p.m.; June–Aug daily 11:30 am–5:30 p.m. House and garden only open Sept–Oct daily 11:30 a.m.–5:30 p.m. Suggested visit: 2 hours or more.*

Other cool things to see and do

✔ **County Sligo Golf Course:** This course challenges even top players, but dabblers can have fun playing it, too. It's set between striking Atlantic beaches and the hill of Benbulben.

Location: Rosses Point, County Sligo. ☎ **071-917-7134.** www.countysligogolfclub.ie. Par: 71. Fees: High season €75 ($120) weekdays, €90 ($144) weekends; low season €40 ($64) weekdays, €50 ($80) weekends. Visitors welcome daily.

✔ **Fishing:** What's your poison (or should I say "poisson"?) — salmon, trout, pike, perch? Contact the North West Regional Fisheries (☎ **096-22788;** www.northwestfisheries.ie) for information about Sligo and Mayo's many places to fish.

✔ **The Quiet Man Heritage Cottage:** In the movie *The Quiet Man,* American John Wayne comes back to his birthplace in Ireland and falls in love with Maureen O'Hara. In the movie, Wayne's character tells a local that he was born in a thatched-roof cottage, just like the seven generations of his family before him, and the local makes a wisecrack about Wayne's buying the place to turn it into a tourist attraction. Ironically, you can now visit a replica of the original house — and yes, they do charge a small fee to the tourists. Unfortunately, no movie memorabilia remains, so all there is to see is the house. If you are a die-hard *Quiet Man* fan, you can take a tour of locations in which the movie was filmed every day at noon from June to August.

Location: Circular Road, Cong, County Mayo. ☎ **094-954-6089.** Admission: €5 ($8) adult, €3 ($4.80) children, 4.50 ($7.20). Open: Daily 10:30 a.m. to 4:30 p.m. April to October. Suggested visit: Thirty minutes.

✔ **Sligo County Museum:** Arise and go now, W.B. Yeats fans and Countess Constance Markievicz fans, to see this collection of photographs, letters, prints, portraits, drawings, and broadsheets that relate to Yeats and Markievicz.

Location: Stephen Street, County Sligo. ☎ **071-914-1623.** www.sligolibrary.ie. Admission: Free. Open: June through September Tuesday through Saturday 10 a.m. to noon; year-round Tuesday through Saturday 2 to 4:50 p.m.

✔ **W. B. Yeats's Grave:** Yeats died in France, but, in 1948, his remains were brought to rest in Sligo — the place he always considered home. His grave in the Drumcliffe churchyard is near a beautiful Celtic high cross. On the grave is an epitaph Yeats wrote: "Cast a cold eye on life, on death. Horseman pass by." Look out for an installation in front of the church incorporating Yeats's poem *He Wishes for the Cloths of Heaven.*

Location: 8km (5 miles) north of Sligo on the main Donegal road (N15). Suggested visit: A few minutes.

✔ **The Yeats Statue:** One of the more interesting statues in Ireland is a cartoonish likeness of Sligo's famous poet near the banks of the Garavogue River, in Sligo Town. Scrawled over his entire figure are the words of his own verse.

Location: On Stephen Street, just across Hyde Bridge in Sligo Town. Suggested visit: A few minutes.

Shopping

The locally famous Foxford wool tweeds, rugs, blankets, and much more are all at **Foxford Woolen Mills Visitor Centre,** Foxford, County Mayo (from Westport N5 northeast to N58 north; ☎ **094-925-6104**). As the name implies, you can tour the working mill. **Pat Sweeny and Son,** Achill Sound, Achill Island, County Mayo (follow signs from Louisburgh off the R335; ☎ **098-45-211**), is a fascinating example of a local trading store, dating back to 1870. It has "everything from a needle to an anchor" and all the gifts, clothing, fishing gear, food, and petrol in between. **The Cat and The Moon,** 4 Castle St., Sligo Town (☎ **071-914-3686**), sells gorgeous Irish handcrafted jewelry, contemporary art, Celtic-inspired home furnishings, and more. Check out the connected art gallery. Stop into **Kate's Kitchen,** 3 Castle St., Sligo Town (☎ **071-914-3022**), for picnic food: meats, cheeses, salads, pâté, homemade bread, Irish chocolates, and preserves. The store also has soaps and potpourri.

Hitting the Pubs

Before a Sligo Town pub crawl, you may want to take in a performance at **The Factory** (☎ **071-917-0431**; www.blueraincoat.com) or at **Hawk's Well Theatre** (☎ **071-916-1518**; www.hawkswell.com). The performance schedule at The Factory is diverse, offering everything from West African music to the excellent production of the Sligo-based Blue Raincoat Theatre. At the Hawk's Well, you'll find professional and local drama, ranging from classic Irish plays to new dance works.

Furey's (Sheela na gig)
Sligo Town, County Sligo

Created by members of the traditional Irish music supergroup Dervish, this pub has great *craic* (fun) and music every night of the week.

Bridge Street. ☎ **071-914-3825.**

Matt Molloy's
Westport, County Mayo

If you like traditional Irish music, this traditionally decorated pub is worth visiting. It was started by the flutist from the famous band The Chieftains, who are often credited with the revival in Irish folk music. The back room features music nearly every night — Molloy himself sometimes stops in for a session when he's in town.

Bridge Street. ☎ **098-26-655.**

Yeats Tavern
Drumcliffe Bridge, County Sligo

Just a short walk from the grave of poet W. B. Yeats, this pub is a popular watering hole for locals and visitors alike. Inside, you find plenty of Yeats memorabilia and quotes from his works. This place features good pub grub as well as a restaurant for more formal dining.

Drumcliffe Bridge. Go 8.1km (5 miles) out of Sligo Town on the main Donegal road. ☎ **071-916-3117.**

Fast Facts: Counties Mayo and Sligo

Area Codes

071 and **074** for County Sligo; **092, 094, 096, 097,** and **098** for County Mayo.

Emergencies/Police

Dial ☎ **999** for all emergencies.

Genealogy Resources

Contact the Sligo Heritage and Genealogy Centre, Temple Street, Sligo (☎ 071-914-3728); the North Mayo Heritage Centre, Castlehill, Ballina (☎ 096-31-809); or the South Mayo Family History Research Centre, Main Street, Ballinrobe (☎ 094-954-1214).

Hospital

Sligo General Hospital is on The Mall (☎ 071-917-1111).

Information

Tourist offices are located at Temple Street in Sligo Town (☎ 071-916-1201; www. irelandnorthwwest.ie); and on Bridge Street in Westport, County Mayo (☎ 098-25-711; www.visitmayo.com). Both are open year-round.

Internet

Cafe Online, 1 Calry Court, Stephen Street, Sligo Town (☎ 071-914-4892), is a comprehensive Internet cafe.

Post Office

Lower Knox Street, Sligo (☎ 071-915-9273), and North Mall, Westport (☎ 098-25-219).

Chapter 20

County Donegal

County Donegal is often ignored by visitors, which is a shame because the county has natural beauty in spades, plus several areas where Gaelic culture thrives (especially the Atlantic Peninsula and the peninsula north of Donegal Bay). The county has many different faces. The **peninsula north of Donegal Bay** is stunning, with mountains, rolling pastureland, charming little towns, and the towering sea cliffs of **Slieve League.** The towns on the south side of Donegal Bay are seaside resorts frequented mostly by Irish vacationers, and some, such as Bundoran, are pretty tacky. **Glenveagh National Park** boasts forests, several sparkling lakes, a castle, and a whole herd of red deer. The Atlantic Highlands (in the north) and the **Inishowen Peninsula** are wild landscapes, vast and breathtaking, with mountains, woodland, cliffs, and the ever-present crashing of the ocean.

There isn't one specific area known for human-made sights; instead, you'll come across a variety of attractions, including a prehistoric fort and a house packed with art treasures, as you explore this little-visited corner of the country.

The largest town in the county, **Donegal Town,** is a nice, walkable village along the River Eske. There are no big attractions in town (other than the castle), so it is not worth spending more than a morning or afternoon exploring, but it makes a good point of departure for touring the coast clockwise.

Getting to and around County Donegal

Local flights come into Donegal airport, Carrickfinn, Kincasslagh (☎ 075-954-8284; www.donegalairport.ie), located 65km (40 miles) from Donegal Town. If you come by car, you can take the N15 north from Sligo. **Bus Éireann** (☎ 1-850-366-222; www.buseireann.ie) travels

County Donegal

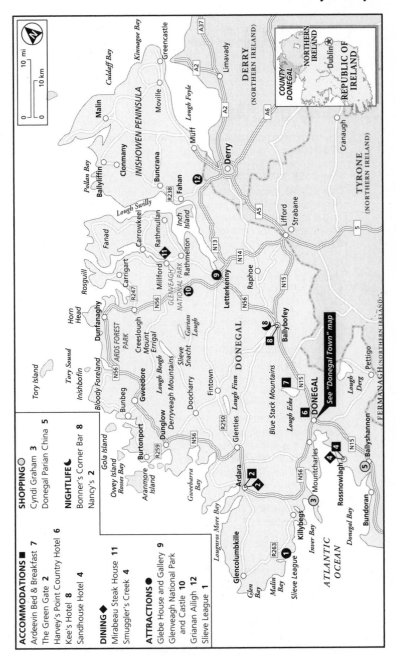

ACCOMMODATIONS ■
Ardeevin Bed & Breakfast **7**
The Green Gate **2**
Harvey's Point Country Hotel **6**
Kee's Hotel **8**
Sandhouse Hotel **4**

DINING ◆
Mirabeau Steak House **11**
Smuggler's Creek **4**

ATTRACTIONS ●
Glebe House and Gallery **9**
Glenveagh National Park
  and Castle **10**
Grianan Ailigh **12**
Slieve League **1**

SHOPPING ○
Cyndi Graham **3**
Donegal Parian China **5**

NIGHTLIFE ☾
Bonner's Corner Bar **8**
Nancy's **2**

year-round to Donegal Town, Ballyshannon, Ardara, Letterkenny, and other towns in County Donegal.

There's no local bus service in Donegal Town, but you can easily walk through and around the town if you don't have a car. It is best to explore County Donegal with a car (or a bike if you are a strong biker) because one of the biggest draws is traveling through the natural scenery.

Spending the Night

For total luxury, check out the new **Solis Lough Eske Castle** (☎ 074-972-5100; www.solislougheskecastle.ie), which opened as this book went to press. If you are staying right in Donegal Town, the **Central Hotel** (☎ 074-972-1027; www.centralhoteldonegal.com) is a fine (if overpriced) place to stay. Doubles run from €95 to €160 ($152–$256). However, if possible I encourage you stay outside town, where you will find a great assortment of charming and often inexpensive B&Bs. If you are interested in renting a cottage, house or apartment, call ☎ 087-619-0240 or visit www.donegalselfcatering.ie.

Ardeevin Bed & Breakfast
$ Lough Eske (outside of Donegal Town)

Perhaps angsty teens should be required to spend a night at Ardeevin, where it seems impossible not to be cheerful. The spacious, airy rooms are furnished in a bright, sweet country style with Victorian touches such as an antique vanity sporting a Victorian-era brush, comb, and mirror set. Your friendly, very professional hosts serve breakfast (one of the tastiest Irish breakfasts I've ever had) in a dining room decorated with polished dark-wood furniture, small sparkling chandeliers, and pink glassware. Be sure to check out the views of Lough Eske from the front of the house.

Take the N15 from Donegal Town, towards Letterkenny and Derry, for 4km (2.5 miles). Take the 2nd left turn after the Skoda car dealership, and then follow the signs for Ardeevin. ☎ *074-972-1790.* http://ardeevin.tripod.com. *Rates: €65–€70 ($104–$112) double. No credit cards.*

The Green Gate
$$–$$$ Ardara

If you want Jacuzzi bathtubs, 800 thread count sheets, and bright reading lamps, this is not the place for you. However, if you are interested in a truly unusual, bohemian lodging, with stunning views of green hills and ocean, this just may be your kind of place. Follow the slightly enigmatic symbols of a green gate from the town of Ardara to the remote hilltop location, where you'll be warmly greeted by Paul Chatenoud, an eccentric, kind, sometimes flirtatious character who was drawn to Donegal from Paris 20 years ago. Meeting Paul, who is full of stories and tips on the best-kept secrets of Donegal, is half of the reason to come here. The other half of the

Donegal Town

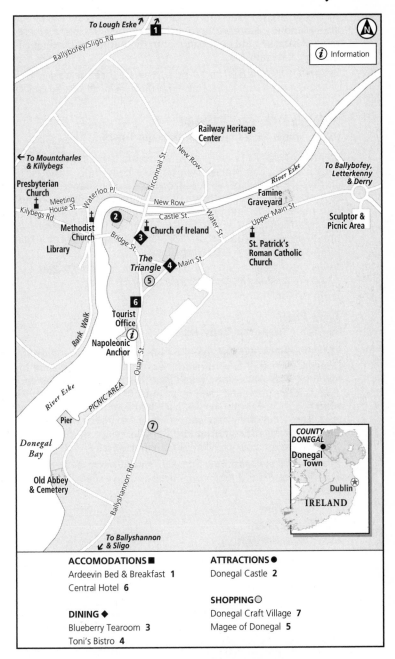

ACCOMODATIONS ■
Ardeevin Bed & Breakfast **1**
Central Hotel **6**

DINING ◆
Blueberry Tearoom **3**
Toni's Bistro **4**

ATTRACTIONS ●
Donegal Castle **2**

SHOPPING ○
Donegal Craft Village **7**
Magee of Donegal **5**

reason is to sleep in a real live cottage (one with a traditional thatched roof and one with an old slate roof), and to appreciate the spare but artistic design of the rooms and property: breakfast is served outside on a tree stump and my room featured a ship's lantern set into a recess in the wall and a haikulike note on the mirror in the bathroom reading: "The water is brown . . . It is normal."

Ardara. To reach the B&B from Ardara, follow the Green Gate signs. ☎ *074-954-1546.* thegreengate.eu. *Rates: €90–€110 ($144–$176) double. No credit cards.*

Harvey's Point Country Hotel
$$$$ Lough Eske (outside of Donegal Town)

Mention Harvey's Point to anyone around these parts and they'll answer with a smile. This well-known hotel is beautifully situated right on the shores of Lough Eske, with water views in abundance. Rooms remind me of those that you see on tours of manor houses, with gorgeous wallpaper, four-poster beds, and opulent furnishings. And everything is kept in tip-top condition (I dare you to find a chip in the paint). There is a great attention to detail — turndown service leaves a small box of chocolates on your pillow, and the service is exceptional.

Lough Eske. Follow signs from Donegal Town. ☎ *074-972-2208.* www.harveys point.com. *Rates: €250–€360 ($400–$576). AE, MC, V.*

Kee's Hotel
$$–$$$$ Stranorlar/Ballybofey

This charming historic coaching inn is in a great location for exploring Donegal. The staff is warm and friendly, and the rooms are big and comfortable, with views of the grand Blue Stack Mountains. Guests can use the gym and the pool, and then relax in front of one of the hotel's open fireplaces. The restaurant serves excellent food, and bikes are available for rent. The hotel often runs special deals, so check the Web site. Be aware that the towns of Stranorlar and Ballybofey are small and quiet, so you'll definitely want a car or bike for transportation.

Take the N15 northeast from Donegal Town to where it meets the N13. ☎ *074-913-1018. Fax: 074-913-1917.* www.keeshotel.ie. *Rates: €84–€160 ($134–$256) double. MC, V.*

Sandhouse Hotel
$$$$ Rossnowlagh

This oceanside fishing lodge-turned-four-star hotel boasts a marine spa, an outdoor hot tub, and a panoramic elevator with sea views. When you're not sleeping like a log in your overstuffed bed, you can take a walk along the cliffs, play some golf at one of the three nearby courses, or just take in comforts of the hotel itself — the rooftop garden, warm fires, fresh flowers, and homemade scones and pies. It's worth it to splurge on a room with a view of the Atlantic Ocean and Donegal Bay.

Rossnowlagh Beach (off the R231 about 8km/5 miles northwest of Ballyshannon). ☎ *071-985-1777. Fax: 071-985-2100.* www.sandhouse-hotel.ie. *Rates:* €*170–* €*250 ($272–$400) double. AE, MC, V.*

Dining in County Donegal

Nancy's (see "Hitting the Pubs" later in this chapter), in Ardara, serves excellent seafood dishes.

Blueberry Tearoom
$ Donegal Town   IRISH/CAFE

Decorated with plates and teapots, this cute and cozy restaurant has the feel of a cottage tearoom out in the countryside. Dishes are simple and fresh, and the menu runs the gamut from a grilled goat-cheese salad to a sandwich of turkey, stuffing, and cranberry sauce on brown bread. For the very hungry, hearty specials such as a roast beef dinner with Yorkshire pudding are served.

Castle Street. ☎ *074-972-2933. Main courses:* €*7–*€*12 ($11–$19). No credit cards. Open: Mon–Sat 9–7 p.m.*

Mirabeau Steak House
$$ Ramelton   STEAK

With the most courteous of service, and a setting that feels as if you are in someone's dining room, this restaurant seems to be a portal to a kinder, more decorous time. The menu includes nice dishes such as duck *á l'orange* and grilled lamb cutlets, but it's the juicy, perfectly cooked steaks that are the real stars here. I particularly recommend the peppered fillet with garlic butter, grilled medium-rare. Sides (which are big enough to feed at least two) are terrific versions of dishes that you'd find in many American households circa 1950: Waldorf salad, dauphine potatoes, cauliflower mornay, and the like. Everything is served at a leisurely pace in a burgundy room featuring a richly colored tapestry, a fire in the hearth, candlelight, and a wall-to-wall Persian carpet.

The Mall, Ramelton. ☎ *074-915-1138. Main courses:* €*12–*€*20 ($19–$32). MC, V. Open: Wed–Sun 6–10 p.m.*

Smuggler's Creek
$$$ Rossnowlagh   SEAFOOD/IRISH

The view itself is enough to make a meal at Smuggler's Creek memorable. From the conservatory dining room, which sits atop a cliff, you can look out at Donegal Bay, and if your timing's good, you may catch a fantastic sunset. Inside, the stone building is decorated with wooden stools, lobster pots, and porthole windows. Not surprisingly, seafood is a specialty here. The fish specials change depending on what's fresh, but lobster is almost always available (and very popular). Landlubbers will find many options, including the excellent steak with mushrooms, onions, and a creamy pepper sauce. Even the bar menu is a notch above, with Atlantic seafood chowder and a Donegal seafood platter amid the usual soup and sandwiches.

About .5km (¼ mile) off the R231, off the main Sligo-Donegal road (N15). Take the little, no-name side road from the R231 to get closer to the water. Signs won't let you miss the turnoff. ☎ 071-985-2366. Main courses: €15–€23 ($24–$37); lobster is more. AE, MC, V. Open: May–Sept daily noon to 11:45 p.m. or so; may close Mon–Tues during the rest of the year. Nov–Feb open weekends only.

Toni's Bistro
$ Donegal Town

Donegal Town tends to have a plethora of expensive, decent restaurants for dinner, but doesn't do very well in the less expensive realm. If you're looking for filling, inexpensive food, head down Main Street to Toni's for sandwiches, soups, burgers and salads. A cross between a coffee house and a diner, this place has exposed stone walls and features photos of Ireland.

Main St. ☎ 097-25-682. Main courses: €11–€14 ($18–$22). MC, V. Open: Mon–Sat 9:30 a.m.–9 p.m., Sun 10:30 a.m.–9 p.m.

Exploring County Donegal

In Ardara, you can rent bikes from **Byrne's,** West End (☎ 074-954-1658). In Letterkenny, **Church Street Cycles** (☎ 074-912-6204) is located on Church Lane off of Main Street.

The top attractions

Donegal Castle
Donegal Town

Built in the 15th century by the O'Donnell chieftain, this impressive castle sits beside the River Eske. Inside, lovely furnishings include Persian rugs and French tapestries — 17th-century additions from the last owner, Sir Basil Brooke, who also added an extension with ten gables and a large bay window. Free half-hour guided tours are available.

Off the Diamond in Donegal Town. ☎ 074-732-2405. Admission: €3.70 ($5.90) adult, €2.60 ($4.20) seniors, €1.30 ($2.10) children and students. Open: Mid-Mar to Oct daily 10 a.m.–6 p.m. (last admission at 5:15 p.m.); Nov to mid-Mar Thurs–Mon 9:30–4:30 p.m. (last admission 3:45 p.m.). Suggested visit: 1 hour.

Exploring the Donegal Bay coastline

The peninsula north of Donegal Bay is one of my very favorite places in all of Ireland. It has gorgeous rolling green pastures, wild mountains, thatched roof cottages, stunning sea cliffs, sweet and friendly little towns, and excellent traditional music. What more could one want? I recommend taking the N56 west from Donegal Town, and then linking up with the R263 to loop around the peninsula. Though the roads are very narrow (one car-width only) and twisty, you'll be rewarded with splendid panoramas and a real feel for rural Irish culture. For stops along the way, definitely check out **Slieve League,** the highest sea cliffs in Europe. The town of **Glencolumbkille,** way out on the peninsula, has an atmosphere infused with Gaelic culture. Most people here speak both Gaelic and English, and the traditional music is fabulous. At the **Glencolumbkille Folk Village Museum** (☎ 074-973-0017), you can live life as it was in the rural Ireland of centuries past. For my money, the best-kept secret in Ireland is **Port,** a small abandoned farm town perched on green hills overlooking the sea. To get to Port from Glencolumbkille, go to the top of the main street, and turn left. When you get to a T-junction, turn right, and start to look for the signs for Port. You can also get to Port by taking N56 south of Ardara, and the taking a right turn after Bracky Bridge. A nonlooping coastal walk at Port provides dazzling views of small cliffs and waves crashing against rock formations. You could end your day in the cute town of Ardara, which has many craft and tweed shops, and **Nancy's,** a cozy little specimen of a pub (reviewed later in this chapter).

Though you could drive the peninsula in one day, I'd recommend two. If you are an experienced hiker, you can also hike around the perimeter of the peninsula in two days. If you prefer a shorter walk you can join up with the coastal trail at several places along the coast, including Glencolumbkille, Port, and Magheera. Another option for the strong-legged is to explore the peninsula by bicycle (you can rent bikes at **Byrne's** in Ardara; ☎ 074-954-1658).

Glebe House and Gallery
Churchill, Letterkenny

This house was the pride of artist, art collector, and world traveler Derek Hill, who filled his space with over 300 works of art. The collection is eclectic, ranging from paintings of Mt. Fuji by famed Japanese painter Hokusai, to Tiffany lamps, and from costume designs by Cecil Beatton to a Renoir painting. Decorative details, including William Morris wallpaper and curtains, pull the collection together. Don't miss the paintings by James Dixon, a celebrated self-taught painter from Ireland's remote Tory Island, and check out the call bells in the kitchen, left over from the time when the house was a hotel. If the weather is nice, you many want to explore the surrounding grounds. You can only see the house on guided tours, which leave every half hour. Across from the house is a gallery that features temporary exhibitions.

Off the R251, about 18km (11 miles) west of Letterkenny. ☎ *074-913-7071. Admission: €2.90 ($4.60) adult, €2.10 ($3.40) seniors, €1.30 ($2.10) children and students. Open: June–Sept daily 11 a.m.–6:30 p.m. (last tour leaves at 5:30 p.m.). Suggested visit: 1½ hours.*

Glenveagh National Park and Castle
Churchill, Letterkenny

This National Park is a beauty, with more than 16,000 hectares of wilderness encompassing valleys and glens, lakes, dense woodlands, bogland, and the highest mountain in Donegal: Mount Errigal. Encounters with flora and fauna are often highlights of a visit; keep an eye out for a herd of red deer, an array of plant life, and all sorts of birds, including golden eagles.

The park is centered on an impressive castle built in 1870 by John George Adair, who obnoxiously decided to kick 224 tenants off the land to create his estate. Tours take you through the grand rooms, which contain the furnishings left by the last owner, Henry McIlhenny, an American philanthropist and art collector. Near the castle is an assortment of well-designed, themed gardens, some featuring exotic plants and flowers. The tea room at the castle is a charming spot for a warm drink and some light food.

The visitor center has an audiovisual show about the park and information on the various trails. If you only have time for one trail, I recommend the View Point Trail, which goes through forest and opens onto a picturesque panorama of the castle and sparking Lough Veagh. If you are visiting in the summer months, either take bug spray or purchase some from one of the machines in the archway leading to the gardens.

Northwest from Letterkenny, on the main road to Kilmacrennan (N56). ☎ *074-913-7090. Admission: Park free; shuttle bus to castle €2 ($3.20) adults, €1 ($1.60) children and students. Tours of the castle cost €3 ($4.80) adults, €2 ($3.20) seniors, and €1.50 ($2.40) children and students. Open: Park year-round daily; visitor center and castle Mar–Oct daily 10 a.m.–6:30 p.m. (last admission at 5 p.m., Nov–Feb daily 9 a.m.–5 p.m. (last admission at 4 p.m.). Suggested visit: 3–4 hours.*

Slieve League
Southwest County Donegal

The movie poster slogan for the cliffs of Slieve League (pronounced sleevleeg) would read: "If you liked the Cliffs of Moher, you'll love the cliffs of Slieve League." These are the highest sea cliffs in Europe. At Carrick, you can turn off to gaze at their immensity from the Bunglas viewing point and decide if you want to take the challenge and walk the ridge. The hike, which starts at the Bunglas viewing point, is narrow and steep, and requires good balance and good hiking boots. It takes about four to five hours round-trip. If you'd like to see the cliffs from the ocean, call ☎ **087-628-4688** to arrange a boat trip with **Nuala Star Teelin.** Boats depart from Teelin pier every two hours from 10 a.m. to 6 p.m. and at other times by appointment.

View point is off N56 in Carrick. Admission: Free. Suggested visit: A few minutes for the view; the walk takes at least 4–5 hours.

Other cool things to see and do

✔ **Climbing Mt. Errigal:** A climb up Donegal's highest peak rewards you with gorgeous views of the surrounding area. Call the **Glenveagh National Park Visitor Center** at ☎ **074-913-7090.**

✔ **Driving the Inishowen Peninsula:** It's wild and woolly country up here, with lonely mountains, windswept pastureland, and panoramic sea views. You need a good solid day (and a good map) to make the loop around the coast of the peninsula.

✔ **Grianan Ailigh:** History and myths surround this ancient burial site and stone ring fort.

Location: Off the N13, northeast from Letterkenny, or west from Derry, in Burt, Inishowen. ☎ **074-936-8080.** Suggested visit: 20 minutes.

Shopping

At **Donegal Craft Village,** on the Ballyshannon-Sligo Road in Donegal Town (☎ **074-972-2225**), a collective of artisans create and sell a range of crafts: glass, jewelry, paintings, weavings, batik, and more. **Magee of Donegal,** on the Diamond in Donegal Town (☎ **074-972-2660**), is the best source for famous Donegal tweed.

At **Donegal Parian China,** on the main Bundoran Road (N15), just south of the town of Ballyshannon (☎ **072-985-1826**), you can watch as crafts-people create this thin china, decorated with shamrocks and other Irish plants and flowers, before you purchase items in the shop. **Cyndi Graham,** whose studio is located right next to the Castlemurray House Hotel, St. John's Point, off the N56 outside of Dunkineely (☎ **074-973-7072**), hand weaves all sorts of items featuring colors inspired by the surrounding land and sea.

Hitting the Pubs

Bonner's Corner Bar
Ballybofey

If you're hankering for a pint and some conversation, go to Corner, with its warm and comfortable brick interior. This is a no-nonsense Irish pub, where you can find plenty of friendly locals engaged in lively chats.

Main Street at Glenfinn Street. ☎ *074-913-1361.*

Nancy's
Ardara

Hobbits would feel right at home at Nancy's, a warren of cozy, warmly lit rooms that are packed to the gills with knickknacks, copper kettles and pots, and an eclectic assortment of tables, benches, stools, and chairs (my favorite being the old sewing-machine table). Pub ownership has passed through seven generations of the same family, and the crowd is always a jovial, talkative mix of locals and visitors. Excellent seafood is served here, including oysters, crab claws in garlic butter, and Charlie's Supper, a dish of shrimp and smoked salmon in a chile, garlic, and lemon sauce.

Front Street, Ardara. ☎ *074-954-1187.*

Fast Facts: County Donegal

Area Codes
Area codes (or city codes) are **071, 073,** and **074.**

Emergencies/Police
Dial ☎ **999** for all emergencies.

Genealogy Resources
Contact Donegal Ancestry, The Quay, Ramelton, Letterkenny (☎ 074-915-1266; www.donegalancestry.com).

Hospital
Donegal Community Hospital is on Ballybofey Road (☎ 073-21-019).

Information
For visitor information, go to the Donegal Tourist Office, Quay Street, Donegal Town (☎ 074-972-1148; www.donegal.ie).

Internet
Try the Internet cafe over the Blueberry Tearoom, Castle Street, Donegal Town (☎ 074-972-2933).

Post Office
Donegal Post Office, Tirconnail Street (☎ 074-972-1024).

Part VI
Northern Ireland

In this part . . .

Northern Ireland has as much splendor and beauty as the Republic with a fraction of the visitors, making it an excellent choice for travelers who don't like crowds. The green folds of the Mourne Mountains (Chapter 23) beg to be hiked, and travelers from all over the world come to clamber over the strange six-sided columns of basalt at the Giant's Causeway (Chapter 22). The North Antrim coast (Chapter 22) is a dramatic landscape of cliffs, beaches, and sea. Farther south, County Fermanagh (Chapter 21) boasts a giant lake with many islands.

In addition to natural beauty, Northern Ireland offers two exciting cities, Belfast (Chapter 22) and Derry (Chapter 21). Belfast has a burgeoning arts scene, a bunch of excellent restaurants, and some gorgeous architecture. Being a university town, Belfast also has no lack of places to party, from old-world pubs to trendy clubs. After many years of religious strife, Derry is enjoying peace and is emerging as a city with a lot to offer, including quite a few historical sights, a burgeoning nightlife scene, and a growing calendar of theatrical, literary, and musical events.

Chapter 21

Counties Derry, Fermanagh, and Tyrone

. . . .

In This Chapter

▶ Exploring Derry's walls and the Bogside murals
▶ Living in 19th-century Ireland and America: The Ulster American Folk Park
▶ Checking out Belleek china
▶ Touring the Marble Arch Caves

. . . .

*T*hese three counties offer diverse attractions, a rolling landscape filled with lakes, and a warm welcome from residents who are excited that many travelers are now visiting the North. This is an ideal place for those who have seen some of the major attractions of the North and the Republic and wish to have a leisurely, relaxing vacation without crowds.

It's a very exciting time to be in Derry/Londonderry City, as the city is experiencing a rebirth after the Troubles. You'll find many historical sights, great pubs, and an up-and-coming arts scene. The pretty county of Tyrone, with its farmlands, cottages, and gentle mountains, is known mainly for the excellent Ulster American Folk Park. County Fermanagh offers a huge and peaceful lake with 154 islands, and the bustling little town of Enniskillen.

Getting to Counties Derry, Fermanagh, and Tyrone

The **City of Derry (Eglinton) Airport** (☎ 028-7181-0784; www.cityof derryairport.com) is 12km (7 miles) from the city and served by **British Airways** (☎ 0844-493-0787 in the U.K., and ☎ 1-890-626-747 in Ireland; www.britishairways.com) and **Ryanair** (☎ 01-249-7791 from outside of Ireland; www.ryanair.com). The easiest way to get to Derry from the airport is to take a cab. The fare is £12 ($24) to the city center.

To get to Derry by car from Donegal, take the N15 to Strabane, and then take the A5 north. To get to Enniskillen from Sligo, take the N16 (which

Counties Derry, Fermanagh, and Tyrone

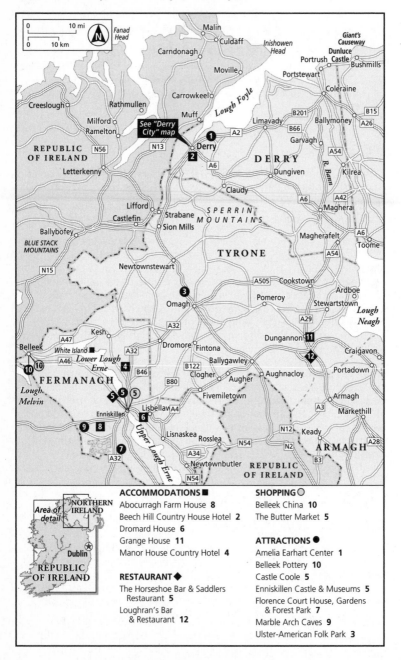

ACCOMMODATIONS ■
Abocurragh Farm House **8**
Beech Hill Country House Hotel **2**
Dromard House **6**
Grange House **11**
Manor House Country Hotel **4**

RESTAURANT ◆
The Horseshoe Bar & Saddlers
 Restaurant **5**
Loughran's Bar
 & Restaurant **12**

SHOPPING ○
Belleek China **10**
The Butter Market **5**

ATTRACTIONS ●
Amelia Earhart Center **1**
Belleek Pottery **10**
Castle Coole **5**
Enniskillen Castle & Museums **5**
Florence Court House, Gardens
 & Forest Park **7**
Marble Arch Caves **9**
Ulster-American Folk Park **3**

becomes the A4 in Northern Ireland) east. To get to Omagh from Derry or Strabane, go south on the A5; from Enniskillen, go north on the A32. If you're driving from the Republic into Northern Ireland, make sure you notify your rental-car company; extra insurance is occasionally required.

Northern Ireland Railways (☎ **028-9066-6630;** www.nirailways. co.uk) services Derry year-round, and **Ulsterbus** (☎ **028-9066-6630;** www.ulsterbus.co.uk) travels year-round to Derry, Omagh, Enniskillen, and other major towns in Counties Derry, Tyrone, and Fermanagh.

County Derry

Inhabited since the sixth century, **Derry/Londonderry City** is one of the oldest cities in Ireland. This small city has seen its share of turmoil and heartbreak, from the siege led by Catholic King James' army in 1688, to the many Irish emigrants who set out from Derry for America in the 18th and 19th centuries, to the horrors and violence of the Troubles in the 20th century. Things have been peaceful in Derry for a while now, and the city is becoming a fun and vibrant place on its way up, with burgeoning nightlife, a cultural scene that's getting more and more vibrant, and many restored historical sights.

Spending the night in County Derry

The "Derry/Londonderry City" map can help you locate accommodations and attractions. Be aware that there are not as many accommodations in Derry/Londonderry City as there are in cities in the South, so be sure to book as far in advance as possible.

Abbey Bed & Breakfast
$$ **Derry/Londonderry City**

Click your heels three times and you may find yourself at the Abbey, which feels like your own comfortable home in Derry City. Your hosts are friendly and helpful, and the individual rooms are decorated in a warm, contemporary fashion, with such cute touches as a beautiful vase in one room and funky striped comforters in another. You'll be right in the Bogside neighborhood, near the walls and near Waterloo Street, one of Derry's best pub streets (though the house remains blissfully quiet).

4 Abbey St. ☎ *028-7127-9000.* www.abbeyaccommodation.com. *Rates: £60 ($120) double. AE, MC, V.*

The Beech Hill Country House Hotel
$$$–$$$$ **Derry/Londonderry City**

This elegant 1729 country house is the perfect place for relaxation. Stroll the gorgeous wooded grounds, and then curl up before the fire with a cup of tea. Or hit the sauna, steam room, or Jacuzzi after working out in the

Derry/Londonderry City

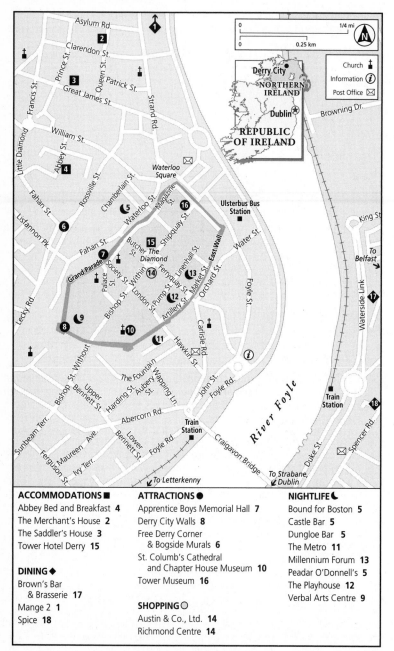

ACCOMMODATIONS ■
Abbey Bed and Breakfast **4**
The Merchant's House **2**
The Saddler's House **3**
Tower Hotel Derry **15**

DINING ◆
Brown's Bar
& Brasserie **17**
Mange 2 **1**
Spice **18**

ATTRACTIONS ●
Apprentice Boys Memorial Hall **7**
Derry City Walls **8**
Free Derry Corner
& Bogside Murals **6**
St. Columb's Cathedral
and Chapter House Museum **10**
Tower Museum **16**

SHOPPING ○
Austin & Co., Ltd. **14**
Richmond Centre **14**

NIGHTLIFE ☾
Bound for Boston **5**
Castle Bar **5**
Dungloe Bar **5**
The Metro **11**
Millennium Forum **13**
Peadar O'Donnell's **5**
The Playhouse **12**
Verbal Arts Centre **9**

fitness room. About half of the 28 rooms are decorated in Georgian style; the other half feature modern furnishings. The Ardmore Restaurant features dishes made with locally caught seafood and home-grown seasonal vegetables. The hotel is just outside Derry/Londonderry City, within easy driving distance of the region's biggest attractions.

32 Ardmore Road. Take the A6 south out of the city toward Belfast and follow the signs. ☎ **028-7134-9279.** *Fax: 028-7134-5366.* www.beech-hill.com. *Rates: £85–£110 ($170–$220) double. MC, V.*

The Merchant's House
$ Derry/Londonderry City

Owned and run by the same people who do such a fine job with The Saddler's House (see the next review), The Merchant's House is an elegant, beautifully restored Georgian B&B within walking distance of the city center. The home has high ceilings and intricate plasterwork, and the bedrooms are spacious and painted in warm, vivid colors. Flames in the fireplace flicker on the walls of the comfortable parlor. Having breakfast in the polished Georgian dining room, you may think you've slipped back in time. Your hosts are incredibly knowledgeable about the city and can help you plan an itinerary that will suit your needs and interests.

16 Queen St. ☎ **028-7126-9691.** *Fax: 028-7126-6913.* www.thesaddlershouse. com. *Rates: £55 ($110) double. MC, V.*

The Saddler's House
$ Derry City

You'll feel right at home in this cozy Victorian B&B, with its guest common room, selection of books in each bedroom, and tasty breakfasts served in a light-flooded space. Rooms aren't huge, but they're certainly big enough to move around in and charmingly furnished in a way that makes them seem more like rooms in someone's home than rooms in a guest lodging. The location is terrific, within a ten-minute walk of the heart of the city.

36 Great James St. ☎ **028-7126-9691.** *Fax: 028-7126-6913.* www.thesaddlers house.com. *Rates: £55 ($110) double. MC, V.*

Derry or Londonderry?

During the Troubles, what you called the city depended on where you stood politically. Unionists (who wish to remain under the English crown) called it Londonderry, while Nationalists (who want to become part of the Republic of Ireland) called it Derry. You'll notice that Derry is usually the name used for the city in the Republic of Ireland, while Londonderry is more commonly used in Northern Ireland. Newscasters often try to avert trouble by calling the city "Derry/Londonderry" (said as "Derry-stroke-Londonderry" since the slash sign is known as a "stroke" here). Recently, many people have taken to calling the city "Stroke City."

Tower Hotel Derry
$$ **Derry City**

This branch of the Irish Tower Hotel chain boasts a terrific location within Derry/Londonderry's medieval walls. The rooms are typical chain-style — nothing fancy, but spacious and comfortable and quite a deal for this rate. The hotel has a gym and sauna, and the staff is always ready to help. The Tower Hotel's central location and business center make it an especially good choice for business travelers. Be aware that breakfast is not included at this hotel.

Butcher Street (just off the Diamond in the center of town). ☎ **028-7137-1000.** *Fax: 028-7137-1234.* www.towerhotelderry.com. *Rates: £55–£90 ($110–$180) double. MC, V.*

Dining in County Derry

Brown's Bar and Brasserie
$$$ **Derry/Londonderry City** **NEW IRISH/INTERNATIONAL**

This sleek, modern restaurant, decorated with neutral colors, zebra-print curtains, modern art, and a stalk of bamboo on every table, serves some of the most innovate cuisine in these parts, made with the freshest ingredients. Groups of friends and couples come to feast on dishes such as sirloin with bacon, mushrooms, Cashel blue cheese, and tomatoes; honey-glazed lamb with mint jus and a tomato, mint, and mozzarella tart; and the fabulous vegetarian Turlu Turlu — leeks, zucchini, and eggplant in a flavorful Middle Eastern sauce. Don't miss the "kick-ass olives" appetizer. The menu changes every eight weeks, so you never know what kind of delicious new offerings you'll find.

1 Bond's Hill, Waterside. ☎ **028-7134-5180.** *Main courses: £11–£20 ($22–$40). AE, MC, V. Open: Tues–Fri noon–2 p.m. and 5:30–10 p.m., Sat 5:30–10:30 p.m.*

Mange 2
$$$ **Derry/Londonderry City** **NEW IRISH**

This place is just what the city center needed: a hip, friendly, and casual restaurant serving inspired and playful dishes using fresh Irish ingredients. The menu changes often; gems on a recent menu included a whole boned sea bass, filled with vegetables and served with mint-apple chutney and chive crème fraiche; and an appetizer of fried-coconut-and-phyllo-coated brie, served with raspberry, blackberry, and chile jams.

2 Clarendon St. ☎ **028-7136-1222.** *Main courses: £12–£21 ($24–$42). MC, V. Open: Daily noon to 3 p.m. and 5:30 to late.*

Spice
$$$ **Derry/Londonderry City** **ASIAN FUSION/NEW IRISH**

This well-named restaurant weaves Asian flavors seamlessly into dishes made with the best in Irish meats, fish, and vegetables. The chile and coriander lamb shank has a great depth of flavor, and the kick of the Szechuan chicken is offset by the leeks and roasted beets that accompany the dish. Even the mashed potatoes get an Asian twist, with cilantro and coconut milk turning them into an addictive side dish. The atmosphere is elegant and unpretentious, and the service is excellent. Couples and groups of friends relax in the dusky-purple room, which is graced with contemporary art and oversized vases of dried flowers. If it's on the menu, the Malteser Hot Toffee Meringue is a must-try mess of sugary goodness!

160 Spencer Road, Waterside. ☎ *028-7134-4875. Main courses: £11–£17 ($22–$34). Open: Mon–Sat 12:30–10 p.m., Sun 5–9 p.m.*

Exploring County Derry

Most of the attractions to be seen in County Derry are in **Derry/Londonderry City.** Walking and bus tours are the best way to get to know the city and its complicated background. In my opinion the best tour of the city walls and the Bogside murals is offered by **Derry City Tours** (☎ 028-7127-1996 or 077-129-37997; try to get Martin as your guide). Tours leave at 10 a.m., noon, and 2 p.m. every day from the Tourist Information Centre at 44 Foyle St., and cost £4 ($8) Another great walking-tour option is **McNamara's Famous Guided Walking Tours** (☎ 028-7134-5335 for schedules, prices, and meeting spots). Finally, **Open Top Tours** (☎ 077-4024-9998; www.opentoptour.com) takes you to sights throughout the city, March through October daily, every hour between 10 a.m. and 4 p.m. Departures are from the Tourist Information Centre located at 44 Foyle St. (☎ 028-7137-7577); and tours cost £8 ($16) for adults and £7 ($14) for seniors, students, and children.

Amelia Earhart Centre
Ballyarnet

Amelia Earhart landed in Derry in 1932, becoming the first woman to fly solo across the Atlantic. To find out more about her historic flight, visit the Earhart Center in Ballyarnett.

North of Derry City 4.8km (3 miles) on the A2. ☎ *028-7135-4040. Admission: Free. Open: Mon–Thurs 10 a.m.–4 p.m., Fri 10 a.m.–1 p.m. Suggested visit: About an hour.*

Digging into an Ulster Fry

What's the difference between a traditional Irish breakfast in the Republic and an Ulster Fry? Well, along with your fried egg, sausage, bacon, black pudding, fried tomatoes, and toast, you often get *soda farls* and *potato cakes.* Soda farls are pieces of soft bread, fluffed with soda and buttermilk; potato cakes are made with mashed potatoes, flour, and butter. They're both fried up with the rest of the breakfast and are delicious.

Apprentice Boys Memorial Hall
Derry/Londonderry

During the Siege of Derry in 1689, thirteen young apprentice boys locked the gates of the Derry walls, keeping King James II's army at bay for more than one hundred days. The Apprentice Boys has become a worldwide organization with over 10,000 members who commemorate this historic event. History buffs should be intrigued by this small museum, which tells the story of the Apprentice Boys and the Siege, from the point of view of the organization, through text, pictures, and a few objects.

13 Society St. (right off the walls). ☎ 028-7126-3571. Admission: Free. Open: June–Aug Mon–Sat 10 a.m.–5 p.m.

Derry City Walls
Derry/Londonderry City

Derry is one of the few European cities that still has intact city walls. The walls, 7.9m (26 ft.) high and about 9.1m (30 ft.) thick, were built in 1618 and succeeded in keeping Derry safe from many attacks. In fact, the walls have never been breached, earning Derry the cheeky nickname "The Maiden City." I highly recommend walking the city walls. You can walk the parapet on your own (a few staircases at different points along the walls take you to the top), or you can take one of the excellent tours described in the preceding "Exploring County Derry" section.

Free Derry Corner and the Bogside Murals
Derry/Londonderry City

Bogside is one of the Catholic neighborhoods in Derry that has seen the worst of the Catholic–Protestant conflict. In 1969, a local man painted the words "You are now entering Free Derry" on a wall at the corner of Fahan and Rossville streets. This act and the slogan became a symbol of resistance to British Rule. The Bogside Murals (also known as the People's Gallery) were created by a collective of three artists who began working together in 1993. These murals depict events in Derry/Londonderry since 1968, and include, among others, a mural of Annette McGavigan, the first child victim of the Troubles; a mural of a young petrol bomber; and mural depicting the events of Bloody Sunday, when 13 civil-rights marchers were shot by British soldiers.

Bogside area. The best way to see the murals is with the artists who painted them. The artists give tours and talks about the murals from their studio at 7 Meenan Sq. Call ☎ 028-7137-3842 to arrange a tour or talk. Tour companies that give tours of the city walls also cover the murals. Suggested visit: 30–60 minutes.

St. Columb's Cathedral and Chapter House Museum
Derry/Londonderry City

This Gothic Protestant cathedral — named for Saint Columb, founder of Derry — towers above the city walls. It houses many memorials and relics from the 1688 to 1689 siege of Derry, when the city's Protestant population held out against the forces of Catholic King James I for 105 days, helping secure the throne for Protestant King William III. Points of interest include the stained glass that tells the story of the siege, and the tremendous mortar ball that King James fired over the city walls embedded with a note asking the people of Derry to surrender (they refused). The Chapter House Museum displays artifacts of the city's history, including the original keys to the city gates, and shows an audiovisual presentation relating the history of the city.

London Street. ☎ *028-7126-7313. Admission: £2 ($4) per person. Open: Apr–Sept daily 9 a.m.–5 p.m.; Oct–Mar daily 9 a.m.–1 p.m. and 2–4 p.m. Suggested visit: 45 minutes.*

Tower Museum
Derry/Londonderry City

This well-done museum really gets at the heart of Derry history, covering events and daily life from prehistoric times to the present day. You'll find everything from Stone Age tools recovered in the area, to a life-size diorama of a woman creating the shirt collars — a task that kept many families financially afloat during the early 20th century. In addition, the museum has added an excellent exhibit focused on artifacts recovered from a Spanish Armada ship that wrecked nearby. Part of a cittern, olive oil jugs, and ship fittings are just some of the objects that you'll find in the display. The museum is housed in the O'Doherty Tower, a replica of the 16th-century medieval fort that stood on this spot.

Union Hall Place. ☎ *028-7137-2411. Admission: £4 ($8) adults, £2.50 ($5) children and seniors. Open: July and Aug Mon–Sat 10 a.m.–5 p.m. and Sun 10 a.m.–2 p.m., Sept–June Tues–Fri 10 a.m.–5 p.m. Suggested visit: 1 hour.*

Shopping in Derry/Londonderry City

The best shopping is found in the inner city, in the **Richmond Centre,** a modern mall facing the Diamond in the center of town and featuring more than 30 shops and boutiques.

The Victorian-style department store **Austin & Co. Ltd.,** The Diamond (☎ **028-7126-1817**), is a city landmark, specializing in clothes, perfume, china, crystal, and linens. The coffee shop on the third floor has a great view of the city.

A story of hope

For many years, the mural depicting Annette McGavigan, the first child victim of the Troubles, had a black and white butterfly representing the unsure future of the peace process. In the summer of 2006, the artists decided to add vivid colors to the butterfly to symbolize their confidence in the continuing success of the process and their delight in the city's revitalization.

Nightlife in Derry/Londonderry City

The Playhouse, 5–7 Artillery St. (☎ **028-7126-8027;** www.derryplay house.co.uk), presents local, national, and international plays and dance. The **Verbal Arts Centre,** Mall Wall and Stable Lane, Bishop Street (☎ **028-7126-6946;** www.verbalartscentre.co.uk), is an incredible place, dedicated to literature in all of its forms. It hosts all sorts of readings, classes, and storytelling events. The **Millennium Forum,** Newmarket Street (☎ **028-7126-4455;** www.millenniumforum.co.uk), offers a program of plays, dance, and musicals, including children's shows.

Hitting the pubs

Want to hear traditional Irish music in Derry/Londonderry? Head to **Waterloo Street,** just outside the city walls in front of Butcher and Castle Gates. Some of the best pubs for informal sessions lie along this route. In particular, the **Dungloe Bar** (☎ **028-7126-7716**), **Bound for Boston** (☎ **028-7127-1315**), **Castle Bar** (☎ **028-7126-6018**), and **Peadar O'Donnell's and The Gweedore Bar** (tel **028-7137-2138**) are great places to have a pint.

The Metro
Derry/Londonderry City

Plenty of little alcoves and mementos from across the globe make the Metro an interesting stop. The pub sits in the shadow of the old city walls and serves a mean beef Guinness stew.

3–4 Bank Place. ☎ *028-7126-7401.*

Counties Fermanagh and Tyrone

Island-studded **Lake Erne** is the centerpiece of County Fermanagh, serving as a destination for boaters and anglers, while County Tyrone is home to what is arguably Ireland's finest outdoor-living museum.

Spending the night in Counties Fermanagh and Tyrone

Abocurragh Farm Guesthouse
$$ Letterbreen, Enniskillen, Fermanagh

On my last visit to this welcoming country guesthouse, I stood outside in the dusk talking about international politics and conflicts with one of my hosts as he fixed his tractor. It was a peculiar feeling to be chatting about such things in this setting, which is incredibly peaceful. The house is located in the middle of the mountains on a working dairy farm. Rooms are bright and clean, combining contemporary pine furnishings with Victorian and country-style touches, and many have beautiful views of the house gardens and the mountains. Foodies will love the breakfast options, which range from cinnamon-flavored porridge with honey, cream, or Irish whiskey, to oak-smoked salmon with scrambled eggs.

Letterbreen. Take the A4 out of Enniskillen through Letterbreen. Go 3.2km (2 miles) out of Letterbreen, and you will see a sign on the left for the guesthouse; turn left. ☎ *028-6634-8484.* www.abocurragh.com. *Rates: £60 ($120). MC, V.*

Dromard House
$ Tamlaght, Enniskillen, County Fermanagh

A warm welcome, a tranquil setting overlooking a valley with grazing cows, and sweet, simple country-style rooms . . . what more could you want from a countryside bed and breakfast? Your friendly hosts Sharon and Clive can point you towards all the best attractions in the area, or you can just relax on the property, taking a walk through the woods, curling up on the giant porch swing overlooking the valley, and watching a movie in the cozy sitting room. Your hosts have kids of their own and are happy to accommodate families.

Tamlaght. Take the A4 southeast from Enniskillen towards Tamlaght. ☎ *028-6638-7250.* www.dromardhouse.com. *Rates: £50 ($100) double. AE, MC, V.*

Grange House
$$$ Dungannon, County Tyrone

Oh, the porridge. Perhaps half of the reason to stay at this grand former Quaker meetinghouse is the Bushmills porridge offered for breakfast. This heavenly concoction is made with Bushmills whiskey, heavy cream, and a topping of brown sugar. Delicious. The other reasons to stay here are not too shabby either: kind and professional hosts, beautiful grounds, the charming floral rooms (dolls and doilies abound), and the inn's proximity to the excellent Ulster American Folk Park.

7 Grange Rd. One mile from M1 Junction 15 on the A29 to Moy/Armagh. ☎ *028-8778-4212.* www.grangelodgecountryhouse.com. *Rates: £80–£89 ($160–$178). MC, V.*

Manor House Country Hotel
$$$–$$$$ Killadeas, County Fermanagh

This Victorian mansion offers wonderful views of Lough Erne. The house is beautifully furnished with antiques, and rooms are traditional, with floral fabrics and dark wood furniture. Kids will love the swimming pool and minigolf course.

Killadeas is off the B82, north of Enniskillen. ☎ *028-6862-2200.* www.manor-house-hotel.com. *Rates: £110–£162 ($220–$324) double. AE, MC. V.*

Dining in Counties Fermanagh and Tyrone

Loughran's Bar & Restaurant
$$ Moy, County Tyrone   IRISH-EUROPEAN

Groups of friends and couples come here for some of the best food in this countryside area. Dishes feature fresh ingredients and the chefs aren't afraid to take a few risks. Recent offerings include seabass with spicy ratatouille and pesto sauce, and spinach-and-ricotta-stuffed pasta with a red pepper sauce. The space is both elegant and casual, with high-beamed ceilings, brick arches, a color scheme of creams and browns, and jazz and pop playing in the background. The ice cream plate makes a superb cap to dinner.

3 Killyman St., off The Square, Moy. ☎ *028-877-89-881. Main courses: £10–£18 ($20–$36). AE, MC, V. Open: Wed–Sat 5–9 p.m., Sun noon–3 p.m. and 5–9 p.m.*

The Horseshoe Bar & Saddlers Restaurant
$–$$$ Enniskillen, County Fermanagh   EUROPEAN

Horse lovers will delight at the equestrian décor here. The food is hearty, delicious, and varied at both the restaurant and the pub, but I recommend dining in the pub, which is a real locals' place, with groups of friends discussing the news, older men who seem to live on their bar stools, and kids running around. Steaks are the specialty at both the pub and the restaurant, and with good reason — their filet with garlic butter could give Peter Luger a run for their money. At the pub, you'll find lasagna; chicken, fish, and lamb dishes; and salads. The restaurant serves standards plus more adventurous dishes such as a pork filet pan-fried in cream sauce with peaches and caramelized apples; and monkfish with a vanilla dressing. A new wine bar and bistro is open daily from 5 p.m. until late and on Sunday from noon to 4 p.m.

66 Belmore St. ☎ *028-6632-6223. Main courses: Pub £3–£14 ($6–$28), restaurant £9–£16 ($18–$32). MC, V. Open: Pub daily 11 a.m.–11 p.m.; restaurant Mon–Sat 5:30–11 p.m., Sun noon to 10 p.m.*

Exploring Counties Fermanagh and Tyrone

Erne Tours (☎ **028-6632-2882**) offers a boat tour of Lower Lough Erne River aboard the 56-seater *Kestrel*. The trip is fully narrated and covers a good deal of the nature and history of the lake. It includes a half-hour stop at Devenish Island, where you can get off and explore monastic ruins dating to the sixth century, including a beautifully preserved round tower. Trips last about one and three-quarter hours and depart from Round "O" Jetty, at Brook Park in Enniskillen, signposted off A46. Tours operate daily in July and August at 10:30 a.m., 12:15 p.m., 2:15 p.m., and 4:15 p.m.; in June daily at 2:15 p.m.; and in May, September and October Tuesday, Saturday, and Sunday at 2:15 p.m. Prices are £9 ($18) for adults, £8 ($16) for seniors, and £6 ($12) for children under age 12.

The Fermanagh Lakes yield loads of salmon and trout. **Trevor Kingston,** 18 Church St., Enniskillen (☎ **028-6632-2114**), can set you up with information and tackle.

For canoeing, sailing, and windsurfing on the lakes, contact **Lakeland Canoe Centre,** Castle Island, Enniskillen (☎ **028-6632-4250**).

Hikers will want to explore Florence Court Forest Park (described later in this chapter).

Belleek Pottery Tours
Belleek, County Fermanagh

Belleek is Ireland's oldest and most famous pottery works. Here, you can watch highly trained craftspeople create and decorate the famous fine bone china (guided tours are given every 30 minutes on weekdays) and explore a museum covering the history of Belleek pottery. If you want to take some pottery home with you, the showroom stocks the complete range of Belleek products.

Main Street in Belleek. Take the A46 northeast from Enniskillen. ☎ *028-6865-9300. Admission: Visitor Centre free. Tours: £4 ($8) adults, £2 ($4) seniors, children under 12 free. Open: Visitor Centre July–Oct Mon–Fri 9 a.m.–6 p.m., Sat 10 a.m.–6 p.m., Sun noon to 6 p.m.; Mar–June Mon–Fri 9 a.m.–6 p.m., Sat 10 a.m.–6 p.m. and Sun 2–6 p.m.; Jan–Feb Mon–Fri 9 a.m.–5:30 p.m.; Nov–Dec Mon–Fri 9 a.m.–5:30 p.m., Sat 10 a.m.– 5:30 p.m. Tours: Every half-hour Mon–Fri 9:30 a.m.–12:15 p.m. and 1:45–4 p.m. (last tour on Fri 3 p.m.). Suggested visit: 1 hour (including tour).*

Castle Coole
Enniskillen, County Fermanagh

This 18th-century neoclassical-style house was completely refurbished by the state. Most of the stone fittings and fixtures are from England, and extraordinarily, almost all the original furniture is in place. The opulent State Bedroom has a bed that was specially made for King George IV to use during his 1821 visit to Ireland. Other highlights are a Chinese-style sitting room and gorgeous woodwork and fireplaces throughout. Save some time to explore the surrounding 600-hectare (1,500-acre) woodlands. Keep an eye out for the current Earl of Belmore, who still lives in one wing of the house.

Off the Belfast-Enniskillen road (A4) about 1.6km (1 mile) out of Enniskillen. ☎ *028-6632-2690. Admission: House £5.50 ($11) adults, £2.50 ($5) children; grounds £2.50 ($5) per car. Open: House Apr–May and Sept Sat–Sun 1–6 p.m., June Fri–Wed 1–6 p.m., July–Aug daily noon to 6 p.m., Mar varying days/hours, call or check website for details; grounds Apr–Sept daily 10 a.m.–8 p.m., Oct–Mar daily 10 a.m.–4 p.m. Suggested visit: 1 hour.*

Enniskillen Castle & Museums
Enniskillen, County Fermanagh

This 15th-century castle, once the stronghold of powerful Irish chieftains, sits majestically in the west end of town, overlooking the River Erne. The castle contains a county museum with exhibits on the area's history, wildlife, and landscape, as well as a museum about the Royal Inniskilling Fusiliers — a town militia who fought against James II in 1688.

Castle Barracks at the west end of town, across Castle Bridge from the A4. ☎ *028-6632-5000. Admission: £2.95 ($5.90) adults, £2.50 ($5) seniors and students, £1.95 ($3.90) children. Open: May–June and Sept Mon and Sat 2–5 p.m., Tues–Fri 10 a.m.–5 p.m.; July–Aug Sat–Mon 2–5 p.m., Tues–Fri 10 a.m.–5 p.m.; Oct–Apr Mon 2–5 p.m., Tues–Fri 10 a.m.–5 p.m. Suggested visit: 1½ hours.*

Florence Court House, Gardens & Forest Park
Enniskillen, County Fermanagh

Fans of Georgian houses will want to make a stop at Florence Court House, which was built in the mid-18th century for the lord of this area. Highlights include the rococo plasterwork in the dining room, the many family heirlooms and portraits, and the majestic staircase. You can see the house by guided tour only.

The extensive grounds are a gorgeous place for a hike, with trails through a contrasting collection of landscapes, from open mountain to bogland to forest to old estate woodland. Trails range from an easy stroll through the woods to an 8km (5 mile) forest trek.

Signposted off A32 south of Enniskillen. ☎ *028-6634-8249. Admission: Tour £5.50 ($11) adults, £2.50 ($5) children; grounds Mar–Sept £3.50 ($7) per car. Open: House Mar 17–Mar 30 daily 1–6 p.m., Apr–May Sat–Sun 1–6 p.m., June Wed–Mon 1–6 p.m., July–Aug daily noon to 6 p.m., Sept Sat–Sun 1–6 p.m.; grounds Apr–Sept daily 10 a.m.–8 p.m., Oct–Mar daily 10 a.m.–4 p.m. Suggested visit: About an hour for the house, longer if you want to explore the grounds.*

Marble Arch Caves
Florencecourt, County Fermanagh

Exploring the Marble Arch Caves is like traveling to another world. Guides lead you on foot through the winding passages and echoing chambers of the caves, pointing out stalactites, stalagmites, curtains, and all sorts of other mineral formations, and offering detailed information on the natural history of the caves. For much of the way you'll follow the bends of an underground river; my favorite part of the tour is seeing a collection of stalactites reflected perfectly in the still water below like a lost city. The short boat ride at the beginning of the tour is another highlight, as you glide silently through some of the smaller chambers.

The Marble Arch Caves are very popular, so it's wise to book ahead. Also, it gets pretty chilly down under, so bring a sweater. If there's been heavy rain, the caves occasionally close for safety reasons, so call if there's been bad weather. Finally, it's important to wear comfortable shoes and to be in decent shape, as you will be walking and climbing stairs for the bulk of the tour.

Marlbank Scenic Loop. Off the A35, 19km (12 miles) south of Enniskillen. When you're in the village of Florencecourt, near the border of Northern Ireland and the Republic, there is a loop road that takes you out to the caves, with plenty of signs to point the way. ☎ *028-6634-8855. Admission: £8 ($16) adults, £5.25 ($11) students and seniors, £5 ($10) children under 18. Open: Mid-Mar to June and Sept daily 10 a.m.–6 p.m. (last tour leaves at 4:30 p.m.); July–Aug daily 10 a.m.–6:30 p.m. (last tour leaves at 5 p.m.). Suggested visit: About 2½ hours.*

Ulster American Folk Park
Castletown, County Tyrone

This immensely interesting outdoor folk park features actual rebuilt 18th- and 19th-century buildings from Ireland and America, from a Pennsylvania log farmhouse to an Irish-Catholic mass house (a home used as a church). Costumed interpreters are stationed throughout to illustrate and explain life during these times. You begin your tour in Ireland and then board a replica of a 19th-century ship bound for America. When you exit, you're in the America of the 18th and 19th centuries. I recommend tagging along with a school group so that you can watch the interpreters role-play everyone from a 19th-century Irish schoolteacher to an American saddler.

The Folk Park has an excellent lineup of events, including American Independence Day celebrations in July, an Appalachian and Bluegrass music festival in September, and a Halloween Festival in October.

Mellon Road. Off the A5, 4.7km (3 miles) north of Omagh. Look for the signs. ☎ *028-8224-3292.* www.folkpark.com. *Admission: £5.50 ($11) adults; £3.50 ($7) students, seniors, and children. Open: Oct–Mar Mon–Fri 10:30 a.m.–5 p.m. (last admission 3:30 p.m.); Apr–Sept Mon–Sat 10:30 a.m.–6 p.m. (last admission 4:30 p.m.), and Sun 11 a.m.–6:30 p.m. (last admission 5 p.m.). Suggested visit: 2 hours.*

Shopping in County Fermanagh

The **Butter Market,** on Down Street in Enniskillen (☎ **028-6632-3837**), has studio workshops where craftspeople make and sell all sorts of local items, including ceramic jewelry, screen prints, Celtic-inspired statuary, and leather goods.

Fast Facts: Counties Derry, Fermanagh, and Tyrone

Area Code

The area code (or city code) for Derry, Fermanagh, and Tyrone is **028**.

Emergencies/Police

Dial ☎ **999** for all emergencies.

Genealogy Resources

In County Derry, contact The Genealogy Centre, 10 Craft Village (at Shipquay St.), Derry (☎ 028-7126-9792). For Counties Tyrone and Fermanagh, contact Heritage World, 26 Market Sq., Dungannon (☎ 028-8772-4187).

Hospital

Altnagelvin Hospital (☎ 028-7134-5171) is on Glenshane Road, in Derry.

Information

In Derry, go to the tourist office at 44 Foyle St., Derry (☎ 028-7137-7577); open year-round. In County Tyrone, contact the Omagh Tourist Information Centre, Townhall Square, Omagh (☎ 028-8224-7831). The Fermanagh Tourist Information Centre is located on Wellington Road, Enniskillen (☎ 028-6632-3110).

Chapter 22

Belfast and County Antrim

- -

In This Chapter

▶ Going back to the early 1900s at the Ulster Folk Museum
▶ Experiencing Belfast's many pubs and clubs
▶ Climbing on the amazing Giant's Causeway
▶ Bringing out your inner adventurer on a rope bridge

- -

*Y*ou get the best of both worlds in this county: an energy-filled city with great dining, lodging, and nightlife options, and the awesome beauty of the cliffs, glens, and ocean of the North Antrim coast.

Belfast and the Surrounding Area

Belfast is a hopping city, full of university students and, thus, full of hot restaurants and hotels and even hotter clubs and bars. Queens University plays a large role in the arts scene here, which is becoming stronger and stronger. Belfast is also a beautiful city, with many examples of Victorian, Edwardian, and Georgian architecture.

Getting to Belfast and County Antrim

Continental, bmibaby, easyJet, and more airlines fly into **Belfast International Airport** (☎ 028-9448-4848; www.belfastairport.com), about 31km (19 miles) from Belfast. The **George Best Belfast City Airport** (☎ 028-9093-9093; www.belfastcityairport.com) handles flights within the country. To get to the city center from Belfast International Airport, take the Airport Express Bus 300, which leaves every ten minutes during peak times and every half hour between 5 a.m. and 6:20 a.m., and between 7 p.m. and 11:30 p.m. The fare is £7 ($14). From Belfast City Airport, take a cab (the fare should be about £6/$12), or the Airlink Bus (Route 600), which departs every 20 minutes between 6 a.m. and 11:30 p.m. and costs £1.50 ($3) round-trip.

If you're coming to Belfast from Britain or Scotland, consider the ferry. **Norfolk Line Irish Sea Ferries** (☎ 0844-499-0007 in Britain, ☎ 01-819-2999 in Ireland; www.norfolkline-ferries.co.uk) takes eight hours from Liverpool, and **Stena Line** (☎ or ☎ 08705-70-70-70 in Britain and ☎ 08705-204-204 in Northern Ireland; www.stenaline.com) runs ferries from Stranraer, Scotland to Belfast that take a little less than two hours.

County Antrim

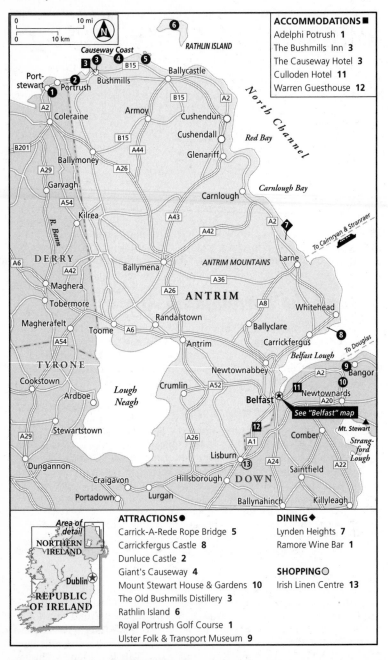

0   10 mi
0   10 km

ACCOMMODATIONS ■
Adelphi Potrush **1**
The Bushmills Inn **3**
The Causeway Hotel **3**
Culloden Hotel **11**
Warren Guesthouse **12**

RATHLIN ISLAND
Causeway Coast
Ballycastle
Port-stewart
Portrush
Bushmills
Coleraine
Armoy
Cushendun
Cushendall
Red Bay
Glenariff
North Channel
Ballymoney
Garvagh
Carnlough
Carnlough Bay
Kilrea
R. Bann
To Cairnryan & Stranraer
DERRY
Ballymena
ANTRIM MOUNTAINS
Larne
Maghera
Tobermore
Magherafelt
Randalstown
ANTRIM
Whitehead
Toome
Ballyclare
Carrickfergus
To Douglas
Antrim
Belfast Lough
TYRONE
Cookstown
Crumlin
Newtownabbey
Bangor
Ardboe
Lough Neagh
Belfast
Newtownards
See "Belfast" map
Mt. Stewart
Stewartstown
Comber
Strang-ford Lough
Dungannon
Lisburn
Craigavon
Hillsborough
DOWN
Saintfield
Portadown
Lurgan
Ballynahinch
Killyleagh

Area of detail
NORTHERN IRELAND
Dublin
REPUBLIC OF IRELAND

ATTRACTIONS ●
Carrick-A-Rede Rope Bridge **5**
Carrickfergus Castle **8**
Dunluce Castle **2**
Giant's Causeway **4**
Mount Stewart House & Gardens **10**
The Old Bushmills Distillery **3**
Rathlin Island **6**
Royal Portrush Golf Course **1**
Ulster Folk & Transport Museum **9**

DINING ◆
Lynden Heights **7**
Ramore Wine Bar **1**

SHOPPING ○
Irish Linen Centre **13**

If you're coming by car from Dublin, take the M1 to the N1 (which becomes the A1) north to Belfast. To get to the Antrim Coast from Belfast, take the A2, which runs along the entire coast. If you're driving from the Republic into Northern Ireland, make sure you notify your rental-car company, because extra insurance may be required.

Irish Rail (☎ **1850-366-222;** www.irishrail.ie) and **Northern Ireland Railway** (☎ 888-BRITRAIL or **028-90-66-66-30;** www.nirailways.co.uk) trains travel from Dublin's Connolly Station to Belfast's Central Station daily and connect many towns in Northern Ireland.

Ulsterbus (☎ **028-9066-6630;** www.translink.co.uk) runs buses to and from towns all over Northern Ireland, including Belfast, Larne, Ballycastle, Bushmills, and several other towns. Ulsterbus also provides service between Belfast and Dublin.

Getting around Belfast and the surrounding area

You can easily navigate Belfast by bus and on foot, so you may want to park your car while you explore or forgo a car altogether. A bus service, **Metro** (☎ **028-9066-6630;** www.translink.co.uk/Metro.asp), operates throughout the city. Most buses depart from Donegall Square in the city center. Smartlink multijourney tickets are available at most newsagents (look for the *Smartlink* sign). If you're going to be moving around the city a lot, it makes sense to buy an all-day ticket. See "Exploring Belfast and the surrounding area," later in this chapter, for information on bus tours in Belfast.

You can also get around Belfast and the area by bike. **Life Cycles,** 36–37 Smithfield Market (☎ **028-9043-9959;** www.lifecycles.co.uk), rents bikes and provides helmets, locks, and maps.

If you need a cab, look for the **taxi ranks** at Central Station, both bus stations, and at City Hall. The metered cabs in Northern Ireland are standardized London-style black taxis with yellow discs on the windshield. I recommend that you take the standard cabs rather than nonmetered cabs. If you do take a nonmetered cab, ask for the price of the journey when you first enter the cab so that you don't get taken for a monetary ride in addition to a taxi ride. If you need a cab, try **Gransha Taxis** (☎ **028-9060-2092**).

Spending the night in Belfast and the surrounding area

Ash-Rowan Town House
$$$ Belfast

This beautiful Victorian row house, on a quiet, tree-lined avenue, is a comfortable and serene place to stay. All four stories are decorated with

Belfast

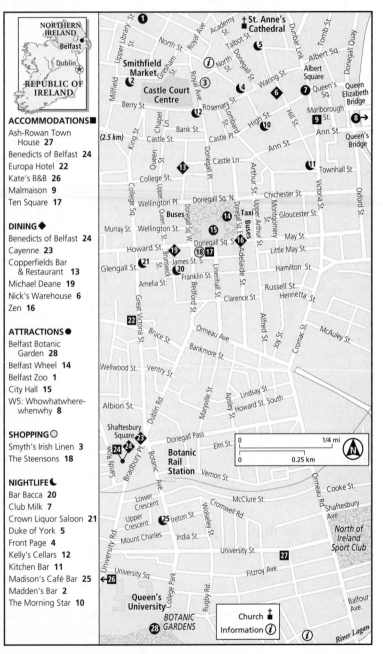

ACCOMMODATIONS ■

Ash-Rowan Town
    House **27**
Benedicts of Belfast **24**
Europa Hotel **22**
Kate's B&B **26**
Malmaison **9**
Ten Square **17**

DINING ◆

Benedicts of Belfast **24**
Cayenne **23**
Copperfields Bar
    & Restaurant **13**
Michael Deane **19**
Nick's Warehouse **6**
Zen **16**

ATTRACTIONS ●

Belfast Botanic
    Garden **28**
Belfast Wheel **14**
Belfast Zoo **1**
City Hall **15**
W5: Whowhatwhere-
    whenwhy **8**

SHOPPING ○

Smyth's Irish Linen **3**
The Steensons **18**

NIGHTLIFE ☾

Bar Bacca **20**
Club Milk **7**
Crown Liquor Saloon **21**
Duke of York **5**
Front Page **4**
Kelly's Cellars **12**
Kitchen Bar **11**
Madison's Café Bar **25**
Madden's Bar **2**
The Morning Star **10**

NORTHERN
IRELAND
Belfast
Dublin
REPUBLIC OF
IRELAND

St. Anne's
Cathedral
Smithfield
Market
Castle Court
Centre
Buses
Taxi
Buses
Botanic
Rail
Station
Shaftesbury
Square
Queen's
University
BOTANIC
GARDENS
North of
Ireland
Sport Club

Church ✝
Information ⓘ

0   1/4 mi
0   0.25 km

River Lagan

country-style furniture, Victorian antiques, and fresh flowers from the garden in back. Breakfasts are terrific.

12 Windsor Ave. From the city center, follow Bedford Street south past Queen's University and make a right on Windsor. ☎ *028-9066-1758. Fax: 028-9066-3227. Bus: 69, 70, or 71. Rates: £98–£110 ($196–$220) double. AE, MC, V.*

Benedicts of Belfast
$$ **Belfast**

Funky, trendy Benedicts is at the center of everything, near some of Belfast's top attractions and hottest eateries and nightspots. Rooms on the second floor are brightly decorated, while rooms on the third floor are sleekly minimalist. The beds are unbelievably comfortable. The staff is friendly, and the Gothic-style bar and restaurant serve up excellent Continental fare in a lively atmosphere.

7–21 Bradbury Place, Shaftsbury Square. From the Westlink (M1), take Grovesnor Road toward City Hall; go right on Great Victoria Street. ☎ *028-9059-1999. Fax: 028-9059-1990.* www.benedictshotel.co.uk. *Bus: 1, 29, 71, 83, or 84. Rates: £80 ($160). AE, MC, V.*

Culloden Hotel
$$$$ **Holywood, County Down**

The Culloden, located near the Ulster Folk and Transport Museum, is a government-rated five-star hotel — and it deserves every point on those stars. A former 19th-century mansion, the hotel is surrounded by almost 5 hectares (12 acres) of beautiful, secluded gardens and the picturesque Holywood Hills. Bedrooms are nicely decorated with modern furnishings, and public rooms are filled with stunning antiques, Louis XV chandeliers, and decorative plasterwork. A terrific spa offers all sorts of treatments. Service is impeccable. Would British Prime Ministers Tony Blair and John Major have stayed here if it wasn't?

Bangor Road. On the A2 northeast of Belfast. ☎ *028-9042-1066. Fax: 028-9074-8152.* www.hastingshotels.com. *Rates: £230–£250 ($460–$500) double. AE, DC, MC, V.*

Europa Hotel
$$$$ **Belfast**

The spacious rooms in this world-class high-rise hotel are decked to the nines — huge beds and sofas, luxurious fabrics, and beautiful mahogany furnishings. But you probably won't be spending much time in your room, given the hotel's fabulous location. It's in the heart of Belfast, right next to the Grand Opera House and near the bustling Golden Mile, which is lined with historic buildings. The guests here tend to be cosmopolitan and elegant.

Great Victoria Street. From the Westlink (M1), take Grovesnor Road toward City Hall; go right on Great Victoria Street. ☎ *028-9027-1066. Fax: 028-9074-8152.* www.hastingshotels.com. *Bus: 82, 83, 84, 85, or Centrelink (100). Rates: £200 ($400) double. AE, DC, MC, V.*

Kate's B&B
$ **Belfast**

Step right up, folks, for one of the best deals in town. The seven good-size rooms here are decorated in cozy Victorian style and get a lot of light through their large windows. You can't beat the location: near the university, the Botanic Gardens, and loads of funky restaurants and hopping clubs. Proprietor Kate Boyd will fortify you for the day with her "heart attack on a plate" breakfast and help you plan an itinerary for exploring the city.

127 University St. (east of Westminster St.). ☎ *028-9028-2091.* katesbb127@hotmail.com. *Rates: £50 ($100) double. No credit cards. Bus: 8.*

Killead Lodge
$ **Belfast**

Craving a country hideaway while you explore Belfast? Located about 20 minutes from Belfast and right near Belfast International Airport, Killead Lodge could be summed up in the word "cheerful." Rooms, painted lemon yellow, feature comfortable beds and flat-screen TVs, and several cats frequent the back garden. Breakfast is ample and satisfying, and your hosts are willing to help with anything. If you stay here, definitely check out Spice, an excellent Indian restaurant down the road.

25 Killead Rd., Aldergrove, Crumlin. ☎ *028-9445-9896.* www.killeadlodge.com. *Rates: £65 ($130). MC, V.*

Malmaison
$$$–$$$$ **Belfast**

This trendy, sophisticated lodging is the definition of a boutique hotel. It's housed in converted 1867 grain warehouses that retain gorgeous architectural details, and it offers incredibly friendly, professional, and personal service. The spacious rooms are decorated with warm tones in a hip, modern style (the hotel calls it "rock-and-roll" style), and are designed to anticipate every need, with height-of-comfort beds, minibars (rare in these parts), and heated towel racks. The city center is a five-minute walk away.

34–38 Victoria St. From the M3, take the Queen's Bridge across the river, and make a right onto Victoria Street. ☎ *028-9022-0200. Bus: 8, 13, 13B, 21, 155, 160, 161, or Centrelink (100). Rates: £150–£170 ($300–$340). AE, DC, MC, V.*

Ten Square
$$$$ **Belfast**

The designers of this Asian-style, minimalist hotel in central Belfast wouldn't know the meaning of the word "clutter." Rooms are a study in simple elegance, with vases of fresh flowers, and low beds covered with white comforters. I must admit, however, that the hotel is resting on its laurels a bit; a few minor facelifts would put it back in the big leagues. You don't have to go far for nourishment; the hotel restaurant, The Grill, serves up great food.

10 Donegall Sq. S. ☎ **028-9024-1001.** Fax: 028-9024-3210. www.tensquare.co.uk. Bus: 82, 83, 84, 85, or Centrelink (100). Rates: £119–£170 ($238–$340) double. AE, MC, V.

Dining in Belfast and the surrounding area

See also Benedicts of Belfast, mentioned in the previous section.

Cayenne
$$$ Belfast   FUSION

This wonderful restaurant was one of the first stars in Belfast's constellation of excellent fusion eateries. It's still going strong, serving dishes that combine ingredients in unexpectedly delicious ways, such as the appetizer of cinnamon quail with carrot, honey, and ginger salad. You can't go wrong with any of the main courses, from rabbit with fresh pasta, black olives, rosemary, and pancetta to lobster with black-bean vinaigrette and steamed basmati rice. Service is friendly and professional, and the decked-out crowd is always in high spirits.

7 Ascot House, Shaftesbury Square. ☎ **028-9033-1532.** Reservations recommended. Bus: 1, 29, 71, 83, or 84. Main courses: £17–£24 ($34–$48). AE, DC, MC, V. Open: Mon 5–10 p.m., Tues–Thurs noon to 2:15 p.m. and 5–10 p.m., Fri noon to 2:15 p.m. and 5–11 p.m., Sat 6–11 p.m., Sun 5–9 p.m.

Copperfields Bar and Restaurant
$–$$ Belfast   IRISH

Come to Copperfields for a satisfying meal at a good price. The hearty dishes are varied, but the highlights are the excellent steak and fish choices. Specials change daily and are always creative, sometimes borrowing Mexican and Asian influences, and all ingredients are fresh and local. What makes this place so popular, in addition to the food, are the comfy sofas and cozy booths.

9 Fountain St. From the Westlink (M1), take Divis Street to Fountain Street, and turn right. ☎ **028-9024-7367.** Bus: 30, 31, 32, or Centrelink (100). Main courses: £8–£15 ($16–$30). AE, MC, V. Open: Daily Sun–Wed noon to 5:30 p.m., Thurs noon to 8 p.m., Fri–Sat noon to 6:30 p.m.

Michael Deane
$$$$ Belfast   NEW IRISH

This baroque-looking restaurant is a temple to upscale Irish cuisine, with dishes that make use of local ingredients. The menu changes all the time; the last time I visited choices included local lamb with vine tomatoes, ratatouille, rosemary crumble, and niçoise jus; and veal with sage-and-apple risotto, crushed organic carrots and horseradish, and a bordelaise sauce. If you want to experience Michael Deane's recipes without having to take out a second mortgage, try the casual Deane's Deli, at 44 Bedford St. (☎ **028-9024-8800**).

38–40 Howard Place. ☎ *028-9033-1134. Bus: 58, 59, 69, 69A, 70, 71, 89, 90, 91, 92, 95, or Centrelink (100). Main courses: £17–£23 ($34–$46). 7-course prix-fixe £65 ($112). AE, DC, MC, V. Open: Mon–Sat noon to 3 p.m. and 6–10 p.m.*

Nick's Warehouse
$$–$$$ Belfast   INTERNATIONAL

Set in an old warehouse, this restaurant exudes charm; and, despite the size of the place, it feels quite intimate. The service is wonderful (I recommend letting the staff choose something for you if you can't decide). The menu changes frequently and gathers inspiration from cuisines all over the world, but you won't be disappointed with the options, from grilled tuna with sweet-pepper-and-chile sauce to a butternut squash risotto with Jerusalem artichokes and toasted cashews.

35 Hill St. From the Westlink (M1), take Divis Street; turn left on Skipper Street. ☎ *028-9043-9690. Bus: 8, 13, 13B, 21, 155, 160, 161, or Centrelink (100). Main courses: £11–£22 ($22–$44). AE, DC, MC, V. Open: Tues–Fri noon to 2:30 p.m., Tues–Sat 6–9:30 p.m.*

Zen
$$–$$$ Belfast   JAPANESE

Calling all sushi-holics: This hip spot is the place to get your raw-fish-and-vinegared-rice fix in Belfast. Bartenders shake martinis behind the glass bar, lit with blue lights, and club-gear-clad 20-somethings strut through the high-ceilinged, dramatic space, which is decorated with carved Japanese wooden screens, black lacquer tables, and a large shiny Buddha. I always order sushi here, but the menu also features an array of cooked Japanese dishes, from vegetable curry to chicken teriyaki.

55–59 Adelaide St. ☎ *028-9023-2244. Bus: 58, 59, 69, 69A, 70, 71, 89, 90, 91, 92, 95, or Centrelink (100). Main courses: £10–£16 ($20–$32). AE, DC, MC, V. Open: Mon–Fri noon to 3 p.m. and 5–11:30 p.m., Sat 5 p.m.–1 a.m., Sun 1:30–10 p.m.*

Exploring Belfast and the surrounding area

City Sightseeing Belfast (☎ 028-9045-9035; www.belfastcitysight seeing.com) operates one-and-a-half-hour hop-on/hop-off history tours of Belfast that stop at Belfast's top attractions (you can hop off the bus and join another bus later at each attraction). Knowledgeable guides do an excellent job of explaining the city's history from the 18th century up until the present day. From May through September, tours depart daily every half-hour between 9:30 a.m. and 4:30 p.m. From October through April, tours depart daily every hour between 10 a.m. and 4 p.m. All tours leave from Castle Place (across from McDonald's) in Belfast's city center. Prices are £11 ($22) adults, £9 ($18) seniors and students, and £5 ($10) children ages 4 to 12.

Local experts lead two terrific 90-minute walking tours that depart from the Belfast Welcome Centre (the main tourist information office), at 47 Donegall Place. On the **Historic Belfast Walking Tour** your guide will relate over 300 years of Belfast history as he or she takes you through the city, pointing out everything from *Titanic*-related sights to the extravagant Victorian city hall. The tour departs on Wednesdays, Fridays, Saturdays, and Sundays at 2 p.m. year-round. To book in advance, call ☎ **028-9024-6609.** The **Blackstaff Way Tour** is the best introduction to the heart of Belfast, taking in most of the city's main streets, including Great Victoria Street, the main thoroughfare. The tour departs at 11 a.m. every Saturday. To book in advance, call ☎ **028-9029-2631.** Both tours cost £6 ($12).

The **Belfast Black Taxi Tours** (☎ **028-9064-2264;** www.belfasttours. com) or **Belfast's Original Political Tours** (☎ **080-8127-1125**) are the best way to get a sense of the rocky history of the city, which saw much of the violence during the height of The Troubles in the 1970s, '80s, and early '90s. Your guide will explain ins and outs of The Troubles as you view the many political murals found in the hearts of the sectarian neighborhoods, including Protestant Shankill Road and Catholic Falls Road. Tours cost £25 ($50) for one or two passengers, or £ 8 ($16) each for three or more passengers.

The top attractions

Belfast's Murals
Belfast

Northern Ireland has a tradition of public mural painting that dates to the early 1970s. Though some murals are not political or religious in nature, most depict Republican or Loyalist political beliefs. The most compelling of Belfast's murals are found along Republican (and primarily Catholic) Falls Road and along Loyalist (and primarily Protestant) Shankill Road and Sandy Row. Both of these areas are currently quite safe for visitors; in fact, residents are used to the interested sightseers who come to visit these areas. If you'd like to view the murals with a guide, contact Belfast Black Taxi Tours or Belfast's Original Political Tours (see earlier in this chapter).

To reach Falls Road from the center of the city, head north on Donegall Place, turn left on Castle Street, go straight ahead down Divis Road and cross Westlink to Falls Road. To find Shankill Road, head north on Donegall Place and Royal Avenue, turn left on Peter's Hill and cross Westlink Road. To find Sandy Row, go south on Great Victoria Street, make a right on Donegall Pass Road, and then another right up Sandy Row.

Belfast Wheel
Belfast

What could be a better introduction to Belfast than sailing high over the city in the pod of a giant Ferris wheel? The Belfast wheel trip lasts about 12 minutes and gives you a running commentary on what you are seeing. Those who are feeling extravagant can indulge in the VIP car, complete with tinted windows and champagne service.

East side of Belfast City Hall. ☎ *028-9031-0607. Admission: £6.50 ($13) adults, £4.50 ($9) children 3–12 years, free for children under 3. Open: Sun–Thurs 10 a.m.–9 p.m., Fri 10 a.m.–10 p.m., Sun 9 a.m.–10 p.m.*

Belfast Zoo
Belfast

This excellent zoo, which boasts a fantastic view of Belfast Lough, features many endangered animals, a Children's Farm, an island of spider monkeys, an enclosure for primates and other African animals, a polar bear canyon, pools for penguins and sea lions, and many other attractions. Several baby animals are born each year as part of the zoo's extensive breeding program. You can have lunch in the Ark Restaurant.

Antrim Road. Take Donegall Street from the city center north, and go right on Antrim Road. ☎ *028-9077-6277. Bus: 45, 46, 47, 48, 49, 50, 51. Admission: Apr–Sept £8.10 ($16) adult, £4.30 ($6.90) child 4–18, children under 4 free; Oct–Mar £6.70 ($13.40) adult, £3.40 ($6.80) child 4–18, children under 4 free. Open: Apr–Sept daily 10 a.m.–7 p.m. (last admission 5 p.m.); Oct–Mar daily 10 a.m.–4 p.m. (last admission 2:30 p.m.). Suggested visit: 2 hours.*

City Hall
Belfast

Modeled on St. Paul's Cathedral in London, Belfast's City Hall was built in 1888 after Queen Victoria conferred city status on Belfast. The building is made of Portland stone, with a central copper dome that rises 52m (173 ft.) into the sky and is visible for miles. In front, there are a statue of the queen and a memorial to the victims of the *Titanic*, which was built in a Belfast shipyard.

Donegall Square. ☎ *028-9027-0456, ext. 2618. Bus: 58, 59, 69, 69A, 70, 71, 89, 90, 91, 92, 95, or Centrelink (100). Admission: Free tours of the interior available. Tours are given throughout the week; call for exact times. Other times by appointment. Reservations required for all tours. Suggested visit: 45 minutes.*

Mount Stewart House and Gardens
Newtownards, County Down

Though its interior is just grand, with a fabulous entrance hall and the famous George Stubbs painting *Hambletonian*, this impressive 18th-century mansion almost pales in comparison with the spectacular gardens surrounding it. There's a fabulous Shamrock Garden, which has an Irish harp–shaped topiary and a flowerbed shaped like a red hand (the emblem of Ulster) enclosed in a hedge shaped like a shamrock. Spanish and Italian gardens are in the back, and a colorful sunken garden sits in the east yard.

On the A2, 5km (3 miles) southeast of Newtownards, along the Ards Peninsula. ☎ *028-4278-8387. Admission: House and garden £7 ($14) adults, £3.50 ($5) children; gardens only £5.35 ($8.70) adults, £2.70 ($5.40) children. Open: House and garden hours vary throughout the year, so definitely call to confirm. Generally, the house is open May–Sept Wed–Mon 10 a.m.–6 p.m., Sept–Oct and Mar–Apr weekends noon to 6 p.m. Closed: Nov to mid-Mar. Garden open daily year-round at 10 a.m.; closing time varies from 8 p.m. in summer to 4 p.m. in winter. Suggested visit: 1 hour.*

Ulster Folk and Transport Museum
Holywood, County Down

This is one of those attractions that kids and adults both love. This truly excellent museum is composed of two very different parts: In the giant Transport Galleries is a stunning collection of trains, cars, buses, trams, motorcycles, and bicycles, featuring all sorts of gems from a Victorian bicycle to a section of the first railway in Ireland to a DeLorean car (that famous *Back to the Future* vehicle), along with interesting text and displays about the various forms of transportation. A highlight is climbing inside to explore some of the buses, trams, and trains. An exciting recent addition to the transport section of the museum is a flight exhibit, which explores the history and science of flight using interactive science displays, artifacts related to the history of flight (including some actual aircraft), and a popular eight-person flight simulator.

The other half of this attraction is an extremely well-done living museum of Ireland in the early 1900s. The museum has re-created a town and a rural area, rebuilding actual period buildings from all over Ireland on this site. Costumed interpreters carry out the tasks of daily life in these buildings — you can watch them cook over an open hearth, spin wool, work metal, print the town newspaper, make lace, and so on; and often, you can try your hand at these activities with them. Don't miss the sweet (in both senses of the word) candy store in the town area. The museum hosts all sorts of events year-round.

Off the A2, 11km (7 miles) east of Belfast. ☎ *028-9242-8428. Admission: Folk museum and transport museum individually £5.50 ($11) adults, £3.50 ($7) seniors, students, and children, free for children under 5; combined admission £7 ($14) adults, £4 ($8) seniors, students, and children, free for children under 5. Open: Mar–June Mon–Fri 10 a.m.–5 p.m., Sat 10 a.m.–6 p.m., Sun 11 a.m.–6 p.m.; July–Sept Mon–Sat 10 a.m.–6 p.m., Sun 11 a.m.–6 p.m.; Oct–Feb Mon–Fri 10 a.m.–4 p.m., Sat 10 a.m.–5 p.m., Sun 11 a.m.–5 p.m. Suggested visit: 3½ hours.*

Other cool things to see and do

✔ **Belfast Botanic Gardens:** These lovely gardens are home to grassy grounds, a particularly colorful and large rose garden, and one of the first conservatories ever built of cast-iron and glass.

Location: Between Botanic Avenue and Stranmillis Road, Belfast (☎ 028-9032-4902). Admission: Free. Open: Grounds daily from 8 a.m. to sunset; conservatory April through September Monday to Friday from 10 a.m. to noon and 1 to 5 p.m., Saturday and Sunday 1 to 5 p.m.; October through March Monday to Friday from 10 a.m. to noon and 1 to 4 p.m., and Saturday and Sunday 1 to 5 p.m. Suggested visit: Forty-five minutes.

✔ **Carrickfergus Castle:** During this impressive, well-preserved castle's 800-year history, it grew from a small castle to an unequaled Norman fortress. Tours are self-guided, with strategically placed information boards bringing the castle's exciting history to life. A highlight is a walk along the parapets, looking out to sea. During the first two weeks of August, the castle and grounds are home to a lively medieval fair and crafts market.

Location: Marine Highway, Antrim Street, Carrickfergus, County Antrim (☎ 028-9335-1273). Admission: £3 ($6) adults and £1.50 ($3) children and senior citizens. Open: April through May and September Monday to Saturday from 10 a.m. to 6 p.m. and Sunday from 2 to 6 p.m.; June through August Monday to Saturday from 10 a.m. to 6 p.m. and Sunday from noon to 6 p.m.; and October through March Monday to Saturday from 10 a.m. to 4 p.m. and Sunday from 2 to 4 p.m. Suggested visit: Two hours.

✔ **W5: Whowhatwherewhenwhy:** Jutting out over the city's waterfront, this flashy interactive science and art museum has all sorts of things to do, hear, and see, from an exhibit where you can create your own animation to a display that challenges you to create your own wind turbine.

Location: 2 Queen's Quay, Belfast (in the Odyssey Center). ☎ 028-9046-7700. www.w5online.co.uk. To get there, cross Queen Elizabeth Bridge from city center, make the first left, and follow instructions on parking. Bus: 94. Admission: £7 ($14) adult, £5.50 ($11) seniors and students, £5 ($10) children ages 3 to 15, children under age 3 are free. Open: July and August Monday through Saturday 10 a.m. to 6 p.m., Sunday noon to 6 p.m.; September through June Monday through Thursday from 10 a.m. to 5 p.m., Friday and Saturday 10 a.m. to 6 p.m., and Sunday from noon to 6 p.m. Last admission is always one hour before closing time. Suggested visit: Two hours.

Shopping in Belfast

Belfast's City Hall is a perfect landmark for the shopping district, which is just across the street. There, you'll find posh (and expensive) British department stores, Irish shops, and some North American chains.

The Steensons, in Bedford House, Bedford Street (☎ 028-9024-8269), sells celebrated contemporary gold and silver jewelry made by Christina and Bill Steenson. **Smyth's Irish Linens,** 65 Royal Ave. (☎ 028-9024-2232), sells a full stock of Irish linens. Much more than just a shop, the **Irish Linen Centre,** Market Square, Lisburn (about 16km/10 miles from Belfast; ☎ 028-9266-3377), exhibits the history of the famous Ulster linen and conducts hand-weaving demonstrations — and, of course, sells plenty of Irish linen, from coats to clothes.

Enjoying nightlife in Belfast

Belfast has a hot and happening nightlife, with lots of club action in addition to the usual pubs.

Hitting the pubs

Belfast has some of Ireland's finest pubs, many authentically Victorian. The company that produces the famed Bailey's Irish Cream hosts a good **Belfast Pub Tour** that covers six of the best pubs in the city, most with traditional music. The tour lasts about two hours and meets May through October Thursdays at 7 p.m. and Saturdays at 4 p.m., above The Crown Liquor Saloon, at 46 Great Victoria St. To ensure a spot on the tour, call ☎ **028-9268-3665** in advance. Tours cost £6 ($11).

Crown Liquor Saloon

Unquestionably the most famous pub in Belfast, and perhaps the most beautiful in Ireland, the Crown is owned by the state (by the National Trust, to be exact). The traditional interior is gorgeous, with hand-painted tiles, carved wood, brass fittings, and gas lamps — truly a perfect Irish watering hole. The local Strangford Lough oysters are excellent. You may want to find a seat early — The Crown fills up most evenings.

46 Great Victoria St. ☎ _**028-9027-9901**. Bus: 82, 83, 84, 85, or Centrelink (100)._

Kelly's Cellars

Not only is this the oldest continuously used licensed pub in Belfast, but Kelly's was also the popular meeting place for the United Irishmen, who organized the 1798 Rebellion. The name is misleading; Kelly's Cellars is a two-storied building with a stone-floored bar downstairs, decorated with all sorts of memorabilia, and a restaurant upstairs. Despite its popularity, Kelly's remains a locals place, filled with interesting characters and often featuring great traditional music. If you get hungry, try the incredible Black Velvet Steak Pie.

30 Bank St. ☎ _**028-9024-6058**. Bus: 80, 81, or Centrelink (100)._

Madison's Café Bar

One of the city's newest and most stunning bars, Madison's is named for the modern hotel in which it's housed. Featuring an Art Nouveau theme and sporting a striking copper-and-ceramic bar top, it's a sophisticated and hip gathering place for young professionals and students. There's an over-25 club downstairs that's great for dancing.

59–63 Botanic Ave. ☎ _**028-9050-9800**. Bus: 82, 83, 85, 89, 90, 91, or 92._

The Morning Star

You have to go down an alley between High and Ann streets to find this historic pub, but you can't miss its striking green-and-red facade, and anyway, it's worth the hunt. The Star serves up the best pint of Caffrey's (Belfast's hometown brew) in town. That's reason enough to go, but the comfortable interior and unique horseshoe bar are attractions as well.

17–19 Pottingers Entry. ☎ _**028-9032-3976**. Bus: 8, 13, 13B, 21, 155, 160, 161, or Centrelink (100)._

Best pubs for traditional music

Some of the best pubs in Belfast to get those toes a-tappin' include **Madden's Bar,** Berry Street (☎ **028-9024-4114;** music Thurs–Fri and Mon–Tues); the **Duke of York,** 11 Commercial Court, off Lower Donegall Street (☎ **028-9024-1062;** traditional music on Thurs); **Front Page,** 106–110 Donegall St. (☎ **028-9032-4924;** schedule changes, so call to find out what's on); Kelly's Cellars (see earlier in this chapter), and **Kitchen Bar,** 16 Victoria Sq. (☎ **028-9032-4901;** traditional music Sat afternoon).

Striking a pose: Club life

Bar Bacca

This place is full of unpretentious locals hanging out and enjoying good drinks and music, from acid jazz to house.

48 Franklin St., behind City Hall. ☎ *028-9023-0200. Bus: 82, 83, 84, 85, or Centrelink (100).*

Club Milk

This is a gorgeous club with gorgeous people enjoying hip-hop, house, R&B, funk, classics, and more.

10–14 Tomb St. ☎ *028-9027-8876. Bus: 8, 13, 13B, 21, 155, 160, or 161.*

North Antrim

North Antrim is a place of dramatic beauty, with sheer sea-pounded cliffs, pristine green valleys, and the spectacular weirdness of the Giant's Causeway. Outdoorsy folks will have a ball. I recommend driving the coastal route along the Antrim Glens, starting at the town of Larne and heading north. The drive takes you along sleepy seaside towns, picturesque crescents of sand, and stunningly green fields, and deposits you at most of the top sights in this area.

If you don't have a car, take advantage of the Antrim tour run by **CitySightseeing Belfast** (☎ 028-9031-5333; www.belfastcitysight seeing.com). The tour takes you to the Giant's Causeway, Carrick-A-Rede Rope Bridge, Dunluce Castle, and the Bushmills Distillery. Tours depart daily at 9:15 a.m., returning at 6 p.m., and cost £18 ($36) for adults, £12 ($24) for children.

If you are interested in taking a guided overnight bike tour of Antrim, check out the offerings at **Irish Cycle Tours** (☎ 066-712-8733 [number is in the Republic]; www.irishcycletours.com).

Spending the night in North Antrim

Adelphi Portrush
$$ Portrush

The Adelphi is located in the center of bustling Portrush, a vacation town if there ever was one, with amusement centers and a semi-permanent amusement park. The Adelphi itself is calm and composed, with every detail well thought out by its proprietors, who are passionate not only about giving guests a great experience but also about making their hotel ecofriendly. This attention to detail is evidenced in the heated stones on the floor of the Jacuzzi area, the laden breakfast table, the extensive menu of treatments at the spa, and the earth-friendly LEDs that light much of the hotel. The rooms have the feel of a business hotel, with plush red carpeting and finely crafted pine furniture, and many have great views of either town or sea. Try to score a room on the fourth floor, where several rooms showcase the hotel's original oak beams. The Giant's Causeway, Dunluce Castle, Carrick-A-Read Rope Bridge, and several golf courses are easily accessible by car from the hotel.

61–71 Main St. ☎ *028-7082-5544.* www.adelphiportrush.com. *Rates: £70–£108 ($140–$216) double. MC, V.*

The Bushmills Inn
$$$–$$$$ Bushmills

The warm glow of a turf fire greets you when you enter this fantastic inn, with its grand staircase, gas lamps, and many antiques. You have a choice between the quaint, individually decorated rooms in the Coaching Inn and the much larger and newer rooms in the Mill House. The cozy library and the oak-beamed loft living room may tempt you to skip sightseeing for a day and curl up by the fire with one of the inn's excellent Irish coffees (made, of course, with premium Bushmills whiskey). Tasty Irish and New Irish cuisine is served in the restaurant (see p. 430).

Located on the A2 (called Main St. in Bushmills), on the banks of the Bush River. ☎ *028-2073-3000.* www.bushmillsinn.com. *Rates: £138–£168 ($276–$336) double. AE, MC, V.*

The Causeway Hotel
$$ Bushmills

Located right next to the famed Giant's Causeway, this hotel's view of the spectacular coast cannot be beaten. This old, family-run hotel dates back to 1836, and although it's been restored and has modern conveniences (rooms have just been outfitted with flat-screen HD TVs), it hasn't lost its old-fashioned feel and sense of hospitality. The rooms are large and clean, but generally unremarkable. That won't matter, though, because you'll be spending all your time gazing at the amazing scenery rather than the draperies.

40 Causeway Rd. Off the A2; follow signs to Giant's Causeway. ☎ *028-2073-1226. Fax: 02-2073-2552.* www.giants-causway-hotel.com. *Rates: £70–£85 ($140–$170) double. MC, V.*

Dining in County Antrim

Bushmills Inn Restaurant
$$ Bushmills IRISH

Located in the venerable Bushmills Inn, this restaurant has an elegant feel, with whitewashed walls, garnet tablecloths, and warm lighting. Maybe you'll go for the maple-glazed filet of salmon, served with savory cabbage, bacon, and a chestnut-mushroom cream sauce; or perhaps you're more in the mood for the grilled sirloin steak served with red-onion marmalade and blue-cheese butter. You can't go wrong; every dish is beautifully prepared. For dessert, the sticky toffee pudding is legendary.

Bushmills (on the A2). ☎ *028-2073-3000. Main courses: £13–£20 ($26–$40). AE, MC, V. Open: Daily noon to 9:30 p.m.*

Lynden Heights
$$$–$$$$ Ballygarry IRISH

Situated on the southern end of the Glens of Antrim, this restaurant probably has the best view of any restaurant on the Northern Coast. The staff is friendly and chatty, and the wine list is as good as it is long. Regional dishes such as duck, pheasant, and salmon fill the menu, and everything's made with as many fresh local ingredients as possible. This is a wonderful stop for anyone driving the coast road, both for a delicious meal and a chance to see the view at leisure. Try the John Dory if it's on the menu.

97 Drumnagreagh Rd. On the Antrim Coast Road, off the A2, on the B148. ☎ *028-2858-3560. Main courses: £15–£17 ($30–$34). AE, MC, V. Open: Fri–Sat 5–9 p.m., Sun 12:30–3:30 p.m. and 4:30–7 p.m.*

Ramore Wine Bar
$$ Portrush NEW IRISH

Pack yourself in with what feels like the rest of the town of Portrush for some casual, well-done grub. You'll find everyone, from couples on dates to families, at the pine bistro tables, chowing down on such options as burgers, a lamb kabob with peppers and onions, and an excellent Thai green curry. Try to get a seat at one of the large windows, which overlook the hustle and bustle of the oceanfront and harbor. And don't miss the Banoffee Pie for dessert — a concoction of toffee, bananas, and meringue.

Ramore St. ☎ *028-7082-4313. Main courses: £6–£13 ($12–$26). Open: Mon–Thurs 12:15–2:15 p.m. and 5–9:15 p.m., Fri 12:15–2:15 p.m. and 5–10 p.m., Sat 12:15–2:15 p.m. and 4:45–10:15 p.m., Sun 12:30–3 p.m. and 5–8:45 p.m.*

Exploring North Antrim

I highly recommend taking the A2, a spectacular coastal drive along sea-splashed cliffs and by small coastal towns with picturesque harbors. Major attractions along the road include the Giant's Causeway, the Dunluce Castle ruins, and the Carrick-A-Rede Rope Bridge (all reviewed later in this section).

Walkers will want to check out the **Ulster Way,** the **Moyle Way,** and the **Causeway Coast Path;** all three are long-distance hikes, but of course you can do part of any as a day- or half-day hike. Check out *Walk Northern Ireland,* available at most tourist offices and as a PDF on www.discovernorthernireland.com (click on Walking, under the "Things to See & Do" tab, for trail maps and details).

Ardclinis Activity Center, 11 High St., Cushendall (☎ **028-2177-1340;** www.ardclinis.com), offers outdoor activities from rock-climbing to rafting. Their programs can be as short as a half-day to as long as a week.

Golfers will certainly want to try **Royal Portrush,** Dunluce Road, Portrush, County Antrim (☎ **028-7082-2311;** www.royalportrushgolf club.com). The excellent 18-hole **Dunluce Course** offers amazing seaside views of the northern Antrim Coast, while the underrated **Valley Course** has beautiful inland views. To get there from Belfast, take the M2 north to Ballymena and then the A26 to Ballymoney. At the roundabout, follow the sign to Portrush (about 16km/10 miles down the road). Par is 72 on both courses. From April through October, fees for the Dunluce Course are ₤120 ($240) during the week and ₤135 ($270) weekends; November through March, they're ₤60 ($120) from Sunday through Friday. From April to October, fees for the Valley Course are ₤35 ($70) during the week and ₤40 ($80) on the weekend; November through March they're ₤25 ($45) Monday through Friday. The courses are open daily from 9:30 a.m. to noon and 2 p.m. onward. Guests are welcome daily except for mornings on Mondays and afternoons on Wednesdays, Fridays, and Saturdays. Book in advance.

Carrick-A-Rede Rope Bridge
Larrybane

Here's one for the Indiana Jones in all of us! This heart-stopping rope bridge, spanning a chasm 18m (60 ft.) wide, is not for the fainthearted: It wiggles and shakes underfoot as the sea crashes 24m (80 ft.) below; and, no matter how brave you are, you're in for a scare. It's worth it though — the views of coastal cliffs and the sea from the area are dazzling, and on a clear day you can see all the way to the coast of Scotland! Seabirds nest on the cliffs of the island, and you can often see them hovering in the wind. There is a 1km (0.62 mile) walk to the bridge.

Off the B15 (look for the signs). ☎ *028-2076-9839. Admission: £3.70 ($7.40) adults, £2 ($4) children. Open: Mar–May 25 daily 10 a.m.–5:15 p.m.; May 25–Aug daily 10 a.m.– 6:15 p.m.; early Sept–Nov 2 daily 10 a.m.–5:15 p.m. Suggested visit: 30 minutes.*

Dunluce Castle
Bushmills

These gorgeous castle ruins, mostly dating from the late 16th century, perch precariously over the sea (so precariously, in fact, that part of the main house plunged into the sea below in 1639). You can explore at will, discovering ruined fireplaces, round towers, and picture windows that frame the sea and sky, and imagining the lives of the powerful Scottish family that lived in this dramatic place. I recommend getting an information sheet from the visitor center before entering the ruins; it's full of interesting details about the different areas of the ruins. Guided tours of the castle can be arranged with advance notice.

Dunluce Road. Take the A2 about 5.6km (3½ miles) east of Portrush. ☎ *028-2073-1938. Admission: £2 ($4) adults, £1 ($2) seniors and children over 4. Open: Apr–Sept daily 10 a.m.–5:30 p.m.; Oct–Mar daily 10 a.m.–4:30 p.m. Suggested visit: 45 minutes.*

Giant's Causeway
Bushmills

This is one of Ireland's strangest and most awesome sights. The Giant's Causeway is a 4.8km (3-mile) stretch of roughly 40,000 tightly packed, mostly hexagonal basalt rock columns of varying heights — some up to 12m (40 ft.) tall — that jut up from the foot of a cliff and eventually disappear under the sea. Experts will tell you the causeway was formed by the quick cooling of an ancient volcanic eruption, but according to legend, Finn MacCool built the causeway as a path across the sea to reach his girlfriend on a Scottish island. (An aside: In 1842, the writer William Thackeray noted in his *Irish Sketch Book,* "Mon Dieu! And I have traveled a hundred and fifty miles to see that?" Just goes to show, even the eighth wonder of the world can't please everybody!) You can either walk or take the shuttle bus to the biggest concentration of columns.

Off the A2 along the North Antrim Coast. ☎ *028-2073-1855. Parking £5 ($10), shuttle bus £1 ($2). Open: Visitor center July–Sept daily 10 a.m.–7 p.m.; Oct–June daily 10 a.m.– 5 p.m. You can hike the Causeway at any time (no admission fee). Suggested visit: 1–1½ hours.*

The Old Bushmills Distillery
Bushmills

A thorough and well-guided tour of the world's oldest distillery, which still produces whiskey, awaits you at Bushmills. One highlight: a room so heady with whiskey fumes that the workers have to get a ride home at the end of the day because they've inhaled so much alcohol. (No fear; a couple of minutes won't affect you.) The shop has every Bushmills product you can imagine, from fudge to golf towels and, of course, every kind of whiskey the distillery makes. The tour ends with a taste test.

Main Street. On the A2 along the North Antrim Coast. ☎ *028-2073-3218. Admission: £6 ($12) adults, £5 ($10) seniors and students, £3 ($6) children. Open: Mar–Oct Mon–Sat 9:15 a.m.–5 p.m., Sun noon–5 p.m. (last tour at 4 p.m. on all days). Tours run about every 30 minutes. Suggested visit: 2½ hours.*

For the birds: Rathlin Island

Rathlin's strategic position between Ireland and Scotland made it the site of many battles over time.

Today, the tiny, boomerang-shaped island off the coast of Ballycastle is a peaceful place and the home of thousands of seabirds, including puffins, and only about 100 people. Storytelling, song, and music flourish here, and islanders are always happy to welcome visitors.

On the eastern end of the island is Bruce's Cave, where the Scottish King Robert the Bruce hid after being defeated by the English. For information on the ferry schedule, contact the Rathlin Island Ferry ticket office (☎ **028-20-769-299;** www.rathlin ballycastleferry.com).

Fast Facts: Belfast and County Antrim

Area Codes

The area code (or city code) for County Antrim is **028.** From the Republic of Ireland, dial **048.**

Emergencies/Police

Dial ☎ **999** for all emergencies.

Genealogy Resources

Ulster Historical Foundation, Balmoral Buildings, 12 College Sq. E. (☎ 028-9033-2288; www.ancestry ireland.com).

Hospital

The Belfast City Hospital is at 51 Lisburn Rd. (☎ 028-9032-9241).

Information

For visitor information, go to the Belfast Welcome Center at 47 Donegall Place (☎ 028-9024-6609; www.goto belfast.com).

Internet

Check out Revelations Internet Cafe at 27 Shaftesbury Sq. (☎ 028-9032-0337).

Post Office

The main post office in Belfast is located at Castle Junction, at the top of High Street (☎ 08457-223344 for information).

Chapter 23

Counties Down and Armagh

● ●

In This Chapter

▶ Hiking in the Mourne Mountains
▶ Rock-climbing, canoeing, and more
▶ Golfing at Royal County Down
▶ Exploring St. Patrick's old haunts

● ●

*T*he stars of **County Down** are the velvety green and purple Mourne Mountains. The Mournes are the highest mountains in Northern Ireland, their rounded peaks reaching over 610m (2,000 ft.). They are a hiking and walking paradise — the mostly uninhabited mountains are threaded with trails that run from easy riverside strolls to strenuous boulder scrambles. This just may be the Irish and Northern Irish country landscape that you pictured before you got here, with weathered stone walls and farmhouses, sheep gamboling in the folds of the hills, lazy cows, windswept mountain gaps, and winding rivers. The stone Mourne Wall, built between 1904 and 1922, connects the 15 mountain peaks, snaking gracefully over rocky cliffs and up heather-covered crests.

The mountains roll down to the coastal area, where tacky-though-charming seaside towns, such as Newcastle, invite lolling on the sandy beaches, sauntering down the street with an ice cream cone, and rattling the bones of your traveling companions in bumper cars at the many amusement complexes.

Northeast of the Mourne Mountains is the land of St. Patrick, the patron saint of Ireland and Northern Ireland, who planted the first seeds of Irish Christianity here in the fifth century. Born in Britain around A.D. 389 and brought to Ireland as a slave, Patrick spent four years as a shepherd for a Druid. During that time, his spiritual life flourished, and after escaping slavery, Patrick trained for the priesthood, probably in France. He returned to Ireland as a missionary, sure that God was directing him to spread Christianity in the pagan land, and began the task of converting the Irish and establishing churches. St. Patrick's Day (Mar 17) is a holy

Counties Down and Armagh

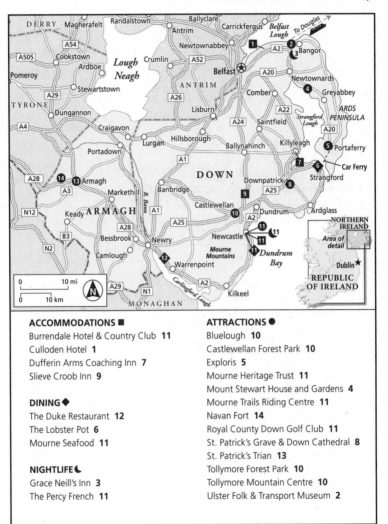

ACCOMMODATIONS ■
Burrendale Hotel & Country Club **11**
Culloden Hotel **1**
Dufferin Arms Coaching Inn **7**
Slieve Croob Inn **9**

DINING ◆
The Duke Restaurant **12**
The Lobster Pot **6**
Mourne Seafood **11**

NIGHTLIFE ☾
Grace Neill's Inn **3**
The Percy French **11**

ATTRACTIONS ●
Bluelough **10**
Castlewellan Forest Park **10**
Exploris **5**
Mourne Heritage Trust **11**
Mount Stewart House and Gardens **4**
Mourne Trails Riding Centre **11**
Navan Fort **14**
Royal County Down Golf Club **11**
St. Patrick's Grave & Down Cathedral **8**
St. Patrick's Trian **13**
Tollymore Forest Park **10**
Tollymore Mountain Centre **10**
Ulster Folk & Transport Museum **2**

day in much of Ireland. People attend Mass; businesses and schools are closed; and until recently, pubs were closed, too.

South and west of County Down is little **County Armagh,** where the city of Armagh is also heavily associated with St. Patrick, who built a stone church and preached Christianity here. The city is still a religious center, home to the seats of both the Catholic and Anglican archbishops. A visit to Armagh City makes a good daytrip from County Down.

Getting to Counties Down and Armagh

The nearest airports are in Belfast, which is also the destination for fer-ries from England and Scotland: See Chapter 22 for information on those methods.

If you're coming by car from Dublin, take the M1 to the N1 north to Newry (N1 becomes the A1 in Northern Ireland). From Newry, take the A28 to Armagh. To get to the coast from Newry, take the A2 southeast (the A2 runs along the entire coast). If you're driving from Ireland into Northern Ireland, make sure you notify your rental-car company because extra insurance may be required.

Irish Rail (☎ 1850-366-222; www.irishrail.ie) and **Northern Ireland Railways** (☎ 028-90-66-66-30; www.nirailways.co.uk) serve Newry, Portadown, Lurgan, Lisburn, Bangor, and other towns year-round. **Ulsterbus** (☎ 028-90-66-66-30; www.ulsterbus.co.uk) travels year-round to Newry, Portadown, Armagh City, and other major towns in Counties Armagh and Down.

County Down

I include the reviews for Culloden Hotel, Mount Stewart House & Gardens, and the Ulster Folk and Transport Museum, which are actually in County Down, in Chapter 22 because they are easy side trips from Belfast, so check that chapter also.

Spending the night in County Down

Burrendale Hotel & Country Club
$$$$ Newcastle

This modern hotel is great for families. The clean, up-to-date rooms are nothing special in the décor department, but the amenities and location are perfect for kids. There is a nice restaurant with plenty of kid-friendly dishes, a large indoor pool, and a hot tub. The town of Newcastle seems made for families, with plenty of ice cream shops and amusement com-plexes. Work off that ice cream while hiking the Mourne Mountains, walk-ing along the sandy beaches, and visiting the two nearby parks. Golfers will also be thrilled with the location: There are 15 courses nearby — including one of the best on the island, Royal County Down. Check online for the hotel's frequent packages and deals.

51 Castlewellan Rd. (off the A2 toward Downpatrick). ☎ *028-4372-2599. Fax: 028-4372-2328.* www.burrendale.com. *Rates: £120–£140 ($240–$280) double. AE, DC, MC, V.*

Dufferin Coaching Inn
$–$$ Killyleagh

This charming inn is located in the shadow of Killyleagh Castle in the little town of Killyleagh, on the road between Downpatrick and Belfast. It has bright, comfortable rooms with beautiful wooden furniture — some rooms even have four-poster beds. The inn is much larger than it looks from the outside, with three pubs, a library, and a guest lounge, plus a restaurant that features Irish cooking and occasionally hosts medieval feasts. Service is warm and friendly.

31–33 High St. (Killyleagh is off the A20). ☎ *028-4482-1134. Fax: 028-4482-1102.* www.dufferincoachinginn.com. *Rates: £50–£70 ($100–$140) double. AE, MC, V.*

Slieve Croob Inn
$$ Castlewellan

If you aren't stirred by the setting of this lodging, restaurant, and bar complex, surrounded by verdant rolling hills, you need to check your pulse. Located where an old farmhouse used to stand, the modern inn has a simple mountain-lodge look to it, with pine furniture, landscape prints, and doors painted forest green. Rooms and bathrooms are ample and sparkling clean. But it doesn't really matter what the rooms look like when there are trails and lanes that virtually begin at the front door, some leading to vistas of Newcastle Bay. The cozy bar and restaurant has gorgeous views; the food is fine as hiking fuel, but it's nothing special. They do, however, make a mean poached egg for breakfast.

Seeconnell Centre, 119 Clonvaragham Rd. Look for signs 1.6km (1 mile) north of Castlewellan, on the A25. ☎ *028-4377-1412. Fax: 028-4377-1162.* www.slievecroobinn.com. *Rates: £75 ($150) double. MC, V.*

Dining in County Down

The Duke Restaurant
$$–$$$ Warrenpoint INTERNATIONAL/NEW IRISH

Fresh, flavorful produce is at the root of the zingy dishes served at this busy, jovial restaurant. Main courses range from meat dishes to vegetarian options, and the seafood choices, such as grilled turbot with wilted bok choy and prawn bisque cream, are especially delicious.

Above the Duke Bar, 7 Duke St. Warrenpoint is 9.7km (6 miles) southeast of Newry, on the A2. ☎ *028-4175-2084. Main courses: £13–£19 ($26–$38). MC, V. Open: Wed–Sat 6–9 p.m., Sun 5:30–8:30 p.m.*

The Lobster Pot
$$$$ Strangford SEAFOOD-IRISH-EUROPEAN

Lobster is, not surprisingly, the house specialty here, served three different ways. Plenty of excellent Irish and classic European dishes are served, but seafood is the highlight of the menu. The interior is comfortable and casual, furnished with blond wood and warm recessed lighting. When the weather's nice, you can drink your aperitif in the lovely beer garden.

9–11 The Square. ☎ *028-4488-1288. Main courses: £17–£20 ($34–$40); lobster £30/$60. MC, V. Open: Mon–Fri noon to 9 p.m., Sat noon to 9:30 p.m., Sun noon to 8:30 p.m.*

Mourne Seafood
$$ Newcastle   SEAFOOD-IRISH

Being by the sea always puts me in the mood for fresh seafood, and this restaurant proved the perfect answer to my cravings. Seafood dishes abound, from the simple (divine mussels in a white wine sauce) to the more complex (a caramelized filet of salmon with fried crab linguini, chile, and chorizo oil). Those who are not seafood fans should be pleased with the steak and chicken options. The restaurant has a casually elegant feel, with contemporary art gracing the walls and spherical red paper lamps hanging from the ceiling. The service is exceptional.

107 Central Promenade. ☎ **028-4372-6401.** Main courses: £12–£14 ($24–$28). MC, V. Open: Mon–Fri 11:30 a.m.–8:30 p.m., Sat–Sun 9:30 a.m.–10 p.m.

Exploring County Down

Be sure to lace those walking shoes tightly, because County Down is a playground for nature lovers, with myriad hiking trails, all sorts of outdoor activities, and a dreamy setting of rivers, woods, and purple-green mountains. The Down Cathedral and the Aquarium are good rainy-day options.

The Mourne Mountains

In my opinion, the finest way to see this beautiful area is to take a hike along one of the many trails. You can access the Mourne Mountains along the A2, getting off at Newcastle, Kilkeel, Rostrevor, Warrenpoint, or any other town in the area. There is also a road that passes the 15 summits of the mountains.

Be aware that the word *walk* is used instead of *hike* in Ireland and Northern Ireland. Anything from a gentle ramble to a tough scramble over boulders may be called a *walk,* so ask for specifics.

Stop by the **Mourne Heritage Trust,** 87 Central Promenade, Newcastle, County Down (☎ **028-4372-4059;** www.mournelive.com); it's open Monday through Friday 9 a.m. to 5 p.m. Check out their terrific Web site before exploring the mountains. They offer all sorts of maps and information, present a series of talks on various facets of the area, and run guided weekend hikes. I recommend picking up the *Mourne Country Outdoor Pursuits Map,* published by the Ordnance Survey of Northern Ireland, which is a detailed topographical map that has many trails marked. I also recommend purchasing *Mourne Mountain Walks,* a packet of ten laminated cards featuring maps and detailed instructions for ten of the area's best hikes.

One of my favorite routes is the **hike to Hare's Gap,** which takes you on a gentle, winding path uphill, with a scramble over large boulders before you reach the gap and a section of the graceful Mourne Wall. There are breathtaking views of the countryside as you ascend, and Hare's Gap is the starting point for a number of other excellent trails that take you higher and deeper into the mountains. Find the route at the parking lot along Trassey Road at the northern foot of Clonachullion Hill. Turn left upon exiting the parking lot, and you see the gate and stile that mark the beginning of the hike. The round-trip hike should take about three and a half hours; good shoes are essential.

Another popular trail leads from the fishing village of **Kilkeel** to the parking lot at the Silent Valley Information Centre to **Silent Valley,** where a section of the Mourne Wall encloses the reservoir that provides water for the residents of County Down. You can pick the route up in Kilkeel or join up at the parking lot in Silent Valley. The walk is easy, leading you through woodlands and moorlands between two giant granite peaks. If you don't wish to walk, you can catch the shuttle bus that travels the route between the Silent Valley Information Centre and the peak of nearby Ben Crom Mountain daily in July and August and on weekends May, June, and September (£1.50/$3). To get to Kilkeel, take the A2. To get to the Information Centre parking lot, drive 6.5km (4 miles) north of Kilkeel on Head Road. The **Silent Valley Information Centre** number is ☎ **028-9074-1166,** and the center and grounds are open daily Easter through September from 10 a.m. to 6:30 p.m., and October through Easter from 10 a.m. to 4 p.m.

If you want to develop or improve upon your hiking skills, **Tollymore Mountain Centre,** Bryansford, Newcastle (☎ **028-4372-2158;** www.tollymoremc.com), offers a range of instructional courses geared to everyone, from beginner to experienced hikers.

You can do more than just hike in the Mourne Mountains. Here are some more options for outdoor activities.

- ✔ In addition to courses in hiking, **Tollymore Mountain Centre,** Bryansford, Newcastle (☎ **028-4372-2158;** www.tollymoremc.com), offers numerous rock-climbing, canoeing, and kayaking instructional courses in the area, ranging from one to three days.

- ✔ For information on **canoeing** here and in other areas of Northern Ireland, you can contact the **Canoe Association of Northern Ireland** (☎ **087-0240-5065;** www.cani.org.uk).

- ✔ **Bluelough,** The Grange Courtyard, Castlewellan Forest Park, Castlewellan (☎ **028-4377-0714;** www.mountainandwater.com), is geared more toward fun than skill-building, offering rock-climbing, canoeing, kayaking, hiking, archery, and much more.

- ✔ Little traffic and gorgeous vistas make the Mournes, especially around Castwellan, prime **cycling** territory. **Ross Cycle,** 44 Clarkhill Rd., signposted from the Clough-Castlewellan Road outside

Castlewellan (☎ 028-4377-8029 or 079-3410-8145), rents bicycles (you can park and ride or get the bike delivered to you).

✔ Point your putter in the direction of the excellent **Royal County Down Golf Club,** 36 Golf Links Rd., Newcastle (☎ **028-4372-3314;** www.royalcountydown.org), a links course full of sand dunes and surrounded by the stunning Mourne Mountains. Visitors are welcome on the Championship course on Mondays, Tuesdays, Thursdays, Fridays, and Sundays, and on the Annesley links every day except Wednesday. Fees for the Championship course are £75 to £80 ($150–$160) during the winter and £140 to £175 ($280–$350) during the summer. Fees for the Annesley links are £30 to £35 ($60–$70) winter and £35 to £40 ($70–$80) summer.

✔ The **Mourne Trails Riding Centre,** 96 Castlewellan Rd., Newcastle (☎ **028-4372-4351;** www.mournetrailridingcentre.com), offers horseback riding on local trails.

Other top attractions in County Down

Castlewellan Forest Park
Castlewellan

This 460-hectare (1,137-acre) wooded park just begs you to stroll around, enjoying the trout-filled lake, wooded paths, and views of a Scottish baronial-style castle on the grounds. The highlight is the gorgeous Annesley Garden and Arboretum, a splendid collection of trees and flowering shrubs from around the world, studded with fountains, ponds, and greenhouses. Don't miss the Peace Maze, the longest and largest hedge maze in the world. Give yourself lots of time — I was in there for a couple of hours. The Grange Coffee House is a sweet little spot for a light lunch and sells heavenly bite-size apple tarts. There is an area for tent campers and for trailers (called *caravans* in Ireland) if you wish to spend the night.

Entrance is across from the marketplace in the town of Castlewellan. ☎ *028-4377-8664. Admission: £2 ($4) per adult pedestrian, £.50 ($1) per child pedestrian, £4 ($8) per car. Open: Daily 10 a.m. to sunset. Suggested visit: 2½ hours.*

Exploris
Portaferry

Exploris is Northern Ireland's only public aquarium, giving a fish-eye view of life in the Irish Sea, with displays of the saltwater environment in Strangford Lough (the lake that Exploris borders) and the environment of the Irish Sea. You can watch thousands of specimens of local sea life doing their thing and hang out with the aquarium's popular seals.

The Rope Walk, in Portaferry. On the A2 on the tip of the Ards Peninsula. ☎ *028-4272-8062. Admission: £7 ($14) adults, £4 ($8) children under 17 and seniors. Open: Apr–Aug Mon–Fri 10 a.m.–6 p.m., Sat 11 a.m.–6 p.m., and Sun noon to 6 p.m.; Sept–Mar Mon–Fri 10 a.m.–5 p.m., Sat 11 a.m.–5 p.m., and Sun 1–5 p.m. Suggested visit: 2 hours.*

St. Patrick's Grave and Down Cathedral
Downpatrick

Sitting atop the Hill of Down is Down Cathedral, a small and austere church built in the 18th and 19th centuries in the style of its 13th- and 16th-century predecessors (buildings of religious significance have stood here for the past 1,800 years). Legend has it that the little churchyard here contains the remains of Ireland's patron saint, St. Patrick. A rock slab with the word *Patric* across it marks the spot. To find out more about St. Patrick and the interesting history of this area, walk over to the **Down County Museum,** on the Mall in Downpatrick (☎ **028-4461-5218**), open Monday through Friday from 10 a.m. to 5 p.m., Saturday and Sunday from 1 to 5 p.m. (free admission).

Down Cathedral, 33 Cathedral St. ☎ 028-4461-4922. Admission: Free. Open: Mon–Sat 9:30 a.m.–4:30 p.m., Sun 2–5 p.m. Suggested visit: 20 minutes, unless you're also visiting the Heritage Centre.

Tollymore Forest Park
Newcastle

A range of wildlife, from foxes to badgers to otters, roams this pleasant 480-hectare (1,200 acre) forest park. Amble along the river, perhaps stopping for a picnic, or break a sweat on one of the mountain trails.

Tullybrannigan Road. Follow the signs from B180, 3.2km (2 miles) north of Newcastle. ☎ 028-4372-2428. Admission: £2 ($4) per adult pedestrian, 50p ($1) per child pedestrian, £4 ($8) per car. Open: Daily 10 a.m. to dark. Suggested visit: ⅓ hours, depending on what you want to do.

Hitting the pubs in County Down

Grace Neill's Inn
Donaghadee

Many pubs claim to be the oldest in Ireland, but this one really is. Don't believe me? *The Guinness Book of World Records* says so, and those people know their pubs. The old part of the tavern practically defines what an Irish pub should look like, and even though it's been extended to include a lounge and conservatory, the whole place keeps the old-school style. The pub grub here is great.

33 High St. (Donaghadee is off the A2, near Bangor). ☎ 028-9188-2553.

The Percy French
Newcastle

Drop into this Tudor-style pub for lunch or dinner (they offer a full menu of Irish classics), or just to have a pint and take in the jovial atmosphere.

Downs Road. ☎ 028-4372-3175.

County Armagh

Tiny County Armagh packs a historical punch, containing the royal, pre-Christian Navan Fort as well as several sights associated with St. Patrick. The attractions in Armagh City are easily seen in a morning or afternoon, so I don't include accommodations or dining options.

Exploring County Armagh

Navan Fort
Armagh

Located just outside the city of Armagh, Navan Fort once pulsed with pre-Christian religious and royal activity. In myth, it is said that legendary Queen Macha had her palace here and that the great warrior Cuchulainn housed his armies here. Only mounds remain today.

The Navan Centre, 81 Killylea Rd., 3km (2 miles) west of Armagh on A28. ☎ 028-90-56-9584. There is open access to the site year-round (the visitor center is open June–Aug Mon–Sat 10 a.m.–5 p.m., Sun noon to 5 p.m.; Apr–May and Sept Sat 10 a.m.–5 p.m., Sun noon to 5 p.m. Suggested visit: 30 minutes.

St. Patrick's Trian
Armagh

This attraction presents the rich religious and secular history of Armagh. Engaging exhibits relate the story of Armagh's earliest roots; the history of St. Patrick, who chose to base himself in Armagh while preaching Christianity; and the tale of *Gulliver's Travels,* featuring a giant figure of Gulliver among tiny Lilliputians (this part of the display may seem a little random until you know that Jonathan Swift spent time in Armagh). The museum also displays the Book of Armagh, written in A.D. 807 and linked with St. Patrick. This is a good place to get a sense of what you'd like to see in town, including St. Patrick's Cathedral (Church of Ireland), located in Cathedral Close (☎ 028-3752-3142) and St. Patrick's Cathedral (Roman Catholic), located on Cathedral Rd. (☎ 028-3752-2802).

40 English St., off Friary Road. ☎ 028-3752-1801. Admission: £5 ($10) adults, £4 ($8) seniors and students, £3.25 ($6.50) children. Open: July–Aug Mon–Sat 10 a.m.–5:30 p.m., Sun 2–6 p.m.; Sept–Jun Mon–Sat 10 a.m.–5 p.m., Sun 2–5 p.m. Suggested visit: 1–1½ hours.

Fast Facts: Counties Down and Armagh

Area Codes

The area code (or city code) for counties Down and Armagh is **028**. When calling from the Republic of Ireland, dial **048**.

Emergencies/Police

Dial ☎ **999** for all emergencies.

Information

For visitor information in Down, go to the tourist office at 53a Market St., Downpatrick, County Down (☎ 028-4461-2233), or on the Central Promenade, in Newcastle (☎ 028-4372-2222). In Armagh, go to the visitor center at St. Patrick's Trian, at 40 English St. (☎ 028-3752-1801).

Part VII
The Part of Tens

The 5th Wave   By Rich Tennant

"Douglas, it's time we talked about this beer paraphernalia hobby of yours."

In this part . . .

I give you a couple of fun extras. You can skip this part completely and still have a great trip, or read on for some bonus information.

In Chapter 24, I list ten traditional Irish dishes and beverages that you shouldn't miss, from home-baked brown bread to Guinness.

If you're wondering what to bring home from Ireland, check out Chapter 25. I describe some of the best and most authentically Irish products sold on the island and point you towards the finest places to buy them.

Chapter 24

Top Ten Traditional Irish Dishes and Drinks

. . . .

In This Chapter

▶ Breaking some brown bread
▶ Digging into a traditional breakfast
▶ Sipping Guinness

. . . .

Though most Irish cities now offer everything from sushi to margaritas, you'll have no trouble finding these quintessential delicious Irish dishes and beverages.

Apple and Rhubarb Tarts

The world would be a happier (and plumper) place if everyone sat down a few days a week to a rhubarb or apple tart, served with a cool dollop of fresh cream.

Brown Bread

Earthy wheaten brown bread is the perfect vehicle for creamy fresh Irish butter, as well as the ideal implement for scooping up the dregs of your soup or stew.

Guinness

Does the thick black stuff really need an introduction? See Chapter 2 for more about the lifeblood of Ireland.

Hard Cider

Sweet and refreshing, a glass or pint of cider is the perfect way to cool down on a warm, lazy evening.

Irish Breakfast

You won't need lunch after chowing down on a traditional Irish breakfast. In its most complete form, the Irish breakfast in the Republic features bacon, eggs, sausages, fried tomatoes, fried mushrooms, black pudding (a sausage that gets its color from pig's or cow's blood), and white pudding (another sausage, but without the blood). You may also find baked beans staring up at you from the plate. In the North, the traditional breakfast plate (called an Ulster Fry) boasts two kinds of breads — soda bread and potato bread — in addition to everything else.

Irish Farmhouse Cheeses

Smoky Gubbeen cheese from County Cork, creamy Cashel blue cheese, all kinds of goat cheese (many pubs serve it fried — yum!) — I could go on and on. . . .

Irish Stew

The cornerstones of hearty, stick-to-your-ribs Irish stew are juicy pieces of lamb, cubed potatoes, and onions, but you could spend a lifetime cataloging the subtle variations in recipes across the country — a sprinkling of parsley in this pub, a handful of carrots in that restaurant, and so on.

Irish Whiskey

Irish whiskey is different from Scotch whisky in several ways. The malt barley for Scotch is dried using peat smoke, but the malt barley used in Irish whiskey is dried in a warm closed oven, preserving the integrity of the barley flavor. In addition, Irish whiskey is distilled three times, giving it a smoothness that connoisseurs claim is unrivaled.

Potatoes (and Curry Chips)

It wouldn't be a book about Ireland without mention of the humble tuber that served as a staple on the island for centuries. The Irish have created a number of delicious potato-based dishes, including *champ* (potatoes mashed with milk and green onions or leeks) and *boxty* (grilled potato pancakes). My favorite potato-related dish is chips (french fries) dipped in curry sauce, available at many fish and chip shops.

Seafood

The Irish have embraced the fact that they are surrounded by waters rife with delicious creatures. The shellfish is spectacular, and the catch of the day is sure to be delicious (I have developed a love for brill). A standout is Irish salmon — you can find it in a variety of forms, from simple smoked slices to moist filets bathed in dazzling sauces.

Chapter 25

The Top Ten Items to Buy in Ireland

Sure, a handful of travelers come back from their trip with nothing more than a few rolls of film and a notebook full of observations and sketches, but most people are a bit more acquisitive than that. Ireland is a wonderful place to indulge your inner shopper, offering a plethora of items (many handmade) that are uniquely Irish.

China

The Belleek Factory, in Northern Ireland, produces wafer-thin porcelain pieces, often decorated with small painted shamrocks or flowers. You can find Belleek pottery all over Ireland, but the Belleek Factory is a force to be reckoned with, selling the entire line of pottery and some unique factory-only items (see Chapter 21).

Crystal

Ireland makes some of the world's finest crystal — pieces that seem to glow and sparkle from within. If Waterford Crystal is on your to-buy list, head to the Waterford Crystal Factory (see Chapter 14) for the widest selection. Don't dismiss the lesser-know crystal factories; some of them produce crystal that is just as beautiful as Waterford.

Irish Whiskey

Just think: You can sit back and sip the smooth water of life while recalling your trip to Ireland. If you get to the Old Jameson Distillery (see Chapter 11), you can even have a bottle personalized. Whiskey fudge makes the perfect thank-you present for dog-sitters and plant-waterers.

Jewelry

Ireland is home to numerous talented silversmiths and goldsmiths, many of whom incorporate ancient Celtic motifs into their designs. One of the most popular souvenirs from Ireland is the Claddagh ring — a ring with two hands clasping a heart that's topped with a crown. Thomas Dillon's, in Galway (see Chapter 18), is one of the best places to find one.

Lace

In the 1860s, poor Clare nuns in Kenmare began teaching local girls to make lace in hopes of helping the struggling economy. The beautiful needlepoint lace is now famous worldwide. In Kenmare, hit The White Room for a huge selection (see Chapter 16).

Linen

You can find the famous snow-white Irish linen in all sorts of forms, from tablecloths to bed sheets to summer dresses.

Musical Instruments

I can't think of a better souvenir from Ireland than a tin whistle. It's inexpensive, truly Irish, easy to bring home on the airplane, and relatively easy to play (buy a tutor book or tape along with it). If you are more of the percussive type, you may want to look into buying a *bodhrán,* the ancient goatskin frame drum. Roundstone Musical Instruments (in Chapter 18) is *the* place for *bodhrán*-hunters, while Custy's Traditional Music Shop (in Chapter 17) sells all sorts of instruments, from fiddles to concertinas.

Pottery

It seems that every road in Ireland bears a sign pointing to a pottery studio. And the amazing thing is that the pieces at most of these places are of the highest quality. Design runs the gamut from the country-style painted pottery of Nicholas Mosse (see Chapter 14) to unglazed modern pieces.

Sweaters

You can thank all those sheep for Ireland's beautiful sweaters. There is a breathtaking range of offerings, from chic cashmere turtlenecks to thick oatmeal-colored Aran sweaters. Check the label to determine whether the sweater was handweaved.

Tweed

Like those battered tweed hats that many farmers wear? You can find them all over Ireland, along with tweed jackets and suits. If you're searching for the perfect tweed, you may want to head up to County Donegal, the birthplace of the famous Donegal tweed, where you'll find tweed-heaven at Magee of Donegal (see Chapter 20).

Irish clothing sizes

The United States and Ireland have different systems for measurements (except for men's shirt and suit sizes, which are the same in both countries). Use the following charts only as guides to steer you toward a near fit — sizes can vary among manufacturers and from store to store.

Women's Coats and Dresses

United States	4	6	8	10	12	14	16	18
Ireland	6	8	10	12	14	16	18	20

Women's Shoes

United States	5	6	7	8	9	10
Ireland	4	5	6	7	8	9

Men's Shoes

United States	7	8	9	10	11	12
Ireland	6	7	8	9	10	11

Appendix

Quick Concierge

● ●

Fast Facts

American Express

Dial ☎ 1-800-924-868 in the Republic or ☎ 0800-587-6023 in Northern Ireland to report lost or stolen traveler's checks.

ATMs

ATMs (called *service tills* or *cash points*) are located all over the country, even in the smallest towns. The major networks are Plus (☎ 800-843-7587; www.visa. com) and Cirrus (☎ 800-622-7747; www.mastercard.com).

Credit Cards

Visa and MasterCard are the most commonly accepted credit cards, followed by American Express, then Diner's Club. If your credit card is lost or stolen, call one of the following emergency numbers from Ireland: For American Express, call 1-336-393-1111 (call collect) in the Republic and in Northern Ireland; for Master Card, call ☎ 1-800-55-7378 in the Republic or ☎ 0800-96-4767 in Northern Ireland; for Visa, call ☎ 1-800-55-8002 in the Republic or 0800-89-1725 in Northern Ireland; and for Diner's Club, call ☎ 303-799-1504 (call collect) from the Republic of Ireland or ☎ 0-870-1900-011 in Northern Ireland.

Customs

You can't bring firearms, ammunition, explosives, narcotics, poultry, plants and their immediate byproducts, domestic animals from outside the United Kingdom, or snakes into Ireland. Also, you may bring in no more than 200 cigarettes, 1 liter of liquor, and 2 liters of wine.

Travelers from European Community countries may bring home as many goods as they like, as long as they are for personal use. For information on U.S. Customs restrictions on what you can bring home from Ireland, read the brochure *Know Before You Go,* at www.customs.gov, or request a printed brochure from U.S. Customs and Border Protection, 1300 Pennsylvania Ave. NW, Room 54D, Washington, DC 20229. Canadian travelers can find out about customs by writing for the booklet *I Declare,* issued by Revenue Canada, Revenue Canada, 333 Dunsmuir St., Vancouver, BC, Canada V6B 5R4 (☎ 800-461-9999 or 506-636-5064; www.ccra-adrc.gc.ca). Australian travelers can obtain a *Know Before You Go* brochure from consulates or Customs offices. For a brochure, write to Australian Customs Services, GPO Box 8, Sydney NSW 2001 (☎ 02-9213-2000; www.customs.gov. au). New Zealanders can get the *New Zealand Customs Guide for Travelers* from New Zealand Customs, 50 Anzac Ave., P.O. Box 29, Auckland (☎ 09-359-6655; www.customs.govt.nz).

Dentists and Doctors

If you need to see a dentist or physician, ask the concierge or host at your hotel or guesthouse for a recommendation.

Otherwise, consult the Golden Pages of the Irish telephone book or the Yellow Pages of the Northern Ireland telephone book, or contact your local consulate for a recommendation. Many emergency rooms have walk-in clinics. Expect to pay for treatment up front and to be reimbursed by your insurance company after the fact.

Driving

You must have a valid driver's license from your home country to drive in Ireland. The speed limit in the Republic is 120kmph (75 mph) on motorways and 100kmph (60 mph) on open nonurban roads. Speed-limit signs have a red circle with the limit written inside in black. In Northern Ireland, the speed limit on motorways is 113kmph (70 mph) while the speed limit on other roads is 100kmph (60 mph).

The Irish drive on the left side of the road. For more on driving in Ireland, turn to Chapter 7.

Drugstores

Drugstores are usually called *chemists* or *pharmacies*. Look under "Chemists — Pharmaceutical" in the Golden Pages of the Irish telephone book or "Chemists — Dispensing" in the Yellow Pages of the Northern Ireland telephone book.

Pack prescription medications (in their original-label vials) in your carry-on luggage. Bring along copies of your prescriptions, in generic form rather than under a brand name, in case you need to get a refill.

Electricity

The standard electrical current is 220 volts in the Republic of Ireland and 250 volts in Northern Ireland. The Republic and Northern Ireland use three-pronged plugs. If you bring non-Irish appliances, you need both a transformer and a plug adapter (available at many hardware stores and

sometimes airports). Many new laptops have built-in transformers, so check before you buy one.

Embassies and Consulates

The American Embassy is at 42 Elgin Rd., Ballsbridge, Dublin 4 (☎ 01-668-8777); the American Consulate is at 14 Queen St., Belfast BT1 6EQ (☎ 028-9032-8239). The Canadian Embassy is at 7–8 Wilton Terrace, Dublin 2 (☎ 01-234-4000); the British Embassy is at 29 Merrion Rd., Dublin 4 (☎ 01-205-3700); and you can find the Australian Embassy at Fitzwilton House, Wilton Terrace, Dublin 2 (☎ 01-664-5300).

Emergencies

For the Garda (police), fire, ambulance, or other emergencies, dial ☎ **999.**

Information

See "Where to Get More Information," later in this appendix.

Internet Access and Cybercafes

Cybercafes and library Internet access, in addition to Wi-Fi access, are all over Ireland. Check the Fast Facts section of each destination chapter.

Liquor Laws

You must be 18 or older to be served alcoholic beverages. You can purchase alcoholic beverages by the bottle at liquor stores, pubs displaying *off-license* signs, and most supermarkets. Ireland has very severe laws and penalties regarding driving while intoxicated.

Maps

If you're driving, a good driving map is essential. My favorite is the Ordnance Survey Ireland's *Ireland Touring Map.* Other great choices are Collins Maps, AA Maps, and Philip's Maps. For local maps, the tourism or visitors' offices in each area are your best bet.

Police

A law enforcement officer is called a *garda* or guard; in the plural, it's *gardai* (pronounced *gar*-dee) or simply *the guards.* Dial ☎ **999** in an emergency in both the Republic of Ireland and Northern Ireland.

Post Office

Post offices in the Republic are called *An Post* (www.anpost.ie for general information) and are easy to spot: Look for a bright-green storefront with the name across it. Ireland's main postal branch, the General Post Office (GPO), is on O'Connell Street (☎ 01-705-8600), in the heart of Dublin. From the Republic, mailing an airmail letter or postcard to North America costs €.82 ($1.30).

In Northern Ireland, post offices are called Post Offices, and the offices and post boxes are bright red. The main post office in Belfast is located at Castle Junction, at the top of High Street (☎ 08457-223344 for information). The cost to send a letter to North America starts at 50p ($1).

Restrooms

Public restrooms are usually called *toilets* and marked with international symbols. Some toilets use the Gaelic words *fir* (men) and *mna* (women). Gas stations normally do not have public toilets.

Safety

For many years, violent crimes in Ireland were rare. Unfortunately, that seems to be changing. Though Ireland's large cities are still generally safer than those in the United States, reasonable precautions are needed. It is a good idea to take a taxi back to your hotel after pubs close, especially in Dublin, and be on the alert in deserted areas at night. In addition, leave your passport and other important documents in your hotel room, always lock car doors, and don't carry loads of cash. If you

want more detailed information on safety, pick up the brochure *A Short Guide to Tourist Security,* published by the Garda (police) and available at most tourist offices in the Republic. Thankfully, political violence has been on the wane in Northern Ireland since the Good Friday Agreement in 1998 and has practically ceased since the IRA (Irish Republican Army) decommissioned their weapons in 2005. For up-to-date safety recommendations for Northern Ireland, check the U.S. Department of State Travel Warning section at http://travel.state.gov.

Smoking

In the Republic and in Northern Ireland smoking is banned in pubs, restaurants, clubs, stores, public transportation, and taxis. Some B&Bs and smaller guesthouses do not allow smoking; check before making a reservation.

Taxes

Sales tax is called *value-added tax* (VAT) and is often already included in the price quoted to you or shown on price tags. In the Republic, VAT rates vary — for hotels, restaurants, and car rentals, it's 13.5 percent; for souvenirs and gifts, it's 21 percent. In Northern Ireland, the VAT is 17.5 percent across the board.

Travelers can have their VAT refunded for souvenir purchases. For information on VAT refunds, see Chapter 5. If you choose to ship items directly home from the store, your purchase is automatically VAT-free.

Telephone

To call Ireland from anywhere in the world, dial the international access code (011 from the United States and Canada, 0011 from Australia, and 00 from the United Kingdom and New Zealand) and then the country code (Ireland is 353; Northern Ireland is 44), followed by the city code without the initial zero (for example, you dial 1 for the Dublin city code, even though it is listed in this book as 01) and the number. *Two exceptions:* When calling Northern Ireland from the United Kingdom, dial 028 and the local eight-digit number. When calling Northern Ireland from the Republic, replace the 028 prefix with 048.

Public phones in Ireland take coins or cards. To make a phone call from a card phone, you must purchase a *callcard* in the Republic or a *phonecard* in Northern Ireland. Both types of cards are available at post offices and newsagents.

To call locally in the Republic of Ireland and Northern Ireland, just dial the number direct. You need to include the city code when calling from town to town in the Republic; in Northern Ireland, you can just dial the eight-digit local number.

As mentioned before, to call Northern Ireland from the Republic, omit the country code and dial 048 and then the local eight-digit number. To call the Republic from Northern Ireland, dial 00-353 and then the city code and number.

To make international direct calls from the Republic of Ireland and Northern Ireland, dial the international access code (00), followed by the country code (1 for the United States and Canada, 44 for the United Kingdom, 61 for Australia, and 64 for New Zealand), the area or city code, and then the local number. So, to call the U.S. number 718-000-0000, you'd dial 00-1-718-000-0000.

From the Republic of Ireland, dial ☎ 11818 for international directory assistance and ☎ 114 for operator assistance with international calls. From Northern Ireland, dial ☎ 153 for international directory assistance and ☎ 155 for operator assistance

with international calls. For local operator assistance in Ireland, dial ☎ 10 in the Republic and ☎ 100 in Northern Ireland. From the United States, the (toll) number to call for directory assistance is ☎ 00353-91-770220.

Calling-card access phone numbers are as follows: In the Republic of Ireland, call ☎ 1800-55-0000 for AT&T, ☎ 1800-55-1001 for MCI, and ☎ 1800-55-2001 for Sprint. In Northern Ireland, call ☎ 0500-89-0011 for AT&T, ☎ 0800-279-5088 for MCI, and ☎ 0800-89-0877 for Sprint.

If you plan to call home a lot while in Ireland, you may want to open an account with Swiftcall (toll-free in Ireland ☎ 0800-929-224; www.swiftcall.com). Its rates offer you considerable savings, not only from Ireland to the United States but vice versa.

If you know that you will have Internet access, you may also want to check out SKYPE (www.skype.com), an Internet-based phone service.

Time Zone

Ireland is five time zones ahead of the eastern United States (when it's noon in New York, it's 5 p.m. in Ireland). Ireland observes daylight saving time.

Tipping

For porters or bellhops, tip €1 ($1.20) per piece of luggage. For taxi drivers, hairdressers, and other providers of service, tip an average of 10 percent to 15 percent.

Tip at least 10 percent or 15 percent at a restaurant. However, check to see whether a service charge (10 percent) has been added to the bill before paying. If the service charge has been added, you may want to round up the amount to 15 percent if you received good service.

It is not customary to tip bartenders at pubs. For waiter service at a bar, leave about €1 ($1.20).

Weather Updates

The best site on the Web for Ireland's weather forecasts is www.ireland.com/weather.

Toll-Free Numbers and Web Sites

AirlinesAer Lingus
☎ 800-474-7424 in the U.S.
☎ 0818-365-000 in Ireland
www.aerlingus.com

Air Canada
☎ 888-247-2262
www.aircanada.ca

American Airlines
☎ 800-433-7300
www.aa.com

BMI
☎ 800-788-0555 in the U.S.
☎ 0870-607-0555 in the U.K.
www.flybmi.com

British Airways
☎ 800-AIRWAYS (247-9297)
☎ 0844-493-0787 in the U.K.
www.british-airways.com

CityJet
☎ 01-605-0383 in Ireland
www.cityjet.com

Continental Airlines
☎ 800-231-0856
www.continental.com

Delta Air Lines
☎ 800-221-1212
www.delta.com

easyJet
☎ **0871-244-2366** (call this U.K. number from all areas)
www.easyjet.com

Lufthansa
☎ 800-645-3880 in the U.S.
www.lufthansa.com

Northwest and KLM Airlines
☎ 800-225-2525
www.nwa.com

Ryanair
☎ 0818-30-30-30 in Ireland
☎ 0871-246-0000 in the U.K.
☎ 353-1-249-7791 (call this number from outside the U.K. or Ireland)
www.ryanair.com

United Airlines
☎ 800-538-2929
www.united.com

Virgin Atlantic Airways
☎ 800-821-5438
www.virgin-atlantic.com

Car-rental agencies

Alamo
☎ 800-462-5266
www.alamo.com

Argus
☎ 01-499-9601 in Ireland
www.argus-rentacar.com

Avis
☎ 1-800-331-1084
www.avis.com

Budget
☎ 800-472-3325
www.budget.com

Dan Dooley
☎ 800-331-9301
www.dan-dooley.ie

Europcar
☎ 01-614-2888 in Ireland
www.europcar.ie

Hertz
☎ 800-654-3001
www.hertz.com

National
☎ 1-800-227-7368
www.nationalcar.com

Where to Get More Information

National Tourist Information Offices

Tourism Ireland (the tourist board for the Republic and Northern Ireland alike) has tons of helpful informational literature; comprehensive B&B, farmhouse, and hotel directories for a nominal fee; and a friendly staff that's eager to answer your questions. Tourism Ireland has an excellent Web site, at www.discoverireland.ie, or you can contact them at ☎ **800-223-6470** in the U.S.

In the United States

Tourism Ireland: 345 Park Ave., New York, NY 10154; ☎ **800-223-6470** within the United States.

In Canada

Tourism Ireland: 2 Bloor St. W., Suite 1501, Toronto, ON, M4W 3E2; ☎ **800-223-6470.**

In the United Kingdom

Tourism Ireland: Nations House, 103 Wigmore Street, London W1U 1Qs; ☎ **020-7518-0800.**

In Australia

Tourism Ireland: 36 Carrington St., Fifth Level, Sydney, NSW 2000; ☎ **02-9299-6177.**

In New Zealand

Tourism Ireland: Level 6, 18 Shortland Street, Private Bag 92136, Auckland 1; ☎ **09-977-2255.**

Other sources of information

For more restaurant, accommodation, and attraction options, pick up a copy of *Frommer's Ireland* (Wiley Publishing, Inc.).

Index

BUSINESS, CAREERS & PERSONAL FINANCE

Accounting For Dummies, 4th Edition*
978-0-470-24600-9

Bookkeeping Workbook For Dummies†
978-0-470-16983-4

Commodities For Dummies
978-0-470-04928-0

Doing Business in China For Dummies
978-0-470-04929-7

E-Mail Marketing For Dummies
978-0-470-19087-6

Job Interviews For Dummies, 3rd Edition*†
978-0-470-17748-8

Personal Finance Workbook For Dummies*†
978-0-470-09933-9

Real Estate License Exams For Dummies
978-0-7645-7623-2

Six Sigma For Dummies
978-0-7645-6798-8

**Small Business Kit For Dummies,
2nd Edition*†**
978-0-7645-5984-6

Telephone Sales For Dummies
978-0-470-16836-3

BUSINESS PRODUCTIVITY & MICROSOFT OFFICE

Access 2007 For Dummies
978-0-470-03649-5

Excel 2007 For Dummies
978-0-470-03737-9

Office 2007 For Dummies
978-0-470-00923-9

Outlook 2007 For Dummies
978-0-470-03830-7

PowerPoint 2007 For Dummies
978-0-470-04059-1

Project 2007 For Dummies
978-0-470-03651-8

QuickBooks 2008 For Dummies
978-0-470-18470-7

Quicken 2008 For Dummies
978-0-470-17473-9

**Salesforce.com For Dummies,
2nd Edition**
978-0-470-04893-1

Word 2007 For Dummies
978-0-470-03658-7

EDUCATION, HISTORY, REFERENCE & TEST PREPARATION

African American History For Dummies
978-0-7645-5469-8

Algebra For Dummies
978-0-7645-5325-7

Algebra Workbook For Dummies
978-0-7645-8467-1

Art History For Dummies
978-0-470-09910-0

ASVAB For Dummies, 2nd Edition
978-0-470-10671-6

British Military History For Dummies
978-0-470-03213-8

Calculus For Dummies
978-0-7645-2498-1

Canadian History For Dummies, 2nd Edition
978-0-470-83656-9

Geometry Workbook For Dummies
978-0-471-79940-5

The SAT I For Dummies, 6th Edition
978-0-7645-7193-0

Series 7 Exam For Dummies
978-0-470-09932-2

World History For Dummies
978-0-7645-5242-7

FOOD, GARDEN, HOBBIES & HOME

Bridge For Dummies, 2nd Edition
978-0-471-92426-5

Coin Collecting For Dummies, 2nd Edition
978-0-470-22275-1

Cooking Basics For Dummies, 3rd Edition
978-0-7645-7206-7

Drawing For Dummies
978-0-7645-5476-6

Etiquette For Dummies, 2nd Edition
978-0-470-10672-3

Gardening Basics For Dummies*†
978-0-470-03749-2

Knitting Patterns For Dummies
978-0-470-04556-5

Living Gluten-Free For Dummies†
978-0-471-77383-2

Painting Do-It-Yourself For Dummies
978-0-470-17533-0

HEALTH, SELF HELP, PARENTING & PETS

Anger Management For Dummies
978-0-470-03715-7

**Anxiety & Depression Workbook
For Dummies**
978-0-7645-9793-0

Dieting For Dummies, 2nd Edition
978-0-7645-4149-0

Dog Training For Dummies, 2nd Edition
978-0-7645-8418-3

Horseback Riding For Dummies
978-0-470-09719-9

Infertility For Dummies†
978-0-470-11518-3

**Meditation For Dummies with CD-ROM,
2nd Edition**
978-0-471-77774-8

Post-Traumatic Stress Disorder For Dummies
978-0-470-04922-8

Puppies For Dummies, 2nd Edition
978-0-470-03717-1

Thyroid For Dummies, 2nd Edition†
978-0-471-78755-6

Type 1 Diabetes For Dummies*†
978-0-470-17811-9

* Separate Canadian edition also available
† Separate U.K. edition also available

Available wherever books are sold. For more information or to order direct: U.S. customers visit www.dummies.com or call 1-877-762-2974.
U.K. customers visit www.wileyeurope.com or call (0)1243 843291. Canadian customers visit www.wiley.ca or call 1-800-567-4797.

INTERNET & DIGITAL MEDIA

AdWords For Dummies
978-0-470-15252-2

Blogging For Dummies, 2nd Edition
978-0-470-23017-6

**Digital Photography All-in-One
Desk Reference For Dummies, 3rd Edition**
978-0-470-03743-0

Digital Photography For Dummies, 5th Edition
978-0-7645-9802-9

**Digital SLR Cameras & Photography
For Dummies, 2nd Edition**
978-0-470-14927-0

**eBay Business All-in-One Desk Reference
For Dummies**
978-0-7645-8438-1

eBay For Dummies, 5th Edition*
978-0-470-04529-9

eBay Listings That Sell For Dummies
978-0-471-78912-3

Facebook For Dummies
978-0-470-26273-3

The Internet For Dummies, 11th Edition
978-0-470-12174-0

Investing Online For Dummies, 5th Edition
978-0-7645-8456-5

iPod & iTunes For Dummies, 5th Edition
978-0-470-17474-6

MySpace For Dummies
978-0-470-09529-4

Podcasting For Dummies
978-0-471-74898-4

**Search Engine Optimization
For Dummies, 2nd Edition**
978-0-471-97998-2

Second Life For Dummies
978-0-470-18025-9

**Starting an eBay Business For Dummies,
3rd Edition†**
978-0-470-14924-9

GRAPHICS, DESIGN & WEB DEVELOPMENT

**Adobe Creative Suite 3 Design Premium
All-in-One Desk Reference For Dummies**
978-0-470-11724-8

**Adobe Web Suite CS3 All-in-One Desk
Reference For Dummies**
978-0-470-12099-6

AutoCAD 2008 For Dummies
978-0-470-11650-0

**Building a Web Site For Dummies,
3rd Edition**
978-0-470-14928-7

**Creating Web Pages All-in-One Desk
Reference For Dummies, 3rd Edition**
978-0-470-09629-1

**Creating Web Pages For Dummies,
8th Edition**
978-0-470-08030-6

Dreamweaver CS3 For Dummies
978-0-470-11490-2

Flash CS3 For Dummies
978-0-470-12100-9

Google SketchUp For Dummies
978-0-470-13744-4

InDesign CS3 For Dummies
978-0-470-11865-8

**Photoshop CS3 All-in-One
Desk Reference For Dummies**
978-0-470-11195-6

Photoshop CS3 For Dummies
978-0-470-11193-2

Photoshop Elements 5 For Dummies
978-0-470-09810-3

SolidWorks For Dummies
978-0-7645-9555-4

Visio 2007 For Dummies
978-0-470-08983-5

Web Design For Dummies, 2nd Edition
978-0-471-78117-2

Web Sites Do-It-Yourself For Dummies
978-0-470-16903-2

Web Stores Do-It-Yourself For Dummies
978-0-470-17443-2

LANGUAGES, RELIGION & SPIRITUALITY

Arabic For Dummies
978-0-471-77270-5

Chinese For Dummies, Audio Set
978-0-470-12766-7

French For Dummies
978-0-7645-5193-2

German For Dummies
978-0-7645-5195-6

Hebrew For Dummies
978-0-7645-5489-6

Ingles Para Dummies
978-0-7645-5427-8

Italian For Dummies, Audio Set
978-0-470-09586-7

Italian Verbs For Dummies
978-0-471-77389-4

Japanese For Dummies
978-0-7645-5429-2

Latin For Dummies
978-0-7645-5431-5

Portuguese For Dummies
978-0-471-78738-9

Russian For Dummies
978-0-471-78001-4

Spanish Phrases For Dummies
978-0-7645-7204-3

Spanish For Dummies
978-0-7645-5194-9

Spanish For Dummies, Audio Set
978-0-470-09585-0

The Bible For Dummies
978-0-7645-5296-0

Catholicism For Dummies
978-0-7645-5391-2

The Historical Jesus For Dummies
978-0-470-16785-4

Islam For Dummies
978-0-7645-5503-9

**Spirituality For Dummies,
2nd Edition**
978-0-470-19142-2

NETWORKING AND PROGRAMMING

ASP.NET 3.5 For Dummies
978-0-470-19592-5

C# 2008 For Dummies
978-0-470-19109-5

Hacking For Dummies, 2nd Edition
978-0-470-05235-8

Home Networking For Dummies, 4th Edition
978-0-470-11806-1

Java For Dummies, 4th Edition
978-0-470-08716-9

**Microsoft® SQL Server™ 2008 All-in-One
Desk Reference For Dummies**
978-0-470-17954-3

**Networking All-in-One Desk Reference
For Dummies, 2nd Edition**
978-0-7645-9939-2

**Networking For Dummies,
8th Edition**
978-0-470-05620-2

SharePoint 2007 For Dummies
978-0-470-09941-4

**Wireless Home Networking
For Dummies, 2nd Edition**
978-0-471-74940-0